# HOMILIES
## ON THE SUNDAY GOSPELS

In Three Cycles,
with Holy Days of Obligation

## Rev. Thomas L. Kemp

OUR SUNDAY VISITOR, Inc.
NOLL PLAZA, HUNTINGTON, IN 46750

*Nihil Obstat:*
Rev. Alphonsus J. Mueller
Censor Librorum

*Imprimatur:*
✠Leo A. Pursley, D.D.
Bishop of Fort Wayne-South Bend
January 23, 1976

ISBN: 0-87973-883-9
Library of Congress Catalog Card Number: 76-675

Cover Design by James E. McIlrath

First Printing, May 1976
Second Printing, July 1976
Third Printing, January 1977
Fourth Printing, August 1977

Published, printed and bound in the U.S.A. by
Our Sunday Visitor, Inc.
Noll Plaza,
Huntington, Indiana 46750

883

# TABLE OF CONTENTS

| Cycle of the Liturgical Year (20-Year Calendar) | Year A (1978-81-84-87-90-93-96) | Year B (1976-79-82-85-88-91-94) | Year C (1977-80-83-86-89-92-95) |
|---|---|---|---|
| Ascension | 47 | 161 | 282 |
| 7th Sunday of Easter | 49 | 162 | 284 |
| Pentecost | 51 | 164 | 286 |
| *Solemnities of the Lord* | 53-55 | 166-169 | 288-291 |
| Trinity Sunday (Sunday After Pentecost) | 53 | 166 | 288 |
| Corpus Christi (Body of Christ) | 54 | 167 | 290 |
| *Season of the Year* | 55-114 | 169-229 | 292-355 |
| 1st Sunday (see Baptism of the Lord) | 24 | 138 | 253 |
| 2nd Sunday of the Year | 55 | 169 | 292 |
| 3rd Sunday of the Year | 57 | 171 | 294 |
| 4th Sunday of the Year | 58 | 173 | 296 |
| 5th Sunday of the Year | 60 | 174 | 298 |
| 6th Sunday of the Year | 61 | 176 | 300 |
| 7th Sunday of the Year | 62 | 178 | 302 |
| 8th Sunday of the Year | 64 | 180 | 304 |
| 9th Sunday of the Year | 65 | 181 | 306 |
| 10th Sunday of the Year | 67 | 183 | 308 |
| 11th Sunday of the Year | 69 | 185 | 310 |
| 12th Sunday of the Year | 71 | 186 | 312 |
| 13th Sunday of the Year | 73 | 188 | 313 |
| 14th Sunday of the Year | 75 | 189 | 315 |
| 15th Sunday of the Year | 77 | 191 | 317 |
| 16th Sunday of the Year | 79 | 192 | 318 |
| 17th Sunday of the Year | 80 | 194 | 320 |
| 18th Sunday of the Year | 82 | 196 | 322 |
| 19th Sunday of the Year | 84 | 198 | 324 |
| 20th Sunday of the Year | 86 | 199 | 326 |
| 21st Sunday of the Year | 88 | 202 | 328 |
| 22nd Sunday of the Year | 90 | 203 | 330 |

| Cycle of the Liturgical Year (20-Year Calendar) | Year A (1978-81-84-87-90-93-96) | Year B (1976-79-82-85-88-91-94) | Year C (1977-80-83-86-89-92-95) |
|---|---|---|---|
| 23rd Sunday of the Year | 92 | 205 | 332 |
| 24th Sunday of the Year | 94 | 206 | 334 |
| 25th Sunday of the Year | 95 | 208 | 335 |
| 26th Sunday of the Year | 97 | 211 | 337 |
| 27th Sunday of the Year | 98 | 213 | 339 |
| 28th Sunday of the Year | 101 | 214 | 340 |
| 29th Sunday of the Year | 102 | 216 | 343 |
| 30th Sunday of the Year | 104 | 219 | 345 |
| 31st Sunday of the Year | 106 | 221 | 347 |
| 32nd Sunday of the Year | 108 | 223 | 349 |
| 33rd Sunday of the Year | 110 | 225 | 351 |
| 34th Sunday of the Year (Christ the King) | 112 | 227 | 353 |
| *Additional Major Feasts* | 114-119 | 229-234 | 355-361 |
| Dec. 8: Immaculate Conception | 114 | 229 | 355 |
| Aug. 15: Assumption | 116 | 231 | 357 |
| Nov. 1: All Saints | 117 | 232 | 359 |

# Year A

# Year A

## "A"    First Sunday of Advent

*Matthew 24:37-44*

In the early nineteen hundreds a man named Lieutenant Ernest Shackleton was exploring the Antarctic regions when his ship went aground on Elephant Island near the continent of Antarctica. Altogether twenty-nine men were marooned there.

Lieutenant Shackleton took five of these men and, in a small boat which they constructed, set out in the stormy and ice-laden Antarctic seas to obtain help. For more than seven hundred miles they battled the elements. But finally they arrived at a whaling station. After rest and refreshments a ship was fitted out to return and pick up the twenty-three marooned sailors. But this first relief expedition failed. They were driven back by the terrible storms of the forbidding Antarctic.

A second expedition was organized, but, like the first, it failed. Still a third time they attempted to bring help to the marooned men, and a third time they failed. But a fourth attempt succeeded. A relief ship succeeded in penetrating the icy waters to arrive off the shore of Elephant Island.

To their happy surprise they found the twenty-three survivors alive. Their struggle to stay alive had been a difficult one. Their only supplies during this time had been matches and salt, their only food penguins and seals. Yet their faith in their captain never faltered. They were sure, they said, that if he himself were still alive he would come back to save them. He did come after four long months.

Compare this thrilling rescue to the season of Advent. Christ is our captain. Those marooned are the entire human race. But God has promised to send relief; this he promised right after the fall of Adam, when the whole human race was left to suffer the consequences of original sin. But from the time of the promise to the time of the fulfillment was four thousand years. These were years of longing, hoping and praying for his coming. The story of the Old Testament is the story of that wait. We may call it his Advent.

The word "Advent" means coming. During the season of Advent we prepare for the coming of Christ. The four weeks of Advent represent the four

9

thousand years the people of the Old Testament waited for the coming of our Savior.

Holy Mother the Church has a purpose in instituting the season of Advent. Her purpose is to take us back to the Christ-less, Redeemer-less years before Bethlehem. Her purpose is to make us realize, by contrast, how cold and barren, how hungry and miserable man was, and can be even now, without Christ.

The longing in the hearts of those awaiting the Redeemer is brought home to us in many ways during the Advent season — by the somber purple vestments worn by the priest, by the plaintive cry of the prayers of the Mass. Holy Mother the Church points out that longing should fill our hearts.

The world before the coming of Christ was in a pitiful condition. History records that even the Jews, the chosen race, suffered miserably. King David in his Fifth Psalm records that there is no truth, no mercy and no knowledge in the land. Lying, cursing, killing and theft abound. Because of these conditions he prayed most fervently.

Holy Mother the Church in her liturgy encourages us to prepare during these four weeks of Advent in four ways for the coming of Christ. The first of these ways is by penance. In this regard she holds out to us St. John the Baptizer as a model to imitate. During his lifetime St. John took the vow of a Nazarite; he shaved his head and went off into the desert and lived on wild locusts and honey. He preached a baptism of penance for the forgiveness of sins.

The second way Holy Mother the Church exhorts us to prepare for the coming of Christ is by prayer. Prayer was naturally easy for the twenty-three men marooned on Elephant Island. It was naturally easy for the Jews, when they were in bondage in Egypt or wandering for forty years in the Sinai desert. The heart prays when it is oppressed by much trouble and suffering.

The third means of preparation is by performing acts of mercy. There are countless opportunities to perform both the spiritual and corporal works of mercy. The sick in the hospitals, the poor throughout the world are crying for our help.

The fourth and final means the Church exhorts us to put into practice during these four weeks is to meditate on Christ's birth. She wishes to think seriously and prayerfully on the meaning of his coming. By his coming Christ reopened the gates of heaven which the sin of Adam had closed. He brought peace and love and light into a world filled with darkness, hate and war.

There once was a nun who had a most beautiful way of preparing her class in school for the Advent season. She would ask them to make various acts of sacrifice. When Advent drew to a close she would ask each child to tell the class what he or she had done. Then Sister would decide which acts of sacrifice were the greatest. She would allow each child to place one figure in the Christmas crib — the greater the sacrifice, the more prominent the figure.

During this Advent season let us heed the warning of Holy Mother the Church and prepare for Christ's coming by penance, by prayer, by acts of mercy and by meditation. Greet the Christ Child on Christmas day with these as your gifts. For he is your captain who has come back to rescue you from a world of suffering and sin. God bless you.

# "A"    Second Sunday of Advent

*Matthew 3:1-12*

The gospel read at this Mass is most appropriate for it speaks of St. John, the Baptizer, the precursor of Christ. St. John was a striking character. Scripture tells us that he dressed in a garment of camel-hair and lived in the desert on locusts and wild honey. This manner of life was in imitation of the prophets of the Old Testament in the early days of the Jewish nation. But all this happened centuries before John the Baptizer lived upon the earth.

In fact, there had not been a major prophet for nearly five hundred years prior to John. Hence John, in assuming this dress and living in this manner, was leaving himself open to criticism and ridicule. He lived in a manner far different from the custom of his age.

In the fifteenth year of the reign of Tiberius Caesar, the word of God came to John in the desert, and John went forth into the regions about the Jordan, preaching a baptism of repentance which led to the forgiveness of sins. This fifteenth year of the reign of Tiberius Caesar is calculated to be about 28 or 29 A.D. Thus John began to preach and baptize around the Jordan about two years before Christ began his public life.

The baptism which John administered was not the Sacrament of Baptism. Rather, it was a temporary rite which admitted men to some new spiritual privileges. It prepared them to become Christians, but it did not make them so. John's baptism was the dividing line between the Old and New Testaments, the partition between the Law and the Gospel. It symbolized the taking away of the stain of sin.

Many Pharisees and Sadducees came to hear John. But once they heard him, they refused to be baptized, for they denied any need of penance on their part. The baptism of John was a figure of the sacrament which Christ was later to institute.

John's mission, in the words of the prophet Isaiah, was to "prepare . . . the way of the Lord, make straight in the wilderness the paths of our God." In John's time, as is true today, men's minds were filled with materialism. They were not disposed to hear Christ's message. Love and charity were missing from their hearts. They were not ready to forgive their neighbors. John, the precursor of Christ, went before him to prepare his way. He endeavored to thaw their hearts. The entire Old Testament was a remote preparation for the coming of Christ. But John's preaching was a proximate and immediate one.

John's work was most necessary, for the pagan world was ill-prepared to receive its creator. Materialism was rampant on every side. Pride and hypocrisy confronted one so frequently. Temporal values so beclouded the minds of the Jewish people that they wrongly expected the Messiah, who was to come, to be a temporal ruler and reign over an earthly kingdom.

The valley of immorality was also one of great depth. John the Baptizer met up with it at every turn. He labored ceaselessly to overcome it. He did not hesitate to tell King Herod that he was guilty of mortal sin in living with his brother's wife. But this brave act of righteousness cost him his life.

My dear people, on this second Sunday of Advent, Holy Mother the Church holds before us the great St. John the Baptizer as one worthy of emulation. St. John went forth to prepare the way for the coming of Christ. She bids us prepare in a similar way for coming feast of his birth.

St. John is no longer with us to lead us in preparation for Christ's coming. But the story of his deeds bids us to act in a similar manner. Let not blatant materialism nor the desire for this world's possessions lead us astray. Let our first concern be for the glory of God and the state of sanctifying grace in our souls.

Let us follow in the footsteps of St. John the Baptizer. His path is not an easy one. Rather it is a difficult one, one which leads us through suffering in this life. But virtue and true happiness will be found at its end. God bless you.

# "A"      Third Sunday of Advent

*Matthew 11: 2-11*

In the Old Testament the prophet Malachi wrote in the third chapter of his book, "Behold I send my angel, and he shall prepare the way before my face." He wrote these words about John the Baptizer, who was to live many centuries later, the subject of today's gospel.

John the Baptizer was the son of Elizabeth and Zechariah; he was the cousin of Christ. It was he whom Christ called the precursor, the one sent to prepare his way. Some two years before Christ began his public life, John went into the desert region around the Jordan and began to preach a baptism of repentance for the forgiveness of sin.

John was a courageous man. When the immoral life that King Herod was living came to his attention, he fearlessly spoke out against him. Herod imprisoned him for daring to raise his voice against his king.

It was from his prison cell that John heard of the works of Christ. He wondered if Christ were the Messiah. Therefore, he sent a message by his disciples to ask him, "Are you 'He who is to come' or do we look for another?"

John's question is indicative of his humility. He had been asked by the Jews if he were the Messiah. John emphatically denied that he was. He said, "The one who will follow me is more powerful than I. I am not even fit to unfasten his sandal."

It is not surprising that John did not know Christ personally. They had lived far apart in different corners of Palestine. Their paths had not crossed until Christ approached John near the Jordan River and asked to be baptized

by him. John's role of preaching the coming of the Redeemer was inspired solely by the Holy Spirit.

Jesus answered the question of John by saying, "Go back and report to
John what you hear and see: the blind recover their sight, cripples walk, lepers
are cured, the deaf hear, dead men are raised to life, and the poor have the
good news preached to them." In making this answer Christ made no claim for
himself. Instead he pointed to his actions, for actions speak louder than words.

The importance of actions is reiterated frequently in the Bible. St. James
writes, "A man who listens to God's word but does not put it into practice is
like a man who looks into a mirror. . . ."

Consider the actions which Christ pointed to — the blind recover their
sight, cripples walk, lepers are cured, the deaf hear, dead men are raised to life.
Thse are actions of charity, actions of compassion. They are the actions by
which Christ chose to identify himself. They are actions motivated by love.
Love was the underlying virtue Christ wished to inculcate above all others in
his Church.

Christ identified himself with the poor. He said, "The poor have the good
news preached to them." Christ wished to have his name identified with poverty. He chose to be born in the poverty of a stable. He lived the life of a poor
person here on earth. In no better way could he tell the poor that he loved
them.

The marks that Christ points to, love for his fellow man and compassion
on the poor, are marks that distinguish his doctrine. They are the marks that
distinguish his Church and his doctrine today.

Some years ago in the heart of the Congo in Africa a group of natives were
converted to the Catholic faith. They told how various missionaries had visited
their people and preached the gospel. The first group to arrive preached the
evil of sin and the need of penance. The natives listened politely, but they were
not convinced. Others came preaching a similar message and met with a similar
result.

Later two Catholic missionaries came to their village. At first they did not
preach at all. Instead they lived with the natives. They performed acts of charity for them. They bandaged up the wounds of an injured man and gave medicine to the sick. They bathed the wounds of a leper and helped to dress his
sores.

By the time they started to preach the gospel, they had already won many
converts. But they won them by their acts and deeds of charity, not by their
powerful preaching. These missionaries exemplified in their lives the teaching
Christ put into practice years ago in Palestine. They showed love and concern
for the sick and the poor.

Let us resolve to practice these virtues in our own lives. Let it be a distinguishing mark of us today. In the early Church it was said, "Look at these
Christians: see how they love one another." Let us display this same love today
for the world to see. God bless you.

# "A"    Fourth Sunday of Advent

*Matthew 1: 18-24*

In today's gospel St. Matthew reveals the details of the marriage of Mary and Joseph. In ancient times Jewish marriages involved three steps. The first step was the engagement. An engagement was often made when the couple were only children. It was usually made by the parents, or other guardians entrusted with the authority to do so. Frequently it was made without the couple's ever seeing one another. It was felt by the Jewish people that marriage was too important a step to be left to the dictates of human passion and the human heart. Therefore, the parents or responsible adults arranged a marriage years in advance.

The second step in the marriage ritual was the betrothal. This is called the ratification of the engagement by the couple themselves. A girl always had the privilege of refusing to marry a certain man. If she did refuse, then the engagement was broken and there was no betrothal. The period of betrothal lasted for one year. It was legally and morally binding under law once it was agreed to by the future bride and groom. This was the period in which Mary and Joseph found themselves in today's gospel story.

The third and final step in the marriage ritual was the marriage ceremony itself. This took place at the end of the year of betrothal.

The terms husband and wife were generally used in referring to two people who were betrothed and not yet married. Thus Joseph is called the husband of Mary in today's gospel, but St. Matthew goes on to explain that they had not yet lived together.

Joseph, the betrothed husband of Mary, was faced with a problem. Mary was found to be with child. Joseph knew he was not the father of Mary's child. He was puzzled at what course of action to follow.

St. Matthew calls Joseph an upright or just man. Indeed he was! But a just man is also a loving man. A just man is free from cruelty. He is not a false accuser.

Mary herself might have attempted to explain matters — declaring her child to be the Son of God, conceived through the Holy Spirit. But this would be a delicate matter; it would be difficult for Joseph to understand fully. Therefore, Mary said nothing; she had faith in God. God had placed her in this situation and God would show her a way out.

Joseph was faced with at least three possibilities. The first was to press for a charge of adultery against Mary. But Joseph was a just man, a loving man. This he refused to do. He could not and did not believe that his humble, pure and loving wife-to-be was guilty of such a sin.

Joseph could have proceeded with the marriage ceremony. But then with the birth of a child either before or immediately after the marriage ceremony, there would be false suspicions or accusations. People would wrongly conclude that Mary and Joseph did not respect the Jewish year of betrothal. This too he decided against.

Joseph chose another course of action. He decided to put her away quietly

— to send Mary to a distant place. After a year's time had elapsed, when the period of their betrothal came to an end and they did not marry, then Joseph could ask for an annulment of their betrothal. This would free Mary to be betrothed and to marry someone else if she so chose. This course of action would give Mary a choice in the matter. Joseph considered it the loving and gentlemanly thing to do.

But once Joseph had decided upon this course of action, almighty God intervened. He sent an angel to Joseph to tell him, "Joseph, son of David, have no fear about taking Mary as your wife. It is by the Holy Spirit that she has conceived this child. She is to have a son and you are to name him Jesus because he will save his people from their sins."

Joseph's mind was greatly relieved. Mary's faith in God, by keeping silence, was justified. Mary's purity and virginity had been attested to by an angel of God. Joseph's faith and trust in Mary had been vindicated. Joseph had been divinely shown what course of action to follow. Joseph obeyed the angel's command. He proceeded with the marriage ceremony and took Mary into his home as his wife.

St. Joseph has been called the silent saint. His name is only mentioned on four occasions in all of Scripture. This incident is the first. The birth of Christ in Bethlehem was the second. The flight of the Holy Family into Egypt is the third mention of Joseph in Scripture, and the finding of the child Jesus in the temple when he was twelve years old is the fourth. Yet on none of these occasions is there recorded a single word that Joseph ever spoke. Next to the Blessed Virgin Mary, Joseph is honored more than any other saint in the Catholic Church.

Joseph's greatness stems from the fact that he was the guardian of the Christ Child here on earth. Christ, the Son of God and Second Person of the Blessed Trinity, humbly subjected himself to Joseph here on earth. He was obedient to Joseph's commands. He was respectful of his wishes. He worked alongside Joseph at his carpenter bench.

Joseph was the head of the Holy Family. He was the breadwinner for Christ, the God-man, and of Mary, the Mother of God. Because of his exalted position and the holy manner in which he fulfilled it, Joseph was chosen as Patron of the Universal Church.

But surprisingly Joseph was the forgotten saint for many centuries. Despite his well-established place in Holy Scripture, it was not until 1481 that Pope Sixtus instituted the feast of St. Joseph. It was not until modern times that St. Joseph came into his own. In 1937 Pope Pius XI declared him to be the model of Christian workers. In 1955 Pope Pius XII established the feast of St. Joseph the Worker.

As Joseph was obedient to the commands of God, let us follow his example. Let us dress our souls in sanctifying grace; let us make our tongues and hearts a fitting manger for the Christ Child on Christmas day. God bless you.

# "A"     Christmas

*Luke 2:1-14, 15-20 or John 1:1-18*

The most beautiful story ever told is the story of Christ's birth. It is a divine story inspired by God himself. In its most beautiful form it is recorded in the Gospel of St. Luke, who had heard it from the lips of our Blessed Mother, years after our Savior's death.

It is a story which only Mary could have related with its abundance of love — a story which Mary had long treasured in her heart, but which God decreed she should tell to St. Luke, so he might record it and reveal it to the world.

While Quirinius was governor of Syria, a decree was published by Caesar Augustus ordering a census of the whole world. Everyone went to register in the town of his birth.

In obedience to Caesar's decree Joseph set out with Mary, his espoused wife, from their home in Nazareth to Bethlehem, the city of David, some sixty miles away. This journey was a difficult one. It would take Mary and Joseph three or four days of walking and riding on their donkey to make it.

Bethlehem in those days was a small village nestled at the feet of the Judean mountains. To the east of it stretched the Judean desert. It was a stopping-off place for travelers crossing the desert. On the edge of the town was a large inn.

The inn of Bethlehem was a square open area surrounded by a high wall. A single door entered into it. Animals spent the night in the central courtyard. Their owners slept on a platform surrounding it. Alcoves were available along this platform for a modest price.

Joseph undoubtedly sought shelter for Mary and himself in one of these small alcoves or rooms, for Mary was with child and the time for her to be delivered was near. But Joseph was told that with so many travelers stopping there, the inn was full. All that was available was to sleep in the stable with the animals. This was the shelter Joseph was forced to accept.

Here it was in the stable that Mary gave birth to her first-born son. She wrapped him in swaddling clothes and laid him in a manger. Thus was the Savior of the world born in Bethlehem.

A multitude of angels hovered around the stable and their singing filled the air with heavenly music, "Glory to God in high heaven, peace on earth to those on whom his favor rests."

The angels brought the good news of our Savior's birth to the shepherds in that locality, living in the fields and keeping night watch by turns over their flocks. The angel of the Lord appeared to them as the glory of the Lord shone around them. The angel said to them, "You have nothing to fear! I come to proclaim good news to you — tidings of great joy to be shared by the whole people. This day in David's city a savior has been born to you, the Messiah and Lord. Let this be a sign to you: in a manger you will find an infant wrapped in swaddling clothes."

The birth of Christ was an event that had different meanings for different people. To Mary and Joseph and to the shepherds who came to adore, it was an occasion of love.

The barrenness of the stable was more than compensated by the warmth of their love. The shepherds were rugged outdoor men. They daily fought to protect their flocks against wolves and robbers. They spent long hours in patient watching over their sheep in the fields.

Shepherds were often the outcasts of fortune; they barely eked out an existence in the fields. But they loved their flocks and endured many dangers to protect them. Hence love was a part of their life. Their hearts swelled with love and joy when the angels led them to see the tender infant child lying in the manger.

But there were others who had different emotions. King Herod in Jerusalem heard of our Savior's birth from the wise men. But his heart was filled with malice and greed. He saw in the birth of the infant Savior a rival for his earthly kingdom. Hate swelled within his heart and he sought to kill the Christ Child, putting to the sword all children in Bethlehem two years of age or under.

We too shall find in the stable what we are looking for. If our hearts are filled with worldly cares, if we are concerned only about material goods, then our attention will center on the bleakness of the stable and its poverty. But if our hearts are open and receptive to love, then the greatest love story of all time will warm our hearts. It will prompt us to love the Infant Savior who came into this world for love of us. It will prompt us to show love to our fellow man.

Over a hundred years ago the Civil War was raging on our American soil. Confederate forces of the South had penetrated into Pennsylvania but were repelled at Gettysburg. They retreated into the Shenandoah Valley. In this no man's land in 1863, Union and Confederate cavalry forces were approaching each other. Anger and bitterness were in their hearts.

But as the two forces drew near each other, both sides spotted a moving object in the road between them. It was a small child crawling in the dirt. Both forces raised white flags of truce and went out to help the infant. For that one Christmas Eve of 1863 a small child had brought peace between two warring armies.

The Christ Child who comes today, born in a stable, will bring us peace also. But we must first prepare our hearts to receive him. We must rid our hearts of hatred and greed. We must let love take their place. Then when we come forward to unite our hearts to his at the Communion rail, the love of the Christ Child will fill them to overflowing. The love which radiated from his crib will bring happiness to the world. God bless you.

# "A" Sunday After Christmas (Holy Family)

*Matthew 2:13-15, 19-23*

Some years ago Pope Leo XIII was looking for a saint to declare to be the protector of the Universal Church. The lives of many saints were examined: the lives of great popes and bishops, the lives of the Apostles and missionaries. The sufferings of martyrs were reviewed; the writings of learned fathers were read and discussed. But after all was said and done, Pope Leo chose a saint who led a most ordinary life, one who never preached a sermon — one who was not a martyr — one whose life was quiet and uneventful.

He picked St. Joseph. The reason he gave was that God had chosen him to be the head of the Holy Family. Certainly if the Christ Child had entrusted his life into St. Joseph's hands on earth, Pope Leo could not go wrong in entrusting the Church to his care.

St. Joseph was not a rich man; he could not provide luxuries for Mary and the child Jesus, but Christ did not want these. When Joseph went to Bethlehem to register for the census which Caesar ordered, the best shelter he could find for Mary and himself was a stable. It was here that Christ was born.

St. Matthew takes up the narrative from this point in his gospel read at today's Mass. He tells us that the Lord suddenly appeared in a dream to Joseph with the command, "Get up, take the child and his mother, and flee to Egypt. Stay there until I tell you otherwise. Herod is searching for the child to destroy him."

Joseph was instantly obedient to the Lord's command. We can imagine Joseph bundling up his few worldly possessions and Mary riding on the donkey, holding the Christ Child in her arms. Egypt had been the customary place of refuge for the Jews from the time of the Maccabees, who fled there when Greece conquered Palestine. Because of previous flights of refugees, Jews could often be found living in most Egyptian cities and villages.

The flight from Palestine to Egypt was a long and difficult one. It took several days and carried one through a desert region. There one had to endure the oppressive heat of the sun on desert sands and cold nights wet with dew. Traveling through the desert meant long stretches to travel between wells or streams where one could drink.

Scripture is silent on the period of exile that the Holy Family spent in Egypt. We neither know the place where they lived nor how long the exile lasted. Our best indication comes from the writing of St. Matthew in today's gospel, who tells us that Joseph stayed there until the death of Herod. Historians think he died around the year 4 A.D. During his time in Egypt one might imagine that Joseph lived in an Egyptian village practicing his trade as a carpenter.

After Herod's death, the angel of the Lord appeared in a dream to Joseph in Egypt with the command: "Get up, take the child and his mother and set out for the land of Israel. Those who had designs on the life of the child are dead." Again Joseph instantly obeyed the command of the angel.

King Herod had ruled over all of Palestine, but this was a large kingdom for the Romans to allow one man to rule. He knew that none of his sons would be allowed to inherit this large domain. He divided up his kingdom in his will, leaving each of his three sons a part of it. He left Galilee to his son Herod Antipas, northeastern Palestine to Philip, and Judea to Herod Archelaus.

Archelaus was a tyrant, exceeding the cruelty of his father. Upon his ascent to power he put to death three thousand of the most influential Jews in Judea. The Romans allowed him to rule only a few years before they exiled him to Gaul.

Joseph feared living under the reign of Archelaus; again he was warned in a dream to go to the region of Galilee. There he settled in a town called Nazareth. In fleeing from Egypt Joseph fulfilled the prophecy of Moses in the Old Testament.

Joseph's life was guided by command from heaven. He had first been directed by an angel not to fear to take Mary as his wife. A second command in Bethlehem warned him to flee into Egypt. A third command in Egypt told him to return to Israel, and the fourth to live in Galilee. Joseph faithfully accepted these divine commands and obeyed them without question.

Scripture is silent about the events of the lives of the Holy Family in Nazareth. Nothing more is heard of them until the mention of Christ being lost in the temple at the age of twelve. Following this one incident a cloak of silence again surrounds the Holy Family until Christ began his public life at about the age of thirty.

The Holy Family is the model for all families to follow. As Joseph and Mary were obedient to the commands of God, all parents should be obedient to the Ten Commandments of God and the precepts of the Church. All parents should imitate Mary and Joseph in the good example they give their children.

Christ too as a child gave us a model to follow in the perfect obedience he showed to Mary and Joseph. He obeyed them while living as a member of the Holy Family in Nazareth. He obeyed the will of his Father in heaven while leading his public life.

Christ shows us the importance of family life through his life here on earth. He spent only three years of his life in his public ministry, but he spent thirty years, ten times that long, living as a member of the Holy Family.

Let us resolve to model our family life on that of the Holy Family. Let us make the members of the Holy Family our models to live by. Let love reign in your home as it did in the home of Jesus, Mary and Joseph. True happiness will enter your family life in proportion to the degree that you model it on that of the Holy Family. God bless you.

# "A" January 1 (Solemnity of Mary, Mother of God)

*Luke 2:16-21*

When Abraham the patriarch was ninety-nine years old, God appeared to him and announced that he would seal a covenant with him and his offspring. As a sign of this covenant every male child descended from Abraham should be circumcised when he was eight days old. Hence circumcision became a symbol of the covenant of Abraham and the Jewish race with God.

Among the Jews circumcision was a solemn rite. Ten relatives or friends were invited to be present as witnesses. Either the father of the child or the "mohel" who acted in his place performed the rite. It was at the circumcision of St. John the Baptizer that Zechariah regained the gift of speech which he had lost. On this occasion he spoke the beautiful words of praise, the Benedictus.

Just where and how the circumcision of Jesus took place Holy Scripture does not tell us. Very possibly it may have taken place at Bethlehem with St. Joseph performing the rite. But of this we cannot be certain.

Circumcision may well be regarded as the first step in Christ's great work in redeeming mankind. In the act of circumcision the first drops of our divine Savior's blood were shed. It was the first sacrifice he made on our behalf. Christ's whole life was a life of sacrifice, but this sacrificial life began with his circumcision. Hence the circumcision of Christ may be called the beginning of our redemption. Therefore, it is most fitting and proper that we begin our new calendar year on the day that Christ began to redeem us.

A further rite of the ceremony of circumcision was the conferring of a name upon the newborn child. We are told in today's gospel that the name "Jesus" was given the new infant Christ Child. This was the named commanded by the angel in his appearance to Mary at the Annunciation. Gabriel told Mary that she would bring forth a child and would call his name "Jesus."

In ancient times a name meant far more than it does today. Each name generally had a special meaning it itself. A name often revealed the nature of a person. The name of "Jesus" means "Savior." In sacred history there was one man who had this name. It was Joshua, whose name meant "Savior" the same as Jesus. Joshua was a savior for his people for he led them into the promised land.

But Christ was a different kind of a savior. It was not his purpose to restore the earthly kingdom of David or free the Jews from foreign bondage. His purpose was to save his people from their sins.

Circumcision may well be compared to baptism. For what circumcision was to the Old Testament, baptism is to the New. As a Jewish male child was presented for circumcision eight days after birth, a Christian child is presented for baptism shortly after birth. As a meaningful name was bestowed on a child in the Old Testament, the name of a Christian saint is bestowed on a child in baptism.

But baptism surpasses circumcision, for baptism is a sacrament, while circumcision was not. Baptism confers sanctifying grace on the soul of the child receiving it. Baptism is the completion and fulfillment of this rite; circumcision was its forerunner and type.

On this first day of a new calendar year, it is most appropriate that we should honor Mary and her infant son. The first day of the calendar year commemorates the day on which Christ began our redemption — the day on which he shed the first drops of his blood on our behalf. Let Christ's sacrifice be meaningful to us.

In making resolutions for the New Year, let us show our appreciation of Christ's sacrifice. Let us make some sacrifice in turn. Let us avail ourselves of the river of grace which Christ offers us. Let us resolve that his sacrifice on our behalf will not be in vain. God bless you.

# "A"     Second Sunday of Christmas

*John 1:1-18*

"In the beginning was the Word; the Word was in God's presence." With these words St. John begins his gospel, the last of the four to be written. St. John wrote it in the year 97 A.D. when he was an old man. When St. John speaks of the "Word," he is speaking of Jesus Christ, Second Person of the Blessed Trinity.

In all of Scripture this is the only reference to Christ as the "Word." But St. John has a good reason for using it — when Christ was on earth, he spread the good word of the gospel.

St. John proceeds to list the attributes of Christ. He tells us that the Word was God. Thus he makes Christ the equal of the Father and the Holy Spirit. He says, "He was present to God in the beginning." These words refer to the eternal nature of Christ. He always was and always will be. He had no beginning and will have no end.

St. John then relates the role Christ played in creation. He says, "Through him all things came into being." Christ along with the Father and the Holy Spirit created the universe. He shared in the creation of the sun and the moon and the stars. He helped create the world itself and all the forms of life that abound in it.

He calls Christ the source of life when he writes, "Whatever came to be in him, found life." As Christ created the world itself, he also created all the forms of life that exist on it.

Only after he lists these attributes of Christ, does St. John state the purpose of his gospel. He writes it to prove that Jesus Christ is God and that salvation is to be obtained through his name.

Each of the other three Evangelists begins his gospel in a different way. Matthew, Mark and Luke all describe the birth of Christ in Bethlehem. They tell of the beautiful events that led up to his birth in the stable and of King Herod's persecution of the Christ Child. But St. John is noticeably different; he is silent on these topics. Perhaps he felt that the three Evangelists had described it sufficiently and repetition was unnecessary. Instead St. John concerns himself only with Christ's public life. He describes Christ as the author of life and calls him "The Light" that "shines in the darkness."

By the term "light" St. John means the light of faith. Faith is the root of the Christian religion, the root of all other virtues. Faith is the virtue by which we express our belief in God and the truths which Christ revealed about him. We believe these truths on the authority of Christ, who revealed them.

His authority for revealing these truths is the greatest possible. Christ fulfilled all the prophecies of the Old Testament about the Messiah. Through his miracles he proved his divine power. This gives us good reason to believe that Christ is God and is speaking the truth. We can readily accept the teachings he gives us.

Faith comes to our souls at the time of baptism. It is infused along with sanctifying grace. Many Catholics, baptized at birth, have possessed the gift of faith nearly all their lives. But at times those who have always possessed it fail to appreciate it as much as converts or those who receive it much later in their lives. "Cradle Catholics" sometimes take their faith for granted without giving it much thought. Faith is a gift we should continually be grateful for.

Faith means taking God at his word. It embraces all the truths Christ taught concerning our salvation. Faith grows stronger when we support its beliefs through actions and deeds. It often moves us to prayer and prompts acts of charity. It supports many other virtues.

A young Chinese girl was converted to the Catholic faith. She was captured by government troops. They laid a crucifix on the floor and ordered her to walk on it. She reverently picked it up and kissed it. She walked around the spot where it had been. A volley of bullets crumpled her body to the ground, but the example she gave of her faith led ninety others to become converts. As St. John tells us of Christ, "Any who did accept him he empowered to become children of God." God bless you.

# "A"    Epiphany

*Matthew 2:1-12*

Today Holy Mother the Church celebrates the feast of the Epiphany of our Lord. It is one of the most important feasts in the Church year. In some eastern countries it is celebrated with more solemnity than is Christmas itself. On Christmas day Christ revealed himself to the Jews, but on the feast of the Epiphany Christ revealed himself to the Gentiles in the person of the Magi. The very word "Epiphany" itself means "showing."

The Magi may well be called astrologers for they were skilled in the study of the stars. They came from the East, from a Median tribe. Basically they are men of mystery. They appear on this one occasion in Holy Scripture and then are never heard of again.

The purpose of the visit of these astrologers was to adore the Christ Child and bring him gifts. They declare this in their own words, for having asked where they can find the newborn king of the Jews, they say, "We observed his star at its rising and have come to pay him homage."

One may conjecture that their journey was a long and difficult one. Coming from the East, they had to cross the Judean desert. Very possibly they left families and loved ones behind them. But sacrifice, danger and hardship meant nothing to them once they had received God's revelation about the birth of the Christ Child.

The star which guided them was no ordinary star in the heavens. Some have called it a meteor or comet which appeared at that time. No adequate explanation of it has yet been given that has satisfied everyone. Yet for the astrologers the star was a sign that notified them of our Savior's birth. It disappeared when they approached Jerusalem, but then reappeared when they left Herod. It guided them to the stable where Christ was born.

Bethlehem was a small town. It had but one central inn. The astrologers would be regarded as important visitors. One can well imagine the innkeeper scurrying around to give them the best of accommodations. This is ironical for the same innkeeper had turned away Mary on Christmas eve, the mother of the Christ Child they had come to adore.

St. Matthew tells us that the astrologers found the Christ Child with Mary his mother. They prostrated themselves and did him homage. Then they opened their coffers and presented him with gifts of gold, frankincense, and myrrh.

Gold signified royalty. By offering gold to the newborn Savior the astrologers recognized him as a king or leader. Incense was used in showing worship to God. In giving frankincense to the infant Christ Child, they acknowledged his divinity.

The third gift, myrrh, was an aromatic balm used in burials. The Jews used to sprinkle it on corpses. By offering myrrh to the Christ Child, the astrologers acknowledged that one day he must die. They were acknowledging the human nature of Christ as well as his divine nature. They were telling him he was man as well as God. Myrrh was a reminder of his cross.

These events took place in Bethlehem over nineteen hundred years ago. The visit of the astrologers to his crib marks the manifestation of Christ to the Gentile nations. It was the day on which the good news of man's salvation was made known to foreign nations.

The star that guided the astrologers to Bethlehem lingers on in the memory of man. It is symbolized by the sanctuary lamp which burns before the altar in church today. The burning light announces to us that the Christ Child is present in church in our midst behind the tabernacle door. He is present here in church in a true physical sense, just as truly as he was present in Bethlehem so many centuries ago.

As the astrologers left all things to go and adore him, we should be inspired to act in a similar manner. We should frequently drop into church and pay a visit to Christ in the Blessed Sacrament. As they brought gifts of gold, frankincense and myrrh to his crib, we too should honor him with gifts.

As they offered him gold, we should acknowledge him as our king by offering him our love. As they gave him frankincense to acknowledge his divinity, we should acknowledge him to be our God by offering him our worship. As they offered him myrrh, we should offer him our sorrow or contrition for sin, to make recompense for the sins of our human nature.

Do not let it be said of you that you saw Christ's star in the heavens and you refused to come to his crib. Do not let it be said that you came to his crib empty-handed. Come bearing your gifts of your love, your adoration and your sorrow. Come and greet him in a manner befitting his role as our Lord and Redeemer. In this way we can truly show our joy that Christ has revealed himself to the Gentile world, to us. Christ's manifestation to the world will then have true meaning in our lives. God bless you.

# "A"  Sunday After Epiphany (Baptism of the Lord)

*Matthew 3:13-17*

In the Old Testament in the Second Book of Kings we read of a great Syrian general, Naaman, who was brave and good. He was well-liked by all. But this most capable general contracted the dread disease of leprosy. Now in Syria at this time there was a young Jewish girl who was a servant in Naaman's household. One day this young girl told the general about a prophet in her country named Elisha who had the power to cure people of the dread disease of leprosy.

Naaman resolved to go and see this renowned prophet, and thus he set out on a journey to Israel. Arriving there with his escort, he was led to see Elisha, who immediately commanded the general to go down to the river Jordan and wash in its waters seven times.

This command at first angered Naaman, for the Syrians had been taught that the rivers of their own country were far more pure than the rivers of Israel. But nevertheless he obeyed. No sooner had he finished his seventh washing than he noticed his flesh again taking on its normal color. His leprosy had disappeared.

This miracle, the cleansing of Naaman in the Jordan, was a type of the Sacrament of Baptism. His cleansing prefigured the power of the sacrament to wipe away sin. His being a Gentile typified that one day baptism would be given to the Gentile people.

Several centuries later Christ was to go down to the Jordan with St. John the Baptizer and there ask to be baptized by him. St. John at first protested, "I should be baptized by you, yet you come to me!" Finally he consented to our Lord's request when Christ insisted on it.

We must realize that Christ was free from all stain of sin. He did not need baptism in any way. Still he consented to it to teach us its necessity. He instituted the Sacrament of Baptism. He commissioned his disciples to administer it, "Go, therefore, and make disciples of all the nations. Baptize them in the name of the Father, and of the Son, and of the Holy Spirit."

Baptism is the one sacrament that is absolutely necessary for salvation. It is the only way we have of removing original sin from our souls. It completely wipes away this and all other sins that may be on the soul of the baptized. It takes away any actual sins a person may be guilty of, along with all temporal punishment due to them. It is truly one of Christ's great gifts to man.

Baptism infuses the gift of sanctifying grace in the soul. When sin is removed, grace flow in. It illumines the soul with a new brilliance. It makes one's soul pleasing in the sight of God. Through baptism one's soul becomes supernaturally alive. It bestows on a soul the infused virtues of faith, hope and charity.

Baptism imprints on the soul an indelible mark — one that will remain on it for all eternity. For those who save their soul this mark will be for their greater glory and happiness; for those who lose it, this mark will be for their everlasting shame. Because this mark is indelible, baptism can never be repeated. It can only be received once.

The ordinary minister of the Sacrament of Baptism is the priest. He administers it solemnly in church using baptismal water and conferring the ceremonies which surround it. But in an emergency anyone can baptize. All that is necessary in an emergency is that one pour plain water over the head of the person to be baptized and say while pouring it, "I baptize you in the name of the Father and of the Son and of the Holy Spirit."

A most interesting story of the power of baptism occurred in the life of St. Genesius, the patron of actors. Famed as an actor and jester, Genesius was chosen to perform for the Roman Emperor Diocletian. He decided to make a mockery of the ceremonies of baptism. Genesius had someone baptize him publicly in the Roman amphitheater.

Immediately he felt a change in his heart. He was powerless to continue with his performance. He stood before the emperor and declared he felt himself to be truly a Christian and intended to live as a Christian from then on. The emperor grew angry. He ordered Genesius to be tortured. Roman soldiers beat him with clubs, stretched him on the rack and scorched him with fire, but Genesius remained steadfast in his new faith. Finally he was beheaded. The grace of baptism brought him the crown of martyrdom. Today Genesius is honored as a saint in the Church and is the patron saint of actors.

Baptism brought salvation to St. Genesius and to countless millions. Let us thank God for the gift of this sacrament. Let us guard closely the baptismal grace within our souls. God bless you.

# "A"     First Sunday of Lent

*Matthew 4:1-11*

Most people would be surprised to hear that our Lord was a mountain climber and an adventurer. Yet the Gospel of St. Matthew, read at today's Mass, bears this out. It tells us that the Holy Spirit led our Lord into the desert and there he fasted forty days and forty nights and following this he was tempted by the devil.

The desert into which Christ was led was undoubtedly the Palestinian desert which lies to the east of Palestine. On the western edge of this desert there lies a mountain whose sides are pock-marked with caves. Tradition tells us that it was in one of these caves of the mountain that Christ slept and spent much of his time during the forty-day fast. In fact, the mountain has been given the name Quarantania, which means forty days' fast. This name was given to the mountain by Christians in honor of our Lord.

Mount Quarantania is very steep, and many mountain climbers today consider it great sport to scale its sides and explore its caves. If tradition is correct, it was here that Christ spent his forty days of fasting. He must have possessed great athletic ability to scale the mountain's sides.

Living in the desert or in these mountain caves was also very dangerous. In the time of Christ and right up until about a century ago, the entire region was wild and uninhabited. Lions and leopards and other wild animals roamed this country. It was only a century ago that the last of the lions in the region was killed off. Lions have often been seen on Mount Quarantania itself.

But Christ was God and the Creator of all life including animal life. Therefore he had nothing to fear from any wild animals.

During his forty days Christ had very little to eat. St. John the Baptizer, who fasted before him, had subsisted on grasshoppers and wild honey. Most probably our Lord did the same.

The devil realized how hungry Christ was; so he came and tempted him to change stones into bread. This was a double temptation; it was a temptation to give in to the wants of the body and undo the good mortification had built up. It was also a temptation to perform a useless and unnecessary miracle. Previously when Christ had performed miracles, it had always been to illustrate his teachings or to show the power and majesty of God. But never had he performed one simply to show his power. Christ rejected this temptation, saying, "Scripture has it: 'Not on bread alone is man to live but on every utterance that comes from the mouth of God.' "

The devil would not admit defeat. He made use of his spiritual powers to take Christ to the pinnacle of the temple and asked him if he were the Son of God to throw himself down and have his angels take care of him. This was a temptation of vainglory or presumption. Again Christ rejected it, saying, "Scripture also has it: 'You shall not put the Lord your God to the test.' "

The devil now had an indication that Christ was the Son of God, but in his audacity he continued to tempt him a third time. Again making use of his spiritual powers, he took Christ to the summit of a very high mountain and displayed before him all the kingdoms of the world in their magnificence. He offered Christ all those riches if Christ would prostrate himself before him.

This third temptation was probably the strongest. The devil was tempting Christ with worldly possessions. It is a temptation the devil persists in using today; he tries to get one to deny his faith for worldly gain. But Christ rejected this temptation also, saying, "Away with you, Satan! Scripture has it: 'You shall do homage to the Lord your God; him alone shall you adore.' "

There are many lessons to be learned from the temptations of Christ. First we may say that if Christ, who was God, permitted Satan to tempt him, certainly we, his creatures, cannot expect to be immune from temptation. The power of the devil is indeed very great.

Secondly, we learn from Christ the way to overcome temptation. That is through mortification of the body. Christ was God and all-perfect. He had no need to go into the desert and fast for forty days. Yet he did fast to teach us the necessity of practicing mortification of the body.

Fasting is a work that is most pleasing to our Lord. By fasting one's soul is strengthened and one's body is brought into subjection to his will. The devil has long regarded the flesh as his best ally. In conquering the flesh by fasting, we lessen the devil's power over us.

Fasting was practiced in the Old Testament. God sent the prophet Jonah to the wicked city of Nineveh to predict its end and destruction in forty days. When the king heard Jonah speak, he put aside his royal robes and dressed in sackcloth and proclaimed a fast by all the people in the city. This fasting and penance moved God to spare the city.

Fasting has won sainthood for many. Despite the relaxation of the universal law of fasting during Lent, one should voluntarily practice it. Deny yourself dessert at dinner or a second helping of food. Give up something that you particularly like. Give up candy or smoking cigarettes. Deny yourself your favorite TV show or some recreation.

If Christ, who was all good, could fast for forty days, we have an obligation to follow his example. St. Paul has told us that prayers and fasting shall pierce the clouds. Let us make use of these means to overcome temptation in our lives. God bless you.

# "A"     Second Sunday of Lent

*Matthew 17:1-9*

Today's gospel tells us of the Transfiguration of Christ, which took place before the three Apostles Peter, James and John. The Transfiguration played an important part in Christ's ministry and was well timed. Already St. Peter had acknowledged Christ to be the Son of God, as revealed to him by God the Father. Just a week before the Transfiguration Christ had predicted his coming passion and death.

The Apostles believed that Christ was the Son of God, the Messiah. But they still held to the mistaken idea of the Jews that the Messiah would found an earthly kingdom on earth and would liberate the Jews and lead them in conquest over their enemies. The lack of any concrete steps to establish such a kingdom and the prophecy of his passion and death had depressed the Apostles. They were in need of some consolation. The Transfiguration proved to be just that.

Christ took with him Peter, James and John, the leaders of the Apostles. He led them up a high mountain, which tradition tells us was Mt. Tabor. There his face became as dazzling as the sun, his clothes as radiant as light. This great glory was something that could not occur because of human power. It was something that could be done by the hand of God alone. It was another substantial proof of Christ's claim to be the Son of God.

Suddenly Moses and Elijah appeared conversing with Christ. The appearance of these two holy men is of great significance. They are the two principal personalities of the Old Testament. Moses represents the Law, for it was to him that the Ten Commandments were given. Elijah represents the prophets, for he was the greatest of the Old Testament prophets. Their appearance with Christ showed the connection between the Old and New Testaments. But yet in their presence Christ was given the place of honor. It showed that he was the Messiah or Redeemer, whom the Old Testament had long awaited.

The three Apostles were overcome with admiration. Without weighing his words, Peter spoke up and exclaimed, "Lord, how good that we are here! With your permission I will erect three booths here, one for you, one for Moses, and one for Elijah." The booths of which he spoke were simply leafy huts which the nightwatchers of the vineyards set up for themselves to protect themselves from the wind, rain and the elements. His remark was ill-timed for such a glorious occasion, but it came from a generous impulse.

Peter was still speaking when suddenly a bright cloud overshadowed them. Out of the cloud came a voice which said, "This is my beloved Son on whom my favor rests. Listen to him." When they heard this, the disciples fell forward on the ground, overcome with fear. This occasion, with the voice of God the Father, is one of three occasions during which he revealed himself to man. The first of these occasions was at the baptism of Christ in the River Jordan. The second was here at the Transfiguration and the third shortly before Holy Thursday night.

Jesus came toward them and, laying his hand on them, said, "Get up! Do not be afraid." When they looked up they did not see anyone but Jesus. As they were coming down the mountainside, Jesus commanded them, "Do not tell anyone of the vision until the Son of Man rises from the dead." The Apostles did not understand what he meant by his rising from the dead. Nevertheless, they blindly obeyed him. Later they would fully understand.

Christ transfigured himself to give his Apostles encouragement and hope when they would see him later nailed to the cross. But he also did it to teach us a lesson. He wanted to show us that at the end of the world our bodies will be glorified at the General Judgment. At the end of the world Christ will call the good to his right hand and reward them with eternal happiness. His Transfiguration is a pledge of our own resurrection. It is a ray of hope to sustain us in times of trial and tribulation.

Christ by his Transfiguration meant to show us the great glory that awaits us in the kingdom of heaven. Theologians tell us that the greatest happiness in heaven is the Beatific Vision, the glory of seeing God face to face. The Transfiguration is a foretaste of this great glory that awaits those who serve God faithfully on earth.

Walter, a little boy of Jamaica, was dying of a fatal disease. His sufferings were intense; his body twitched with pain. Yet he would not pray to become better. A short time before he had made his first Holy Communion. He remembered well the words which his sister had told him about the great glory that awaited the just in the kingdom of heaven. Walter's one prayer was that he wanted to go to God. Finally God did take Walter to himself.

The Transfiguration is a promise of our future glory. Let it be an inspiration for us as it was for St. Peter and the other Apostles. Let us resolve to live in God's grace and do all things well so that one day we too may see God face to face. God bless you.

# "A"     Third Sunday of Lent

*John 4:5-42*

In today's gospel, St. John relates the encounter of Christ and a Samaritan woman at the well of Jacob. Samaria lay in the central part of Palestine. To the north of it lay Galilee; to the south of it, Judea. In traveling from Galilee to Judea or vice versa, the shortest route was through Samaria. Since Jewish law required that all Jews spend the feast of the Passover in Jerusalem, the Galilean Jews had to make this journey annually.

Today's gospel story finds Christ returning home from Jerusalem to Galilee. On his way he had to pass through Samaria. Ordinarily, this was a two-day journey with the usual stopping point around Sychar or Schechem.

But there was an animosity between the Jews in Samaria and those in the rest of Palestine. Their quarrel dated back seven centuries. In 720 B.C., the Assyrians invaded Samaria. They captured and subjugated it. They carried off 27,000 Samaritans and made them slaves in their native land. In their place they sent a large number of Babylonian colonists to till their soil and live in their homes.

Jewish law forbade a Jew to marry anyone of another faith or nationality. Nevertheless, the remaining Samaritans finally did accept the Babylonian colonists over the centuries and did intermarry with them. Jews in the other parts of Palestine resented this.

Later still, Judea was overrun and conquered by Babylonians. But the Judean Jews were faithful to their marriage laws. They stubbornly refused to intermarry with the Babylonians. In time, they returned from their Babylonian captivity and in the year 450 B.C. attempted to rebuild the temple in Jerusalem.

The Jews in Samaria, who had held to the other beliefs of the Jewish religion, offered their help in rebuilding the temple, but their help was refused. A bitter quarrel broke out. Although this occurred in the year 450 B.C., the bitterness and ill-feeling still persisted in the time of our Lord.

Ordinarily, Jews did not speak to Samaritans. In addition, the custom prevailed in Palestine that men did not speak to women, especially rabbis or men in high places as Jesus was considered. Thus when Jesus, who was tired and thirsty, stopped at the well in Shechem which had been drilled by Jacob, the holy man of the Old Testament, and a Samaritan woman came to the well to draw water, it astounded the woman that a Jewish man should speak to her and ask her for a drink of water.

In reply to her astonishment, Jesus said that if she had recognized God's gift, she would have asked him instead for living water. The Samaritan woman did not understand what Jesus meant by living water. She assumed he meant the water in the well. Observing that Jesus did not carry the leather bucket or cord of goat's hair to haul the water from the hundred-foot well, she replied, "You don't have a bucket, and this well is deep. Where do you expect to get this flowing water?"

Jesus replied that everyone who drank water from the well would get thirsty again, but those who drank of the living water he would give them would never be thirsty again.

The woman responded, "Give me this water, sir, so that I won't grow thirsty and have to keep coming here to draw water." Christ then said to her that the hour was coming soon when people would worship, not just in Jerusalem as did the Jews nor on that mountain as did the Samaritans, but anywhere and everywhere.

The woman then realized that Christ to whom she was speaking was a great prophet. She went to spread the news to the rest of the townspeople, who flocked out to hear him. They were also much impressed with the preaching of Christ. They begged him to remain with them, and Christ did for a few days' time.

When Christ was leaving their midst, they admitted that "we know that this is really the Savior of the world." Christ had offered the gift of faith to the people of Shechem. They had accepted it; they believed in Christ and acknowledged him to be their Redeemer and Savior.

The nature of Christ's Church was becoming apparent. Christ had broken with Jewish tradition in speaking to Samaritans, their enemies. He had dared to speak to an unescorted woman in public. Christ was abandoning the customs and traditions of the Old Testament and establishing the New.

Christ was offering salvation to men and women alike, to all peoples of all nations. Following his resurrection, Christ would commission his Apostles to go and teach all nations. He would make his Church truly Catholic and open to all.

This same faith he is offering to us. Let us receive it as did the Samaritan woman at the well, and as did the people of the village of Shechem. For a strong and living faith is the first step toward the salvation of our souls. God bless you.

## "A"    Fourth Sunday of Lent

*John 9:1-41*

Today's gospel according to St. John tells of a miracle Christ performed in restoring the sight of a blind man. The man had been blind from birth. Christ proceeded to spit on the ground and make a mixture of mud from the dirt and saliva and smeared it on the blind man's eyes.

On two other occasions Christ restored sight to the blind simply by telling them that they had the power to see. But in this instance Christ chose to use a roundabout method. The miracle was effected when the man washed the mud off his eyes.

Still on another occasion Christ chose to use saliva in touching the ears and mouth of a man who was deaf and dumb in order to restore his hearing and his speech. Christ used this method of curing undoubtedly because it was a common belief, although a false one, that there were curative powers in saliva. Modern-day eye doctors and specialists tell us that there aren't curative powers in mud and that such a mixture placed on one's eyes would irritate them more than it would help them.

After placing mud on the blind man's eyes, Christ told him to go and wash in the pool of Siloam. This was a landmark in Jerusalem. Originally, there was no natural water source in Jerusalem. One of the early Jewish rulers, Hezekiah, realized that in case of siege from an invading army, Jerusalem was very vulnerable becasue its citizens and defenders had no water source inside the city.

Therefore the king ordered that an underground conduit or channel be chiseled from the brook of Kidron outside the city walls to a pool inside the city. A conduit six feet high was cut through sheer rock for 583 years. The pool, into which it emptied inside the city, was the pool of Siloam. A staircase of 33 stairs led down to it from the street level. The channel was a great engineering feat in its day.

Once the blind man had washed the mud off his eyes in the pool, his sight was restored. This miracle created a great stir and consternation among his friends and acquaintances in the city. Some of them refused to believe it was the same man. They ended up taking him to the Pharisees.

The Pharisees questioned him at length. In response to their questions, the man cured of blindness replied very directly: "He put mud on my eyes. I washed it off, and now I can see." These verses of St. John, describing the reaction and thoughts of the Jews, are the finest description of varying attitudes and reaction in the gospels.

Some of the Pharisees refused to believe the man had ever been blind, blindly trying to deny that Christ had miraculous powers. Others said that he had violated the Sabbath — that he had violated it in two ways: first, by mixing saliva with mud, which was servile work and was forbidden; and second, by curing the blind man, which was practicing medicine and was also forbidden.

The Pharisees charged that Christ could not be from God because he did not keep the Sabbath. But the simple question was asked them—how could he perform such works if he were not from God? The Pharisees had to retreat from their position in confusion.

In desperation, the Pharisees groped around for some explanation to belittle Jesus or explain his miracle. They finally asked the man cured of blindness what he had to say about Jesus. The man replied without hesitation, "He is a prophet."

The answer which the cured man gave was direct, honest and logical. In the Old Testament, many of the prophets proved their identity by performing miraculous acts. The prophetic words of Moses were proved when the many plagues came upon Pharoah and Egypt. Elijah proved his prophetic ability by performing deeds the prophets of Baal could not do. Jesus was doing the same.

The common sense answers of the blind man confounded the Pharisees. They had no logical explanation that could discredit him and disprove the miracle which Christ had performed. Therefore, they resorted to insults and threw him bodily out of the synagogue.

Expulsion from the synagogue was perhaps the one punishment the Pharisees had at their command. It meant social ostracism. It would cause many of his friends to turn their backs on him. The blind man must have been aware of this and realized the Pharisees would resort to it because of their hatred of Christ. But still he answered their questions truthfully and bravely, not fearing the consequences. Expulsion from the synagogue was a small price to pay in comparison with the gift he had received from Christ, receiving his sight.

When Christ heard of his expulsion, he sought out the cured man and asked him if he believed in the Son of God. Again he responded sincerely, "Who is he, sir, that I may believe in him?" Jesus replied, "You have seen him; he is speaking to you now." And the man affirmed his belief and bowed down to worship him.

Because this man had stood up to the Pharisees and told the truth, Christ bestowed on him a second gift and favor, the gift of faith. It was as spectacular as the gift of sight, but in terms of spiritual values, a gift even more precious and meaningful.

In this gospel narrative there is related a beautiful progression in the blind man's idea of Jesus. At first he called him the man who rubbed mud on his eyes. Later, before the Pharisees, he called him a prophet. Later still, when Christ met him a second time and revealed his true identity, the man worshipped him and acknowledged him to be the Son of God.

From Christ's hands he was the recipient of a twofold gift. He was granted the gift of seeing the light of day and, later, the light of faith. Let us learn from and follow the example of this blind man. Let us reaffirm our faith in Christ as the Son of God. The light of faith in this world leads to the enjoyment of eternal light and happiness in the next. God bless you.

# "A"    Fifth Sunday of Lent

*John 11:1-45*

With the exception of his own resurrection, to which it led, the raising of Lazarus from the dead has been called Christ's greatest miracle. Certainly it was the most decisive one he performed. It led the Sanhedrin to decree Jesus' death.

At this time Jesus was teaching in the district of Perea, on the Eastern side of the Jordan River. A messenger arrived to tell him that his friend Lazarus was critically ill. Lazarus lived in Bethany with his two sisters, Mary and Martha. Our Lord had no home of his own, but the home of Lazarus was probably more like home for Christ than any other place he visited. As the gospel states, Christ loved Lazarus and his sisters very much.

But even after receiving this message, which Christ certainly knew anyway through his divine knowledge, he lingered for two more days in Perea, preaching and carrying out his divine mission. He said, "This sickness is not to end in death; rather, it is for God's glory. . . ."

Finally, after two days had elapsed, he said to his Apostles, "Let us go back to Judea." Bethany is located in Judea, only two miles east of Jerusalem. Christ and his Apostles arrived there to learn that Lazarus had died and that his body had been buried for four days.

In Palestine and other surrounding countries with hot climates, it was customary to bury a person the same day that he died. In those times there was no way to preserve the body for any length of time, and decomposition began very quickly. But even though burial took place on the day of death, the period of heavy mourning lasted for a week. Hence, many friends and acquaintances were still to be found at the home of Lazarus and his sisters.

Martha, who acted as spokesman for the family, spoke to Christ: "Lord, if you had been here, my brother would never have died." The reputation of Christ had preceded him; he was known as the healer of the sick. No sickness or degree of suffering had stumped him. When he told a sick man that he was healed, the sickness disappeared regardless of its intensity or nature.

Martha continued, "Even now, I am sure that God will give you whatever you ask of him." Martha's faith was strong enough to hope that Christ could raise her brother from the dead even though he had been buried for four days. On two previous occasions Christ had raised the dead to life. He had raised to life the daughter of Jairus, but in that instance the girl had just then died.

The second such miracle was the raising to life of the only son of the widow of Naim. In this second instance, Christ and his disciples had met the burial procession. They were about to place his body in a tomb when Christ took the boy by the hand and he sat up and Jesus gave him back to his mother.

But both these previous miracles had been performed on the same day as death occurred. Lazarus had been dead for four days. Christ certainly was aware of this even before he came to Bethany. He certainly knew from the very beginning what he intended to do.

Christ may have waited these few additional days before performing this miracle to make the prediction of his own resurrection more realistic. It was a symbol or type of the time that his own body would remain in the tomb.

Christ said to Martha, "I am the resurrection and the life; whoever believes in me, though he should die, will come to life; and whoever is alive and believes in me will never die. Do you believe this?"

The life to which Christ was referring, of course, was the life of the soul. He was stating that our souls would continue to live even after our bodies had died. He was saying that our souls would live eternally after death.

Martha affirmed her belief in this when Christ asked her and she went on to declare her belief that Christ was the Son of God, the long-awaited Messiah who would redeem the world.

Following her affirmation Christ proceeded on his plan of action. He asked to see the body of Lazarus. He wept true tears of compassion. This caused the Jews to remark, "See how much he loved him!"

As was customary in those days, the tomb of Lazarus was a cave in the rock. A large stone had been rolled to the entrance to it to seal the tomb. Christ asked that the stone be rolled away. At this Martha protested that he had already been buried for four days and that his body would have begun to decay. She added that "surely there will be a stench." But this protest of Martha's only went to point out the greatness of the miracle Christ was about to perform, that he raised to life a decaying body.

When the stone had been rolled away Christ prayed aloud saying, "Father, I thank you for having heard me." Frequently in performing miracles, Christ first gave thanks to God. Christ was teaching us how to act — when asking for favors of God we should pray to him and thank him for all the benefits he has bestowed upon us.

Then Christ called loudly, "Lazarus, come out!" The dead man came out, bound hand and foot with linen strips, his head wrapped in a cloth. Christ had raised to life his friend Lazarus who had been dead for days, whose body had begun to decompose. It was the greatest miracle he had performed so far. It was a foreshadowing of his own resurrection to come. This miracle caused many of the Jews to believe in Jesus and his doctrine.

But in meditating on this miracle of Christ, let us realize that death eventually will be the lot of us all. Some day death will claim our souls. Some day each one of us will face God in judgment. Our destiny hangs in the balance. If death comes upon us while we are in serious sin, death will be for us our entry into eternal punishment. This we should strive to avoid at all costs.

We should strive to live in the state of sanctifying grace. Death, then, will not mark for us the beginning of everlasting punishment; rather it will mark the beginning of eternal happiness. God bless you.

# "A"  Passion Sunday (Palm Sunday)

*Matthew 26:14 — 27:66*

Today is Passion or Palm Sunday. This is the day on which our Lord Jesus Christ entered the city of Jerusalem on a triumphal march more than nineteen hundred years ago. Christ, who had been preaching in Galilee, determined to celebrate the feast of the Passover in Jerusalem. As he drew near to the city, he sent his disciples ahead to procure a donkey.

They brought the animal to Jesus and laid their garments on it, and Jesus rode it into the city of Jerusalem. A great multitude of people gathered to meet our Lord. They kept shouting: "Hosanna! Blessed is he who comes in the name of the Lord!" They cut palm branches and laid them in his way. The people were rejoicing, for this was the Christ who raised Lazarus from the dead. This was the same Christ who multiplied the loaves and fishes to feed five thousand people. This was the Christ who gave sight to the blind and cured the lepers. They were manifesting their admiration for him.

But alas, how fickle was their acclaim! Where would these same people be on Friday of that week when Christ was being tried before Pontius Pilate? Many of these same people would be found in the crowd that on Friday would shout, "Crucify him!"

Perhaps you may think that if you had personally been present in Jerusalem during these stirring days, your faith would have remained strong. You would not have weakened or gone along with the crowd. But the crowd did demand his death.

Consider what Christ did for you on the first Holy Thursday. He took bread into his hands, blessed it and broke it and gave it to his Apostles, saying, "Take this and eat it; this is my body." Then taking a chalice of wine, he blessed it and gave it to his Apostles and told them "this is my blood, the blood of the covenant, to be poured out in behalf of many for the forgiveness of sins." By these words Christ changed bread and wine into his body and blood.

Christ perpetuated this sacrament when he told his Apostles, "Do this as a remembrance of me." He gave to them and their successors in the Church the power to do what he had done, to change bread and wine into his body and blood. He established the Holy Eucharist as a sacrament.

Following the Last Supper, Christ led his Apostles to the Garden of Olives to pray. There, anticipating the sufferings he was about to undergo, he suffered a bloody sweat. Finally after three hours of prayer and agony, one of his Apostles betrayed him to the Jews with a kiss. For thirty pieces of silver he betrayed our divine Savior to the soldiers who led him away.

Christ was taken before Caiaphas, the high priest, to be judged. A parade of false witnesses was then brought forward. After much false testimony Christ was led before the Sanhedrin. His captors began to spit on him and to buffet him. Throughout the long night Christ was mocked and maltreated.

Early on Good Friday morning they led him bound to Pontius Pilate. When Pilate learned that he was a Galilean, he sent him to Herod Antipas.

Herod in turn treated him with contempt and clothed him in a bright purple robe and sent him back to Pilate. Pilate admitted to the chief priests and people that he found no guilt in Christ, but as a means of appeasement, he asked the crowd whom they wished released to them, Christ or the known criminal Barabbas. They chose Barabbas. When Pilate asked what they wished him to do with Christ, they replied, "Crucify him!"

Pilate then delivered Christ up to be scourged and crowned with thorns. What great pain those sharp thorns must have caused him as they were pressed down deeply into his head. The scourging left his body bloody and torn. But Christ willingly endured this torment because he wished to redeem us. But then Pilate saw that even this cruel and unjust punishment of Christ did not satisfy the Jews. They would be satisfied with nothing short of his death. Casting justice aside, Pilate gave in to their wishes and handed Christ over to them to be led away and crucified.

Leading Christ along the way from Pilate's courtyard to Mt. Calvary outside of Jerusalem, the soldiers nailed him to the cross and left him there to die the terrible death of crucifixion. This was the most painful death known to the ancient world. The weight of one's body was suspended by a few nails and ropes. The contracture of the muscles caused one to want to move, but each movement brought a new torture. A burning thirst seemed to consume one's whole body. Finally after three hours of this agony Christ succumbed in death.

Holy Week, which commemorates all these events, comes only once each year. It is a time to gain many and great graces. By next Sunday Holy Week will be a thing of the past. What will it have meant to you? How will you spend these important days this week? Do not pass by this opportunity of grace. Attend Mass and the services in your parish church. Make it a truly holy week in your own life. God bless you.

# "A"    Easter Sunday

*John 20:1-9*

Once while preaching in Galilee, Christ made a claim about himself. He said, "Destroy this temple, and in three days I shall rebuild it." The temple he referred to was his body.

Still on another occasion he said, "An evil and adulterous generation seeks a sign, but no sign shall be given it except the sign of Jonah the prophet. As Jonah was three days and three nights in the belly of the whale, so shall the Son of Man be in the earth three days and three nights."

Jewish leaders remembered these prophecies of Christ even after they had put him to death. Therefore, with Pilate's permission, they placed a guard around his tomb. But the guard they placed there only served as witnesses of his glorious resurrection.

Early on Easter Sunday morning the two Marys, Mary Magdalene and Mary the mother of James and Salome, brought spices to the tomb in order that they might anoint the body of Jesus. They asked one another who would roll back the stone for them. But upon coming to the tomb, they beheld the stone was rolled back and a young man sitting on the right side clothed in a white robe. He directed the women to tell Peter and the other disciples that Jesus had risen from the dead — he was not there but he would precede them into Galilee.

The two women immediately carried the good news to the disciples. At once Peter and John started running for the tomb. As St. John mentioned in his gospel, he outraced Peter to the tomb. They both beheld that it was empty.

Later Mary Magdalene returned. She saw two angels sitting where Christ had been laid, and she began to weep. A voice asked her why she was weeping. She thought at first that it was the gardener, but then when he spoke her name, she recognized him as Christ himself. Jesus told her that he must ascend to his Father. Mary carried the good news to the Apostles.

That same evening Christ appeared to two disciples on their way to Emmaus. At first they did not recognize him, but later, when he broke bread with them at their evening meal, they realized who he was. Then suddenly he vanished. Christ appeared to the Apostles in Jerusalem, Thomas being absent. He appeared again a week later when all were present.

Christ proved beyond any shadow of a doubt the falseness of the rumor the elders and chief priests spread about him — that his followers had stolen his body. He appeared many times to many people. On one occasion he appeared to more than five hundred people.

Christ's resurrection was a shock to some of the Jewish people. It was a source of embarrassment. They were at a loss as to what to do about it. They could not seize him a second time and put him to death. He made them look foolish by proving he had power over life and death itself.

Their consciences prompted them to go to Christ and confess their guilt — to admit they were wrong in not believing him and beg his forgiveness for having put him to death. But their pride was too great to permit them to do this. They were perverse in their sin.

Christ's resurrection was conclusive proof that he was the Son of God as he had claimed. He showed that he had power over life and death itself, a power which only God possesses. It was a fulfillment of the prophecy he had made. It was the sign of Jonah — the rebuilding of the temple. The guards at the tomb and many others attested to this.

His resurrection was his greatest miracle — the miracle upon which the Christian religion depends. He had foretold it. If Christ had been proven wrong in this one instance, his Church would have crumbled. His followers would have fallen away. But this was not to be.

Christ's resurrection confirmed the faith of his followers. It convinced many of the truth of his teachings. But there still remained many whose hearts were hardened, who rejected this undeniable proof of his divinity.

During the Roman persecutions by the Emperor Hadrian in the year 132 A.D., orders were given to heap a mound of earth upon the Holy Sepulchre and to plant a grove of trees atop it. These orders of the emperor were carried out.

But in the fourth century when the persecutions ended, St. Helena, the mother of the Emperor Constantine, ordered the grove of trees cut down and the ground cleared away. The Holy Sepulchre was uncovered and opened for veneration. St. Helena was also responsible in the same manner for finding the cross on which Christ was crucified.

On Easter Christ did not disappoint us. He rose as he said he would. Let us renew our faith this Easter Sunday morning. As the souls in Limbo rejoiced when Christ came to preach to them on Good Friday when his soul left his body, let us rejoice that he has risen from the dead. Let his resurrection be a source of inspiration and hope for us. It is a pledge of our own resurrection to come. God bless you.

# "A"     Second Sunday of Easter

*John 20:19-31*

In the year 212 B.C. the armies and navies of the great Roman Empire set siege to the Greek city of Syracuse on the island of Sicily. For two years the Romans continued this siege, making little or no progress against the unusual and ingenious defense of this city. For behind the defense was the brilliant and inventive mind of the scientist Archimedes.

When the Roman ships attacked the city from the sea, giant machines hurled down rocks upon them and sank many ships. Still other ships were seized in giant pincers and carried off through the air. Huge glasses were used to concentrate the rays of the sun on the attacking wooden ships and set them on fire at distances of half a mile away.

When events were reported back to Rome, the leaders and learned men there were incredulous. They laughed at these stories and would not believe them. Some of them demanded to be brought to Syracuse to see these events with their own eyes. These Roman leaders were lacking in faith.

But as faith is a necessary virtue in a natural sense, it is even more important in the spiritual realm. Faith is the underlying and basic virtue in the Catholic religion. A shining example of the lack of faith and then of its strong profession can be seen in the life of the Apostle St. Thomas.

The death of Christ was a heavy blow to Thomas; his faith was so shattered he refused to believe the report of the other Apostles that Christ had risen from the dead and was alive. His answer to them was, "I will never believe it without probing the nailprints in his hands, without putting my finger in the nailmarks and my hand into his side."

A week later the disciples were once again gathered together, and this time Thomas was with them. Christ again appeared to them and invited Thomas to do as he had requested — to take his finger and examine his hands and put his hand into his side. Immediately Thomas fell down in adoration before Christ and said in response, "My Lord and my God!"

This is the fullest and most explicit expression of faith recorded in the gospels. It is doubly an expression of Christ's divinity. It is a sublime admission of the Messianic character of Christ. St. Thomas went on to become a great missionary, winning the martyr's crown in India.

Faith is one of the three theological virtues. It is a virtue by which we believe all those things God has revealed. St. Paul tells us that faith is the root of all virtues.

Faith comes to us in the Sacrament of Baptism. The priest in baptizing an infant brings faith into his soul along with sanctifying grace. Faith begins to grow as one reaches the age of reason and learns the revealed truths of our religion.

Faith does not depend on our completely understanding the revealed truths of our religion. It is not founded on seeing or knowing them fully. Rather faith concerns itself with many things which do not appear to our senses. By faith we place our belief in such mysteries as the Holy Trinity and the Incarnation.

In the supernatural sphere faith plays a role comparable to that of reason in the natural sphere. It has been called the staff which supports reason. Faith never requires us to believe anything contrary to our human reason, for God is the author of both and, being all-truthful, cannot contradict himself. Faith concerns itself with mysteries above and beyond the grasp of reason.

When one makes and act of faith, his authority for believing is that of God himself, who tells us what we must believe to be saved. He is the greatest authority possible. Practically every day we make acts of human faith. We believe newspaper accounts of space flights and bombings. But the human authority which reports these events can be mistaken. Not so with God! God is all-knowing and all-truthful. He can never deceive nor be deceived.

Faith is a most necessary virtue to obtain salvation. St. Paul tells us that without faith it is impossible to please God. Faith is the life of the just man and the strength of his soul. Faith enlightens our understanding; it infuses a love of God within us.

Faith is a gift of God — a gift he gives to those whom he loves. It is not something to be taken for granted. Therefore, we should be grateful to God for bestowing this gift upon us, this gift which so many millions on this earth do not possess today.

Let us each day make an act of faith in God. Let us ask St. Thomas to strengthen our faith, so that on the day of judgment, our faith will be a brightly burning beacon to illumine our way into the kingdom of heaven. God bless you.

# "A"  Third Sunday of Easter

*Luke 24:13-35*

The body of Christ was no longer in the tomb! Jerusalem was buzzing! The miracle man, the great preacher, the man who had been so kind to everyone, but whom the Scribes and Pharisees envied because of his popularity, had been put to death. One of his own Apostles had betrayed him for thirty pieces of silver. He had been brought to trial on trumped-up charges. Even Pilate was aware of his innocence but had allowed him to be crucified to curry the favor of the crowd.

Because he had said he would rise again on the third day, Pilate had stationed a guard around his tomb. But the guards were helpless as two men in white rolled away the stone from it. They were probably angels, but the Pharisees wouldn't admit this. They didn't believe in angels. The guards had been paid to say the Apostles took his body away. But everyone knew this wasn't true. The Apostles were scared and frightened, as the Jews wanted them to be. Only one of them had dared to come to Calvary and stand beneath his Master's cross.

But then, one of the two women who came to the tomb early on Easter Sunday morning claimed she saw angels who told her Christ had risen. This was the same Mary who had once been a public sinner, but had turned over a new leaf and reformed. But even so, how could this be, for no one had ever risen on his own from the dead before?

This was the tenor of the talk as Cleopas and his companion walked along the road heading west from Jerusalem toward the small village of Emmaus. As they went along their way to this village only seven miles distant from the Holy City, a stranger joined them. Their eyes were fixed on one another, and they did not recognize him.

Cleopas and his companion could not understand why the stranger did not know of these things. But then the stranger surprised them. He began with Moses in the Old Testament and quoted all the hundred or more passages which referred to the Messiah or Redeemer. He quoted for them passages which they were familiar with, which said that the Redeemer would be a great leader and free his people Israel. But then, he also quoted passages for them which said the Messiah would be delivered up to the Jews and would suffer for them and be put to death. These were passages which they had overlooked and did not think about. As Cleopas said later, "Were not our hearts burning within as he talked to us on the road and explained the Scriptures?"

When they arrived at their destination, the stranger said he would go on, but Cleopas and his companion begged him to stay with them as the time of day was so late, and he acquiesced.

Scripture is silent on who Cleopas and his companion actually were. Tradition tells us, however, that Cleopas was the brother of St. Joseph, the foster-father of Christ, which would make him the uncle of Christ. Tradition tells us that his son, Simeon, succeeded St. James as bishop of Jerusalem when the former was martyred. Tradition also tells us that the companion was St. Luke, the writer of today's gospel, which relates all the details of this marvelous event. But in the true spirit of humility, he does not mention his own name in Scripture.

Having disguised his true identity so that he would not be recognized, Christ accepted the invitation of these two disciples and entered with them into a house in Emmaus. At the evening meal, when the stranger broke bread and distributed it to them, their eyes were opened and they recognized him to be Christ himself.

Scarcely had the disciples recognized the Savior when they no longer saw him. He disappeared from their sight, thus revealing to them the nature of the glorious body which he now possessed, the conditions of whose existence were unlike those of other men.

Our Savior had opened their eyes. They had recovered their hope. The effect was as sudden as it was deep. Immediately they set out on the road back to Jerusalem, despite the fact that it was dusk and night would soon be upon them. They woke the Apostles and other disciples from their sleep and broke the good news to them. They had seen the Lord.

Their faith, which had been shaken by Christ's crucifixion, was now restored. The cloud of doubts which had enshrouded them had now disappeared. They had received the personal verification which they were seeking. Christ had furnished it for them.

But just as Christ was with these two disciples and they did not recognize him, sometimes he is present with us and we do not recognize him. We are unaware of his presence. The disciples were preoccupied; their thoughts were on many other things.

How often are our thoughts and attention centered on material things around us? The work and activities of everyday life cloud out the presence of God. God dwells in the hearts of the faithful through his gift of sanctifying grace. Frequently he prompts us with actual graces. He comes to us bodily and physically when we approach the Communion rail. He is present in each one of us through his creative actions. He not only made us, but his continual creative act keeps us alive every day we spend here on earth. God watches us, too, by sending a guardian angel to watch over us.

God is with us in these many ways. Let us believe in him and think of him often. Then we shall see him through the eyes of faith. As he finally revealed himself to his two disciples in Emmaus, he shall make known his presence to you. God bless you.

# "A" Fourth Sunday of Easter

*John 10:1-10*

One group among the Jews that constantly followed our Lord and kept track of his teachings was the Pharisees. Their reasons for following him were not always the best. They were jealous of his following and were constantly looking for ways of trapping him in his speech. Christ pointed out on various occasions that they were hypocrites, but he was generally most kind and considerate to them.

In today's gospel of St. John, Christ addresses to them one of the most beautiful parables of all time, that of the Good Shepherd. He said, "I am the good shepherd." He then proceeded to distinguish the difference between a good shepherd and a hireling. A good shepherd will lay down his life for his sheep, but the hireling, whose own the sheep are not, sees the wolf coming and flees. Christ literally did lay down his life for his sheep on the cross.

The first duty of a shepherd is to know his flock. He is familiar with all the sheep that belong to him, and they are constantly on his mind. He counts their number frequently to see that none are missing or have strayed from the flock. He watches and observes that none are sick or suffering in any way. As our Good Shepherd, Christ knows our temptations, our struggles and our failings. He is aware of our safety and well-being at all times.

The second duty of a shepherd is to feed his flock. A shepherd must lead his flock to streams to drink and to green pastures to graze. He must keep them away from poisonous weeds which would harm or kill them. As our Good Shepherd, Christ nourishes us with his own body and blood. He has given us the sacraments as a constant source of life and grace.

The third duty of a shepherd is to protect his flock. He must not lead them near dangerous cliffs or ravines. He must protect them from the dangers of wolves or other predators. As our Good Shepherd, Christ surrounds the soul of each of us with a mantle of grace. He gives us sufficient grace to ward off any temptation. In time of danger we need only to pray to him, and he will not fail to hear and help us.

As members of Christ's flock, we have an obligation to know and follow our Shepherd. We come to know him through instruction in Christian doctrine, through our formal classes in religion. We know our Shepherd through the Sunday gospels and sermons in Church. We know him by reading Catholic newspapers and periodicals.

Once we know our Shepherd, we have the obligation to follow him also. We are obliged to obey the Ten Commandments of God and the precepts of the Church. We must place our life and well-being in his fatherly care and follow where he will lead us.

No one would doubt for an instant that Christ is our Good Shepherd. But in the divine plan of redemption, Christ returned to heaven and entrusted his flock into the hands of other shepherds to care for. Through the priesthood he has made other men shepherds of his flock. Among a multitude of good shepherds, one who fits the description of the Good Shepherd was Father Damien, the leper priest. A century ago when lepers in the Hawaiian Islands were exiled to Molokai, Father Damien volunteered to care for their spiritual needs.

At first the lepers on the island were skeptical of him. But then they saw how he helped care for their wounds and their sickness. They watched him lay pipeline to bring them fresh drinking water. They listened as he explained God's loving care for each of them. They observed that he would bring the Holy Eucharist to the very ill who could not come to Church to receive it.

Observing how well Father Damien came to know, feed and protect his flock, the lepers gave him an affectionate nickname. They called him the "Good Shepherd." They saw him as a true follower of Christ, who took care of his flock. Needless to say, the lepers of Molokai proved to be docile sheep in his fold.

From today's gospel, let us learn a lesson. Let us recognize Christ as our Shepherd, our leader. Let us be grateful for the excellent care he gives us. Let us resolve to be docile sheep in his fold. God bless you.

# "A"     Fifth Sunday of Easter

*John 14:1-12*

The Gospel of St. John is different from the other three gospels in the New Testament. It was the last of the four to be written. St. John wrote it about the year 97 A.D. when he was an old man. Undoubtedly he had read and was familiar with the gospels of Matthew, Mark and Luke. He purposely did not repeat many of the miracles and parables which they had told so well.

But St. John did have something important to write. For example, five chapters of his gospel, chapters thirteen through seventeen, deal with the beautiful discourse Christ gave to his Apostles following the Last Supper on Holy Thursday night. This is only briefly mentioned by the other three evangelists. It is a part of this beautiful discourse that is contained in the gospel read at today's Mass.

Christ said to his Apostles, "Let not your heart be troubled. You believe in God, believe also in me." Christ with his divine knowledge knew that he was about to be arrested that same night and led off to face the Sanhedrin and Pontius Pilate and be put to death. Christ knew that the world of the Apostles, who had followed him for the past three years and believed in him, would be a world of chaos. He was giving them an anchor of hope that would stabilize them in the sea of trouble which would soon engulf them.

Christ made a beautiful and consoling statement, "In my Father's house there are many mansions." In our troubled world, where we hear of overcrowding in some of our cities and overpopulation in some countries, it is pacifying to hear that God has prepared a mansion — an eternal dwelling place in the kingdom of heaven — for each one of us. There will be room for everybody in the world to come. This is where God wants and wishes every one of us to go.

Earthly hotels and inns are built to accommodate limited numbers. When they're filled to capacity, travelers are turned away. But not so in heaven. There God is the divine architect who built it. With divine knowledge he has built heaven large enough to accommodate all who earnestly try to enter.

Christ lovingly adds, "And if I shall go and prepare a place for you, I will come back and take you to myself. . . ." Christ was saying that although he had come on earth on a divine mission, he would return to his heavenly kingdom. It was his desire to lead his Apostles and all of us to enjoy this paradise with him.

But let us not deceive ourselves. It is not easy to follow Christ. The path along which he would lead us would be a path of suffering and death. The very night he told of his love for his Apostles, he would be cruelly scourged and crowned with thorns. If we are to follow Christ, we too must expect to suffer for him on this earth. But Christ will be a guide to us in time of suffering; he will be a pioneer to lead men to eternal happiness.

At this point in his discourse St. Thomas, one of the Twelve, interrupted him. Thomas will never be called a great thinker or theologian. He bluntly confessed his ignorance: "Lord, we know not where you go; and how can we know the way?" Yet Thomas did have an admirable quality in him; he was honest and sincere.

In answer to Thomas' doubt, Christ made one of the most meaningful and descriptive replies concerning himself that is to be found in all of Holy Scripture. He said, "I am the way, and the truth, and the life."

In the Old Testament the Jews struggled for each of these goals separately; for instance for forty years Moses sought the way to the promised land, wandering through the desert of Sinai. But now Christ said he was the embodiment of the way.

In the Old Testament the Psalmist wrote in the twenty-fifth psalm, ". . . teach me your paths. Direct me in your truth. . . ." Philosophers and scholars have been seeking truth for endless centuries, but now Christ said he was simply "the truth."

The Old Testament psalmist petitioned, "Will you not . . . give us life . . .?" But here again in response to these centuries of longing and praying, Christ was answering their prayers. He declared himself to be the embodiment of all three goals — the way, the truth, and the life.

In the Middle Ages the religious writer Thomas à Kempis paraphrased this expression. He wrote, "I am the way you must follow, the truth that you must believe and the life that you must hope for." His sentiments ring true; they are so obvious. Christ is the road that we must follow to reach the Father. He is the channel through which truth and life come to us. But then the simpler and more profound statement of Christ implies all this also.

The Apostle Philip then interrupted him; he asked Christ to show him the Father. His request was a logical one. It flowed from the Jewish belief in monotheism — namely that there is only one God. All neighboring nations around Palestine believed in many gods.

Philip was trying to reconcile in his mind his belief in one God and the words of Christ, telling of two persons, the Father and the Son. Once again Christ patiently answered his question. He said, "I am in the Father, and the Father in me. . . ."

Christ did not attempt to explain the mystery of the Trinity. However, he did offer a motive for believing in it. He said to "believe for the sake of the works themselves."

The Apostles knew that Christ had performed many miracles; he had cured the sick, the lame and the blind. Christ promised them that faith in him would allow them to perform miracles also. Christ foresaw that their faith in him would be challenged. He wanted them to fortify their faith and be prepared to repel any attack made against it.

Christ is asking that each one of us have a strong faith also. There will be days when the trials of life will test our faith. But whatever tribulations assail us, let us realize that Christ loves us. He has prepared a mansion in heaven for each of us. We must believe in him. He is the way, the truth, and the life. Only he can lead us to our heavenly home. God bless you.

# "A"    Sixth Sunday of Easter

*John 14: 15-21*

Although today is the sixth Sunday of Easter, the gospel read at today's Mass is taken from the discourse that Christ delivered to his Apostles on Holy Thursday night immediately following the Last Supper. St. John treasured these words in his memory and related them many times. Finally he set them down in writing some sixty years later in his gospel.

In the early days of his public life, Christ spoke to his Apostles about his heavenly Father. Only much later did he speak of the Holy Spirit. But now following the Last Supper Christ speaks freely of both the Father and the Holy Spirit.

Christ said, "I will pray the Father and he will give you another Counselor." By the term "another" Christ meant a third person like unto the Father and himself — a person who would also have divine power.

Christ continued to list some of the divine attributes of the Paraclete. He said he would be with them always. Christ meant that he would have eternal existence. There would be no end to his existence on earth or his co-dwelling with the members of his Church.

Christ likewise calls him the "Spirit of truth." By this term he means that the Holy Spirit will be a Counselor who will be with them and guide them along the path of truth. Not only will the Spirit of Truth abide with the Apostles but also with their successors. He will abide with his Church forever to guide it along a truthful course.

Christ testifies that the indwelling of the Holy Spirit, the Spirit of Truth within his Church, may be hidden, but it will be real and perpetual. Christ said,

"I will not leave you desolate. . . ." Since Christ had already declared himself to be the Truth, then the Spirit of Truth will perform his office by bringing to the disciples a remembrance of all that Jesus said and did.

Christ performed his mission well in teaching about the Holy Spirit. His name is mentioned three hundred times in Holy Scripture. But not only did Christ teach about the Holy Spirit, but the Spirit himself manifested his presence here on earth on three different occasions.

At the baptism of Christ in the River Jordan, the Holy Spirit appeared in the form of a dove, the emblem of love and purity. Again at the Transfiguration of Christ on Mt. Tabor, the Holy Spirit appeared in the form of a bright cloud. A third time he appeared on Pentecost Sunday.

This third coming was the one which Christ had foretold so well. On this occasion the Holy Spirit appeared in the form of fiery tongues and descended upon the Apostles and the Blessed Virgin present in the upper room in Jerusalem. His appearance in the form of fiery tongues was symbolic of the effect he was to have upon their souls. The Holy Spirit confirmed the Apostles in their faith. He gave them spiritual strength and courage.

Christ imparted to the Apostles a knowledge of the faith in his lifetime. But even while possessing this knowledge, they remained timid and afraid. On Holy Thursday night when Christ was arrested by Jewish leaders, St. Peter, the leader of the Twelve, denied three times that he knew Our Lord. When Christ was crucified, only one Apostle, St. John, remained beneath his cross. The others fled in fear.

Following Christ's ascension into heaven, the Apostles again gathered in fear in the upper room in Jerusalem in the absence of their leader, Christ. They hid themselves from the Jewish people. But following the descent of the Holy Spirit, their conduct was far different.

They openly and bravely preached the Christian faith. On the first Pentecost Sunday four thousand converts were baptized and brought into the newly formed Christian Church. The Apostles literally fulfilled the command of Christ to go and make disciples of all nations. Sts. Peter and Paul went to Rome, St. James to Spain, St. Thomas to India. All but one met with the death of martyrdom.

The missionary zeal of the Apostles is a direct testimony to the presence of the Holy Spirit within the Church. He worked a moral miracle in their souls. He transformed the Apostles from fearful followers into brave and zealous missionaries. The Holy Spirit was with the Church in its infant years and is with it still. He has inspired and guided it throughout the centuries.

The Holy Spirit had a profound effect upon the life and conversion of one of the great leaders of the Catholic Church of the last century — Henry Cardinal Manning. As a young man Henry Manning became an Anglican minister and published a book of sermons. His book was widely acclaimed, but then one day a friend stopped him and made a criticism of it. He said that in the entire book there was not a single mention of the Holy Spirit.

This omission was not intentional; it was something that young Manning was unaware of. For the next two years he studied and read all he could about the Holy Spirit. The result of this study was his conversion to Catholicism.

Later still he became a Catholic priest and rose to be a cardinal in the Church. Throughout his life his special devotion was to the Holy Spirit. The Spirit of Truth brought him to membership in the Church and through him worked much good.

Let us learn through the example of this holy man — let us learn through the teaching of Christ himself in today's gospel of the important role the Holy Spirit plays in the Church. He is our advocate and our protector. Let us pray to him frequently. Let us ask his aid in strengthening our faith. The Holy Spirit, the Spirit of Truth, whom Christ promised to send us, is with us forever. Never will he desert us. God bless you.

# "A"  Ascension

*Matthew 28: 16-20*

Visitors to the city of Jerusalem are inevitably impressed with the panorama of hill country surrounding the city. Looking to the east the summit of Mount Olivet commands your view. To reach it one must cross a small stream, the Brook of Kidron. Then one ascends a small plateau, the Garden of Olives. Beyond this the road from Jerusalem divides into two forks. The left fork leads one to the summit of Mount Olivet.

This was the road along which Christ led his Apostles on the fortieth day after his resurrection from the dead. During these forty days Christ had appeared to many people. He had appeared to Mary Magdalene and to the two disciples on their way to Emmaus on Easter Sunday. Later he had appeared to ten Apostles in Jerusalem, Thomas being absent. A week later he appeared to them again, this time Thomas being present. Christ had returned to Galilee and appeared to many there. Once he had appeared to a crowd of five hundred people.

Now on the fortieth day following his resurrection, Christ led his mother and Apostles to Mount Olivet. He stopped to address them, "All authority in heaven and on earth has been given to me." He was explaining that the power he had received from his heavenly Father was unlimited.

Thereupon he commissioned them, "Go therefore and make disciples of all nations, baptizing them in the name of the Father and of the Son and of the Holy Spirit, teaching them to observe everything I have commanded you. . . ."

On a previous occasion Christ had sent his Apostles out to preach, but he had cautioned them to preach only to the lost souls of the house of Israel — that is, the Jewish people. Now his command to them is to make disciples of all nations. He is sending them to the Gentiles as well as the Jews. He is sending them to teach and baptize all men. He is excluding no one from the good news of his gospel. He is establishing one of the four marks of his Church, that of being catholic, of teaching all men.

After speaking these words to his Apostles, Christ ascended from the ground where he was standing. He rose into the sky above and disappeared from their view. The Apostles were gazing upward, trying to follow his path of ascent, when two men dressed in white, obviously angels, appeared on the scene and asked, "Why do you stand looking into heaven?" They announced that Christ had ascended to his heavenly Father.

Christ in ascending into heaven was simply returning to his heavenly home. He had always dwelt in heaven with God his Father. For a few brief years Christ had taken on the body of man and come down here to earth. He had come on a specific mission — to redeem mankind and reopen the gates of heaven which had been closed by the original sin of our first parents. But now his mission was completed. He had accomplished his intended task. He had redeemed mankind. With his mission completed, Christ was now simply returning home.

In ascending into heaven, Christ brought with him the souls of the Old Testament who had been waiting for him in Limbo — the souls who for all these many centuries had died but could not enter heaven — the souls who had waited so many centuries for the Messiah to come and save them.

Now at last their longing and their prayer were answered. The Messiah had come, Christ, in reentering heaven, opened the gates of heaven to all mankind. Now once again man could attain eternal happiness. He led a glorious procession of saints of the Old Testament into heaven with him. Among them was St. Joseph, his foster father, who had died some time before.

One may call the feast of Christ's Ascension the dividing line between the Old and New Testaments. The gates of heaven, which had been closed by the original sin of our first parents, had been reopened by Christ's Ascension. With heaven open, man could again directly save his soul.

Christ is our mediator in heaven before the throne of his Father. He ascended into heaven with his human body. He dignified our nature by returning in human form to heaven's heights. As the possessor of a human nature, Christ can act as our mediator and intercessor. He can intercede for man before the throne of God, as one human for another.

His ascension into heaven with a human body is a pledge of our own ascension on the day of the last judgment. As heaven is now the home for his human body, we can rely on his promise that it will become the home for ours on the day of general judgment.

Down through time, God has seen fit to bless certain individuals with special supernatural gifts. One such person so blessed this century was Theresa Neumann, a German woman. Theresa was granted the stigmata, the imprint of nails in her hands and feet, and at various times was granted heavenly visions. Such a vision occurred on the feast of the Ascension in 1939 in Konnersreuth, Germany.

Theresa Neumann described in detail to her parish priest what she saw on this occasion. She beheld the original scene on Mount Olivet where Christ left his Apostles and ascended heavenward. She observed that Our Blessed Mother was there and that she was leaning on the shoulder of St. John for support. When Christ ascended, Mary looked to the ground, and there she beheld the footprints of her Divine Son in the rock where he had been standing before he ascended. Theresa was privileged to see these footprints herself.

Let us recall that the Ascension of Christ has brought many benefits to us. It means that the gates of heaven are now open for us to enter. Christ now resides in heaven as our mediator and friend. He is willing and anxious to help us. Let us adore the risen Christ. Let us beg of him the favors we need. Let us pray to him that one day our bodies may share with him the gift of eternal glory. God bless you.

# "A"    Seventh Sunday of Easter

*John 17: 1-11*

How frequently in the gospel pages of the New Testament is Christ to be found at prayer! Today's gospel is no exception. Taken from the seventeenth chapter of St. John, this gospel passage is part of the long and beautiful discourse which Christ addressed to his Apostles on Holy Thursday night following the Last Supper in Jerusalem.

This particular section of it is called the "High-Priestly Prayer" because in it Christ prays for his disciples. He prays aloud, and this serves as an instruction for his followers. He prays for himself and then prays for the Apostles whom the Father has entrusted to him.

Christ begins, "Father, the hour has come; glorify your Son. . . ." Glory is well-deserved praise. Christ has merited this glory or praise from his heavenly Father for performing his mission here on earth so well. Christ has already given glory to his Father by preaching his gospel. He has honored him through the many miracles which he performed.

In effect, Christ was saying he has finished the work his heavenly Father has assigned to him — he has finished it save for the final and most important step of enduring a cruel crucifixion. Having completed his mission so well, Christ is asking in prayer that his Father glorify him. This glory which he would receive would be a benefit for his Apostles and followers.

Having prayed for himself, Christ then prays for his Apostles and followers. He asks his Father to bestow on them the gift of eternal life. He asks that they be granted eternal salvation. He proceeds to give four reasons why they should receive this reward. He tells his Father that the Apostles are their common possession; they belong to the Father equally as much as to himself.

The second reason he gives in asking this favor is that his disciples have glorified the Father themselves by being obedient to his word. They have believed the doctrine he has taught them. They have preached about the Father to other men. On Christ's testimony they have believed that it was the Father who sent him to them.

Still another reason why Christ asks his Father to reward his disciples is that they will soon find themselves without a guide or shepherd. The earthly career of Jesus is fast coming to an end. The next day he will be crucified. Henceforth, the Father must keep them.

Finally he asks that his Father glorify them, for they will soon be exposed to the hatred of the world for believing in his doctrine and following his teachings. Christ says, "I have given them the words you gave me, and they have received them. . . ." Indeed before long all of them will be asked to suffer most grievously for the sake of Christ and his Father. Most of them will die a martyr's death for their faith. For this reason Christ asks this favor of his Father.

Notice that Christ does not pray to his Father to shield them from this danger or persecution or take it from them. He does not pray for their being removed from the world but simply that they be preserved from evil and that they will come to enjoy eternal life.

Christ, in a sense, was praying for the successors of the Apostles also, for their successors in the priesthood. The work of a priest is to serve as a mediator between God and man. In the name of his congregation a priest offers up prayers to God in heaven. He prays in their behalf whenever he offers the sacrifice of the Mass. He represents his people before the throne of God.

A priest also represents God before his people. He dispenses God's sacraments to them. He brings them God's grace for the first time in the Sacrament of Baptism. He gives them forgiveness of their sins in confession. He offers them Christ's body and blood in Holy Communion.

Christ could have brought salvation to men in the myriad of ways. From an unlimited number of possibilities, he chose that of ordaining certain men as priests. Because they possess human nature, they are not perfect. Even among the original Twelve, one betrayed our Lord. Their leader, St. Peter, denied our Lord three times.

Christ tells us that his Father in heaven loves his priests and will glorify them for the good work they have done in following him and spreading the gospel. Christ prays that they will enjoy eternal life. Since Christ is God, we know his prayer is efficacious — it will be heard and bring about the result he is praying for. The large number of good priests found in the Church in every century and every generation bears this out.

A century ago in this country when a missionary was needed to administer to the needs of the Navajo Indians in the West, Father Anselm Weber, a Franciscan priest, left his teaching position to undertake this task. He was dedicated to his assignment. Not only did he preach to them and care for their needs, but when he saw injustice being done them by the government, he went to Washington and pleaded in their behalf. He bargained with the leaders of the Santa Fe Railroad, who were treating the Indians in a shameful manner.

In each and every way he worked for their benefit. He brought the Indians closer to God and brought God to them through the Holy Eucharist. When Father Weber died, he was praised by all. Even the government and railroad officials, with whom he had disagreed, were forced to admit the good he had accomplished.

Let us join our voice to that of Christ as he prays his priestly prayer. Let us ask God to continue to bless the priests in his Church. The priesthood is the means by which God's graces are brought to the members of his Church. It is the means by which your sacrifices are offered to God. In the words of St. John Chrysostom, "When you see a priest offering the sacrifice of the Mass, it is the hand of Christ invisibly stretched forth." God bless you.

# "A"    Pentecost Sunday

*John 20:19-23*

Pentecost Sunday is the feast of the Holy Spirit. In the words of today's first reading from the Acts of the Apostles, "And suddenly a sound came from heaven like the rush of a mighty wind, and it filled all the house where they were sitting. And there appeared to them tongues as of fire, distributed and resting on each one of them. And they were all filled with the Holy Spirit. . . ." Thus did the Holy Spirit confirm and strengthen the Apostles, the leaders of Christ's newly founded Church.

But Christ had involved the Holy Spirit on other occasions. On Easter Sunday evening Christ appeared to the Apostles. He breathed on them and said, "Receive the Holy Spirit. If you forgive the sins of any they are forgiven; if you retain the sins of any, they are retained." By these words Christ instituted the Sacrament of Reconciliation. He gave his Apostles the power to forgive or retain sins. But he gave this power not only to them, but also to their successors, the bishops and priests in the Catholic Church.

One of the commandments of the Church obliges every Catholic to go to confession once a year; another requires every Catholic to receive Holy Communion during the Easter time, that is, between the first Sunday of Lent and Trinity Sunday, which occurs next Sunday. These two commandments taken together are called one's "Easter Duty."

Holy Mother the Church imposes these commandments not for the purpose of making us do something unpleasant but rather because she realizes we need the graces of these sacraments, Penance and Holy Eucharist, so very much. She feels that if we neglect them for over a year very grave spiritual harm will befall us.

Christ, in instituting the Sacrament of Reconciliation, did not intend it to be a means of spiritual torture. Next to the Eucharist, it is God's greatest gift to mankind. It is the sacrament of the second chance — a second opportunity to gain heaven. Christ intended that we should keep forever the grace we gain in Baptism. But in case we should lose it, he gives us an opportunity to regain it through Penance.

On one occasion the agonized parents of a small dying boy called for Don Bosco to come and see their son. But to their great grief, the boy died before the saint arrived. But Don Bosco told the parents their son was only sleeping.

Shaken gently, the boy awoke and said, "Don Bosco, I have been calling you for so long. I wish to go to confession. I was going to go to hell for a sin I never confessed." With this the saint heard the boy's confession and then said,

"Would you rather stay on earth or go to paradise?" The boy answered, "To paradise." Don Bosco whispered, "Good-bye, my son," and the boy passed away to his eternal reward.

Penance is a sacrament of God's love. God so loved mankind he did not wish to abandon him even after he had offended him by mortal sin. Hence he gave us this means of regaining his grace. But despite this, Penance is one of the most widely misunderstood and least appreciated of all the sacraments.

When a priest sits in the confessional, he takes the place of Christ. The words of absolution which he pronounces have the same effect as those Christ spoke to Mary Magdalene. Through his words a great change takes place in the soul of the penitent. The soul blackened with mortal sin is made white as snow. It is clothed with the garment of sanctifying grace. The change that occurs in the soul is far more wonderful than Christ's healing of the leper. Sin is far worse than leprosy of the body.

Confession is a natural remedy for any soul stained with sin. One would not hesitate to see a doctor if he were seriously ill. Likewise one sick with sin should seek the healing powers of this sacrament. Yet for some reason many people have an aversion about entering the confessional.

In the early centuries of the Church this was not so. In early times penances were often long and severe, and some were performed publicly. Still people appreciated the Sacrament of Reconciliation and went regularly without much urging.

But finally in the year 1215 Pope Innocent found it necessary to make it obligatory under pain of mortal sin for Catholics to go to confession at least once during the year. But why was this law necessary?

Some may say that going to confession is humiliating. To a certain extent it is, but our sins are no secret from almighty God. Others may object that they dislike confessing their sins to another human being, even though he is a priest. Let us remember that the lips of the priest are sealed with the seal of confession. A priest would commit a grave sin if he were to reveal what he heard in the confessional. Many priests have suffered greatly by keeping it. St. John of Prague was martyred rather than break it.

Brother Leo, a companion and friend of St. Francis of Assisi, once saw in a vision a turbulent river and a multitude of people trying to cross it. Some sank before they had gone very far from shore. Others sank in midstream. Still others sank near the opposite bank. Very few reached the other shore in safety.

When he relayed this vision to St. Francis, the saint told him what it meant. The river is the current of the world. People start out in it with the grace of baptism. But unfortunately many sink into mortal sin — some in childhood — others in middle life — some in their old age. Very few preserve their baptismal innocence to the end, without added help. That help is the Sacrament of Reconciliation.

Let us, therefore, view Penance as a sacrament of God's love — a means to help us attain the kingdom of heaven. Let us resolve to receive it frequently. If we have not made our Easter Duty this year, let us resolve to do so this coming week. God bless you.

# "A"    Trinity Sunday
# (Sunday after Pentecost)

*John 3:16-18*

The first book of the Bible, the book of Genesis, quotes God as saying, "Let us make man in our image, after our likeness. . . ." The Jews of the Old Testament correctly believed that there was only one God while nearly all of the nations around them believed in a multiplicity of gods. Yet in this biblical passage, God is speaking in a plural voice, "Let *us* make man . . . after *our* like- ness. . . ."

This plural form is indicative that there is more than one person in God. The Old Testament did not fully reveal the mystery of the Holy Trinity to the Jewish people, but from time to time did give some indications of it. One such indication was God's revelation to Abraham in the valley of Mambre. Here three young men appeared to Abraham and all began to speak. However, they spoke with one voice.

When Christ came to earth, he refrained from teaching the Blessed Trinity as an article of faith in the earliest days of his public life. He developed and revealed this mystery only gradually; for example, in today's gospel Christ speaks to Nicodemus, "God so loved the world that he gave his only Son. . . ." Here Christ speaks of two persons of the Blessed Trinity, the Father and the Son. These words to Nicodemus Christ spoke early in his public life.

Only later did Christ begin speaking of the Holy Spirit to his Apostles. He said he would send the Holy Spirit, the Spirit of Truth, the Sanctifier, upon them. After he had risen from the dead, he told them that he must return to his heavenly Father or the Holy Spirit, the Paraclete, would not come to them. At the Last Supper Christ said, "I will pray the Father, and he will give you another counsellor. . . ."

When St. John the Baptizer baptized Christ in the Jordan River, the three persons of the Blessed Trinity manifested themselves here on earth. St. John said he saw the heavens open and the Spirit of God descending as a dove. Then he heard a voice from heaven say, "He on whom you see the Spirit descend and remain, this is he. . . ." In this instance God the Father was heard speaking from the cloud. God the Son was being baptized, and God the Holy Spirit was seen in the form of a dove.

On one occasion Christ asked Peter who he thought him to be. Peter an- swered that he was the Christ, the Son of God. Christ responded, "Blessed are you, Simon Bar-Jona! For flesh and blood has not revealed this to you, but my Father who is in heaven." Christ revealed that God the Father had com- municated with St. Peter and disclosed Christ's true identity. When Christ was transfigured on the mountain before Peter, James and John, God the Father again spoke out of a cloud.

The Holy Spirit manifested himself on Pentecost Sunday in visible form. He descended on the heads of the Apostles gathered in the supper room in Jerusalem in the form of fiery tongues. They felt a great spiritual transformation within their souls. They bravely went forth after this to preach the gospel.

Before Christ ascended into heaven he said to his Apostles, "Go therefore and make disciples of all nations, baptizing them in the name of the Father and of the Son, and of the Holy Spirit. . . ." Here Christ commanded them to administer the Sacrament of Baptism and to give it in the name of the Blessed Trinity. His command has been literally carried out.

But despite these revelations, the nature of the Trinity itself remains a mystery. No theologian ever has understood or ever will understand how there can be three persons in only one God. Its essence is beyond the power of our minds to grasp.

St. Patrick made use of a simple analogy in teaching the Blessed Trinity to the Irish people. He picked a three-leafed shamrock and showed it to them. He asked them how many shamrocks he held in his hand and they replied one. He asked how many leaves it contained and they replied three. He said in similar fashion there was one God in three divine Persons.

Let us thank God for revealing the mystery of the Blessed Trinity to us. Let us pray that one day we may enjoy the presence of all three Persons in the kingdom of heaven. God bless you.

# "A"    Corpus Christi

*John 6:51-58*

In the institution of the Holy Eucharist one can discern four steps or stages Christ took in establishing it:
  1) the Preparation,
  2) the Promise,
  3) the Fulfillment of the Promise, and
  4) the Acceptance of the Eucharist by the Apostles and men in every age.

The first step, the preparation, took place at Bethsaida in Galilee, where Christ took five barley loaves and two fish and multiplied them and fed five thousand people. This miraculous multiplication of the loaves and fishes was a preparation for the Eucharist, for Christ showed he had the divine power to create it.

The promise of the Eucharist occurred only one day later at Capernaum, a village only four miles distant from Bethsaida. The crowd that had been fed by the multiplication of the loaves and fishes had followed him to Capernaum. The words of the promise are contained in today's gospel, "If any one eats of this bread, he will live forever. . . ."

No sooner had Christ made the promise — of giving people his body to eat and blood to drink — than a murmur went through the crowd asking how could he do this. In reply Christ said that "unless you eat the flesh of the Son of man and drink his blood, you have no life in you. . . ." Thus he made the reception of Holy Communion a necessary condition for spiritual life.

The third step in establishing the Eucharist was the fulfillment of the promise on Holy Thursday. It occurred at our Savior's last meal with his Apostles before his crucifixion. He took bread and wine into his hands and said, "This is my body. . . . This is my blood. . . ." With these words he actually changed bread and wine into his body and blood. Then he passed this power on to his Apostles by saying, "Do this as a remembrance of me."

The fourth and final step in the establishment of the Eucharist is the acceptance of the sacrament by men. The Apostles and early members of the Church readily accepted it; they embraced it lovingly. It even became a custom in the early Church to communicate each and every time Holy Mass was offered.

But what was needed was a continual acceptance of the Eucharist. Unfortunately in the Middle Ages this devotion to the Blessed Sacrament began to wane. In the early thirteenth century an Augustinian nun, St. Juliana of Cornillon, knelt at prayer in chapel. She beheld a vision. It was a vision of the Church under a full moon. But in the moon was one dark spot.

Our Lord then appeared to St. Juliana and told her: "Juliana, what disturbs you is that a feast is wanting in my Church, which I desire to establish. It is the feast of the Most High and Most Holy Sacrament of the altar. At present the celebration of this mystery is observed only on Maundy Thursday; but on that day my sufferings and death are the principal objects of consideration; therefore, I desire another day to be set apart in which it shall be celebrated by the whole of Christendom. And you, Juliana, are chosen to give the opportunity for the establishment of this feast."

St. Juliana made our Savior's wishes known, and within half a century the Holy Father established all over the world the glorious feast of Corpus Christi, the feast we celebrate today, to give honor to the Holy Eucharist.

To complete Christ's plan for the acceptance of the Eucharist in every age, public honor must be paid Christ in the Eucharist. Let us who live in the twentieth century pledge our acceptance of it to Christ. On this feast of Corpus Christi let us renew our faith in Christ's body and blood present on our altar. Let us offer our adoration to Christ present behind the tabernacle door. Let us resolve that we shall frequently receive him in Holy Communion. Christ has promised that "if anyone eats of this bread, he will live for ever." God bless you.


# "A"    Second Sunday of the Year

*John 1:29-34*

In today's gospel St. John relates an event that took place in the beginning of our Lord's public life, a meeting, the meeting of Christ and St. John the Baptizer. John had already begun his public life; he was preaching and baptizing in the region around the Jordan River. Christ came to him and asked to be baptized. Up to this time the two had never met. They had lived in distant places and never had the opportunity of meeting before.

Under ordinary circumstances John would have granted the request of any stranger to be baptized. But with Christ he hesitated. He protested that it was Christ who should baptize him. John had received a special revelation from the Holy Spirit saying he would recognize the Messiah when the Holy Spirit descended on him in the form of a dove.

When Christ asked for baptism, the Holy Spirit descended on him. John knew immediately Christ was the Messiah. For this reason he protested his unworthiness to baptize Christ. When Christ protested, John did as he wished and proceeded with the ceremony. John's baptism was not a sacrament, but only a rite symbolizing the forgiveness of sins.

John proceeded to give the purpose for his preaching and baptizing. He said, "I myself did not know him; but for this I came baptizing with water, that he might be revealed to Israel." John's whole purpose was to make Christ known to the Jewish nation — to reveal his identity and to prepare his way.

The next day John caught sight of Jesus and said, "Behold, the Lamb of God, who takes away the sin of the world!" John's description of Christ as a lamb was something new in idea and comparison. Lambs are gentle animals; they allow themselves to be shorn and to be slaughtered without a murmur.

In calling Christ a lamb he was attributing these same qualities to him. Truly Christ was a meek and gentle person. At the conclusion of his public life Christ would allow himself to be led away to be slaughtered — willingly enduring the death of crucifixion.

In the Old Testament lambs were used for sacrifice. God instructed Moses that a lamb without blemish be slaughtered by each Jewish family before the Exodus from Egypt. Lambs were sacrificed at the feast of the Passover. In calling Christ the "Lamb of God," John indicated that the life of Christ was to be offered as a sacrifice and that God himself was to offer it.

From the time of the original sin of our first parents the gates of heaven had been closed to mankind. God had been offended by the sin of men. No one of sufficient dignity had made a sacrifice to God worthy enough to take away the guilt of this original sin. But now God's own divine Son was to be the sacrificial victim, the lamb to be offered up.

Christ's death was according to God's eternal plan. It was to be predetermined. From the moment of creation, God knew that man would fail the test he gave him. He foresaw the disobedience of our first parents. He saw that it would be necessary for his own Son to come to earth and die for the sins of mankind.

In the sixteenth chapter of the book of Leviticus, Moses described a scapegoat who would carry away all men's sins to an uninhabited land. Christ would fulfill this prophecy.

From the words of today's gospel, let us realize the great sacrifice Christ made on our behalf. He offered his life to redeem us. Let us show him our appreciation and our gratitude for this great act of redemption. Let us resolve to be faithful members of his flock. Let us honor him through the reception of the sacraments of his Church. In this way the blood of the Lamb will wash away our sins and lead us to eternal salvation. God bless you.

# "A"    Third Sunday of the Year

*Matthew 4:12-23*

In today's gospel St. Matthew tells us that when John the Baptizer was arrested by King Herod, Christ withdrew from the area of the Jordan where they had been together. Christ made his way north to the Sea of Galilee and in particular to the village of Capernaum, where he took up his residence.

Capernaum was the largest and most prosperous of the nine villages located on the lake. The Sea of Galilee was the center of life and activity in that region. It was thirteen miles long from north to south and eight miles wide from east to west. The lake has an oval shape and is wider at the north end than at the south.

In the time of our Lord the lake was thick with fishing boats. A fishing expedition on the lake would often have two hundred boats or more. Fish were plentiful in the lake. Fishing was generally done with nets. A large bell-shaped net, weighted on the ends, was thrown into the water between two boats. The boats would generally row together and encircle a large quantity of fish.

This was the manner in which Peter and his brother Andrew were fishing when Christ came upon them. Christ simply said to them, "Follow me, and I will make you fishers of men." Immediately they left all and followed Christ. In a similar manner he called two other brothers, James and John, the sons of Zebedee. They also gladly left all and followed Christ.

In this simple and direct way Christ summoned his Apostles. He beckoned them to enter upon a new manner of living. Their lives would be radically changed. Eventually their preaching and their activity would cost them their lives. They would die as martyrs. But the life to which he summoned them earned for each of them the crown of eternal happiness.

One may well ask, why did Christ choose these particular individuals to be his Apostles? As fishermen they were not well educated. Yet they had mastered the fundamentals of reading and writing. Five of their number wrote books in the New Testament.

The Apostles were not rich men. Yet as fishermen they were able to make a living. Except for John they were married men and also had to provide for their families in some way in going off to follow Christ. Despite their problems and obligations, they readily responded to Christ's call.

Each of these individuals had his own faults and failings. St. Peter was boastful and tempestuous. He rose to fight the guard trying to arrest Christ in the Garden of Olives and cut off his ear. Christ had to restrain him and tell him to put away his sword. James and John were ambitious men. Thomas was a skeptic.

We might imagine Christ would have chosen men with greater talents to be his followers — men who were better educated, men who were gifted speakers, men with more pleasing personalities. Christ, using his divine knowledge, chose imperfect men, men with failings. Christ chose them deliberately. He wanted to show that the success of his Church, which he was to found on them, did not depend on any individual's gifts or talents. The success of his Church would be determined by the Holy Spirit, who would guide and direct it.

We may say that the Apostles were merely tools in the hands of Christ. Christ often used a poor tool to achieve a great result. This proves the divinity of Christ and his Church.

Even today many of those who receive vocations to the priesthood or religious life are not always the richest or smartest or most talented of people. Christ uses weak tools today to show that his Church is divine — that its success is determined by the guiding hand of the Holy Spirit.

In the ordination ceremony of a priest the young ordinand stretches out at full length on the floor of the sanctuary, face down, like a corpse. He remains in this position a long time. The symbolism of this ceremony is that the future priest is yielding his body to be the instrument of Christ. When he arises, he will renounce his own life. His life in the future will be an extension of the life of Christ. His will will be to will what Christ would will.

The vocation to follow Christ, to become a fisher of men, is indeed a high one, the highest on earth. But the price demanded is also high. Persecution and even death can await the disciples of Christ.

Let us thank God for giving us this means of spreading his Church on earth — that he gave us good and zealous Apostles. Let us pray often for the priests of his Church. Let us pray that God will continue to send good and holy priests to be shepherds of his flock on earth. God bless you.

# "A"    Fourth Sunday of the Year

*Matthew 5:1-12*

The public life of Christ lasted three years. It began when he was publicly baptized by John the Baptizer in the River Jordan. Christ then went into the desert and fasted forty days. Shortly after this he began to preach and gather his Apostles and disciples around him. At Cana he performed his first miracle, changing water into wine.

Christ made his way to Capernaum and made the city his temporary home, his base of operations for his preaching around Galilee. It was in the second year of his public life in the vicinity of Capernaum, on a mountainside, believed by many to be Karn Hattin or the "Horns of Hattin," that Christ delivered his most frequently quoted sermon — his Sermon on the Mount. Modern scripture scholars believe St. Matthew to have grouped teachings from other occasions together and placed them in this one sermon. But the truth and beauty of Christ's teachings stand out regardless of the incidents of the time and place of their delivery.

Christ enunciated eight benedictions or blessings which have come to be known at the eight Beatitudes. He said, "Blest are the poor in spirit; the reign of God is theirs." In the pagan world of the Roman Empire in which Christ lived, happiness was measured in material wealth. The person who experienced great pleasure was considered happy. The person who possessed great wealth was considered a blessed person; so also, one possessing great power.

But now Christ is enunciating a new concept. He is presenting a new idea of what constitutes happiness. He is setting forth a new set of values to live by. Christ says that those who are not covetous of the goods of this earth, the poor in spirit, possess a greater happiness than those who are; they possess the reign of God.

Christ gives eight Beatitudes or sources of happiness and a corresponding reward for each of them. To the sorrowful, he promises consolation. To the lowly he promises inheritance of the land. To those seeking holiness, he promises them their fill.

These first four Beatitudes outline a road for one to follow to reach eternal happiness. They are concrete earthly steps which one must follow. They are the conditions for entrance to the kingdom of heaven. These conditions of humility, detachment, sympathy and a desire for holiness lead to true happiness. Christ was showing the people that poverty was neither a disgrace nor a punishment; it can be a blessing in disguise.

In the last four Beatitudes Christ speaks of the crowning reward and joy of those who practice them. In them he blesses the merciful, the single-hearted, the peacemakers and the persecuted. He lists their subsequent rewards. They shall obtain mercy; they shall see God, be called the sons of God and enjoy great reward in heaven.

By the merciful, Christ referred to those who feel compassion in their hearts for the sufferings of others. By the single-hearted, Christ means those whose heartfelt goal is to please and serve God. Their hearts are not diverted toward the pursuit of other goals — pleasure or wealth or glory. They have no double goal or ambition in life. Their single purpose is to obey and please God.

Christ said, "Blest are the peacemakers." Peace is an elusive virtue. It is hard to find and hard to preserve. The complexities and irritations of everyday living seem to gnaw away at peace and leave one irritated and anxious. Thomas à Kempis, a spiritual writer of the Middle Ages, said, "Think that God and you are alone in the world, and you will then have peace in your heart." The secret of peace is to pray deeply and shut yourself off from the irritations of the world.

Christ blessed those who suffer persecution for his sake. There are many who suffer in this world, but they complain against God in their suffering. Suffering, to be beneficial, must be endured for the sake of Christ. Suffering for the sake of Christ will merit reward.

The Beatitudes of Christ were a new and startling revelation. They were the blueprint of a divine plan to govern our everyday actions. The Beatitudes guarantee us blessing or happiness in this life. In addition they promise us a reward in the life to come. Their reward is twofold.

Worldly rewards pass away with death. The goal of a true follower of Christ is different; his goal extends beyond death to the world hereafter. The Christian goal is a heavenly crown. To attain it one must study and practice the Beatitudes. The reward for practicing them is a double one — happiness in this life and an eternal crown in the next. God bless you.

# "A"    Fifth Sunday of the Year

*Matthew 5:13-16*

A little Chinese girl was a close observer of the missionary priest in her village. She watched him pray in church; she listened to him preach; she noticed how he visited the sick and how he stopped to greet people and always had a smile and kind word for everyone.

One day this little girl visited a neighboring village. She listened in on a catechism class where a nun was describing the virtues of Christ to her class, although she did not mention his name. She told about a man who was always good and kind. Noticing her little visitor, the nun stopped to ask her if she knew about whom she was talking. The small girl replied, "Yes, he's the missionary father in our village."

This was a splendid tribute to the missionary priest. He was called to mind when the virtues of Christ were described. This truly is the goal of every priest — to be another Christ. In the ordination ceremony the young man being ordained is called an "alter Christus" — another Christ.

In the ordination ceremony the future priest lies face downward on the floor of the sanctuary. He lies there stretched out at full length and motionless as a corpse. He lies there as if he had no life, no will of his own. In the former rite, his hands were tied together with a white cloth called a maniturgium. This symbolized that he was a captive of Jesus Christ. In the future he will think as Christ would think; he will act as Christ would act. He will be a tool in the hands of Christ; he will be an instrument to bring Christ's grace into the hearts of men. He will carry God's graces to men, and in turn, men's prayers to God.

In the words of Christ in today's gospel, Christ calls his disciples the salt of the earth. Christ's use of this term is not unusual. Salt has been used for centuries as a preservative for food. It is often mentioned in the Old Testament. The Jews used to rub salt on the skin of a new-born child to purify and harden the skin. They also dedicated land to God by sprinkling salt on it.

When Christ calls his disciples the salt of the earth, he means that they are to be saviors or preservers of the human race as salt saves or preserves food. The power of the priesthood is the greatest honor that can be bestowed upon a human being. St. John Chrysostom often remarked that the power of the priest far exceeds that of kings, for as a king rules over the bodies of men, priests rule over their souls. St. Francis of Assisi used to say that if he met a priest and an angel, he would greet the priest first. For priests have power over the body and blood of Christ; they can call Christ down from heaven under the appearance of bread and wine, which angels cannot do.

Priests are entrusted with great responsibility — that of hearing the most intimate secrets of one's heart in the confessional. They are recipients of the greatest honor — that of daily offering Holy Mass. A priest may hold Christ in his hands at the Consecration of the Mass some twenty thousand times in the course of his life.

Frequently one is asked, how does a vocation come? The answer is that God ordinarily uses ordinary signs. In the case of Peter and some of the other

Apostles, Christ directly called them to follow him. But this is not usually the case. A vocation may often come simply through a liking for spiritual things. It may come through a simple desire to help one's fellow man. If one suspects he or she has a vocation, one should talk it over with a parish priest or confessor.

A further step is to pray — pray to the Holy Spirit to enlighten your mind to know your vocation in this life. Let us pray to him daily. Let us ask of him the grace to know our vocation and the courage to follow it, once we know it. God bless you.

# "A"    Sixth Sunday of the Year

*Matthew 5:17-37*

In today's gospel Christ quoted a commandment of the Old Law, "You shall not kill; and whoever kills shall be liable to judgment." But then he extended it, "But I say to you that every one who is angry with his brother shall be liable to judgment; whoever insults his brother shall be liable to the council, and whoever says, 'You fool!' shall be liable to the hell of fire [Gehenna]."

At first appearance it would appear that our Lord was giving the Jews a new law — far more strict and complicated than that contained in the Old Testament, the law of Moses. But his real purpose was not to give them a new law composed of outward signs — rather to give them a new sense of righteousness.

Christ spoke in legalistic terms because the Jews were familiar with them. The council or Sanhedrin was the Jewish court, composed of seventy-two judges, which judged criminals and handed down verdicts that included the death penalty, although that sentence was reserved to the Romans. Gehenna was a valley to the south of Jerusalem, where rubbish and the carcasses of dead animals were burned. There was a constant crackling fire there which reminded one of the fires of hell.

Such things as growing angry with one's brother or using abusive language were not forbidden by Jewish law. The Pharisees in their interpretation of the Fifth Commandment held that only murder itself was wrong; animosity was frequently found among them and was not condemned. Fraternal charity had no place in their religion.

They were closing their eyes to the law of love. Even without the Ten Commandments they should have known this. For not only does the natural law forbid murder, but also it commands us to be charitable to our neighbor as well. In fact, for this very reason, the hardness of their hearts, God gave Moses the Ten Commandments on Mount Sinai.

On one occasion a young man asked Christ which was the greatest commandment of the Law. Christ replied, ". . . you shall love the Lord your God with all your heart, and with all your soul, and with all your strength, and with all your mind. . . . You shall love your neighbor as yourself." Truly if one loves his neighbor as himself, he will naturally refrain from killing him or doing anything to harm him. This was the idea which the Pharisees failed to see. Fraternal charity is a most important commandment. Christ gave us the spiritual and corporal works of mercy as means of practicing it.

There once lived a charitable widow who supported her two daughters by taking in sewing. She owned two sewing machines, an old hand model and a new electric one on which she did most of her work.

The poor widow learned that the Sisters at her local parish convent desired a sewing machine. She decided to donate one of hers to them. She thought first of giving them her old one, but then realized that they could make great use out of her new electric one. Therefore, she gave them her new electric machine, which she had depended upon for her livelihood.

God rewarded her generosity almost immediately. The very afternoon the Sisters received the machine they kept the girls after school to begin a sewing class. That same afternoon a large trailer truck crashed into a bridge near this poor widow's house. It was the bridge that her daughters had to cross to go to school. The time of the accident was the time they would ordinarily be crossing it. The poor widow realized that her act of charity had most probably been responsible for saving her daughters' lives.

Let us remember that the message of love is the basic teaching of Christianity. We must look for God in our neighbor. We must realize that God has made our neighbor to his image and likeness. Let our actions be governed by this belief. God bless you.


# "A"    Seventh Sunday of the Year

*Matthew 5:38-48*

In the Hebrew language the word "talion" means the law of revenge. In the Old Testament and in ancient times this law protected individuals by obliging the next of kin to avenge injury or the murder of one's kinsman. The first five books of the Bible place many restrictions on this "talion" or law of revenge. These laws try to make sure that the injury inflicted by the avenger does not exceed the damage done by the aggressor.

When Christ came to earth, this was the spirit and the feeling of the Jewish people — revenge and hatred smoldered within them. The meekness displayed by Christ and the doctrine of love that he preached was something strange and foreign to their ears. Christ quotes for his listeners the verses of Exodus and Leviticus which say, "An eye for an eye and a tooth for a tooth." But now Christ, who is speaking as the Messiah and the Son of God, contradicts and changes this command. He says, "Offer no resistance to injury." He lays down a new law for the New Testament.

Christ then enumerates four areas of non-resistance. The first of these is physical violence. He says, "When a person strikes you on the right cheek, turn and offer him the other." The second area is legal action; he says, "If anyone wants to go to law over your shirt, hand him your coat as well."

The third area is that of forced labor or service. Ancient governments were legally empowered to require their subjects to do certain forced labor or work; for example, Simon of Cyrene was ordered to help Christ carry his cross to Calvary. An expression synonymous with this was "to walk a mile." Thus Christ says, "Should anyone press you into service for one mile, go with him two miles."

The fourth area of non-resistance is that of giving and lending money. Christ instructed his followers to give to the beggars and to lend to the borrower.

In listing these areas of non-resistance, Christ is not contradicting or denying the virtue of justice. One can be justly required to give of his property, time or labor. What Christ is saying is that what is required by law should not be the measure of our giving. We should give beyond that. He is saying there is another law above the law of justice — the law of charity. Through charity we do not measure what we give; we give generously without measure.

Christ again quotes the book of Leviticus, "You shall love your countryman but hate your enemy." Christ by his divine authority changes this commandment to: "love your enemies, pray for your persecutors." In the Old Testament the Jews were a very nationalistic people. Their religion was confined to their nation; they were forbidden by law to intermarry with foreign peoples — with Gentiles. Hence they felt no obligation to foreigners or Gentiles in any way. Hating or harming them was not considered wrong.

Christ was jarring their established set of values. He was upsetting their standard by which they had lived for many generations. Jewish life and culture had been centered within their own nation; now Christ was lifting that protective veil. He was showing them that those who lived beyond their national borders were also their neighbors. He was telling the Jews they had an obligation to love these people too.

Christ even told them they must pray for their persecutors. This was the real test of their good will. When we pray for a person, we ask God to shower his graces upon them, which is the greatest good that can befall one here on earth.

Christ went on to ask them a question, "If you love those who love you, what merit is there in that? Do not tax collectors do as much?" By asking this question Christ was pointing out that it is common to return love to others when love is shown to us. This was done by the Gentiles and pagans who had no religion at all. To love one's friends and family was an ordinary action, and no extraordinary reward should be expected for it.

But to love foreigners, the enemies of one's nation, was no ordinary thing. How was it ordinary to love one's personal enemies — those who had attempted to harm one in some way? Love in these situations does not spring from natural inclinations. Christ meant that his followers should love their enemies, and this for a supernatural motive. This is the distinguishing mark of a Christian — that he act out of supernatural motives rather than natural ones.

To love one's enemies in our modern world means that one must pray for them. When he meets them publicly, he must be civil toward them. He must refrain from talking about them when their back is turned. This is the minimum expected from a true Christian.

Christ gave us an example of how to love our enemies. When he was condemned to death by Pilate, the Roman soldiers led him away to crucify him. This was part of their duty as soldiers, to execute criminals and those condemned to death. Most probably they had been called upon to execute hundreds of others before this. Their taunting and prodding, their blows and their jeers came as second nature. Yet when hanging upon the cross, Christ said of them, "Father, forgive them; they do not know what they are doing." Christ was putting into practice most beautifully his command to love his enemies.

Let us imitate this example of Christ in forgiving and loving our enemies. Christ has shown us that to love our enemies is proof that we are sons of our heavenly Father. God bless you.

# "A"    Eighth Sunday of the Year

*Matthew 6:24-34*

Today's gospel according to St. Matthew is perhaps one of the most consoling sermons Christ ever preached. He tells us, "Look at the birds in the sky. They do not sow or reap, they gather nothing into barns; yet your heavenly Father feeds them. Are you not more important than they?" It illustrates in a very down-to-earth manner the providence of almighty God. Through it God directs all things to their final end.

Through divine providence God directs not only the activities of man but likewise the activities of the animal world and of nature as well. Every plant on this earth was created for a purpose. Every star in the sky serves an important function. The law of nature, with its intricate workings of the processes of life, is a part of God's plan. The solar system follows his direction.

But among all the creations of the universe and all the forms of life, God's primary concern is for man. Man is the chief creature of God's creation. If God is concerned about the birds in the air and the animals in the field, he is more concerned about us.

At times the providence of God is doubted or called into question by worry over many temporal matters. There is a just reason for concern over certain problems that arise. But worry causes unjust concern. Worry calls into question God's providence. Worry expresses doubt that God will direct all things for the good of man.

Worry is really foolish when we consider what God does for us. He gives us food to sustain our lives, water to drink, air to breathe. God provides us with all the necessities of life. In fact, if God should cease to care for us for a single instant, we would die; we would cease to exist.

God knows more about us than we know about ourselves. Elsewhere Christ tells us that even the hairs in our head are numbered. What human being knows this about himself? God's Providence extends even to the smallest details of our life.

Not only does God care for us in a natural sense, but in a supernatural sense as well. God's concern was so great that when Adam committed original sin, God sent his own Divine Son down to earth to redeem mankind. Christ, who was truly God, took on a body like ours. He died on the cross for men, thus showing us what great love he has for us.

Christ said, "There is no greater love than this: to lay down one's life for one's friends." Christ literally did this for us. In addition he left us a means of grace, the sacraments, to sustain our spiritual life.

Despite his loving care, there are those who call his providence into question. They ask, why does God permit sickness? Why does God permit wars? Why does God permit fires, floods, earthquakes and other tragedies?

The answer to such questions is not always clearly evident. God frequently does not manifest his reasons to us. But we can be sure that good may come out of them. God may permit a person to suffer with cancer or some incurable disease to incite contrition in his soul.

In regard to suffering we can do no better than to follow the example of Christ himself. Although he was God, Christ was not immune from suffering here on earth. In the Garden of Olives he suffered a bloody sweat. Later he was crucified. He prayed to his Father, "Father . . . not my will but yours be done."

Christ has said the time will come when he will ask the Father to grant us an understanding of his providence. This will come on the day of General Judgment, at the end of the world. Until then we must accept the advice he gives us in today's gospel, "Stop worrying, then, over questions like, 'What are we to eat, or what are we to drink, or what are we to wear?' . . . Your heavenly Father knows all that you need. Seek first his kingship over you, his way of holiness, and all these things will be given you besides." God bless you.

# "A"    Ninth Sunday of the Year

*Matthew 7:21-27*

In the gospel of today's Mass, taken from St. Matthew, Christ tells his listeners, "None of those who cry out, 'Lord, Lord,' will enter the kingdom of God but only the one who does the will of my Father in heaven." Christ is saying in effect that to be a Christian, it is not enough simply to believe in his teachings, but one must live a Christian life. One must live according to the will of Christ as manifested through the Ten Commandments and the precepts of his Church. One's belief must be accompanied by good deeds.

Christ then employs the example that those who received miraculous powers — those who prophesied, exorcized demons and made miraculous cures — will not automatically be saved. They must also cooperate with God's grace. Otherwise on the day of judgment Christ will say of them, "I never knew you. Out of my sight, you evildoers!"

Christ concludes his remarks by telling a parable — the parable of the solid foundation. He told of the wise and foolish men who built their homes in different places, one on a rock foundation and the other on sandy soil. In building a home in ancient Palestine it was all-important to build near a water supply.

Most frequently men would build near a wadi, a small running stream. But then in the rainy season a wadi would turn into a rapid torrent. It would overflow its banks and cause a flash flood. Any home that was built on the sandy bottom near the bank of the wadi would be washed away. A prudent man would always build on higher ground on a rocky foundation. It meant having to carry water a longer distance to his home, but it meant more security in the rainy season.

The meaning of this parable is that our Christian faith must have a firm foundation. It is not difficult to hear the word of God, but it is difficult to put his word into action in our life. Hearing his word without practicing it is like building on a sandy foundation. What is needed is good works and action along with our belief. This is like a rock foundation for our house.

In the first reading from today's Mass, taken from the Book of Deuteronomy, Moses told the Jewish people to take God's words to heart, to wear them on their wrists and on their foreheads. Many Jews understood Moses literally. They made small boxes called Philacteries and placed within them a parchment containing key texts from Exodus and Deuteronomy. They unfortunately did not interpret Moses figuratively — they did not make the words of Moses a part of their lives.

St. Paul brings home a similar point in his epistle read in the second reading at today's Mass. He says in effect that a mere formal observance of the Jewish law does not guarantee our salvation.

All three Scripture readings of today's Mass present us with a challenge. They want us to make the teachings of Christ a part of our life. They want our faith to be a firm faith which will carry over into what we say and do. We must live Christianity every day of our life.

Into the lives of each of us will come a rainy season. Winds will buffet us. The stream of trouble will overflow its banks and assail the foundations of our Christian faith. To withstand this storm of temptation, our faith must be deeply rooted. It must be founded on rock.

Faith is a gift of God. It comes to us through the sacrament of baptism. It becomes stronger as we reach the age of reason and make acts of faith through our own will. St. Augustine calls it our most solid treasure.

Christ said, "Whoever disowns me before men I will disown before my Father in heaven." But he likewise promised rewards to those whose faith is strong: "Whoever acknowledges me before men I will acknowledge before my Father in heaven." Let us make an act of faith each day. Let us regard our faith as an uncut jewel, which we shall hone and polish and display for all men to see. God bless you.

# "A"    Tenth Sunday of the Year

*Matthew 9:9-13*

If there was ever anyone qualified to describe Christ's call to Matthew to become an Apostle, it was Matthew himself. It is his own account of Christ's call to him that we read in today's gospel. However, in his humility he describes it in only five short verses in his gospel.

Matthew was a publican, a tax collector. As a group the Jews despised and hated tax collectors, even though they were members of their own race and nation, as much as they did foreigners. This was due in part to the corrupt system the Roman government used in farming out taxes. They would sell to the highest bidder the right to collect taxes in a certain area. The man winning the contract was then responsible for turning over to the Roman government a specified sum of money. Anything he could collect over and above this amount he was allowed to keep for his own private gain.

Needless to say, many tax collectors were unscrupulous. They collected far more taxes than were needed in a certain area. They grew personally wealthy through such unjust means. The citizens had no way of knowing how great a tax they owed in justice. In time they came to think of all tax collectors as unjust men.

Taxes were collected on practically every conceivable phase of life. They were levied on all goods imported or exported from the country. They were levied on the number of pack animals one owned. They were levied on the number of wheels and axles on one's cart. There was a sales tax on practically all goods bought and sold. It was estimated that between 10 and 20 percent of all produce and wealth was paid out in taxes. You might say that taxes in Palestine were as bad, almost, as they are in our state and nation.

The hatred for the tax collectors was almost fanatical. People rashly assumed that all tax collectors were dishonest and classified them as sinners. They spoke of them in the same breath as they would of thieves and murderers.

St. Matthew was a tax collector in the seaport town of Capernaum. He was not the chief tax collector of the area, but rather one of the subordinates who did the actual collecting from the Jewish people. Being engaged in this occupation, he was an outcast of Jewish society.

When Christ came to the place where Matthew was collecting taxes, his eyes perceived the goodness of his soul, and Christ said, "Follow me." Matthew immediately got up and followed him. There was no hesitation or delay in the response of Matthew in accepting Christ's invitation. Matthew was to display many virtues in his character. His goodness was to show the Jews guilty of rash judgment in calling all men of his occupation sinners.

Undoubtedly, in choosing Matthew, Christ knew he would someday inspire Matthew to write a gospel. Tax collectors were required to be able to read and write well; they needed this talent in their work. The other Apostles, who were fishermen, did not. Christ was to put his literary ability to great use.

Matthew later invited Christ to dine in his home. Present at the dinner were other tax collectors, friends of Matthew. When the Pharisees observed this, they asked other disciples of Christ, "What reason can the Teacher have for eating with tax collectors and those who disregard the law?" By asking such a question they showed their perversity in continuing in their rash judgment.

But Christ overheard their question and answered it himself. He said, "People who are in good health do not need a doctor; sick people do." The tax collectors and others present at the dinner were only too well aware of their sins and defects. In accepting Christ they were seeking a means to overcome them.

Christ, in giving this answer, was using an analogy. He was comparing the Pharisees to people in good health. For outward appearances the Pharisees observed the minutest items of the law. They gave the appearance of great holiness, but inwardly they were filled with pride and guilty of rash judgment in condemning others.

Christ added the command, "Go and learn the meaning of the words, 'It is mercy I desire and not sacrifice.' " Here he was quoting from the prophet Hosea, who lived and wrote in the Old Testament in the 8th century B.C. At that particular time in Palestine there was political division in the country, and the Israelites were forbidden to go to Jerusalem and offer sacrifice. Almighty God sent many prophets to them to encourage them to lead a good life despite their inability to offer sacrifices in the holy city as they wished. Among them was Hosea, who wrote that God desired mercy of them.

Christ concluded his remarks to them by saying, "I have come to call not the self-righteous, but sinners." Christ was simply announcing his mission here on earth — he had come to save sinners. But one necessary condition was that sinners recognize their sin—that they admit their evil deeds. Once they admitted their guilt, then Christ would remove it from their souls. But the Pharisees would not do this. They were self-righteous. They would not admit that they were guilty of any sin. They would not avail themselves of the help Christ was offering them.

Christ was later to institute the Sacrament of Reconciliation. This would take away the sins of men once he had departed into heaven. But even here the penitent had to first accuse himself of sin. He must admit his guilt to God and to the priest to whom he is confessing. Then and only then will forgiveness be given.

From Christ's choice of Matthew as an Apostle, let us learn of his love for the lowly and oppressed. From his words and teachings let us learn of his mercy and forgiveness. Let us avail ourselves of his mercy and grace by acknowledging our sinfulness. Let us wash away any pride or arrogance in our lives and humbly beg his pardon. God bless you.

# "A"   Eleventh Sunday of the Year

*Matthew 9:36—10:8*

The time was the second year of our Lord's public life. The place was the remote countryside of Galilee, in northern Palestine. Large crowds had come out from the towns and villages to see and hear our Lord, to hear him preach, and some to beg for miraculous cures for their sicknesses. St. Matthew tells us in his gospel that at the sight of the crowd, Jesus was moved with pity.

The emotion of pity that our Lord expressed was in marked contrast with the harsh treatment they were accustomed to at the hands of their own religious leaders, the scribes and Pharisees. They viewed the common people as chaff to be destroyed. Although they were the official religious teachers of the people, they did not want to be contaminated by them. They frequently avoided them and, when forced to deal with them, often treated them harshly and rudely. But this harsh treatment does not surprise one, knowing the pride and arrogance that filled their hearts.

In following Christ through Galilee, many of the crowd were near exhaustion. They were like sheep without a shepherd. Christ on observing this remarked, "The harvest is good but laborers are scarce. Beg the harvest master to send out laborers to gather his harvest."

Although Christ had gathered a number of disciples around him, he was saying that their number was small in comparison to the number of souls to be harvested. The harvest master to whom he referred was almighty God. The advice he had for his Apostles is as true today as it was then. He told them they should pray for laborers to gather in the harvest — as we should pray today for vocations, for priests and Sisters to help lead souls to Christ.

Then from the many disciples and followers Christ chose twelve men in particular and made them Apostles. He commissioned them to go forth and preach his gospel. He said, "Make this announcement: 'The reign of God is at hand!' "

He bestowed upon them many special powers — power to cure the sick, to heal lepers, to expel demons and even to raise the dead. All these miracles Christ had performed himself, and he passed on this miraculous power to his Apostles. Unfortunately, Scripture does not describe in any great detail how they used this power, but the Acts of the Apostles mention how Peter and John cured a man who had been crippled from birth near the gate of the temple in Jerusalem. At Lystra Paul cured a cripple, and at Troas he raised young Eutychus to life after he had died in a fall from a building.

It is interesting to note that at the time of this gospel Christ had not yet bestowed full powers upon the Apostles. He had not yet established the Holy Eucharist. He did not give them the power to forgive sin until Easter Sunday night. Nor did he commission them to baptize until shortly before he ascended into heaven. At this point, he only empowered them to preach and cure the sick.

Notice, too, that Christ placed limitations on the territory where they were to preach. He said, "Do not visit pagan territory and do not enter a Samaritan town." He was confining their mission to Jewish people only. In the time of Our Lord, Palestine was divided into three major parts: Galilee to the north, Samaria in the central part of the country, and Judea to the south.

The Samaritans were not recognized as Jews by their fellow citizens. Centuries before, when Samaria had been overrun by the Babylonians and Syrians, the Samaritans had disobeyed the Jewish law and intermarried with their conquerors. Hence a new strain of people developed who were disowned and not recognized as Jews by their remaining fellow countrymen. For the time being, Christ respected this Jewish political division. Only later, after his resurrection, would he commission his Apostles to preach the gospel to all nations.

It is interesting to note the identity of the Twelve Apostles and what they accomplished in their lifetime. The first of them Christ called, the one he was to make their leader, was St. Peter. Peter was later to bring the Christian religion to Rome and there be martyred around the year 67 A.D. by being crucified upside down.

Christ also chose Peter's brother, Andrew. St. Andrew was crucified in about the year 60 A.D. in Achaia. Christ also chose their fishing partners and another set of brothers as Apostles, James and John, the sons of Zebedee. Since Christ chose two men named James as Apostles, the first of these, the brother of John is called James the Greater. St. James the Greater was beheaded by King Herod Agrippa.

His brother, St. John, was the youngest of the Twelve Apostles. John alone, of the Twelve Apostles, was brave enough to stand beneath the cross of Christ and witness his crucifixion. The others had fled in fear. It was to St. John that Christ entrusted the care of his Blessed Mother when dying on the cross. St. John's life was miraculously preserved on several occasions. He survived a wreck at sea. He drank poison and was unharmed. Also he emerged unharmed when thrown into a cauldron of boiling oil. St. John was to write the fourth gospel and three epistles.

St. Philip was the fifth Apostle chosen. He was a quiet and kindly man. It was he who brought Nathaniel or Bartholomew to meet Christ. St. Philip was martyred in Hierapolis. Bartholomew, whose name had been changed from Nathaniel, carried the gospel to India. India at the time, however, meant any land to the east of Palestine. Tradition tells us that he was beheaded there; his relics were carried back and now are in the Church of St. Bartholomew on an island in the Tiber River.

St. Thomas, the doubting Apostle, also carried the gospel to India. He was killed by a spear being thrust through his body. His remains are at Malipur in India.

St. Matthew was a tax collector. As a Jew, he helped collect taxes for the Romans. Because of this he was despised by his fellow Jews. Matthew was well-educated and most probably a man of means. He was the author of the first gospel. He was martyred somewhere in the vicinity of Persia.

St. James, the son of Alphaeus, was called James the Less. He was the brother of Thaddeus, who was also called Jude. James the Less was the first bishop of Jerusalem. He was martyred by being thrown headlong from the top of the temple in 62 A.D. His brother, St. Jude or Thaddeus, wrote one of the epistles. He preached the gospel in Arabia, where he was martyred.

St. Simon was supposedly a member of the Zealot party. The Zealots were men dedicated to making Palestine a free nation. They hated the Romans and all foreign rulers and would go to any extreme to get rid of them, even murder. Thus if Simon the Zealot were to have met Matthew, the tax collector for the Romans, under ordinary circumstances, they would have been mortal enemies. But yet as Apostles of Christ they lived peacefully together.

The last Apostle was Judas Iscariot. Judas was the apostle who betrayed our Lord for thirty pieces of silver. Christ undoubtedly knew what Judas would do when he chose him to be an Apostle but chose him anyway. At the time of his selection, Judas was most probably a good man and had good intentions. He succumbed to the temptation of greed much later on. St. Matthias was chosen to replace him after his death.

The Apostles as a group were just ordinary men. Eleven of them were fishermen and one a tax collector. Eleven of them became great saints in the Church; they achieved this great sanctity because they followed the vocation Christ gave them and cooperated with his graces.

One of the great marks of the Church is its apostolicity — the Church was founded by and through the Apostles. The Pope in Rome is the direct successor to St. Peter, the first Pope. The bishops of our Church are the successors of the other Apostles.

Let us thank God for giving to his Church such holy and zealous men as the Apostles. For it is through their efforts that we have the gift of faith today. God bless you.

# "A"  Twelfth Sunday of the Year

*Matthew 10:26-33*

Back in the days of World War II when Hitler was at the height of his power, the President of our country, Franklin D. Roosevelt, met with the Prime Minister of Great Britain, Winston Churchill, on a battleship in the middle of the Atlantic Ocean. They drew up the Atlantic Charter. They guaranteed four freedoms to the world. One of these was freedom from fear. But in writing about and describing freedom from fear they were simply stealing a page from St. Matthew's gospel.

In this passage of St. Matthew, read as the gospel for today's Mass, Christ is quietly and privately instructing his disciples. Three times he bids them not to be afraid. He says, "Do not let men intimidate you." He is preparing them for the dangers and trials they will face when he leaves them, when they go forth to preach his gospel to mankind. He does not want to disillusion them into thinking that success and popularity will be their lot. It will be just the opposite. It will be suffering and persecution and sometimes even death.

Their lot in life will resemble that of Jeremiah the prophet, from whose book in the Old Testament the first reading of today's Mass is taken. Jeremiah lived and wrote during the troubled times when the Babylonians ruled over Palestine. As a prophet, he was inspired by God to speak out against the abuses taking place in the temple and the disloyalty of the Jewish people to God. Because he dared condemn their evil practices, Jeremiah was imprisoned. Then the leaders of the Jews decided to kill him. He was dropped in a cistern but rescued by a friend. The Jews forcibly took him to Egypt and murdered him there.

Jeremiah was simply preaching the word of God; for this he was tortured and killed. Christ warns his apostles that despite the persecution that lay ahead, they should not fear to proclaim his gospel. "What I tell you in darkness, speak in the light." By "darkness," he was referring to the one small corner of Galilee in which he was instructing them. By "light," he meant they should preach this doctrine in all churches all over the world.

Christ said, "What you hear in private, proclaim from the housetops." In ancient Palestine and in other eastern countries, the roofs of houses were generally terraces. There the members of the family would gather in the cool of the evening and carry on conversation. From one rooftop to another the news of the day would quickly spread. It was here, where people were atuned to speaking and listening, that they should preach the doctrine he was teaching them.

In his second caution against fear, he says, "Do not fear those who deprive the body of life but cannot destroy the soul." He was pointing out to his Apostles that to die was the common lot of all men. No human power could do more to a man than nature itself would eventually accomplish. Therefore, they should not fear death for a good cause. There were greater evils in this world than the death of one's body.

But then he cautions them that there is something that they should be fearful of: "Rather, fear him who can destroy both body and soul in Gehenna." He tells them they should fear almighty God, for he has the power to cast their souls into the fires of hell or Gehenna. We should not abandon God in the face of persecution, for the suffering God could inflict on those who abandon him in the world to come is far worse than the worst imaginable suffering in this life.

Christ asks, "Are not two sparrows sold for next to nothing?" The smallest coin in the Jewish monetary system was the assarion. It was worth only 1/16 of a denarius. Its value would be about half a cent. This was what two sparrows sold for in Christ's time, one assarion.

But then Christ hastened to add, "Yet not a single sparrow falls to the ground without his consent." Here Christ is teaching his disciples that the providence of God extends even to the sparrows of the air. Certainly, then, he is far more concerned about human souls. Christ adds, "You are worth more than an entire flock of sparrows."

Christ gives an example of God's concern for man. He says, "As for you, every hair of your head has been counted." He is showing that God knows far more about us than we know about ourselves. God created each one of us; he gave us life. God, by a continuous act of his providence, keeps us alive. His love and concern are manifest in many ways. He gives us our food to eat, the air to breathe, the water to drink.

Because God provides for us so well and is so concerned for our welfare, Christ cautions his Apostles a third time, "So do not be afraid of anything." There is no human person or force that can harm us that greatly. Our only fear should be about the loss of our immortal soul.

Christ concludes with the words, "Whoever acknowledges me before men I will acknowledge before my Father in heaven. Whoever disowns me before men I will disown before my Father in heaven." Christ implies that men have free will. They can use their free will either to acknowledge or disown God. We should be most concerned about making the right choice in this regard.

One can disown Christ by his words — by speaking disrespectfully of him or denying him. He can disown Christ by his silence — by refusing to pray to him, by neglecting to worship him on Sundays. He can disown Christ by his deeds — by doing violence to his fellow man, by not respecting his property or rights.

On the other hand we acknowledge Christ when we do not fear to speak the truth. We acknowledge him when we do not fear to use good and decent language. We acknowledge him when we do not fear to be honest in all our business dealings — when we cheerfully get up on a Sunday to attend Holy Mass.

These are the ingredients with which saints are made. It was said of the martyrs that they feared God so much they had no fear of any man. Let us prayerfully hope the same can be said of us. God bless you.

# "A"      Thirteenth Sunday of the Year

*Matthew 10:37-42*

St. Matthew tells us in the gospel read at today's Mass that our Lord said to his Apostles, "Whoever loves father and mother, son or daughter, more than me is not worthy of me." Already some of his Apostles had left their families to follow him; for example, James and John, the sons of Zebedee, had left their father in the fishing boat when Christ called them and followed him immediately.

Christ in saying this was not tearing down the Fourth Commandment, which commands us to "honor your father and your mother." Rather, he is saying that there is a higher claim on the love and services of his followers. The higher claim is that of almighty God. When one has chosen to follow him, his service must come first above all else.

Consider the sacrifice of St. Perpetua, who suffered martyrdom in 205 A.D. by being thrown to the raging lions in the Roman Empire's persecution of the Church. A convert to Christianity, she loved her religion dearly. When arrested, she refused to deny it even though threatened with death. During her time in prison, her father came to visit her. He was still a pagan. He carried Perpetua's tiny infant in his arms. He pleaded with her to renounce the Christian faith. But even the love she had for her father and her baby boy was not strong enough to make her renounce her faith.

Our Lord continued, saying, "He who will not take up his cross and come after me is not worthy of me." This was one of the many veiled references Christ made during his public life to his forthcoming crucifixion. But this allusion as did all others went over the heads of the Apostles. Only after his crucifixion took place did they begin to fit all the pieces together and realize that he was speaking about that.

They did realize that crucifixion was the ordinary form of capital punishment used by the Romans. It was the cruelest death they knew of. A man condemned to be crucified was forced to carry the beam of his cross to the place of execution. To carry one's cross meant to make the supreme sacrifice. Hence, Christ was saying that to be worthy to be his follower one had to be willing to make the supreme sacrifice, even suffering death for his sake.

Christ added, "He who seeks only himself brings himself to ruin, whereas, he who brings himself to naught for me discovers who he is." To seek to satisfy the pleasures and whims of one's body is a fruitless pursuit. The body is never satisfied with any amount of pleasure; it craves only more and more. It is a pursuit doomed to failure, for the body is dissatisfied and in the end grows old and decrepit and dies. The only way to save the body is to deny it; deny it for a higher good — the service of Christ.

Christ then, in speaking to his Apostles, addresses them in three different titles. He calls them prophets, holy men and disciples. The Jews understood a prophet to be one who spoke in place of another. Indeed the Apostles were also holy men and disciples. They were all of these. Christ sent them forth to speak in his place.

Christ said, "He who welcomes a prophet because he bears the name of prophet receives a prophet's reward." In the first reading of today's Mass, we have an example of that. The prophet Elisha was welcomed by the lady in Shunem when she recognized him as being a holy man of God. She fed him and provided him with a bed to sleep in. She was rewarded when Elisha told her that she would bear a son in her old age.

Our Lord tells his Apostles that the people who welcome them into their homes and are kind to them will be rewarded. The Apostles are going forth in the name of Christ and preaching his gospel. They are his representatives here on earth. Christ said directly, "He who welcomes you, welcomes me." In his lifetime, Christ bestowed many spiritual blessings on those who were hospitable to him while here on earth — for instance, on Mary and Martha, on Lazarus and Zacchaeus. Christ will continue to bestow many similar blessings on those who welcome those who preach his gospel today — his priests and religious.

In effect, to aid those who preach the gospel of Christ makes one a missionary for Christ. One of the great joys in heaven for those who help Christ's successors will be the gratitude of the saints, whose souls were saved by religious they have aided.

Christ concludes by promising, "Whoever gives a cup of cold water to one of those lowly ones because he is a disciple will not want for his reward." Even the smallest of kindnesses, as exemplified by the cup of cold water, will not go unrewarded. Those who aid the disciples sent by Christ, even in the smallest way, are doing something pleasing to Christ our Lord, something for which he has promised them an eternal reward.

The second Vatican Council has decreed that the laity should go forth as powerful proclaimers of the faith — that the laity can and should perform a work of great value for the evangelization of the world. This is a duty and responsibility laid at the feet of every lay Catholic.

One practical way that the laity can fulfill this obligation of aiding Christ's disciples is by joining parish societies. You can lend your name, your time and your efforts to these practical means of extending Christ's kingdom here on earth.

The Church founded by Christ, using the authority Christ gave it, has seen fit to divide his kingdom on earth into parishes for the care of the souls living therein. As members of this parish, we urge you to take pride in this membership. Support parish activities. Give of yourself, your time and your energy. This is the spirit of Christ.

One factor, more than any other, that has stifled the growth of the Church in this country and in the world has been the indifference of lay Catholics. Once they have attended Sunday Mass, they consider their duties as Catholics to have ended for the week. Their attitude is, leave it to the priests and Sisters to teach and spread the Catholic faith. They smugly refuse to lift a finger for a parish activity, to attend a parish society meeting. But their attitude is wrong.

The second Vatican Council has pointed this out. The words of Christ in today's gospel tell them they should aid the disciples who preach his gospel. My dear people, examine your conscience in this regard. What have you done to aid those who preach Christ's gospel? What have you done to support your parish activities? If you cannot answer these questions affirmatively, then resolve to turn over a new leaf. Become a lay apostle. If you do, Christ has promised that you shall not want for a reward in heaven. God bless you.

# "A"     Fourteenth Sunday of the Year

*Matthew 11:25-30*

Christ had just finished his tour of preaching in Galilee. Although large crowds had turned out to hear him and brought to him many of their sick to be cured, still they did not believe in him or follow him. Christ had pronounced judgment on some of these Galilean cities. Christ said that there were more hardened sinners in Chorazin and Bethsaida in Galilee than there had been in Tyre and Sidon in the Old Testament. He said that Sodom would fare better on the day of judgment than Capernaum.

Christ then gave praise to his heavenly father for revealing to the merest children what he had kept hidden from the learned and the clever. His reference here to the learned and clever undoubtedly is to the spiritual leaders of the Jews, the scribes and the Pharisees. By the merest children Christ was referring to his Apostles, disciples and other followers. His Apostles were simple fishermen; his faithful followers in general were from the lower and poorer classes of Jewish society.

It is most ironical that those who knew most about the law of the Old Testament are the least disposed to his messianic revelation which would supersede it. A knowledge of the law of the Old Testament seems to be an obstacle to following the law of the New.

He points out in his prayer to his heavenly Father that he willed this situation to be. Thus, the beneficiaries of this new revelation are the humble, the lowly, those who possess a childlike simplicity. Humility becomes a necessary virtue for receiving the revelation.

Christ then tells his followers that all authority and power has been given to him by his Father in heaven. He then asserts that he and his heavenly Father have a thorough knowledge of one another. He then tells them that he is at liberty to reveal a knowledge of his Father to whomever he wishes.

Christ then issues an invitation to the weary and the overburdened to come to him and he will refresh them. The love that Christ holds in his heart for the poor and the afflicted clearly manifests itself. Christ is our God and Creator. He is the author of life and grace. He tells the poor and suffering in the world that he has love for them. When the rest of the world casts them out and suppresses them, he will help them. This is the greatest help and refreshment possible, from the author of life itself.

He invites the weary and the burdened to take his yoke upon their shoulders. In Palestine, the Jews were accustomed to using wooden yokes on their oxen. An ox was measured and a yoke to fit him was carved out of wood. After it was carved, it was then tried on the ox again and then planed and sanded so it would be smoother and would not chafe or irritate the skin of the ox in any way.

Making a yoke was the work of a carpenter. Joseph was the local carpenter in Nazareth, and Christ was his helper. Undoubtedly, in his lifetime, Christ had carved many yokes for oxen. A pious tradition tells us that the young Jesus carved the best ox-yokes in all of Galilee, and farmers came from many miles away to have him make their yokes — his love and understanding of animals was so great.

Christ has reference here to placing a light and well-fitted yoke on their shoulders, to the heavy burden the scribes and chief priests were wont to put on them. On another occasion Christ told the Jewish religious leaders how they delighted in placing heavy burdens on their followers, burdens which they themselves refused to carry.

In contrast to this heavy burden imposed by the Jewish leaders, the yoke or burden Christ asks us to carry is light and well-fitted to us. For as Christ had love for the oxen of the field, he has even greater love for us. He never overburdens any of his flock. He fits the burden he asks us to carry to our needs and our abilities. He tells us directly that his yoke is easy and his burden is light.

Not only is his burden light, but he gives us a new motive for bearing it —

Pope Benedict XVI

# *Joseph Alois Ratzinger*

Born: April 16, 1927

Ordained Priest: June 29, 1951

Ordained Bishop of Archdiocese
of Munich and Freising: May 27, 1977

Elevated to Cardinal: June 27, 1977

Elected Supreme Pontiff: April 19, 2005

Installed as Supreme Pontiff: April 24, 2005

Father of providence,
look with love on Benedict, our Pope,
your appointed successor to St. Peter
on whom you built your Church.
May he be the visible center and foundation
of our unity in faith and love.
Grant this through our Lord Jesus Christ, your Son,
who lives and reigns with you and the Holy Spirit,
one God for ever and ever.

ICEL © 1973

ARCHDIOCESE OF MILWAUKEE

that is, the motive of love. Christ is no longer concerned with the jealousies and bickering and pride of the scribes and Pharisees. He is concerned that his followers have love for God in heaven and for their fellow men. For if love pervades their hearts, then their burdens, no matter how heavy, will be easy to bear.

Christ said to learn from him for he is gentle and humble of heart. Considering the burden which Christ bore himself, there is no burden or yoke that can begin to compare with the cross he carried to Calvary. It was the instrument of his death. It was weighted down with the sins of all men of all ages.

The burden he was asked to carry, he carried willingly and without complaint.

Christ reveals himself as being gentle and humble of heart. His gentleness was evident day after day when the sick and helpless and ill were brought to him from all the towns of Galilee. His heart went out in sympathy to each and every one of them. He cured the lepers and made them whole. He gave sight to the blind and hearing to the deaf. He told the cripple to take up his bed and go into his house. When the crowds that came to hear him grew hungry and weary he multiplied the loaves and fish to feed them.

In the midst of this great charity and love which he manifested, Christ was humble. Every so often he cautioned the poor whom he cured to tell the miracle to no one. When the crowds wanted to make him king by force, he fled into the mountains alone. He avoided every earthly honor. Christ was born in the poverty of a stable. When preaching the gospel in Palestine, it was said, he had no place to lay his head.

Christ has made himself the friend of the poor and the oppressed by word and example. He has invited us, "Come to me." Therefore, why not accept his invitation? He loves us with an immeasurable love. Therefore, pray to him often. Beg of him the help and grace you need. He is our closest friend. He is eager and anxious to help us. God bless you.

# "A"     Fifteenth Sunday of the Year

*Matthew 13:1-23*

In today's gospel Holy Mother the Church presents for our consideration the parable of the seeds. It was a parable that had great meaning to the Jewish people, for farming was one of their major occupations. When the autumn rains came in November, they would begin to break up the soil with a kind of rough plowing and set out their seed.

Christ mentions in the parable that some seed fell on a footpath. The typical Jewish farm was criss-crossed by many footpaths; they were a common sight. The birds in Palestine, especially the sparrows, are most voracious. Frequently a sower can be seen being followed by a swarm of birds ready to eat any seed he may drop behind him.

The second type of soil on which the seed fell was rocky ground. This too is very typical of Palestine. The ground there is a thin layer of humus soil with large patches of limestone showing through in many places. The seed that would fall on this limestone would soon wither away after it had sprouted.

The third type of soil on which the seed fell was among thorns. Thorn bushes were a constant menace to the Palestinian farmer. His light plow was unable to cope with the heavy briers and thorns that infested his fields. Seed that fell among these thorns would naturally be choked off.

The last type of soil mentioned was good soil. Seed landing there grew and yielded grain a hundred- or sixty- or thirtyfold.

Christ taught this parable to the Galileans while seated in a boat only a short distance from shore. He did not explain its meaning to them at the time. However, when the disciples were with him alone, they asked him its meaning. Christ went on to explain.

The sower is almighty God. The seed is God's message to men. The footpath on which some seed fell represents the man who heard God's message but did not understand it. The birds, representing the evil one, stole it away from him.

The seed falling on patches of rock signifies the man who hears the message and at first receives it with joy. But he has no roots, so he soon withers. When trouble comes along, he falls away.

The seed sown among the briers represents the man who hears the message, but worldly anxiety and the lure of money choke it off. Such a man produces no yield. The seed sown on good soil represents the man who hears the message and takes it in and bears fruit giving a yield of a hundred- or sixty- or thirtyfold.

To draw a moral lesson from this parable, ask yourself what kind of soil your heart represents. How do you receive God's message? Is your heart like a hardened footpath where God's message cannot take root? Is your heart like rocky soil where God's message will wither? Does worldly anxiety and the lure of money choke off God's message when it comes to your heart, as did the thorns and briers?

The message of God can take root and grow only in good soil. We must make sure that our heart is fertile soil for God's word. We must try to understand it for what it is. We must allow it to take root; we must put aside the briers of worldly concerns that would choke away its life. Only in this way can God's message take seed and grow.

A century ago there were no Catholics in the village of Newton Grove, North Carolina. The village doctor, Dr. Monk, ordered a package of medicine from New York City. It arrived wrapped in a newspaper containing a sermon preached in St. Patrick's Cathedral. Dr. Monk read the sermon and became very interested in it.

He sat down and wrote a letter to any Catholic priest or bishop in North Carolina, especially the city of Wilmington, which was nearby. There it was delivered to Father Gibbons, the local pastor. Father Gibbons paid a visit to Dr. Monk and soon began instructing him in the faith. Dr. Monk not only became a Catholic, but a lay apostle as well. He did not keep quiet about his newfound faith, but told his patients and friends how much it meant to him. He was personally responsible for bringing hundreds of others into the Catholic Church. His heart proved to be fertile ground in which the seed or message of God could take root and grow. Remembering Dr. Monk, let us resolve that our hearts too will be fertile soil to receive God's message. God bless you.

# "A"    Sixteenth Sunday of the Year

*Matthew 13:24-30, 36-43*

On the occasion of today's gospel, Christ was teaching the Jewish people from the shore of the Sea of Galilee. The crowd was so anxious to hear him that they kept pressing him back into the water. Our Lord stepped into a boat and, sitting down, taught the crowds from there.

On this occasion he preached to them the parable of the "weeds." He told them the reign of God is like a man who sowed good seed in his field. While he was asleep, his enemy came and sowed weeds among his wheat, and then made off. When the crop began to mature, the weeds made their appearance as well. His servants asked him if they wanted them to pull up the weeds, but he answered no, lest they pull up the wheat along with it. He told them to let them both grow until harvest time and gather the weeds to burn and the wheat to store in his barn.

Later that day when the crowds had left Christ, his disciples asked him the meaning of the parable. He explained that the farmer sowing seed was the Son of Man. The field was the world, and the good seed, the citizens of the kingdom. The enemy is the devil, and the weeds are the followers of the evil one. The harvesters are the angels. The harvest is the end of the world. As they threw the weeds into the fire to burn at harvest time, so too at the end of the world the evil ones, the followers of the devil, will be cast into the fiery furnace.

It is evident that the kingdom of God, as it exists here on earth, is a mixture of both good and evil. Both good and evil exist side by side. But if God permits good and evil to exist side by side in this world, it does not mean that the evil will never be punished. On the contrary, the punishment of the evil will be very severe. Their punishment is only postponed until harvest time.

One lesson we may learn from the parable is that both good deeds and evil habits have small beginnings. They both grow from a tiny seed. Great sins all have a small beginning. They grow from temptations to commit small sins. Once consented to, the temptations grow larger. Therefore, one must be careful to see that no bad habits take root in his life. It is far easier to get rid of a sinful habit when it first begins to take root than later when it has grown and produced great sin.

If the weeds of neglecting our prayers have taken root in our lives, we should be quick to root them out. Each evening before retiring we should get down on our knees and recite an act of contrition. Each morning upon arising we should recite a morning offering, offering to God all that we do that particular day.

So also with the weeds of dishonesty, or impurity. Dishonesty in small matters can easily lead to dishonesty in much larger ones. Dishonesty shows a lack of respect for the rights of others. Purity is a virtue with which there is no compromise. Impurity in any form can readily cause one to lose his soul.

Profanity is another sin which begins with a small beginning. Unless it is routed out immediately, it will readily grow and multiply.

Mortification and penance become necessary tools in our battle to free our souls from the weeds of sinful attachments. Penance can kill the weeds that rob our souls of grace. Penance can restore a soul to its former state of grace.

One saint who purified her soul by penance was St. Margaret of Cortona. For nine years Margaret lived with a man who was not her husband. One day she found him murdered in the woods. The sight of his decaying body made her realize the end she was coming to herself. It prompted her to do penance. She spent much time in prayer and began to perform many acts of charity. Through the Sacrament of Penance she was reinstated in grace and began to lead a holy life. One day St. Mary Magdalene appeared to her and told her that her penance was most acceptable in the sight of almighty God.

Like St. Margaret, let us root out the weeds of sin in our own lives. Let us make our souls fertile soil on which to receive the message of Christ. In this way his message will take root in our souls and grow and lead us to an everlasting reward. God bless you.

# "A"     Seventeenth Sunday of the Year

*Matthew 13:44-52*

The gospel of St. Matthew read at today's Mass contains three separate and distinct parables. Yet all three of these parables which Christ preached in his native Galilee have a common thread of meaning. All of them pertain to the kingdom of heaven and the means Christ gave us to attain it, membership in his Church. All three parables were down to earth and full of meaning for the Jewish people. In addition, it was natural for Christ to use this literary form of a parable to teach the Jewish people.

In the first of these parables Christ says the reign of God is like a buried treasure which a man found in a field. In our modern age this parable may at first have or seem to have an unnatural or stilted meaning. Yet it was very clear and meaningful to the Jews who heard it.

We must realize that in the time of Christ there were no banks as we know them today for the deposit of money. In ordinary everyday practice people considered the safest way of guarding their money was to bury it in the ground. The knowledge of the place of burial was their guarantee of safety.

We must realize, too, that Palestine was the most fought-over country in the world. In the course of history it had been conquered and reconquered by the Jews, the Babylonians, the Assyrians, the Persians, the Greeks, the Romans and several other peoples. In time of war when people fled their homes, whatever wealth they could not conveniently take with them they buried in the ground, hoping that when their homeland was reconquered they could dig up their treasure and repossess it. Sometimes this did not come about. Sometimes the conquest would last for a long period of years and the original buriers would never return. It was not an uncommon thing for a man to find a buried treasure on his land. The owner of a piece of land could claim any treasure found on it.

Here Christ is comparing the reign of God, or the kingdom of heaven to buried treasure. As a man would naturally try to acquire title to the land of the treasure, so, too, would one who realized the greatness of happiness in heaven would try to become a member of Christ's Church and attain this great happiness.

In the second parable Christ compares the kingdom of heaven to a merchant's search for fine pearls. To better understand this parable, one should realize that the most valuable and treasured jewel or possession known to the ancients was a fine pearl. Diamonds and other stones were relatively unknown and were not treasured as highly. Hence to Jews living in the time of Christ, a fine pearl was the finest treasure one could possess.

Thus Christ was using a most natural comparison between these two. He was comparing their greatest known treasure to the kingdom of heaven.

But there is more implied in this parable. Christ tells us that to buy or obtain the pearl, the man who discovered it went back and put up for sale all that he had. He took whatever action was necessary to obtain the treasure. In comparing the pearl to the kingdom of heaven, one should take the necessary means to acquire heavenly happiness. This means one must believe in the teachings of Christ and obey his commandments. This is the action that is necessary — the equivalent of selling one's goods to obtain the treasure.

In the third parable, Christ compared the reign of God, or the kingdom of heaven, to a dragnet thrown into the lake which collected all sorts of things. This was a meaningful and natural comparison to make. The Apostles of Christ were fishermen. They made their living by fishing from the sea. Since they were fishing for a living and not just for the sport of it, the means they used to fish with was not a fishing rod but a dragnet.

They ordinarily used a large net, or at times a series of three nets, supported either from a boat or from buoys. Their net was weighted from the bottom, so that it would come close to the bottom of the lake. They would suspend the net in the lake between their boats. They would beat the water with their oars to scare the fish into it and then drag the net to shore.

By fishing this way with a dragnet they would not only enclose the fish but at times old shoes and bottles and other refuse that had been thrown into the lake. Once they had dragged the nets to the shore they would begin the task of sorting the fish from the refuse taken with them.

The net can be compared to the Church of Christ here on earth. The items collected in it are the members of his Church. They include the good, bad and indifferent. Christ compared the sorting of the fish and junk collected to the day of judgment which will take place at the end of the world. He said at that time angels will separate the wicked from the just and hurl the wicked into the fiery furnace.

We must realize that in the world God permits the good and bad to live side by side. He does not separate them here on earth. Neither does he reward or punish them. That will come later. In fact, it is the use we make of our free will that makes us good or evil.

Frequently we may hear the question, why does God permit this or that evil to exist in the world? Here we have the answer to it. God does not intend this life to be a place of reward or a place of punishment. That will come later. He intends it to be a place of trial.

In all three parables Christ is speaking about the kingdom of heaven. This is the goal God has intended all of us to reach. This is our intended final destination. But to attain it, we must make some effort of our own. We must acquire title to the land; we must sell what we have or rid ourselves of our earthly possessions; we must sort out the good from the evil in our lives. But since this is our intended goal, it is worth any effort we are required to make to achieve it. Let us remember that heaven is an eternal reward — one to which there is no end. Therefore, no matter what the price or effort, it is more than worth it. Let us realize that heaven is the goal of our personal lives; let us work diligently to attain this end. God bless you.

# "A"    Eighteenth Sunday of the Year

*Matthew 14:13-21*

Father Timothy Dempsey, a priest from the diocese of St. Louis, has often been called "the Apostle of the down-and-out." Born in Ireland, Father Dempsey suffered hunger in one of Ireland's potato famines. But after studying for the priesthood, Father Dempsey came to the United States and was stationed in St. Louis. There he worked among the poor and underprivileged.

When the depression of the 1930's hit this country, Father Dempsey saw many people go hungry. So he set out to secure food for them and feed them. He started a free lunch station that fed some six million meals to the poor during the depression. On one day alone in 1932 more than 13,500 people were fed.

But in doing this charitable work, Father Dempsey was doing no more than imitating our divine Savior himself. In the miracle mentioned in today's gospel, our Lord and his Apostles were gathered on the northwest shore of the Sea of Galilee. The Apostles had just returned from a tour of preaching in the small towns and hamlets of Galilee. A large crowd had assembled to hear our Lord preach and witness his performing miracles.

Our Lord had gratified the crowd. But then, wishing to obtain a little rest and peace and quiet for himself and the Apostles, he put out to sea in a boat with them. They set sail for the eastern bank of the Sea of Galilee, for Bethsaida. But the crowd, sensing what the destination of Jesus and his Apostles might be, set out on foot and walked around the northern shore of the lake to this place. Some of the crowd arrived on foot even before our Lord and the Apostles were able to make the trip by boat.

But again our Lord had compassion for the crowd. He spoke to them as they had requested. He healed those who were sick. But it was now evening, and one of his disciples came to our Lord and mentioned to him that the people had had nothing to eat. He suggested that the multitude be dispersed so that they would go back to their homes and villages and obtain something to eat.

But our Lord had already determined on a course of action. He intended to work another miracle. On previous occasions he had performed miracles only when requested to do so, but this time Christ took the initiative. He told the Apostles there was no need for them to send the people away. But they protested that the only food they had was five loaves of bread and two fish.

Christ asked that they be brought to him and then he bade the crowd to sit down on the grass. Christ took the five loaves and two fish, looked up to heaven, blessed and broke them and told the Apostles to pass them out to the multitude.

The Apostles did as our Lord commanded. But there seemed to be no bottom to the basket of food. They passed them out and continued to pass them out. No matter how much they passed them out, they could not empty the basket of food of its contents. Everyone had enough to eat.

When they had finished eating, the Apostles began to gather up the fragments of food so that nothing would be wasted, and they filled twelve baskets with the fragments of the loaves and fish that were left over. They had more fragments left than the amount of food they had originally started with.

St. Matthew goes on to tell that the number of people that our Lord miraculously fed that day numbered about five thousand.

There are several important lessons we can learn from this miracle that Jesus performed on the shore of the Sea of Galilee. We should notice that before he broke the bread or distributed it, he blessed it first. This was an old Jewish custom. No Jew would sit down to eat without first blessing his food. This, too, is a Christian custom.

Whenever we sit down to eat, we should realize that the food before us has been given us by almighty God. Everything we have in this world has been given to us by almighty God. God has not only given us our life, but also gives us each day the means to sustain it. In teaching the Apostles how to pray, in teaching them the Our Father he taught us: "Give us this day our daily bread."

Since our food comes to us through the goodness and creation of almighty God, we owe him a debt of gratitude. This debt we can fulfill by reciting our grace before and after meals.

A second lesson we can learn is the great compassion Christ showed for the crowd despite his being tired. Despite his having preached to them earlier that day and being eager to find rest and quiet, he cheerfully consented to speak to them again and to perform a miracle for their benefit when he saw their need. This charity and compassion are synonymous with Christ. It is a virtue which predominated in his life; it is a virtue which he tried both by word and example to instill into his followers.

Charity and compassion have marked the true followers of Christ down through the ages. Following World War II, some of the charitable work of Pope Pius XII has been brought to light. During the war and the Nazi occupation of Rome, the food situation in the capital city became very acute. The Pope realized this and made noble efforts to relieve it.

He pooled the Vatican resources and was able to gather together a fleet of 100 trucks. These he sent daily to northern Italy to the farm regions and the grain-growing belt. Each day these 100 trucks would return to Rome loaded with flour and other types of food. The flour was turned over to the bakers of Rome who baked bread for the Pope.

Each day some 200,000 people were fed at the Vatican. Bread and hot soup was the usual fare plus whatever else they could obtain. There was a nominal charge of two lire for the food (the equivalent of half-a-penny in our American money), but the poor were never turned away when they did not have it. As the food situation grew worse, the number of people who were fed by the Vatican grew to 400,000 each day.

In this instance, Pope Pius XII showed himself to be a true follower of Christ. He showed charity and compassion on the multitude when they were in need. He practiced a corporal work of mercy in feeding the hungry.

In our lives so let us resolve to imitate our divine Savior in the practice of charity and compassion. Let us resolve that we will say grace before and after every meal. Let us show our gratitude to almighty God for the food he gives us. God bless you.

# "A"     Nineteenth Sunday of the Year

*Matthew 14:22-33*

The Sea of Galilee is shaped like a pear; its wide end lies to the north. It is 13 miles long and seven miles wide. In elevation it is very low; it is located 682 feet below sea level. Both to the east and west of it lies the Galilean mountain range. It fills a broad valley in the midst of this range.

Ordinarily, it is calm and placid; its surface resembles that of a sheet of glass. But then at times, without any previous warning, turbulent wind currents will pour over the mountains and churn the sea into a raging frenzy. This was the case in today's gospel after Christ had told his Apostles to sail across it.

Christ had just finished multiplying the loaves and fishes and feeding a crowd of some five thousand people. The response of the people to this miracle was a natural one, but one that Christ was not anxious to see. The people wanted to seize Christ and make him their king or temporal ruler. This was not a part of Christ's plan for redemption. Christ was truly a king, but a spiritual one only.

Realizing the Apostles would be no help to him in this situation, he insisted that they sail in their boat to the other side of the lake. Many of them, too, dreamt of Christ's establishing a temporal kingdom upon this earth. Then too, Christ in his divine knowledge knew that a storm would suddenly arise that night at sea and provide him with the opportunity to perform the miracle described in today's gospel. Christ made his way into the nearby mountains alone, choosing this way to avoid the crowd.

The Apostles had only sailed a few hundred yards from shore when one of the sudden storms, for which the Sea of Galilee is famous, broke upon them. Their sails were useless. Even rowing with their oars failed to gain them any headway. They were at the mercy of a violent sea, and fear came upon them.

Minute after minute and hour after hour went by. The Apostles huddled in their boat, always fearing that the next wave might be the one to upset them and claim their lives. But then suddenly, about three o'clock in the morning, in the eerie blackness of the stormy night, they all plainly saw Christ walking on the water and coming toward them. They were terrified. Some cried out, "It is a ghost!"

But then the gentle voice of Christ reassured them. "Get hold of yourselves! It is I. Do not be afraid!" While saying this, the waves passed under his feet and around him. He appeared not even to be wet. He walked as smoothly as he would have on dry land.

As might be expected, Peter, the natural leader and spokesman for the Apostles, had something to say on this occasion also. "Lord," he said, "If it is really you, tell me to come to you across the water." Christ, who was completely honest and frank at all times, said to him, "Come!"

Peter was an impulsive person. He would not take time to think out a situation. He would say or do the first thing that came into his head. At the time of the Transfiguration, when Moses and Elijah appeared together with Christ on Mt. Tabor, Peter spoke up and wanted to build three grass huts to commemorate the appearance — three small temporary shelters which would have been down within the year. This was the first empty thought that came into his head.

At the Last Supper, Christ quoted the prophet Zechariah as saying, "I will strike the shepherd and the sheep of the flock will be dispersed." Peter spoke up and said, "Even though I have to die with you, I will never disown you." Yet the same night Peter denied that he knew our Lord on three different occasions.

Later that same evening when Christ was arrested in the Garden of Olives by the Roman soldiers, Peter drew his sword and cut off the ear of one of them. Such an assault on the ruling Romans might well have caused his own arrest. It might even have prompted them to draw their swords in turn and injure or slay Peter. But here again Christ intervened to save him, as he did in the incident in today's gospel. Christ healed the wounded soldier.

In today's gospel Peter got out of the boat and started to walk on the water moving toward Jesus. But then the impulsive Peter became frightened and began to sink. He cried out, "Lord, save me!" Jesus at once stretched out his hand and caught him. Christ reprimanded him, "How little faith you have!"

Christ climbed onto the boat, and immediately the wind died down. The

Apostles in the boat paid him reverence and declared, "Beyond doubt you are the Son of God."

Christ had come to help his Apostles. He came to help them in two ways, first by calming the storm and helping them in a physical sense. But he came also to help increase and strengthen their faith. He revealed his glory to them — his power and control over the forces of nature, his ability to walk on the water, his ability to calm the storm.

Picture Christ, if you will, extending his hand to Peter and saving him from the raging sea. Despite Peter's rashness, despite his impetuosity, Christ was to choose him to be his successor on earth, the first visible head of the Church, the first Pope.

One of the teachings of the Catholic Church today is that the Pope enjoys infallibility. In matters of faith and morals, when the Pope speaks from his official position of the chair of Peter to the entire Church, we have Christ's guarantee that he is speaking the truth. Christ had promised that he will be with his Church always until the end of the world. He has promised also that the jaws of death will not prevail against it. But these conditions can only be true when the Pope teaches faithfully and truly the doctrine of Christ.

As Christ extended his saving hand to Peter on the Sea of Galilee, so Christ extends his saving hand to Peter's successor, the Pope in Rome, to guide him on the course of truth and preserve him from perishing in the sea of errors that surround him.

Let us be grateful to Christ, our Lord, for the saving hand he extends to us and to his Church. Christ is kind and compassionate. He is filled with love for us.

For, like Peter, we are filled with human failings and weaknesses. Whenever we stumble and fall, let us not fail to cry out as he did, "Lord, save me!" Christ, who is all-powerful and all-loving, will not fail to hear and help us. God bless you.

# "A"  Twentieth Sunday of the Year

*Matthew 15:21-28*

In the first reading at today's Mass, the prophet Isaiah writes in the 56th chapter of his book that foreigners will join themselves to the Lord. This prophecy was literally fulfilled through the events mentioned in today's gospel or third reading. St. Matthew tells us in his gospel that Christ had journeyed into the district of Tyre and Sidon. This territory was in the country of Phoenicia; it was to the north of Galilee and was inhabited by Greeks.

This was the first journey of Christ into a foreign land since Mary and Joseph had taken him as an infant and fled into Egypt to escape the wrath of Herod, who was trying to kill him. Then, after Herod had died, Mary and Joseph had returned to their native Palestine and dwelt there. This Phoenician trip was also to be Christ's last journey to a foreign country.

Christ, once each year, had passed through Samaria in going from his native Galilee in the north of Palestine to celebrate the Passover in Jerusalem, located in Judea in the southern section of the country. Samaria lay in between the two, in central Palestine. Geographically, Samaria was a part of Palestine, yet the Jews in Jerusalem and Galilee did not regard the Samaritans as true members of the Jewish people. Years before, the Jews living in Samaria had intermarried with the Syrians and Babylonians, contrary to Jewish law, giving birth to a new nation not purely Jewish.

Christ's reasons for going to Phoenicia were threefold. He was looking for a place to escape temporarily from the plots of his adversaries, the Pharisees and the Sadducees. He was looking for a place to rest from the large crowds which followed him everywhere in his native Galilee and gave him no rest at all. Also, and perhaps most important of all, he wanted to bring his Apostles and close disciples to an isolated place to teach them and complete their training as his followers.

But Christ did not find the isolation and solitude he had hoped for. His reputation as a great preacher and miracle-worker had preceeded him. A Canaanite woman approached him and asked him to heal her daughter, who was possessed by a demon. Although a gentile and a pagan, she addressed Christ politely with the title Son of David. But St. Matthew tells us that Christ gave her words no response. He ignored her. He kept walking along the road with his Apostles.

Never before had Christ taken such a hard line as he did with this pagan woman. He allowed her to continue to follow him down the street, imploring him as she went, but gave her no recognition. Even the disciples began to grow weary of hearing her pleas. They asked Christ to get rid of her, as she was beginning to annoy them. At this point Christ said simply, "My mission is only to the lost sheep of the house of Israel." He announced that he was confining his preaching and miracles to the Jewish people.

But this Canaanite woman would not take no for an answer. Again she pleaded, "Help me, Lord." At this point, Christ responded, "It is not right to take the food of sons and daughters and throw it to the dogs." By sons and daughters Christ was referring to the Jewish people, and by dogs he meant gentiles. But we should not misconstrue this figure of speech in referring to the gentiles as dogs to be an insult. It was customary for eastern people to speak to each other using figures of speech. The term "dog" did not have the insulting or derogatory connotation in the Aramaic language, which Christ spoke, that it does to us.

Christ was telling her that his mission was to preach to and heal the Jewish people. He bore no hatred or ill-feeling toward the gentiles, but their time had not yet come. Much later, just before his Ascension, he would commission his Apostles to go and teach all nations. The Jews were to have the first opportunity to obtain salvation; the gentiles would have their turn later. Christ had not come to Phoenicia to preach publicly or perform miracles, but merely to be alone with his Apostles and to instruct them.

The woman understood well what Christ meant and took no offense from it. She replied, using the same figure of speech which Christ had used himself:

"Please Lord, even the dogs eat the leavings that fall from their master's table." She declared herself willing to accept any small favor Christ might give her over and above what he was bound to give the Jews.

Christ complimented her, saying she had great faith, and then granted her request. He worked a miracle at a distance. Even though her daughter was not present, she recovered that very moment.

From this miracle of Christ we can learn an important lesson — perseverance in our prayers. The Canaanite woman persevered in her request, even when the Apostles wished to silence her and even when Christ had told her his mission was to aid the Jews. She persevered because of the love she had for her daughter. Her love and perseverance were rewarded.

When we pray to God, he certainly hears our prayers. If he delays in answering them, there is a good reason for the delay. Perhaps it is to strengthen our faith — to cleanse our souls more fully, to make us more humble. Perhaps, in his divine knowledge, he knows that what we are praying for is not good for us. In such a case, he will answer our prayers in another way and give us something better in its place.

No prayer remains unanswered. God will hear us and grant us what is best for us in the light of eternity. We may not see or realize the manner in which he is answering us; that may remain a secret until the day of final judgment. God is most kind, most loving, most generous. He is pleased that we pray to him for help. Remember, he will not be outdone in generosity. He has said that he will reward a hundredfold a cup of cold water given in his name. God bless you.

# "A"     Twenty-first Sunday of the Year

*Matthew 16:13-20*

Among the twenty-seven books in the New Testament, two are epistles written by St. Peter. The first of these epistles St. Peter wrote from the city of Rome in the year 64 A.D. or later. He addressed it to the people of Cappadocia and other neighboring people in Asia Minor.

St. Peter writes this epistle with an air of authority. He makes the claim to be an Apostle of Jesus Christ. He writes orders for the presbyters and disciples of the Church in Asia Minor. He directs their activities even though hundreds of miles away.

In this instance St. Peter, as always, acted as chief of the Apostles and was so acknowledged by them. It was Peter who spoke in the name of the other Apostles on Pentecost Sunday. It was Peter who first received converts into the newly founded Church. It was Peter who moved for the choice of another Apostle to take the place of Judas. It was Peter who defended the other Apostles before the Jewish Tribunal.

It was Peter who received the first gentile into Christ's Church. It was Peter who summoned and presided over the Council of Jerusalem, the first council of the Church.

There is a good reason for these events. After Christ had risen from the dead he said to Peter, "Simon, son of John, do you love me more than these?" Peter replied, "Yes, Lord, you know that I love you." Christ said to him, "Feed my lambs." Again Christ asked him if he loved him, and again Peter affirmed that he did. Christ responded, "Tend my sheep."

A third time Christ asked Peter if he loved him. The repetition of this question for a third time grieved Peter. He answered, "Lord, you know everything. You know well that I love you." Christ said, "Feed my sheep."

By telling Peter to feed his lambs and feed his sheep, Christ gave St. Peter authority to rule over his Church on earth. He made St. Peter the visible head of his Church on earth. He placed him over the other Apostles. He gave him the office that we call today by the title of Pope.

On a previous occasion, as mentioned in today's gospel, Christ promised this power to St. Peter. He said to him, "You are 'Rock,' on this rock I will build my church, and the jaws of death shall not prevail against it." Christ changed Peter's name from Simon to Peter, which means rock. He promised to make Peter the rock or foundation on which He founded his Church. This promise he fulfilled when he told him to feed his lambs and feed his sheep.

Peter's authority over the other Apostles was readily recognized by them. St. Matthew clearly states in his gospel that St. Peter was first among the Twelve. Christ prayed for Peter that his faith fail not, and once confirmed, he would confirm his brethren in faith. Their faith was to be governed by him.

St. Peter was the spokesman for the other Apostles whenever the occasion arose. It was St. Peter who baptized Cornelius, the first Gentile to be received into the Church. It was St. Peter who decreed that Gentiles might become Christians simply by being baptized.

St. Peter went to Rome and there presided as its bishop in the year 44 A.D. For twenty-five years he filled this post as bishop of Rome. It was here in Rome in 65 A.D. that Peter wrote his first Epistle to the Cappadocians. After reigning as the bishop of Rome for some twenty-five years, Peter was finally put to death there by the Emperor Nero; crucified upside down in the year 69 A.D.

Because Peter chose Rome as his see or bishopric, the bishop of Rome today is regarded as his successor as Pope in the Catholic Church. St. Linus succeeded St. Peter, and it was he who was regarded as Pope. St. Clement succeeded him. In the year 90 A.D. a dispute arose in the Church at Corinth. The dispute was settled by St. Clement, even though St. John, the Apostle, was alive and dwelling in Ephesus at the time.

From the time of St. Peter, there has been an unbroken line of successors in the Papacy, 263 of them, right down to our present Pope Paul VI. He reigns in Rome as Pope today, the direct successor to St. Peter.

The list of Popes, numbering among them 76 canonized saints, is a list of learned and saintly leaders of the Church. No country on earth can boast of such a long line of distinguished leaders.

Let us thank God, my dear people, for giving us this means of ruling his Church on earth; let us thank Christ that he has left us a visible head of the Church to rule in his place here on earth. Let us recognize our Holy Father as the successor of Jesus Christ on earth. Let us honor him with the greatest respect. For in honoring the leader of Christ's Church, we are honoring Christ himself. God bless you.

# "A" Twenty-second Sunday of the Year

*Matthew 16:21-27*

One of the great saints in the Catholic Church in the last five centuries is St. Ignatius Loyola. Born of Spanish nobility, Ignatius as a young man chose military service in the army of his native country as his career. He earned fame and honor for his gallantry as a soldier. When war broke out between France and Spain, he was entrusted by his country with the defense of Navarre. But misfortune struck the gallant leader.

A cannon ball from the French artillery richocheted off the stone wall of the fortress, striking and breaking his right leg. The loss of Ignatius, their leader, threw panic into the ranks of the Spanish troops, and they soon surrendered to the French. But the victors treated Ignatius with honor. They recognized his rank and ability as a soldier. They escorted him home to his native Loyola. There he heard disappointing news.

His leg had been set improperly on the battlefield. A bone was protruding; it had to be sawed off. His leg had to be rebroken, reset and painfully stretched. He was told that even if all went well, one leg would always be shorter than the other; he would henceforth walk with a limp. His days of military leadership were at an end. Ignatius accepted all this with the courage and patience of a veteran soldier.

While it was all taking place and he was lying idly in bed, he looked around for something to occupy his mind. There was but one book available at Loyola; that was a life of Christ. This he read and reread. But there was one sentence in the book, one question which Christ asked, which stuck in his mind — a sentence taken from today's gospel: "What profit would a man show if he were to gain the whole world and ruin himself in the process?"

This sentence contains a world of meaning. It provides food for thought for each one of us. Picture, if you will, a giant balance scale. On one side is piled all the riches of the world, the gold, the silver, the precious jewels, the riches of every nation of every age. On the other side of the scales is placed your immortal soul. Which means more to you? Which is of the greater worth? Which would you prefer — the pleasure and enjoyment of those riches for a few short years or the salvation of your soul and happiness for all eternity?

Ignatius pondered this question well. He realized that his whole world had been the military rank and honors he had achieved; he had cared little for spiritual things. But he resolved to change. Leaving Loyola, he made a retreat at Manresa. He placed his sword on our Lady's altar at her shrine of Montserrat. He went forth to found the Jesuit order in the Church — a religious order which has given us many great saints and scholars.

Today's gospel depicts Christ preaching to his disciples in their native Galilee. He tells them that in a little while he must go to Jerusalem. There he must suffer greatly at the hands of the elders, the chief priests and the scribes. The chief priests were predominantly the Sadducees in Jerusalem; the scribes were mostly of the Pharisees. They, together with the elders, the respected leaders of the people, made up the Sanhedrin, the court and ruling body in Jerusalem under the Roman governor Pilate. He said these men would put him to death.

At this point, St. Peter, the natural leader and spokesman for the Apostles, spoke up. Peter loved Jesus and did not want to see him hurt. He said, "God forbid that any such thing should ever happen to you."

Imagine Peter's surprise when Christ rebuked him for showing concern that harm should come to his master. He said, "Get out of my sight, you satan! You are trying to make me trip and fall." Peter shared the misconception of nearly all the Jews of his time, that the Messiah to come would be a temporal ruler and rule over a temporal kingdom. He would lead them to great successes on the field of battle.

The reason for the rebuke was that Peter, though unintentionally, was urging Christ to do the same thing the devil was urging him to do — to seek an easy way out, to escape the sacrifice on the cross. Christ told him he was judging by man's standards and not by God's. Matters seen in the light of eternity often look far from those seen in a material way.

Christ then spoke his beautiful discourse on self-denial which has been so often quoted and written about by spiritual writers. "If a man wishes to come after me, he must deny his very self, take up his cross, and begin to follow in my footsteps." He prefaced this sentence with the words, "If a man wishes." This means that to follow Christ must be an act of free will.

To deny oneself means to say no to oneself and yes to God. It means one must dethrone himself and enthrone God. It means that we must cease making our pleasure the motivating force of our life, and instead make God's honor and glory the chief motivating force of our life. Self-denial means that God must be number one with us in everything we do.

Christ said we must take up our cross. All his listeners knew that the cross was the instrument of death. The person sentenced to die by crucifixion was forced to carry the cross-beam of his cross to the place of crucifixion. Therefore, Christ meant that those who would follow him must be able to endure any suffering, even death, for his sake.

He added that only by losing our life for his sake will we find it. He clearly meant that to lose our earthly life for his sake will be the means of gaining eternal happiness in the life to come in heaven.

Then he asked the question which made St. Ignatius think so deeply. "What profit would a man show if he were to gain the whole world and ruin himself in the process?" Here, Christ was weighing worldly values against eternal values. If a man were to possess the greatest treasure on this earth, or even all the treasures of the earth together, he would possess it for but a single instant of time, when compared with the length of eternity, which is forever.

Even the smallest reward in heaven would be of far greater value than the greatest treasure as a reward on this earth. There can be no true or accurate comparison between the two — no more of a comparison that can be made between time and eternity. Eternal values surpass temporal ones in every case.

Lest any man choose in any other way, Christ had one final word of warning. "The son of Man . . . will repay each man according to his conduct." There will come a day of judgment when everyone will have to answer for his choices and his actions. Everyone will be rewarded or punished according to the good or evil that he had done. Judgment is inescapable. If there is no other thought or consideration that will prompt one to do good, then this alone should more than suffice. The alternative is untold suffering for all eternity.

My dear people, these words of Christ wrought a great change in the life of St. Ignatius. But what effect will they have on yours? Perhaps they may not cause you to change your state of life, but at least they should make you more conscious of eternal values. They should cause you to weigh your life and your conduct in the light of eternity. They should make us realize that heaven is the true goal of us all. God bless you.

# "A"     Twenty-third Sunday of the Year

*Matthew 18:15-20*

One of the greatest of all Americans was Benjamin Franklin. In the year 1787 he became alarmed at a situation that developed in the Constitutional Convention in Philadelphia. Its members failed to open its sessions with prayer as had been done all through the Revolutionary War. Benjamin Franklin voiced a protest against it:

"I have lived a long time, eighty-one years — and the longer I live the more convincing proof I see of this truth, that God governs the affairs of men. And if a sparrow cannot fall to the ground without His notice, is it probable that an empire can rise without His aid? We have been assured by Sacred Writings that except the Lord build the house, they labor in vain that build it. . . . I therefore beg leave to move that thenceforth prayers imploring the assistance of heaven be held in this assembly every morning before we proceed to business."

One reason why men should pray is because of the power of prayer. Christ has said, "Where two or three are gathered in my name, there am I in their midst." Hence prayer recited in a group has the power to call down God from heaven in the presence of men.

During World War II Captain Eddie Rickenbacker was one of eight men flying over the Pacific Ocean in a transport plane. The plane developed engine trouble and crashed into the ocean. But all the men managed to scramble onto a rubber life raft. Their only possessions were four oranges and a Bible. Soon the oranges were gone. The men faced the threat of starvation.

The men decided to pray publicly together. Following their prayers, two fish escaping from a school of barracuda leaped into their boat. After that there were no skeptics left in the boat.

Then they prayed for water. Suddenly a rain storm came up, and the men had their fill of fresh water. But even with the rainstorm and the few fish they caught, they felt the pangs of hunger. They prayed to be rescued. Finally after twenty-one days of drifting, a scouting plane saw them and brought help. Following their rescue Captain Rickenbacker and his crew gave public testimony to their belief in the power of prayer.

The power of prayer is so great it has been called the key to heaven. When Christ was crucified on Mount Calvary, he was crucified between two thieves. The thief on his right, St. Dismas, begged mercy of Christ, saying, "Jesus, remember me when you enter upon your reign." Christ replied, "I assure you: this day you will be with me in paradise." This single prayer of a dying thief gained him eternal salvation. Scenes like this occur frequently.

Prayer has opened the gates of heaven and saved more souls from hell than man can number. An act of perfect contrition has the power to remove mortal sin from one's soul. Prayer can gain one sanctifying grace. It can bring the triune God from heaven into the souls of men.

Prayer can satisfy in whole or in part for the temporal punishment due to sin. Prayer has the power to release souls from purgatory. The suffering of the souls there is most terrible. The tragic part is that the souls detained there are helpless to help themselves. They must depend on the prayers of the Church Militant, those of us here on earth. When one realizes that his prayers can free a soul from such great suffering, he can grasp some idea of the power of prayer.

Prayer plays on the heartstrings of almighty God. Prayer is like the broadside salvo of a battleship, a salvo which the gates of heaven cannot withstand. Prayer can stay or move the hand of God to act. Prayer can change the course of history. It can make a lasting mark in eternity. Hence one ought to pray to make known his needs to God, and because of the power of prayer.

When one prays, he should pray with devotion. Prayer is more than lip service. There once was a parrot that could recite the fifty-six words of the Our Father perfectly, but the parrot could not know the meaning of the words. Too many people pray like the parrot without realizing the meaning of what they are saying. We should mean what we say in prayer and pray with devotion.

One too should pray with resignation to the will of God. Far too often people pray only that their own will be done. They forget that God is all knowing and all wise. Christ gave us the example in this regard when he prayed in the Garden of Olives, "Father . . . not my will but yours be done."

Lastly, St. Paul advises we should pray without ceasing. This means we should pray daily — every morning upon arising and every night before retiring. Every day we should make an act of contrition for our sins. It means too we should make our every action a prayer to God. One can do this by reciting the Morning Offering each morning.

Truly if one prays in this manner, with devotion, with resignation and without ceasing, he will be exalted in heaven. Christ has said, "Ask and you shall receive, that your joy may be full." God bless you.

# "A"    Twenty-fourth Sunday of the Year

*Matthew 18:21-35*

The greatest writer in the English language is William Shakespeare. One of his best known plays is the "Merchant of Venice." A frequently quoted passage of this play is Portia's answer to Shylock, who is demanding a pound of flesh,

"The quality of mercy is not strained.
It droppeth as the gentle rain from heaven
Upon the place beneath; it is twice blest;
It blesseth him that gives, and him that takes;
'Tis mightiest in the mightiest: it becomes
The throned monarch better than his crown; . . ."

But the idea which Shakespeare expresses here is not new. It comes directly from the teaching of Christ, which is beautifully illustrated in the gospel read at today's Mass.

Christ taught the parable of the merciless official during his last days in Galilee. A certain king decided to settle his accounts with his officials. One official owed him a very large amount. Since he had no way of paying the debt, the king decided to sell him and his family. But then the official prostrated himself before the king and begged for patience, promising to repay the whole debt. The king relented and forgave him his debt.

This same official went out and met a servant who owed him only a fraction of what he had owed the king. He refused his fellow servant's plea for mercy and had him thrown into jail.

When his fellow servants saw what had happened they were badly shaken, and went to their master to report the whole incident. His master sent for him and said, "You worthless wretch! I cancelled your entire debt when you pleaded with me. Should you not have dealt mercifully with your fellow servant, as I dealt with you?" Then in anger the master handed him over to the torturers until he paid back all that he owed.

Christ then gave the moral teaching of the parable, "My heavenly Father will treat you in exactly the same way unless each of you forgives his brother from his heart." Christ was here extolling the virtue of mercy or forgiveness.

On still another occasion Christ was questioned by his disciples as to how many times one must forgive those who sin against them. They asked if they must forgive seven times as stated in the Jewish Law. He answered, "I say to you not seven times but seventy times seven times." Our Lord meant we must forgive indefinitely.

Christ not only preached mercy on this earth, but he practiced it as well. He forgave Mary Magdalene; he forgave the sins of the woman accused of adultery. He forgave the sins of the paralytic at Capernaum, the man sick with palsy. Even while suffering the cruel torments of crucifixion, he forgave the sins of the good thief hanging beside him on the cross.

One of Christ's greatest gifts to man was the Sacrament of Penance, or of Reconciliation. As Christ had forgiven sinners, he wanted to pass this power on to his successors in the Church so that sinners of all times might avail themselves of the benefits of his sacrament.

Crucifixion was the cruelest death known in the Roman world. Inevitably the victim suffered so much pain and agony he would begin to blaspheme and revile his executioners. This was almost expected. But Christ was different. Instead he said, "Father, forgive them, for they know not what they do."

The virtue of mercy is nothing more than an extension of the second great commandment of God — "Love your neighbor as yourself." True love wishes the good of the one who is loved. True love of our neighbor would be willing to forgive him any offenses he might have committed against the lover.

When St. Thomas Moore was about to be beheaded by the orders of King Henry VIII, he was asked if he were not angry at the king. He replied he was not. He replied he wished to imitate St. Stephen, who forgave Paul and the others who stoned him to death.

Let us imitate their example. Let us practice forgiveness of those who have harmed us. In so doing we shall be imitating Christ himself. Forgiveness of others makes us worthy of God's forgiveness. It will make us worthy of eternal reward hereafter. God bless you.

# "A"     Twenty-fifth Sunday of the Year

*Matthew 20:1-16*

In the gospel read at today's Mass, St. Matthew relates the parable of the laborers in the vineyard. The conditions Christ gives for hiring laborers are most timely; they could occur today in the Holy Land, so little have conditions changed. Vineyards are still cared for by hand. Owners of estates still go into the marketplace to hire workmen for the day.

The estate owner, either because time was pressing to harvest the crop of grapes or because he was generous, went out several times during the day to hire workmen. He hired workers at dawn, midmorning, noon, midafternoon and late afternoon. He reached an agreement on wages with those he hired at dawn. With those he hired later in the day he told them only he would pay them what was fair. To all of these workers at the end of the day he gave a full day's pay.

The estate owner represents God. The workmen are the souls he calls to his service. The wages he pays them are their eternal reward. The hour of payment represents the hour of death. The varied trips to the marketplace represent the varied times of life God may give the gift of faith.

St. Matthew concludes this gospel passage with the sentence, "Thus the last shall be first and the first shall be last." Scripture scholars see the first here as representing the Jewish people. They were the first called to the faith, but many rejected the call. The gentiles were the last to be called, but many of them accepted the call, and they shall be first.

The moral lesson to be derived from the parable is that the call to the faith comes to different people at different times. There is no priority given to any nation or any race. The accident of birth does not mean that one will be saved automatically, nor does it mean that one will automatically be lost. The parable beautifully illustrates the catholic or universal nature of the Church.

Christ commanded his disciples to "go, therefore, and make disciples of all nations." Christ died on the cross for all men. On the first Pentecost Sunday, people from many different nations, speaking many different languages, all understood the Apostles speaking their own tongues and were baptized in the Church. Thus the birth of the Church on Pentecost had the mark of catholicity about it. The first person to describe the Church of Christ as "Catholic" was St. Ignatius of Antioch in 400 A.D. The name has been used ever since.

During World War II, two boys entered the army together, a Catholic from Brooklyn and a Methodist from Kansas. They were assigned to the same outfit overseas and were captured together by the Germans. While they were in prison camp a German chaplain came to say Mass for the prisoners. The non-Catholic boy was amazed to see his Catholic friend and a German soldier kneeling side by side at Mass. His friend later explained to him that the Church is the same all over the world. This led to the soldier's conversion when he was freed.

The Catholic Church is the largest single denomination in the world. It claims over four hundred million members spread throughout the world. Its missionary activities are legendary. The growth of the Church in our country can be traced to such missionary labors. Of the thirteen original colonies founded by England, one of them, Maryland, was established for religious freedom for Catholics. It was a Catholic priest, Father Hennepin, who discovered Niagara Falls. Father Marquette, a Jesuit missionary, was the first to explore the Mississippi. The city of St. Louis was named after a king of France and a saint in the Catholic Church — so also cities in nearly every state in the union.

A Catholic priest was with Columbus when he discovered America. St. Augustine, Florida, was the first permanent settlement in the continental U.S.A. and was named for a saint. Franciscan missionaries helped settle our western coast and found such cities as San Francisco, named after St. Francis, and Los Angeles, which means city of the angels.

We owe a double debt of gratitude to these Catholic missionaries. We should thank them for the gift of faith which they have left us. We are obligated to them for settling our country.

Christ's love for men knows no bounds. As the estate owner went out five times to bring workmen into his vineyard, Christ down through the centuries has gone out countless millions of times to bestow the gift of faith on souls. No matter at what hour we have been called, whether we have been Catholics right from birth or are converts to the faith, let us resolve to make our faith a strong and living one. Let us strive to be worthy of the reward Christ has promised to those who believe in him. God bless you.

# "A"     Twenty-sixth Sunday of the Year

*Matthew 21:28-32*

The time was Tuesday of Holy Week — the last week of our Lord's life on earth. The place was the city of Jerusalem in the outer precincts of the temple. Christ had been hailed only two days before on Sunday as the Savior of the people. They had greeted him with shouts of Hosanna. Since that time they had not ceased to follow him. But around him at the moment was a group of the chief priests and scribes of the temple.

Therefore he took this opportunity to address to them the following parable: A man who owned a vineyard had two sons. He told the first son to go out and work in the vineyard. The son addressed his father politely as "sir" and promised to go right away. However, he never went. The father gave the same command to the second son, but the son refused. Later, however, he repented and did go out and work.

Jesus asked the crowd of scribes and chief priests which of the sons did as the father wanted. They naturally replied the second. Christ then said to them that the tax collectors and prostitutes were entering the kingdom of God before them.

The meaning and application of this parable are quite obvious, and nearly all Scripture scholars are in agreement on its meaning. The son who said he would obey his father, and then did not, represents many of the Jewish people. They were the chosen people, pledged to look for the coming of Christ. Their prophets and leaders throughout the Old Testament spoke about and prepared for his coming. Abraham's covenant with God was their promise, but their refusal to accept Christ when he did come was their refusal to go into the vineyard.

The son who at first refused to go into the vineyard and then repented and went represents the gentile nations. For centuries they were the lost souls. They were without God's revelation or special help. They had nothing beyond the natural law of their consciences to guide them. The fact that they repented and finally went into the vineyard represents their future acceptance of Christ's teaching.

After Jesus tells them the parable he puts a question to them. He asks which of the two sons did what the father wanted. They are compelled to give the obvious answer — namely, the second. Then Jesus, speaking directly to the chief priests and elders, said that tax collectors and prostitutes were entering the kingdom of God before them. He directly pointed out to them that they were exemplified by the first son, who did not obey.

The two groups Christ mentioned, the prostitutes and tax collectors, were among the most despised groups of Jewish society. Christ was using them as examples of some who would enter heaven before them. He adds that these groups were among those who put faith in the teachings of John the Baptizer, whereas their leaders did not.

St. John's message to the Jewish people was to preach repentance for sin.

But repentance was one virtue many refused to practice or follow. The second son is the parable showed repentance for his refusal to obey his father. Having repented, he then obeyed.

One may say that the primary purpose of this parable is to show that true obedience consists in deeds rather than in words. One's actions speak louder than — and are far more important than — the words one speaks. Performance will far outweigh promises.

Obedience is a most necessary virtue. We all realize that it is necessary to have authority. Without it there would be disorder and chaos. Yet when someone in authority gives us a command that is difficult or distasteful, our natural reaction is to rebel against it. Here we must use the power of our wills to do what we know is right, despite its difficulty. We must obey.

As Christians, we should look upon a command from a lawful superior as an opportunity of gaining grace. The Catholic Church teaches us that one of the graces God gives us is *actual* grace; this is a passing help to do what is good and pleasing in God's sight and avoid evil. There is no set pattern for our receiving these graces. God gives them freely when he deems the time to be appropriate.

The father's calling the son to work in his vineyard is an example of such a grace. Fulfilling the duties of one's state in life may also be such a grace. For a father, it may mean going off to the factory or office each day. For a mother, it may mean the housework, the cooking of meals and many other details. For a child, it may mean going to school day after day.

Perhaps the son, in refusing to go into his father's vineyard, was thinking of the monotony of his work, row after row of grape vines. Each one of them had to be weeded. It was a grueling, back-breaking job. To one looking down the rows of vines, they seemed endless. Perhaps, too, we may dread the monotony of the job we are forced to perform. Because of the drudgery, we too may be tempted to refuse or reject this offered grace, to refuse to perform our duty.

But as Catholics we should not refuse or pass up these graces offered to us by almighty God. There is a limit on his generosity and the graces he gives us. The particular grace he is offering us now may never be offered again.

Let us resolve to use these graces and to use them wisely. Let us accept the graces offered by God whenever they are presented to us. For it is only by working in the vineyard of our Lord that we can hope for salvation. God bless you.

# "A"     Twenty-seventh Sunday of the Year

*Matthew 21:33-43*

Some of the parables our Lord taught are contained in the one or two of the gospels of the Four Evangelists. But the particular parable, that of the tenants, is contained in three of them — Matthew, Mark and Luke. The particular gospel of St. Matthew is read at today's Mass.

Tenant farms and vineyards were a common thing among the Jews in the time of Christ. Frequently in secular writings Jews are depicted as having to face the problem of dealing with absentee landlords. In this particular parable read at today's Mass, Christ depicts the landowner as having put a lot of energy and labor into the development of his farm. Christ shows him as having put a hedge around it, dug a vat and erected a tower.

In the time of Christ a hedge consisted of a line of cactus plants or a loose stone fence around property. At times a closely spaced row of thorn bushes was erected. This was designed to keep out the wild boars, who would gore and tear up the grape vines, and also thieves who might steal the grapes.

The landowner dug a vat; this was for the winepress which was to be found in every vineyard. The press consisted of two vats or troughs, one above the other but connected to each other. The grapes were pressed in the upper vat, and the grape juice would run down into the other. The vats were generally made of stone or brick.

And finally he built a tower. Towers were generally built of stone and covered with roofs of branches. A tower provided shelter for those entrusted with running the vineyard and also was a place from where they might watch for thieves or anyone doing harm to the vineyard.

After building all these things in his vineyard, the landlord leased it out to tenant farmers. In the time of our Lord tenant farmers were entitled to a certain share of the crop, and the rest they were obliged to turn over to the owner of the vineyard.

The owner of the vineyard went away, but at harvest time he sent his servants to the tenants to obtain his share of the grapes. The tenants beat one servant, killed a second and stoned a third. He sent more servants with similar results. Finally, he sent his son to collect the rent. The tenants, knowing his son would inherit the vineyard, killed him too, hoping they would come into possession of his inheritance.

Christ related this parable in the city of Jerusalem to a group of chief priests and elders of the temple. His meaning was obvious. The landowner was almighty God. The wicked tenants were his listeners, the chief priests and elders to whom he was addressing the parable, in particular, as well as the Jewish people in general. God had made them the chosen people and entrusted them with the duty of preparing the world for the coming of Christ.

The servants whom he sent to collect his share of the crop were the prophets of the Old Testament. The killing, beating and stoning of these servants refers to harsh treatment the prophets of the Old Testament had received at the hands of the Israelites.

The son of the landowner, whom the tenants also killed, represented Christ. Christ delivered this parable in the Holy City on Tuesday of Holy Week, the last week of his public life. In a few days' time, on Thursday night following the Last Supper, the listeners would send soldiers to arrest Christ and bring him before the Sanhedrin and Pontius Pilate. The following day they would crucify him.

When Christ had finished the parable he asked the chief priests and elders what the landowner would do to the evil tenants. They answered, "He will bring that wicked crowd to a bad end. . . ." But in their false piety, they could not bring themselves to believe that Christ was referring to them. Some may have imagined that he was referring to the Romans, who then ruled over the Holy Land, or to some other group of evil people.

Christ then quoted for them a passage from the Old Testament, from the Book of Psalms: "The stone which the builders rejected has become the keystone of the structure." This prophetic passage referred to the Christ who was to come and be rejected by the Jews; it referred to Christ who was talking to them.

Then lest there be any doubt about his meaning, Christ pointedly told them that the kingdom of God, namely the position they held as teachers and leaders of the Jewish religion, would be taken from them and given to others — to a nation that would yield to a rich harvest.

In language that was crystal-clear, Christ was prophesying their downfall. He said their place would be taken by others, namely the gentiles; by others who would return a fair share of the harvest to the landowner. They would be God's chosen people in the New Testament to come.

In reflecting on this parable, we must admire the patience of the landowner. He sent two groups of servants and then his own son to collect his portion of the crop that was justly his. For many centuries God was patient with the Jews, sending many prophets to warn them and then his own divine Son to preach to them. But finally, following the death of his Son, a new order was established. The vineyard was entrusted to others — to the gentiles.

We who are Christians today are successors of the first gentile followers of Christ. The care of God's vineyard has been entrusted to our hands. Eventually, at the time of harvest, an account of our trust will be made of us. What answer will we be able to make to God in judgment?

Will we be able to answer that we have lived a good Christian life? Will we be able to say that we have worked loyally and faithfully in his vineyard? Will we be able to answer that our faith has brought forth good fruit? Will we be able to answer that the needs of our life have enhanced the honor and glory of God — the reason for which he placed us in his vineyard?

Ask yourself the question — what fruit or good works have you produced in your life to show honor to God? If you cannot give a definite and positive answer to this question, then perhaps it is time to turn over a new leaf. It is time to make a change in our lives and begin to pay tribute to God.

God is most patient. But despite his patience the day of judgment will eventually come. Only those who have returned to him a just harvest will be admitted to his eternal home in heaven. God bless you.

# "A"     Twenty-eighth Sunday of the Year

*Matthew 22:1-14*

In today's gospel St. Matthew relates the parable of the wedding banquet. The king in the parable invited many guests to this banquet which he gave for his son. But when the banquet was ready, the guests refused to come. A second time he sent his servants, reminding the invited guests that his bullocks and corn-fed cattle were killed and everything was ready. Still they refused to come. One went to his farm, another to his business. Some laid hold of his servants and insulted them, and some even killed them.

At this the king grew furious. He sent his army to destroy those murderers and burn their city. After this he sent his servants into the byroads and invited anyone they came upon to fill up the wedding hall. The king, coming to the banquet, caught sight of a man not properly dressed for the occasion. He had his servants bind him hand and foot and cast him into the darkness outside.

Theologians are in common agreement as to the meaning of this parable. The king giving the banquet is almighty God. The wedding banquet to which he invited them is membership in Christ's Church. Those first invited, who refused to come, were the majority of the Jewish people. The murder of his servants represents the crucifixion of Christ and the martyrdom and sufferings inflicted on his disciples. The guests brought in from the byways represent the gentile peoples. The person lacking the proper dress represents the member of his Church coming to the sacraments in the state of serious sin rather than in sanctifying grace.

Consider the greatness of this invitation to the wedding banquet which we have received. From the day of our birth we are slaves to sin, sold into this slavery by the original sin of our first parents. We have become spiritual beggars. But now we have received an invitation to the wedding banquet — an invitation to partake of spiritual life. This invitation is a ray of grace and hope. It is an invitation for us to become saints of God — an invitation to enter the kingdom of heaven.

We are invited to partake of a banquet given by almighty God. We are offered a means to rise above the material kingdom in which we live and to become citizens of a heavenly kingdom. It is a privilege we have not earned, a privilege we are not worthy of; yet this privilege is offered us because of God's generosity and love.

St. Matthew's sequel to the story tells of a guest entering the banquet without the proper dress. This could only mean that his soul was not in the state of sanctifying grace — that instead he was in the state of serious sin. Early commentators on Holy Scripture thought this referred to Judas Iscariot, one of the original Twelve, who betrayed our Lord.

However, in a broader sense, it could be any Christian who had grave sin upon his soul. Any Catholic who would attempt to approach the Communion rail to receive Christ's body and blood in serious sin would be lacking the wedding garment. The actions of such a Catholic show his indifference to Christ's crucifixion, to the torments Christ endured to free us from sin. Such a person would be making a sacrilegious Communion.

God grant that such an unworthy reception of Communion would never take place. But if it should, we know the harsh penalty that will be inflicted. The king ordered the man bound hand and foot and thrown into the night to wail and grind his teeth. The punishment for sacrilege is eternal torment.

One saint who in her lifetime prayed often for those guilty of sacrilege was St. Thérèse of Lisieux, the Little Flower. As a child, St. Thérèse once heard of a hardened criminal about to be executed. Although a Catholic, the criminal spurned all religious assistance. He ridiculed the sacraments. Thérèse prayed for him fervently. Before his death he relented and asked to see a priest.

All of us are invited to the wedding banquet. Let us gladly accept this invitation, but let us make sure that we are all wearing the wedding garment — that our souls are clothed in sanctifying grace. God bless you.

# "A"     Twenty-ninth Sunday of the Year

*Matthew 22:15-21*

When Jesus entered Jerusalem for the third and last time in his public life, the Jews sought a way of trapping him and putting him to death. On Tuesday of Holy Week a group composed of Pharisees and Herodians approached him with a trick question. They asked, "Is it lawful to pay tax to the emperor or not?"

The Herodians, who proposed the question, were a political group among the Jews. They were supporters of King Herod, who in turn had pledged his loyalty to Rome. Many Jews, on the contrary, were openly opposed to Roman rule. But the Herodians, while not loving the Romans, acknowledged their authority and were willing to abide by it.

The question they asked our Lord appeared to be a simple one, but it was not. If our Lord answered yes, he would lose his status in the eyes of the Jewish people of being a liberator, the role the Jews expected the Messiah to play. But on the other hand, if he answered no, the Herodians would denounce him to the Roman authorities as being opposed to their government.

But our Lord saw through their trick. He saw the implications of their question and did not fall into their trap. Instead he called them hypocrites and asked them to show him a coin of tribute. When he asked them whose head and inscription were on it, they replied, "Caesar's." Then Christ said, "Then give to Caesar what is Caesar's, but give to God what is God's."

By this answer our Lord was indicating there are two separate fields of authority, the civil authority and religious authority. He indicated that man owes allegiance to both the state and the Church.

Sometimes it is charged today that a Catholic cannot be a good American — that he cannot show full loyalty to the federal government and to the

Catholic Church as well. Such a charge is false; it is absurd. There is nothing to prevent a good Catholic from being a good American.

In fact, the very opposite of this charge is true. Being a good Catholic can aid one in being a good American. Following the commandments of God in one's spiritual life makes one truthful and honest. All these are qualities a good citizen should possess. A good citizen should have respect for his neighbor's property; he should be honest; he should be truthful and morally good.

Being a good Catholic is an aid to being patriotic and civic-minded. This is not only true in principle but has proven to be true in actual practice as well.

During World War II in Waterloo, Iowa, there stood a certain house in whose window there hung a flag containing five blue stars. It was a proud house, the house of the Sullivan family. Their five sons were serving in the United States Navy. But following the battle of the Solomon Islands, those five blue stars were changed to gold stars. All five sons were killed in action. The Sullivans were a fervent Catholic family, and at the same time they were genuinely patriotic.

Delving back into American history, one becomes aware that Catholics and the Catholic Church played a large part in winning independence for the United States. One man responsible for helping America win her freedom was Bishop John Carroll, the first Catholic bishop of the United States, the bishop of Baltimore.

When America first declared her independence and revolted against Great Britain, Congress sent Benjamin Franklin to France to help secure that nation's aid in America's cause. But at first Franklin was unsuccessful in his efforts. Washington sent him an urgent note saying that unless America secured French aid, the cause would fail. Great Britain had won a continuous series of victories since the war began, and most people considered it but a matter of time before the revolution collapsed.

America needed arms and ships and trained leaders and supplies of many types. It was at this time that Bishop Carroll, then Father Carroll, petitioned the Pope in Rome to use his influence to secure French aid. The Pope in turn sent a papal nuncio to the King of France. The King of France granted the request of the papal nuncio and promised to send the French army and navy to aid America.

The papal nuncio then told Benjamin Franklin that it was through the intercession of Father Carroll that this aid was being sent. George Washington himself later said that Bishop Carroll did more to insure the success of the American Revolution than any other man. In England he was referred to as "the rebel bishop."

The foreign soldiers who came to America's aid in the Revolutionary War were predominantly Catholic. Lafayette was a Catholic. So too was John Barry, the father of the American Navy. Kosciusko and Pulaski, the Polish volunteers, were Catholics. It was actually through the aid of these soldiers that the Revolution was won. The French navy blockaded Cornwallis by sea at Yorktown, prevented his escape and caused him to surrender.

Down through history the contributions of Catholics to the United States have been great indeed. We as Catholics can be proud of the contribution of our faith and its members to the government of this country.

Let us realize that we have a twofold duty — a duty to our God and to our country. In being good Catholics, we are likewise being good citizens. God bless you.

# "A"    Thirtieth Sunday of the Year

*Matthew 22:34-40*

The incident related in today's gospel occurred when a group of Pharisees surrounded our Lord for the purpose of trapping him in his speech. Our Lord had just finished answering a group of the Sadducees, who had been unable to catch him in anything he had said.

A lawyer was the spokesman for the group that addressed him. He asked our Lord which commandment of the law was the greatest. Christ replied, " 'You shall love the Lord your God with your whole heart, with your whole soul, and with all your mind.'. . . The second is like it: 'You shall love your neighbor as yourself.' "

In giving these two commandments Christ did not attempt to give a summary of the Ten Commandments God had given to Moses on Mount Sinai. Rather he gave the motives for keeping the Ten Commandments. The first great commandment our Lord enunciated was to love God.

The first three of the Ten Commandments are based on this. The first obliges us to worship God; the second forbids us to take his name in vain; the third, to attend Mass and keep holy the Lord's day. Certainly the person who truly loves God will do all these things.

We have the greatest of motives for loving God. God is our creator. He has given us our life and everything we possess. We depend upon him for the food we eat each day, the air we breathe, for the clothes we wear, for the roof over our heads. God constantly, day after day, showers his blessings upon us.

Because of his goodness, man has a serious obligation to love God. He can show this love through daily prayer and by obeying God's commandments. Man can show his love for God by praising and glorifying God, by willingly accepting all that comes from his hand.

The second great commandment — to love our neighbor — flows from the first. One should see in his neighbor another creature made by God. Our neighbor is the handiwork of God's creation — one whom God has made to his image and likeness — one upon whom God has bestowed the gift of life.

The account of our Lord's giving these two great commandments of love is contained in St. Matthew's gospel, as read in today's Mass. However, two other evangelists, St. Mark and St. Luke, in their accounts throw additional light on this event. St. Mark points out that the lawyer's motive in asking the question was not the best; he was trying to trip Jesus up verbally. But when he heard our Lord's answer, he was completely satisfied by it. His bad dispositions changed to good ones.

He answered Christ, "Excellent, Teacher . . . 'to love . . .' is worth more than any burnt offering or sacrifice." Our Lord congratulated him and said, "You are not far from the reign of God."

All three evangelists are quick to point out that love is the most important virtue in the Christian religion. Without it, it is impossible to please God. When love is present, the commandments of God are easy to obey. They become a living reality. They become a part of our life.

Christ stressed love more than any other virtue in his teachings. It was the predominant virtue in his life upon earth. It was love that prompted him to humiliate himself and come to earth and take on the body of man.

It was love that prompted Christ to perform so many miracles — to heal the lepers, to give sight to the blind. It was love that prompted him to multiply the loaves and fishes and feed the multitude on the mountainside. It was love that prompted him to endure the terrible torments of crucifixion. Unless Christ had loved us, he would never have redeemed us.

Christ gave us the perfect example to follow in showing love to God and to our neighbor. He showed us love both by his teaching and his example.

God has even made our future place in the kingdom of heaven dependent upon the degree of love of God in our hearts. The greater the love of God in our hearts in this life, the greater will be our happiness in the next. Love is the deciding factor in our place in eternity.

It is the love of God that has won heaven for so many saints. St. Nicholas of Tolentino is an example of a saint who loved God deeply. Born in the thirteenth century, St. Nicholas found his greatest happiness in visiting Christ in the Blessed Sacrament and pouring out his heart in love to him.

As a young man he determined to become a monk. This he did. He was stationed at the city of Tolentino for over thirty years. There it was his duty to preach daily to the people. His sermons were frequently marked by conversions to the faith and great evidence of grace. He touched the hearts of all who heard him.

His life was a continual display of love for God and his fellow man. It dominated his life. It brought much happiness into the lives of all around him. In the end it brought him eternal happiness in heaven as a saint of God.

Love can do the same for you if only you will let it. Christ loves each one of us with an immeasurable love. If we only return a small fraction of this love back to God, we can attain to indescribable heights in the kingdom of heaven. Love can change your life. God bless you.

# "A"    Thirty-first Sunday of the Year

*Matthew 23:1-12*

The place was the city of Jerusalem, in the outer precincts of the temple. The time was Tuesday of Holy Week, the last week of our Lord's life here on earth. On the previous Sunday Christ had entered the holy city in a triumphal procession riding on a donkey, with palm branches strewn before him and the crowds shouting, "Hosanna in the highest!"

Since he had entered the holy city crowds had not ceased to follow him and beg to hear him preach. Someone from the crowd brought up the subject of the scribes and the Pharisees. Christ did not hesitate to speak about them.

But to the surprise of many, Christ backed up the authority of their teachings. He said they had succeeded Moses as teachers. He admitted the authenticity of their doctrine. He admitted that they taught with authority — that their teachings were correct and authentic. He told the Jewish people to observe everything they commanded them to.

This was shocking news to some of the Jews, who had observed the evil lives that some of the scribes and Pharisees were leading. They had falsely reasoned that since they were leading evil lives, it was unnecessary to follow their teachings. Christ quickly contradicted this idea.

Christ then added in explanation that while their words were bold, their deeds were few. They placed heavy burdens on other men's shoulders but refused to carry any burden themselves. He said that they performed their good works to be seen by others.

Christ then gave them two concrete examples. He said they widened their phylacteries and wore huge tassels. Phylacteries were small wooden boxed containing copies of certain prayers found in the Old Testament, which the Jews fastened to their left arm and their forehead by means of leather straps whenever they prayed. Some, by wearing larger or more ostentatious phylacteries than others, would try to make themselves seem more pious in the eyes of their fellow Jews. Still another custom some fell into as a false sign of piety was to put them on a long time before prayer service and wear them for a long time after prayer service had ended.

The second means Christ pointed out by which they showed false piety was to lengthen their tassels. In the Old Testament the books of Numbers and Deuteronomy describe God commanding the Jews to wear fringes on the border of their garments that they might remember the commandments of God. As a false sign of piety some of the scribes and Pharisees began to lengthen these tassels on their clothing and to brighten their colors. They tried to convey the idea that the longer their tassels the more faithful they were in observing the Ten Commandments. But in reality this was but another sign of their pride and hypocrisy.

Christ continued. He pointed out that they tried to take the places of honor at a banquet. At any formal gathering the place of honor was the seat to

SEASON OF THE YEAR / 107

the immediate right or left of the host, or as close to him as possible. These were the seats they constantly sought for themselves.

They also coveted the seats of honor in the synagogue. According to Jewish tradition, children and unimportant people sat in the rear seats of the synagogue. The more important people sat in the front. The choicest seats of all were those of the elders, which faced the congregation. These they prized above all others.

Christ pointed out that they were fond of being called rabbi and father and teacher. These titles were a form of flattery among them. There was but one true father; that was God the Father in heaven. There was but one true teacher; that was the Messiah, whom Christ claimed to be.

Christ said the greatest among them was not the man who made the greatest show of outward piety before others; rather the greatest was he who serves the rest. To be truly great, Christ pointed out, one must serve another as a servant serves his master.

Christ concluded his thoughts on the subject with this statement, "Whoever exalts himself shall be humbled, but whoever humbles himself shall be exalted." Christ preached humility in all things, but it is especially applicable in prayer, the subject Christ was discussing.

Prayer is in itself an act of humility, for in prayer we testify to our dependence upon almighty God, and the need we have of his help. In prayer we take the position of a beggar knocking on the gates of heaven, asking for help. A beggar cannot be proud; otherwise he is contradicting himself in what he is asking for.

Prayer is talking to almighty God, In talking to God we cannot put on any airs or false disguises. God is all-knowing and all-wise; He cannot be deceived. He clearly sees through our pretense or disguise. Rather than obtaining what we want, we are turning God against us by our attempt to deceive him.

Pride and prayer are incompatable. The prayer of a proud person is an empty shell; he is using prayer as but another means to display his pride before others. To pray with pride is to be dishonest with God; it is an insult to him. It is to invite God's wrath and punishment rather than his favor. As Christ said, "Whoever exalts himself shall be humbled. . . ."

Let us heed these words of Christ; let us heed the example he has give us — of being humble of heart. At the Last Supper, before giving us his body and blood in the Eucharist, he washed the feet of his Apostles.

While Christ rejected the prayer of the proud Pharisees, he heard the prayers of the humble. He granted forgiveness and many graces to the repentent Mary Magdalene, who poured precious oil on his feet and wiped them with her hair. He granted salvation to the humble prayer of the good thief. All this bears true testimony to the statement of the ancient writer in the Book of Sirach who said, "The prayer of the humble pierces the clouds." God bless you.

# "A" Thirty-second Sunday of the Year

*Matthew 25:1-13*

In the light of modern-day customs the parable of the ten virgins seems unrealistic, but it is unfair to judge these parables in the light of modern customs. They must be judged in the light of the customs in the time of ancient Palestine. In this light the parable is very realistic.

In the time of our Lord a wedding ceremony was an occasion for widespread celebration. A whole village would turn out for the ceremony, and the ensuing festivities might continue for a week or more.

Contrary to our custom, the bride and groom would not go away on a honeymoon trip. Instead they stayed at home and held open house for a week or longer. Secular Jewish historians testify to the fact that it was a common practice when a wedding was planned that ten virgins would keep the bride company until the groom arrived at her house. Also it was customary when traveling after dark in Palestine to carry a lighted lamp for there was no kind of street lighting to be found.

In view of these facts the parable takes on a new glow of reality. Christ tells us in this particular parable that of the ten bridesmaids waiting for the groom to come during the night, five were foolish and five were wise. The foolish virgins neglected to take any oil for their lamps; the five wise ones had brought oil, but only enough to keep their own lamps burning.

The groom delayed his coming until after midnight, and the lamps of the five foolish virgins began to go out. Therefore, they went off to the oil dealer to buy more oil for their lamps. While they were gone, the bridegroom arrived and took the five wise bridesmaids into the house for the wedding ceremony.

When the five foolish virgins returned, they cried to the master of the house to unbar the door for them. But he replied that he did not know them and refused to let them in.

In the case of most of his parables, Christ does not explain the meaning. He leaves it up to the hearer to draw his own application. But down through the centureis theologians and Scripture scholars have agreed upon a common application of this parable of the ten virgins.

They look upon the wedding feast as the kingdom of heaven. The bridegroom represents Christ, and the bride, the Church. The bridesmaids or virgins represent the faithful members of the Church. The light in their lamps represents the light of faith. The oil that feeds the lamps represents everything that helps us preserve sanctifying grace. As long as the lamp is burning the soul is alive with sanctifying grace. When the lamps go out, our souls are darkened with serious or mortal sin.

As the bridegroom finally did come at some hour after midnight, so too death will someday claim us all. The five wise bridesmaids who had oil in their lamps and were taken inside by the bridegroom represent those souls found with sanctifying grace in their souls at the hour of death. They will be taken into the kingdom of heaven. The five foolish bridesmaids, who were found without oil in their lamps, represent those who lost their light of faith through serious sin. Being left outside by the bridegroom represents their being excluded from the kingdom of heaven, of being condemned to the punishment of hell.

Although Jesus did not usually explain the meaning of the parables he taught, he departed from his custom and stated a moral lesson for this one. He said, "Keep your eyes open, for you know not the day or the hour." The moral as stated by Christ lends support to the application made by Scripture scholars. We should always be prepared for the day of judgment by keeping the light of faith alive in our souls, by remaining constantly in the state of sanctifying grace. This we should do at all times, for we know not the day nor the hour of our death. We do not know the time or occasion when Christ, the bridegroom, will come and call us.

On the day of judgment we must all face Christ. On that day we won't be members of a large group. There will be just you and Christ, alone, together. This will be your particular judgment. Christ will judge you that day as king and ruler. He won't be wearing the crown of thorns as he did before Pilate; rather he will be wearing a crown of eternal glory.

But Christ will be a just judge. He will not condemn us to hell for something we did not do. God does not want us to choose an eternity of suffering for ourselves; he did not make us for that reason. He made us for heaven. He will only condemn to hell those who have stubbornly disobeyed his laws, who refused to put on the wedding garment of sanctifying grace. He will condemn to hell only those who have deliberately and willingly and knowingly chosen to act contrary to his laws.

When we appear before Christ to face judgment, our prosecutor, the one who will accuse us of serious sin, will be the voice of our own conscience. No matter how much we have tried to smother or drown it or stifle its speaking out, it is there! It will be heard on judgment day. In the presence of an all-knowing God we cannot conceal the truth through a lie. We will not be able to color or hide the truth of its testimony. We will not be able to plead ignorance for things we have knowingly done.

With our own conscience to accuse us, we shall not be able to call Christ unjust for any punishment he does mete out. We ourselves will be the first to admit that we deserve any punishment that he inflicts.

Judgment may come suddenly as the prophet Daniel testified it did for King Belshazzar in the Old Testament. King Belshazzar gave a sumptuous banquet for over a thousand people. At this banquet there was much drinking, idolatry and immorality. While the banquet was still in progress, a hand became visible which wrote three words on the wall beside the king's throne. They were, "Mene, Tekel and Peres."

Neither the king nor any of his party could solve their meaning, until the king called Daniel forward to translate them. Daniel revealed their meaning, saying God had measured Belshazzar's kingdom and would put an end to it — that the king had been judged and found wanting. That very night King Belshazzar was killed.

We may not be as fortunate to receive a warning as did this evil king, but death will surely come to us all. It will come when we least expect it. It will come like the bridegroom in the night. Therefore, let us imitate the five wise bridesmaids. Let us prepare for it by continually keeping our soul clothed in the garment of sanctifying grace. Then Christ, instead of locking us in the darkness outside, will lead us with him into the wedding feast of eternal happiness. God bless you.

# "A"    Thirty-third Sunday of the Year

*Matthew 25:14-30*

The place was the city of Jerusalem. Our Lord had just made his way there after traveling south from Galilee through Jericho and Judea. The time was the last week of his life prior to his crucifixion. It was his third and final visit to the holy city during his public life.

Large crowds were gathering to hear him preach. They hung on his every word. Never before had they heard a speaker with his knowledge and his authority. They were aware of his claim to be the long-awaited Messiah or Redeemer. Many approached him with skepticism, but the longer they listened the more convinced they were that he spoke the truth.

On this occasion Christ related the parable of the silver pieces. He told them that a man was going away. He summoned his servants, and to one he entrusted five thousand silver pieces; to a second, two thousand, and to a third, one thousand. Then he went away for an indefinite period of time.

This parable which our Lord preached in the holy city made a great deal of sense to the Jewish people and touched on a common occurrence. It was common in eastern nations for wealthy men, when going away on long trips to entrust their property to trusted servants. Written records found in Egypt and Assyria testify that this practice was common in their countries as well as in ancient Palestine.

Also in ancient times, interest rates were exceedingly high. A man investing his money over a long period of time could easily double it. Money lenders charged high rates of interest in loaning money to others, but they likewise paid high rates to those investing money with them.

One item of interest in this parable is that the master entrusted different amounts of money to different servants. He had formed a previous judgment of the business ability of his various servants; he entrusted his wealth to them in proportion to the ability he judged them to have.

Scripture scholars and theologians agree almost unanimously in their interpretation of this parable. They view the liberal master as representative of almighty God. They see in the varying amounts of money entrusted to the servants as representing the gifts, skills and talents of different people.

As the master expected his servants to use their entrusted money for his benefit, so God expects us to use our skills and talents for his benefit. We are expected to use our natural gifts for his greater honor and glory.

It goes without saying that God has bestowed different talents and gifts on different individuals. But the more talents he has given a person, the more honor and glory he expects in return.

On the day of judgment God will not judge us on the amount of talent or skill we have been given in our lifetime, but rather to what use we have put the talent or skill which we were given. God is not interested in the results obtained by our work, but rather in the effort and zeal we put into our work.

To the first two servants, who had doubled their five thousand and two thousand silver pieces, the master said, "Well done, you are industrious and reliable servants. Since you were dependable in small matters, I will put you in charge of larger affairs. Come, share your master's joy!"

Like the master in the parable God will reward abundantly those who use their natural talents to do good and promote his honor on this earth. Their reward will be exceedingly great in the world to come.

But the master had harsh words of punishment for the servant who hoarded his silver and did not put it to good use. In a narrow sense, Scripture scholars view this slothful servant as representing the scribes and Pharisees. Their attitude was to keep the law of the Old Testament exactly as it was — to build a fence around it. Christ condemned them for their narrowness, for their refusal to help others.

But in a broader interpretation, this slothful servant can represent anyone entrusted with talent by almighty God who refuses to use that talent for the benefit of God and his fellow man.

In the parable the slothful servant readily admitted his master was a harsh man — that he reaped where he did not sow and gathered where he did not scatter. Through his own admission of guilt, the master punished him. He took away the money previously entrusted to him and cast him out of his house into the darkness outside.

Note well, it was not for losing or destroying what was entrusted to him that the slothful servant was punished; it was only for neglecting to use it. So it will be on judgment day. It will be for one's failure to make an effort to serve God that one will be punished. It will be for wasting our time and talents and neglecting our eternal end.

There are so many ways in which we can honor God. When we recite the prayers at Mass with the congregation we honor God. God is not concerned with the quality or the loudness of our voice. He is not concerned with your accent or enunciation. He will not judge you on whether your voice is sweet and melodious or raucous and hoarse. He merely wants you to use it to show him honor.

The same is true with the hymns we sing at Mass. God is not concerned with whether you have a tin ear or perfect pitch. He simply wants you to use your voice, no matter what it may be, to show him honor.

Again God wants us all to pray. In addition to the public prayers of the Church he wants us to make use of silent or mental prayer. He wants us to tell him in our own words how sorry we are for offending him; he wants us to pray for our needs and our wants. He will never punish us for using incorrect grammar in our prayers nor for the foolish things we pray for. He will only punish us if we neglect to pray at all.

We may correctly judge ourselves to be in the category of the least talented servant. We may be slow to learn and devoid of any skill. But this is not what counts. The important thing is that we use the few talents we have to show honor to God in our own poor way.

Let us resolve to use the short time we have on earth and the few meager talents we possess to please and honor God. Then God will be able to say on the day of judgment, "Well done, you are an industrious and reliable servant. Share your master's joy." God bless you.


# "A"     Thirty-fourth Sunday of the Year (Christ the King)

*Matthew 25:31-46*

The day was Christmas. The year was 800 A.D. The place was St. Peter's Basilica in Rome. On that day Charlemagne, King of the Franks, who ruled over modern-day France and Germany and all of central Europe, had journeyed to the Eternal City. He witnessed the services conducted in St. Peter's by Pope Leo III before a numberless crowd of people.

In the ensuing ceremonies, Pope Leo summoned Charlemagne to the altar. He placed on his head the crown of the Caesars, the rulers of the Roman Empire. He addressed him with the title of "Augustus," the title given to the Emperors of the Roman Empire in past centuries. Pope Leo had crowned Charlemagne as King of the Roman Empire.

But Charlemagne was a good Christian. If you were to ask him who was his king, he would have replied without hesitation, "Christ." Christ too was once hailed as a king. The day was Palm Sunday, the Sunday before his crucifixion. The place was the city of Jerusalem. Christ had come to the holy city to observe the feast of the Passover as required by Jewish law.

Christ rode on a donkey. In royal procession the donkey was the beast upon which kings and royal personages were accustomed to ride. The people of the city cut palm branches from trees and strewed them in his path. They greeted him with cries, "Hosanna to the son of David." Since David had been king of the Jews, to call Christ his son was to acknowledge his kingship.

Hence Christ was not only proclaimed by the Jewish people as their king. Even the Roman rulers acknowledged his kingship. When criminals were condemned to death in the Roman empire, the name of the crime was placed above the cross. In the case of Christ, who was guilty of no crime, as Pontius Pilate, the Roman governor, himself admitted, a sign was placed above his head declaring, "Jesus of Nazareth, King of the Jews."

Besides the Jewish people and the Roman governor proclaiming Christ's kingship, Christ himself admitted it. When asked by Pilate if he were king of the Jews, Christ answered, "As you say." This was the answer given by the Son of God, Second Person of the Blessed Trinity, who was all-truthful and who could not lie.

In the gospel of St. Matthew read at today's Mass, we see Christ sitting as judge over all the peoples who have ever lived, sentencing them to heaven or hell, depending on their deeds in this life. But to judge others is the function of a king or ruler. Christ will be judging the kings of other nations. He will be exercising his authority as the king of kings.

The kingship of Christ was proclaimed centuries before his birth. It was prophesied by the holy men in the Old Testament. Isaiah, Daniel, King David and many others foretold that Christ would reign as king. When the Angel Gabriel announced his coming birth to Mary, he said her child would sit upon the throne of King David. The Magi who came to adore him in his crib at Bethlehem announced as their purpose to adore the newborn king of the Jews.

On occasions in his public life Christ was proclaimed a king. Nathaniel acknowledged him to be the son of God and king of Israel. When Christ multiplied the loaves and fishes, the people wanted to seize him and make him their king. Two of the Apostles, the brothers, James and John, both sought for high places of honor in his kingdom. By these numerous proclamations, the kingship of Christ is beyond doubt.

Thus it came as no surprise to the world when on December 11, 1925, Pope Pius XI issued the encyclical "Quas Primas" on the subject of the Kingship of Christ. He enumerated in it many reasons for calling Christ our king. Among them he reaffirmed Christ's right to rule all nations of the earth. He established Christ's right to teach all the nations of the world, to make laws for them and to rule over people in regard to the things that pertain to their eternal salvation.

Pope Pius protested against the restrictions made by so many human rulers infringing on the rights of the Church to proclaim the religion of Christ. He protested the widespread indifference and neglect of honor shown Christ. He asserted that as king of the universe, Christ commanded the respect and obedience of all men.

Pope Pius XI was largely motivated to institute the feast of Christ the King as a means of bringing peace to the world. He had personally witnessed the death and destruction of a World War and of a revolution in Russia and eastern Europe. It was the hope and desire of this holy Pope to establish the reign of Christ the King over the hearts and minds of men. He knew that if this were accomplished, Christ who is all just and all loving would bring a reign of peace upon this earth.

In the renovation of the Church calendar following the Second Vatican Council, the feast days of many saints were surpressed and changed. The Feast of Christ the King was retained, but its date of celebration was changed. Whereas it was formerly celebrated on the last Sunday of October, it is now celebrated as the last Sunday of the Church year. It is the feast we celebrate today.

Let us in our own hearts acknowledge Christ to be our king. Let us acknowledge him as our creator and the ruler of the universe. Then truly by honoring him as king in our life on earth, when the day of judgment comes, as St. Matthew relates, he in turn will claim us as his subjects. He will direct us to join those on his right hand to enter into eternal life. To acknowledge Christ as our king upon this earth is to insure his reign over us for all eternity in the kingdom of heaven. God bless you.

# "A"     Dec. 8: Immaculate Conception

*Luke 1:26-38*

When Moses was driving the sheep of Jethro to the foot of Mt. Horeb, he perceived on the summit of this mountain a flame of fire in the midst of a bush. Yet the bush was not consumed by the fire. His curiosity was aroused to the point that he went to see it at close range.

On December eighth, the feast of the Immaculate Conception, Holy Mother the Church invites us to contemplate the Blessed Virgin Mary in a similar prodigy. Like a raging fire, the original sin of our first parents has engulfed the world. It has darkened the soul of every creature ever born, with but one exception, the Blessed Virgin Mary. Mary stands out like the burning bush, unscathed and untouched by the flaming sea of sin around her. This privilege of Mary's we call her Immaculate Conception.

Holy Scripture does not tell us openly that Mary was conceived immaculate, but it does give us good indications of it. One such indication is the judgment passed on the serpent after he had tempted Adam and Eve to commit original sin. God said to him, "I will put enmity between you and the woman and between your offspring and hers; he will strike at your head while you strike at his heel."

The serpent to whom God referred was the devil, who had tempted Adam and Eve to sin. The woman referred to was Mary. Her offspring was her son, Jesus Christ. The enmity between Mary and the devil was Mary's sinlessness.

The day of the Immaculate Conception dawned at long last. It appeared to be no different than any other day. The angelic choir did not descend from heaven to announce it. No wise men were beckoned by a star. No shepherds were summoned from the hills to come and rejoice. But the Immaculate Conception did occur. The life of grace had entered the world once again. Supernatural life sprang alive. Promise was given of our redemption.

The Immaculate Conception had taken place, but yet it remained a secret, hidden even from Mary herself. Mary, the humble virgin, never gleaned or suspected that God had blessed her in such a way. It remained a secret until one day Mary was at prayer. Suddenly the angel Gabriel appeared to her and greeted her with the words, "Rejoice, O highly favored daughter! The Lord is with you. Blessed are you among women."

What a startling revelation for Mary to be called highly favored by an angel of God and to be told the Lord was with her. It was the first time such a greeting had been given to any human being since the sin of our first parents.

There is good reason why God should bestow this privilege upon the Blessed Virgin Mary. From all eternity God had chosen her to be the mother of Christ, the mother of the God-man. Her innocence, her virtue and her goodness had been foreseen by God. It would not have been fitting that his own divine Son be born of a mother whose soul was in sin. It was inconsistent that the Mother of God be tainted by a sin of Satan. Therefore, God decreed that Mary should enter this world with her soul bright in the state of sanctifying grace.

Because Mary's sinlessness is not explicitly proclaimed in Scripture, it was not until the fifth century that the Greeks began to proclaim it. The Latin-speaking nations followed their lead in the seventh century. Perhaps the theologian loudest and most outspoken in proclaiming Mary's praise and sinlessness was Duns Scotus of the Middle Ages. From his time on, the belief in Mary's Immaculate Conception has become a litany.

In the year 1849 Pope Pius IX began to contemplate the declaration of Mary's Immaculate Conception as a doctrine of faith. Questionnaires and circulars were addressed to all the bishops and leading theologians of the world, asking them their opinion on this question. His approach to the question was similar in many respects to the approach of the popes to the Second Vatican Council. After long and assiduous study, Pope Pius IX ascended to the Chair of Peter and spoke officially as Pope for all the world to hear — he declared the Immaculate Conception of the Blessed Virgin Mary to be an article of faith.

We know that Pope Pius acted wisely, for only four years later, Mary herself confirmed this doctrine. On eighteen different occasions our Blessed Mother appeared to a poor French peasant girl, Bernadette Soubirous, in the small village of Lourdes in France. Bernadette described the lady as one of exceeding beauty. She and Bernadette prayed the rosary together. After several requests from Bernadette as to her identity, the lady answered most sweetly, "I am the Immaculate Conception." In confirmation of Mary's apparition, a spring of fresh water began to flow from the spot and untold miracles have been performed in its waters.

Through Mary's Immaculate Conception, a beacon of light has illumined the world. Mary has become a shining star. She is a model for men to live by; she is a ray of hope to inspire men in their battle with the powers of evil. The glory of Mary's Immaculate Conception is a reflection of God's glory in heaven.

It is no wonder that the bishops of the United States a century ago chose Mary under the title of her Immaculate Conception as the patroness of our country. A beautiful basilica has been built in her honor in our nation's capital. It is only fitting and proper that as citizens of the United States we honor Mary on this, her national feast day. Let us pray to Mary, our sinless mother, and beg of her the grace to avoid sin in our own lives. God bless you.

# "A"     Aug. 15: Assumption

*Luke 11:27-28*

When the Second Vatican Council was announced back in 1959, many people besides the bishops and theologians were invited to attend it. These included non-Catholics, whose doctrines and beliefs were known to exclude belief in the Blessed Virgin Mary.

With so many non-believers attending, the question was asked, how would the Vatican Council treat the subject of the Blessed Virgin Mary? Would Vatican II downgrade devotion to our Blessed Mother? Would Vatican II take away some of her honors?

The answer to all these questions was a resounding NO! In fact, the exact opposite was true. If anything, Vatican II confirmed and strengthened the position of Mary in the Church. It devoted one entire chapter of the Constitution on the Church to the Blessed Mother — twelve full pages of doctrine and explanation. It held her in a high and exalted position.

Mary herself stated in the beautiful words of the Magnificat that "all ages to come shall call me blessed. God who is mighty has done great things for me. . . ." The truth of these words has been borne out in all the councils of the Church, from the earliest at Ephesus to Vatican II; all have praised and honored her.

Vatican II makes a distinction between the honor we show Mary and the honor we show to God himself; we adore God alone, but the honor we show to Mary is above the honor we show to any other saint.

The Council tells us that true devotion to Mary consists of three things. The first of these is a recognition of Mary's excellence. This is not difficult to recognize, for Mary is the Mother of God. She is the Mother of Jesus Christ, the God-man.

God had good reason to choose Mary as his mother. Never did she tarnish her soul with any stain of sin. God likewise preserved her from the stain of original sin as well. Mary practiced virtues to an eminent degree. Her humility was outstanding. In her humility she deemed herself unworthy of obtaining the honor that was the dream of all Jewish girls — of becoming the mother of the Messiah. Instead Mary took the vow of virginity. Perfect obedience to God's will was another of her outstanding qualities.

The second step in true devotion to Mary is a real love for Mary. Loving Mary is not difficult. Christ gave her as a mother to all men, and she loves each of us with a mother's love. She loves us with a deep and abiding love. We should feel privileged to return this love to her.

The third and final step in true devotion to Mary, as pointed out by Vatican II, is imitation of her. Mary is so easy to imitate because she is so completely human. Mary has been the model for Sisters and religious from the very beginning of the Church.

Mary's virtues lend themselves to imitation very easily because they are simple virtues. While the greatest of all human beings and possessing the greatest honor of our race, Mary was also the most humble. She was always kind and considerate and faithful to her duty. She was concerned about others. Her concern for the bride and groom at Cana prompted Christ to perform his first miracle.

One cold spring morning at the turn of the century, the Ohio River became swollen by rain and began to overflow its banks. The water rose rapidly, and people living along its banks were forced to leave their homes to save their lives. One elderly widow left her modest cottage and fled on foot to the nearest town.

She had no shelter and no place to stay. Passing by a Catholic Church, she stopped in for a visit. She knelt in adoration before the Blessed Sacrament and began to say her rosary. Time after time she mentioned Mary's name in prayer. Her Hail Marys became a melodious stream of prayer. As evening drew near, this elderly lady left the Church, wondering where she would find shelter for the night. As she walked along the street, a lady of evident wealth drove by in a beautiful car and stopped. She offered the elderly woman shelter for the night, which she gladly accepted.

Later that evening the elderly lady began to reveal some of the sorrows of her life. She told how her husband had died at an early age, leaving her to raise a large family alone — of how one daughter had run away from home and was never heard of again. As she told her story and began to mention names and supply small details, tears began to fill the eyes of her host.

Finally the rich lady burst forward and threw herself in the widow's arms and sobbed, "Mother!" With tears of sorrow she besought her mother's forgiveness for leaving home many years before. Gladly was she forgiven.

This poor widow's prayers to Mary had been heard and answered. Mary not only found her shelter for the night, but she likewise restored to her a long-lost daughter.

Let us heed the words of Vatican II. On this the feast of her Assumption let us show her true devotion. Let us recognize her excellence. Let us come to love and imitate her. Let us pray to her often. Mary, who loves us with a mother's love, will not fail to hear and answer our prayers. God bless you.

# "A"  Nov. 1: All Saints

*Matthew 5:1-12*

One of the most beautiful spots on this earth is the Italian Riviera. The natural beauty of the Mediterranean Coast, combined with an enjoyable climate the year around, makes it a pleasant place. Luxurious mansions dot the cliffs overlooking the shoreline. But in examining these mansions, one of the most luxurious of all is named "Reliquenda," which means, "The things that have to be left behind."

The man who named this estate was probably a good Christian, for the name is a reminder that death will separate us from all our earthly treasures. It is a reminder not to become too attached to our possessions in this life.

The first two days of November are two important feast days in the liturgy of the Church. November 1st is the feast of All Saints on which day we honor all the saints in heaven having no special feast day of their own. November 2nd is All Souls Day, the day the Church sets aside to pray for the souls suffering in purgatory.

The souls suffering in purgatory are members of the Church Suffering. They, together with the Church Triumphant, the saints in heaven whom we honor on November 1st, and the Church Militant, those of us struggling to save our souls here on earth, form the Communion of Saints.

The souls suffering in purgatory are in need of help. During the month of November the Church urges us to pray for them in a special way. The month of November is dedicated to them. The Church's desire that we pray for the departed souls has a long-standing tradition. In the Book of Maccabees in the Old Testament we read that it is a holy and wholesome thought to pray for the dead that they may be loosed from their sins.

The Church's doctrine is a most reasonable one. We know that only those guilty of mortal sin will be punished by the fire of hell hereafter. But we also know that nothing defiled will enter the kingdom of heaven. Hence those guilty of venial sin or with temporal punishment — or sin that has not been satisfied — cannot enter immediately into heaven. Hence it is most reasonable that there be a place of temporal punishment in the world to come.

But despite the reasonableness of the Church's doctrine on the existence of purgatory, it has been bitterly assailed by the enemies of the Church. Leaders of the Reformation attacked it strongly. To relieve any doubt on this matter, the Council of Trent officially declared that there is a purgatory. It stated that the souls detained there are aided by our prayers and sufferings, especially by the Holy Sacrifice of the Mass.

The doctrine of purgatory is a most consoling doctrine, for it shows the mercy of almighty God. The souls suffering there are nonetheless happy, for they know that someday they shall enter heaven. Still their sufferings are hard and severe. They suffer a pain of loss in being separated from God, the source of all happiness.

They also suffer a pain of sense. St. Thomas Aquinas tells us that even the least suffering in purgatory exceeds the greatest suffering in this world. In purgatory it is our soul that suffers, while on this earth we can experience only bodily suffering.

The tragic thing about the souls suffering in purgatory is that they are unable to help themselves. Their period of meriting and demeriting is over. They can only wait and suffer. But we, members of the Church Militant on earth, can help them. The Council of Trent tells us that the souls in purgatory are aided by our sacrifices and prayers, especially by the Mass.

Most certainly any souls in purgatory will be eternally grateful to us for any sacrifice we can make to help them. Christ said, "Blest are the merciful for they shall obtain mercy." Any soul we can free from purgatory by our prayers or sacrifices will be our benefactor in the kingdom of heaven. The souls in purgatory are the future saints of heaven. Once in heaven, they can pray for us.

During this month of November, pray often for the Poor Souls. Consider that purgatory may possibly be our future home; we will then want others to pray for us. Let us make it our special goal this month by our prayers, our sacrifices and our Masses to help free a soul from this fiery prison and bring it to eternal happiness in heaven with God. God bless you.

# Year B

# Year B

## "B"    First Sunday of Advent

*Mark 13:33-37*

My dear people, a most appropriate wish for me to extend to you today from this pulpit would be to wish you a Happy New Year. For today is the first Sunday of Advent, the beginning of the ecclesiastical or Church year.

A great amount of attention is paid to the beginning of a new calendar year, but too little to the beginning of the new Church year. The change is noted, though, in the Church's liturgy. The green vestments of the Pentecost season have been put away, and the purple ones of the penitential season of Advent are now being worn.

The Church aims to create a new atmosphere, a new disposition in our souls. She creates a mood of expectancy, of waiting, of preparation. She gives indication that something great is at hand. The very word "Advent" means coming. The coming that is so eagerly awaited is the coming of the Christ Child.

The four weeks of Advent represent the thousands of years the world awaited the coming of the Messiah. It was a period of darkness, but it was not unillumined by stars. The chosen people had kept before themselves the promise of a Redeemer. They nourished their spiritual life on this hope. In the words of St. Mark, it was time to watch and pray.

In Advent the Church lives again through a period of hope and expectation. She employs her liturgy to sharpen our desire, to mold our thoughts and spiritually prepare us for the coming of Christ. It is to one's spiritual advantage to prepare well for his coming.

The just people of the Old Testament sighed and longed for four thousand years for the coming of the Messiah. Immediately after Adam and Eve had committed original sin, God spoke words of punishment to the serpent who had tempted them, "I will put enmity between you and the woman, and between your offspring and hers. . . ."

The woman referred to was the Blessed Virgin Mary, Her offspring was Jesus Christ, her Son. The enmity God referred to was his sinlessness, his crushing of Satan's power over the world.

121

It was prophesied that Christ would be descended of the house of David. We read in Psalm 132, "The Lord swore to David a promise from which he will not withdraw: 'Your own offspring I will set upon your throne.' " Micah prophesied the place of Christ's birth as Bethlehem. Daniel prophesied the time of his birth.

David prophesied many details of Christ's sufferings. In the Twenty-second Psalm he wrote, "I can count all my bones. They look on and gloat over me; they divide my garments among them and for my vesture they cast lots."

But all these prophecies prepared men for the one big event, the birth of Christ in Bethlehem on the first Christmas day. The many prophecies of the Old Testament served as a preparation for this major event.

Yet it would profit us little to speak of the coming of Christ if he were to have come and then suddenly to have departed this world. But this was not the case. Christ came to earth and perpetuated his coming in the hearts of men by establishing his Church and a means of grace, the sacraments. Christ left open a door by which he might come into the soul of every individual.

Let us resolve to prepare well for the coming of Christ during this holy season of Advent. As the master in today's gospel ordered the man at the gate to watch with a sharp eye, let us too be watchful in this time of preparation. Let us purify our souls from any stain of sin by receiving the Sacrament of Penance. Let us physically unite ourselves to Christ through our reception of the Holy Eucharist. Let us be spiritually on watch and alert to the means of grace Christ is offering us at the beginning of this new Church year. God bless you.

# "B"     Second Sunday of Advent

*Mark 1:1-8*

It is interesting to note that in her liturgy the Church only celebrates three birthdays: that of our Lord, our Blessed Mother and St. John the Baptizer. Ordinarily when celebrating the feast day of a saint, the day of his death is the day that is celebrated.

There is a special reason for celebrating the birth of St. John the Baptizer, for St. John was born without original sin on his soul. Shortly after the Annunciation, Mary went to visit her cousin Elizabeth. Scripture tells us that "the baby leapt in her womb. Elizabeth was filled with the Holy Spirit." Thus St. John, along with Christ and Mary, was born without the stain of original sin on his soul. Hence the date of his birth is celebrated as a feast day in the Church.

St. John was no ordinary person. His birth had been foretold by the archangel Gabriel, who appeared to Zechariah and told him that his wife Elizabeth would bear a son in her old age. When Zechariah doubted the angel's word, he was struck dumb. He remained mute until after John was born and he was asked his name. He took a tablet and wrote that his name was John. At that moment he regained his gift of speech. His first words were the beautiful words of the prayer often called the Benedictus; "Blessed be the Lord, the God of Israel, because he has visited and ransomed his people."

In obedience to the command of the angel, Zechariah dedicated his son to be a Nazarite; that is, he would not take any wine or strong drink. When John grew to manhood, he led a life of mortification and penance. He went into the desert and there fasted and prayed a great deal. His food was locusts and wild honey.

Finally in the fifteenth year of the rule of Tiberius Caesar, the word of God came to John in the desert. He went forth into the region around the Jordan proclaiming a baptism of repentance which led to the forgiveness of sins. A large crowd began to follow John. Some even wondered if he were not the promised Messiah, but to this John responded, "One more powerful than I is to come after me. I am not fit to stoop and untie his sandal strap."

John's mission here on earth was to prepare the way for the coming of Christ. Christ approved of John's work by coming to the Jordan and asking to be baptized by him. The baptism which John administered, however, was only a symbol of the sacrament Christ was later to establish.

Perhaps the outstanding event in John's life was his courage in proclaiming the gospel of Christ and denouncing sin. He told the well-to-do that they must share their clothes with the poor. He instructed the tax-collectors to collect no more than that which was actually owed them. He warned the soldiers not to bully anyone and to be content with their pay. John did not fear to tell King Herod that it was unlawful for him to live with his brother's wife.

This bravery in denouncing was to cost John his life. Herodias, with whom Herod was sinfully living, asked for the head of the imprisoned John. Herod gave in and granted her her wish.

The sinlessness of John, his love of good and hatred of evil, is something we can all strive to achieve in our own lives. Let us endeavor to rid our souls of whatever might tend to lessen God's grace in us. Let us imitate St. John in viewing sin as the greatest of evils. Let us imitate his moral courage in avoiding whatever is displeasing to almighty God. God bless you.

# "B"  Third Sunday of Advent

*John 1:6-8, 19-28*

When St. John the Baptizer was preaching in the desert, a delegation of priests and Levites was sent from Jerusalem to ask him who he really was. This delegation which approached him was a highly official one. The priests were the guardians of the temple and the Levites might be called temple police. This delegation put to John a very pointed question, "Who are you?"

Certainly many of these who asked him knew that he was the son of Zechariah and Elizabeth, but they still realized that John was no ordinary person. His birth had been announced by the Archangel Gabriel, who appeared to his father Zechariah and told him that his wife Elizabeth would bear a son in her old age. When Zechariah doubted the angel's word, he was struck dumb. He remained dumb until the birth of John. The first words that he spoke thereafter were the beautiful words of the Benedictus, "Blessed be the Lord, the God of Israel, because he had visited and ransomed his people."

In obedience to the Archangel Gabriel, Zechariah dedicated his son John to be a Nazarite, which meant he would not take any wine or strong drink. When John grew to manhood, he led a life of mortification and penance. He went into the desert and there fasted and prayed a great deal to prepare for his great mission.

Finally in the fifteenth year of the reign of Tiberius Caesar, the word came to John in the desert. John went forth into all the regions about the Jordan and began to preach a baptism of penance for the forgiveness of sins.

Word came back to the Jews in Jerusalem about the preaching and wonderful works of John. Hence they sent the priests and Levites to find out who he really was. They first suspected John was the Messiah or Redeemer, who had long been expected. This John denied outright. He said, "I am not the Messiah."

When John thus squelched their unspoken suspicions, they questioned him further. They vaguely believed that some prophet would come as the precursor of the Messiah, so they asked him: "Who, then? Elijah?" John denied again, saying, "No." This brief and positive answer was indicative of his humility.

As a last possibility they asked him, "Are you the Prophet?" Again John answered briefly, "No." Having exhausted all the possibilities of who he might be, they asked him what he had to say for himself. John answered, "I am 'a voice in the desert crying out: Make straight the way of the Lord!' "

John wished by his testimony to give witness to the person of Christ. He declares his duty to be to prepare the way for the Lord. He testifies that Christ, who is to come after him, is to be preferred before him, the strap of whose sandal he is not worthy to unfasten.

John announced that God was on the point of inaugurating his reign, in fulfillment of centuries of longing. This was a message the Jewish people were pleased to hear. For centuries they had been under the rule of the Persians, Egyptians and Syrians. Presently they were under the domination of Herod and the Roman government. Despite all their oppression, they still clung to the belief that God had not abandoned his people. John's message of the Messiah's coming was music to their ears.

Many people received John favorably. They praised him and flattered him. But John remained unaffected by the praises and blessings showered upon him. Neither did the abuse or criticism he received bother him. His sole purpose, to which he adhered without any deviation, was to preach the coming of Christ.

St. John in a sense is the symbol of Advent so prominent in today's gospel. Why is his mission spoken of so prominently? As John the Baptizer went abroad to announce the coming and public life of Christ, the Church bids us to prepare for the coming of Christ in another way.

The whole season of Advent is a preparation for the coming of Christ, for his birth into this world on Christmas day. The word Advent itself means coming. The season of Advent marks the beginning of the Church year. It is most fitting that the season which prepares for the birth of Christ into this world should so begin the Church year.

Just as the Church is preparing for the birth of Christ at Christmas, so too the world around us is preparing for the coming of Christmas. But yet the manner in which the world around us is preparing for Christmas is entirely foreign to and oblivious of the true meaning of Christmas. The world is preparing to celebrate Christmas in a materialistic and almost a pagan manner.

Observe your own conduct, my dear people, during this approaching Christmas season. Amid all the hustle and bustle, the writing of Christmas cards, the wrapping of presents, and plans for holiday trips, ask yourself if you have prepared for the coming of Christmas in a spiritual way. Has the holy season of Advent prompted you to do anything special in a spiritual way for the celebration of Christ's birth. John the Baptizer preached a gospel of penance for the remission of sin. Has Advent, my dear people, prompted you to practice any penance for the ensuing feast?

What sacrifice has Advent prompted you to perform? What prayers has it prompted you to say? Can you say that you have really prepared for the celebration of Christ's birth in a spiritual way? If you cannot give an affirmative answer to these questions, then you too have been swept along in the current of materialism. You have heeded the call of the world instead of the call of John the Baptizer.

But still Advent is not over. There yet remains time to prepare for the Infant Savior's birth. There still is time to open the door of your soul and make it a fitting place to receive the Christ Child. When you come to visit him in His crib this Christmas, do not come empty-handed. Make a mental list of the gifts that you will offer him.

Mark high on that list the reception of the Sacrament of Reconciliation. The absolution of the priest in confession can take away the stain of mortal sins and dress it in the robe of sanctifying grace — a garment far brighter than the glitter of Christmas tinsel.

Mark high on your list also the reception of Holy Eucharist — the sacrament which contains the body and blood of Christ. List also the performances of small penances in preparation for your sins. Offer them up in honor of the cold the Christ Child suffered in his crib at Bethlehem and the indignity he endured in being turned away from the inn.

Offer up some small sacrifice in adoration of the Infant Savior. Let your prayers ascent as the incense of the Magi at our Savior's crib.

Resolve my dear people, that the message of St. John the Baptizer will not fall on deaf ears, but will root and flower within your souls. Resolve to prepare for the coming of Christ this Christmas. God bless you.

# "B"    Fourth Sunday of Advent

*Luke 1:26-38*

The greatest event in the history of the world! The Messiah had come to redeem mankind. The Redeemer was about to be born! An Archangel was sent from God to announce this good news to men! Yet all the circumstances concerning this great announcement convey a note of simplicity.

The place of this great announcement was Galilee, the forgotten part of Palestine, and Nazareth was one of its most insignificant small villages. And the person to whom this announcement was made was a poor and humble orphan girl named Mary. Mary was born when her parents, Ann and Joachim, were in their old age. Tradition tells us that they died shortly after Mary's birth and she was an orphan at an early age.

Jewish law required all children twelve years of age or over to celebrate the feast of the Passover in the temple in Jerusalem. From this age forward they were regarded as adults. Mary being an obedient and respectful Jewish girl, complied with this law. Tradition tells us it was at this time that the High Priest Zechariah, then on duty in the temple in Jerusalem, arranged for her betrothal with Joseph.

Betrothals were a serious agreement among the Jewish people, far more serious than our present engagement is today. They were generally arranged by the parents or guardians of a boy and girl. Often they were arranged years in advance of their taking place. Betrothals were as binding as the marriage covenant itself; they were almost never broken unless, of course, death or some natural cause intervened.

In the case of Mary, it was sometime between her betrothal and actual marriage to Joseph that the angel Gabriel appeared to her with this great and startling news. God's selection of the archangel Gabriel reveals the importance of the message he bore. It was the same Gabriel who in the Old Testament had appeared to the prophet Daniel to tell him the secret of the seventy weeks of years which would end in the coming of the Messiah. Now that the seventy weeks of years, or 490 years had passed, Gabriel was sent once again to announce the forthcoming birth of the Savior.

Gabriel greeted Mary with the words, "Rejoice, O highly favored daughter! The Lord is with you. Blessed are you among women." St. Luke tells us that Mary was deeply troubled by these words. Mary was not indeed frightened by the appearance of an angel, but rathered she was troubled by the words he spoke. To be called "blessed among women" by an angel of God was startling. In her humility she regarded herself only a poor orphan girl, unworthy of the honors this angel was trying to bestow upon her.

But the angel reassured her, "Do not fear, Mary." Then came the great and startling announcement mankind had awaited for thousands of years. "You shall conceive and bear a son and give him the name Jesus." Then Gabriel told her he would be the son of the Most High — that he would ascend to the throne of David and his reign would have no end.

Such a great and startling honor would have overwhelmed any ordinary person, but not the humble virgin Mary. She simply asked the angel Gabriel, "How can this be since I do not know man?" Mary, even though betrothed, was still a single person. Undoubtedly by this time, she and Joseph, her future husband, had come to a common agreement to live as single people, even though they would be legally married. Joseph would respect the vow of virginity she had taken.

Immediately Gabriel answered her question with an explanation, "The Holy Spirit will come upon you and the power of the Most High will overshadow you . . . the holy offspring . . . will be called Son of God."

By her question Mary showed her concern for safeguarding the vow of virginity she had taken. She was asking only what she must know to conform herself to the divine will of God. Gabriel's answer gave her this necessary knowledge. He revealed to her that she had been chosen to be the Mother of the Son of God. He then told her that her cousin Elizabeth had conceived a son and was now in her sixth month.

Now, having delivered his message, Gabriel had only to wait for Mary's answer and consent. Mary had free will and had the right to refuse, but as God foresaw from all eternity, she would not refuse. She replied, "I am the servant of the Lord. Let it be done to me as you say." It was at this instant that the Incarnation took place. It was at this precise moment that Christ, the Second Person of the Blessed Trinity and true God, took on the body of man. He entered the womb of the Blessed Virgin Mary.

St. Louis of Granada once wrote, "Just as the sun must be wrapped in clouds if we are to gaze upon it with eyes undimmed, so God wrapped Himself in flesh as in a cloud, so that the eyes of our soul might bear to look upon Him." Christ in his divine nature had come down from heaven; He took upon himself a human nature. He was at one and the same time both God and man. He, who was one person, now had two natures, divine and human.

Thus in this way the mystery of the Incarnation was brought about. The promise God made to his people many centuries before, to redeem his people, had now been fulfilled.

The Incarnation of the Son of God was necessary to make satisfaction to the injured majesty of God. God, who was infinitely perfect, had been offended by the sin of our first parents. The graveness of this injury can only be measured by the dignity of the person offended. Since God is infinitely perfect, the offense of sin was infinitely grave. Man, if left to himself, could never make satisfaction for this sin, because man was so far inferior to God in dignity. Thus only one equal to God in dignity could make recompense for it. Thus it became necessary for man's salvation for Christ to assume the body of man and make satisfaction for man's sin.

Christ, by coming to earth in bodily form, never lost any of his divine dignity. He remained God and Second Person of the Blessed Trinity all the while he lived on earth as man. As St. Ambrose said of him, the divinity of Christ was not destroyed but only hidden for a while by his human nature.

In fact, instead of losing dignity by coming to earth, Christ gave a new dignity to the human race. He elevated our human nature by assuming it himself. He, who was God, lived with our nature and elevated it.

When Mary said to the angel Gabriel, "Let it be done to me as you say," the Christ Child was conceived in her womb by the Holy Spirit. At that moment she truly became the Mother of God. Mary, by her words of consent, brought to the world the greatest joy of all time: the long-awaited Redeemer had entered the world to save mankind.

But this great news was to remain a secret until it was revealed in a stable in Bethlehem by a choir of angels. In a few days' time we celebrate that great event. Let us be thankful to Christ for assuming our nature. Let us be thankful to Mary for consenting to be his Mother. With that humble virgin in the small insignificant town of Nazareth, an event took place that has changed our world. God bless you.

# "B"    Christmas

*Luke 2:1-14, 15-20 or John 1:1-18*

Once more, dearly beloved in Christ, the Church calls upon us to celebrate with all joy and thanksgiving the birthday of our Savior, that great day, foreordained from the beginning, when the glory of the Lord was revealed that all flesh might see the salvation of God — that great day when man first beheld the Word made flesh and saw his glory, the glory, as it were, of the only begotten of the Father, full of grace and truth.

In her solemn offices at this holy season the Church puts before us in detail the story of the birth of God made man; that sweet story which, though it has been familiar to us from earliest childhood, tells of a mystery so profound, of a pity so divine, and of hopes so glorious that we never tire of hearing it, or of contemplating the loving mercy of God revealed to us.

And in those days there went out a decree from Caesar Augustus ordering a census of the whole world. But there also went out a decree from the Throne of God that the Savior of the world should be born.

The sacred narrative continues: "Everyone went to be enrolled each to his own town. And so Joseph went from the town of Nazareth in Galilee to Judea, to David's town of Bethlehem. . . ."

That this was to be the place of the Redeemer's birth was known for many centuries, for Micah had prophesied, "But you Bethlehem-Eprathah, too small to be among the clans of Judah, from you shall come forth for me one, who is to be ruler in Israel." Thus in that obscure little town, in the despised land of the Jews, in the dead of night on a winter's eve, with no shelter but a stable overhead, the Lord of life was born, a helpless infant.

The moment decreed from all eternity had come; Jesus lies upon his Mother's robe. The world, which he had come to save, went heedlessly on as before, ignorant of the great event which had come to pass.

But for us, dear friends, we shall say with the shepherd, "Let us go over to

Bethlehem and see this event which the Lord has made known to us." Let us keep our thoughts fixed on this wonderful scene in the stable. Had the inhabitants of Bethlehem but known what had come into their midst, they would have rivaled each other for the honor of sheltering their Lord. They would have come singing psalms and with the smoke of incense to bring their Lord into his temple.

But the Son of God did not will to come into this world amid pomp and majesty. The Prince of Peace revealed himself only to a chosen few — Mary and Joseph, the shepherds, the wise men from the east. These were the few to whom He revealed his birth — the few who came to adore Him. Christ chose these few because of their purity and humility of heart. He chose them because of their love and purity; neither wealth nor worldly position meant anything to God, who could see men's souls.

Let us fix our gaze more closely on the Christ Child and his mother: the mother, a virgin most pure; the child, none other than the God who made her. He is the Eternal Word, but he is mute; he is omnipotent but is bound in swaddling clothes. The Creator of the world has taken the form of a creature. His glory is hidden in lowliness, his majesty in weakness, and his Love for man in an infant's heart.

But Christ had a purpose in coming in this manner. He veiled his glory in the crib so that He might win our hearts by love. He concealed his omnipotent power that he might banish fear. He was born among the lowly to establish Christian charity.

Love, mercy, charity — these are the virtues that permeate the Christmas season. Countless acts of mercy and charity have been performed in Christ's name since that first memorable Christmas day. But the pattern of helping the poor and unfortunate was then determined. Pity for the poor has its source in the Babe of Bethlehem.

Nothing ever did so much to loosen the devil's hold upon the world. Nothing ever struck such a blow for peace. A beacon was lit in the darkness of a troubled world.

Dear friends, let us rejoice on this happy occasion. God so loved the world that he sent his only-begotten Son to redeem it. But let us remember it is the same Christ who was born in a stable, who will come to judge the world in majesty. So let us love Him as an infant so that we may face him without fear on judgment day. God bless you.

# "B" Sunday after Christmas (Holy Family)

*Luke 2:22-40*

The Jews had many ritualistic and religious laws. Among these was the Law of Purification. This law declared every mother who gave birth to a male child to be legally unclean for seven days. At the end of this time the child was to be circumcised.

Following the circumcision the mother was to remain in her home thirty-three days. She could not enter the sanctuary of the temple until this time. On the fortieth day a mother presented her son in the temple, offering a yearling lamb for a holocaust. However, in the case of the poor an offering of two turtledoves was acceptable. This was the offering that Our Blessed Mother made.

Actually Our Blessed Mother was not bound by this law, for she became the Mother of Christ while still remaining a virgin. However, Mary voluntarily complied with it; she wished to avoid giving scandal to her friends.

On duty in the temple at this time was the aged Simeon. The Holy Spirit had promised this holy man that he would not die until he had seen the Messiah.

Immediately upon entering the temple holy Simeon realized the Christ Child was the Messiah. Taking Christ into his arms, he said, "Now, Master, you can dismiss your servant in peace; you have fulfilled your word. For my eyes have witnessed your saving deed. . . ."

Simeon proceeded to bless both the Child and our Blessed Mother. Then he proceeded to utter the prophetic words, "This child is destined for the downfall and the rise of many in Israel. . . ."

Christ was not to cause the fall of anyone directly. Rather, he occasioned the fall of only those who heard his doctrine and refused to believe it. In this sense their disbelief caused their own fall.

Christ instead came for the resurrection of many. Christ came with the intention of saving all men — of offering to all the way of salvation. He came to reopen the gates of heaven and to men a way to eternal paradise.

Holy Simeon then said that Christ was destined for the downfall of many. Down through the ages some heretics have denied that Mary was a virgin; others, that Christ was God, and others still that Christ possessed human nature.

Some have denied that Christ truly died on the cross; others that he truly rose from the dead. They have denied that Christ fulfilled the prophecies; that he founded the Catholic Church. Practically nothing has escaped their contradiction. But yet their downfall itself fulfills this prophecy and points to the divinity of his message.

Simeon then directed his words to our Blessed Mother and prophesied that "you yourself shall be pierced with a sword." One of the titles of Mary is Our Mother of Seven Dolors or Seven Sorrows. The first of these sorrows was to come in a matter of days. For an angel appeared to Joseph and told him to take Mary and the Christ Child and flee into Egypt for Herod was trying to kill him.

Mary was to suffer the sorrow of losing her divine Son when he was twelve years old for three days in the temple. She was to suffer the sorrow of meeting her divine Son carrying his cross on the way to Calvary. She was to watch him flung upon it and see his hands and feet pierced with nails and then raised aloft to hang suspended on the cross for three hours of agony before he died upon it. Mary was to witness his body being taken down from it and laid in her arms — the inspiration for the Pietà of Michelangelo. Mary was to suffer the agony of seeing her divine Son being laid in the tomb. Mary's burden of sorrow would indeed pierce her heart.

But no sooner had holy Simeon uttered these prophecies than the holy woman Anna, who lived at the temple and spent her time in prayer and fasting, came forward. Although wrinkles lined her face, prudence showed therein. Bowed by the infirmity of years, she was vigorous in the knowledge of God. Widowed after only seven years of marriage, she had spent the remainder of her life at the temple with her prayers and pious actions.

Anna publicly began to praise the Christ Child in the temple and publicly proclaimed for all around to hear that this child was the redeemer of Israel. God had rewarded Anna's holiness by allowing her to recognize Christ as our Redeemer. Seized by joy at this occasion and her soul being filled with grace, she could not constrain herself from declaring for all to hear that the Christ Child was our Lord — the Redeemer of mankind.

These events at the Presentation of Christ in the temple — the prophesy of Simeon and the praise and preaching of Anna — are an immediate preparation for the mission of Christ. The entire Old Testament with its many prophecies and writings is a remote preparation for the coming of Christ.

But now the remote preparation has ended. Christ has been born. An immediate preparation must be made for his mission of redemption. The prophecy of Simeon and the praise of Anna are one step in a series, in preparing for his mission. Other steps in preparation were to come later, like the preaching of St. John the Baptizer.

The importance of Christ's mission is pointed out by all the preparation that was made for it. In fact, if anything is important, it is worthwhile preparing for. The necessity of preparation is an important lesson we can learn from the gospel story of today — that of our Lord's presentation.

The most important moment in our life is the moment of our death. An interesting story concerning the importance of preparation is found in the life of the Emperor Henry of Germany. In his early life Henry was a devout Catholic and had a great devotion to St. Wolfgang. He frequently visited his tomb. One day St. Wolfgang appeared to him and pointed to two words written on the wall: "After six."

Henry began to wonder what these words meant. He concluded that they meant in six days he would die. He made a general confession, gave a large sum of money to the poor and spent much time in prayer. But after six days he was still very much alive. Then he thought they meant that he would die in six months. He continued to lead a very holy life for the next six months, but they came and went and he was still living.

Then he thought they could only mean that he was to die in six years. And so for the next six years he led a very holy life. But still he lived on. Thinking still more about the words, he concluded that the meaning of the apparition was this that he should be prepared to die at all times — this was the best way to live.

Let today's gospel — Christ's presentation — teach us the importance of preparation. Let us prepare as did holy Anna to receive him with a pure heart and pure mind. Purify our hearts by confession — purify our minds by prayer and banishing distractions. Preparation will allow graces of redemption to fill our souls and lead us to eternal happiness. God bless you.

# "B" January 1 (Solemnity of Mary, Mother of God)

*Luke 2:16-21*

A generation ago it was customary to reserve a certain door in the home to measure the height of the children. In many a home, a door or panel filled with such marks was a common sight. Once each year Dad would line up Johnny and Mary and Billy and Susan and mark off their height, and beside the mark he would put an initial and the date. In painting the house, one was careful to leave that side of the door untouched.

Keeping such a record served many purposes. Johnny and Susan could refer to it at any time and see how much they had grown. It encouraged them to stand straight and grow tall. It made them eager to show progress in their bodily growth.

But what is even more important than keeping track of our bodily growth is to note our spiritual development. New Year's Day, the Octave of Christmas and the beginning of a new calendar year, is an excellent time to measure ourselves spiritually.

Instead of feet and inches, we use other means to check on our spiritual growth. We can take check on our knowledge of God and the study of our religion. We can measure the increase of charity and other virtues. We can observe the frequency with which we have received the sacraments.

Unfortunately many Catholics never grow very tall in the knowledge of their religion. When they leave school, they cease to study and learn about their faith. They neglect to subscribe to or regularly read any Catholic paper or periodical.

Ask yourself this question — how much Catholic reading have you done this past year? How many Catholic papers come into your home? How often do you bring home a pamphlet from the pamphlet rack?

If you were unable to answer these questions satisfactorily, then make it a

New Year's resolution for this year that you will begin to read regularly some Catholic paper or periodical. Make it a resolution that you will subscribe to or bring home regularly some Catholic paper or magazine.

A second means of measuring your spiritual growth during this past year is to see how you have increased or grown in the practice of the virtue of charity. How many acts of kindness did you practice this past year? Was it more than during the previous year? Count the times you showed some extraordinary courtesy either to your family, the neighbor next door or your co-worker on your job. Measure yourself in this regard with some charitable person you know.

Make plans now to grow taller in the practice of the virtue of charity during this coming year. Think of some circumstance in which the practice of a small sacrifice on your part would bring great happiness to those around you. Resolve to see Christ in your neighbor during this coming year. Do for him what you would do for Christ himself. Make this coming year one in which you will advance in charity and the love of God.

Ask yourself too how often you have received the sacraments this past year. Was it more or less frequently than in past years? Did you come to the Communion rail as often as you could have? How often did you go to confession and obtain absolution for your sins? If the answers to these questions are not "frequently" or "often," then why not?

The sacraments are the ordinary means Christ has given us to gain grace. Nothing is more pleasing to Christ than to have someone receive his body and blood in the Eucharist frequently and devoutly. The Eucharist is our greatest treasure here on earth. Christ himself is present within it.

Regardless of your past performances, make frequent Communion — yes, even weekly Communion — a major New Year's resolution for this year. Make this year a banner year in your life for the reception of our Lord's body and blood.

Today, besides being the beginning of a new calendar year, is also a holy day in the Catholic Church. It is the Octave day of Christmas and the feast of Christ's circumcision. In obedience to Jewish law Christ was circumcised on the eighth day following his birth. On this occasion the first drops of his blood were shed for mankind. His innocent flesh was wounded, and he began his suffering for mankind on this day.

Christ's later life was to be a life of sacrifice and suffering. But his suffering began on New Year's Day, the Feast of the Circumcision. Hence today is a feast day or anniversary of Christ's first suffering for man.

The circumcision ceremony was an acknowledgement of man's sinful nature. Hence it was an act of humility for Christ to endure — Christ who was all good and free from all taint of sin himself. It was a humiliation for Christ, the God-man, to undergo a ceremony acknowledging the sinfulness of man.

Therefore, in beginning this new calendar year, let us measure ourselves and our spiritual life by comparing ourselves with him, our Redeemer. Let us stand up against his cross. Let us see how our charity or practice of virtue compares with his.

Let us resolve to try to lessen this gap. Let us act during this coming year as Christ himself would act in similar circumstances. Let us make this year a banner year for spiritual growth. Let us resolve that the end of this year will find us giants in the grace of God. God bless you.

# "B"     Second Sunday after Christmas

*John 1:1-18*

The gospel read at today's Mass is the beginning of the Gospel according to St. John. In the days prior to the Second Vatican Council, this particular gospel passage was read at every Mass. It came at the end of the Mass and was known as the Last Gospel. It was read, of course, in the Latin language.

St. John wrote his gospel when he was a very old man. Scripture scholars tell us that he wrote it about the year 97 A.D. He wrote it on the island of Patmos. When he wrote it, St. Peter had been dead for many years. St. John had also witnessed the destruction of the city of Jerusalem which Christ had prophesied. St. John's purpose in writing it was to prove that Jesus Christ was God and that salvation is to be obtained through his name.

One characteristic of St. John's gospel that is very pronounced is his symbolism — a symbolism that is not only pronounced but intentional. St. John begins his gospel by speaking of Christ, but he refers him by the term, "the Word," spelled with a capital W. The other Evangelists speak of Christ in the conventional way, referring to him as our Lord Jesus Christ. They tell of his birth in Bethlehem and the circumstances which surround it. But not St. John.

Since St. John was the last to write a gospel, he had undoubtedly seen and read the other gospels. Perhaps he thought their explanation of Christ's origin in the world was sufficient and a further account of his birth was unnecessary. Perhaps John referred to Christ as the Word because he, Christ, was to bring the word of the gospel to earth. He was to reveal the word of God to mankind. St. John does not explain his reasons. All this is part of his symbolism.

But St. John does go on to say, "The Word was in God's presence, and the Word was God." St. John's intention here is to reveal the eternity and divinity of Christ. By saying that Christ, or the Word, was in God's presence, John is saying, in effect, that he existed from all eternity along with God the Father. By saying that the Word was God, John is stating that Christ, the Second Person of the Blessed Trinity, is truly God along with the Father and the Holy Spirit.

St. John then asserts, "He was present to God in the beginning. Through him all things came into being, and apart from him nothing came to be." Here St. John wishes to show that the Son shared the work of creation along with the other two Persons of the Blessed Trinity. He was co-creator of the universe. Everything in the universe came into being through him.

St. John implies here that Christ, the Word, possesses the quality of infinite wisdom. Infinite wisdom is an attribute demanded of a creator, and since

Christ created all things, he must possess this infinite wisdom. He has supreme intelligence.

St. John introduces the thought that Christ is the author of life. He says, "Whatever came to be in him found life. . . ." Christ is life itself and the principle of all natural life.

Next St. John calls him the creator of light — the light of men — light that illumines the path of man on earth. He calls him "The light" that "shines on in darkness, a darkness that did not overcome it." Light here represents that which is good, as opposed to evil. It represents the good, the wholesome and the true. Light stands for immortality as opposed to death and the end of life. This light comes to man through the gospel, which is the means of spreading light. Hence Christianity is light. The good news of the gospel is light. They flow from Christ, who is the author of light. They serve to dispel the darkness of sin and ignorance.

The beginning of St. John's gospel is symbolic. But at the same time it is also sublime. It is a meditation on creation and eternity and the greatness and the qualities of God. But then in the midst of this reflection on Christ's greatness and eternal qualities, St. John abruptly changes his train of thought. He introduces a new topic. He begins to talk about St. John the Baptizer. This other St. John was sent into this world to be the precursor of Christ, to prepare the way for his coming on earth.

The Baptizer was to be a witness to testify to the light — St. John, the son of Zechariah and Elizabeth in their old age. His name was given him by an angel of God. At his birth he was dedicated to be a Nazarite, to fast often. While John was fasting in the desert, the word of the Holy Spirit came to him and prompted him to begin to preach a gospel of repentance for sin. St. John's message alerted the people concerning the coming of Christ, the Messiah. It prepared his way. It gave testimony to the light.

But then after introducing the topic of St. John the Baptizer and his mission on earth, of preparing the way for the Messiah, St. John again returns to the subject of Christ. St. John says, "To his own he came." Here he is referring to the Jewish people. The great and crowning privilege of the Israelites or Jews was that it was prophesied that the Messiah was to be one of their race. This prophecy was fulfilled in the birth of Christ. In fact, St. Matthew opens his gospels by tracing the lineage and genealogy of Christ, from his foster-father Joseph back to King David and the Israelite offspring of Abraham, Isaac and Jacob.

St. John does not take the time or trouble to do this. Perhaps he thinks that St. Matthew and the other gospel writers did it well enough before him. St. John simply states that his own did not receive him. He ever so briefly tells us that most of the Jewish people did not believe the teachings of Christ. They did not follow his teachings. They refused the privilege of becoming members of his Church upon earth.

St. John quickly passes over their rejection to say that those who did receive and accept him he empowered to become children of God. Christ gave the gifts of supernatural life and light to those who did believe in his teaching and accept his gospel. He brought salvation to them. He opened to them the way to the kingdom of heaven.

St. John implies he is writing for those who accepted his teaching. He states that we have all had a share of his fullness. That enduring love came through Jesus Christ. As Christ is the author of light and of life, so too he is the author of love — love that will last and endure.

St. John concludes his prologue or the beginning of his gospel on a note of hope. He states that only Christ, the Word, has seen God. It is his privilege to extend this vision to others. And Christ has so extended it. But our only hope of seeing God or enjoying the Beatific Vision of heaven ourselves is through the Church of Christ.

But if we avail ourselves of the teaching of Christ, if we believe in his gospel, if we practice his teachings, then there is hope — hope that someday we too shall enjoy the Beatific Vision ourselves and enjoy the happiness of heaven hereafter. God bless you.

# "B"      Epiphany

*Matthew 2:1-12*

Today on the Feast of the Epiphany, St. Matthew tells us in the gospel read at today's Mass that astrologers came from the east after Jesus' birth in Bethlehem and inquired, where could they find the "newborn King of the Jews?" In the old translation of this gospel the word "Magi" was used to describe these men from the East. This term "Magi" is a literal and accurate translation in Latin. But then in the Middle Ages someone confused the term "Magi" with kings. This meaning is incorrect. They were not kings.

"Magi" might be translated as a mature scientists, students of the stars or as astrologers as we now have it. Actually they are men of mystery. We know only that they were not Jews; they were from the East. Probably they were of a Median tribe that lived a nomadic life somewhere in Persia.

They speak only two sentences in all of Holy Scripture. They ask, "Where is the newborn king of the Jews? We observed his star at its rising and have come to pay him homage." We do not know how they came to know of the birth of Christ, whom they called the newborn king. We do not know how they came to associate his birth with a star. Most probably this knowledge was given them through a direct divine revelation.

The star which they followed has also created many scriptural questions. The astronomer Kepler has shown from scientific data that at this particular time in history the three planets Mars, Jupiter and Saturn were very closely aligned in the eastern sky. Their alignment would cause one to judge with his naked eye that it was a single large bright star. Still others think the star that guided them was a comet that entered the earth's atmosphere at that particular time.

The arrival of these three Magi or astrologers in Jerusalem with their questions about a newborn king was a matter of grave concern to King Herod. Summoning the chief priests and the scribes he learned of them the prophecy of Micah: "But you Bethlehem-Eprathah, too small to be among the clans of Judah,/From you shall come forth for me one who is to be ruler in Israel."

Aided with this new information and having given a promise to King Herod to convey to him any new information they might gain, they set out from Jerusalem to Bethlehem. King Herod had asked that they report their findings to him so that he might also pay the newborn king homage. But his real motives were far different.

After leaving Jerusalem, the star which had guided the Magi reappeared and led them to Bethlehem to the place where the child was. Entering the house, they found the Christ Child with Mary, his Mother. They prostrated themselves and did him homage.

The Magi did not come empty-handed, as Orientals scarcely ever paid a visit to a superior without offering gifts. This visit was no exception. They opened their coffers and presented him with gifts of gold, frankincense and myrrh.

Gold was a gift given only to royalty. But in giving gold to the Christ Child they acknowledged his kingship, his majesty, his reign over men. Incense was a gift offered only to God. In giving incense to the Christ Child, they acknowledged his divinity. Myrrh was a balm used to anoint the bodies of the dead. In giving him myrrh they acknowledged that someday he must die — that he possessed a human nature and must die as do all men. Hence in bestowing these particular gifts to Christ, they acknowledged him to be king, God and man. (We are not even sure of the number of Magi who came to Bethlehem. From their three gifts it has been presumed there were three — possibly more.)

The stay of the Magi, or the astrologers, at Bethlehem was probably not a long one. Possibly no more than overnight. Any long delay would have aroused the already distrustful Herod. But they received a message in a dream not to go back to Herod. So they went back to their country by another route. From Bethlehem a seven- or eight-hour trip by camel would bring them beyond the Jordan and beyond the jurisdiction of King Herod.

The Magi disappear from the pages of Holy Scripture as quickly as they entered them, and they are never heard of again. They are men of mystery. They bring to mind many questions which are unanswered.

But the Magi, we can be certain, are not Jews; they are foreigners from another land. They are the first gentiles to whom God manifested the presence of his divine Son here on earth. Hence they represent the gentile nations. The revelation of the birth of Christ our Redeemer was made to the Jews on Christmas even when the angels announced his birth to the shepherds in the field and they came to adore him.

Then through the guidance of the star in the east his birth was made known to the gentiles in the persons of the Magi on the Feast of Epiphany. Hence for us the Feast of the Epiphany is one of great importance. The Epiphany is one of the ten major holy days or highest feasts in the Catholic Church. In some countries, for instance Canada, when it was formerly celebrated on January 6th, it was one of their six holy days of obligation.

God has revealed his presence here on earth to many men in many different ways. Some men have been converted to Catholicism through the good example of other Catholics; some through their study of history and the faith, others in assorted ways. In whatever way the faith has come to us, let us thank God for it. Let us rejoice on this Feast of Epiphany, the feast of the revelation of his birth to the gentile nations. Let us kneel in adoration before him as did the Magi. Acknowledging the kingship, the divinity and humanity of Christ can bring us great rewards. God bless you.

# "B"  Sunday After Epiphany (Baptism of the Lord)

*Mark 1:6-11*

The River Jordan, in which Christ was baptized, flows south through the country of Palestine, dividing the country in two parts. It connects the Sea of Galilee to the north with the Dead Sea to the south; its current is very swift. Its banks are lined with a dense jungle growth of willow and poplar trees and clinging creeper vines. Its banks are too high and steep to permit any irrigation or agriculture.

It was in the country of Bethany beyond the Jordan where John the Baptizer was baptizing and where Christ came to him. He came on a winter's day. Despite the fact that they were cousins, Christ was not personally acquainted with John. John had lived in the desert regions, and Christ, who had lived at Nazareth, was just about to begin his public life.

John had clearly announced his mission here on earth. He was the precursor of the Messiah. He was to prepare his way. The Messiah, who would follow him, would be more powerful than he and would baptize with the Holy Spirit.

The Holy Spirit had promised John a sign — that he would descend upon the Messiah as a dove when he came. When John saw this sign, he recognized Christ immediately as the Messiah — the Redeemer whom he had long awaited. Then also a voice came from the heavens: "You are my beloved Son. On you my favor rests." God the Father in heaven manifested his presence here on earth and gave approval of Christ's mission.

Christ himself was true God and true Man. He was all good and perfect. He had no need of any baptism for his own sake. Nevertheless his baptism by John served a divine purpose. It was a public announcement for the world to hear that Christ was the long-awaited Messiah. His baptism marked the beginning with clear divine approval of the public ministry of Christ upon this earth. It was an announcement to man that his redemption was close at hand.

The Incarnation did not take place at this time. In fact, it had taken place some thirty years earlier in a stable at Bethlehem, where Christ was born. But his baptism served as the occasion at which God solemnly introduced his beloved Son in his Messianic role.

Through his baptism by John, Christ taught us the necessity of baptism. He taught us the importance of receiving this sacrament of the new law. Christ said, "Unless a man be born again of water and of the Holy Spirit, he shall not enter the kingdom of heaven." Christ made baptism the single most necessary sacrament of the new law. By allowing himself to be baptized, he set an example for us to follow.

Baptism sets us free from the stain of original sin with which we are all born. It is the magna carta of our freedom from the bondage of sin. Through natural birth we are born into this world; but through baptism we are born into the spiritual world. Through baptism we are made children of God and become heirs to heaven. Through baptism the gift of sanctifying grace is bestowed upon our souls.

The ordinary minister of the Sacrament of Baptism is the priest, who administers it solemnly in church. To administer it he uses baptismal water which he pours over the head of the child while saying the words, "I baptize you in the name of the Father, and of the Son, and of the Holy Spirit."

But because baptism is so necessary, Holy Mother the Church did not want it to depend exclusively on the availability of a priest. Therefore, in case of emergency she had given permission to everyone to baptize. All one need do is take ordinary water and pour it over the head of the person or child while saying the necessary words. Baptism is a sacrament which all Catholics should know how to administer in case of necessity.

Baptism is the doorway to supernatural life; it is the key to the kingdom of heaven. It is the means God chose to bring supernatural life to mankind. Christ entrusted its administration to his Apostles when he said, "Go . . . make disciples of all nations. Baptize them in the name of the Father, and of the Son, and of the Holy Spirit."

Baptism is the sacrament by which men and women are granted membership in the Church of Christ. They are incorporated into Christ's mystical body. They are entitled to further reception of other sacraments, especially the Holy Eucharist, and many other spiritual benefits. Through baptism they are given a new dignity. The Holy Trinity comes to dwell within their souls in the form of grace. They become temples of the Holy Spirit.

Through baptism not only original sin, but any other sin an adult may have previously committed, is washed away. Temporal punishment to sin is likewise remitted. Baptism is such a holy and great sacrament, it can only be received once in one's lifetime. An indelible mark is placed upon the soul of the person who receives it. This mark is for one's greater glory and happiness in the kingdom of heaven or for one's greater punishment in hell hereafter.

In the Second Vatican Council a Liturgical Commission was set up to make appropriate changes in the liturgy of the Church. These changes have been made not only in the Mass but in the ceremony of baptism as well. Many beautiful and meaningful ceremonies surround the sacrament. Before its administration the child is anointed on the breast and back with the oil of catechumens. This is a sign of spiritual strength.

Following the baptism the child is anointed on the forehead with holy chrism. This anointing signifies that the baptized Christian is a member of the body of Christ. The child is then covered with a white garment. This signifies the outward sign of Christian dignity. The Easter or baptismal candle is lighted and handed to the parents and godparents of the child. This signifies the light of faith. The priest touches the mouth and ears of the baptized child. This symbolizes the child's willingness to proclaim the faith he has now received.

The Sacrament of Baptism is one of God's greatest gifts to men. It is a sacrament in which we are born spiritually; a life of grace enters our soul. St. Francis de Sales was accustomed to say that the place he enjoyed visiting more than any on earth was the church of his baptism. It was on that spot that the life of grace began within his soul and the Holy Trinity took up its abode with him.

Let our sentiments be the same. Let us thank God for instituting this sacrament to bring spiritual life to us. Let us resolve that we shall try to preserve this baptismal grace within our souls untainted by the stain of sin. God bless you.

# "B"    First Sunday of Lent

*Mark 1:12-15*

The strongest man in our Revolutionary army was a man named Begordius Hatch. The marker above the grave of this Atlas of George Washington's army had begun to decay, and the school children of Lebanon, New York, contributed a penny each to restore the monument. For this strong and brave soldier had served in every campaign with the Father of our Country.

His reputation as the strongest man in the first army of the United States was established when he picked up a cannon and walked away with it on his shoulder. Tall and muscular Hatch boasted that no one had ever thrown him in wrestling since he was fourteen.

Even at the age of sixteen he was robust. On one occasion, at a barn-raising bee, his farmer neighbors agreed not to lift at all when they and Begordius Hatch were to carry a heavy beam together. Hatch carried the heavy beam alone.

But as Begordius Hatch was a soldier in the army of George Washington, so you and I are soldiers in an army. We are soldiers in the army of Christ. We have been inducted to serve under his standard, the sign of the cross. We were made the children of God by the Sacrament of Baptism, and when we attained our spiritual manhood we were made his soldiers by the Sacrament of Confirmation.

Today's gospel depicts for us a battle scene. In it we see our leader, Jesus Christ, engaged in deadly battle with the enemy of God, the leader of the forces of evil, with Satan. In this battle we see our divine Savior victorious, for soon afterwards he casts out the devil from the dumb man who has been possessed, and he begins to speak.

But do not deceive yourself, the devil is a strong and fearful foe. He has an intellect far superior to ours. He has been called a roaring lion going about seeking whom he may devour.

Although defeated by God himself, the devil, still powerful, has changed his tactics. He has directed his attack towards us. He knows very well that God loves each one of us personally. Because of that love, the devil in turn hates us. His goal is to bring each one of us down into the torments of hell.

Sometime in our life, we don't know when, we shall come in conflict with the devil. There will be no shirking of the battle. We shall be forced to declare ourselves a follower of Christ or succumb to Satan. For as Christ tells us elsewhere in the gospel, "He who is not with me, is against me; and he who does not gather with me scatters."

Rest assured, Christ will not desert us. His grace is always with us to help us when we need him most. If we fail, it is not because Christ has failed us, but rather because we have failed Christ.

And how should we prepare for this battle? We should prepare by increasing our spiritual strength so as to be able to repel the devil's temptation at any time. In Christ's own words, this may be accomplished by prayer and fasting.

This season of Lent is a special time to build up our spiritual armor — to increase our spiritual strength. It is the time to renew our allegiance to Christ our Lord and to nourish ourselves on the graces which he offers us.

Certainly it would not be too much to expect to make a daily visit to our Lord in the Blessed Sacrament or to make the Stations of the Cross. For those whose work does not keep them from it, there could be nothing better than to attend daily Mass and receive our Lord in Holy Communion. Christ, whom we receive in Holy Communion, is the source of all grace.

To deny ourselves is important — first of all by abstaining on Fridays and fasting on Good Friday, which is imposed on all those 21 through 58 who are of good health and able to do it. Denying ourselves in other ways — whether it be by giving up smoking, television or some other pleasure — would be an excellent means of fortifying ourselves against temptation.

Let us resolve to be strong soldiers in the army of Christ, as was Begordius Hatch in the army of George Washington. Remember that we have been inducted into the army of Christ. The battle with the enemy of your soul lies ahead. There is no way out but to resist him. The stakes are high: eternal happiness in heaven or eternal suffering in hell.

Today Christ is offering you the weapons — prayer and fasting, grace and the sacraments. Seize them, for there is no substitute for victory in this battle of life. God bless you.

# "B"    Second Sunday of Lent

*Mark 9:2-10*

Today on the Second Sunday of Lent, Holy Mother the Church places before us St. Mark's account of the Transfiguration of our Lord. Gathering details from this account and from similar accounts in the gospels of St. Matthew and St. Luke, Scripture scholars generally believe the Transfiguration took place on Mount Tabor.

Christ had led Peter, James and John up to this mountain, and they were the witnesses of this great miracle. Before their eyes his face grew brighter than the sun and his clothes became dazzling white.

The Old Testament tells us that on one occasion Moses on Mt. Horeb appeared in a brilliant light. But it adds that he only reflected divine light. Christ shone with a radiance all his own.

When Christ was transfigured, there appeared with him Moses and Elijah; the two were in conversation with Jesus. Their appearance is significant, as they are the two chief figures of the Old Testament. Moses represents the Law, and Elijah was the greatest of the prophets.

Their presence with Christ shows the connection between the Old and New Testaments. Yet among them Christ had the place of honor. It was clear to the three Apostles that Christ was the long-awaited Messiah. Moses and Elijah spoke with Christ concerning his forthcoming death.

All three Apostles were overcome with awe and surprise. They hardly knew what to say. Nevertheless Peter found some words: "Rabbi, how good it is for us to be here! Let us erect three booths on this site, one for you, one for Moses, and one for Elijah."

The booths that Peter spoke of were simply leafly huts which the night-watchers of the vineyards set up for themselves for protection against the wind, the rain and other inclement weather. These leafy huts were generally poorly constructed and were not expected to last any more than a season. Such booths would have been most inappropriate memorials for so glorious an event. Nevertheless, Peter's remark showed that he grasped the importance of this occasion.

No sooner had Peter made his comment, when a cloud overshadowed them and a loud voice was heard, "This is my Son, my beloved. Listen to him." It was the voice of God the Father speaking in praise of his Son. The First Person of the Blessed Trinity was manifesting his presence here on earth.

On two other occasions God the Father was to manifest himself to man. The first occasion was at the baptism of Jesus by John the Baptizer in the River Jordan. The other which was yet to come was around Holy Thursday, sometime before the Last Supper.

Upon hearing the voice of God the Father, the three Apostles fell to the ground in fear. Jesus came and touched them and bade them arise. Looking around they no longer saw anyone with him. The apparition was over. They started down the mountain together, but Jesus strictly enjoined them not to tell anyone what they had seen, before the Son of Man had risen from the dead.

The Apostles were uncertain about what Christ meant when he said, "risen from the dead"; this they discussed among themselves. Nevertheless they were obedient to his command in not telling of the Transfiguration to others at that time.

Christ transfigured himself before the three Apostles to give them encouragement and hope, for soon they would see him undergo the agony of crucifixion. He wanted them to have a source of consolation when they would see him suffer.

The Transfiguration of Christ was a proof of his divinity. The glory he showed them was something only God could possess. The presence of Moses and Elijah, the leading figures of the Old Testament, confirmed Christ's claim to be the Messiah. The voice of God the Father from the cloud added credence to these beliefs.

The Transfiguration has a meaning for all men. It is pledge of our own future resurrection. On the day of General Judgment our bodies and souls will be reunited. Christ will then bestow on the just the joys of eternal happiness in heaven.

The Transfiguration of Christ should be a source of hope and consolation for all men. The thought of it should sustain us in time of trial and tribulation. Let us beg of Christ the spiritual strength to preserve his grace in our souls throughout our life — grace that will endure until we see the transfigured Christ in all his glory in the world to come. God bless you.

# "B"     3rd Sunday in Lent

*John 2:13-25*

Many centuries ago King David sat with his harp composing psalms in praise of almighty God. In the 10th verse of the 69th Psalm he wrote, ". . . zeal for your house consumes me. . . ." But little did he dream that this particular verse would be quoted centuries later by the Apostles in describing the actions of Christ.

The temple in Jerusalem was a very sacred place to the Jews. The first temple was built by King Solomon. It took seven years to construct and was dedicated in the year 961 B.C. It served the Jews in their worship for nearly three hundred years. But the temple was finally destroyed when the Persians overran Palestine and led the Jews away as captives to Persia.

When the Jews were freed from their Babylonian captivity they returned to the Holy Land. Under the leadership of Zerubbabel the temple was reconstructed and dedicated in the year 516 B.C. It continued in use again until the year 169 B.C., when the Syrian leader Antiochus II captured Jerusalem and plundered the temple in 169 B.C.

Just a century later the city of Jerusalem was again captured in war — this time by the Roman General Pompey in the year 63 B.C. The Romans placed Herod upon the throne in Israel. Under the Roman rule the Jews set about once again to rebuild the temple, their task taking some 46 years.

The temple consisted of an inner chamber, called the Holy of Holies, within the temple building itself. Surrounding the temple building were two courts; the inner court was the court of the priests, and the outer court was called the Court of the Gentiles.

It was in this outer court, the Court of the Gentiles, that on festive occasions the merchants set up their business stalls. Thus cattle and sheep and all kinds of food and other goods were to be seen. Jewish law forbade such activity, but yet it was tolerated by the priests.

Jewish law likewise required every adult Jew to celebrate the feast of the Passover in the city of Jerusalem. Mary and Joseph first brought Christ to Jerusalem for this feast day when he was twelve years old, and he had come every year since then. By now Christ had begun his public life. He came to the city of Jerusalem for the Passover with a retinue of his disciples.

When Christ entered the temple on this occasion he saw a sight that displeased him greatly. The merchants and others were desecrating the temple. Therefore Christ made a whip of cords. He upset their money stands and booths. He drove the merchants out of the temple saying, "Get them out of here! Stop turning my father's house into a market-place!"

The Levites were entrusted with the duty of keeping public order in the temple. They were abashed and staggered by this bold act of Christ. Christ had done in a dramatic act what they were supposed to do but had failed to do for so many years. They were too embarassed to stop Christ in what he was doing, for they knew he was right. But after a few minutes they reacquired some of their composure and together with some other Jews challenged him, "What sign can you show us authorizing you to do these things?"

Christ could have asserted his divine authority at this time. He could have pointed out he was doing the duty which they had neglected. But instead, he used this occasion to make a prophecy. He said, "Destroy this temple . . . and in three days I will raise it up."

The Jews obviously misunderstood Christ from the answer they gave him. They mentioned the forty-six years it had taken them to build the temple originally. Even his disciples did not know the meaning of his words at the time. Actually he was referring to the temple of his body and the time he would take to rise from the dead.

Only after Christ had been put to death and his body laid in the tomb did these words come to mind and their meaning sink in.

The Sacrament of Holy Orders, which makes a man a priest, was once conferred in seven steps of orders. The first four steps or orders were called minor orders. They were known as porter, lector, exorcist and acolyte.

The order of porter was the first to be administered. In bestowing this order upon a young man, the bishop handed to him the keys of the church and said "Fulfill your office to show that you know that you will account to God concerning the things that are locked away under these keys." Thus through the order of porter a young man was made the guardian of the church and its contents. This is one of the duties of every priest.

One of the great saints of the Church was St. Francis of Assisi. Out of humility, St. Francis refused to accept the order of the priesthood. However, he did receive the minor orders and the other parts of Holy Orders up through the order of deacon. During his lifetime he once went to a deserted, run-down country church. When he was scheduled to preach no one came to hear him.

Therefore he decided what was needed was to exercise his order of porter. In the next few weeks he did a lot of manual labor in the church. He swept and scrubbed it. He repaired the stone and masonry. He repaired its altar and its steps and made it a clean and beautiful church as it once had been.

St. Francis did not preach a word in it. But the people of the community observed his diligent work in repairing the church, making it a suitable house for our Lord to dwell in in the Blessed Sacrament. The story of his hard work spread quickly. When next Mass and devotions were scheduled in the church, it was filled to overflowing, because St. Francis had exercised his order of porter in beautifying God's church.

Let us take pride in our own parish church. Let us give it what we can, not only through the collection but also in time and effort to help make it a suitable house for God to dwell it. Let us be grateful to our janitor, the ladies of the Altar and Rosary Society and all those who give of their time and energy to help keep it clean and beautiful.

Whatever we do in beautifying God's home on earth, God will reward by bestowing upon us a beautiful mansion in the kingdom of heaven. God bless you.

# "B"     Fourth Sunday of Lent

*John 3:14-21*

The Gospel of St. John read at today's Mass tells us a conversation Christ had with Nicodemus. Nicodemus was one of the leading citizens of the city of Jerusalem. He was one of the seventy-two members of the Sanhedrin, the governing body of the city and surrounding nation. His status would be comparable to that of a federal judge or congressman in our country today.

Nicodemus had heard of Christ, his teachings and his miracles. He wanted very much to meet him. But he was a timid soul. He feared to come to Christ openly in the daytime. He feared the criticism of his colleagues in Jerusalem if they knew he was a follower of Christ. Therefore he arranged to meet and talk with Jesus secretly at night. Only a few of the Apostles knew about this meeting.

Nicodemus was extremely cautious in arranging this meeting with Jesus, but his motives were obvious. He wanted to know the objectives and nature of the kingdom whose coming John had announced and whose actual presence

Jesus was now preaching. Jesus could read men's hearts. He knew that Nicodemus was honest and sincere.

Nicodemus complimented our Lord when he first met him by saying that he knew that he came as a teacher from God — that no one could work the signs Christ worked unless God was with him.

Christ began to instruct Nicodemus: "Just as Moses lifted up the serpent in the desert, so must the Son of Man be lifted up." The Book of Numbers in the Old Testament tells us that when a number of the Jews had been bitten by poisonous serpents in the desert, Moses lifted up a bronze serpent upon a pole as a divine remedy to heal them.

When Christ referred to himself, the Son of Man, as being lifted up, he referred to his crucifixion. But neither Nicodemus nor the Apostles understood this at the time. Only later would they come to a true realization of the words.

Christ continued, "God did not send the Son into the world to condemn the world, but that the world might be saved through him." Thus we have Christ, the Messiah, speaking to Nicodemus, a leader of the Jews, a member of their governing body. Christ revealed to Nicodemus his mission here on earth, and Nicodemus believed in him. One might believe that Nicodemus would publicly support our Lord and help persuade his fellow members of the Sanhedrin of the truth he taught. But this was not to be the case.

Nicodemus was a timid man. He had lacked the courage to meet Christ publicly in the daytime. He lacked the courage to stand before his peers in the Sanhedrin and tell them the Messiah had come to earth. A fearful battle raged in his soul. The social pressure of his position prevented him from declaring his true beliefs.

Consider how his soul must have been rent when Christ was led before the Sanhedrin on Holy Thursday night. One of his Apostles, Judas Iscariot, had betrayed him for thirty pieces of silver. False witnesses were brought forward to testify against him. His fellow members of the Sanhedrin were seeking a way to put Christ to death. Nicodemus knew that Christ was the Son of God and the charges made against him were entirely false. Yet he still lacked the moral courage to stand up and say so. He feared to declare his beliefs in public.

How deeply troubled was his soul! In later life what remorse must have flooded his being! How keenly must he have regretted his timidity and cowardice! What would he not have given for another opportunity to free Christ and declare to all the world that Christ was their Redeemer, completely innocent of all the charges made against him. But Nicodemus did not do this when the opportunity presented itself. Instead he sat silently listening to the false charges made against him; he acquiesced when the Sanhedrin sent him bound to Pilate.

It was only after Christ had died on the cross that Nicodemus took some action. Together with another wealthy and influential friend, Joseph of Arimathea, Nicodemus asked Pontius Pilate for the body of Christ; Pilate granted their request. Together they anointed the body of Christ with myrrh and aloes and placed it in the tomb of Joseph.

Nicodemus was a believer in our Lord but a timid one. It took the death of Christ to prompt him to action. History records nothing more about him except that his name is listed in the Roman martyrology and he is declared a saint. His feast day is August 3rd. It could well be that when the Roman government publicly persecuted the Christian Church, Nicodemus did publicly proclaim his faith and was martyred for it.

From the story of today's gospel, let us learn to be strong and courageous in proclaiming our faith. Nicodemus at the time of these incidents did not have the benefit of the Sacrament of Confirmation. He had not received the Holy Spirit to make him a strong and perfect Christian and soldier of Jesus Christ.

But we do have the benefit of this sacrament of strength. Therefore, let us be proud of our faith. Let us never hide it. When the occasion demands, let us proclaim it openly. Christ has said, "He who acknowledges me before men, him will I acknowledge before my heavenly father." God bless you.

# "B"    Fifth Sunday of Lent

*John 12:20-33*

In the gospel of today's Mass, St. John tells us that there was a group of Greeks who wished to see Jesus. They had heard of his miracles and of his wonderful teachings and were anxious to see him. They approached two Apostles, Philip and Andrew, who in turn relayed the message to Jesus.

These Greeks had come to Jerusalem to celebrate the feast of the Passover. In the Old Testament only circumcized Jews were permitted to be members of the Jewish religion and take part in the religious services in the inner temple. However, certain gentiles who conformed to the external practices of the Jewish religion, like fasting, pilgrimages to Jerusalem and the observance of the Sabbath, were permitted to enter the outer courts of the temple. These Greeks were among that number. Our Lord gladly received them.

This incident in the early public life of our Lord is an indication of the nature of his future Church. It would not be open only to Jews, but gentiles as well would be received into it. Christ had come to earth to save all men without exception.

Christ took this opportunity to begin to instruct the Apostles and those around him on the doctrine of the Blessed Trinity. He unveiled a part of this mystery or great truth. He spoke of the Father, the first person of the Trinity. Christ said, "Anyone who serves me, him the Father will honor."

Again he added, "What should I say — Father, save me from this hour?" Christ as a person was praying out loud. As a person he was speaking to his heavenly Father. He said again, "Father, glorify your name!"

At this a voice came from the sky: "I have glorified it, and will glorify it again." God the Father in heaven spoke to men on earth. He manifested his presence. He spoke to men in response to the prayer and request of Christ, his divine Son.

The mystery of the Blessed Trinity is one of the great dogmas or articles of our Christian faith. It is a teaching that the Jews of the Old Testament were unaware of. God did not reveal it to them. It was something new that Christ was teaching men.

Christ's manner of teaching it was to reveal it gradually, step by step. If Christ had revealed it fully, all at one time, they would undoubtedly have rejected it. Those who heard it would have fled from Christ and would not have listened to him any longer. Christ presented to the crowd only as much truth as their minds were able to digest at one time.

Speaking to the crowd about God the Father was not difficult. Christ associated the Father with God himself, with Yahweh, whom the Jews knew from the Old Testament. This the Jews readily accepted.

Then after preaching to the Jews for a year or more, Christ began to identify himself, claiming to be the Son of God. He claimed to be the Messiah or Redeemer. On one occasion he said, "I am who am." He was claiming eternal existence which belongs to God alone. The Jews understood him clearly, for they took up stones to throw at him. Stoning was the penalty for blasphemy, the sin of falsely claiming to be God.

The difference in the claim of Christ was that his claim was true. He proved throughout the three years of his public life that truly he was the Son of God, by his miracles, his resurrection and other signs. He proved His divine nature.

Christ on later occasions in his public life also spoke of the Third Person of the Blessed Trinity, the Holy Spirit. Christ promised that after he ascended into heaven he would send the Spirit, the Paraclete, down upon the Apostles to teach them all things. He said also that unless he ascended into heaven, the Spirit would not come upon them.

Both the Father and the Holy Spirit manifested their presence in visible fashion here on earth to give support to Christ and his teachings. The Father spoke out of heaven in the words contained in today's gospel. He had spoken twice before out of a cloud — at the river Jordan and on the occasion of Christ's Transfiguration.

The Holy Spirit appeared in the form of a dove at the baptism of Christ in the river Jordan by St. John the Baptist. He appeared again on Pentecost Sunday as Christ prophesied he would, in the form of fiery tongues which came and sat on the head of each Apostle. On this occasion the Holy Spirit gave spiritual strength to all whom he confirmed in the faith.

Christ spoke on occasion of all three persons together. Before His Ascension into heaven He commissioned His Apostles, "Go therefore and make disciples of all nations. Baptize them in the name of the Father and of the Son and of the Holy Spirit."

The Holy Trinity is one of the chief doctrines of our faith. Yet it remains a mystery for us. None of us can clearly understand how there can be three distinct persons in one and the same God. But because it is a mystery we should not refuse to believe it. We find many mysteries in the world of nature around us. We cannot fully understand the nature of electricity or atomic power, but we believe in their existence. We believe in the Trinity because of the testimony of Christ, who proved his divinity by his many miracles.

The mystery of the Blessed Trinity was preached by the Apostles and the early Fathers from the very beginning of the Church. It is contained in the Apostles' Creed and the Nicene Creed recited at Mass. Devotion to the Blessed Trinity has won spiritual reward for many saints.

One saint known for his devotion to the Blessed Trinity was Venerable Bede, His favorite prayer which he said many times a day was, "Glory be to the Father, and to the Son, and to the Holy Spirit."

Let us heed the words of Christ in today's gospel in speaking to his heavenly Father. Let us express our belief in the Blessed Trinity. Let us pray in adoration to our triune God. Belief and worship in the three persons in God can bring us eternal reward. God bless you.

# "B" Passion Sunday (Palm Sunday)

*Mark 15:1-39*

Christ entered this world as a baby in Bethlehem, but even then he was God. He knew all things and could foresee the future. All through the thirty-three or more years he lived on earth, Christ in his divine nature foresaw the death he was to die. During the joy of the wedding feast of Cana and in the midst of all the miracles of curing the blind and the lame, the vision of his cross never disappeared from before his eyes.

Even when Christ was transfigured on Mount Tabor, even when the Jews greeted him with shouts of "Hosanna" and wanted to make him king, the knowledge of his impending crucifixion was never absent. It hung as a shadow over his entire life.

By enduring such great sufferings in his lifetime, Christ showed us how we should view suffering in our own. Christ did not view suffering as an evil inflicted by God. The only real evil in this world is the sin which we commit ourselves. Christ used suffering as a means to redeem mankind. We, in turn, can use suffering in our own lives as a means of gaining grace and obtaining salvation.

Man has striven hard to alleviate suffering whenever possible. He has surrounded himself with comfort, warmth and softness. He has discovered pills to relieve the pain of an aching head. He has even covered these pills with sugar to make them sweet-tasting to the tongue. He has invented nerve-deadeners to make durable the hours spent in the dentist's chair. It provides anesthetics for persons going into the operating room. He has made great strides to alleviate suffering, but he shall never totally eliminate it.

Christ's crucifixion teaches us how we can endure suffering. We can offer it up as a sacrifice for our own sins and imperfections. Christ said, "If anyone will be perfect, let him take up his cross and come after me."

Christ's attitude toward suffering can be expressed in no better way than in the seventh and final word he spoke from his cross. It was the final sentence he spoke on earth before his death. In the midst of his terrible agony he looked upward toward heaven and said, "Father, into your hands I commend my spirit."

These last words were nothing new. They were centuries old when Christ spoke them. They are a direct quotation from the Thirty-first Psalm of King David, written centuries before.

Where did Christ learn this psalm? Why did he recite it as the last word before his death? The answer is — he learned it at his mother's knee. Mary taught it to him when he was a child. This was the psalm customarily said by the Jewish people as their night prayer before going to bed.

Picture Christ learning this psalm from our Blessed Mother. See him kneeling to pray each night to God his Father. It is no wonder then that he made these words the last words he spoke in his lifetime. He was simply repeating the words Mary, his mother, had taught him. He was repeating what he was accustomed to say every day.

Think of how Mary must have felt upon hearing them. The work she had done silently through the years bore fruit before her eyes. These words were now immortalized. They are an inspiration to all parents who teach their children to pray.

In his prayers each night Christ had offered his life and work to his Father. Now in death he was offering him his sufferings. His example is so clear, so easy to follow. Christ did not merely tell us how to suffer; he showed us.

The lesson on how to suffer is one which the saints of God learned well. One example of a saint who suffered well is St. Bernadette Soubirous, to whom Mary revealed herself at Lourdes, France. Our Blessed Mother told Bernadette to scratch some muddy soil and swallow it. Bernadette obeyed her. From this muddy soil a spring of miracle-working water began to flow.

Later in life Bernadette entered the convent. Later still she contracted a painful incurable disease. On one occasion when suffering greatly, her mother superior came to her and suggested that she return to the spring at Lourdes to seek a cure for her own illness.

To this Bernadette replied, "No, the spring is not for me." She felt that although she had won healing for other people, it was her business to suffer for Christ.

Each of us has some small cross to bear, some suffering to undergo. It is most important that we accept it willingly as did Christ. Only in this way can we be sure that we shall be drawn to Christ. Only in this way can we be sure of meriting an eternal reward. God bless you.

# "B"  Easter Sunday

*John 20:1-9*

It has been said that except for the Blessed Virgin Mary, his mother, no one on earth loved our Lord more dearly than did Mary Magdalene. Mary was a repentant sinner. She loved our Lord so dearly because he had forgiven her so much. She showed her love for Christ when she bathed his feet with a flask of precious oil, worth a great deal of money, and wiped them with her hair.

What reason other than love would prompt her to be up before dawn and make her way to his tomb the second day after his death, hoping to anoint his dead body? Imagine her surprise when she found the stone had been moved away from the mouth of the tomb, and she peered into it, to discover that his body was not there.

Eagerly did she run back and tell Peter and the other disciple whom Jesus loved that the tomb was empty. Only three days before Peter had denied three times that he knew our Lord, but he repented his denial. His position as leader of the Apostles was not questioned or challenged because of it.

St. John, the author of today's gospel does not identify Peter's companion, the disciple whom Jesus loved, by name. Yet other Scripture sources do identify him as John himself. It is reasonable to assume that John did not mention his own name out of a sense of humility.

When Peter and John heard this startling news, they began immediately to run to the tomb. John the younger and more agile of the two Apostles, outraced Peter to the empty tomb. He bent down to peer into it and saw the wrappings lying on the ground. This was strange indeed! No tomb-robbers would have bothered to unwrap a corpse they were stealing away. Stranger still, the wrappings were lying there in their folds, as though the body of Christ which they enclosed had come out of them without disturbing them. No tomb-robbers could have put them back in this manner. To begin with, how could any tomb-robbers have gotten past the soldiers on guard at the entrance of the tomb?

As John mulled over these and similar thoughts, Peter came up behind him and entered the tomb. John followed him in. As yet neither of the two Apostles understood the Scripture that Jesus had to rise from the dead. But little by little everything began to point to the fact that Jesus had left the tomb under his own power. Still puzzled and wondering, the two Apostles went away to where they were staying.

The tomb had actually been opened that morning by an angel of the Lord. Following a mighty earthquake, an angel descended from heaven and rolled back the stone and sat upon it. In appearance he resembled a flash of lightning, while his garments were as dazzling as snow. The guards grew paralyzed with fear of him and fell down like dead men. The guards later re-entered the city and reported to the chief priests what had happened. The elders then convened and bribed the soldiers to lie and say that the Apostles had come and stolen the body away while they were asleep.

Meanwhile, Mary Magdalene, after telling the startling news to Peter and John, had returned to the tomb accompanied by Joanna and Mary the mother of James. Mary stood beside the tomb weeping. A man approached her and asked, "Why are you weeping? Who is it you are looking for?" Mary imagined him to be the gardener, but he spoke again to her pronouncing her name, "Mary." Mary then recognized him to be Jesus himself. He directed her to go and tell his disciples that he was ascending to his Father. Again Mary hurried off.

The resurrection of Christ can be called his rebirth. On Easter Sunday Christ assumed human nature for a second time. He arose from the tomb, body and soul, alive, radiant and glorious. On Easter Christ began a new life — a short life — one that only lasted forty days, but an active one. He was to appear to his Apostles later that evening and give them the power to forgive sin. He was to establish the Sacrament of Penance. He was to appear to many other people on various occasions.

But his resurrection from the dead ranks as the most important event in the history of the world. He owed it to himself. On one occasion when he was preaching to the scribes and Pharisees, they demanded a sign or miracle of him. He answered, "An evil and unfaithful age is eager for a sign! No sign will be given it but that of the prophet Jonah. Just as Jonah spent three days and three nights in the belly of the whale, so will the Son of Man spend three days and three nights in the bowels of the earth." Because of this prophecy the Jews had posted a guard around his tomb, but Christ had not fulfilled it.

Christ rose from the dead for many reasons. His resurrection is an irrefutable proof of his divine power — that he is the Son of God, as he claimed. He rose from the dead to continue his work here on earth. He had yet to commission his Apostles to make disciples of all nations and to baptize them.

He rose too for our justification. His resurrection confirms our faith. It sustains our hope. It is a stamp guaranteeing our resurrection in the world to come. Christ had said, "He who eats my flesh and drinks my blood shall have life everlasting and I shall raise him up on the last day." If Christ did not rise from the dead, his promise would have been made in vain, but now that he did rise, his resurrection becomes a pledge of our own.

On this Easter Sunday, let us rejoice with the risen Lord. Let us pray to him the victor over sin and death. Let us physically unite ourselves to him in the Holy Eucharist. Let us share his life of grace. In all the trials and tribulations that beset us, let us draw the courage to face them from the vision of the risen Christ. God bless you.

# "B"    Second Sunday of Easter

*John 20:19-31*

The Resurrection is the greatest of all miracles. It is the central point in the Catholic religion. All else hangs upon it. In the words of St. Paul, if Christ had not risen from the dead, vain would be our faith.

But yet the Resurrection is a reality. Christ did rise from the dead. And because he did, the Catholic Church is in existence today.

The Resurrection is no ordinary event. No man before Christ ever rose from the dead. No man has risen since. It was the greatest miracle ever. It showed that Christ had power over life and death themselves.

In a natural sense, one cannot blame the Apostle Thomas too greatly for being skeptical of Christ's Resurrection. In a natural plane, one cannot censure him too harshly for his temporary doubt.

When the other disciples told Thomas they had seen the Lord, he responded, "I will never believe it . . . without putting my finger in the nail marks and my hand into his side." This was his doubting frame of mind when Christ appeared to him a week later and invited Thomas to do as he had requested. Thomas fell in adoration before him exclaiming, "My Lord and my God!"

These words of Thomas are the fullest and most explicit expression of faith recorded in the gospels. It is double confession of Christ's divinity. It is a sublime admission of the Messianic character of Christ.

Thomas doubted on this one occasion, but only this once. From here he went forth to perform great deeds for Christ. He preached the gospel among the Medes and the Persians. He preached in Ceylon and Sumatra. He was finally martyred in India. His tomb was believed discovered at Mylapore in India by the Portuguese in 1523. During his lifetime he displayed strong faith in Christ.

Faith is one of the theological virtues. It is a virtue by which we believe all those things that God has revealed. St. Paul calls faith the root of all virtues.

Faith comes to us in the Sacrament of Baptism. It is the key to everlasting life. It is infused in our souls along with sanctifying grace. It grows in our souls as we learn and are disposed to believe the revealed truths of God.

Faith does not depend on our complete understanding of the revealed truths of our religion. It is not founded on our seeing or knowing something fully. Rather, faith concerns itself with many things which do not appear to our senses. In faith we believe such mysteries as the Holy Trinity and the Incarnation. It has Divine Revelation as its object.

In the supernatural sphere faith plays a role comparable to that of reason in the natural sphere. Faith never requires us to believe anything contrary to our human reason, for God is the author of both and cannot contradict himself. Faith concerns itself with mysteries above and beyond the grasp of human reason.

When one makes an act of faith, his authority for believing is that of God himself. He is the greatest authority possible. Practically every day of our life we make acts of human faith. We believe the scientists who tell us about the atom and the solar system.

We make many acts of faith every day based on human authority. Yet such human authority can be mistaken. The greatest human authority cannot begin to compare with God, who can never be mistaken or deceived. God also is eternal truth.

Faith is a gift of God — given to those whom he loves. It is not something to be taken for granted. God bestows it on us out of his benevolence. It is a treasure we should thank God for possessing. We should regard ourselves as privileged when we see so many millions deprived of this gift and so many millions not allowed to practice it.

Faith is necessary to eternal salvation. St. Paul reminds us it is impossible to please God without faith. He calls it the life of the just man. Faith enlightens our understanding. It infuses confidence and love of God into our souls.

Not only does faith manifest itself inwardly, but outwardly as well. It works upon the Christian to manifest itself in good deeds. The Christian whose soul is filled with faith will also live by it. He will pray diligently; he will avoid occasions of sin. He will show his faith through prayer and adoration to God.

As faith worked miracles of grace in the life of St. Thomas, it can help us as well. Its effects are as visible today as they were in the time of Christ.

Pray daily for an increase of faith. Pray that God will give you a strong faith, a faith able to withstand any temptations against it. Pray the prayer of St. Thomas, "My Lord and my God!" Let faith permeate your life. As St. Paul says, "The just man lives by faith." Let this be true in your life. God bless you.

# "B"      Third Sunday of Easter

*Luke 24:35-48*

Christ rose from the dead glorious and immortal on Easter Sunday morn. He remained on earth for forty days before ascending into heaven. During that time twelve different appearances are recorded in Holy Scripture. His first was to St. Mary Magdalen on Easter Sunday morning; his last on Ascension Thursday.

His appearance recorded in today's gospel is one of his later appearances. The Apostles on this occasion were gathered in an upper room in Jerusalem when miraculously the risen Christ appeared in their midst. The Apostles immediately recognized our Lord; there was no doubt in their minds that it was he. But still they doubted their senses. They thought perhaps they were only seeing an apparition.

But Christ soon dispelled this doubt in their mind. He said to look at his hands and feet. Our Lord retained the imprint of the five wounds he had received in his crucifixion, the holes made by the nails in his hands and feet and the hole in his side pierced with a lance, as a proof of his identity. They were also a sign of victory over death. The wounds of Christ were a reminder of the great price he paid for our redemption. When our Lord invited his Apostles to look at and touch his wounds, there was no doubt that it was really he.

But our Lord went further still. He asked the Apostles if they had anything to eat, and they put before Him some cooked fish. Our Lord began to eat. No ghost or spirit lived on food. Thus our Lord, in eating in front of them, proved that he was present in a true physical sense.

Our Lord's presence in the upper room was no mere subjective experience for the Apostles, but a physical one as well, for the Apostles could touch and feel our Lord and he could eat food.

His body was a glorified body; in this sense he enjoyed impassibility or freedom from suffering. No longer could he be scourged and crucified. He enjoyed the gift of agility — the ability to move quickly from place to place, which accounts for his sudden appearance in the middle of the upper room in Jerusalem. Also his body was in complete subjection to his soul. But these gifts of the glorified body of Christ will be the same gifts that the bodies of the just will possess after the last judgment.

The first greeting that Christ extended to his Apostles upon entering the upper room in Jerusalem was one of peace. "Peace be to you." This greeting of peace has a special meaning for us as Christians. Peace in a true Christian sense, is more than merely the absence of war or violence. It is a virtue in itself. It is tranquillity of mind and soul. Peace cannot be possessed in this true sense by one in a state of serious sin, for such a person has no tranquillity of soul. His soul is at war with God.

Hence sanctifying grace is a necessary prerequisite for true Christian peace. As the angels sang at our Savior's birth in Bethlehem, "Peace on earth to men of good will." The author of peace is God himself; peace is one of the fruits of the Holy Spirit that comes to us in Confirmation. Peace was the greeting and gift Christ gave to his Apostles the night of the Last Supper.

Our Lord concludes his address to his Apostles by explaining to them the Scriptures and enlightening their minds. He shows them how it was fitting that He should suffer death and then rise again. St. Luke describes this preaching of Christ with only these few words. We wish that he had recorded them all. But then Christ did not deem this necessary or essential for our salvation. It is our belief that God inspired St. Luke and the other three evangelists to write down in Sacred Scripture all those things necessary for our salvation, and since these were not included, we have to be satisfied not to know them.

Christ concludes his greeting with the words, "Of these things you are witnesses." A witness is one who bears testimony or furnishes evidence. Hence our Lord after appearing to his Apostles in his glorified body, sent them out as witnesses to all the world that he had truly risen from the dead. He sent them out to bear testimony to all the things he had taught them. He sent them to furnish evidence to all that he had come on earth to redeem mankind and give man a way to salvation.

This testimony we have heard and we are hearing again today from this reading of Sacred Scripture. Let us take this testimony to heart and help to spread the good news of the risen and glorified Christ. God bless you.

# "B" Fourth Sunday of Easter

*John 10:11-18*

One of the most beautiful and inspiring parables which Christ preached upon earth is the parable of the Good Shepherd. Christ said, "I am the good shepherd." Christ held himself up as the good shepherd who leads souls to their eternal destiny.

After making this claim he gave the qualifications of a good shepherd. A good shepherd is one who lays down his life for his sheep. Such a one loves his flock and is willing to make a sacrifice for them. He is willing to take pains to guard them, to bring back to the right way the sheep who are lost.

Christ did all of this. He freely laid down his life for his sheep upon the cross. He endured every type of poverty and suffering. He went to the farthest extreme to bring back the lost souls.

Christ in his Incarnation gave up the happiness of heaven and the bright choirs of angels for the hardships of this earth. He assumed our nature that we might learn to follow him. In his public life he sought out the poor and the suffering to heal and cure them. He preached to the lost souls and showed them a hope for salvation. To those hungry for spiritual nourishment, he offered his own body and blood as our food and drink. He endured a bloody passion and died on the cross that we might live.

Contrast to these actions of Christ those of a hired hand. A hired hand is not a shepherd; he does not own the sheep. When the wolf comes, the hired hand runs away. How different the actions of Christ, who willingly handed himself over to the officials to lift the burden of sin from men's shoulders.

Christ wishes all men to be members of his flock, for he is the God and creator of all. When danger threatens his flock, Christ, the Good Shepherd, does not flee. He is there to support us with his grace. He gives sufficient grace to all men to overcome sin. To the soul that succumbs to sin, Christ is there to offer him the gift of pardon.

Christ said, "I know my sheep, and my sheep know me." Christ knows us, for he is God and knows all things. He knows even our most secret thoughts, words and actions. He knows us far better than we know ourselves. Christ in turn allows us to know him.

We come to know Christ through the teachings of his Church. He commissioned his Apostles to make disciples of all nations. This they and their successors have literally done. They have carried the gospel to the far corners of the earth.

But there are many sheep who belong to Christ that are not in his true fold. There are many souls outside of his Church. These souls Christ earnestly desires to have. He said, "I must lead them too."

How will Christ bring these souls to himself? Christ himself has given us this answer. He said, "They will hear my voice." He will speak to them through his Church. The natural result of this is that they will hear and follow the voice of their master. Christ added, "There shall be one flock then, one shepherd."

This is the goal that Christ seeks — that all men be united in his Mystical Body — that they will become members of his Church, his fold. That is the reason he commissioned his Apostles to make disciples of and to baptize all nations.

We who are members of his flock may ask what is our duty in all of this. Our duty is a very definite one. We must be loyal and faithful members of the flock of Christ. We must follow him; we must imitate his actions. We must acknowledge him to be our shepherd and leader.

It is the nature of sheep to flock together. Human beings are likewise prone to this gregarious instinct. Therefore as members of his flock, his Church, we must give good example to others. We must attend Mass on Sunday and live up to the other obligations of our faith.

We should strive to keep our souls continually in the state of sanctifying grace. We should frequent the sacraments often; the sacraments are the means of making this grace grow in our souls. If we do this, then Christ, our Good Shepherd, will lead us into the pasture of eternal happiness. God bless you.

# "B"    Fifth Sunday of Easter

*John 15:1-8*

Christ often spoke to the Jewish people in figures of speech. He used many parables to convey the truth of his gospel. He used metaphors. Today's gospel from St. John is an example of a pure allegory. It is the veiled expression of a truth that is not expressly stated. It conveys a message with a hidden meaning.

Christ calls himself the vine and his heavenly Father the vine-dresser. Although he does not expressly say so, he implies that the Jewish people to whom he is speaking are the vineyard. But yet this figure of speech finds its origin in the Old Testament. Both Jeremiah and Ezekiel had reference to it.

Christ next refers to the branches of the vine that bear fruit. Although he does not describe them explicitly, he means that his Apostles and the priests of his Church are the branches that bear fruit. He says that the branches that do not bear fruit will be taken away. Some scholars think there that he had a special reference to Judas who betrayed him.

He adds that the branches that bear fruit he will clean and prune that they may bear more fruit. Pruning a branch or cutting away dead twigs allows more life to go into the fruit-bearing branches, and they produce a great yield of fruit.

Scripture scholars believe that here Christ was referring to the other Apostles and disciples who were faithfully carrying out his mission.

Christ then says that they are already clean because of the word he has spoken to them. Christ refers here not just to the sermon he was preaching on this one occasion, but also to all of the former instructions he had given them in the past.

Christ then advises his Apostles and hearers to abide in him, adding that the branches have no life in themselves unless they are attached to the vine. They cannot bear fruit of themselves unless they are attached to the vine.

Then Christ explicitly says, "I am the vine, you are the branches." This one passage in Scripture, perhaps more than any other, comes close to explaining the Mystical Body of Christ. We are the members of His body; we have life through him. If we are to bear fruit, we must abide in him and he in us. And he adds, "Without me you can do nothing." The Council of Orange in the early Church quoted this passage of Scripture in explaining that all grace we possess comes to us through Christ — sanctifying grace as well as the passing actual graces which we receive.

Christ, after giving us the source of life and grace, lists the consequences of being detached from him. "If anyone does not abide in me, he shall be cast outside as the branch and wither. And dead branches are good for nothing but to be gathered up as firewood and burned."

In the sense of allegory, one may conclude that these dead branches are those Christians who voluntarily separate themselves from the vine by their own choice — that is, by the commission of sin. Hence the sinner is the dead branch, for he has separated himself from the source of life and grace; he has separated himself from Christ. And as dead branches are gathered up and burned in the fire, so sinners will be gathered up at the last judgment and will suffer in the fires of hell.

Christ then promises that if we abide in him we should ask him for whatever we wish in prayer, and our request will be granted. Asking favors of God is nothing other than a prayer of petition. Christ promised to hear the prayers of those united to Him through the life of grace. He promised that the prayers of the just would be efficacious — that they would be heard and answered.

In the concluding verse of today's gospel, Christ says that his Father is glorified by those who abide in him and become his disciples and bear much fruit. Hence being united to Christ through grace and doing his will is a means of giving glory to God. God is honored and pleased with those who are true disciples. He in turn will reward them with an eternal reward.

This then is the goal that Christ holds before us — to attach ourselves to him through a life of grace. Our lives then will bear much fruit, and we shall earn an everlasting reward. An example of this is brought out in the life of Francis Libermann, who was born in the early 19th century in France the son of Alsatian rabbi. As a young man Francis learned of the Catholic religion and became a convert to it. He decided as a young man to enter the seminary and become a priest.

But Francis was stricken with epilepsy, which hindered him and prevented his ordination. For fourteen years he prayed constantly to our divine Savior and he miraculously recovered from it. God had plans for that branch of St. Francis to bear much fruit. After his ordination to the priesthood in 1841 he founded a religious society to spread the gospel to the natives in the heart of Africa. His society later came to be known as the Holy Ghost Fathers, and Francis was their first superior general.

He was one of an original group of seven men, missionary priests who set off into the heart of Africa to bring Christ's gospel to the natives. That first year his six companions died from disease and other causes. But Francis persevered. He was later joined by other missionaries. His work did bear much fruit.

Today there are over 800 priests in the Holy Ghost Fathers. They are aided by several hundred more Brothers, Sisters and catechists. They care for nearly two million souls won to the faith by the efforts of the Holy Ghost Fathers throughout the last century. The story of Father Francis Libermann, a convert and crippled epileptic, is the story of a branch that bore abundant fruit. God bless you.

# "B"    Sixth Sunday of Easter

*John 15:9-17*

In 1674 Christ appeared to a pious French nun, Sister Margaret Mary Alacoque. He revealed his Sacred Heart to her and said it was bursting with love for men. A second time he appeared to her. On this occasion flames were emanating from His Sacred Heart. He said these flames represented his love for men but this excess of his love for men met with coldness and rebuff on every side.

The excess of the love of Christ for men is seen on every side. On Easter Sunday evening Christ walked along the road to Emmaus with two of his disciples and he explained the passage of Scripture relating to his death and resurrection. And the gospel tells us that their hearts burned within them as they heard him talk. He conveyed to them the message of love that he bore for men.

Today's gospel begins with the words, "As the Father has loved me, I also have loved you." Christ continues to give the measure of his love for men. He says, "Greater love than this no one has, that one lay down his life for his friends." This was the exact measure of the love Christ had for us. He did lay down his life for us upon the cross. His love and his sacrifice for us could be no greater; he gave us his very life. He endured the cruelest of suffering, mocking and scourging, crowning with thorns, ending with crucifixion.

But then after this great testimony of love, Christ gave us one command. It was, "Love one another as I have loved you." His command was to love — to love one another. And the measure of the love we should show was the measure of his love for us. This means our love for one another should be limitless. As Christ loved us with an infinite love, so should we show such a similar love to others.

The command of God alone is more than sufficient reason to show this love for our neighbor. But there are additional reasons why we should do it:

God has implanted in our hearts a natural love of self; we should extend this love to include our fellow human beings, our neighbors. We should love our neighbor because we have all descended from the same first parents; we are all members of the same human race.

We should love one another because each of us is a creature created by God Himself and placed here on earth. Each of us is made to God's own image and likeness. Each of us has an immortal soul. Each of us was destined for eternal life. Each of us shares in Christ's redeeming body and blood. Each of us shares in the benefits of his cross.

There are many means we can choose to show this love. St. Paul tells us we should rejoice with him when he rejoices and be sad with him when he is sad. We should bear his burdens with him and so fulfill the law of Christ. We should give patience to the elderly, understanding to the young. We should show compassion to the suffering and unfortunate.

We should pray for our neighbor. We should ask almighty God to bestow upon him the graces he needs for his spiritual and temporal welfare.

We should practice toward him the corporal and spiritual works of mercy. We should help feed the hungry, we should visit the sick and help bury the dead. We should help instruct the ignorant, and counsel the doubtful. In all things we should consider the great indulgence and kindness Christ showed to us and should try to return it in some small way to our neighbor.

Back in the early days of the Roman Empire, there lived a young Roman soldier named Martin. Martin was proud of his rank of tribune. Martin's father had been a soldier before him, and Martin was nobly following in his father's footsteps.

But Martin was by nature a charitable person. His regiment had been ordered to Amiens in France. One winter day Martin was riding his horse along an icy road, when he met a beggar. The poor man was thin and shivering in the wintry cold. Martin stopped and asked himself what he could give this beggar. He remembered he had given all the rest of his money to others who were in need.

As he watched him shiver in the cold he decided what he would do. He took off the nice warm cloak which he was wearing. He withdrew his sword from its scabbard and cut his cloak in two parts giving one to the freezing beggar.

Martin spoke kindly to the beggar and then rode away.

Later that night while sleeping Martin had a strange dream. There appeared to him a man wearing half of his cloak, but it was not the beggar to whom he had given it. Instead it was Jesus. Our Lord spoke to Martin, "My servant, Martin, you are not yet baptized, but yet you have clothed me."

After this vision Martin inquired more deeply into the Christian religion and asked for the Sacrament of Baptism. He later still became a priest and bishop in the Church and is now canonized a saint.

Consider too the gift made by a Catholic priest, Father John Washington, who had been the assistant priest at St. Stephen's Church in Arlington, New Jersey. In World War II he enlisted as a chaplain in the army. He was sent overseas across the Atlantic on a troop ship, but on its voyage the ship was torpedoed in the north Atlantic.

Father Washington raced around the sinking ship, praying with some and consoling others, helping in any way he could. He finally ran across one fearful soldier who had lost his life jacket. Without hesitation Father Washington took off his own and handed it to the soldier. The ship soon sank in the waves, and Father Washington was drowned. He had made the supreme sacrifice. He had laid down his own life for his neighbor. He had acted in a very Christ-like manner.

He had fulfilled to an eminent degree the command of Christ: "Love one another as I have loved you." Let us take this command to heart and imitate the example of St. Martin of Tours and Father Washington in our own lives. God bless you.

# "B"     Ascension

*John 20:1-9*

The readings of today's Mass describe in detail the Ascension of Christ into heaven. Immediately following his resurrection Christ travelled with his Apostles into Galilee. During this time he appeared to them many times. On one occasion he appeared to a crowd of five hundred people. He left no doubt in anyone's mind during these forty days that he had truly risen from the dead.

But after three weeks Christ led his Apostles back to Jerusalem. On the fortieth day after his resurrection, Christ had dinner with his Apostles in the upper room in Jerusalem. Following the dinner he led them to the summit of Mount Olivet, a short distance from the city on the road to Bethany.

He commissioned them to go and make disciples of all nations. He was then lifted up before their eyes into a cloud which took him out of their sight. Two young men with white garments appeared and announced to the Apostles that Christ had ascended into heaven.

It is interesting to observe the various views held concerning the Ascension down through the centuries. In the Middle Ages there was a common belief that the sky was a canopy of crystal which covered the earth. Paintings of the Ascension during this age depict Christ rising through a cloud to the other side of this canopy. God the Father is seated there awaiting his arrival.

Our knowledge of the universe has progressed greatly since the Middle Ages, but the basic fact of the Ascension remains the same. The Ascension of Christ is the crowning glory for the Old Testament. From the time of our first parents the gates of heaven had been closed to man through original sin. All who died in the Old Testament were denied the sight of God.

But Christ's Ascension changed all this. When he ascended into heaven, he reopened heaven to all mankind. He led into heaven a triumphant army of souls. He led the prophets and the many holy men of the Old Testament to their eternal reward.

Christ's Ascension was the Old Testament's day of triumph. It climaxed centuries of waiting. It was their day of reward. It was the dividing line between the New and the Old Testaments. It was the day that Joseph, the foster father of Christ, and Moses and Daniel were united with God. It was the day they saw God face to face and began to enjoy the happiness of heaven.

By entering heaven Christ was returning to his true home. Christ had been living on earth for some thirty-three years. He had performed miracles and established a Church. He had come to earth on a special mission, but now his mission was over. He had come to redeem mankind, and this he accomplished. Now he was returning to his true home.

But while on earth Christ had promised us that we too could enter heaven. He promised that all who were baptized and believed in his teachings and obeyed his commandments would enjoy heaven too. His entrance into heaven is a pledge of our own future resurrection. His Ascension marks the opening of heaven to all mankind.

The Ascension also marks the first time a human body entered heaven. When Christ came down to earth he assumed a human body. In ascending into heaven, he ascended with this body. He reentered heaven with his human nature as well as the divine.

When the holy bishop St. Martin of Tours was dying, he suffered great agony. He lay on his deathbed staring straight up. Those around him would turn his body and try to relieve his sufferings. He asked them to please not disturb him as he was meditating on the path Christ took in going to heaven. This was of far greater importance than trying to relieve his sufferings.

Let us imitate St. Martin in this regard. Let us frequently think of heaven and realize it is the home God created for us. Let us work and pray that one day we may attain it as Christ did. God bless you.

# "B"      Seventh Sunday of Easter

*John 17:11-19*

Christ instituted the priesthood on Holy Thursday night at the Last Supper. Following the Last Supper, while still in the Cenacle or upper chamber in Jerusalem, he gave his Apostles a beautiful discourse. Down through the centuries this beautiful discourse or talk came to be known as "The Priestly Prayer." It is contained in the 17th chapter of St. John's gospel. Part of this priestly prayer is contained in the gospel for today's Mass, verses 11-19.

In these verses Christ is praying for his Apostles, and in a broader sense for all the future priests of his Church. He prays for them to God the Father in heaven. He mentions four reasons why he is praying for them. First he mentions he is praying for them because they are his own; God the Father has entrusted them to him. And he goes on to say they are God the Father's, for he says, "All I have is yours."

The second reason for his prayer for them is that they have given glory to God the Father. They have glorified the Father by obeying the Son. They have kept our Lord's word. They have acknowledged that everything they have has been given them by God the Father. They have believed that God the Father sent his Son to men.

His third reason for praying for them is that the Apostles shall soon find themselves alone in the world. Our Lord is leaving them; he will no longer remain in the world. The Apostles will soon find themselves without a guide and without a shepherd. Hence it is now up to God the Father to keep them. He prays his Father to let none of them perish.

His last reason for praying for them is that they are about to be exposed to the hatred of the world for having believed God's word. The world will hate them for they do not belong to the world, just as Christ himself is not a part of the world.

Our Lord makes a careful distinction here, "I do not ask that you should take them out of the world, but that you should keep them clear of what is evil." To take them out of the world would mean the end of their apostolate, and that Christ does not want at this time. Rather he prays that they not be contaminated by the dangerous environment in which they live.

Our Lord, after giving the four reasons why he is praying for his Apostles and his priests, then makes a request of the Father. He asks the Father to consecrate them in truth, to make them holy in truth. The meaning of the word "consecrate" or "make holy" goes back to the Old Testament. To consecrate in the Old Testament means to separate something from profane uses, to set it aside entirely to God. For example, Moses sanctified Aaron and his sons to devote them to the service of the altar. The vessels in the temple were consecrated by using them for sacrifice and nothing else.

Earlier that evening Christ had instituted the Holy Eucharist. Earlier that evening too, he had instituted the priesthood. He had conferred upon his Apostles the power to celebrate Mass, to offer up the Eucharist. Now he is asking his heavenly Father to consecrate the Apostles in their priestly work of preaching the gospel and celebrating the Eucharist. Their apostolate will not be effective without a corresponding increase in grace to help them.

The consecration Christ prays for in behalf of his Apostles is an internal blessing. It is a grace or blessing so that the Apostles, while remaining in the world and conducting their mission in the world, will not be contaminated by it . . . that their goal and interest will be centered in heaven.

Our Lord in praying for his Apostles brought attention to the continuity of his mission on earth — the mission given him by the Father and passed on by him to his Apostles and by them to their successors, the priests and bishops of his Church today. Hence the mission of the Church today is truly God's mission.

Forty-five times in the course of his discourse on Holy Thursday evening our Lord invoked the name of his Father. Truly he and his Apostles were fulfilling the mission of God the Father. Three times during Christ's life on earth, God the Father manifested his presence to men. The first was at the baptism of our Lord in the river Jordan by St. John the Baptist. The second was at Our Lord's transfiguration. The third was here in Jerusalem, not long before Christ prayed this priestly prayer.

Christ prayed aloud, "Father, make your name known." And that time a voice like peals of thunder came from heaven, "I have made it known and will yet make it known." Hence God the Father confirmed our Lord's mission and signified he would grant his prayerful requests.

Our Lord's prayer was an efficacious prayer. Since He is himself God and Second Person of the Blessed Trinity, he has all power within his own right. Whatever he prayed for was as good as granted. When he prayed that the mission of his Apostles and priests be sanctified, we know that it was.

It is inconceivable in a human sense to imagine one living in the midst of the world and not being infected to some degree with a worldly spirit, but because Christ prayed that his Apostles be immunized from a worldly spirit, while preaching the gospel to it, we know that this is so.

Let us, in meditating on this priestly prayer of Christ's, join our prayer to his. Let us pray that he will send an abundant supply of priests to work in his vineyard. Let us pray that they will effectively preach the good news of his gospel. Let us pray that they may work in this world and yet not be infected by it. God bless you.

# "B"    Pentecost

*John 20:19-23*

Christ said, "The hour is coming for everyone who kills you to think he is offering worship to God." One might expect that when Christ was leaving his Apostles to return to heaven, he would have promised them success in their mission and happiness here on earth. But instead he promised them only suffering and persecution. He even said they would be put to death for his name's sake.

The Apostles realized the truth of the words Christ spoke to them. When he ascended into heaven, they became fearful. They gathered together in the upper room in Jerusalem and bolted the door for protection and began to pray.

Christ heard their prayers and answered them. On Pentecost Sunday, ten days after Christ's Ascension, the Holy Spirit descended upon them in the form of fiery tongues. He imprinted an indelible character upon their souls.

A great change occurred in the souls and hearts of the Apostles and others gathered in the room. Previously all but John had fled from beneath the cross of Christ. Saint Peter had denied our Lord three times. But no longer were the Apostles fearful.

On Pentecost Sunday the Holy Spirit came down in parted tongues of fire which appeared over the head of each of them. He moved St. Peter to preach to the crowd assembled in Jerusalem, people from many different countries. There were Parthians, Medes and Elamites, inhabitants from Mesopotamia, Judea and Cappadocia, citizens from Pontus, Phrygia and Pamphylia, from Egypt, Libya and Cyrene. That first Pentecost Sunday three thousand souls were converted and baptized in the Christian faith.

Pentecost has rightfully been called the birthday of the Catholic Church.

It was the day on which the first converts were taken into it. But the Holy Spirit did not come down on the Church on this one occasion to desert it. He remains with it still. Christ said he would ask the Father to "give you another Advocate, who will dwell with you forever."

The Holy Spirit comes down upon each of us in an individual manner in the Sacrament of Confirmation. In the Acts of the Apostles we read that Philip, the Deacon, baptized several people in Samaria and then called upon Saints Peter and John to confirm them with the Holy Spirit.

In a similar manner when Saint Paul was passing through Ephesus, he met twelve followers of John the Baptizer. He instructed them further, baptized and confirmed them. We are told in the nineteenth chapter of the Acts of the Apostles, "As Paul laid his hands on them, the Holy Spirit came down on them and they began to speak in tongues and to utter prophecies."

In early Christian times, the Roman leader Julian was converted to the Christian faith. Later he fell away from the faith and was known as "Julian the Apostate." Later still he became Emperor of Rome. To make his denial of the faith complete he decided to profess idolatry at a public ceremony. Great preparations were made for this celebration by the pagan priests. With all possible pomp they prepared to offer sacrifices to the false idols.

When the moment came to conduct this pagan festival, the priests found themselves paralyzed. They could not move to conduct it. Their sharp knives would not cut the flesh of the sacrificial animals. The fire on their altar went out. They began to look around for the cause of their paralysis.

Then a young Christian man stepped forward and bravely proclaimed, "I am a Christian. Only a few days ago I was anointed with the oil of confirmation to strengthen me in the struggle for my Savior. In my heart I called upon the name of Jesus, and your devils lost their power. In the name of Jesus Christ, who is true God, the demons have been put to flight."

The emperor was confused and filled with terror. He feared the punishments of an offended God. Without another word the sinful service broke up. The grace of confirmation stood out most clearly in this incident. Armed and fortified with the grace of this sacrament, this young Christian was able to stop a pagan service.

In the Sacrament of Confirmation, the Holy Spirit abides in the souls of those who receive it. He strengthens one's soul and enables one publicly to profess his faith without fear.

Let us remember that although Christ prophesied persecution for his Church, he has likewise given us a means of bearing up under it. That means is the Holy Spirit, who comes to us in confirmation. If we follow the inspirations of his grace, the path to salvation lies within our reach. God bless you.

# "B" Trinity Sunday (Sunday After Pentecost)

*Matthew 28:16-20*

On the last of his voyages to the American continent Christopher Columbus ran into a hurricane, a terrific storm at sea that tossed and turned his boats. Many of the sailors became extremely ill; all were terrified. Columbus went to the bow of his boat. He drew his sword from his scabbard and with it made the sign of the cross on the mounting waves.

Suddenly the storm began to subside and the waves lost much of their momentum. The sign of the cross is but a simple sacramental in the Church. Yet it is a most powerful prayer.

The sign of the cross expresses our belief in two of the most important mysteries of our faith — our Redemption and the Blessed Trinity.

The sign of the cross is used to begin and to end other prayers. The priest uses it to confer the Sacrament of Reconciliation. He pours water over the head of an infant in baptism and baptizes in the name of the Trinity.

The Bishop in conferring the Sacrament of Confirmation makes the sign of the cross with Holy Chrism on the forehead of the children and confirms in the sign of the Blessed Trinity. Likewise, in the anointing of the sick, the priest anoints the senses of the sick person in the name of the Blessed Trinity, making the sign of the cross as he does.

Today is the feast of the Most Blessed Trinity. The Holy Trinity is the foundation stone of our faith. It is at the bottom of all the things we believe.

The Trinity expresses our belief that there is one God but in God there are three separate and distinct Persons, the Father, Son and Holy Spirit. These three Persons are separate and distinct Persons, yet each Person has the same divine nature.

Each of the three Persons is all-powerful or omnipotent. Each is eternal. Each Person is omniscient — knows all things. Each of the three Persons is absolutely perfect.

All three Persons are responsible for the work of creation of the world. All three persons brought about the sanctification of men.

Our motive for believing in the Trinity is not that we fully understand it. In fact it is a mystery which is beyond our capability of understanding.

Actually there are many mysteries in nature which we cannot understand. We cannot fully comprehend the nature of electricity. We cannot understand the full nature of atomic power.

On one occasion St. Augustine was contemplating the Blessed Trinity and wondering how there could be three persons in one God. As he thought about this, he walked along the seashore. He saw a small boy who had dug a hole in the sand and was trying to fill the hole with water from the ocean. He stopped and asked the boy what he was trying to do. The boy replied that he was trying to put the ocean in the hole.

St. Augustine laughed and told the boy that was impossible. But the boy replied that he could do that long before he could understand the Blessed Trinity. With that the boy disappeared, and the saint knew that he was an angel sent by God to tell him he would never fully understand the mystery of the Trinity.

One of the big reminders we have of the Blessed Trinity is the sign of the cross. Each time we make it we invoke the names of the three Persons. We profess our belief that these three Persons are but one God.

A few years ago a non-Catholic man stopped at a Catholic rectory and asked the priest whom he met there some questions about Catholic liturgy. One of the questions he asked was what those senseless circles were that Catholics so often made on their breast.

At first the priest was puzzled, but then he came to realize that by these senseless circles the man had seen were a few Catholics making the sign of the cross carelessly — perhaps even disrespectfully.

Perhaps if you take time to observe too, there are far too many Catholics who do bless themselves carelessly. From the way in which many bless themselves it is hard to recognize what they are doing as the sign of the cross.

Let us resolve that when we make the sign of the cross we shall make it fervently. Let us resolve that for us the sign of the cross will indicate our belief in the Holy Trinity. God bless you.

# "B"      Corpus Christi

*Mark 14:12-16, 22-26*

St. Juliana of Cornillon was born in Belgium in 1183. At an early age she sought admission into the Augustinian order and was accepted. As a nun, St. Juliana had one great love — the Blessed Sacrament. It was her hope and desire that someday there would be a special feast dedicated to the Blessed Sacrament.

One day while at prayer Juliana had a vision. She beheld the Church beneath a full moon. But in the moon there was one dark spot. Our blessed Lord appeared to her and explained that what was missing was a special feast to honor the Holy Eucharist — this was the meaning of the dark spot on the moon.

Our Lord said, "Juliana, what disturbs you is that a feast is wanting in my Church which I desire to establish. It is the feast of the Most High and Most Holy Sacrament of the altar. At present the celebration of this Mystery is observed only on Holy Thursday; but on that day my sufferings and death are the principal objects of consideration; therefore I desire another day to be set apart in which it shall be celebrated by the whole of Christendom. And I desire it for three reasons:

"First, that faith in this divine mystery which is beginning to be attacked and will in future times be further menaced, may be more confirmed and reassured.

"Secondly, that the faithful who believe and seek the truth may be fully taught and convinced, and enabled to draw from this well of life the strength necessary to carry them on in the way of virtue.

"Thirdly, that reparation may be made for the irreverence and impiety shown towards the Divine Majesty in the Blessed Sacrament, by a sincere and profound adoration of this feast.

"And you, Juliana, are chosen to give the opportunity for the establishment of this feast." Juliana in turn made this revelation known to her superiors and the local clergy in her section of Belgium. The wheels of ecclesiastical approval then began to grind, at first ever so slowly, but still surely. Finally the Bishop of Liège granted permission for a procession to honor the Holy Eucharist. Then came others.

Within fifty years' time, in 1264, Pope Urban IV instituted the Feast of Corpus Christi to be celebrated following Trinity Sunday. He authorized a procession to be held in parish churches in honor of the Blessed Sacrament.

Our Holy Father, too, wanted to increase devotion to the Blessed Sacrament.

His goal was threefold. He wished a greater adoration of the Blessed Sacrament. He wanted Catholics to visit the Blessed Sacrament more frequently in their parish churches. He wanted the faithful to receive our blessed Lord in the Holy Eucharist more frequently.

Consider for a moment the effects of receiving Christ in the Blessed Sacrament.

First, Holy Communion *physically unites* us with Christ himself. We actually receive, into our own bodies, Christ's body and blood. There is a physical union between Christ and the person who receives him. Christ actually remains physically present in our bodies for about fifteen minutes — that is, until the sacred host dissolves.

Second, Holy Communion increases *sanctifying grace* within our souls and makes us more pleasing to almighty God. It gives us special actual graces.

Third, Holy Communion affords us *spiritual delight*. Napoleon, who had conquered nearly all Europe, said later, when exiled to St. Helena, that the happiest day of his life was the day of his first Holy Communion. I am sure that all of us at some time in our lives have felt a similar joy in receiving our blessed Lord.

Fourth, Holy Communion is a *pledge of our future resurrection* from the dead. Christ said, "He who eats my flesh and drinks my blood has life everlasting, and I shall raise him up on the last day."

Fifth, Holy Communion has a special effect of overcoming *concupiscence* or passion in us. St. Philip Neri once had a penitent come to him who had contracted a serious habit of sin from which he seemed unable to free himself. St. Philip asked him, "Did you ever commit this sin on the day of your communion?" "Not as far as I can remember," said the man. "Then communicate every day," was the saint's answer; the man did, and he overcame the sinful habit.

Sixth and lastly, it has the effect of cleansing our soul from *venial sin* and the *temporal punishment due to sin*.

On a warm, sultry day in Jamaica a priest was driving his carriage along the road toward his mission church on Montego Bay when he heard a voice call, "Fader! Fader!" He stopped his carriage and saw a young black boy walking along the road. He recognized him as a member of the mission and offered him a ride to church, as they had more than five miles to go.

In the course of the conversation the boy told the priest that he had already walked about eight miles over the mountains and was fasting to receive Holy Communion. The priest realized then that the boy lived over thirteen miles away from the mission chapel, since they still had five miles to go. He realized that, with a thirteen-mile walk each way, the boy had to travel 26 miles to go to Mass, and in addition he was fasting to receive Holy Communion.

The sacrifice we make to receive Holy Communion is small indeed in comparison to the sacrifice made by this Jamaican boy. Yet the benefits to be derived from it are immeasurable.

On this Feast of Corpus Christi let us kneel in adoration before the Blessed Sacrament. Let us renew our faith in his real presence in the Holy Eucharist. Let us resolve that we will receive our Lord frequently at the altar rail. Let us help illuminate the one dark spot in the moon shining down over his Church. God bless you.

# "B"     Second Sunday of the Year

*John 1:35-42*

Scripture scholars have long noted the difference between the gospels of Saints Matthew, Mark and Luke on one hand and that of Saint John on the other. Instead of being an orderly and chronological account of our Lord's public life as are the first three, the gospel of St. John is fragmentary. But yet these fragments are precious ones.

In today's gospel, for example, St. John recalls his first meeting with Christ. He had formerly been a follower of St. John the Baptizer. One day he and his companion St. Andrew were walking with the Baptizer in Bethany, on the east bank of the Jordan River, when Christ walked by. The time of day was about four o'clock in the afternoon.

Through divine revelation St. John the Baptizer recognized who Christ was. He cried out, "Look! There is the Lamb of God!" Immediately John and Andrew left St. John the Baptizer and started to follow Christ. Jesus noticed them and turned around and said, "What are you looking for?"

The two disciples addressed our Lord using the term "Rabbi," which means "teacher," and asked: "Where do you stay?" Christ extended to them an invitation, "Come and see." The Apostles accepted the invitation and went with our Lord to the place where he was staying.

Scripture doesn't tell us exactly where Christ was staying on this occasion. Most probably it was a reed hut, a temporary shelter that travelers threw up hastily to shield themselves from the rains and weather. Christ was a carpenter by trade and could easily have done this.

In fact, Scripture only mentions two places where our Lord actually did lodge for a night. The first was in the house of Zacchaeus and the other was in the home of Mary, Martha and Lazarus. Elsewhere it mentions he had nowhere to lay his head.

But for Andrew and John the place of Christ's lodging was not important. They had heard St. John the Baptizer call him the "Lamb of God." They were curious to learn more about him, to hear what he had to say. Their feelings toward Christ probably bordered between curiosity and admiration. His invitation to come to his dwelling must certainly have pleased them. No doubt they spent the rest of the day with him; perhaps, even the night also.

The first act of St. Andrew, when he found where Christ was staying, was to go and call his brother, Simon Peter. Here he is fulfilling a role that he will fill other times in Sacred Scripture; he is the "introducer." He introduced St. Peter to our Lord. Later he would introduce Christ to a young boy who had five barley loaves and two fishes. Later still he would introduce some Greeks to Christ. Andrew was as quiet as his brother Peter was talkative. Yet he was a faithful and courteous disciple.

When Andrew brought his brother Peter to our Lord, Christ's first statement to him was: "You are Simon, son of John; your name shall be Cephas. . . ." Cephas is the Greek form of an Aramaic name, "kipha" in the language which Christ and his Apostles spoke. It meant "rock." Christ chose this name in particular for he knew even then that he would one day make Peter the head of his Church. He would be the rock on which it was founded. Translated into Latin his name is Petrus, and in English it is Peter.

The question asked by the two disciples, Andrew and John, "Rabbi, where do you stay?" is an echo of a similar question asked of King David in the Old Testament centuries before. David was fleeing from King Saul and had no home, no place to stay. In this sense David was a type of our Lord.

We can ask the same question of Christ today: "Where do you stay?" Christ's permanent and eternal home is in heaven, where he has existed from all eternity. Yet on earth Christ has set up for himself a temporary dwelling place. It is in the tabernacle present in every Catholic Church.

After each Mass that is celebrated, the consecrated hosts remaining after Communion, which truly are Christ's body and blood, are placed in the tabernacle. The sanctuary lamp burning before the tabernacle reminds us of his presence there.

The tabernacle is a humble home — a rectangular box with a metal door protecting it. Such a humble home is in keeping with the humility Christ displayed while living here on earth. He was born in a stable and lived in the humble home of Joseph the carpenter.

Christ extends to us an invitation similar to the one he gave Andrew and John: "Come and see." He invites us to come to church — to kneel before him in his home in the tabernacle — to offer him homage and praise! He is inviting us to visit him often and spent some time with him. What is our response?

Some day we shall be knocking on Christ's door. It is inevitable. We shall

all face him in judgment on the day of death. We shall seek admission to his permanent home in heaven.

Will Christ know us? Will he recognize us from our visits to him here on earth? Lest the heavenly door be closed upon us and we be turned away, let us resolve to be frequent visitors at his home here on earth. God bless you.

# "B"   Third Sunday of the Year

*Mark 1:14-20*

In the gospel read at today's Mass, St. Mark tells us that St. John the Baptizer had been arrested. The reason for his arrest was that he had denounced King Herod for living with his brother's wife. St. John the Baptizer and our Lord had both been preaching in Judea, in the vicinity of Jerusalem. But at the time of St. John's arrest the Jews there had grown very hostile. Therefore, Christ with his followers journeyed north into the country of Galilee.

In Galilee Jesus proclaimed the good news that the Messianic kingdom foretold by the prophets was at hand. The time of fulfillment had come. Christ's message to the Jews was similar to that of St. John ahead of him: "Reform your lives and believe in the good news."

As Jesus was making his way along the Sea of Galilee, he observed Simon and his brother Andrew casting their nets into the sea. He called both of them to follow him, saying, "Come after me; I will make you fishers of men." In a similar manner he called James and John, the sons of Zebedee. They immediately left their father and went off in the company of Jesus.

However, Christ's call to these two sets of brothers to be his Apostles was not his first meeting with them. Previously Andrew and John had both been followers of St. John the Baptizer. John the Baptizer, upon seeing Christ, had called him the Lamb of God, and both disciples left to follow him. Andrew, in turn, had brought his brother Peter or Simon to meet Christ.

Hence these four disciples were acquainted with Christ. They had followed him, more or less at a distance, for a month's time or better. But now that John the Baptizer had been imprisoned, Christ extended a formal invitation to these two sets of brothers to become his Apostles. He extended to them a vocation to the religious life.

At the beginning of this world, God had a purpose in creating every creature in it — even in creating the wild animals of the field. Every insect or bird that flies through the air was created by God with some particular reason in mind. But if God had a purpose in creating the animals and birds, he had an even greater purpose in creating man.

God does not give the same graces or the same calling to all. Some he calls to the married state of life — to be the fathers and mothers of families. Some he calls to be doctors, lawyers, and professional people. Some he calls to be school teachers. And to some he calls to be priests and Sisters, to enter the religious life.

The highest call of all is that to the religious life. Not everyone accepts it as did Peter and Andrew, James and John in today's gospel. Some choose to reject this calling of Christ. On one occasion, when a young man came to Christ and asked him what he had to do to gain eternal life, Christ said if he wanted to be perfect to go sell everything and come follow him. The gospel tells us that the young man found this difficult to do because he was very rich.

Even today there are some who reject the call of Christ. They reject the great blessings of a vocation, for they are too attached to the pleasures and riches of this world. The vows of poverty, chastity and obedience are too difficult to assume.

Consider how these three virtues help one attain perfection. In the vow of poverty one voluntarily renounces the temporal goods of the world in order to follow Christ. The religious, of course, is always given what he needs to live on and fulfill his duties. But this vow removes from one's life many concerns over material goods that might stand in the way of one's perfection.

The vow of chastity is a priceless jewel. It is a vow of perpetual virginity. By renouncing the right to marry, one may give up human attachment all of one's lifetime and render love to God alone. Thus by the vow of chastity one's love remains undivided. This vow is most pleasing to God. It is a vow which both Mary and Joseph took to please God. By this vow St. John the Evangelist pleased our Lord.

Obedience is the vow by which one submits his or her will to that of a superior. Thus one obtains religious merit for any action he is ordered to perform. One may always know that through obedience he is doing the will of God. Although these virtues may seem difficult to practice, our Lord rewards their practice most bountifully.

On one occasion Christ appeared to St. Francis of Assisi and asked him to give him three gifts. St. Francis protested that he would give him his heart if he wished, but he knew not what to give him. Our Lord told St. Francis to put his hand into his cloak and there was a large beautiful gold coin, far more precious than anything he had ever seen before. This he offered to Christ. A second time he bade him do the same thing and a third. Our Lord told St. Francis that these three gold coins represented the virtues of poverty, chastity and obedience — that they were the gifts most pleasing to Him.

Remember that to whomever Christ gives a vocation he will give a corresponding grace to fulfill the duties he is called upon to perform. At times the duties assigned may be great, but God always gives more than sufficient graces to carry out those duties.

We should be thankful that we live in a free country — a land where one is free to follow a vocation without persecution of any type. This is not true in many parts of the world today. A few years ago the people of Nova Huta, Poland, rose up in revolt, for the Communist leaders of their country had closed down the seminary. These good Christian people knew that without a seminary there would be no more young men ordained priests to say Mass in their churches. God has blessed our country with the freedom to follow one's vocation. The first step in choosing one's vocation, my dear people, is to pray to the Holy Spirit. We should ask him to enlighten our minds to know what our vocation in life is — to show us in some way what he wants us to do in life.

God may not appear to you and reveal your vocation to you by a direct positive revelation. Frequently he only gives you a desire or liking for spiritual things ... an ambition to do something good in life. If you have the least inkling or desire in this regard, be sure to talk it over with your confessor or parish priest. He will always help you interpret this desire and direct you on what course to follow.

Pray also that once you know your vocation God will give you the grace to follow it. Christ said, "Everyone that has left home, or brothers or sisters, or father or mother, or wife or children for my name's sake shall receive one hundredfold and shall possess life everlasting." God bless you.

# "B"    Fourth Sunday of the Year

*Mark 1:21-28*

Today's gospel tells us that Jesus entered the synagogue on a sabbath and began to teach. The Saturday synagogue service provided Christ with his best opportunity to address a large crowd of the Jews. On the other days of the week they were working in their fields or vineyards.

The ruler or chief priest in each synagogue had the authority to invite a member of the congregation to address those present. Such an invitation generally went to the better educated and more eloquent among the Jews. It was through such invitations as this that Christ had several opportunities to speak in various synagogues.

St. Mark points out that the people who heard him preach were spellbound. He taught with authority and not like the scribes. The customary method of preaching among the scribes was to quote the ancient rabbinical teaching and gave the most popular opinions on a subject. They generally refrained from giving definitive answers to questions proposed to them. In contrast to this, Christ taught with authority. He answered questions directly and positively.

There was present in the synagogue on this occasion a man possessed with an unclean spirit, who cried out, "What do you want of us, Jesus of Nazareth? Have you come to destroy us? I know who you are — the holy One of God." The devils had come to recognize that Christ had power to expel them. But at this early point in his public life, Christ had not yet claimed to be the Son of God or the Messiah.

Christ quickly ordered the devil to come out of the man and to be quiet. The devil convulsed the man violently and with a loud shriek came out of him. The Jews were dumbfounded at how the devil obeyed Jesus. In the Old Testament from the time of King Solomon exorcism rites came into use. Frequently the high priest or exorcist would put a ring on the possessed person. He would give him a mixture of herbs to drink and recite certain prayers. But more often than not, it had no effect on the person.

How different it was when Christ expelled them. The devils obeyed instantly. His power and authority were evident. Christ used this power of expulsion on several occasions. He even passed the power on to his Apostles and followers.

This power has been passed down to the priests and bishops of the Catholic Church today. It is a part of the Sacrament of Holy Orders, the order of exorcist. It was one of the four minor orders when the sacrament consisted of four minor and three major orders.

A priest uses this power of exorcism each time he baptizes solemnly. He reads a prayer over the child he is baptizing. This does not imply that an unbaptized child is possessed; it implies rather that there is no room for the devil in the soul of a baptized Christian. There is no room for the devil in the soul when the Trinity dwells there in the form of sanctifying grace.

At other times when exorcism is conferred, it is with prayers, holy water and the sign of the cross. Holy water has great power against the powers of the devil. The Blessed Sacrament is not used in the rite because of danger of irreverence to the sacrament.

Exorcism was used in the early Church far more than it is today. Writers like Tertullian, Origen and Justin speak of it frequently. But even though it is less common today, we should realize that the devil does possess great powers.

One of the devil's great powers today in tempting people is that many are unaware of his powers. Some do not believe in his existence. Being aware of his existence and his power is a large part in the battle of overcoming him. The other part is prayer and good works. Therefore, let us be on guard against him. Let us pray frequently, even daily, for the strength and will power to reject his temptations when they come along. God bless you.

# "B"    Fifth Sunday of the Year

*Mark 1:29-39*

There is an old saying that there is only one joke in the entire New Testament — that is, when Christ cured St. Peter's mother-in-law. Some people may take the circumstances of the miracle as a joke, but in all actuality they were not intended to be.

St. Peter's mother-in-law was truly sick with a very high fever. When Christ left the synagogue at Capernaum, he went to Peter's house. At this point Peter and his brother Andrew, along with their good friends and fishing partners, the two sons of Zebedee, James and John, asked Christ to cure her.

Once this request was made known to Christ, he immediately took action. He went over to the bed where she lay. Christ took her hand and helped her sit up and immediately the fever left her. Immediately she got up and began to wait on them.

According to our modern American humor, you don't see many mothers-in-law who would get out of a sickbed and begin to wait on a son-in-law and his friends. But Peter's mother-in-law did just that.

Frequently you hear the question asked — how many of the Apostles were married men and how many were single? We know from this Scripture passage that St. Peter was married. We know only that Sts. Paul and John were single. Concerning the others, we are not told, but we would probably be right in assuming that the majority of them were married.

The further question was asked — why don't priests marry today? Why do they live single lives? Why do we have priestly celibacy? The best answer we can give to this question is to say that priests lead single lives in imitation of Jesus Christ, who led a single life here upon this earth. When Christ began his public life, he devoted himself to it unreservedly. He gave it his entire time and energy. He did this as a single person. In the 19th chapter of St. Matthew, Christ recommended a single life for his disciples. He spoke of those who remained single for the love of the kingdom of heaven and he recommended those practice it who could.

St. Paul speaks on this subject in his first epistle to the Corinthians. He says: "I say to the unmarried and to the widows, it is good for them if they so continue, even as I. . . . He that is without a wife is solicitous for the things that belong to the Lord, how he may please God. But he that is with a wife is solicitous for the things of the world, how he may please his wife, and he is divided."

Many of the early Fathers and leaders of the Church practiced celibacy and recommended it for all priests and clerics. Among those who so recommended it were Sts. Eusebius, Jerome and Cyril. Hence from the earliest times in the Church there were to be found a large number of unmarried priests.

The first Church law on this subject came from the country of Spain in the year 300. That country at the Council of Elvira decreed that all bishops, priests and clerics should lead a celibate life. Following the lead of Spain, certain other countries and provinces followed suit and made similar declarations.

In 747 King Pepin of Germany was perplexed. He saw single and celibate priests in some places and married ones in others. He petitioned Pope Zachary to legislate on the subject and make some common rule. But the Pope declined to do so at the time. He said he left it up to the rulers of the various countries and regions to make the decision.

However, the Church let it be known that it favored single or celibate priests. It disinherited the children of priests, for example. Problems had arisen in some certain cases — where some priests owned a church in their own name. When they died their sons inherited it, sons who were not priests themselves. This abuse was ended.

The Church likewise declared that the son of a priest could not become a priest himself. The Church wished to prevent a dynasty from developing in the priesthood. It wanted a vocation to the priesthood to be strictly a grace from almighty God. It wanted, too, to discourage priests from marrying.

This was the history of celibacy for the first thousand years of the Church. It was strongly encouraged by the Church and was the law in some countries. But in 1123, at the first Lateran Council, celibacy was made the law for the entire Western Church or Latin rite. This law was reaffirmed at the Council of

Trent, and within our own lifetime at the Second Vatican Council.

Vatican II says on the subject: "Through virginity or celibacy observed for the sake of the kingdom of heaven, priests are consecrated to Christ in a new and distinguished way."

Even since the Second Vatican Council, our present Holy Father, Pope Paul VI, in June, 1967, issued an encyclical on "Priestly Celibacy." He calls it a brilliant jewel that has been guarded by the Church for centuries. He points out that priests live a life of chastity not out of disdain for the gift of life, but because of a greater love for Christ and his Church.

Pope Paul points out that Christ promised a great reward to anyone who would leave home, family, wife and children for the sake of the kingdom of God. This is what the priests of the Catholic Church have done. He calls priests the voluntary captives of Jesus Christ. He points out that priests have voluntarily given up the pleasures of married life here in this life for the hope of a greater reward hereafter.

Pope Paul answers several objections that are raised against priestly celibacy. To the argument that it is impossible for a large group of men constantly to live a chaste life in our world, he adds that it becomes possible when they are fortified with the grace of Jesus Christ and the Sacrament of Holy Orders.

To the argument that his life is lonely, Pope Paul answers that the solitude of a priest is not lonely because it is filled with God.

Priestly celibacy has been most beneficial to the Church. Not long ago a leading Protestant church official stated that a married deacon of his church and his family were sent to Japan to do missionary work. He pointed out that with the salary and expenses incurred, seven Catholic missionaries were sent to Japan for the same amount. Even then he admitted that the single or celibate Catholic missionary could more easily mix with the people, live their life, and be closer to them.

Pope Paul says in his encyclical that priestly celibacy is a treasure that belongs to the whole Church — a treasure from which all the laity benefit. He points out that they should receive their priests with love and respect. They should cooperate with them in their undertakings. He urges that the laity pray and work for vocations. God bless you.

# "B"    Sixth Sunday of the Year

*Mark 1:40-45*

St. Mark tells us in today's gospel that when our Lord was preaching at Capernaum a leper approached and asked Christ to cure him. Lepers were the outcasts of Jewish society; leprosy was a common and dreaded disease at that time.

Leprosy was a fatal disease. It ate away one's flesh. Within a few years a leper would see his hands and feet, his nose and ears rot away. He would lose his power to move about. His flesh would loosen from the bone. His joints would no longer function. In the last stages of the disease a leper would pray for death.

In the Old Testament, the book of Leviticus prescribed laws and regulations concerning lepers. A leper had to leave his home and live in the countryside. If he approached a healthy person on the road he was required to cry out "Unclean!" as a warning. Should it ever happen, which it seldom did, that a person was cleansed of leprosy, he would have to present himself before the priests to be declared clean. Only then could he return to his home and live among society.

The leper in today's gospel was actually breaking the law in approaching Christ, a healthy person. But having heard of his miracles, he had a great desire to be cleansed. He implored our Lord for help.

The heart of Christ was filled with charity and love for his fellow man; he granted the leper's request. He touched the leper and said, "I will do it. Be cured." Immediately the leper's body was restored to perfect health. His hands and feet were whole again. Christ then ordered him to present himself to the priest to be declared clean. He also cautioned him, "Not a word to anyone. . . ."

It was natural that when the leper presented himself to the priest and was declared clean, people would ask him how his cure came about. The inquisitive officials, friends and the man's family would pursue their questions until he acknowledged that it was Christ who cured him. It would be next to impossible to keep quiet about this miracle.

Christ had done something no other man could do. He had cured a leper. He showed that he possessed divine power. It was a means of proving the truth of the gospel which he was preaching. It made Christ extremely popular. No longer could he approach a town without crowds milling around him.

Christ performed this miracle as he did so many others out of a motive of mercy or compassion. His heart went out in sympathy for the sufferings of this poor leper. But the mercy displayed by Christ brings to mind the life of another virtuous priest who dedicated his life to the care of lepers. This priest was Father Damien Joseph de Veuster, whose name has been introduced into the process of canonization.

Father Damien was born in Belgium in 1840. It was his desire since boyhood to become a missionary priest. He entered the seminary and was ordained a priest. His assignment after ordination was to the Hawaiian Islands. There as a young priest he worked in poor parishes on Oahu. But in 1873 his bishop called a meeting of the priests of the islands. He explained that an epidemic of leprosy had broken out in the Hawaiian Islands. The lepers were being exiled to the island of Molokai. The bishop wanted a priest to volunteer to take care of them.

Immediately four priests jumped to their feet. Father Damien was one of them. From the four the bishop chose Father Damien; his strength and good health were a determining factor in his choice.

Arriving on Molokai, Father Damien found conditions in a deplorable state. The lepers had no sanitary drinking water. Immediately Father Damien organized a work crew of lepers able to work. He drilled a well in the mountains and piped in fresh water for the lepers to drink. With their help he built a chapel and began to celebrate daily Mass.

Father Damien proved to be a tireless worker both for the physical and spiritual good of the lepers. He became their civic leader in the absence of any other. He functioned as a doctor and health officer. He arranged for burials for those who died. He helped them build cottages to live in. He dressed the wounds of the sick. He saw that the helpless and the invalids were cared for. He became a spiritual father to every leper on the island.

Father Damien brought the sacraments to the sick and the dying. But one thing he insisted on — those who were able must attend Sunday Mass. Each Sunday Father Damien would address the congregation with the words, "My dear lepers." This he did for twelve years. But then one Sunday he addressed them with the words, "My fellow lepers." A great cheer broke out in the church which lasted many minutes.

In this way the lepers learned that Father Damien had himself contracted the dread disease that they themselves had. But even while afflicted with it, he continued his administration to them for the next three years. He finally died in 1888. His last words were, "God's will be done. My work with all its faults and failures is in his hands."

As Christ had compassion on lepers here on earth, Father Damien, his priest and follower, imitated the charity of his Master. Let us too imitate his example. Let us have compassion on the sick and the suffering with whom we come in contact.

Let us pray to Father Damien and beg his intercession with almighty God. God bless you.

## "B"    Seventh Sunday of the Year

*Mark 2:1-12*

St. Arnould of Metz was once bothered exceedingly by the thought of a sin he had committed years previous as a youth. He was tormented by the thought that the sin was too great for God to forgive. One day, while deep in despair, he walked across the bridge over the Moselle River. Taking his ring off his finger, he threw it in the river, saying, "If I ever find that ring again, I will believe that my sins are forgiven."

Some weeks later St. Arnould was seated at dinner. Fish was served him for the meal. Cutting into the fish he struck a hard object. It was the ring he had thrown in the river weeks before. St. Arnould was convinced that his sins were forgiven. He was sorry for having despaired of God's mercy.

God does not always perform miracles to make known his mercy, but he told us of his mercy in Holy Scripture on many occasions. When we say the Our Father, the prayer that Christ himself taught us, we beg God's forgiveness. We pray, "Forgive us our trespasses as we forgive those who trespass against us."

When God forgives us, the advantage is all on our side. When God forgives us, he does not injure himself. We alone are the losers if we refuse to take advantage of his mercy.

God's mercy is well displayed in the gospel read at today's Mass. When the paralyzed man was let down through the roof at Capernaum, Christ said to him, "My son, your sins are forgiven."

Some of the scribes began to murmur against him saying, "Why does the man talk in this way? He commits blasphemy! Who can forgive sins except God alone?"

Christ said in answer to them, "Why do you harbor these thoughts? Which is easier to say to the paralytic, 'Your sins are forgiven,' or to say, 'Stand up, pick up your mat, and walk again'? That you may know that the Son of Man has authority on earth to forgive sins, I command you: Stand up! Pick up your mat and go home."

The man stood and picked up his mat and went outside in the sight of everyone. Christ had proved conclusively that he had the power to forgive sin.

But Christ was not content to forgive the sins of one man. He wanted all men in all ages to have a means of having their sins forgiven. Thus he gave us the Sacrament of Penance or Reconciliation.

On Easter Sunday night Christ appeared to his Apostles in Jerusalem and said, "Receive the Holy Spirit. If you forgive men's sins, they are forgiven them. If you hold them bound, they are held bound." By these words he gave to his Apostles and their successors in the Church the power to forgive sins. He instituted the Sacrament of Reconciliation.

When a priest sits in the confessional, he takes the place of Christ. The words of absolution he pronounces have the same effect as those which Christ spoke to the paralytic. Through these words a great change takes place in the soul of the penitent. The soul stained with mortal sin becomes as white as snow. It is cleansed of sin and clothed in the garment of sanctifying grace.

Confession is a natural remedy for any soul dead with sin. If one were ill he would not hesitate to see a doctor; likewise, the soul sick with sin should not hesitate in seeking the healing powers of the confessional.

Penance is a sacrament of God's love. If one should lose sanctifying grace through serious sin, Penance gives him the chance to regain it.

But despite the many benefits of this sacrament, it is widely misunderstood. It was bitterly attacked at the time of the Reformation. People began to avoid it. In 1215 Pope Innocent III found it necessary to make it obligatory under pain of mortal sin to go to confession at least once a year.

Why is it people so dislike confession? Some say it is humiliating. In one sense this is true, but then God knows all our sins long before we confess them.

Some say they dislike confessing their sins to another human being even though he is a priest. But a priest would commit a serious sin himself if he revealed what he heard in the confessional. Priests have been known to give up their lives rather than reveal what was told them in the confessional.

This was the case of St. John Nepomucene, a holy priest who lived in Prague in the fourteenth century. The cruel emperor questioned this saintly priest on what he had heard in the confessional, but the priest refused to reveal any confessional matter. A long imprisonment did not force him to change his mind. Neither did torture nor the promise of great reward have any effect on him. Finally in exasperation the emperor ordered the holy priest drowned in the river at night. But a heavenly light hung over the spot where his body lay. It was covered and venerated. Many miracles were worked through his intercession. Today St. John Nepomucene is a saint in the Church.

If Satan can keep one from going to confession, he feels he has gained a great victory. The correct view of confession is to regard it as a sacrament of God's love. Therefore, resolve to receive it regularly. God bless you.

# "B"     Eighth Sunday of the Year

*Mark 2:18-22*

In the gospel text of today's Mass, our Lord has been invited to a banquet. The banquet was given by Saint Matthew in our Lord's honor. He and his Apostles were present. But because of the many miracles he had performed, Christ was a public figure. He had no privacy. Crowds followed him everywhere. This banquet was no exception. Some scribes and Pharisees even followed him to Matthew's house.

Observing Christ and his disciples at this joyous occasion, they compared him with John the Baptizer, who continually preached and practiced fasting. They asked him why John and his followers fasted and he did not.

Our Lord answered their question and veiled criticism of his conduct by asking a question in turn, "How can the guests at a wedding fast as long as the groom is still among them?" He answered the question himself by saying that they cannot fast as long as the bridegroom is with them. But they will begin to fast when the groom is no longer with them.

Christ was referring to himself as the bridegroom. He implied that being with the Apostles was an occasion for festivity. Later times would change. He would be taken away from them and this would be the appropriate time to fast.

Our Lord was in no way denying the benefits of fasting. Fasting played an important part in both the Jewish religion and our Christian religion today. The very first command God gave to man was a command to fast — not to eat the fruit of the forbidden tree.

The New Testament affords many examples of fasting. Besides John the Baptizer, Christ himself fasted for forty days before beginning his public life. The Apostles fasted for ten days after Christ ascended into heaven.

Christ not only practiced fasting, but preached it as well. He said to his Apostles, that certain devils could be driven out only by prayer and fasting. In today's gospel he tells us that fasting will come when the bridegroom will leave us.

From the earliest times fasting was imposed upon the members of Christ's Church. For many centuries the season of Lent was the season for fasting.

Only within the last few years since Vatican II has the obligation of fasting been reduced. Obligatory fasting is limited to two days, Ash Wednesday and Good Friday. Throughout the rest of Lent fasting is recommended but not commanded.

Fasting consists of eating only one full meal a day and two other light lunches, not equal to a second full meal. The Church does not intend that one should injure his health through fasting or be impaired from performing his ordinary work. The sick are excused from it.

Fasting helps curb our bodily appetites. It is an excellent way of building up our spiritual will power. Most frequently the temptations that come to us come through our bodily appetites. Fasting gives us the spiritual will power to say no when such a temptation comes along.

Fasting is a means of mortification. It mortifies the body and brings it into subjection to the soul. The early Fathers of the Church add that we can tame our bodies through fasting as wild animals are tamed. Fasting inclines a man to prayer. It leads to a high degree of virtue. Fasting makes one resemble the angels, who neither eat nor drink.

The devil regards the flesh as his greatest ally. Fasting deprives him of his greatest weapon. It puts him in chains.

Fasting can even lead to an improvement in bodily health. The dieting fad, which is so popular today, is only another form of fasting — fasting from certain fat-producing foods. But in fasting one has the additional advantage of not eating for a religious motive and thus gaining grace through it.

Fasting counteracts the sin of gluttony. In gluttony one gives free reign to bodily appetites. One reduces himself to acting like an animal rather than listening to the dictates of his intellect and will. Fasting opposes the desires of the flesh. Fasting offers our body with all its powers and senses to God.

Christ said the time for fasting would come. That time has arrived. Let us not neglect to fast in our own individual lives. To enjoy the banquet with the bridegroom hereafter, we must fast when he is not with us. God bless you.

# "B" Ninth Sunday of the Year

*Mark 2:23—3:6*

The gospel of St. Mark read at today's Mass, records the first incident of conflict between our divine Savior and the leaders of the Jewish people, the scribes and the Pharisees. This was over the question of observance of the Sabbath.

Our Lord was preaching in Galilee in the vicinity of the small fishing village of Capernaum. The day was the Sabbath, and he and his disciples were walking through a field of grain. As they walked along, some of his disciples picked a few ears of grain and shelled them and ate them. Possibly our Lord did this also; they did this because they were very hungry.

The Pharisees observed this action on the part of our Lord's disciples and reprimanded Christ, their leader, for it. They were not accusing our Lord or his disciples of stealing, for it was an oriental custom to permit travelers to pick and eat figs, grapes, olives and other fruits they chanced upon in their journey.

The Mosaic Law expressly sanctioned this custom, for we read in the book of Deuteronomy: "If you go into your neighbor's vineyard, eat of the grapes as many as it pleases you, but take them not away with you. If you go into his field, you may pluck the ears with your hand, but you may not reap them with a sickle."

Rather, the Pharisees reprimanded our Lord for breaking the law of the Sabbath which forbade the reaping or threshing of grain. The Jewish Talmud states that to pick a piece of fruit or grain is to harvest, and to shell it is to winnow. Hence the Pharisees were protesting that our Lord broke the law of the Sabbath on these two counts, the reaping and the winnowing of grain. The Jews also had another law which forbade walking more than 1,000 yards from the walls of the city or the farthest homes.

Our Lord had no wish to argue with the Pharisees on any questions of the interpretation of the Law. Instead he raised the questions to a higher level. He proved to them by an example that the observance of the Sabbath is a matter of positive effect and therefore admits of exceptions, and that it should yield to necessity, in this case hunger.

Our Lord quoted for them the story of King David, who was fleeing with a band of 400 followers from the tyranny of King Saul. David and his band fled to Nob, where the tabernacle was kept at the time, and David asked the high priest Ahimilech for some badly needed food. The high priest then questioned David to learn whether he and his men were legally pure and when he found they were, he gave them loaves of proposition from the temple.

Jewish Law stipulated that these loaves of proposition might be eaten by the priests of the temple a week after they had been presented there, and it forbade others from eating them. Nevertheless, in this case, the high priest (Ahimilech) made an exception to the law because of the extreme hunger of David's troops. Once he learned they were legally clean, he gave them the loaves of proposition to eat.

By this story Christ raised the question as to whether it was permissible to perform a good deed on the Sabbath when the Mosaic Law forbade it or whether one should observe the law and allow some evil to happen. And our Lord gives the answer to this question by saying that the Sabbath was made for man and not man for the Sabbath.

The Jews themselves know that Christ was right in teaching them this. They could easily remember learning in their history and religion classes how the Jews of the Old Testament had fought vigorously to defend themselves when the tyrant Antiochus had attacked them on a Sabbath. Fighting in battle and conducting war were expressly forbidden by Jewish Law. Yet in this instance the Jews did fight on a Sabbath, for it was necessary to do so to save their lives.

Christ's answer of this question meant that the law of abstention from work on the Sabbath should not be so rigid as to exclude the law of charity or necessity.

St. Mark continues with a further incident in his gospel dealing with this same question. Whether this incident happened on the same day or some weeks or months later on another occasion, he does not say. He only mentions that on a Sabbath Christ went into a synagogue and there met a man with withered hands.

Upon seeing him, Our Lord proposed a question to the Jews present in the synagogue, whether it was permissible to do a good deed on the Sabbath. St. Mark tells they sat there in silence. Christ had placed them in a dilemma they could not answer.

The Jewish leaders had taken a dislike to Christ. They were jealous of his popularity and following. They were anxious to accuse him of breaking the law of the Sabbath. So not being able to give him a good answer, they kept silent.

Our Lord had already determined what he was going to do on this occasion. He was determined to cure the sick man. He told him to stretch out his hands, and when he did, Christ restored them to perfect health. He cured him.

After this miracle, the Pharisees attempted to plot with Herod and the civil rulers to do away with Jesus. Their hatred and jealousy were even beginning to lead them to the depths of committing murder.

In our present Church law, we too have a commandment which forbids unnecessary servile work on Sunday. Nevertheless, the law of necessity and the law of charity supersede it. The law is meant to set Sunday aside as a day of rest to give honor to God. But, where necessity or the law of charity demand it, they take precedent over it.

Let us resolve in our own lives to give honor to God by the proper observance of his day, but especially let us show him honor by practice of the virtue of charity. God bless you.

# "B"  Tenth Sunday of the Year

*Mark 3:20-35*

The incidents related in St. Mark's gospel read at today's Mass occurred in the village of Capernaum. It occurred during the early part of Christ's public life. Christ had left his carpenter's bench in Nazareth. He had given up a comfortable and secure livelihood to become a wandering preacher.

During his public life Christ had no place to lay his head. He threw away any security he may have had. He had to depend on the charity of his listeners and followers for his next meal. In the eyes of his relatives and acquaintances he was doing a foolish thing — something no sensible person would do. In addition, the Pharisees and religious leaders in Jerusalem had heard reports of him and had sent a delegation to Capernaum to oppose him in his teachings.

His family and friends attempted to persuade him to renounce this life he was leading and return to Nazareth and his carpentry trade. Finding themselves unable to persuade him or force him in any way to return, they could only draw conclusions about him. They said, "He is out of his mind." Little did they realize the divine mission he was undertaking.

A group of scribes had arrived from Jerusalem; their mission was to oppose Christ. They grasped at whatever incident they could to belittle him. It so happened that Christ had just cured a demoniac. The possessed man whom Christ cured had been dumb and blind. Christ not only cast the devil out of the man but restored his sight and his power to speak.

These facts the scribes could not deny. However, they did make a charge against him, "He expels demons with the help of the prince of demons." It was the beginning of many attacks they would make upon him.

But Christ easily refuted their charge with a commonsense answer. He asked, "How can Satan expel Satan? If a kingdom is torn by civil strife, that kingdom cannot last." Christ was showing them that their charge was ridiculous and illogical. He continued, "If a household is divided according to loyalties, that household will not survive. Similarly, if Satan has suffered mutiny in his ranks and is torn by dissension, he cannot endure; he is finished."

Christ was attempting to show the scribes that the expulsion of the devil was a sensible sign of the devil's defeat; it marked the beginning of the fall of his empire. His expulsion of the devil showed that he was stronger than the devil. In reality, Christ was showing divine power in being able to expel the devil.

Christ had shown divine power, but the scribes said he was possessed by a devil. This was blasphemy on their part. Christ had harsh words for them, "I give you my word, every sin will be forgiven mankind and all the blasphemies men utter, but whoever blasphemes against the Holy Spirit will never be forgiven. He carries the guilt of his sin without end." It was a sin of pure malice, a sin of attributing something evil to God.

At this point the mother and relatives of Christ arrived on the scene. They had made the journey from Nazareth to Capernaum. Although the words brothers and sisters are found in Scripture, we must remember that the Aramaic language which Christ spoke had a much more limited vocabulary than our modern English. They used the same word for brother as they would for a cousin or more distant relative. Hence the words brother and sister are used in a much broader sense in Aramaic than in English.

When told that they were outside the house asking for him, Christ gazed around and said, "These are my mother and my brothers. Whoever does the will of God is brother and sister and mother to me." By this answer Christ did not disown his family ties, but he subordinates them to a higher bond of brotherhood.

Christ was showing that the reign of God makes higher demands on the personal commitment of a disciple than do family ties. Love of family is a good thing, but the love of God is greater. If the two obligations conflict, the greater good must be chosen. The duty of being a disciple of Christ must take precedence over any family ties. God bless you.

# "B"  Eleventh Sunday of the Year

*Mark 4:26-34*

Today's gospel according to St. Mark tells the parable of the seed growing by itself. To understand the meaning, it is first necessary to understand the customs and climatic conditions of the Near East. It is customary in this warm climate for farmers to plant grain in their fields in either November or December and then to sit back and relax until harvest time.

An old proverb prevails among them, "Four months to wait, and the harvest will come." The winter rains and the spring sunshine take care of the irrigation of the soil and the ripening of the ear. The farmer has little or no work to do between planting and harvest time.

In this parable, Christ evidently referred to himself in speaking of the Sower or Harvester. The seed is the word of the gospel. The harvest is the membership in his Church. The long period of waiting between the sowing and the harvesting, the night after night and day after day, refers to the impatience of many Jewish converts who were expecting an immediate and glorious manifestation of the kingdom of God.

Some Jews had a mistaken idea of what the messianic kingdom would be like. They expected an immediate and highly dramatic inauguration of its reign. By this parable, Christ wanted to teach them patience and confidence in the mysterious plans of God. He wanted to show them that his Church would grow without any violent revolutionary upheaval or theatrics, that the growth of his Church did not depend on any individual or any nation.

Christ wanted to show by this parable that there was a continuity between his mission, represented by the sowing of the seeds, and the slow and eventual growth of his Church. Even though disappointing to the Jews, his Church would surely grow and would embrace the gentile nations as well.

Christ continued with a second parable. He compared the kingdom of God or his Church to a mustard seed. The particular seed he referred to was that of the black mustard plant cultivated in gardens in Palestine. The smallness of the mustard seed was proverbial. Although actually a plant, its product was frequently called a tree because of its wooden base. It would grow to over seven feet in height and had wide spreading branches, giving the appearance of a tree. When the mustard fruit was ripe, hundreds of sparrows and goldfinches could be found in its branches.

Our Lord could have chosen many other more stately trees, for instance the oak or the cedar, to compare his Church to, but instead he chose the mustard plant because he wished to emphasize the humble beginnings of his Church. In fact, no other organizations ever seemed to have a shakier beginning. He founded his Church with eleven fishermen and one tax collector as its leaders.

Christ allowed himself to be ignominiously put to death. At the time of his crucifixion, his Church numbered only about 120 faithful disciples or members.

But yet before the death of the last Apostle, Christianity had overleaped the frontiers of the civilized world. St. Thomas had set out for India and parts unknown. St. James had gone to Spain. St. Jude and Philip to Ethiopia and parts of Africa. St. Peter was crucified in Rome, the capital of the Roman Empire.

Three centuries of persecution were powerless to check its spread. All the power the Roman Empire could bring to bear against it could not block its growth and progress.

The contrast between its humble beginnings and its miraculous growth is well exemplified through Christ's comparison to a mustard seed. The small mustard seed has today become a tree in whose shade all the nations of the earth may seek shelter.

St. Mark concludes this particular section of his gospel with the statement that Christ spoke to the crowds only in parables, but to the Apostles he explained all things when they were alone. These words seem to imply that the people only partially understood the meaning of Christ's teachings. They seemed to lack the full meaning the Apostles had when Christ unravelled the allegorical meaning of his parables.

It implies too that Christ gave his Apostles a more complete instruction when speaking to them privately. The parables he spoke to the people were only a partial manifestation of the gospel. The complete and full manifestation he saved for his Apostles and the leaders of his Church.

Let us therefore be grateful to the almighty God for the many graces he bestowed upon his Church — for its marvelous and steady growth without the help of any other nation or temporal power, for its rapid and continual growth from such humble beginnings. Let us realize that only the divine guidance of the Holy Spirit could bring about such results. Let us thank God for the gift of faith that we possess and invoke his protection in guarding it throughout our lives. God bless you.

# "B"  Twelfth Sunday of the Year

*Mark 4:35-41*

Today's gospel speaks of a storm which suddenly broke when our Lord was at sea with some of his disciples. But storms such as the one described in today's gospel were a common occurrence on the Sea of Galilee. This body of water is a large lake over 600 feet below sea level. It lies at the bottom of a torrid basin, surrounded on all sides by high hills and mountains. To the north is Mount Hermon, whose peak rises over 9,000 feet in the air.

Violent wind currents frequently blew down from these high peaks engulfing the Jordan valley below. Even today one can set out on the lake in motionless water without so much as a ripple, in water as smooth as a mirror. There will not be sufficient wind to fill a sail. Then without warning the calm waters of the lake will be churned into giant waves by the violent and sudden winds which come up without warning.

It was evidently such a storm as this in which our Lord and his Apostles found themselves on the lake. Our Lord had fallen asleep in the boat. The waves were so great that they threatened to upset the boat, but our Lord slept on. Finally the Apostles were so overcome with fear that they awakened our Lord with the cry, "Lord, save us, we are perishing!"

Our Lord rebuked the Apostles, saying, "Why are you fearful, you of little faith?" He chastised them because they seemed unaware that he, as God, knew all things, that he knew about the violence of the storm even though he was fast asleep. He indicated that their fear was ungrounded.

Fear is a widespread emotion in the world today. So many people are fearful of so many things. The poor are fearful that they will not have the means with which to live. The rich are fearful that they will lose their wealth. The sick are afraid they will not recover their health. The well are afraid they will grow sick. The old are fearful of dying, and the young are fearful of growing old. It is a sad and regrettable situation that supposedly religious people are beset with such vain and empty fears.

A few years ago a hobo hitched a ride on a railroad train. He crawled into a partially empty box car, lay down and went to sleep. He woke up some time later when he felt something crawl across his face. He realized too upon awaking that the train was moving, it was vibrating from side to side and the cars rolled along the rails. The doors of the cars had been locked, and it was pitch dark inside.

The hobo pulled a few matches from his pocket and lit one to look around. When he did so, he discovered he was in a banana car. Then he began to think and to worry that the object that had crawled across his face might have been a tarantula — a poisonous spider. If one of them should bite him in the darkness of the banana car, he thought, he would surely die.

He rushed to the door of the car and began to pound on it violently, but to no avail. There was no one to hear him and open the car door. In fact, it was not until several hours later, when the train stopped, that the car door was opened and the hobo was discovered. By this time he had become a raving maniac. He was taken to a mental institution and was only released several months later. His ungrounded fears had put him in this condition.

Fear is contagious. It spreads to others. Fear can infect a whole crowd of people and cause them to perform actions none of them would think of committing alone.

Fear can even make one cruel, as it did the woman in a half-filled life boat rowing away from the sinking Titanic. When a man who was attempting to save his life appeared at the side of the boat, she picked up an oar and began to beat at his hands until he released his hold and drowned in the ocean.

Instead of giving way to fear in time of danger, we should instead put our trust in almighty God. The Apostles called upon our Lord when the storm threatened to upset their boat. So too should we call upon him in prayer when trouble besets us.

Each and every day upon arising or in saying our night prayers we should renew our faith — we should say an act of faith. Let us ask him to strengthen our faith, day by day, so that on the day of death, it will be a brightly burning beacon to illumine our way into heaven. God bless you.

# "B" Thirteenth Sunday of the Year

*Mark 5:21-43*

The Seneca Indians, part of the Iroquois, had an interesting custom. Whenever a girl died, they captured a bird and placed it in a cage on the grave of the young girl. They would wait until the bird began to sing and then they would open the door of the cage and allow the bird to fly away.

It was their belief that if the bird flew up into the sky, it would continue its journey to the land of the spirits. The song of the bird would convey their sentiments for happiness to the young maiden in the land of the spirits.

Their belief is nothing strange. All tribes of peoples, no matter where or when they have lived, have had some kind of belief in the life hereafter. Today's gospel confirms our belief in the immortality of the soul and life in eternity.

In today's gospel a ruler of the Jewish people approached our Lord. He was not an ordinary citizen, but an official of the synagogue, a respected member of the Jewish community. He made a most unusual request; he asked Christ to come and lay his hands upon his daughter who had just died and raise her to life.

This was unheard of. Everyone knew that death was the end of life and there was no escape from it. Death was final. Everyone around thought this Jewish leader was out of order in asking Christ to restore life to his dead daughter.

Without hesitation Christ followed this Jewish leader to his home. He first observed the flute players who played a mournful dirge to announce the sad news of death to all around. He observed the crowd of mourning Jews.

Christ greeted them with a startling salutation, "The child is not dead. She is asleep." From their experience the Jewish people recognized signs of death, and they were not to be fooled or deceived. They knew the girl was dead. Her body was cold; her pulse had ceased. Her heart had stopped beating. Therefore, they would not believe our Lord.

They began to ridicule him, but he walked past them into the house. One might expect that Christ expected and welcomed their testimony concerning the girl's death to confirm the greatness of the miracle he was about to perform.

Our Lord took the girl by the hand and the girl arose. Life was restored to her. Immediately the people began to spread the report of this great miracle. Many came to believe in Christ because of this miracle.

But Christ performed this miracle, as he did many others, for a specific reason. He performed it to prove his divinity. He wished to give people a reason for believing in the other doctrines which he preached. This miracle has a special lesson for us. It teaches us that the soul is immortal.

The immortality of the soul is a doctrine which Christ taught continually. It is a doctrine that is difficult to prove. Yet all primitive tribes and peoples have believed in a life hereafter. The most learned men of every age have professed their belief in it.

Each of us realizes that we have certain spiritual powers within us. We each have powers that are the property of the soul, which we cannot assign to any certain part of the body — for example, our power to think and reason. Each of us has a will by which we determine to act or not act in a certain situation. These powers are the effect of a spiritual soul — a soul that does not die with the body.

We know too that God is just. He rewards the good and punishes the evil. At times justice is not meted out in this world. We can reason, therefore, that it must be meted out in the life to come.

Therefore, for these many reasons, let us make an act of faith in the immortality of the soul. Let us view the miracle of Christ in raising this girl to life as a pledge of her own resurrection. Let us believe his teaching that we shall live again on the day of judgment. God bless you.

# "B" Fourteenth Sunday of the Year

*Mark 6:1-6*

In today's gospel, St. Mark tells us that our Lord paid a visit to his home village of Nazareth. At this time in his life, he had already begun his public life and gathered several Apostles around him. He had been preaching around Capernaum, a village 20 miles northeast of Nazareth. His purpose in coming to Nazareth was not social, merely to visit relatives or friends, but rather to preach the gospel to the people of Nazareth.

Nazareth, like all the villages of Galilee, had a synagogue. It was customary for the people of the village to gather here on the Sabbath or feast days to pray. The prayer service usually began with a profession of faith. This was followed by a reading from the Books of the Old Testament. These readings were generally made in the Aramaic language, which the people of Palestine spoke instead of the original Hebrew, which few of them understood.

Then would follow a sermon or talk and then a series of eighteen benedictions. Customs permitted that anyone who wished, or those who were the leaders of the synagogue and felt able to do so, could perform the readings or give the sermon. It was only required that the priest on duty in the synagogue give the last benediction.

On this particular Sabbath when our Lord entered the synagogue in his home town of Nazareth, he got up to read the Scripture and give the sermon on it. We even know from St. Luke's account of this incident the particular passage in Scripture that Christ read that day in the synagogue. He read from the sixty-first chapter of the Book of Isaiah, which spoke of the coming of Yahweh.

Then our Lord began to speak to the people of his own home town. He told them something most startling. He said today was fulfilled the prophecy which he had just read to them. He announced in effect to them that he had come to save them, that he was the Messiah or redeemer they had long awaited.

A wave of astonishment swept over his audience. They could hardly believe their ears. They were amazed at our Lord's knowledge of Sacred Scripture; they marveled at his eloquence. Questions entered their minds — wasn't this the son of Mary and Joseph the carpenter? They knew that Jesus had never attended rabbinical school. He had worked in Joseph's carpenter shop. How could he know so much about the Bible?

But the astonishment the people of Nazareth first displayed soon turned to anger and distrust. They were amazed at our Lord's knowledge and ability to speak. But this was not what they expected from him. Reports that Christ had healed the sick wherever he went had preceded his return home. Hence they had lined the synagogue with the crippled and sick of the village. They now besought Christ to heal these crippled people.

But this Christ refused to do. Christ had cured the sick on other occasions but only in support of his teachings, in support of the faith of the people. But in Nazareth, his home town, the people would not put their faith in him. Therefore as a punishment for their lack of faith, Jesus refused to perform a large number of miracles and cure all the sick.

However, to show that he still possessed the miraculous power of healing, he did lay his hands on a few of them and heal them, but not on all as the Jews had requested. He punished them in this way for their disbelief. The Nazarenes, who had grown up with our Lord and knew him as an equal, could not bring themselves to believe that he was a great prophet, that he was fulfilling the prophecy of Isaiah in their very midst. Our Lord quoted for them an ancient proverb: "A prophet is without honor only in his own country."

This visit of Jesus to his home town of Nazareth has a special significance. It marks the end of the first part of his Galilean ministry. Jesus will begin a new phase of his ministry in which his Apostles will play a more prominent part. His rejection by the people of Nazareth marks the first major rejection he has received since beginning his public life. But there will be other ones to follow, culminating in the crowd in Pilate's court shouting for the governor to free Barabbas rather than our Savior.

There have been many rejections of Christ's gospel since that time. Let us resolve in our lives that we will not place ourselves in that number. Let us resolve to receive Christ's message — that we will take it to heart and act upon it, that his gospel will be a living force within our lives. God bless you.

# "B"     15th Sunday of the Year

*Mark 6:7-13*

In today's gospel according to St. Mark, our Lord gathers his twelve Apostles about him and sends them off by twos to preach the gospel. This incident is recorded likewise in the gospels of St. Matthew and St. Luke. St. Matthew supplies the additional detail that he sent them only to the towns of Palestine, forbidding them to go to the towns of the gentiles and the Samaritans. He wished them only to gather the lost sheep of the House of Israel.

It was natural that Christ should send them in pairs. Emissaries of the various synagogues were accustomed to visit the people in rural districts, and they traveled in pairs. Hence to see a pair of men approaching on a religious mission was a common sight to the Israelites.

Our Lord gave them three specific instructions for their mission. First, they were to take nothing special for the journey; no knapsack, no bread, no money, no second coat. They were permitted only a staff and sandals. The details of what they could take are, in themselves, unimportant, but they serve to point out that Christ wanted them to take no more than was absolutely necessary.

He told them secondly that they were to lodge in the house where they first entered, until they left that place. Our Lord did not want his Apostles changing from one house to another as this would lay them open to the charge of inconstancy; it would be likely to cause jealousies and contentions.

However, he cautioned them that if they were not given a welcome and a hearing they were to leave that house and shake off the dust from their feet as a witness against them. In that case those who rejected them would be responsible for their own disbelief.

The mission of the Apostles in preaching to the rural villages of Palestine was to urge them to repent and to announce to them that their redemption was at hand. As a sign of their authority to carry out this mission of preaching, Christ gave them power to cast out evil spirits.

This power they used, for St. Mark tells us that they cast out many evil spirits. He adds also that they anointed many of the sick with oil and cured them. This anointing with oil at this time was not the Sacrament of Extreme Unction or Anointing of the Sick, for Christ had not as yet made the Apostles priests and had not instituted any of the sacraments at this time.

Rather, the anointing that they gave was a gesture to arouse faith in the suffering soul. It was a symbol or type of the sacrament that Jesus was to institute later. It was a prelude to the sacramental rite.

Undoubtedly this anointing was a most effective rite or gesture, as many of the sick were cured by it. The miraculous cure of the sick and the casting out of devils could not have helped but to impress the Jews of Galilee. It announced to them in a most dramatic way that their redemption was at hand. It brought to the forefront their need to perform penance.

This mission of the Apostles in going two by two into the countryside was an essential part of their training. Our Lord taught and trained them well for three years during his public life. Their training might well be compared to the training that a seminarian receives today in a seminary.

After three years of this training, just before he ascended into heaven, Christ gathered his Apostles around him and commissioned them to go forth and teach and baptize all nations. From that point on, their teachings were more meaningful. They could teach the whole of Christianity. Their baptisms could wipe away sin from people's souls. Their anointings then would bring grace into one's soul and prepare one for death.

This mission which Christ gave his Apostles is still being carried out within his Church by priests and bishops of the Church today, the legitimate successors of the Twelve Apostles. They too have a direct commission to teach and baptize and to anoint the sick. This commission was given them through their reception of the Sacrament of Holy Orders.

Hence, my dear people, the gospel that you hear preached to you today is given with the same authority, the same command with which the Twelve Apostles first preached it on the hillsides of Galilee. Therefore, receive it in the same spirit. Listen to it as you would listen to the Apostles. Make it a part of your life.

Do not let it be said that you were among the number that would not welcome them or hear them, and they stamped the dust off their feet as a witness against you. Rather, let it be said that you welcomed them into your home. In accepting the word of God and the successors of the Apostles who preach it, will bring the blessings of true Christian peace upon your home. God bless you.

# "B"      Sixteenth Sunday of the Year

*Mark 6:30-34*

Today's gospel is a continuation of the Gospel of St. Mark. In the gospel read last Sunday, St. Mark told how our Lord had sent the Apostles off in groups of two to preach the gospel in the Galilean countryside. In today's gospel, the Apostles have just returned from the mission. They told our Lord of all they had done and the teaching they had given. They also brought him some bad news. It was at this time that St. John the Baptizer had been beheaded by King Herod.

St. John was the precursor of Christ. He had preached a gospel of repentance for the remission of sin. He had prepared the way for the coming of Christ. Now his mission on earth was finished; he had died a martyr for upholding morality.

In the wake of the hard work and missionary efforts of the Apostles, Christ suggested to them, "Come away into a quiet place by yourselves and rest a little." As this was good advice for the Apostles in their time, the Church considers it good advice for her priests today. She prescribed by Canon Law that every priest make a yearly retreat — that he leave his duties for the better part of a week and devote himself to prayer and meditation.

No priest can impart holiness to others if he is not a holy man himself. No priest can inspire others to prayer if he does not pray himself. Therefore, once each year Holy Mother the Church wants her priests to leave their duties and devote themselves to a period of prayer and meditation. Thus their everyday duties will not becloud their spiritual goals. Their work will not warp or deter them from their heavenly aims.

In a physical sense this rest was necessary too, for St. Mark says, "They had not even the leisure to eat in peace." At times, too, the life of a priest is very busy. Sunday mornings are a good example. Besides his own two Masses, a priest helps in the distribution of Holy Communion at other Masses. He is constantly greeting people — issuing letters of recommendation, writing out baptismal certificates, checking on envelopes, answering phone calls concerning the time of Masses and caring for a hundred other trivia. All these he does gladly because in some small way they help lead souls to Christ.

Hence Our Lord and his Apostles boarded boats at the point where they were near Capernaum, at the northern end of the Sea of Galilee. They set sail for the eastern end of it near the plains of Julias. But in the morning there is little breeze on the lake and progress is slow.

The multitude seeing them depart guessed their purpose. They watched their direction from the seashore and started to follow them by land. They circled the northern shore of the lake and forded the Jordan River a little above its mouth. Many of the crowd covered this distance in quicker time than the Apostles and our Lord could arrive by sea.

When finally our Lord and the Apostles did reach their destined shore, they saw their dream of privacy was shattered. A large crowd already awaited them, and it was swelling with new arrivals.

St. Mark tells us that our Lord had pity on the crowd because they were like sheep without a shepherd. In this Christ fulfilled a prophecy made by Ezekiel centuries before. Christ became the spiritual shepherd of this wandering and lost flock. And as a true shepherd of souls, he began to give them long instructions.

Picture, if you will, a tender and compassionate Christ, despite his physical tiredness, despite all the demands on him, even not allowing him time to eat, granting this crowd their wish, speaking to them of the kingdom of heaven. But as Christ granted the requests of the crowd on the shores of the Sea of Galilee, the same compassionate Christ rules from heaven today. He is still as willing to grant our requests and prayers today.

Let us learn from the crowd which followed Christ. They were eager for spiritual food. Let us, too, be eager for spiritual food. Let us besiege heaven with our spiritual needs. Let our prayers be a constant din upon the gate of heaven. The same compassionate Christ will not fail to hear us and grant us what is for our spiritual good. God bless you.

# "B"    Seventeenth Sunday of the Year

*John 6:1-15*

Today Holy Mother the Church has placed before us for our consideration the beautiful gospel story of the multiplication of the loaves and the fishes. All four Evangelists record this miracle in their gospels, but the beautiful account of St. John has been chosen for today's gospel.

The time of year in which Christ performed this miracle was the springtime — either March or April, for St. John tells us that the Passover was near. The time of day was about four o'clock in the afternoon. The crowd had been with Christ since early morning and had had nothing to eat.

The place where he performed it was a grassy hillside on the eastern shores of the Sea of Galilee.

The crowd that followed our Lord was deeply impressed by his miracles and by his preaching. They believed in him and wanted to follow him. Their hunger for spiritual food was their main concern; they did not consider that it was late in the afternoon and was time for their evening meal. Their bodily hunger did not bother them. They had not thought to make any provision for it.

Christ knew that the crowd was intent upon every word that he was preaching; therefore he had compassion upon them. Whenever he had worked miracles on previous occasions, he had performed them only upon request. However, on this occasion he performed a miracle without being requested. Christ turned to Philip and asked him, "Where shall we buy bread so that these may eat?"

Philip gave a commonsense answer that two hundred days' wages of bread would not be enough for them, even for each one to receive a mouthful. The practical man among the Apostles, St. Andrew, the brother of Peter, went out among the crowd to inquire if anyone had made provisions for bringing food with them. He found one young boy who had five barley loaves and two fish. But then he asked, "What are these among so many?"

One could almost read the minds of the Apostles at this point and hear them say that there was no human solution for the problem and the only practical thing to do was to send the people away. But Christ intervened before anything like this was done. He commanded the Apostles to make the people sit down.

Jesus took the five loaves and, when he had given thanks, distributed them to those reclining, and likewise the fish, as much as they would like. And everyone ate his fill. And when they had finished he told the Apostles to gather up the fragments, which they did. They found that they had twelve baskets of fragments remaining.

Clearly this was a great miracle — to feed 5,000 people with only five loaves and two dried fish. It was something which only God himself could do. In doing this Christ showed that he possessed divine power. He proved that he was God.

But there are other lessons to be learned from this miracle of Christ. One important lesson is the compassion Christ showed in feeding the crowd when they were hungry. When Christ preached his Sermon on the Mount He taught us the corporal works of mercy, the first of which was to feed the hungry.

This lesson is an important one — one that we can practice today. On another occasion Christ said, "The poor you will always have with you." Today, even some twenty centuries after Christ lived upon earth, a large segment of the world's population is suffering from hunger.

All of our recent Popes have written on this question. Half of the world's population still go to bed hungry at night. Malnutrition is still a common cause of death in many parts of the world.

In India rickets disease, caused by a deficiency of certain vitamins in one's diet, is extremely common. The country of India does not produce sufficient food for its people to live on. It is a common sight there to see children roaming the streets rummaging through garbage cans in search of food.

In Bolivia the vast majority of people live in the mountains which cover most of the country. Because of the very high altitude, only a certain few grains and vegetables will grow there. Hence the diet of these people is unbalanced and very meager.

Much of the country is of such an altitude that it is above the timber line where trees will grow. There are very few trees, and consequently there is little wood to burn. Neither is there any other kind of fuel, so their homes are not heated. Even though near the Equator, they are often cold because of the altitude. Likewise, because of a lack of fuel, their meals are not cooked. They eat their food cold.

These stories of hunger and suffering throughout the world are endless. This hunger existed in the time of Christ and it exists now.

When Christ lived on earth he helped relieve it by performing a miracle. This, of course, is impossible for us, but there are other natural ways in which we can help relieve it.

Above all, we should be grateful to God for what he has given us. We should thank him for our living in a land of abundance. This we can do in a special way by reciting our grace before and after each meal.

There are so many homes where an abundance of good food is taken for granted, and God's name is never mentioned in prayer before and after meals. One cannot expect God to continue to shower his gifts in abundance upon us if we never take time to thank him for what he has given us. If the poor and hungry of the world could sit at our tables, they would thank God long and fervently.

As Christ blessed food and thanked his heavenly Father for it before distributing it to the people on the mountainside and multiplying the loaves and fishes, let us learn from his example. Thanking God for temporal goods will prepare us for spiritual blessings in the world to come. God bless you.

# "B"  Eighteenth Sunday of the Year

*John 6:24-35*

The gospel read at today's Mass relates the preaching of our Lord at the village of Capernaum. Only the evening before Christ had fed a crowd of five thousand people miraculously multiplying the loaves and fishes. This miracle he had performed toward evening at Bethsaida, on the northeast shore of the Sea of Galilee. Most of the crowd had slept there that evening on the grassy slopes of the lake.

But the next morning the crowd began to look around for Jesus and his Apostles. They were nowhere to be found. Hence they decided to return to their homes in Capernaum, a four-mile trek along the northern shore of the lake. Upon arriving there, they found to their great joy that Christ and his Apostles had already preceded them there. They asked him, "Rabbi, when did you come here?"

Our Lord could read their thoughts. He answered that "you are not looking for me because you have seen the signs but because you have eaten your fill of the loaves. You should not be working for perishable food but for food that remains unto life eternal. . . ."

It is the unanimous opinion of all leading Scripture scholars that the "food that remains unto life eternal" which Christ referred to is the Holy Eucharist. Christ used this opportunity to promise the Eucharist to the Jewish people and to prepare them for its establishment.

The Holy Eucharist is the heart of the Catholic religion. It is the object of our adoration. The Holy Eucharist as reserved in the tabernacles of our churches throughout the world is the center of our worship — the focal point of our attention.

Because the Eucharist is so important to our religion, it is only fitting and proper that Christ should make adequate preparation for it. The Old Testament made remote preparation for the establishment of the Eucharist through various types and prophecies. One such type was the offering of bread and wine by the holy priest Melchizedek.

Another type was the manna which God fed the Jews wandering in the desert of Sinai. The manna was a white wafer-like substance which miraculously fell from heaven each morning in the desert of Sinai, where the Jews wandered for forty years before settling in the promised land. They would gather up the manner each morning before it melted away and eat it as food.

Their descendants themselves brought up the question of manna to Christ. They said, "Our ancestors had manna to eat in the desert. . . ." Christ solemnly assured them it was not Moses who gave them the bread from heaven, but his Father who gives them the real heavenly bread.

A plea was heard from the crowd to "give us this bread always." It was a spontaneous and sincere wish of those present to partake of the Eucharist which Christ was promising them.

Christ said, "I . . . am the bread of life." With these words Christ began a lengthy discourse on the Eucharist. Today's gospel quotes only the first few words of this discourse. The remainder of it will constitute the gospel read at Mass for the next few Sundays.

In addressing these words to the crowd, "I myself am the bread of life," Christ gradually began to unfold to them the true meaning of the Eucharist which he was later to found. He was making an immediate preparation for its establishment.

Some two years later in the upper room in Jerusalem, Christ would take the bread and wine into his hands and say over them the words, "This is my body," and, "This is my blood." Although the appearance of the bread and wine would remain the same, as well as their taste, the substance would be radically different. They would actually be Christ's body and blood.

The full meaning of this great miracle would not be immediately apparent to the Apostles. It would take time and reflection to bring about its full impact. Only after much thought and prayer would the importance of his promise to give us the Eucharist become apparent. The words that he uttered at Capernaum, "I . . . am the bread of life" would then have a deeper meaning and ring with greater truth.

The real presence of Christ in the Eucharist is the difference between a Catholic church and any other church. Christ in the tabernacle is the center of our worship. The importance of his presence is brought out in an incident in the life of Bishop Mermillod of Lausanne, one of the great preachers of the last century.

One Sunday the bishop had delivered a most eloquent sermon and then, as was his custom after Mass, he knelt in adoration before the Blessed Sacrament for half an hour's time. As the bishop was about to leave the church the timid voice of a lady interrupted him.

The lady explained that she was not a Catholic, but had attended Mass at the invitation of some friends who had told her of the bishop's eloquence. "But frankly," she said, "you failed to convince me. You sounded like a polished lawyer, pleading your case, defending some doctrine of the Church." But then she explained that she remained in Church after the others had left. She hid behind a pillar.

It was then she observed the bishop as he came and knelt before the altar for half an hour's time. "As far as you knew," she said, "the church was empty. There was no one there for you to convince, no one for you to influence. What was it that made you kneel there so long?"

The bishop then explained to her the Catholic belief that Christ is truly in the tabernacle under the appearance of a small white host. When the bishop finished his explanation of the Blessed Sacrament, the lady said she wanted to take instruction in the Catholic faith — she wanted to become a Catholic.

The promise that Christ made at Capernaum, of being the bread of life, is fulfilled every time Holy Mass is offered upon the altar. His presence in the tabernacle exerts a magnetism that has drawn countless thousands of souls to him. Let us too join these ranks and kneel in adoration before him. God bless you.

# "B"    Nineteenth Sunday of the Year

*John 6:41-51*

Today's gospel for the 19th Sunday of the Year is a continuation of the sixth chapter of the Gospel of St. John in which Christ promises the establishment of the Holy Eucharist. On the day preceding this promise, Christ multiplied the loaves and fishes and miraculously fed five thousand people near Bethsaida on the shore of the Sea of Galilee.

The following day he was addressing them at Capernaum, a village some four miles east of Bethsaida. Our Lord told the crowd assembled around him that he is the bread of life, the bread that comes down from heaven.

But the Jews kept saying, "Is this not Jesus, the son of Joseph? Do we not know his father and mother? How can he say that he came down from heaven?"

Christ heard their questions. "Stop your murmuring," he told them. These questions from the crowd indicated some hostile elements among them, some who doubted or did not believe our Lord. Jesus sensed this immediately. He pointed out to them the necessity of the Father drawing those who came to him. Then Jesus simply repeats his previous statement, "I am the bread of life."

Our Lord then refers back to a previous statement the Jews had made only a few minutes earlier about the manna of Moses in the desert. He said, "Your ancestors ate manna in the desert, but they died." He adds that the bread he is referring to is the bread that comes down from heaven, and when a man eats, he will never die.

He then states: "I am the living bread." Up to this point Jesus had been speaking of the living bread and the bread that came down from heaven but had made no mention of eating this bread. Now he mentions it explicitly — bread "for a man to eat and never die."

Christ continues in this same vein of thought: "If anyone eats this bread he shall live forever." The eating he refers to is a physical eating of the bread; yet the result of this physical eating will be eternal or everlasting life. Thus a spiritual reward, that of everlasting life, will result from a physical eating of this living bread.

From the rules of logic or syllogistic reasoning one can readily conclude that this living bread he is inviting the Jews to eat is himself. But lest there be any doubt in the minds of his hearers, Christ explicitly states that "the bread I will give is my flesh, for the life of the world."

Thus he began to clarify ever more and more just what the Holy Eucharist would be. The significance of the Holy Eucharist which Christ promised us lies in its purpose. He gave us the Eucharist to help us in our fight against evil and to aid us in our struggle to do what is good.

In theology, in the study of the sacraments, there is one Latin rule which predominates over all others. It is *sacramenta propter homines,* which means that sacraments are given for the good of men. The Holy Eucharist is no exception to this rule.

Christ did not bestow the Holy Eucharist upon us as a reward for superior virtue. He did not give his body and blood for only the saintly to receive. Rather, he gave us the Eucharist as a help and a remedy against our sinful nature. He gave us the Eucharist as a means of overcoming the habits of sin.

Christ said on another occasion, "It is not the healthy who need a physician but those who are sick." Our Lord showed us his personal concern for the poor sinner in his forgiveness of Mary Magdalen and the good thief on the cross. For the paralytic on the stretcher, Christ both forgave his sins and gave him health of body.

Thus certainly Christ did give us the Holy Eucharist for the good of men.

In his own words, he gave us the Eucharist for the life of the world. The Eucharist is most truly the life of the world, for it gives the life of sanctifying grace to all who receive it. Supposing the recipient to be already in the state of sanctifying grace either through baptism or the Sacrament of Penance, the Holy Eucharist then is the ordinary means of increasing this sanctifying grace within us.

Grace is simply the dwelling of the Blessed Trinity in our souls. God, our creator and maker of all things, comes to make his home within us. It brings into our hearts and souls the greatest treasure ever.

One of the most prominent converts to the Catholic faith of the last century was Cardinal John Henry Newman of England. At the time of his conversion he was a highly paid leader of the Anglican church. Up to the last hours before his reception into the Catholic Church his friends endeavored to dissuade him from taking the step.

As a last resort they argued, "Think of what you are doing. If you become a Catholic you will forfeit your income of four thousand pounds a year." This amounted to $20,000 in pre-inflation American money.

But to this argument Newman had a brief answer. "What are four thousand pounds when compared to one Holy Communion."

Cardinal Newman had in mind Christ's great promise: "The bread that I will give is my flesh for the life of the world." Let us, too, recall it. Christ's body and blood in the Holy Eucharist can bring us to eternal life. God bless you.

# "B"     Twentieth Sunday of the Year

*John 6:51-58*

In the gospel of St. John read at today's Mass, our Lord continues his discourse at Capernaum, in which he promised the Holy Eucharist to the Jewish people. The gospels of the two previous Sundays contained earlier parts of the discourse. Christ said directly, "I myself am the living bread come down from heaven." He affirmed positively what this living bread consisted of, namely, of himself.

Our Lord promised: "If anyone eats this bread he shall live forever. . . ." He states that the eating of the living bread, namely his body, will bring about a spiritual effect, namely eternal life. St. Ignatius of Antioch, writing some ten years after St. John wrote his gospel, called it "the medicine of immortality, the antidote for death."

But once again as they had done a few times during our Lord's discourse, the Jews interrupted him with a question. They said to one another, "How can this man give us his flesh to eat?"

Jesus heard their question and gave them an immediate answer. He answered them in the tone of a threat or punishment: "Let me solemnly assure you, if you do not eat the flesh of the Son of Man and drink his blood, you have no life in you." Thus our Lord made the reception of the Eucharist, the eating of his flesh and the drinking of his blood, a necessary condition for spiritual life; that is, the life of grace in one's soul.

He concluded this threat or promise with the positive condition of receiving the Eucharist, "He who feeds on my flesh and drinks my blood has life eternal, and I will raise him up on the last day."

Theologians have long debated and discussed this necessity. Certainly for an infant, who has not reached the use of reason and who does not know the meaning of the Eucharist, the sacrament is not necessary to be saved. But for adults, the reception of the Holy Eucharist is morally necessary under ordinary circumstances. No adult can long sustain his spiritual or supernatural life if he willfully neglects to receive Holy Communion. Thus every grown, adult Catholic has a moral obligation to receive the Holy Eucharist, at least once a year.

Christ continued, "For my flesh is real food and my blood real drink." By real food and drink Christ meant true food and drink. He means that they had the physical qualities of food and drink . . . that the physical appearance of the Eucharist would be no different than that of any other food. The Eucharist today has the physical appearance of bread and wine.

Christ concludes this particular part of gospel narrative with a pledge that "the man who feeds on this bread shall live forever." Again our Lord promises eternal life, that is, eternal happiness in heaven, as a reward for faithfully and worthily receiving the Holy Eucharist, eating his body and drinking his blood.

In considering Christ's command to eat his flesh and drink his blood, the question has often been asked, how often should we obey this command? How often should one receive the Holy Eucharist? If we look back in the Acts of the Apostles we find that the faithful at Jerusalem received Christ's body and blood every day.

In the early centuries of the Church the faithful were expected to communicate each and every time the Eucharist, or Mass, was celebrated. On some occasions they received even oftener, as the Eucharist was sometimes carried away to their homes where they communicated privately outside of Mass.

This practice of frequent or daily communion continued in the Church up until about the time of Charlemagne — about the year 800. But then a change occurred. People began to receive the Holy Eucharist less frequently.

Looking back into the later middle ages, we have the teachings of Jansen and Arnould, who taught that one should only receive Holy Communion after long and severe penances. They discouraged frequent reception of the Eucharist. But the Church in the course of time has labeled the teachings of these men as false and heretical.

Christ called the Eucharist our food and drink. But food and drink are needed for the body daily. If a person goes without food and drink for more than a day his energy neatly decreases. Thus through this comparison of Christ, we can say that the Eucharist is needed at frequent intervals.

On December 20th, 1905, Pope Pius X issued an encyclical on the subject. He wrote, "Frequent Communion should be open to all the faithful. No one who is in the state of grace and who approaches the holy table with a right and devout intention, can be lawfully hindered therefrom."

Pope Pius explained what he meant by right intention . . . one should not receive out of routine or vainglory or human respect, but for the purpose of pleasing God or being more closely united with him by charity and seek the divine remedy for weakness and defects.

Pope Pius X further instructed parish priests and confessors frequently and with great zeal to exhort the faithful to this devout and salutary practice. A year later he granted a plenary indulgence to anyone who would receive Holy Communion five times a week. In 1907 he wrote, "Frequent Communion is the shortest way to secure the salvation of every individual man as well as that of society."

Church law only obliges Catholics to receive Holy Communion once during the Easter season; that is, from the first Sunday of Lent to Trinity Sunday. Yet it is clearly the mind of the Church that Catholics should receive Holy Communion much more frequently, even daily.

The latest official decree on the practice of frequent Communion is that of the Second Vatican Council. The Constitution on the Sacred Liturgy of Vatican II states: "Hearty endorsement is given to that closer form of participation in the Mass whereby the faithful, after the priest's Communion, receive the Lord's body under elements consecrated at that very sacrifice." Thus Vatican II gives strong endorsement to the practice of frequent or daily Communion.

But in encouraging frequent and daily Holy Communion one can do no better than to repeat the invitation of Christ himself, "He who feeds on my flesh and drinks my blood has life eternal, and I will raise him up on the last day." God bless you.

# "B" Twenty-first Sunday of the Year

*John 6:60-69*

The gospel read at today's Mass is taken from a sermon preached by our Lord at the synagogue at Capernaum. Among those present who heard this sermon were the Apostles and many disciples of Jesus, along with other Jews who were not his followers. At this point in our Lord's public life, he had already performed many miracles. He had also preached to them in parables about the kingdom of heaven.

But now the time had arrived when our Lord made a stern test of the faith of his followers. He promised to give them his body to eat and his blood to drink. Christ demanded an act of faith without reserve from his disciples in these words. He demanded, if they were capable of understanding anything at all about his Church, that they also accept this teaching.

The Apostles, from their existing knowledge of Christ, knew certainly that he was not suggesting cannibalism to them. Neither did they understand in what manner this would come true, as Christ had not explained it. But what Christ was demanding from them was an act of faith without reserve, that in some miraculous way his words would come true and they would actually eat his flesh and drink his blood. After making this statement Christ asked explicitly: "Does this try your faith?"

Then he went on to add, "Only the spirit gives life, the flesh is of no avail." The meaning of the word "spirit" here, according to St. Cyril and other Scripture scholars, means the divinity of Christ; the manner in which Christ gives life to us is through our spirit or soul and not through our flesh. The life Christ referred to was the life of sanctifying grace in our souls, although this the Apostles did not clearly understand at the time.

But Christ through his divine knowledge knew, even as he was speaking, not only that some of his disciples did not understand him, but that they also did not believe him. Their faith was not strong enough to accept his teachings. And St. John in his gospel tells us: "They walked no more with him." They began one by one to leave the synagogue and drift away and return to their former way of life.

The fault in their leaving Christ was not in Christ himself or his teaching or preparation of them. The fault was in the manner they chose to use their gift of free will. Christ presented them with a truth they could not fully understand — how he could give them his body to eat and his blood to drink — and faith was demanded of those who heard it. But faith was lacking in those who walked away.

When these disciples began to leave, Christ did not alter his statement in any way. Neither did he try to prevent their leaving. In fact, their departure left a gap, a void in the ranks of his disciples. What Christ did at this time was to test the faith of those remaining a little more. Jesus turned to them and said, "Would you also go away?"

To answer this question Simon Peter stepped forward and assumed his role as leader of the Apostles in answering Christ. He responded, "Lord, to whom should we go? You have the words of eternal life." Peter had not yet been chosen by Christ to be the head of the Apostles, but he was their natural leader and spokesman. His words are a beautiful expression of faith. Peter felt certain that he was speaking for the other Apostles in responding as he did.

Our Lord was demanding a clear-cut decision from those closest to him. This he received by Peter's reassurance. Christ would strengthen the faith of his Apostles through the gift of grace. He would give them added gifts and added graces. He would test their faith with new trials in future times, culminating in seeing their leader crucified. But Christ was assured of their good faith, their belief in his teaching.

Down through the centuries the followers of Christ would be called upon to profess their faith at various times. For example, in Japan during the 16th and 17th centuries a persecution of the Church broke out. Many Catholics openly professed their faith and were tortured for it and put to death.

But one particular Japanese Christian lacked faith strong enough to endure persecution. Under torture he renounced his faith and his life was spared and he was given freedom to live. But when he did so, a Jesuit missionary priest, Father Mastrilli, bravely came forth from the crowd that had been watching him. He asked if he might take the prisoner's place. He acknowledged that he was a Catholic priest. The Japanese officials arrested him immediately and began an excruciating ordeal of sixty hours of torture, finally executing him by cutting off his head.

The strong faith of this priest was an inspiration to all. It even inspired the apostate who had denied his faith under torture. Many years later as an old man he came back to face the government. He acknowledged that he had sinned against God in denying his faith. He said he had made a grave mistake and that he had once again embraced the Catholic faith. At the age of 80 he was put to death for his faith.

Let us pray that when the test of persecution comes to us, our faith will not be wanting . . . that it will be strong as that of Father Mastrilli . . . that it will resemble the faith of St. Peter and the Apostles. Let us acknowledge the truth of the words of Christ, who promises his body to eat and his blood to drink in the Holy Eucharist. Faith in the Eucharist and faith in Christ can bring us to eternal salvation. God bless you.

# "B"     Twenty-second Sunday of the Year

*Mark 7:1-8,14-15,21-23*

The Pharisees had developed a hostility toward our blessed Lord. They were awaiting an opportunity to attack him. On this occasion mentioned by St. Mark in today's gospel, when his Apostles sat down to eat with unwashed hands, they thought they had found one.

The Jews had a ritual for washing one's hands before eating that dated back to the time of King Solomon. Water had to be poured twice over each hand. Also prescribed were the amount of water that was to be used and how far up on the wrist or arm the hand was to be washed.

In Galilee, where the Apostles came from, there was a shortage of fresh water, and these ritualistic practices were generally overlooked. But the Pharisees of Jerusalem did follow them very closely. It was evidently a group of Pharisees from Judea or the vicinity of Jerusalem who made this criticism of the Apostles.

Our Lord answered them sharply: "You hypocrites! It was a true prophecy Isaiah made of you writing as he did, 'This people does me honor with its lips, but its heart is far from me.' " Our Lord went on to say that they leave God's commandments on the side while holding up as doctrine the traditions of men.

Our Lord took this opportunity to enlarge upon this subject. He called the multitude to him and said to them, "Listen to me, all of you, and grasp this: It is not what enters into the mouth that defiles a man; it is what comes out of the mouth that defiles him."

Christ was enunciating a new doctrine. He was upsetting the entire concept of defilement and wrongness that had been built up in the Jewish religion for some four thousand years. He was tearing down the entire structure of ritualistic purifications.

When questioned on this by his Apostles, he explained it further: "For it is from within, from the hearts of men, that their wicked designs come, their sins of adultery, fornication, envy, blasphemy, pride and folly. All these evils come from within, and it is these which make a man unclean."

Christ was giving forth a whole new moral doctrine. He was making the heart the seat of moral life. He was giving the reasoning behind the Ten Commandments which God gave to Moses long ago on Mount Sinai. He was setting forth the Christian concept of sin.

It is sin that defiles a man. Sin is any willful word, deed or omission contrary to the law of God. Sin must proceed from one's will. Sin occurs when one knowingly and willingly does something wrong.

The Pharisees left our Lord in a shocked and angry state. They had received a most unexpected answer. Christ had rejected their entire system of ritualistic purification and cleanliness. He had set forth new moral principles that had no parallel. For this they were not prepared. Neither the other Jews nor the Apostles fully understood it.

In fact, it was not until years later that the full implication of Christ's statement was grasped. This occurred years after our Lord's ascension when the Church was confronted with the question whether Gentile converts were required to observe Jewish dietary regulations.

Only by restudying Christ's words and applying them to this new situation did their true meaning come forth. Then the Apostles and the young Church began to grasp the full meaning and scope of what Christ had to say on this occasion.

In fact, not just this passage, but all of Christ's words in Holy Scripture are filled with deep and hidden meanings. It requires constant and repetitious study by even the greatest minds to bring forth these new meanings. New applications of these eternal truths are continually occurring.

Let us, therefore, become aware of the meaning of this teaching of Christ. Sin and defilement come from within a man — from his heart and mind. It is the thought and intention behind our actions that will bring us either to eternal punishment or on the contrary, we hope, to eternal reward. God bless you.

# "B"  Twenty-third Sunday of the Year

*Mark 7:31-37*

In today's gospel St. Mark tells us that our Lord was returning to the Sea of Galilee by way of Decapolis. A man was brought to him who was both deaf and dumb. Our Lord took this man apart from the crowd and put his fingers into the man's ears, and spitting, touched his tongue and said, "Ephphatha" which means "Be opened." Immediately the man could hear and speak correctly.

This miracle of Christ is commemorated by the priest in the ceremonies of the Sacrament of Baptism. There the priest makes the sign of the cross on the ears and mouth of the child and repeats the words of Christ.

In performing these many miracles upon earth, Christ did them for a spiritual reason. The baptism ritual brings this out in a beautiful way. It first gives one the gift of grace. It brings one spiritual life and opens one's mind to spiritual things.

God's main purpose in creating our senses was that we should use them to give honor and glory to God. He gave us the gift of speech so that we might praise God and sing his glory. This was exactly what the dumb man in the gospel did when he regained his power of speech; he gave glory to God.

God gave us our gift of hearing that we might hear his praises. He gave us sight that we might see his glory through creation and read what is pleasing to him. We cannot use our senses in any greater way than this.

A few years ago Senator Edward Kennedy was asked to give the commencement address at a school for the deaf. As he did so, one of the graduates stood beside him and read his lips. He conveyed his thoughts to the assembly and graduating class by sign language.

Senator Kennedy told the class that America is still a land of opportunity. He said that their graduating class proved this point — that despite their natural handicap of deafness, they have learned a way to communicate with each other. By using other senses in a special way, lip reading and sign language, they have acquired a knowledge of the things other men learn in natural ways. They have learned how to make their way in the world and take their place in society.

In a similar sense there are many people today who are spiritually deaf and dumb. They are deaf to the pleadings of grace. They refuse to hear the promptings of their guardian angel as to what is right and wrong. They are dumb in the practice of justice and charity in their lives.

They are deaf to the fact that the happiness of heaven is everlasting, for they exchange it for a few moments of passing pleasure. They are blind to spiritual values. They are like Esau, who exchanged his birthright for a bowl of porridge.

A beautiful story of spiritual awareness is told of Cardinal Faulhaber, the renowned Archbishop of Munich. One day he was visiting a home for blind soldiers. He walked through the home and cheered them up. He encouraged them and blessed them. As he came to one blind soldier, he heard him praying, "Lord, I beg you not to take away from me the light of my eyes, but if it is your will, at least leave me the light of my mind, but if it is your will that I be deprived of that, leave me at least the light of my faith."

The cardinal stopped and asked the soldier where he had learned such a beautiful prayer. The man replied he had learned it as a child and had never forgotten it. Certainly the loss of one's sight is a tragic affliction, but the loss of one's faith is a greater one.

Our sentiments should be like those of the blind soldier. If God has given us the gifts of hearing, speech and sight, let us thank God for them. Let us show our gratitude by using these gifts in his honor and praise. Let us imitate the deaf and dumb man Christ cured as mentioned in today's gospel. Let us lift up our voice in praise of God. God bless you.


# "B"     Twenty-fourth Sunday of the Year

*Mark 8:27-35*

The gospel of St. Mark read at today's Mass tells us that Christ and his Apostles had traveled north of the Sea of Galilee to the vicinity of Caesarea Philippi. In this rural pagan district Christ was away from the malicious intrigues and demands of the Pharisees. He could freely discuss with his Apostles the fundamental question of his own identity and his mission.

Our Lord asked his disciples directly, "Who do people say that I am?" Questioned together the Apostles would not naturally have the same answer to give. Among the responses he received were John the Baptizer, Elijah and one of the prophets. Some identified Jesus with the great prophets of the Old Testament. Others, who did not identify him with any particular prophet of the Old Testament, nevertheless recognized him to be a prophet himself and a forerunner of the Messiah. Yet none of them identified Christ as the Messiah himself.

Then after receiving these answers Christ directly asked the disciples themselves who they thought Christ to be. St. Peter answered directly, "You are the Messiah." Still this was not the first time that Christ had been identified as the Messiah here on earth. The demoniacs, those from whom Christ had cast devils, had called him the Son of God. So also had Nathaniel and the disciples whom Christ had saved from the storm at sea called him the Messiah. But Peter's confession is important because this is the first time Christ manifested his true identity to all his Apostles as a group. The gospel account of this incident read at today's Mass is that of St. Mark. But in addition to his account, St. Matthew and St. Luke also speak of the same incident. St. Matthew makes one interesting addition to his account at this point.

Christ turns to Peter and says, "Blessed are you, Simon bar-Jonah, because flesh and blood have not revealed this to you, but my Father, who is in heaven."

Our Lord reveals that Peter's knowledge of his identity was directly given him by God the Father in heaven.

One reason, perhaps, why St. Mark fails to mention this detail in his gospel is that St. Mark was not one of the Twelve Apostles. He was a close friend of St. Peter and one of his companions. St. Mark's gospel is largely the story of Christ's life as seen through St. Peter's eyes and told by him to Mark. Perhaps St. Peter in his humility did not choose to reveal this information about himself to Mark.

But then Christ began to teach them that the Messiah had to suffer and die at the hands of the Jewish leaders. This was to correct a false idea that the Apostles as well as most other Jews had formed concerning the Messiah — that he was to be a temporal ruler and enjoy a triumphal reign on earth.

Hence Christ's image as a suffering Messiah was something strange and foreign to their thoughts. Christ revealed that three distinct groups, the elders, the chief priests and the scribes would altogether reject him. Christ revealed that he must suffer and die, but then on the third day he would rise again. Here is Christ's first prophecy of his resurrection. But at the time the Apostles were so stunned by the idea of Christ's suffering and dying that it meant nothing to them.

Peter then drew our Lord aside from the others and began to remonstrate with him. But our Lord reprimanded him, "Get out of sight, you satan! You are not judging by God's standards but by man's."

By the term Satan, Christ meant that it was Satan, the devil, who was suggesting to St. Peter that Christ could not suffer. Peter willingly admitted that Christ was divine but rejected the idea that Christ could suffer. Peter would have only a half-Christ. This false idea Christ immediately corrected.

St. Peter's two answers to Christ on this occasion showed him to be the natural spokesman and leader of the Twelve Apostles. Hence Christ's selection of Peter as the leader of the Apostles and Pope or head of his Church was a natural choice.

Christ then taught the Apostles a truth he would reiterate on other occasions: "If a man wishes to come after me, he must deny his very self, take up his cross, and follow in my steps."

Christ spoke of the cross, the manner in which he would die. The cross had a special meaning to the Jews, a distasteful one. Crucifixion was the ordinary means of criminal execution in ancient times. The Romans, who then ruled Palestine, used it more frequently than any other means for putting a man to death. The Roman general Varus had ordered two thousand Jews to be crucified at one time. Later still, in the year 70 A.D., when Titus destroyed the city of Jerusalem he had 4,000 Jews crucified at one time. In fact, he encountered a shortage of wood. He could not find enough wood to make all the crosses he desired.

Hence Christ held out the cross, a symbol of suffering and death, as a Christian symbol. He showed the cross to be the reason for his coming. He showed that the plan of his divine Father was that he should carry a cross and die upon it. He showed further that anyone who would be his disciple must be willing to carry a cross.

Suffering would be the way of life of Christians and the cross their trademark. Then Christ concluded his remarks: "Whoever would save his life will lose it, but whoever loses his life for my sake will save it."

Christ made a play of words upon the two kinds of life, one's physical biological life here on earth, and one's spiritual, eternal life hereafter. If one were to spend his physical life here on earth in the pursuit of pleasure, then he would lose his eternal life hereafter. He would be condemned to hell to suffer rather than enjoy the happiness of heaven.

On the other hand, one who would lose his life on earth — walk in the footsteps of Christ and willingly carry a cross — would save his eternal life. He would be rewarded with an eternity of happiness in heaven. Hence, let us learn through these words of Christ that suffering is our lot. To save our souls we must be willing to carry our cross in this life, no matter how large or small it will be. For only in following in the footsteps of Christ in this life can we pass through the doors leading to eternal happiness. God bless you.

# "B"     Twenty-fifth Sunday of the Year

*Mark 9:30-37*

In the Gospel of St. Mark read at today's Mass, our Lord is bringing his ministry in Galilee to an end. He had taken his disciples up on a mountain, where he was instructing them privately. Even upon coming down from the mountain he was trying to keep his whereabouts a secret. He and his Apostles were preparing to make their final journey to Jerusalem together to celebrate the Pasch.

Our Lord prophesied, "The Son of Man is going to be delivered into the hands of men who will put him to death; three days after his death he will rise." Twice before Christ had prophesied his suffering and death. But then on this occasion also, the Apostles failed to realize the meaning of what he was saying. Still they were too afraid to ask him about it.

Then occurred an incident of which the Apostles were not too proud. They fell to quarreling or bickering among themselves. This is something one might expect to find in a large household of children but not among Christ's

Apostles. Nor was this the first time that something like this had occurred. On two occasions the Apostles fell to quarreling or bickering among themselves. The object of their quarrel was who was the most important among them.

Our Lord ended this squabble in a hurry. He sat down along the roadside and called his Apostles around him. He said: "If anyone wishes to rank first, he must remain the last one of all. . . ." He quickly deflated their pride and their pettiness by stressing the importance of the virtue of humility.

There happened at this time to be a small child nearby. Jesus took the child in his arms and placed him in their midst. He then proceeded to teach them a lesson in humility, which if they could not learn alone from the God-man, they could understand from the example of a child. Christ said, "Whoever welcomes a child such as this for my sake welcomes me. And whoever welcomes me welcomes, not me, but him who sent me."

A child, like a grown man, has his faults and may be said to carry within himself the germ of vices which may one day grow into grave sins. But a child possesses a wealth of lovable qualities which are frequently wanting in the adult. A child is simple and docile. He is free from ambition and pretense. He is eager to learn and quick to believe. It was of qualities such as these that Christ was thinking when he took a small child in their midst. And especially a child is humble; he is not consumed by pride.

A humble person is one who acknowledges his own nothingness, his dependence upon God in all things, and who acts according to his convictions. A humble person is one who is keenly aware of the great power and majesty and wisdom of almighty God. And in comparison he is aware of the transitory nature of all earthly things.

A humble person is aware of the insignificance of any individual man when compared to the greatness of almighty God. He knows that the greatest display of power or authority on this earth fades away into nothingness when compared to the limitless power of almighty God. He knows that the greatest wealth and treasure on earth are only infinitely small pieces of God's creation. He knows that the greatest of human knowledge looks like ignorance when compared to the infinite wisdom of almighty God.

And because the humble man is aware of these truths, he does not seek honor for himself. The humble man is not covetous of the goods of others. The humble man is not vain in any knowledge he may acquire. In fact, knowing the worthlessness of worldly honors, the humble man seeks to avoid them.

God loves a humble person. The reason why humility is so highly prized in the sight of God is that humility is akin to truth. Truly all the honors and riches of this world are as nothing when compared to the greatness and power of almighty God.

Christ gave us in himself the outstanding example of humility. He who was the Second Person of the Blessed Trinity and true God humbled himself to come to earth and take on the body of man. He chose deliberately to be born in the poorest of circumstances, in a stable where animals fed. He chose to be raised in the household of Joseph, a poor hard-working carpenter.

When Christ began his public life he chose as his Apostles eleven fishermen, struggling for a living on the Sea of Galilee, and one tax collector. When asked, on one occasion in his public life of preaching, where he lived, he said, "Come and see." During the time of his public life he had no home, he had no bed whereon to lay his head. In this he fulfilled a prophecy made concerning the Messiah centuries before.

As Christ chose the wood of a manger on which to lie in birth; he chose the hard wood of a cross on which to lie in death. Christ chose to enter, to live in and to leave this world without any of its possessions; yet he was the creator of all things. On Holy Thursday, the night of the Last Supper, when he gave us the great sacrament of the Eucharist, the night before his death, he spent his time washing his Apostles' feet. Truly he could say, "Learn of me because I am meek and humble of heart."

Mary, our Blessed Mother, is an outstanding example of humility. In her youth she was too humble to share the dream of all Jewish women, to become the mother of the Messiah. Instead she sought to please God by taking upon herself the vow of virginity. But God saw and recognized her humility by choosing her above all others to be his own Mother.

One saint noted for his humility was St. Anthony of Padua. St. Anthony was a nobleman; his family was among the first of Portugal. Under ordinary circumstances, St. Anthony would succeed his father in serving the throne of that country, but instead he wished to devote his life to serving God. His parents sought for him an appointment as a canon of the cathedral in Lisbon. But he declined this position of honor in the Church.

Instead St. Anthony decided to go to Africa to help convert the Moors, but poor health forced him to return home. But on his return trip he was shipwrecked on the coast of Sicily. In Sicily he sought admission to the Franciscan order and was accepted. He worked as a lay brother in the kitchen of the monastery there, carefully concealing his royal background and education.

On one occasion he was ordered to speak to the monks in the chapel when the scheduled preacher was taken ill. His eloquence astounded all. St. Anthony was then ordered by St. Francis to study for the priesthood. As an ordained priest he was first assigned to teach theology. He later devoted himself to the duties of a missionary preacher. He was in demand everywhere. He won many converts to the faith. He also performed many miracles. His holiness became well known. But despite it all he remained a very humble person.

In our own lives let us imitate the humility of this saint of God. Let us imitate the humility of our Blessed Mother and of Christ himself. As Christ has said, "He who humbles himself shall be exalted." God bless you.

# "B"     Twenty-sixth Sunday of the Year

*Mark 9:38-48*

The second book of Maccabees tells us that when King Antiochus of Syria had conquered Jerusalem he resolved to lead all the Jews away from the worship of the true God. He required them to eat pork meat, which was forbidden by Jewish Law. But this was something Eleazar, an elderly scribe, refused to do. King Antiochus had Eleazar arrested and threatened him with death unless he ate the pork meat.

Eleazar's friends came to him with a plan — they would secretly substitute other meat for the pork and Eleazar would eat it, pretending it was pork. But Eleazar refused to do this. He said there were many young people who would be deceived and think he had become a pagan. Because of his refusal to eat pork, Eleazar was tortured and eventually killed. He said that although he might escape the punishment of man by this trickery, he could not escape the punishment of God.

Eleazar, my dear friends, was afraid of giving bad example, or what we commonly call scandal. His example should be an inspiration for us all to follow.

Scandal is a sin against the Fifth Commandment. The Fifth Commandment states, "You shall not kill." It forbids us to kill or injure another. But there are many ways of injuring another. We may injure another's soul as well as his body. And this is exactly what scandal does; it injures another's soul.

It can be given either by word, by action, or omission. The person who would use profanity in front of a child would give scandal by word. An example of scandal by omission would be missing Mass on Sunday when others know it.

Scandal is a serious sin because it robs almighty God of souls he created for himself — souls he created and intended to enter the kingdom of heaven. Scandal counteracts Christ's redemption and death upon the cross.

Scandal is a great injury to the person to whom it is given. It robs one of his most precious gift, that of sanctifying grace. It is more serious in a sense than seriously harming a person physically. For if one is robbed of his life, he still may save his soul. But if one is robbed of sanctifying grace and dies in that state, he will suffer for all eternity in hell.

Consider, temptation is the work of the devil in this world. Because of his misery and suffering in hell, he tries to induce others to commit sin and be forced to suffer with him. But in giving scandal and leading others into sin, one is doing the work of the devil himself. Consider too that the harm done by scandal may long outlast a person; it may endure long after one is dead.

Scandal is a sin that is most hateful in the sight of God. Christ said, "He who scandalizes one of these little ones that believe in me, it were better for him that a millstone should be hung about his neck and that he be drowned in the depths of the sea."

Scandal is a grave sin, one deserving of severe punishment. Its great evil is clearly brought out by Christ when he says in today's gospel, "It would be better if anyone who leads astray one of these simple believers were to be plunged in the sea with a great millstone fastened around his neck."

The great millstone used by the Jews for grinding grain was so large that a donkey or beast of burden had to turn it; it was too heavy for an ordinary man to turn. The great weight and size of such a stone would surely cause one to drown. Drowning was a means of capital punishment inflicted on rare occasions by the ancient Romans and Jews for only the worst of crimes. It was considered so loathsome or dreadful because the body of the deceased was not available for burial thereafter.

Christ continued to speak on the subject of giving scandal, "If your hand is your difficulty, cut it off! Better for you to enter life maimed than to keep both hands and enter Gehenna with its unquenchable fire." Gehenna was a valley to the south of Jerusalem, which was used as the city dump. There the carcasses of dead animals were burned and one could always find crackling fires there giving off nauseating odors. The Jews frequently compared the fires of Gehenna to the eternal fires of hell.

Christ in speaking of cutting off one's hand or foot or gouging out an eye was not advocating mutilation of one's body. Willful mutilation would be a serious sin. Christ mentions them only in a figure of speech to show that the sin of scandal is far worse then the physical evil of mutilation. Scandal is such a heinous sin that there is no torment in this life severe enough to punish it.

Scandal is the opposite of good example. As scandal is such a despicable sin, so good example can be a tremendous force for good. Giving good example to children can be a most effective way of teaching them to do good and leading them along the road to salvation.

There is a serious obligation on parents and all in a position of authority to give good example to all under their care. Good example fosters the practice of virtue. It teaches a lesson so deep in meaning that thousands of words cannot express it. Good example is the easiest and most effective way of teaching virtuous habits.

Christ said, "Any man who gives you a drink of water because you belong to Christ will not go without his reward." Some years ago in Africa, a group of native porters entered a village on a hot summer day. Because they were of a different tribe, custom forbade offering them a drink of water. But a few children who had studied this Scripture passage, carried out a bucket of water to them. They said they were doing it in the name of Christ.

Indeed the good example they gave in performing this one small act of kindness will earn them an eternal reward. Let us resolve that the example we give will always be good. God bless you.

# "B" Twenty-seventh Sunday of the Year

*Mark 10:2-16*

Weddings at the time of our Lord were occasions of great celebration, greater than they are today. A wedding celebration lasted three or four days, and many were invited to it. Actually it should not surprise us that Christ chose to perform his first public miracle at a marriage feast.

Marriage was established by God as the basis of our society. It is a most important institution. God made marriage for two purposes — to propagate the human race and to provide for the mutual help and love of husband and wife.

Christ in coming to earth did a great deal for marriage. He eradicated several abuses concerning marriage. The story related in today's gospel brings this out clearly. The Pharisees asked Christ if divorce were permissible, pointing out that Moses had permitted it. Christ answered that Moses had permitted this because of the stubbornness of their hearts.

He then added, "At the beginning of creation God made them male and female; for this reason a man shall leave his father and mother and the two shall become as one. They are no longer two but one flesh. Therefore let no man separate what God has joined."

God in instituting marriage laid down certain rules to follow. One such rule is the indissolubility of marriage — that marriage last until death. In the wedding ceremony the bride and groom promise to take each other in good times and in bad, in sickness and in health all the days of their life. Thus the marriage bond binds them together as long as they both live.

This Christian view of the indissolubility of marriage was respected from the foundation of the Church down to the sixteenth century. It was incorporated into the civil law of the Western world. It was respected by all countries alike. But in the sixteenth century there occurred an incident which did great harm to the indissolubility of marriage. King Henry VIII of England sought to have his marriage to Catherine of Aragon annulled by the Catholic Church. The Church's answer to Henry was the same answer that would have been given to any man, be he king or beggar, "Let no man separate what God has joined."

But Henry would not abide by the Church's decision. He attempted marriage outside of the Church and led a whole nation astray. Henry failed to find happiness; he attempted marriage many times. But from his deed, divorce and its evil consequences entered English law. From English law, it was carried across the Atlantic and became a part of American law.

Divorce is something which civil law has no right to grant. Marriage was made by God as a permanent and indissoluble bond. Breaking God's law in this regard can only lead to misery and unhappiness. Great suffering is brought to family life through the divorce court.

Christ did a great thing for marriage in reasserting its indissolubility. But he helped it in other ways too; he raised it to the dignity of a sacrament. From our catechism we know that sacraments are signs instituted by Christ to give grace. Matrimony does exactly this. It gives sanctifying grace to the man and woman who receive it worthily.

In addition it gives a special sacramental grace to the couple to help them fulfill their duties as husband and wife, as father and mother. Many times in life married couples meet with difficulty. These special sacramental graces are available at all times throughout their married life for them to call upon and use.

Marriage sanctifies the love of husband and wife for each other. St. Paul compares this love of husband and wife to the supernatural union of Christ and his Church. He said, "Husbands, love your wives, as Christ loved the church. . . . He who loves his wife loves himself. Observe that no one ever hates his own flesh; no, he nourishes it and takes care of it as Christ cares for the church — for we are members of his body."

Let us be grateful to our Lord for what he did for married life — for making it a sacrament and a means of grace, for restoring it to its original and indissoluble state. Marriage is the state of life in which the large majority of men and women can save their souls. God bless you.

# "B"     Twenty-eighth Sunday of the Year

*Mark: 10:17-30*

In the gospel read at today's Mass, St. Mark tells us how a young man approached our Lord and asked him what he must do to possess eternal life. Our Lord responded that he must keep the commandments — he should not commit adultery, not murder, or steal or bear false witness against any man. He should not wrong his neighbor and should honor his father and mother. The young man replied that he kept all these commandments from his childhood.

The gospel tells us that Jesus fastened his gaze upon him and conceived a love for him and then gave him the greatest gift he can give to any man — he gave him a vocation to follow him. He said to go sell what he had, give it to the poor and come back and follow him.

But this young man's face fell, and he went away sorrowing, for he had great possessions. He refused a vocation to the priesthood, a vocation to follow Christ. The reason he refused it was wealth and earthly possessions. The treasure of this world meant more to him than a call to follow Christ.

Christ gave the call to follow him to others. We should be grateful to God that several accepted this call. Christ called a group of fishermen around the Sea of Galilee, and they accepted. They became the Twelve Apostles.

In the Old Testament God chose Aaron to take care of all things that pertain to the service of the altar. This duty was a serious one. When the sons of Levi sought to usurp this office they were warned by God not to do so under pain of death. When King Uzziah tried to perform the priestly functions, he was stricken with leprosy.

But as the priesthood of the Old Testament was a great honor which God conferred upon men, so the priesthood of the New Testament is a greater honor still. Christ said to St. Peter, "I will give you the keys of the kingdom of heaven. Whatever you shall bind on earth shall be bound also in heaven. Whatever you shall loose on earth shall be loosed also in heaven." Christ gave his Apostles the power to cleanse sins from the souls of men.

He gave them, too, the power to baptize — to remove original sin from men's souls. He gave them the power to bless and to sanctify. He gave them the power to change bread and wine into his body and blood. The power to offer the Holy Sacrifice of the Mass.

The priesthood is the greatest honor God has conferred upon the human race. It is an honor he gave neither to angels nor archangels. Not one of them can ascend the altar each day and call down God from heaven. Not one of them has the power to bind and loose the sins of man. Not one of them is privileged to hold the Christ Child in his hands each morning — no, not even the greatest Seraph.

But Christ, in bestowing such power and honor upon the priesthood, did not promise his priests a life of ease and luxury. On the contrary, he promised them suffering. In his parting message to his Apostles immediately before his passion and death, he said, "They will forbid you in the synagogues; indeed the time is coming when whoever kills you will think he is doing a service to God."

One might expect his departing message to his Apostles to be one of success and happiness, but instead it was a promise of persecution and death.

The Apostles realized the truth and reality in our Savior's words. They returned to Jerusalem after the Ascension full of fear and anxiety. They hid in the upper room in Jerusalem for the next nine days.

Then on Pentecost Sunday the Holy Spirit came down upon the Apostles in the form of fiery tongues. A great change took place in their hearts. They went forth fearlessly and bravely to preach the gospel.

Christ's prophecy of persecution and death remained true after Pentecost as it was before. The change was in the Apostles themselves. No longer did they fear suffering and death. Consider the deaths they met:

St. Matthew — martyred in Ethiopia.

St. Mark — dragged through the streets of Alexandria until he was dead.

St. Luke — hanged on an olive tree in Greece.

St. James the Less — thrown from the pinnacle of the temple in Jerusalem.

St. Philip — hanged from a pillar in Hierapolis in Phrygia.

St. Bartholomew — flayed alive and scourged.

St. Andrew — crucified.

St. Thomas — pierced with a lance.

St. Simon — crucified in Persia.

St. Matthias — stoned to death.

St. Peter — crucified upside down in Rome

St. Paul — five times given forty lashes less one; thrice scourged with rods; three times shipwrecked, once adrift for a day and a night; once stoned; suffered perils from robbers, floods and a dozen more dangers. When arrested in Jerusalem, he tried every means to escape death, even appealing to Rome because of his Roman citizenship; was sent to Rome and there, after a long time in prison, was beheaded.

St. John alone was not martyred — but this was not his fault. He was boiled in oil, but God miraculously saved his life. He later wrote a gospel.

The Church for the first two and a half centuries suffered the greatest possible persecution. The Roman Empire, using the Roman army, the world's greatest known force, utterly failed to wipe out a religion established by Christ using twelve uneducated fishermen. The survival and growth of the Church is unexplainable in any natural sense.

But the persecutors of the Church forget one thing — that their persecution will never succeed. While Christ promised his followers that they would be persecuted, he likewise promised them ultimate triumph: "Behold, I will be with you all days even to the end of the world."

Consider the fate of those who have persecuted the Church:

Pontius Pilate — exiled to France, took his own life.

King Herod, who killed St. James — eaten by worms.

Nero, who martyred Sts. Peter and Paul in Rome — stabbed by a slave.

Julian the Apostate — struck down in the field of battle by a lance; said in his last words, "Galilean, you have conquered."

Napoleon, who imprisoned Pope Pius VII for five years — was imprisoned on St. Helena for the last seven years of his life.

It has been said, "The blood of martyrs is the seed of Christians." The more the Church has been persecuted, the more it has grown.

Eleven thousand priests were martyred in Spain in Communist persecutions and in the Spanish civil war. But today Spain is one of the strongest Catholic countries in the world. Persecutions of the Church in Poland, China and Hungary have only confirmed the faith of these conquered peoples.

Christ sends suffering to those he loves. Christ loves his priests and followers. Consequently, he has sent them suffering. Even his Blessed Mother was no exception to this rule. A sword of seven sorrows pierced her heart.

Christ said, "He who does not take up his cross and follow me is not worthy of me. . . . He who loses his life for my sake shall find it. . . . Blessed are they who suffer persecution for justice's sake, for theirs is the kingdom of heaven."

Let us not refuse to follow Christ as did the young man in today's gospel. But wherever his cross leads, let us willingly follow it. God bless you.

# "B"    Twenty-ninth Sunday of the Year

*Mark 10:35-45*

In the Gospel of St. Mark read at today's Mass our Lord is leading his Apostles out of Galilee toward Jerusalem. His journey there was to be his last, for the Roman governor and Jewish leaders would put him to death on Good Friday. But in making this journey our Lord and his Apostles were obeying the precepts of the Jewish Law which required all Jews to celebrate the feast of the Passover in Jerusalem.

Christ was walking in advance of all his Apostles. But James and John, the sons of Zebedee, caught up with him and made a request of him. They said, "See to it that we sit, one at your right and the other at your left, when you come into your glory."

Our Lord answered them directly, "You do not know what you are asking." But then he asked them a question. "Can you drink the cup that I shall drink . . . ?" In ancient times to drink from the same cup with someone means you were willing to share that person's fortune, good or bad. Only shortly before this, our Lord had prophesied how the chief priests and scribes would torture him and put him to death. Hence it was clear to James and John that our Lord was asking them if they could suffer the same sufferings he was about to suffer. He added, "[Can you] be baptized in the same bath of pain as I?"

Without hesitation they replied, "We can." The two Apostles did not understand precisely what this suffering would be, but Christ respected their good will. He assured them they would drink his cup and be immersed in his bath of pain.

But then Christ told them that "sitting at my right or my left — is not mine to give." This honor was reserved by God the Father from all eternity for others. Christ did not mention her by name, but the human person who was to share the highest position of honor in heaven was his own Blessed Mother. She alone of all womankind was to enter this world free from the stain of original sin. God honored Mary above all other human beings by choosing her to be his mother. Mary has since been honored by being crowned Queen of Heaven.

What James and John were asking for was performent over the other ten Apostles with whom they were equals. But the other ten, upon learning of the request of the two Zebedee brothers, became indignant.

James and John were ambitious. Yet the object of their ambition was in itself a good thing, namely heavenly reward. Christ did not condemn them for this. For heaven should be the goal of all of us. It should be our ambition, also, to attain eternal happiness there. Our Lord was fond of James and John. They along with St. Peter were the three Apostles to whom he revealed his glory at the Transfiguration. Even on this occasion Christ promised them a share in his sufferings.

But our Lord in order to stifle the bad feeling or mild squabble among the Apostles, of the two who sought preferment over the others and the other ten who felt indignant about it, gave the Apostles a lecture on the necessity of service to others. He held up, as an example of how not to act, the gentiles who loved to show authority over others. He said, "It cannot be like that with you."

Christ concluded: "Anyone among you who aspires to greatness must serve the rest; whoever wants to rank first among you must serve the needs of all. The Son of Man has not come to be served but to serve — to give his life in ransom for the many."

Christ held up himself as an example of the service he wished them to give to others. Christ was about to give up his life as the price necessary to redeem mankind and reopen the gates of heaven. This great service of giving up his life was worthy of imitation on their part.

The Apostles were aware that they would have positions of authority in Christ's Church. Our Lord's message to them was that they should not use that authority in a tyrannical way, that rather they should make the service of those entrusted to them the ideal of their office.

Service to others is a virtue that is closely akin to charity; it flows from love of one's neighbor. Service is a virtue that priests are instructed in with their seminary training. Thus a parish priest is at the service of his parishioners. He is at their service in baptizing their children. He serves them in celebrating the Holy Sacrifice of the Mass. The priest serves his parishioners in making himself available in the confessional.

The priest serves his parish in performing marriages. He serves them in responding to a sick call and giving the last rites of the Church. He serves them in giving marriage counseling. He serves them in visiting the sick.

But service to others is a virtue that not only priests but every Catholic should practice. Service should be the mark of a Christian. At the turn of the century at Cambridge University in England, a group of students were attending a lecture. In the middle of the lecture flames shot out from one side of the building and the cry of "Fire!" was heard.

The students reacted instinctly to what they had been told to do in event of such an emergency. They formed a line, a bucket brigade between the building and the River Cam. Bucket after bucket of water was passed along until the fire was extinguished and the building saved with only minor damage.

The professor in charge of the class walked along the line thanking the students for their help. When he came to the end of the line, he noticed one of the smallest boys of the class standing knee deep in the water at the river's edge. The professor asked him why he had chosen that spot. The boy responded he wanted to be of service to others and thought he could best serve there.

This century so far has witnessed a great change in attitude among university students. The fad today is to throw fire bombs and set buildings on fire — then to pelt the firemen with rocks when they come to extinguish it. Instead of service many are showing disservice to others.

John Ruskin in his book "The Stones of Venice" wrote that "education is the leading of human souls to what is best. . . . The training which makes men happiest in themselves also makes them most serviceable to others."

In former times an education meant both a growth in knowledge and a growth in the practice of virtue. Today our store of knowledge about the world is steadily increasing, but, sad to say, our growth in virtue and service to others is not. What is urgently needed in our educational institutions today is a greater stress on the use of knowledge for the service of others.

St. James and St. John learned this lesson Christ taught them on serving others extremely well. St. James was the first bishop of Jerusalem. He was permitted to drink the cup of Christ, for in the year 43 A.D. he was beheaded by King Herod, the first of the Apostles to be martyred.

His brother, St. John, lived in the city of Ephesus for many years, there preaching the word of God and ruling over the Church. He personally cared for our Blessed Mother until her death, a duty entrusted him by Christ on the cross. St. John converted Parthia and part of Persia to the Christian faith. He too drank of our Lord's cup, for in about the year 95 he was arrested in a persecution of the Church and sent to Rome. There the Emperor ordered him thrown into a cauldron of boiling oil. But God miraculously saved his life. In approximately the year 97 St. John wrote the fourth gospel. He died a natural death around the year 100.

St. James and St. John both earned high places in heaven by the service they gave to their fellow men. Let us imitate them in the practice of this virtue. Let us heed the words of Christ. Let the service of our fellow men be a guiding principle in our lives. God bless you.

# "B"    Thirtieth Sunday of the Year

*Mark 10:46-52*

One of the greatest of all Americans was Benjamin Franklin. In 1887 he made a speech before the Constitutional Convention in Philadelphia. He arose to suggest that the daily proceedings be opened with prayer. He said, "I have lived a long time, sirs, 81 years — and the longer I live, the more convincing proof I see of this truth, that God governs the affairs of men. And if a sparrow cannot fall to the ground without his notice, is it probable that an empire can rise without his aid? We have been assured by the sacred writings that 'except the Lord build the house, they labor in vain that build it.' . . . I, therefore, beg leave to move that henceforth prayers imploring the assistance of heaven be held in this assembly every morning before we proceed to business."

Prayer is one thing that belongs to God. Because we are his creatures, we have the obligation to honor him by prayer. The question is frequently asked, "Why should I pray?" One answer is that we should pray to make known our needs to God. The importance of making known one's needs to God is clearly shown by the gospel story of Christ entering the city of Jericho. When Christ entered that city, shortly before his death, the blind beggar Bartimaeus was sitting by the wayside. He cried out, "Jesus, Son of David, have mercy on me." He continued to cry out despite the attempts of the crowd to silence him. Finally our Lord heard him and cured him.

If Bartimaeus had remained silent, Christ would have passed him by and he would never have regained his sight. But because Bartimaeus made known his need to God, Christ cured him. Our state is like that of Bartimeaus. If we do not pray and make known our needs to God, it is foolish to expect God's help.

Another answer on why we should pray is because of the power of prayer. Christ said, "Where two or three are gathered together in my name, there am I in the midst of them." Hence prayer when recited in a group has the power to call down God from heaven into the presence of men.

The power of prayer is so great that it has been called the key of heaven.

When Christ suffered death on Mount Calvary, he was crucified between two thieves. One of them, Dismas, besought his help, saying, "Jesus, remember me, when you enter upon your reign." Christ answered him, "This day you will be with me in paradise." Hence a single prayer had the power of gaining eternal happiness for a dying thief. Scenes like this are re-enacted daily.

Prayer has opened the gates of heaven and saved more souls from damnation in hell than man can number. An act of perfect contrition has the power to remove mortal sin from one's soul. Prayer has the power to gain sanctifying grace; it can bring the triune God from heaven into the soul of man.

Prayer can satisfy in whole or in part for the temporal punishment due to sin. It has the power to release souls from purgatory. The souls there suffer most terribly. Their sufferings are comparable to those of hell except that they will not last forever. A soul in purgatory is powerless to help himself; he must depend upon the prayers of the Church Militant on earth. When one realizes that his prayers can free a soul from such great sufferings, he can grasp some idea of the power of prayer.

Prayer plays upon the heartstrings of almighty God. Prayer taps the inexhaustible source of mercy and love. Prayer is like the broadside salvo of a battleship, a salvo which the gates of heaven cannot resist. Prayer can stay or move the hand of God to act. Prayer can change the course of history; it makes a lasting mark in eternity. Hence one ought to pray for two reasons, to make known his needs to God and because of the power of prayer.

Another question that is frequently asked concerning prayer is, "How should I pray?" The answer is that one should pray with devotion, humility, resignation to God's will and without ceasing.

Since prayer is the elevation of the soul to God, one should pray with devotion. He should mean what he says in prayer. Far too often people regard prayer as a lip service which they render to God. They become like the parrot that could recite perfectly the fifty-six words of the "Our Father." When we pray, we should mean what we say in prayer.

One's prayers should be humble, for it is written in the book of Sirach or Ecclesiasticus, "The prayers of him who humbles himself shall pierce the clouds." Christ taught us this lesson when he preached the parable of the Pharisee and the tax collector. The Pharisee prayed aloud and proudly, while the tax collector, the publican, asked God to be merciful to him because he was a sinner. Christ said this man went back to his house justified rather than the other," for he who exalts himself shall be humbled, and he who humbles himself shall be exalted."

One should pray with resignation to the will of God. Far too often people pray that only their own will be done. They forget that God is all-knowing; he knows our needs better than we do ourselves. Christ gave us the example of how to pray in this regard, for he prayed in the Garden of Olives, "Father . . . not my will but yours be done."

Lastly, in the words of St. Paul, one ought to pray "without ceasing." This means one should pray regularly each day — that is, one ought to pray upon arising in the morning, in the evening before retiring, and before and after meals. Each day one should make an act of perfect contrition for his sins.

But to pray always means more than this. It means we should make our every action a prayer to God. We can consecrate our daily actions by reciting the morning offering each day. Through this simple prayer everything we do becomes a prayer to God. In this way we can pray without ceasing.

Truly, if one prays in this manner, with humility, resignation, devotion and without ceasing, he will be exalted in heaven. Christ has said, "Ask and you shall receive that your joy may be full." God bless you.

# "B"     Thirty-first Sunday of the Year

*Mark 12:28-34*

In the Old Testament the Jewish rabbis listed 613 precepts of the law. There were 248 commands and 365 prohibitions. These were further classified into light and grave. It was a timely topic of discussion among the Jews to debate these precepts of the law and to give one's opinion on the light or grave binding force of many of these laws.

Therefore, the question the scribe asked of Jesus, as mentioned in today's gospel, is not an unusual one. It was not a trick question as were many questions asked of him. Rather it was a serious one. So when he asked our Lord which was the first of all the commandments, Christ gave him a very definite answer.

He said, "You shall love the Lord your God / with all your heart, / with all your soul, / with all your mind, / and with all your strength. This is the second, / You shall love your neighbor as yourself."

The answer that Christ gave pleased the scribe greatly. Christ did not delve into the hundreds of commands and prohibitions of the Old Testament. Instead he gave the motives for observing all these commandments — that is, love of God and love of neighbor.

One may further ask what the love of God consists of. True love of God consists in wishing God all the honor and glory and doing whatever is in our power to secure the honor and glory for him. Christ himself said, "If you love me, keep my commandments." Hence to love God is to live life free from sin and to keep his commandments.

In giving the first of all the commandments, Christ said we should love God with all our heart, all our soul, all our mind and all our strength. This means that the love of God should permeate all aspects of our life. We should have a mental appreciation of placing God above all other aspects, persons or things. Christ said, "He who loves father or mother more than me is not worthy of me; he who loves son or daughter more than me is not worthy of me." This does not mean, for example, that when a young man becomes a priest or a young lady a Sister, they love their parents less than do other children who do not enter the religious life. Very often the opposite is true. Boys and girls with religious vocations may have greater sensible love of their parents than others; it only means they have a greater pure appreciative love of God.

Love of God does not depend on warm affections of the heart nor on a display of emotions. A mother can weep bitterly at the death of a child, while a father may not shed a tear. Yet both love their child deeply.

A true love of God will prompt the soul to do tremendous things for God. It will prompt one to perform virtuous actions. It will prompt one to put his own convenience and pleasure in the background. It will move him to give preference to whatever will promote God's honor and glory.

The love of God is like a flame. It reaches out and ignites anything which it comes in contact with. It thaws the cold and frigid heart. It sheds heat and light on all around. It is contagious. A person burning with it will influence all around him.

The love of God will bring us many benefits. It will benefit us now and for all eternity. It will bring a great flow of God's graces into our soul. It will increase God's love for us.

A love of God will help wipe away our sins. The First Epistle of St. Peter, echoing the Book of Proverbs, tells us that love covers a multitude of sins. Love of God will incite us to virtue. It will be a protection against our enemies. It will merit us a place in heaven hereafter. St. Paul, quoting Isaiah, tells us that eye has not seen, nor ear heard, nor has it entered into the heart of man which things God has prepared for those who love him.

Theologians tell us that the degree of the love of God in a person's heart at the hour of death will determine his degree of happiness in the kingdom of heaven. The love of God is the prime virtue in our Christian religion. Not only the fact of our future happiness in heaven but the degree of happiness depends on it. Therefore the single most important thing we can do in our lifetime is to develop a deep and burning love of God.

There are countless reasons why we should love God. We should love him because of the great and limitless love he has for us. God so loved us that he created us and placed us in this world. He so loved us that he sent his divine Son to redeem us. He loves us so deeply as to keep us alive every moment of our life; he is sustaining the life of each of us at this instant. And for all of this he asks only our love in return.

There are countless hundreds and thousands of ways of showing our love for almighty God. God only infrequently asks the supreme test of love as he did of some martyrs in giving up their lives. Far more often God will test our love by placing some small cross on our shoulders. Perhaps it will be a sickness or a tragedy within our family. Perhaps it will be enduring a life of poverty or a humiliation in front of our friends. Whatever the test, let not our love of God be found wanting.

There are many saints in heaven about whom we hear very little. One of these saints is St. Ives. Yet St. Ives is outstanding because of his deep love for God. The reasons for his saintliness are not difficult to discern.

When he was a child, his mother was often heard to tell him he should strive to be a saint. When little Ives inquired of his mother what a saint was, she replied that a saint was one God created to be happy with him in heaven forever — that a saint is one who loves God above all things and obeys all his commandments.

His father was a source of good example to him also. His father told him, as his mother had taught him, to love God above all things, that he would teach him to love his neighbor. His father accordingly took little Ives with him frequently in performing some deed of mercy or kindness for his neighbor. In this way St. Ives learned to make the love of God and the love of neighbor the guiding principles of his life.

Let us also make them the guiding principles of our lives. Christ has listed the love of God and the love of neighbor as the two great commandments of the law. They are the leading virtues of our Christian religion. They will be the deciding factors on how we spend our life in eternity. God bless you.

# "B"      Thirty-second Sunday of the Year

*Mark 12:38-44*

In today's gospel according to St. Mark, our Lord gives a brief instruction to his Apostles and followers. He had just led them from their native Galilee south into the city of Jerusalem to celebrate the Passover. It was to be our Lord's final celebration of it, for within a week he would be arrested by the priests and led before the court of Pontius Pilate.

On this particular occasion Christ was present within the temple at Jerusalem. He had been observing a group of scribes. He condemned their pride. He pointed out how they paraded around in robes and accepted marks of respect. They took front seats in the synagogues and places of honor at banquets. He pointed out their hypocrisy — that they recited long prayers for appearance's sake and devoured the savings of widows. Christ passed judgment on them. He said because of their pride and hypocrisy they would receive a severe sentence.

But then something else caught the attention of Christ. He and his Apostles were near the temple treasury. They observed the Jewish people making donations to the treasury. Many of them were paying assessments at the thirteen alms-boxes found in the temple treasury hall. Temple priests were on hand during the Passover season to record each of these paid assessments or free will donations. More often than not they would record and call off aloud the donations each one gave.

Many of the Jews gave a large amount of money. But then there came the poor widow who put in two small copper coins worth about a cent. No doubt the priest recorded and announced aloud the amount of her donation. Those standing around undoubtedly knew the smallness of her donation. Perhaps some snickered or gave a contemptuous glance.

But from Christ there was another response. Christ told his disciples that this poor widow had contributed more than all the others who had donated to the treasury. They gave from their surplus wealth, but she from her want. She gave all she had to live on.

Among the Jews in the Old Testament it was customary to pay tithes or give one-tenth of all their possessions to the temple. Tithing began as a custom with Abraham very early in the Old Testament. God made a covenant with Moses and the Jewish people concerning tithing.

Again in the Old Testament God spoke to Malachi. He told him that he was displeased with the Jewish people because they had ceased to obey his laws. But then he added, "Return to me, and I will return to you," and, "Bring all your tithes into the storehouse . . . and try me in this . . . if I open not unto you the floodgates of my mercy." Thus God promised to bless abundantly those who obeyed his laws and paid their tithes.

The Jewish people in general were conscientious in paying their tithes. They continued in this practice right down to the time of Christ. But small abuses did creep in, for instance, the hypocrisy and vanity they displayed in paying their tithes, and the pride the rich took in contributing large sums of money and being praised for it.

In the New Testament Christ sent his Apostles and disciples to the various towns and villages to preach the gospel. He told them not to take any provisions with them. He said that a laborer was worthy of his pay. He meant that the Apostles and disciples should live off the provisions and contributions of those to whom they preached the gospel.

In the New Testament we read in the Acts of the Apostles that Ananias and other Jews made contributions to St. Peter for his support and that of other poor Christians. Thus from the earliest times, in the New Testament as well as in the Old, it was customary to give alms to the Church.

At the present time it is a Church law that all Catholics should contribute to the support of their pastor. Our present Church law does not specify how much should be contributed by any one individual as did the Old Testament in saying that it should be a tithe or one-tenth of one's earnings. However one's contribution should be a generous one, one in keeping with one's means.

Among the nations of the world today, the Church is supported in various ways. In certain countries of Europe, for instance, Italy, it is supported by taxes. When one pays his yearly taxes to the government, a certain amount is given to the Church for its support. Yet in other countries, like our own United States, this is not done. In our country the Church is supported solely by contributions placed in the Sunday or weekly collections. Difficulties sometimes arise when people move from one country where the Church is supported by taxes to a country like our own where it is not so supported. They have to learn to contribute to their Church.

Here in the United States not only our Church but our Catholic schools as well are supported by your voluntary goodwill offerings in the Sunday collections. But because there is no tithe asked of our Catholic parishioners, or no specified amount is assessed them, their contributions frequently are token ones. They do not represent a substantial sacrifice on a wage-earner's part.

Remember that God so loved us that he gave us our life and everything we possess in this world. He has bestowed countless blessings upon us. Therefore in gratitude to almighty God our Sunday contribution should be an expression of the gratitude you feel to him for all these gifts. As God has been generous in bestowing his blessings on you, you should be generous in contributing to his Church.

It is not always the amount that makes your contribution a generous one. While in the temple, Christ witnessed many wealthy Jews contributing large sums of money, yet he only praised the generosity of the poor widow who gave just two copper coins. Christ knows your means; he knows when you are generous. You cannot deceive him.

Your contribution is your secret with Christ. Only he will praise you or blame you for it; just let it be said of you as Christ said of the poor widow, "She gave from her want. . . ." God bless you.

# "B"    Thirty-third Sunday of the Year

*Mark 13:24-32*

The gospel according to St. Mark read at today's Mass is a talk Christ gave to his disciples in the week preceding his death on the cross. Our Lord had led his Apostles into the Holy City of Jerusalem to celebrate the Passover. He had completed his last visit to the temple in Jerusalem. He then led his disciples to Mount Olivet, outside the gates of the Holy City, and proceeded to speak to them about the end of the world.

He mentioned several signs that would be seen before the world came to an end: ". . . the sun will be darkened, the moon will not shed its light, stars will fall out of the skies, and the heavenly hosts will be shaken." Our Lord pointed out these phenomena to us as a sign that the end is near.

He then spoke of his parousia, his second coming, his coming in the general judgment to judge all men. He said, " . . . men will see the Son of Man coming in the clouds with great power and glory. He will . . . assemble his chosen from the four winds, from the farthest bounds of earth and sky."

Holy Mother the Church presents these words of Christ on the end of the world for our meditation today. For just as surely as the world will one day come to an end, so too will the life of each of us come to an end. At some day in the future, the soul of each one of us will depart from our body; it will appear before our Lord and Savior Jesus Christ in particular judgment. The day this will happen is the day of our death.

Death is the separation of body and soul. It is the cessation of bodily life. It is the separation of man from everyone and everything which he holds dear upon earth . . . from home, from father and mother, husband or wife. It is separation from one's friends, from one's life work, from his position in life. It is a curtain drawn down upon the play of life. Death separates us from everything we have or are, save the grace we possess in our souls the moment it strikes. Death comes like a thief in the night.

Death is the punishment for original sin. When Adam committed that first terrible sin of disobedience, God cast him forth from the garden of paradise and said, ". . . you are dust, and to dust you shall return." Adam and Eve did not at first grasp the full meaning of these words; it was not until sometime later when they discovered their beloved son Abel lying dead in a field that their meaning was brought home to them. We can picture Eve shedding bitter tears over her dead son, but death was the final victor, the result of her own first sin.

With death there results the ugly corruption of the body. Beauty fades away, and earth reclaims the dust from which life was taken. The story is told of the great impression of death upon St. Francis Borgia. St. Francis was of Spanish nobility and deeply devoted to his queen — Queen Isabella. Upon her death it fell to the lot of St. Francis to open her casket as a part of her burial ceremony. What he saw was a foul and disgusting corpse. "What!" he exclaimed, "Is this all that remains of my gracious sovereign?" The gruesome sight of a decaying corpse persuaded him to become a Jesuit priest.

Death will come to all; of this we may be certain. St. Paul writes: "It is appointed to all men once to die, and after death to be judged." Reason demonstrates it. Experience proves it. Just as surely as the sun rises and the sun sets, and as the seasons come and go, each of us here in church today will someday meet with death.

Our entire life is a prolonged struggle against death. We are most particular to eat nourishing foods, to get plenty of sleep, fresh air and sunshine, for these things are conducive to good health. But they can only prolong our life for a few years at most, a relatively short time. When we are sick we call a doctor; through his medical care, or sometimes through surgery and hospital care, we cure a particular illness and enjoy good health for a longer time — but still only for a time.

In the end death will claim each of us. No one has ever cheated death, and no one ever will. This very hour that I am speaking to you, in various parts of the world several thousand people will die. Modern statistics say that in the world today tens of thousands of people will die and face God in judgment.

Death is certain. Only the time and place are not. Who knows here at Mass today who will be the next to die? Who knows the next in his family to face death? No one except God knows these answers.

Death has been pictured as something terrible. For those who die in mortal sin, it truly is terrible. For those who have dedicated their lives to sensuality, to those who have lived dishonestly, to those who have refused to worship God at Sunday Mass, death can only mean one thing — the beginning of eternal suffering in hell. For these people have foolishly wasted their lives; they have pursued earthly pleasure; they have entered eternity without making any preparation for it. They shall have forever to regret it.

But for those who die with sanctifying grace on their souls, death holds no fear. For the just man death is but the passing into everlasting happiness. For those who have been obedient to God's laws, the Ten Commandments; for those who have shown love to both God and neighbor, death means but the passing into the beautiful and eternal mansion of heaven. Christ has told us that in his Father's house there are many mansions for those who love him.

Death should not be feared by those in the state of grace. St. Aloysius Gonzaga was playing a game of chess one day when he was asked what he would do if he knew he would die within the hour. He replied, "I would keep on playing chess." These are the sentiments of a saint. These should be the sentiments of anyone who lives in the state of grace and is in the friendship of almighty God.

The lesson death teaches is to be prepared for it at all times, to live each day as if it were going to be your last. In the words of Christ, "Watch and pray, for you know not the day nor the hour."

Christ has given us a special means of preparing for death; these are the last rites of the Church: the Sacrament of Reconciliations of Holy Eucharist, called Holy Viaticum when given at the time of death, and the Sacrament of Anointing of the Sick. These sacraments can take away serious sin, increase or restore sanctifying grace to our soul and prepare us in the last minutes of our life to pass into eternity.

Every time we say the Hail Mary we ask our Blessed Mother to pray for us now and at the hour of our death. St. Joseph has been called the patron of a happy death. But perhaps no better means of preparing for death or forceful reminder of it can be found than the prayer the priest says in the burial service: "O Lord, while we lament the departure of our brother, thy servant, out of this life, we may bear in mind that we are most certainly to follow him. Give us grace to make ready for that last hour by a devout and holy life." God bless you.

# "B"  Thirty-fourth Sunday of the Year (Christ the King)

*John 18:33-37*

During World War II Nazi Germany overran the small country of Denmark. The ruler of this little land at the time was King Christian X. He was a king who loved his people.

For years he had taken a morning horseback ride through Copenhagen, unaccompanied and unprotected. This he continued to do even after the Nazis took power. One morning a Nazi officer met him and asked him where his bodyguard was.

The king replied, "Right here, all around me. All my people are my bodyguard." This king was loved by his people and took delight in going among them as their friend and benefactor.

Today we celebrate the feast of another king — of Christ. Christ is the King of kings — the greatest of them all. His reign extends over the entire world. And his reign shall last until the end of time.

The Kingship of Christ is a relatively new feast in the Catholic Church. It was established in 1925 by the then reigning Pope Pius XI. It is a feast of our present 20th century which has witnessed such great changes in the liturgy of the Church.

But even though the feast of Christ's kingship is a new one, nevertheless the idea of his kingship has its foundation in Holy Scripture. Christ proclaimed his kingship himself while on this earth.

When the Archangel Gabriel appeared to the Blessed Virgin Mary, he told Mary that she was to be the mother of Christ. He told Mary that the Lord God would give the son to be born of her the throne of his father David and that he would be king of the house of Jacob forever and that his kingdom would have no end.

In his last sermon to the people of Jerusalem, just before he was led away to be crucified, Christ proclaimed himself to be king. After he was arrested and led before Pontius Pilate, Pilate asked him, "Are you the King of the Jews?" Christ answered it, "It is you who say I am a king." . . .

But then Christ added a further explanation, "My kingdom is not of this world." But this further explanation neither Pilate nor the Jews understood. The Jew had wrongly expected that the Messiah or Redeemer would be a temporal king. They expected his kingdom to be a worldly one. They expected the Redeemer to free the Jews from their bondage to the Roman Empire.

On one occasion when Christ was preaching to a multitude on a mountainside in Galilee, the crowd was so impressed and taken up with his doctrine that they wanted to seize him and make him their king. Christ had to flee into the mountains alone to escape them.

The people did not understand that Christ did not want subjects to acknowledge his kingship by means of guns and marching armies. He did not wish his power proclaimed by warships on the sea or any might of arms.

Christ instead wanted his kingship proclaimed by worship and prayer. He wanted his kingship proclaimed by a doctrine of love and good works. He wanted his kingship to hold sway in our hearts. He wanted his kingdom proclaimed over our minds and wills.

Christ rules over our minds because his doctrine is truth. it is proclaimed to us through the natural law. It is proclaimed through the pages of Holy Scripture. It is proclaimed through the voice of his Church.

Christ reigns over our wills. We proclaim ourselves to be members of his kingdom whenever we choose good instead of evil, whenever we choose purity over immorality or honesty over dishonesty.

Christ too reigns in our hearts. We proclaim his reign when we show an act of love to our fellow man.

Christ is our king because he is God, the creator of the universe. He is our creator who gave us life. He is the ruler who rules over every moment of our lives. All rulers on this earth derive their power from him.

Christ's power as king was acknowledged from his first days on this earth. While he was a newborn babe in the stable of Bethlehem, the Magi from the east came to see him and adore him. One of the gifts they brought him was gold, a gift given only to kings. When Christ was crucified on the cross a sign was placed over his head entitled, "Jesus of Nazareth, King of the Jews."

One of the first to honor Christ publicly as king was the renowned preacher Savanarola. In the year 1429 he erected a statue to Christ the King in the city of Florence, Italy, and began a campaign of preaching about him to the children of the city. This gave rise to many good works done in his name.

In the year 1913 the people of Silao in Mexico decided to build a thirty-foot statue to Christ the King on the top of a nearby mountain. The statue could be seen for miles around and was a great center of devotion.

But revolutionists at that time sought to overthrow the government. One of their cruel acts was to dynamite this statue and destroy it completely. But very patiently the people began to rebuild it, and a new statue looks down from the mountain today.

In the course of history many have tried to dethrone Christ who reigns as our king. But in this no one ever has succeeded or ever will succeed. Persecutions have come and gone, but Christ our King reigns on. The archangel Gabriel has said his kingdom shall have no end.

Let us today acknowledge Christ to be our King. Let us pledge to be his loyal subjects. Let us pray that all nations will be subject to his rule. Let us acknowledge Christ to be our King upon this earth, so that one day we may be his subjects in the kingdom of heaven. God bless you.

# "B"  Dec. 8: Immaculate Conception

*Luke 1:26-38*

Today we celebrate the Feast of the Immaculate Conception of the Blessed Virgin Mary. Because of the disobedience of our first parents, the guilt of their original sin had engulfed the world. It darkened the soul of every creature descended from Adam and Eve — all but with one exception, the Blessed Virgin Mary. Mary stands out like the burning bush, unscathed and untouched by the flaming sea of sin around her.

Holy Scripture does not tell us openly that Mary was conceived immaculate, but it does give us some indications of it. One such indication is the sentence God passed on the serpent after he had tempted Adam and Eve to commit original sin. God said to the serpent, "I will put enmity between you and the woman,/and between your offspring and hers;/He will strike at your head,/while you strike at his heel."

The serpent to whom God referred was the devil. The woman was Mary and her offspring was her divine Son, Jesus Christ. God promised that Mary would resist the power of the devil which means she would never be stained with sin. She would enter this world immaculate.

After many centuries of waiting, the day of the Immaculate Conception finally dawned. It appeared to be no different than any other day. No angel descended from heaven to announce it, but yet a most important event did occur.

The Immaculate Conception had taken place, but yet it remained a secret, hidden even from Mary herself. But one day while Mary was at prayer, the archangel Gabriel appeared to her and greeted her with the words, "Rejoice, O highly favored daughter!"

There was good reason for God to bestow this favor upon Mary. From all eternity he had chosen her to be his mother, the mother of Christ. Her innocence and goodness had been foreseen by God. It would not be fitting that the Son of God be born of a person whose soul was in sin. It was inconsistent that the soul of God's mother be tainted by a sin of Satan. Therefore he decreed that she should enter this world without sin.

But because Mary's sinlessness was not explicitly proclaimed in Scripture, it was not until the fifth century that the Greeks began to proclaim it; the Latin-speaking nations followed their lead in the seventh century. The theologian who proclaimed it most vociferously was Dons Scotus during the Middle Ages. From his time on the belief in Mary's sinlessness has become a litany.

In the year 1849 Pope Pius IX began to contemplate the declaration of Mary's Immaculate Conception as a doctrine of faith. Questionnaires and circulars were addressed to all the bishops and leading theologians of the world asking their opinion and belief on this question. After five years of research, on December 8, 1854, Pope Pius IX solemnly ascended to the Chair of Peter and officially declared the Immaculate Conception of the Blessed Virgin Mary to be a doctrine of faith.

Pope Pius acted wisely in this, for only four years later Mary herself confirmed this doctrine. On eighteen different occasions Mary appeared to a poor French peasant girl, Bernadette Soubirous, in a small village called Lourdes. Bernadette described her as extremely beautiful. Together she and Bernadette prayed the rosary, but she did not reveal her identity immediately.

After several requests by Bernadette as to who she was, she answered most sweetly, "I am the Immaculate Conception." In confirmation of Mary's statement and apparitions there, a spring began to flow from the spot, and untold miracles have been performed in its waters.

More than a century ago the bishops of the United States met to choose a patron saint for our nation. They chose Mary under her title of Immaculate Conception to be our patroness. A large and beautiful Washington shrine has been constructed in her honor.

Mary, through her Immaculate Conception, has become a beacon of light and inspiration for the world. In the darkness of this sinful world she has become a shining star. She is a model for men to live by; she is a ray of hope for men to grasp in their tedious struggle with the powers of evil. Mary in her Immaculate Conception is a reflection of the glory of heaven.

On this her feast day, let us implore her blessings. Mary is not only our sinless mother, but she is also the patron saint of our country. Let us open our hearts in prayer to her. Mary will not fail to hear and answer them. God bless you.

# "B"    Aug. 15: Assumption

*Luke 1:39-56*

Today's gospel relates the beautiful canticle spoken by Mary to her cousin Elizabeth. In this hymn of praise Mary does not exalt herself, but rather she exalts God. He has kept his promise to mankind after centuries of waiting. He is sending his Son to redeem men from their sins. Mary rejoices that this great event has come about. She says of God, ". . . holy is his name." Mary humbly consents to play her part in it.

All ages of the Church have paid honor to Mary, but they have honored her under different titles and in different ways. In the early apostolic Church Mary's role as Mother of God was emphasized. The doctrine of her truly being God's mother was proclaimed at an early date.

So also the virginity of Mary was early proclaimed. One of her earliest titles was the Virgin Mary. Mary has been honored in other ways in other centuries. One such honor of recent vintage is her sinlessness. It was only slightly over a century age that Mary's sinlessness was declared an article of faith and her Immaculate Conception was given due recognition.

When Christ died on the cross he entrusted the care of his mother to his beloved disciple, St. John. He in turn took Mary into his home in Ephesus. There, tradition tells us, Mary lived on for many years. There finally at an advanced age she met a peaceful death. She was buried in a nearby tomb.

Tradition again relates that one of the Apostles, St. Thomas, was absent when her death occurred. Upon returning to Ephesus and hearing of her death, he asked to see her body. But when the tomb was opened, her body was not there. In its place were sweet-smelling flowers. Knowing that the tomb had not been opened previously since her body had been placed in it, the Apostles concluded that God must have assumed her body into heaven along with her soul.

This conclusion was a reasonable one, for the body of Mary had never been tainted by sin. No stain of sin, either that of our first parents, original sin, or sin of her own commission, had ever defiled her soul. Therefore, since sin had not touched her soul, there was no reason for God to allow her body to return to dust.

From that time until the present it was the common belief in the Church that Mary's body had been assumed into heaven. Yet it was not until 1950 that Pope Pius XII officially declared Mary's Assumption to be an article of faith. He wrote in his proclamation of this doctrine, "Mary was taken up body and soul into heavenly glory. She was exalted by the Lord as the Queen of all, in order that she might be the more thoroughly conformed to her Son."

When the Second Vatican Council convened in 1959, the question of Mary's position in the Church was given great consideration. One aim of the Council was to bring about a union or greater harmony between the Catholic Church and other Christian denominations. Most of these other denominations do not share our belief about Mary. Many of their leading theologians were present at the Council as observers. But the Second Vatican Council affirmed that the Blessed Virgin Mary is a daughter of the Church and indeed its first member. It said she serves the Church in a special way as exemplar of virgin and mother. It reaffirmed the honors and titles she possesses.

The Assumption of Mary into heaven may be called the consummation of all the other honors she has received. It is the birthday of her true greatness and glory. It is the crowning recognition of all the virtues she practiced in her lifetime. It marks her entry into the heavenly honor which was due to her. It marked the reunion of Mary with her divine Son, who loved her so deeply.

From time immemorial Christians have flocked to Mary; they have sought her intercession in time of trial and distress. They have invoked her aid whenever disaster has threatened. Mary has never failed to hear and answer their prayers.

No grace comes to us unless it comes to us through Mary's hands. Mary is our hope and consolation. She is our source of strength. She is the comforter of the afflicted. She is the help of Christians.

Let us honor Mary as our Mother. Let us pray to her daily. It has been said that hell cannot boast of containing a single soul who ever had a true and heartfelt devotion to Mary. A concern to save our souls and a devotion to Mary go hand in hand. Let us honor Mary here in this life as our Mother, so that in the world to come, Mary may claim us as her children.

A midwestern priest recently wrote the story of his vocation to the priesthood. In civilian life he had been the operator of a giant crane used in building construction, lifting steel beams high into the air. One day while he was working on a huge skyscraper high above the ground, the braces supporting his crane broke loose and his crane began to roll off the edge of the building.

He was thrown suddenly forward, but as he fell the chain he wore around his neck, containing the miraculous medal of Mary, caught on the emergency brake handle. The brake action temporarily stopped the fall of the crane and gave him sufficient time to jump off the crane to safety. Our Blessed Mother had saved his life. Therefore, he decided to serve her in a better way — through the priesthood.

On this feast of Mary's Assumption, the day she began to receive heavenly glory, let us honor her as our Mother. Let us give to her some small glory from this earth below. God bless you.

# "B"    Nov. 1: All Saints

In ancient Greece one of the great masterpieces of art was the beautiful marble temple in Corinth. Before it there stretched a sweeping boulevard. It was the custom to inscribe in marble in this temple the names of the winners of the Greek Olympic games. It was the dream of every Greek youth to have his name inscribed there.

To achieve this honor the runners underwent the most rigorous of training. St. Paul speaks of these runners and their rigorous training in his epistle to the Corinthians. The Greeks thought that having their names inscribed in the temple was the greatest honor that could befall one; it was their ideal of immortality.

But as St. Paul points out and as we well know there is a far greater honor that can come to one . . . greater than that of a winner in the Olympics — that of becoming a saint of God . . . of not just having one's name engraved in granite, but rather of enjoying eternal happiness with God in heaven.

Today, my dear people, the first day of November, is All Saints Day, a holy day of obligation, a day on which we may give honor to all the saints in heaven.

We know that relatively few of the saints in heaven are canonized — declared to be saints by the Catholic Church; that besides them there are countless others who have lived lives of virtue and are happy with God in heaven. But these countless saints we do not know — they are the so-called unknown saints in heaven. Some saints have feast days of their own through the year but on All Saints Day we honor these other saints who have no feast days of their own. Undoubtedly this number of saints may well include some souls whom we knew well upon this earth — some parents, relatives, friends who have departed this life.

Back in the early days of Rome the Roman citizens had a custom of preserving in their homes images of their illustrious ancestors of their families. These images consisted of a mask representing the features of the deceased person together with the clothing in fashion in his day and any armor or insignia he may have worn.

At the death of one of the members of the family a weird funeral procession was held. The masks were fitted to the servants of the family, who marched along representing the other deceased of the family, to the family tomb.

This Roman custom of wearing the images of one's ancestors has come down to us today in the festivities generally taking place on Halloween. Even the word Halloween has a Christian meaning. It was originally called the Eve of All Hallows, meaning the eve of All Saints, the day on which the images of God's saints were paraded before us and we showed honor to them.

Therefore, on All Saints Day, let us remember that the saints in heaven can help us. Let us invoke their aid through prayer. Let us pray to them not only on their feast day, but frequently throughout the year. They have great power in interceding with God for us.

Tomorrow, November 2nd, we celebrate another important feast day in the liturgy of the Church, All Souls Day. It is the one day in the year Holy Mother the Church sets aside to pray for the souls suffering in purgatory. The souls suffering there are members of the Church Suffering. Together with the Church Triumphant in heaven and the Church Militant upon earth they make up the Communion of Saints.

In fact Holy Mother the Church dedicates the whole month of November to the Poor Souls and entreats us to pray for them especially during this time.

And on All Souls Day itself a priest is permitted to celebrate three Masses for this reason — one of only two such days in the year when this permission is given.

The suffering of the souls in purgatory is very severe. They suffer the pain of loss for having faced God in judgment and they realize the great loss in being separated from him. They also suffer a pain of sense. St. Thomas tells us that even the least pain in purgatory is more severe than the greatest pain in this world. Venerable Bede tells us that purgatory is more intolerable than all the torments that can be felt or conceived in this life. For in purgatory our souls will suffer and not just our bodies, as on earth.

But the tragic part of the souls who suffer in purgatory is their helplessness. They can do nothing to help themselves. Their period of meriting and demeriting is over. They can only wait and suffer. But we on earth can help them. The Council of Trent tells us that the souls in purgatory are aided by our sacrifices and prayers, especially by Holy Mass.

St. Monica once said to her son, St. Augustine, "Lay this body where you will but only this I beg of you, that you make remembrance of me at the Lord's altar." St. Gregory the Great records in his writings that upon the death of a monk named Justus, he ordered thirty Masses to be sung for him. On the thirtieth day, after the last Mass was said, Justus appeared to his superior and said, "I was in pain, but now I am well."

Praying for the suffering souls is a spiritual act of mercy. Let us remember that any soul whom we may free from the grave torments of purgatory by our prayers or good works, will be eternally grateful to us. He will be our benefactor in heaven for all eternity.

Remember the souls in purgatory are the future saints of heaven. For when a soul has completely satisfied his temporal punishment due for his sins he will be taken up into heaven with God and there will enjoy eternal happiness. If this soul knows that it was your prayers or your good sacrifices that were the means of freeing him from the flames of purgatory, his gratitude will know no bounds.

Therefore, let us resolve to make an extra effort to attend Mass tomorrow for the Poor Souls on their feast day. Let us resolve to pray for them throughout this month. Consider that someday purgatory may be your resting place. Certainly then you would want others to pray for you. Resolve therefore, to help the poor souls in whatever way you can. In their gratitude they will more than return the favor. God bless you.

# Year C

# Year C

## "C"    First Sunday of Advent

*Luke 21:25-28, 34-36*

Toward the end of the first century there lived a beautiful pagan woman named Eudoxia. But this woman was equally as famous for her sins as she was for her beauty.

One night Eudoxia was lodging in a house a short distance from a monastery. As she sat in her room that evening near an open window, she heard a voice coming from the monastery. Eudoxia was curious, so she began to listen. A monk was in chapel reading from a spiritual book about the sufferings of hell and the last judgment.

Eudoxia began to tremble. The unknown voice pierced her to the heart. Never had she heard anyone speak of such a subject before. The reading finally stopped, but Eudoxia could not sleep that night.

The next day Eudoxia sought out a Catholic priest to talk to. She told him she was ready to renounce her sinful life. Soon she began taking instructions in the Christian faith. The life she led from then on was something entirely new and different.

As in the past she had been known as a sinful woman, so now she was known as a woman of great piety and holiness. She became a model for all. Following her death she was canonized and is now known as St. Eudoxia.

But her conversion was brought about by reflection on the last judgment and sufferings hereafter.

Today on this First Sunday of Advent, Holy Mother the Church presents to us for the gospel of the Mass a reflection on the last judgment and signs of the last day. Perhaps this Scripture passage will arouse in us the same sentiments as it did in St. Eudoxia.

Each of us will face God twice in judgment — once immediately upon our death in particular judgment when God will sentence us directly to heaven, hell or purgatory. While our bodies are buried here upon earth, our souls shall live on in eternity.

Then on the last day, when the terrible suffering prophesied in today's gospel comes to take place, God will judge the whole world in general judgment.

Sometimes people ask why a second or general judgment is necessary. It will be held because justice demands it. Frequently in this life good people suffer while the evil are honored and prosper. Justice demands that the evil be publicly exposed and the good rewarded. In all this God's divine wisdom will be exposed in its full splendor and glory.

On the day of general judgment God will reunite our bodies and souls. He will raise up our bodies from the dust of the earth. Our bodies following this resurrection will be glorified bodies. We will not be able to feel either cold or warmth; we won't suffer from hunger or thirst. We shall never have to worry about growing old or suffering from aches or pains. We shall be able to travel quickly from one place to another. While our bodies will be our same bodies, they shall possess many and new qualities.

The manner in which this judgment will take place will not be a long drawn-out discussion. All our thoughts, words and actions will be revealed in a single instant. Our own consciences will be the accuser. Our minds will be flooded with a realization of the good and evil we have done. We will be the first to condemn ourselves.

When judgment is finished Christ will pronounce sentence — the same Christ who stood before Pilate and was forced to endure an unjust judgment of being condemned to death before a tribunal of man. To the good Christ will say, "Come you blessed of my Father, take possession of the kingdom prepared for you from the foundation of the world." To the evil he will say "Depart you cursed into everlasting fire." From this judgment of Christ there is no appeal. His sentence will be pronounced for all eternity.

On the day of judgment there will be great rejoicing for those worthy to enter the happiness of heaven, but there will be much remorse for those condemned to the fires of hell. Those condemned would do anything for a second chance — one more opportunity to right the wrongs they have committed — their repentance would know no bounds. But then it will be too late.

Our Christian teaching on judgment was the theme for the play "Everyman," written many centuries ago, which is regarded as a classic piece of literature. In the first scene Everyman is given a dinner by his friends, but suddenly Death appears and tells him that his time on earth is complete and he must appear before God in judgment. Everyman begs for a few more days, but death refuses. He begs for one more day, but this he also refuses. Finally he begs for one more hour and death relents and grants him one more hour on earth.

Everyman appeals to his friends to go with him and intercede with God for him, but they are not ready to meet God themselves and refuse to go with him. He appeals to his relatives, but they refuse. He appeals to a woman companion, a partner in sin, but she refuses.

Finally in the last scene he hurries to the church to make a final confession; fortified by his last grace he then struggles onward with only a few ragged figures to assist him, the few good deeds he has done in his lifetime, to meet God in judgment. The play closes with Death ushering him off this earth.

From this play, and from the gospel of today which Christ preached on the signs and tribulations of the last day, we can learn an important lesson. Be prepared! Be ready at any hour or any moment to meet God in judgment! We do not know the day or the hour we will have to face God in judgment. Christ said death comes like a thief in the night. We should live always in the state of sanctifying grace, then death will not be able to rob us of eternal happiness hereafter. God bless you.

# "C"    Second Sunday of Advent

*Luke 3:1-6*

The gospel in today's Mass most appropriately speaks of St. John the Baptizer, the precursor of Christ. Almighty God in his providence chose John to precede Christ, to prepare his way. John in fulfilling his mission was a most striking character. Scripture tells us that he was dressed in a garment of camel hair and that he fed on locusts and wild honey. This manner of life was in imitation of that of the prophets of the Old Testament in the early days of the Jewish nation. But all this happened centuries before John the Baptizer lived upon this earth.

In fact, there had not been a major prophet for nearly five hundred years prior to John. Hence John, in assuming this dress and fulfilling this role, left himself liable to criticism and sarcasm. He lived in a manner far different from what was customary for that age.

John the Baptizer was no ordinary person. His birth had been announced by an angel, for the Archangel Gabriel appeared to his father Zechariah and told him that his wife Elizabeth would bear a son in her old age. And when Zechariah doubted the angel's word, he was struck dumb until the time of his son's birth. And the first words that he spoke after regaining his speech was that most beautiful prayer, recited each day by the priest in his Divine Office, the Benedictus: "Blessed be the Lord, the God of Israel, because he has visited and ransomed his people."

Zechariah named his son John and dedicated him to be a Nazarite; that is he would not take any wine or strong drink, in obedience to the instructions of Gabriel. When John grew up he began to lead a life of mortification and penance. He went into the desert and there fasted and prayed a great deal. In this way he prepared for his great mission.

Finally in the fifteenth year of the reign of Tiberius Caesar, in the words of today's gospel, the word of God was spoken to John in the desert. And John went forth into the region of the Jordan, preaching a baptism of repentance for the forgiveness of sins. This fifteenth year of the reign of Tiberius Caesar is calculated to be about 28 or 29 A.D. Thus John began to preach and baptize around the Jordan about a year or two before Christ began his public life.

The baptism which John administered was not the Sacrament of Baptism. Rather, it was a temporary rite with which men under the law were admitted to some new spiritual privileges they did not have before. John's baptism prepared men to become Christians, but it did not make them so. John's baptism has been called the dividing line between the Old and the New Testaments, the partition between the Law and the Gospel. It is called a baptism of repentance which led to the forgiveness of sin, and it symbolizes the cleansing or the taking away of the stain of sin.

Many Pharisees and Sadducees came to John to hear him. But once they heard him they refused to be baptized because they denied the need of any repentance on their part. The baptism which John gave was not a mere human institution, but rather of divine institution. It was a figure as well as a preparation of sacramental baptism.

There was very little doubt regarding John's message. He announced that God was on the point of inaugurating his reign, in fulfillment of the centuries of longing. This was a message the Jewish people were pleased to hear, for centuries they had been under the rule of the Persians, Egyptians and Syrians. And presently they were under the domination of Herod and the Roman government. Despite all their oppression they still clung to the belief that God had not abandoned his people. John's message of the Messiah's coming was music to their ears.

John did not mince words in speaking to the Jews. On one occasion he called them a brood of vipers. He told the well-to-do that they must share their clothes and food with the poor. He instructed the tax-gatherers to collect no more than was justly due them. He warned the soldiers not to plunder anyone and to be content with their pay.

But despite his frank accusations, John was popular with the people. Some were so impressed with his preaching that they believed him to be Elijah, a prophet. A delegation of priests and Levites came to him from Jerusalem to ask him if he were not the Christ. But all of this John firmly denied: he claimed only to be a voice of one crying in the wilderness, making straight the way of the Lord. He remained unaffected by the praises and blessing showered upon him; the abuse and criticism of others did not bother him. His sole purpose, to which he adhered without deviation, was to preach of the coming of Christ. John was most humble in his work.

John is called the precursor, the one who went before the Lord to prepare his way. The entire Old Testament is a remote and mediate preparation for his coming. But John's preaching was a proximate and immediate one. In the words of today's gospel, it was the work of John that every valley shall be filled and every mountain and hill shall be leveled.

John's work was most necessary, for the pagan world that existed at this time was ill-prepared to receive its Creator. There were many mountains of materialism that had to be brought low. There was the valley of pride and hypocrisy which Christ so frequently met. Temporal values so filled their minds that they expected their Messiah to be a temporal ruler.

The valley of immorality was one of great depth, but John labored ceaselessly to overcome this obstacle along with the others. He did not hestitate to tell King Herod that he was guilty of adultery in living with his brother's wife. But this brave act of righteousness cost John his life.

My dear people, on this second Sunday of Advent, Holy Mother the Church holds before us the great St. John the Baptist as one worthy of emulation. As John went forth to prepare the way for the coming of Christ, so Holy Mother the Church bids us to prepare for the feast of the coming of Christ into the world on Christmas day.

The world is far from prepared for our Savior's coming at the present time. Many mountains and many valleys obstruct his path. There is the valley of indifference which needs to be filled. So many people today are forgetful of God. And too, there is the mountain of materialism that needs to be leveled.

The modern world with its blatant advertising holds before us the tinsel and glitter of material things.

John the Baptizer is no longer with us to lead us in preparing the way for Christ. But the gospel story continually puts before us the story of his deeds. It bids us to do in like manner. Let us imitate this great saint in levelling the mountains and filling the valleys so that the Christ Child may come into our hearts. If mortal sin obstructs the path of the Christ Child coming into our hearts, let us resolve to remove it in time to receive the Christ Child worthily. Resolve to frequent the Sacrament of Reconciliation and put your soul in the state of sanctifying grace. God bless you.

# "C"     Third Sunday of Advent

*Luke 3:10-18*

Today's gospel of St. Luke tells of the preaching of St. John the Baptizer. St. John was the cousin of our Lord; he was the son of Zechariah and Elizabeth. He was six months older than Christ. When St. John was about twenty-seven years of age, the Holy Spirit prompted him to go into the desert region about the Jordan River and preach a baptism of repentance which led to the forgiveness of sins.

John was the precursor of Christ, the one who prepared his way. The prophet Isaiah described him in these words: "A herald's voice in the desert, crying, 'Make ready the way of the Lord.' . . ." In his work as precursor, John employed two rites, the rite of baptism and of confession of sins. Neither of these rites were sacraments, but both were symbolic. The baptism of John was a type of the sacrament of baptism which Christ would establish at a later date. Neither was confession of sins, which he advocated, a sacrament. But it led to sincere repentance. The official stamp of approval for John's preaching and work would come later when Christ himself submitted to his baptismal rite.

John had many sincere followers among the Jews. But some who followed him were insincere; among this latter group were the Pharisees and the Sadducees. John was aware of their presence; he called them a "brood of vipers." Thus could John say to the crowds, "Give some evidence that you mean to reform."

John's message centered on the coming of the Messiah in the near future, but not exclusively so. He preached a practical spirituality; he had comments to make on the main social problems of the day. When asked by the Jews how they should act, John could say, "Let the man with two coats give to him who has none. The man who has food should do the same." He was preaching the practice of charity in a very concrete way.

John also had a message for the publicans, the tax collectors of that age. The Romans never made a practice to collect taxes themselves; instead they sold the right to collect taxes in a certain area to the highest bidder, generally a local citizen. Thus the tax collectors in Palestine were local Jews. To them John said, "Exact nothing over and above your fixed amount."

Accompanying the tax collectors on their odious mission of gathering the taxes through the countryside were soldiers. They were not soldiers of the conquering Roman army. Neither were they soldiers in the guard of Herod, the tetrach or ruler of Galilee. Rather they were soldiers whose chief duty was to enforce the collection of taxes. They dealt roughly with any Jew who refused to pay his fair share of the tax burden. To them John said, "Don't bully anymore. Denounce no one falsely. Be content with your pay."

After hearing John preach and observing this austere-living man who dressed in camel's skin, many of the Jews wondered if he were not the long-awaited Messiah. John denied this but then told them the Messiah would come after him, "I am baptizing you in water, but there is one to come who is mightier than I. I am not fit to loosen his sandal strap. He will baptize you in the Holy Spirit and in fire."

John later identified Christ as the promised Messiah, whose way he was preparing. Seeing Christ coming toward him, John said, "Look! There is the Lamb of God, who takes away the sins of the world!" John added, "I saw the spirit descend like a dove from the sky, and it came to rest on him . . . Now I have seen for myself and have testified, 'This is God's chosen One.'"

When John identified Christ as God's chosen One, many of his disciples left him and followed Christ instead. Scripture mentions five who left John to follow Christ and become his Apostles. Among the Twelve Apostles there were probably even more than five who had followed John, possibly even all.

When Christ had submitted to John's baptism and had begun his own public life, the role of John diminished. Still he continued to preach and speak out on the main social questions of the day. It was one such comment that cost John his liberty and finally his life. John publicly condemned Herod for living with his brother's wife, Herodias. Herod arrested John for this and put him in prison.

On the occasion of Herod's birthday, the daughter of Herodias danced for the King. Her dancing so delighted Herod that he swore to give her anything she asked for. Prompted by her mother, she said, "Bring me the head of John the Baptizer on a platter." Herod reluctantly granted her request, and St. John was beheaded.

St. Jerome tells us in his writings that the hatred of Herodias for John was so great that she viciously attacked his head after it was brought to her. Several times she plunged a dagger through his tongue. Christ lovingly extolled John's virtues, for he said of him, "I assure you, there is no man born of woman greater than John."

On this third Sunday of the season of Advent let us heed the words of

John the Baptizer which our Holy Mother the Church presents to us in the gospel for our consideration. John prepared the Jewish people for the coming of the Messiah. During this season of Advent, whose very name means the coming, prepare for the coming birth of our Savior on Christmas day. As John told the soldiers and tax collectors to be honest and live good lives, let us lead good Christian lives by obeying the laws of God and of the Church. Preparation of this type will bear much fruit. God bless you.

## "C"     Fourth Sunday of Advent

*Luke 1:39-45*

The greatest news ever announced to mankind! This would be but a mild description of the message that the Angel Gabriel brought to the young Virgin Mary in her humble home in Nazareth. He brought her news that she was about to become the mother of our Savior — that the long-awaited Redeemer was about to be born into this world and Mary was to be his mother.

This was the news that the world had awaited for thousands of years. The Messiah was to come and redeem mankind. The gates of heaven, long closed by Adam's original sin, were now about to be reopened. Man would once again have a means of saving his soul and gaining the happiness of heaven. Yet this earth-shattering news was made only to one person, to the Virgin Mary herself. But the humble Virgin Mary kept this great news to herself. She did not breathe it even to a soul. In fact it was necessary for an angel to reveal it to St. Joseph, her intended spouse.

While announcing this great news to Mary, the Archangel Gabriel also told her of another event of importance. He told Mary that her cousin Elizabeth was expecting a child in three months' time. This was like an invitation to go and pay her a visit. That is exactly what Mary did. The story of that visit is recorded in the gospel read at today's Mass. Mary went to the hill country of Judah and entered Zechariah's house to greet her cousin Elizabeth.

St. Luke tells us in his gospel, "When Elizabeth heard Mary's greeting, the baby stirred in her womb. Elizabeth was filled with the Holy Spirit. . . ." It is the common opinion of theologians that at this moment the yet unborn soul of St. John the Baptizer was cleansed of original sin and infused with sanctifying grace. Thus in this way Elizabeth was filled with the Holy Spirit.

Elizabeth, too, evidently having been informed by an angel or in some miraculous way that Mary was to be the mother of the future Redeemer, uttered the beautiful words that have been incorporated into the prayer called the Hail Mary, "Blessed are you among women, and blessed is the fruit of your womb."

The Visitation was a most joyous occasion. The Mother of the Savior and the mother of his precursor visited each other. The births of both of them had been foretold by an angel. And Mary and Elizabeth were cousins, blood relatives of each other.

Hence the Visitation is a joyous meeting of two cousins who had not seen each other in a long time. It is a meeting of two future mothers, of the two future mothers whose sons were to play the major role in man's salvation.

At the occasion of the Visitation Elizabeth's greeting to Mary helped form the prayer known as the Hail Mary. Mary's answer to Elizabeth, "My soul magnifies the Lord, and my spirit rejoices in God my Savior," is the prayer which all priests recite daily in their Divine Office. It is called the Magnificat.

Christ in his public life was to meet St. John the Baptizer at the river Jordan and ask to be baptized by him. But in a sense this was not their first meeting. Their first meeting was at the Visitation. It was at the Visitation that Christ brought sanctifying grace to the soul of John.

The feast of the Visitation is celebrated on July 2nd. Yet it is most appropriate that the gospel story of the Visitation be read at today's Mass, the 4th Sunday of Advent, the Sunday before Christmas, the feast of Christ's birth. In chronological order this was the one event which preceded the birth of Christ here on earth, Mary's visit to Elizabeth. Therefore it is altogether fitting and proper that we commemorate that holy event today.

The feast of the Visitation is a fitting preparation for Christ's birth on earth. If the announcement of Christ's birth, the Annunciation, was the greatest news ever announced to man, then the reality of that announcement, the birth of Christ in Bethlehem, the Nativity, was the world's greatest event. In a few days' time we shall celebrate that great event, Christmas day.

Christmas day is a day of joy and happiness. It is a day when all men can rejoice in the knowledge that the Savior of the world has been born. Christ's birth means for men the beginning of their redemption.

But surprisingly enough there have been men at different times who have tried to suppress the meaning and happiness of this day. Even while Christ lay as a small infant in the crib, King Herod tried to suppress this joyous occasion by sending his soldiers to kill the Christ Child, for he viewed him as a rival to his own throne. But Herod failed in his endeavor.

Down through the ages there have been others who have tried but with equally unsuccessful results. In 1647 the British government in the midst of the Protestant Reformation passed a law making it a crime to celebrate the feast of Christmas. Sermons on Christmas were outlawed in all churches. Christmas was called a Popish feast and invention. Christmas trees, yule logs and decorations of any sort were outlawed. Women were arrested for making plum pudding.

Secretly, however, the British people loved Christmas. It was impossible to wipe out the Spirit of Christmas from their hearts. In one village a Christmas wreath suddenly appeared in the village square. No one would admit to hanging it there. All the citizens who were asked, refused to take it down. In order to enforce the law of the land, the mayor of the village had to climb up the tall tree in the village square and take it down himself.

The British no-Christmas law took effect in our own American colonies. In Boston in 1840 a Catholic bookseller closed his shop on Christmas day. Neighbors called on him to see what was wrong — they asked if someone of his family had died or was seriously ill.

But Christmas is too important and too joyous an event to be suppressed. These laws of suppression have long ago faded away, and Christmas has been returned to its original and important position. In a few days' time we shall celebrate this great feast. As the Annunciation and Visitation are events leading up to it, let us also make careful preparation for its coming.

Let us prepare for the coming feast of Christmas by clothing our souls in the state of sanctifying grace. If necessary let us have recourse to the Sacrament of Reconciliation to remove any serious, mortal sin, if we should be guilty of any.

Let us resolve to receive the Christ Child into our body on Christmas day in the form of Holy Communion. Make your heart his crib. In no more fitting way could you celebrate the good news of the Annunciation and Visitation. God bless you.

# "C"    Christmas

*Luke 2:1-14, 15-20 or John 1:1-18*

My dear people, in the history of the world there has not been a more touching scene than the birth of Christ in Bethlehem. Never has there been a more tender or endearing event, and yet so simple and plain.

The birth of Christ is commemorated in a way as is the birth of no other person, be he president or king, champion or hero. The birth of Christ is synonymous with love and with charity. On no other occasion are more presents exchanged or more love shown the world around than on Christmas day.

The birth of Christ is a familiar story, one we have heard from early childhood. Yet it tells us of a mystery both profound and divine. It tells us of hopes so glorious that we never tire of hearing it. It reveals to us the mercy of God.

The birth of Christ is the most important event in the history of the world. Even our calendar takes its origin from it. We say that this is the year 1976 A.D. — *Anno Domini,* or after the birth of Christ.

But why, my dear people, is Christmas so important? The reason is that Christ had planned and made it so. Christ was born around midnight in the sleepy little town of Bethlehem. Seemingly this is nothing out of the ordinary, but yet the planning of Christ becomes evident when we consider that the prophet Micah prophesied centuries before that Christ would be born there: "And you, Bethlehem are not least among the princes of Juda, for out of you will come a leader, who will rule your people, Israel."

And the manner in which this prophecy came true is most amazing, for in those days there went out a decree from Caesar Augustus that the whole world should be enrolled — all were to register in the city of their birth. Mary and Joseph were then living in Nazareth, but Joseph had been born in Bethlehem. Thus he set out for the little town of Bethlehem, along with Mary, his wife, on obedience to Caesar's decree. Bethlehem was some sixty miles distant, a journey of four days afoot. In ordinary circumstances Joseph would simply have registered there and then immediately returned to this home in Nazareth.

Thus it would appear that it was by the slimmest of circumstances that Christ was born in Bethlehem. But these slimmest of circumstances were a part of God's planning. For as Caesar Augustus decreed that a census of the world should be taken, a decree came from the throne of God that the Savior of the world should be born.

The infant Jesus, born in the stable on Christmas day, was no ordinary babe. He was the God-man, Redeemer of mankind, who had come to save the world. But the world went heedlessly on as before, ignorant of the great event which had come to pass.

He had come into this world on a divine mission; from his crib, he began to fulfill it. Not by words did he teach, but rather by the circumstances of his birth. He taught a lesson more powerful than any words could convey.

He taught us a disregard for pomp and majesty, for he revealed his birth to only a chosen few — to Mary and Joseph, the shepherds on the hillside and the wise men from the East. These were the few to whom he revealed himself; these were the few who came to adore him. Christ chose these few because of their humility and purity of heart. He chose them because of their love and purity. Neither wealth nor worldly position meant anything to God, who could see men's souls.

Fix your gaze more closely on the Christ Child and his mother. The mother, a virgin most pure — the child, none other than God, who had made her. He is the Eternal Word, but he is silent. He is omnipotent, but is bound in swaddling clothes. The Creator of the world has taken the form of a creature.

He has come to save the world. His very name, Jesus, means Savior. But did he come to save mankind from poverty, suffering or work as some might imagine? No, he came to bless poverty, for he was born in a stable. He came to bless suffering, for did he not suffer, even as a baby? He came to sanctify labor, for did he not work with his foster-father, Joseph, in his carpenter shop?

Our tiny infant Savior, lifting up his tiny arms from his bed of straw, has a universal appeal. There are hardened sinners whom no amount of preaching or rhetoric can reach. But yet these same hardened hearts are moved by the sight of a cuddling infant.

Not long ago a priest was telling a group of children the beautiful story of Christmas. He emphasized the cold and the suffering Jesus had to endure. When he had finished, he asked the children, "What would you have done if you had been in the stable with the infant Jesus?"

Jimmy was the first to answer. "I'd build him a big bonfire," he said.

Johnny answered next, "I'd wrap my jacket around him."

Margaret suggested, "I'd make him a cup of warm tea."

Then Mary piped up, "I'd take the little baby in my arms, if the Blessed Virgin would let me, and I'd just love him."

This last answer was the best. For what Jesus wants of us is love. Love is the only thing that will satisfy him. Christ entered the world where the hearts of men were filled with hate. He taught us a new lesson. He taught us that love would thaw the hatred of men and bind them together in a Christian family.

Not long afterwards pagans would say, "Look at those Christians; see how they love one another."

Love is the virtue that permeates the Christmas season. Countless acts of love have been performed in Christ's name since the first memorable Christmas day. But the pattern of love was first determined and has its source in the Babe of Bethlehem.

My dear friends, let us rejoice on this happy occasion. God so loved the world that he sent his only begotten Son to redeem it. Let us remember it is the same Christ who was born in a stable who will come to judge the world in majesty. Let us love him as an infant, so that we may face him without fear on judgment day. God bless you.

# "C"    Sunday After Christmas (Holy Family)

*Luke 2:41-52*

There was once a small boy who looked over the hill from his own home. In the light of the setting sun he saw a distant house. Its windows reflected the sun's light back to him in a golden hue. "There is a golden house," he thought. "I will go there and see it." And so off he started toward the distant golden house. But after an eager journey he was very much surprised to find that the house was not golden at all. It was just an ordinary house like any other one. Its windows instead of being golden were just like his own.

And so he turned around towards his own house but then suddenly he noticed that his own home was a golden home. The rays of the sun made it glow with a golden light. Ever so eagerly did he run home.

But there once was a home that truly was a golden home. That was the home of the Holy Family in Nazareth. This home was not built of gold; in fact, it was poorer and smaller and humbler than the other homes around it. Yet it was brighter than all.

It was brighter, for it was the home of the Holy Family. It was filled with an abundance of love. All the members of the Holy Family performed their duties perfectly. St. Joseph was the model father; Mary, the model Mother, and Christ the perfect child. Today, on the feast of the Holy Family, Holy Mother the Church holds them up for us as a model to imitate.

St. Joseph was not a rich man; he could not provide luxuries and comforts for Mary and the child Jesus, but Christ did not want these. When Joseph went to Bethlehem to register, the best shelter he could find for himself and Mary was a stable. It was here that Christ was born.

And only a few days later, to save the life of the infant Christ Child, Joseph had to flee with him and Mary into the strange country of Egypt. There he lived with them in a strange land, providing for them the best he could for a few years' time.

Finally when Herod died, Joseph, Mary and the Christ Child returned to Nazareth in Palestine. Joseph provided for them the best he could working as a humble carpenter. This is the story of the Holy Family. It is a humble story, one of suffering and trials.

Only one incident of the Holy Family in Nazareth is related in Holy Scripture. This incident is mentioned in the gospel read in today's Mass. When Our Lord was twelve years old, Mary and Joseph took him to the temple in Jerusalem to help celebrate the feast of the Passover. It was required that all Jewish men go to Jerusalem for this feast. Custom dictated that the Jewish women go along. When a young boy entered his thirteenth year he too was considered a man and was asked to go along.

But when they started home Jesus remained in Jerusalem, although his parents did not know it. Thinking he was in the caravan, they had come a day's journey before it occurred to them to look for him among their relatives and acquaintances. They returned to Jerusalem looking for him. There they found him in the temple, sitting in the midst of the teachers, listening to them and asking them questions. And all were amazed at his understanding and his answers.

Our Lord returned with Mary and Joseph to Nazareth and there he lived with them until he was about thirty years of age when he began his public life. Christ never preached a sermon during these 30 years of his private life, but yet he did preach most powerfully by his example during this time. Christ spent 30 of his 33 years on this earth in the home of the Holy Family in Nazareth.

By his quiet life of 30 years at Nazareth we learn the importance of family life. The chief ingredient that goes for making a family a holy family is good example. There is no substitute for good example.

When the children of a family see their father and mother going to Mass on a Sunday morning, they will naturally go along. When parents speak of God respectfully, the children will acquire the same habit. When parents are truthful in their speech, the children will learn to be the same.

A family can become a holy family only if they give God the first place of honor in the home. The family that honors him and prays to him as a family unit is a holy family. There is much truth in the saying that "the family that prays together, stays together."

Not long ago a parish priest called at the home of some parishioners, the Smiths. They lived in a small, old house which was somewhat run-down. When Mrs. Smith answered the door, she felt ashamed to have Father see the poverty of their home. But her little daughter Mary did not share this feeling. She said, "Father, we live in the best home ever! Come, I want to show it to you!"

She led Father into the living room. Father did not notice that the carpet was threadbare. Instead he noticed a Catholic magazine lying on the table and some Catholic books on the bookshelf.

From there she led Father into the dining room. Father did not notice that the dining room furniture needed to be refinished; instead he looked at the picture of the Last Supper above the dining room table.

She led Father into the kitchen. Father did not notice the wood piled there next to the antique stove. Instead he noticed the picture of the Sacred Heart on the wall. From there she led Father into the bedroom. Father did not notice the frayed bedclothes. Instead he noticed the crucifix on the wall and the rosary on top of the dresser. Mary opened her dresser drawer and said, "See, Father, here is where I keep my missal."

Father turned to Mrs. Smith and said, "Indeed, you have a beautiful home. I would not want to see it any different."

My dear people, God will bless your home, not in proportion to its beauty or its value. He will bless it in proportion to the place of honor that you give him in it.

Resolve on this the Feast of the Holy Family that you will make your home a truly Christian home. Model it on the home of the Holy Family in Nazareth. Give God a place of honor in your home, and he in turn will richly reward it with his blessings. God bless you.

# "C"    January 1 (Solemnity of Mary, Mother of God)

*Luke 2:16-21*

Five hundred years ago the world was at war. Mohammed II had captured Constantinople; he hoped Germany would be his next prize. He battled his way forward to the walls of Belgrade, then in Hungary. There seemed to be no way of stopping him. But at this time Pope Callistus III in Rome appointed a 70-year-old monk, St. John Capistran, to preach a crusade against the Turks.

St. John took this commission most seriously. He hurried back and forth across Germany and Hungary, to rally thousands to the defense of Christendom, all this despite his age. By the time Mohammed II reached the gates of Belgrade, St. John Capistran did have an army prepared to meet him. Before the battle he gave general absolution to the army and gave them a battle cry to use in going into battle — the cry was the name of Jesus.

The following morning, before the Turks had time to regroup their forces, the Christians rushed to the attack shouting our Lord's holy name. The Turks were completely routed. Their army was forced to retreat in disorder. Before long they were pushed back off the European continent.

The name of Jesus worked wonders for St. John Capistran and his followers. It has worked wonders down through the centuries. The name of Jesus worked miracles for the Apostles. When a crippled beggar asked St. Peter for alms, Peter replied he had none to give him but said, "In the name of Jesus Christ the Nazorean, walk!" And the beggar did just that.

The name of Jesus was given us by the angel Gabriel, who appeared to Mary at the Annunciation and said, "You shall conceive and bring forth a son and you shall call his name Jesus." Mary obediently did as the archangel commanded.

The name of Jesus was officially given to our Lord on the Feast of the Circumcision, eight days after his birth. This was the law of the Jewish religion, that a boy be named at his circumsion a week after birth.

The name Jesus means Savior, but it did not arouse any particular notice among the Jews for it was a common name. St. Paul had a friend named Jesus who was with him when he was a prisoner in Rome.

But because our Lord bore this name it has come to mean more than any other name in history. If we were to ask who was the greatest man in history, one might answer Julius Caesar, Napoleon or George Washington. However, miracles have never been worked in the names of these men, but they have in the name of Christ.

Jesus is the sweetest of all names. It is sweet to the tongue to pronounce; it is sweet for our ears to hear. It brings consolation to the suffering; it brings peace to the disturbed.

Jesus himself spoke of his own name with great respect. He said, "If you ask the Father anything in my name he will give it to you." Thus using his name in prayer makes our prayers powerful. It is the name in which the sacraments are imparted and grace is given.

Because the name of Jesus conveys such power and majesty and respect, we are obliged to say it and use it with reverence and respect. In the Old Testament God's name was given as Yahweh. It was used with the greatest respect. Only one person, the high priest, was permitted to pronounce it and then only once a year. At all other times instead of the name Yahweh or God, the name Adonai which means Master or Lord was used.

The sacred name of Yahweh was engraved in gold and fastened to the mitre or headdress of the high priest. There, open and visible to all, it reminded them continually of the obligation of respect. The Second Commandment of God, "You shall not take the name of the Lord your God in vain," obliges us to do this even now.

In the New Testament other ways of showing respect for His holy name have been found. For example, it is customary for one to bow his head reverently each time he hears the name pronounced. If a man is wearing a hat, it is customary for him to tip his hat when the name is said. St. Paul writes in his epistle to the Philippians that "at the name of Jesus every knee should bend of those in heaven, on earth and under the earth."

For many centuries the name of Jesus was used reverently. But unfortunately in the Middle Ages abuse of the holy name of Jesus began to spread. In 1274 at the Council of Lyons Pope Gregory X made an urgent plea for reverence to the Holy Name.

But it remained for Bishop Diaz of Lisbon, Portugal, in 1432 to take concrete action in this regard. In the midst of the black plague which was sweeping the city, a wave of blasphemy likewise spread through. Bishop Diaz established a society for the reverent use of the Holy Name. He called it the Holy Name Society. The society spread rapidly through the city; the wave of blasphemy was suppressed. And almost immediately the black plague ended — to all it was an evident reward for the new respect shown to our Lord's holy name.

Today the Holy Name Society has spread throughout the world. There are two million members in this country alone. Pope after Pope has blessed and in-dulgenced this society. It is the most highly indulgenced lay organization in the Catholic Church today. A plenary indulgence is given to a man upon the occasion of his joining the Holy Name Society. A plenary indulgence is likewise given on the second Sunday of each month if a Holy Name Society member receives Holy Communion with the society in a body.

Today is the feast of the Holy Name, the Sunday following the Circumcision, the day on which our Lord received this holy name. On this feast day Holy Mother the Church urges us to pledge ourselves to the reverent use of Our Lord's Holy Name. We urge the men of the parish to show their reverence in a special way by becoming members of the Holy Name Society.

Holy Mother the Church has granted an indulgence of 15 days each time one pronounces the name of Jesus. With the reward so great, how can one refuse to say the name of Jesus often and say it reverently?

Not long ago an elderly lady entered the hospital with cancer of the tongue. A doctor diagnosed her case and told her he would have to perform an operation and remove her tongue. Before the operation he asked her if she had any last words to say. Her last words were, "Blessed be the name of Jesus." Truly Christ must have richly rewarded this lady for her love and devotion. Let us pray that our last words can be the same. God bless you.

# "C"     Second Sunday after Christmas

*John 1:1-18*

Today, my dear people, is the Second Sunday after Christmas. It is the Sunday following the Octave of Christmas. It is the Sunday following the feast of the Holy Family. Therefore one might expect the gospel chosen for today's Mass to be somewhat Christmasy — to have some reference to the birth or early life of our Lord. But instead the beginning of St. John's gospel, the first eighteen verses of his gospel are chosen for this Mass.

In one sense it seems strange that St. John, unlike the other three Evangelists, who begin their gospels with the story of Christ's birth in Bethlehem and early life, does not follow suit. And certainly one cannot say that St. John did not know about these events. St. John was one of the original twelve Apostles. And then when Christ was dying on the cross, he turned to St. John and to his Blessed Mother, who were both standing beneath His cross on Calvary and said to them, "Behold your mother. . . . Woman, behold your son."

St. John literally fulfilled that obligation. He took our Blessed Mother into his home in Ephesus, and there she lived with him for the remaining eighteen years of her life. Hence St. John knew our Blessed Mother extremely well. He certainly knew the details of Christ's birth in Bethlehem. But despite all this, he chose to begin his gospel in a different way. He states that his purpose in writing his gospel was to prove that Jesus Christ was God and that salvation is to be obtained through his name.

St. John does begin his gospel by speaking of Christ. But he does it in a roundabout way. He does it by referring to Christ as "the Word." Nowhere else in all of Scripture is Christ or God referred to in this manner or by this title. It is to be found only here in St. John's gospel. By the term "Word" St. John means the "Word of Salvation," who is Christ.

St. John after referring to Christ as "the Word" proceeds to list his attributes. He says that "the Word was God." He proclaims the divine nature of the Word, Jesus Christ, the Second Person of the Blessed Trinity. He makes him equal to the Father and the Holy Spirit.

He then says, "He was present to God in the beginning." By this he proclaims the eternity of Christ. He had no beginning, and he will have no end. He always was and always will be. He then relates his role in the act of creation, "Through him all things came into being." St. John asserts that Christ along with the Father and Holy Spirit had a role in the creation of the Universe. It was he who created the world and the entire universe. It was he, the Word, who made the sun, the moon and the stars. He it was who made the animals that roam the earth. It was he who gave life to man himself. Hence Christ is the author of life or life itself.

But not only was Christ the life of the world, he was its light also. It was he who created natural light, who made the sun. It is he who is the author of the light of wisdom and knowledge, who can dispel the ignorance and confusion of man. It is also he who is the author of the light of grace. For as Adam and Eve, our first parents, lost grace through original sin, it was Christ who restored grace to mankind. It is Christ who brings the light of grace to our soul — grace which is given through Baptism and the other sacraments.

St. John the Evangelist, the Apostle and the author of the last gospel, then gives a short discourse on the other St. John, St. John the Baptizer. He says he came as a witness to testify to the light. St. John the Baptizer testified, "This is he of whom I said, 'The one who comes after me ranks ahead of me, for he was before me.' " St. John the Baptizer was the precursor of Christ. He went before him to prepare his way. He announced to the people that the Redeemer Christ had come into this world. He disposed people to be prepared for his coming and his gospel.

In the concluding words of this gospel prologue St. John gives the theme of the life of Jesus Christ, "Of his fullness/we have all had a share — / love following upon love." Hence it is love that is the theme of Christ's ministry. Love is the theme of the New Testament.

On one occasion when Christ was asked what is the greatest commandment, he replied that it was to love the Lord your God above all things and love your neighbor as yourself. St. Paul says, "There remain these three: faith, hope and love, but the greatest of these is love."

Love is an infused virtue. It comes to our souls in baptism. It is a natural virtue. A baby will naturally develop love for his mother. People generally show love to those who are kind to them. But Christian love must be extended beyond this by the use of one's intellect and will.

St. John wrote, "If anyone says he loves God, but hates his brother, he is a liar. For how can one refuse to love his brother whom he sees and love God whom he does not see?''

Christ went on to give us a new command of love which was foreign to all that had been taught before by others. Christ said, "Love your enemies." The Jews had been taught to hate the Samaritans and the gentiles or all other foreigners, and the feeling was mutual between them. So Christ's command to love one's enemies was something new and different, something to which they were unaccustomed.

An excellent example of Christian love for one's enemies came out of the French revolution. One French revolutionary, a fallen-away Catholic, had developed a great hatred of priests. He had taken a vow that no priest would ever enter his house and live to tell about it — that he would kill any priest who did so enter. For many years he persecuted priests very severely.

But then as he grew older he developed a fatal illness and lay on his deathbed suffering intensely. One of his neighbors told the neighboring parish priest about his illness and at the same time told him about his hatred of priests and his vow to kill any priest who entered his house. But hearing this story did not deter the local parish priest from calling at his house regardless.

When the priest entered the room, the sick man flew into a rage. He asked for a weapon, but none was available for him to use. He then clenched his fist and shook it in the face of the priest and said, "With this hand I have strangled to death twelve of your kind."

"Wrong," said the priest, "It was only eleven. The last one did not die. God kept him alive to save you from hell." With that the priest opened his shirt and collar and exposed the scars on his neck that this very same sick man had inflicted on him. In that instant the dying revolutionist realized the wrongness of his deeds and his hatred. He begged the priest's forgiveness, made a good confession and died in the arms of the Church.

Truly this parish priest displayed the love that Christ spoke of, love for his neighbor, even for his enemies. If he had not, a man's soul would have been lost for all eternity.

St. John tells us in his gospel prologue of today's Mass that "enduring love came through Jesus Christ." Let this enduring love which Christ taught become a part of our lives. Love is the greatest of all virtues. It is the basis of our Christian faith. God bless you.


# "C"    Epiphany

*Matthew 2:1-12*

If you ask any school child how many Magi came to visit Christ in his crib at Bethlehem on the Feast of the Epiphany, his automatic answer would be three. The correct answer is that we really don't know. The Magi as a group gave Christ three presents, but there may have been more than this number in their group. A pious legend, sprung up in the Middle Ages, even assigned names to the Wise Men, but these names have no foundation in fact.

Still another pious but false tradition that has sprung up concerning them is that they were kings. This we are sure that they were not. Because the term "Magi" has been mistakenly associated with kings, our new translation of the gospel read at today's Mass calls them astrologers.

Basically they are men of mystery. They appear this one time, and one time only on the pages of Holy Scripture. We know that they came from the East, most probably from Persia. They were members of a wandering Median tribe. They were students of the stars, amateur scientists, astronomers, or as the gospel calls them, astrologists.

Only two sentences of theirs are recorded in all of Holy Scripture. Arriving in Jerusalem from the East they inquired: "Where is the newborn King of the Jews? We observed his star at its rising and have come to pay him homage."

The question that they asked greatly disturbed King Herod. To hear of a newborn king was very unsettling to the ruling king. King Herod assembled his chief priests and scribes and presented the question to them. A quick study of Holy Scripture brought the answer — in Bethlehem of Judah. Centuries before the prophet Micah had written, "And you Bethlehem, land of Judah, are by no means least among the princes of Judah, since from you shall come a ruler who is to shepherd my people Israel."

The star which guided the Magi to Jerusalem and led them to believe that a newborn king had been born is also a matter of interest to us. Scripture does not explain how a star came to lead these wise man on their search. Perhaps they had received some private divine revelation.

And a star that would change directions and lead them also is a mystery. Some think it may have been a comet appearing in the eastern horizon at that particular time. Still others following the astronomer Kepler think that at that particular time the three planets Mars, Jupiter and Saturn were aligned in the sky in a very rare coincidence. Their alignment would give the appearance to the naked eye of one bright star. Whether the true explanation is either of these two or still another explanation we cannot be sure.

After giving them the information concerning the place of the newborn king's birth in Bethlehem, Herod extracted a promise from the Magi to return to Jerusalem and report to him what they had found giving as the reason "that I may go and offer him homage too." Herod's true purpose was far different from this.

Armed with this information the Magi resumed their journey. The star which had originally guided them reappeared in the sky and led them forward, finally standing still over the place where the child was. Entering the house they found the Christ Child with Mary, his Mother. They prostrated themselves and paid him homage.

The Magi did not come empty-handed. They never paid a visit to a superior without giving a gift. To the Christ Child they brought the most precious products of their country, gold, frankincense and myrrh.

Gold was a gift that was given only to royalty. Hence in giving this to the

Christ Child, the Magi acknowledged him to be a king. Incense was a gift given only in adoration to God. In giving this to the Christ Child the Magi acknowledged his divinity. Myrrh was a balm used in anointing the bodies of the dead and preparing them for burial. In giving this to Christ the Magi indicated that the Christ Child would one day die; they thereby acknowledged his human nature.

From the visit of the Magi, the astronomers, to the crib of Christ there are many lessons which one may learn. One outstanding lesson is this — the Magi were the first non-Jews, the first gentiles, to whom the birth of Christ our Savior was revealed.

On Christmas day when Christ was born the angels announced his birth to the shepherds in the fields, but the shepherds were Jewish, members of the chosen people. His birth remained a secret with the Jews until the Magi appeared on the scene. Hence the Magi can be seen to represent the gentile people. Their visit is a revelation to the gentiles, in fact to all men, that the long-awaited Savior and Redeemer has finally come to earth to save mankind.

The universal nature of his redemptive mission begins to reveal itself. Later in his public life Christ would first present his gospel to the Jewish people. But only after their majority's rejection of it, only after his cruel death on the cross, would he instruct his Apostles to go and baptize and preach to all nations. The visit of the Magi was a sign of his universal mission in the future.

On this Feast of the Epiphany, let us rejoice in Christ's revelation of his mission to all men. Let us rejoice in the revelation of his birth to the gentile people. Let the glad tidings of his birth bring joy into our lives. Let the star announcing his coming illumine the pathways of our life. God bless you.

# "C"  Sunday After Epiphany (Baptism of the Lord)

*Luke 3:15-16, 21-22*

Many centuries ago Pope Eugene IV wrote this encyclical to the Armenians: "Holy Baptism holds the first place among the Sacraments, because it is the door of the spiritual life; for by it we are made members of Christ and incorporated with the Church. . . . The effect of this Sacrament is the remission of all sin, original and actual; likewise of all punishment which is due for sin."

This has been the teaching of the Catholic Church down through the centuries, from the time of Christ and the Apostles. Christ said, "Unless a man be born again of water and the Holy Spirit he cannot enter into the kingdom of heaven."

Likewise immediately before ascending into heaven Christ commissioned his Apostles, "Going therefore, teach ye all nations, baptizing them in the name of the Father and of the Son and of the Holy Spirit."

Baptism is solemnly administered in Church by the priest who pours water over the head of the person to be baptized and says, "I baptize you in the name of the Father and of the Son and of the Holy Spirit." Baptism is the first and most necessary of all the sacraments. It has the effect of washing away the original sin of our first parents from the soul of a child and clothing one's soul in the garment of sanctifying grace.

In the case of adults it washes away not only original sin, but also any actual sins which the baptized person may have committed himself. It takes away all venial sin and temporal punishment of which one is guilty. No stain of any type of sin remains in the soul of the newly baptized person. Should a person die immediately after baptism there would be nothing to keep his soul from ascending directly into God's presence in heaven.

In St. Luke's gospel read at today's Mass we learn that Christ joined the crowd that was receiving baptism from St. John the Baptist in the River Jordan. The River Jordan is one of the world's most rapid streams connecting the Sea of Galilee in the north with the Dead Sea in the south of Palestine. Its banks are lined with willows, poplars and tamarisk trees. The banks of the stream are steep and unfit for cultivation. It was along these banks in the vicinity of Bethany that John administered baptism to Jesus.

The baptism which John administered was not the Sacrament of Baptism. Christ had not yet instituted it. Rather it was external ablution symbolizing repentance. John's baptism had no power to remove original sin from the soul, nor instill the gift of grace. It was merely a type or a prefiguring of the sacrament that Christ was to institute at a later time.

Christ actually had no need of baptism. His soul was untainted by any kind of sin. He was the source of goodness and virtue. He was God himself. Yet he asked for and willingly received this symbolic baptism of John for good reasons. First of all, he wanted to confirm the work and mission of John the Baptist, his precursor. John actually was the son of Zechariah and Elizabeth and the blood cousin of our Lord.

Christ submitted to this ceremony of penitential baptism to show us the importance of the future sacrament. Christ was later to say, "Unless a man be born again of water and of the Holy Spirit he cannot enter into the kingdom of heaven." The importance of these words of Christ is dramatized by his submission to the rite of a symbolical baptism in the River Jordan.

Christ gave us baptism as the magna carta of our liberty from the bondage of sin and Satan. From the time of the original sin of our first parents, all mankind had entered this world with the stain of their sin on their souls. The gates of heaven were barred to man. God had been grievously offended by man's sin; his justice had not been appeased.

Christ gave us baptism as the means of removing this stain of original sin from the soul of man. It was the means of breaking Satan's grip on the world and on men's souls.

When baptism wipes away sin from one's soul, it clothes a child in the state of sanctifying grace — the garment of God's friendship. It makes one a child of God. At the time of conception life enters one's body; but at the time of baptism life comes into one's soul — supernatural life, life that will continue forever — for all eternity. Just as conception quickens the body, baptism gives life to the soul.

Baptism makes one an heir of heaven. When the baptized soul in the state of sanctifying grace departs this life, he has God's promise of eternal happiness in heaven hereafter. Baptism gives him his birthright; it removes the obstacles of sin which would keep him from entering there.

Baptism puts an indelible seal upon one's soul. The saving waters of baptism place an indelible mark upon it which will never be erased. This mark is for one's greater glory in the kingdom of heaven and for one's greater punishment should one lose his soul in the future through serious mortal sin. It is a mark which brands one's soul with the stamp of having the triune God residing within it. St. Clement called this indelible mark the "seal of the Lord."

Baptism prepares one's soul for the reception of future sacraments. It instills the first sanctifying grace in one's soul; the soul is then prepared for the further reception and increase of this grace in the reception of other sacraments, Penance, Holy Eucharist and the like.

Recently a new rite for the Sacrament of Baptism was introduced into the Church. In the prayers of this new rite the priest or celebrant says: "Dearly beloved, this child has been reborn in baptism. He (or she) is now called the child of God for so indeed he/she is. In Confirmation he/she will receive the fullness of God's Spirit. In Holy Communion he/she will share the banquet of Christ's sacrifice."

Baptism thus becomes the passport from a life of sin to a life of grace. It is the spiritual birth of a child. It brings spiritual life into one's soul.

Our Western hemisphere, with the land mass of North, South and Central America was not discovered for the world until Christopher Columbus landed on San Salvador in 1492. The colonization of the New World then began, but colonization brought vices and hardships as well. One of these was slavery. In a little over a century more than two million slaves were brought into North America alone.

One person who realized the moral evil of this practice was a young Jesuit missionary in South America, Peter Claver. He made it his mission to greet these enslaved blacks as their ships landed at the various piers and help them in any way he could. He went into the holds of the slave ships and bound up the wounds of the shackled slaves. He would bathe and put salve on their bone-bruised ankles and wrists.

But in addition to helping them in a physical way, he helped them spiritually as well. He spent long hours preaching the word of God and Christ's gospel to them. He would then baptize all those desirous of becoming Christians, and their number was great. It is estimated that he baptized three hundred thousand blacks. For bringing the gift of grace through baptism to so many souls, he had been canonized a saint. Let us thank God for giving us this saving sacrament. God bless you.

# "C"    First Sunday of Lent

*Luke 4:1-13*

When Jesus Christ, the Second Person of the Blessed Trinity, came to earth and took on the body of man, part of the humiliation he endured in his Incarnation was to allow himself to be tempted by the devil, the enemy of all souls. In today's gospel St. Luke tells us that Christ, after fasting forty days in the desert, was tempted by the devil.

Holy Mother the Church places before us this picture of Christ fasting in the desert on this first Sunday of Lent for an important reason. She wishes to teach us the importance of fasting and performing penance in our own life.

Scripture does not go into detail about the place of our Lord's fast nor what if anything he lived on during this time. Most probably the place of his fast was the Palestinian desert east of the Jordan and the Sea of Galilee. Most probably our Lord subsisted on the few edible things in the desert as did John the Baptizer before him, that is, locusts and wild honey.

But the reason for Christ's fasting is obvious. He was setting an example for us to follow. He wanted to show the importance of submitting the appetites and desires of our body to the command of our will. He wished to point out that the material pleasures of our body should be subservient to the spiritual — that as intelligent human beings we have the will power to say no to our carnal appetites.

St. Paul in his epistles pointed out the training the runners of Greece went through for the Olympic games. We in our own day know the spring training of baseball players, the rigorous training of boxers for a major fight and the training camp of football players. But if training for a human athletic event is so important, then it is infinitely more important to train our minds and our wills for the greater struggle against the forces of the devil that would lead us to commit sin, to train ourselves to resist temptation.

Christ, who was God, suffered the humiliation of allowing himself to be tempted by Satan. Satan undoubtedly knew the identity of Christ, whom he was tempting — he believed him to be the Son of God. Only a short time before his fast and temptation, Christ had been baptized in the River Jordan by John the Baptizer. On that occasion the voice of God the Father spoke from heaven, "You are my beloved Son on whom my favor rests." Then too the devil was aware of many of his miracles which showed divine power.

But the devil wanted to be sure. He wanted to see if he could be led into sin. Hence the devil in his first temptation said to Christ, "If you are the Son of God, command this stone to turn into bread."

Christ certainly had the power to do this. But Christ is using his miraculous power on other occasions had always used it for a good and useful purpose — as a charitable act to help someone or to confirm the faith of those who witnessed it. The devil's purpose on this occasion was to get Christ to use his power in a needless manner. He wanted him to use it merely to prove that he possessed it. This would be giving into pride or vanity.

Christ immediately rejected this temptation. He said, "Scripture has it, 'Not on bread alone shall man live.'"

But the devil persisted in his temptations. Using his spiritual powers, the devil took Christ to the top of a high mountain and showed him the kingdoms of the world and said, "I will give you all this power and the glory of these kingdoms. Prostrate yourself in homage before me. . . ." This was a temptation to covet worldly goods. It was a temptation to attach more importance to worldly goods than to the obligation of adoration that we owe to God alone.

One might wonder why the devil offered Christ so much — all the kingdoms of the world. To this we may say that the devil is a good salesman. He knows his customer, and he doesn't oversell him. To an ordinary person the devil might present a temptation measured in dollars and cents — to steal a specified amount of money. But Christ, he realized, surpassed all others in virtue. Therefore he put his pride very high — all the kingdoms of the world. It was a temptation to ambition.

And Christ rejected this temptation as he did the one before it. He said, quoting Scripture, "You shall do homage to the Lord your God; him alone shall you adore."

But the devil persisted and tempted him a third time. He took Christ to the parapet of the temple in Jerusalem and bid him to throw himself down from there and have his angels catch him. This was a temptation to subject oneself to unnecessary danger — to overestimate one's own strength or ability — a temptation to vainglory.

This is the type of temptation the devil often gives to the young and the foolish — a temptation to drive a car too fast or recklessly — a temptation to subject oneself to an occasion of peril and expect to walk away unscathed or unburned.

Christ realized the danger in what the devil was suggesting and said, quoting Scripture again, "It also says, 'You shall not put the Lord your God to the test.'"

Two of the Evangelists, St. Luke and St. Matthew, give us an account of those temptations of Christ in their gospels. However the order of the second and third is reversed. St. Matthew lists the temptation from the pinnacle of the temple as the second one and the one from the high mountain as third. The order in which they actually occurred is unimportant. They both give the same substantial account of them.

Undoubtedly they occurred when Christ was fasting in the desert alone. No one was present to witness them save the devil, the tempter, and Christ, the tempted. Christ undoubtedly told his Apostles about these temptations at a later time. Christ revealed these temptations for a definite purpose. He wanted to teach men that if he, who was divine, was subject to temptation, then we, the creatures of God, who are human, must also expect to endure it. We cannot expect to escape it. We must face it and fight it.

But in another sense temptation is a sign of God's love. We read in the Book of Tobit: "Because you were acceptable to God, it was necessary that temptation should prove you." God allows temptation to those whom he trusts. Temptation affords us an opportunity of manifesting our loyalty to him.

Temptation is a means of acquiring the rewards God has promised to those who serve him. Temptation should be viewed as a mark of God's favor. The devil never tempts those who are already in his power. He confines his temptations to those whom he envies in the service of God. Temptations are a proof of God's friendship. They arouse us from a tepid state. They cleanse us from imperfections. They allow us to expiate for the temporal punishment due to sin here in this life. They perfect virtue. They are steps on the ladder which leads to heaven.

Christ by enduring these temptations showed us not only that we are to be tempted but also how to deal with temptations and reject them. First of all, we should pray as he did for forty days in the desert. In prayer we are in conversation with almighty God. He will give his help to those who pray to him and seek his aid.

Secondly we should mortify our bodies by fasting and other penance. We must make our bodily appetites obedient to the commands of our will. Our spiritual welfare and the good of our souls should take precedence over pleasures of our bodies.

Remember, God never permits one to be tempted beyond his strength. St. Paul writes in his first Epistle to the Corinthians: "And God . . . will not suffer you to be tempted above that which you are able . . . to bear. . . ." His grace is with us, whenever temptations come our way. No one can ever say the temptation was so strong he was forced to give in. The one who succumbs to temptation does so only through the choice of his own free will and the rejection of God's graces.

Therefore in the beginning of this holy season of Lent let us practice fast and other forms of mortification. Let us be ready to battle against temptation whenever it may arise. Let us view it as an opportunity of ascending a rung on the ladder that leads to the kingdom of heaven. Got bless you.

# "C"     Second Sunday of Lent

*Luke 9:28-36*

Three of the Evangelists, Matthew, Mark and Luke, give an account of the Transfiguration in their gospels. The particular account of St. Luke is read at the gospel of today's Mass.

St. Luke tells us that Christ took three of his Apostles, Peter, James and John, onto a mountain to pray. The mountain to which he took them is not identified in the gospel story, but from its description, from the locality in which Christ was preaching just prior to this, and other evidence, Scripture scholars strongly believe it to be Mt. Tabor.

The three Apostles whom he took with him may well be called the leaders of the Twelve. St. Peter was their natural spokesman. Later Christ was to make him Vicar or Head of his Church here on earth. St. James was to suffer martyrdom, to shed his blood for Christ. St. John was our Lord's closest friend and confidant.

While Jesus was on the mountain praying with his three Apostles, his face changed in appearance. His clothes became dazzlingly white. He was transfigured before them. Christ had a definite purpose in performing this miracle and revealing his glory to his Apostles. He wished to prevent their being scandalized when in the near future he suffered his Passion and allowed himself to be crucified.

Only a short time before, Christ's true identity was made known to them when Peter declared him to be the Son of God. Then too, Christ had immediately prophesied his sufferings and death. This prophecy had depressed the spirit of the Apostles. The Apostles, mistakenly, looked for Christ to establish an earthly kingdom. They could not see how allowing himself to be tortured and put to death would fit into these plans of redeeming mankind. Hence Christ gave them this foretaste of glory which they could recall and look back upon when they saw him hanging on the cross.

But when Christ was transfigured, suddenly two men were talking with him — Moses and Elijah. Their presence with Christ was significant. The Jews had continually accused Christ of being a violator of the law, but here was Moses, the author and originator of the law, talking with Christ. Also, Elijah, the leading prophet of the Old Testament, was present with him. And between them they gave Christ the place of honor.

Their presence gave support to Christ in his mission — he had come to earth not to contradict the law, but to fulfill it.

This, the fact that he could call these holy men of the Old Testament back to life and have them present with him on the mountain, showed his power over life and death. It proved his claim to be the Son of God, God who was the author of life. And Moses and Elijah spoke to Christ concerning his mission and future death in Jerusalem, and they spoke in the presence of Peter, James and John, who heard them.

The Apostles entered a trance, similar to a deep sleep. They were spellbound by the great event they had witnessed. As Moses and Elijah were about to leave, St. Peter spoke up, "Lord, it is good for us to be here. Let us set up three booths, one for you, one for Moses, and one for Elijah." The booths of which St. Peter spoke were small grass huts which the shepherds in the fields used to shelter themselves against the elements of the weather. To erect three such small and temporary structures as grass huts in commemoration of so great an event was a foolish and inane suggestion. But still it showed that St. Peter realized the importance of this Revelation.

But while Peter was speaking, a cloud came and overshadowed them. From out of the cloud there came a voice, "This is my Son, my Chosen One. Listen to him." It was the voice of God the Father, come down from heaven. It was as awesome as thunder. The earth trembled with it. At the sound of it the Apostles fell to the ground.

Thus not only had Moses and Elijah, the two leading figures of the Old Testament, come to life and confirmed the mission of Christ, but God, his heavenly Father, the First Person of the Blessed Trinity, had spoken out of a

260 / HOMILIES: YEAR C

cloud. He too had given his support to his divine Son. He had called him his Chosen One; he commanded the Apostles to listen to him.

When the voice of God the Father fell silent, the Apostles looked up. They then saw no one other than Jesus himself. Moses and Elijah had left him. Jesus was there alone with them. He then made a request of them — not to reveal what they had seen to others until he had himself risen from the dead.

Christ's Transfiguration proved his divinity. It gave his Apostles a fore-taste of the glory that was due him in heaven. But one cannot help but realize the close association of his Transfiguration with his Passion and death. This miracle of Christ took place immediately after Christ had told his Apostles of his approaching sufferings and death. When Moses and Elijah appeared with Christ they talked with him about his approaching Passion.

From all of this we can learn an important lesson in our own lives — through suffering we too can earn an eternal reward. Future glory and honor must be merited by our suffering in this life on earth.

Christ said on another occasion that "the kingdom of heaven suffers vio-lence, and the violent bear it away." He said also, "If any man will come after me, let him deny himself, and take up his cross and follow me."

These words of Christ convey the message that we can only enter heaven the hard way — by doing violence to our flesh — by struggling against our pas-sions — by fasting and penance — by enduring sufferings patiently for the sake of Christ. There is no easy way to enter heaven; heaven must be gained and earned through combat.

This, of course, is not the language of today. This is not the modern way of living. One modern liberal of our times has said, "The idea of a future life poisons this present life." The thought of a future life, of either eternal reward or eternal punishment, dampens one's enjoyment of the pleasures of the pres-ent. If one hesitates to enjoy a certain pleasure, for fear that he may be commit-ting a sin, he may be called a square or a cop-out.

But unless one does battle against temptation, he is exchanging his birth-right for a bowl of porridge, the future happiness of heaven for some fleeting pleasure here on earth. Remember the words of St. Paul to the Romans: "I reckon that the sufferings of this time are not worthy to be compared with the glory to come. . . ." God bless you.

# "C"     Third Sunday of Lent

*Luke 13:1-9*

At the gospel of today's Mass St. Luke's account of the parable of the fig tree is read to us. Christ said, "A man had a fig tree growing in his vineyard, and he came out looking for fruit on it but did not find any. He said to the vinedresser, "Look here! For three years now I have come in search of fruit on the fig tree and found none. Cut it down."

Scripture scholars are in almost unanimous agreement as to the allegorical meaning of this parable. Our Lord himself is the gardener. The fig tree represents the Jewish people. The three years' time the gardener sought fruit from the fig tree represents the three years of our Lord's public life. The judgment to cut down the fig tree represents the punishment to be meted out to the Jewish people for refusing to accept our divine Savior.

This punishment was not long in coming, for in the year 70 A.D. the city of Jerusalem was leveled to the ground by the Roman army as Christ prophesied it would be.

This allegorical interpretation of the parable has found almost universal acceptance among the Scripture scholars. But yet in a broader sense, another application is possible. The barren fig tree can be seen not merely to represent the Jewish people, but anyone who hears the gospel of Jesus Christ and either refuses to believe it or to act upon it.

Unfortunately in the Catholic Church today there are a greater number of lukewarm or tepid Catholics. They are Catholics in name only. The waters of baptism have been poured over their heads. They have received the gift of sanctifying grace. But yet they do not attempt to increase this grace as often as they could or should through the reception of Holy Communion or the other sacraments. They are like barren fig trees.

Several centuries ago when St. Francis of Assisi knelt in prayer Christ spoke to him. He said, "Repair my Church." St. Francis wondered what he meant. He first interpreted Christ's words literally. He began physically to repair the Church of St. Damien in the nearby village which had fallen into disrepair. With stones and mortar he also repaired two other nearby churches. But after performing this labor, St. Francis realized that Christ meant more than to repair his churches in a physical sense. He wanted him to repair them in a spiritual sense also.

In a similar sense Pope John XXIII wanted to repair Christ's Church back in 1959 when he first convened the Second Vatican Council. He wanted to restore the Church in the hearts of men. He wanted men to have a better understanding of the true nature of the Church.

When Pope John assumed the office of Pope in the Catholic Church, he said in his first public talk that he called on all Catholics to be a perfect people for the Lord. In fact, this goal of perfection, he declared, was his chief reason for convoking the Second Vatican Council. His views on this matter are contained in the Dogmatic Constitution on the Church, a major document of the Second Vatican Council.

In this document our Holy Fathers and the Fathers of the Council state that all the faithful are called to perfection. All are called to holiness.

Holiness is a virtue which means conformity to the will of God. It means health of the soul. Holiness is to the soul what health is to the body.

In calling holiness conformity to God's will, we have the example of Christ himself to follow. In the Garden of Gethsemane just prior to his Passion and death, Christ prayed, "Father, if it be possible, let this chalice pass from me, yet not my will, but yours be done." Later while dying on the cross he said, "Father, into your hands I commend my spirit." Christ conformed himself perfectly to the will of his Father in heaven. He is the true picture of holiness.

Christ practiced a doctrine of holiness himself. He taught holiness to others in his preaching. He taught the theological virtues of faith, hope and love. He taught the Ten Commandments.

Christ gave us the means of holiness. He gave us the Seven Sacraments. He gave us baptism, which wipes original sin from our souls. He gave us the Holy Eucharist, which contains his own body and blood and which brings an increase of grace to those who receive it. He gave us the Holy Sacrifice of the Mass — the perfect religious sacrifice.

Christ established a Church as a means of leading men to holiness. From membership in his Church he excluded no one. He told his Apostles to go and baptize and teach the gospel to all nations. Christ wants all men to be saved; he wants all men to be holy. It extends to all men in all ages and all walks of life.

Christ did not intend that only those who enter the religious life to practice holiness. He intended that all members of the laity practice it as well. He intended that the laity as well as the religious obey the Ten Commandments and practice the virtues of charity and love. There are no second-class citizens in the Church of Christ. Baptism has the same effect for all. Each and every Christian has the same right to heaven.

Being holy does not necessarily mean that one must walk around constantly with a long face — that all laughter and pleasure be removed from life. On the contrary, a holy person is very likely to be a happy person. A holy person can find great pleasure in the things around him. It means only that one abstain from unlawful and immoral pleasures. For example, John Bosco was a happy-go-lucky person. He was always laughing. But yet he was a very holy person.

Holiness can be achieved by people who make their living through manual labor — by those who perform hard physical work. It was achieved by St. Isidore, who was a farmer; by St. Martin, who was a soldier. It can be achieved by a housewife in her home. St. Monica achieved holiness and sainthood in this way. Let us remember that Christ himself spent thirty of his thirty-three years on this earth working with St. Joseph, his foster-father, at a carpenter's bench. And Christ is the perfect example of holiness.

Pope John XXIII, who summoned the Second Vatican Council, was a holy man himself. His purpose in convoking it was to achieve greater holiness in the world. Let us learn to practice holiness from his example. Let us learn to practice it from the words of Vatican II. Holiness in this life is the key to happiness in the next. Let us not be a barren fig tree, but rather let us bear fruit abundantly. God bless you.

# "C" Fourth Sunday of Lent

*Luke 15:1-3, 11-32*

The parable of the Prodigal Son is a parable of inspiration. It has no parallel in all of literature. It is a parable of mercy and love; it is the kind of parable no human mind could invent, one that could come only from the lips of our Savior. It is a classic of mercy and forgiveness. It has been suggested by some that instead of being called the parable of the Prodigal Son, it should instead be called the parable of the forgiving father.

Christ addressed the parable to the scribes and Pharisees, who were critical of his association with sinners and tax collectors. He told them about a father who had two sons. The younger came to the father and asked him to give him at that time the share of his estate that he would one day inherit. The younger had assumed that his father would one day will his estate to be divided between his two sons.

This younger son had no regard for his father's rights and ownership of his own property. He thought only of himself. He was guilty of greed, of covetousness. He presumed on his father's love and concern for him. He failed to see that generally when fathers possess property, they retain it and administer it because of foresight. Their experience in the ways of the world equip them with greater ability to govern or run a farm or business.

Undoubtedly the father in today's parable knew the character of his younger son. He recognized his faults, his greed, his impetuousness, his lack of foresight. Had he been a strict father, his answer to his son would certainly have been NO! But instead, being an over-loving or a doting father, he lacked the heart to refuse his son's request. He went against his better judgment and gave in. He divided up his property with his younger son as he had requested.

As one might expect, the younger son squandered and used his newly acquired possessions foolishly. He went off to a distant land and spent his money on dissolute living. He spent his father's hard-earned money in a foolish way. For a short while the money flowed through his hands in a reckless and carefree manner. But soon he found himself with nothing left.

A famine overtook the land where he was living. With his fortune gone, he found himself in dire need. He had no means to make a living. In desperation he sought out the help of a man he had met, the owner of a large amount of property. He in turn sent him to his farm to take care of his pigs.

To the Jews this was the lowest of all occupations. The Jews regarded pigs as unclean animals. They were forbidden to eat pork. Hence to raise pigs was the lowest of all occupations. It was the depth of depravity.

The customary food for hogs back in the time of our Lord was the fruit of the carob tree. The carob tree was a very common type of evergreen that grew throughout Palestine. It produced green pods which were edible but had an unpleasant taste. Even the poorest of the poor refused to eat carob pods; thus they became the staple food for hogs.

The prodigal son began to feel the pangs of hunger. He realized that he was not as well-fed as were the hogs he was taking care of. As formerly he was guilty of greed or covetousness, even now he began to envy the hogs the food that they ate.

Suffering this indignity and being half-starved, the prodigal son began to realize his guilt in leaving his father's house. He repented his sinfulness. He began to reflect that even the servants in his father's house had more to eat and lived better than he did himself. Therefore he resolved to return home and beg his father's forgiveness.

Our Lord tells us that the father caught sight of his son while he was still a long way off. A father sighting his son at such a great distance is not the result of mere chance. It could happen only when a father was looking for his son. It could happen only to a father who had never become resigned to his son's leaving home, who still held out the hope of his return.

Immediately the father ran forward to greet his son. The son had prepared a confession — a confession of humility acknowledging his guilt. But his father never let him finish it. He interrupted him. He wanted only to show his love for his son. He threw his arms around his neck and kissed him.

He ordered his servants to bring the finest robe for his son. It was the custom of all well-to-do families of the Middle East to own a beautiful and expensive robe. This could be worn by any member of the family on festive occasions. And to the father this was a festive occasion, the return of his lost son. Thus he ordered the festive robe to be brought out for him and also a ring for his finger; a ring was the sign of nobility. The father decided that the occasion called for a celebration — that the fatted calf should be killed.

Meanwhile the elder son was out on the land. As he neared the house he heard the sound of music and dancing. When he learned from a servant the occasion of the celebration, the return of his younger brother, the elder brother grew jealous. He refused to go in.

He protested to his father that he had worked long and hard for him, but the father had never given him a party or celebration, such as he was giving now. In saying these things and acting in this manner, the elder son was guilty of the sin of jealousy or envy.

Envy is an old sin. It was the sin which caused Lucifer and some angels of heaven to fall from grace. It was the sin which caused Cain to kill his brother Abel. It is the kind of sin that the devil tempts many people to commit even now.

In response to this outbreak of envy, the father appealed to love. He explained to his oldest son that all he had was his, that he was with him always. He pointed out that there was reason to celebrate because his brother had returned from the dead.

Each of the brothers was guilty of sin: the younger one, of greed or covetousness; the older, of envy or jealousy. In each case the father was merciful and forgiving. His love for his sons went beyond their petty jealousy and greed.

The love of the father in this parable can readily be compared to the love God has for men, his adopted sons. Even despite our sins God has love for us. When Adam sinned, God sent his own Son to redeem us. On the cross Christ said of his executioners, "Father, forgive them for they know not what they do."

God does not prevent our sinning. He gives us free will as the father gave his son free will to leave home. But once we are sorry, he forgives us. He receives us with open arms as the father did his prodigal son. Therefore, let us realize the great love God has for each of us. Whatever sins we may have committed, let us beg his forgiveness. God bless you.

# "C"    Fifth Sunday of Lent

*John 8:1-11*

St. John relates in today's gospel that Christ was visiting the city of Jerusalem. He made his annual trip there to celebrate the feast of the Passover, as required by Jewish law. But the scribes and the Pharisees were envious of our Lord. They attempted to lay a trap for him. One day as he sat teaching in the temple they brought forward a woman who was caught in the sin of adultery.

The ancient Jewish law of Moses required that a woman caught in adultery be stoned to death. However, this particular law had not been enforced in centuries. At the time Christ lived on earth, the death penalty for adultery was considered far too harsh. The Jews called Christ "teacher" and asked him what he had to say about the case.

The Jews were attempting to trip Christ up on the horns of a dilemma. If Christ said she should not be stoned to death, he would be contradicting the law of Moses. In addition stoning a person to death was forbidden by Roman law; hence to obey a Jewish law would be to break a Roman one. On the other hand, if he said she should be stoned and should be put to death, he would be contradicting the principles of love and mercy which he had taught so often. They saw no escape from this dilemma which they were placing before him.

The crime of adultery came under the jurisdiction of the Sanhedrin, the Jewish court of 72 members that ruled over the city of Jerusalem and Judea. Nevertheless they brought this woman to Christ instead in order to test him.

But Christ was more than a match for their cunning and deceit. He answered them nothing at all. He remained silent. Instead he bent down and started tracing on the ground with his finger. Scripture does not tell us what he traced in the sandy Palestinian soil. But we can well imagine.

Remember Christ was God, Second Person of the Blessed Trinity. As God, Christ possessed divine knowledge. He could see the souls of those questioning him. He knew directly what sins each of them had committed and was guilty of. Perhaps among other things he spelled in the sand the hidden sins of which they were guilty. He may have brought to light the most secret sins of which they were guilty.

But then, after scratching his message in silence in the sand, Christ stood erect. He looked the woman's accusers in the eye. In bringing this woman to him and accusing her of adultery, even if the charge were true, they were guilty of the sin of detraction themselves. They were revealing the hidden faults of another. They were publicly robbing her of her good name. They were preparing to rob her even of her life. If their charges were false, then they were guilty of calumny.

They said they had caught her in the act. But how would they know of the private actions of another unless they were spying, or eavesdropping or listening in on the secrets of another. They were invading another's privacy, which is wrong in itself.

Undoubtedly too there were other women present in the crowd. Perhaps they had committed the crime of which they accused this woman. But there they were, standing there, some perhaps with stones in their hands, ready to hurl them at the accused, eager to see blood flow. They were the products of their time, cruel, pagan, barbarous. They were following the example of their conquerors, the Romans, who were noted for their cruelty.

The crowd before our Lord had not yet learned the lesson of love he came to teach them: "Love your neighbor as yourself." If they themselves were guilty of no other crime, then at least they were guilty of a lack of charity.

Christ looking at them said, "Let the man among you who has no sin be the first to cast a stone at her." Then a second time he bent down and wrote on the ground. Again Scripture is silent on the message he wrote or scribbled in the sand with his finger or the twig of a tree. Perhaps he continued writing what he had started to write before — their names and the secret sins on their soul of which they were guilty, sins they thought were safely hidden away. Christ may have revealed them for what they really were.

At this point the message of Christ was beginning to sink in. They realized they could not deceive Christ. Christ had invited the innocent one or sinless one among them to cast the first stone. But not one among this sordid crowd could make this claim. Their evil intent of tripping up Christ, of wanting to see the blood of another spilled upon the sand, had come out in the open.

In humiliation they took the only alternative open to them. One by one, beginning with the elders, they dropped their stones on the ground and began to walk away. Christ had forced them to admit that they also were sinners.

Then finally when the last of the woman's accusers had left, Christ turned and spoke to the woman accused of adultery: "Woman, where did they all disappear to? Has no one condemned you?" "No one, sir," she answered.

It was at this point that the mercy of Christ asserted itself. Christ was sinless. At his own suggestion, he who was without sin might cast the first stone. Christ alone among the entire crowd of the woman's accusers would be able to do this, but yet he would not. Christ came on a mission to teach mercy, love and forgiveness — not hate or revenge.

Jesus said, "Neither do I condemn you. You may go, but from now on, avoid this sin." But Christ's failure to condemn this woman and his display of mercy should not be construed in any way as a condoning of the sin she was accused of. As much as Christ loved man, he hated man's sins.

Christ was able to forgive this woman and send her away for he himself was to assume the burden of her sin on his own shoulders. In the not-too-distant future he was to assume the burden of her sin and the sins of her accusers and the sins of all men on his shoulders. He was to carry a cross up Mt. Calvary. Christ would not condemn this woman because he was to be condemned for her.

Christ's mission on earth was to redeem mankind from the shackles of sin — to reopen to man the gates of heaven. He was to do this by his own sufferings and death — by his passion and crucifixion, a death he voluntarily accepted. By his death he would satisfy God's justice and compensate for the great injury sin had caused him.

Because of this Christ could send the accused adulteress away. Because of his future satisfaction Christ was able to institute the Sacrament of Penance — to give to his Apostles and their successors, the priests and bishops of his Church, the power to forgive the sins of all men of all ages.

Let us thank God for sending his divine Son to redeem us. Let us thank him for the merciful sacrament of forgiveness — the Sacrament of Reconciliation. Let us thank him for this sacrament of a second chance. Let us use this sacrament as often as necessary to keep our souls in the state of sanctifying grace. Let penance be for us a means of gaining eternal salvation. God bless you.

# "C"     Passion Sunday (Palm Sunday)

*Luke 22:14 — 23:56*

The official Roman method of executing criminals was crucifixion. In early Roman times a forked cross in the shape of a "Y" was used. The hands of the victim were nailed to the forked branches. Later two notched beams were laid across one another at right angles and nailed together.

Customarily the hands of the victim were fastened to the crossbeam when the sentence was first passed. He was then led or driven through the streets with a rope tied around his waist. When he reached the place of execution, his feet too were nailed to the vertical beam of the cross, and the two beams were fastened together and the cross erected.

This was the normal method of crucifixion. In some few recorded cases a criminal was pardoned his crime after being crucified. But in each case where a man was taken down from the cross alive he died shortly afterwards.

Crucifixion was considered by the Romans to be the most severe of all punishments. Some Roman officials, among them Cicero, thought it was excessively cruel and wanted to outlaw it, but failed in their attempt. It remained the official method of execution for the Romans for many centuries.

As a general rule the Roman cross was low. The feet of the victim were about a yard from the ground. But when the victim was someone of importance or the Romans wanted to make a special example of him, a higher cross was used. In the case of Christ, his cross was probably higher than those of the two thieves crucified beside him. This is indicated by the fact that when they wished to alleviate his thirst they soaked a sponge in gall and put it on a reed in order to hold it to his lips.

The question has been asked, precisely how does crucifixion cause one's death? Some have thought that it causes one to bleed to death. But science does not bear out this theory. The average body contains about five quarts of blood. One can lose about half this amount and continue to live. It is estimated that in crucifixion, since no vital organs are pierced when the hands and feet are pierced with nails, less than half a pint of blood is lost.

A more reasonable explanation is that of asphyxiation. The hands and the feet are nerve centers of the body. When they are pierced with nails, it causes pain. It causes an infection in the body known as tetanus or lockjaw. This can be contracted when one steps on a rusty nail.

Bacteria or bacilli infect the central nerves in the hands and the feet causing them to contract violently. The muscles are irritated into continuous spasms, and they too contract. And all the while the weight of the body pulls down against the nails which pierce the hands in a suspended position. Frequently one's arms were tied to the cross with ropes so that the nails would not pull through the hands.

The continuous contraction of the nerves and muscles pulling against the nails causes one unbearable pain. Muscle spasms attack the arms and shoulders and then later the back, legs and thighs. These muscle spasms impede the flow of blood to the various parts of the body. Hence the blood is unable to carry oxygen to the parts of the body as it normally does. A very high bodily fever and severe thirst are indications of this condition.

Crucified victims have been known to push down on their feet as hard as they could, even though their feet were also pierced with nails and pushing down caused them untold pain. But this pushing down or attempting to stand as erect as possible relieved the muscle contraction in their arms and chest and allowed them to take a small breath of air and inhale some oxygen in their body.

When the Roman executioners wanted to hasten the death of a crucified victim they would break his legs. This would prevent his pumping for air on the cross and cause him to die more quickly. This was the case of the two thieves crucified beside our Lord. But Christ had been scourged at the pillar and crowned with thorns; he had lost a great deal of blood before his crucifixion. Hence he died more quickly on the cross.

Still another means the Romans used to hasten the death of a crucified victim was to start a brushwood fire beneath the cross. The smoke from the fire would help suffocate the victim on it.

But the end result of the violent muscle contraction and the blood being unable to carry enough oxygen to the various parts of the body brought death through asphyxiation. It sometimes came in a matter of hours; it sometimes took a couple of days. But it never failed.

Crucifixion was the official Roman means of execution; it was the cruelest and most painful death they knew. But consider that Christ endured this torment and death voluntarily. He was God, Second Person of the Blessed Trinity. He had within him the power to come down from the cross at any time he wished. He could have punished or executed his own executioners. Christ said to Peter, who had drawn his sword to protect him from being arrested in the Garden of Gethsemane, "Do you not suppose that I cannot entreat my Father and he will even now furnish me with more than twelve legions of angels?"

Christ endured this cruelest of deaths voluntarily. But why? He did it out of love for man. He did it to free man from the chains of sin, to reopen to him the gates of heaven.

This is the message of Calvary. Christ died out of love for man. He voluntarily submitted to crucifixion to atone for the sin of our first parents. The weight of the cross on his shoulders was the weight of all our sins.

The words Christ spoke from the cross were not the usual threats or curses of a crucified criminal. They were words of love and forgiveness. Of his executioners he said, "Father forgive them for they know not what they do." He spoke consolingly to his mother. He forgave the sins of the penitent thief crucified next to him. These are the words of the crucified God-man.

There is no way we can atone for these cruel torments and death of our Savior. We can only feel remorse for our sins which led him to this end. We can beg his forgiveness for our offenses.

From Calvary we can learn the great evil of sin. We can form a firm resolution to avoid it in our lives. A mortal sin which kills the life of grace in our souls is a far greater evil than the most painful death of our bodies. Mortal sin makes one deserving of the fires of hell, a punishment far more severe than even the pains of crucifixion.

Let us look upon the cross of Christ as a sign of mercy and forgiveness. Let it be the means of blotting out sin in our own lives. God bless you.

## "C"      Easter Sunday

*John 20:1-9; Luke 24:1-12 or 13-35*

During the early 19th century the Emperor Napoleon was at the height of his military power. He had conquered nearly all of Europe. One of the countries he overran was Austria. While subduing this country, he sent one of his generals, Messena, with an army of 18,000 men to capture the village of Feldkirch. There was great consternation in the little town as the invading army approached.

The villagers gathered together to decide what should be done. They agreed on one thing — it was useless to oppose Napoleon's legions — but beyond that they could not come to any common decision. At this point the kindly village pastor arose and said, "My beloved children, this is Easter Sunday. Cannot God, who arose from the dead, protect us in our distress? Shall our first act in this calamity be to forsake him? Let us go to church as usual, and trust to God for the rest."

The people accepted his words hopefully, and the sextons were ordered to ring the bells as joyfully as possible. The people turned out *en masse* to enter the church. They celebrated Easter as joyfully and as gaily as ever. The French armies, upon hearing the bells ring and ring, concluded that it could only mean one thing — that strong Austrian reinforcements had arrived. The French General Messena, not wishing to risk a battle at that time, ordered his army to retreat. Thus the Easter bells of Feldkirch saved the city. Christ would not allow those who were celebrating the glory of his great feast day to be captured and oppressed.

Truly, my dear people, Easter is the greatest feast in the Church calendar. It is the day on which Christ rose from the dead glorious and immortal. It is the feast day of our redemption.

Christ's Resurrection is the logical fulfillment of his teachings. It is the fulfillment of prophecies made centuries ago. It is proof positive that Christ was the Son of God as he claimed to be. It is proof that the Church which he established is the one true one.

Not long ago a wealthy western businessman became concerned over the number of religions in existence today and their diverse claims. He conceived the idea of establishing a universal religion for all to belong to. But before attempting this, he desired to learn more about the Catholic Church. He therefore, contacted a Catholic priest asking him his suggestions.

The priest replied, "I can give you one sure-fire suggestion. Have yourself nailed to a cross and hang there until you die. Let them bury you. Three days later, or the next day, if you prefer, rise from the grave by your own power without the help of anyone. Your success will be certain."

Needless to say, this reply helped dissuade the ambitious businessman from his endeavor. No human could ever do these things. Yet this is exactly what Christ did.

There are many liberalists and others in the world today who hold peculiar notions concerning Christ. They maintain he was a good man who went about doing good for people. But pin such people down. Ask them, precisely what good did Christ do? Did he do the things expected of a good person today? Did he jump in the water to save someone from drowning? Did he give the poor money to buy food with? Did he comfort the sick?

No, he did none of these things. He did things above and beyond the ordinary powers of others. He didn't save anyone in the water; instead he walked on the water. He calmed the storm at sea by his word only. Christ did not give money to the poor to buy food with; instead he multiplied the loaves and the fishes. He didn't simply comfort the sick; he cured them. He made the blind see, the deaf hear, and the crippled walk again.

On three occasions Christ even raised the dead to life. He raised to life the daughter of Jairus, who had been dead a short while. He raised to life the only son of the widow of Naim, who was on his way to being buried. He raised to life Lazarus, who had been dead for several days and whose body had begun to decay.

But Christ's greatest miracle, upon which the Christian religion depends, is his own Resurrection from the dead. At various occasions he had foretold it. He said, "Destroy this temple and in three days I will rebuild it." The Jewish leaders remembered this prophecy of Christ, for they went to Pontius Pilate after they had crucified him and told him of it and asked for a guard for his tomb. This request was granted.

Hence the cross of Christ became the crucial experiment — the challenge. Although he had performed other miracles, the Jews believed that his death would be the end of his life — that his followers would fall away, and that the religion he founded would end.

Christ did not disappoint us. He rose as he said he would. He rose on Easter Sunday morn. The guards at his tomb were powerless to stop him. He even stayed on earth for forty days, appearing to his Apostles and crowds on many occasions and proving that it really was he. He even invited his doubting Apostle, Thomas, to put forth his finger into the wounds in his hands and side.

Christ had conquered death. Sin had been cheated of its greatest punishment. Christ had opened to man the road to eternal life. He proved that he was God.

Let us on this Easter Sunday morning renew our faith in this great teaching of the Church. As the souls in Limbo rejoiced when Christ came there on Good Friday afternoon to preach to them, while his body was in the tomb, let us rejoice on his return to life on Easter Sunday, when he rose from the dead.

Let his Resurrection be for us a source of inspiration and of hope — hope of our own resurrection to come. God bless you.

# "C"    Second Sunday of Easter

*John 20:19-31*

Brother Leo, one of the early followers of St. Francis of Assisi, once saw in a vision a turbulent river and a multitude of people trying to cross it. Some sank before they had gone very far. Others managed to get halfway across and then sank. Still others almost reached the opposite shore before they too sank and drowned in the current. Only a very few reached the safety of the other shore.

Brother Leo asked St. Francis for an explanation of this vision. St. Francis declared that the river is the current of life. Those swimming the river were those trying to preserve their baptismal grace. Those who drowned were those who committed mortal sin and lost their baptismal innocence some time in life — some at an early age, some in middle age, and still others toward the end of their life. Very few preserved it. The meaning of the story is that unless men had the additional help of the Sacrament of Reconciliation, great numbers would indeed perish.

In today's gospel, St. John relates how Christ instituted this sacrament. Breathing on his disciples he said: "Receive the Holy Spirit. If you forgive men's sins, they are forgiven them. If you hold them bound, they are held bound." By these words Christ gave his disciples the power to forgive or retain sin. He gave this power to his Apostles, and to their successors, the priests and bishops in the Catholic Church.

When a priest sits in the confessional, he takes the place of Christ. The words of absolution he pronounces have the same effect as those which Christ spoke to the paralytic or Mary Magdalene. It is as if Christ were sitting in the confessional and speaking through the lips of the priest.

Through these words of absolution a great change takes place in the soul of the penitent. The soul blackened with mortal sin is made white as snow. It is cleansed of sin and clothed with the garment of sanctifying grace. The change that occurs in the soul is far more wonderful than Christ's healing of the leper. Sin is far worse than any leprosy of the body.

Confession is a natural remedy for any soul dead with sin. I am sure you would not hesitate to see a doctor if you were seriously ill. Likewise one sick with mortal sin should seek the healing power of the priest in the confessional.

Yet while people will not hesitate to go to a doctor for the slightest illness, they still have an aversion about entering the confessional. In the early centuries of the Church this was not so. In early times penances were often long and severe, and some were performed publicly. Yet people appreciated the Sacrament of Reconciliation and went regularly without much urging.

But finally in the year 1215 Pope Innocent III found it necessary to make it obligatory under pain of mortal sin for Catholics to go to confession at least once during the year. But why was this law necessary?

What is the reason some Catholics do not go more often today when they have to? Perhaps they may answer that it is humiliating. To a certain extent it is humiliating to have to accuse oneself of doing wrong, but our sins are no secret from almighty God. He knows our most secret thoughts, words and actions.

Others may object that they dislike confessing their sins to another human being, even though he is a priest. Perhaps they do not realize that a priest tries to forget as quickly as possible what he hears in the confessional.

A priest is bound by the seal of confession. He would commit a serious sin himself if he were ever to reveal what he heard in the confessional. On occasion priests have even been known to give up their lives rather than break the seal of confession. In reality there is no good reason for a sinner's hesitating to make use of the Sacrament of Reconciliation.

To make a worthy confession there are only a few brief rules to follow. First, one should examine his conscience. He should try to call to mind what sins he has committed and how often he has committed them. No great length of time is required to do this. The person who makes a daily examination of conscience will have no trouble at all when it comes time for confession. A quick review of the Ten Commandments and the duties of one's state of life can be a great help.

The second step is to elicit contrition for one's sins. This contrition or sorrow should spring from supernatural motives. One should be sorry for one's sins because he dreads the punishment due to sin, the loss of heaven and the pains of hell. This suffices for confession and is called imperfect contrition. A higher type of sorrow, being sorry for our sins because they've offended God, who has been so good to us, is more desirable. Perfect contrition is necessary in danger of death, when one does not have the opportunity of going to confession.

The next step is to confess one's sins to a priest. When Christ forgave the sins of the leper and Mary Magdalene, he could clearly see their souls since he was God. He knew their sins without their telling him. But in the case of a priest this is not so. In order to forgive sins, a priest must first know them. In order for him to know them, the penitent must confess them to him. That is why confession to a priest is necessary. It is the way that Christ ordained it.

Lastly, one should accept the penance which the priest gives him. It would be futile for a sick person to call a doctor and then refuse to take the medicine which the doctor prescribes. Likewise the penance which the priest assigns helps take away the temporal punishment due to sin and makes the soul healthier in the sight of almighty God.

Penance is a sacrament which brings grace to the soul. It should be received regularly. A touching story that reveals the great benefit of the sacrament occurred in the life of Father Damien, the leper priest, whose cause is up for canonization. Father Damien, a healthy man, went into voluntary exile with the lepers on Molokai to take care of them.

Every few months a ship would stop at Molokai to leave off supplies. On one occasion the bishop of Hawaii accompanied this ship. When Father Damien learned this he rowed out to the ship and asked to see the bishop. The ship captain refused. Father Damien pleaded with the captain, saying he only wanted to go to confession for he had not seen a priest in a very long time. But the captain was adamant in his refusal.

The only way the bishop and Father Damien could communicate was for the bishop standing on the bridge and Father Damien in the rowboat below to shout at one another. But yet in this public and humiliating manner, by having to shout out his sins, Father Damien went to confession, so much did he desire to receive the sacrament.

We who have the opportunity of receiving confession so easily, let us resolve to receive it regularly, as often as necessary to keep our souls in the state of sanctifying grace. Confession is a sacrament of God's mercy, the sacrament of a second chance. Should we ever have the misfortune to commit serious sin, let us not hesitate to go to confession and restore sanctifying grace in our souls. God bless you.

# "C"    Third Sunday of Easter

*John 21:1-19*

In the year 1708, the last Catholic priest then living in Japan, a Jesuit, was beheaded. He had been captured five years earlier being smuggled into the island. The Emperor thought that with the last priest in the country put to death, the Catholic religion that had been started there was dead. But he was wrong.

In 1859, after Commodore Perry sailed into Japanese waters and a treaty was signed permitting foreign ships to visit Japanese ports and chaplains to live in the port cities, a few priests once again made their home in Japan.

In 1865 a group of people from a distant village came to see one of the priests. They asked to see the chapel, which evidently met with their approval when they saw the Blessed Sacrament exposed there. Then their leader asked him two questions: "Do you honor the Virgin Mary?" and "Is the Holy Father in Rome the head of your Church?"

To each question the priest answered yes, and the man replied, "Then you believe the same as we do. We are Catholics." To this simple man, whose people had been separated from any religious teaching for 150 years, the rule of the Pope was the distinguishing mark that identified the Catholic Church.

Although not frequently discussed and more often than not taken for granted, the rule of the Pope over the Catholic Church is one of its distinctive marks. It stands for its unity of leadership and unity of rule.

Thus it was at the command of our former Pope, Pope John XXIII, that the Second Vatican Council was summoned. In obedience to his command 2,400 bishops from all over the world convened in Rome.

But after the Council's first session Pope John died. A new Pope was elected to succeed him in a most orderly fashion — Pope Paul VI. And immediately 500 million Catholics throughout the world acknowledged his leadership. And thus it is clear that the power of the Pope does not depend upon the person who holds the office but rather upon the office which he holds.

The reason for this power the Pope holds is a divine one. Many years ago in the city of Caesarea Philippi Our Lord said to St. Peter, the prince of the Apostles, "You are Peter, and upon this rock I will build my Church, and the gates of hell shall not prevail against it."

With these words, Christ changed the name of the leader of the Apostles from Simon to Peter. The name Peter which he gave him meant rock. Henceforth Peter was the rock upon which the Church would be built; Christ promised to make him the foundation of his Church.

Christ kept his promise and actually did bestow the power of the primacy upon Peter; for following his Resurrection Christ said to him, "Feed my lambs. . . . Feed my sheep." With these words he bestowed upon Peter the power to rule over his Church as a shepherd rules over his flock. He gave him the power to teach, rule and govern his Church, and his authority extended over the other Apostles.

Peter used this authority as Pope or Supreme Pontiff of the Church during his lifetime. It was Peter who received the first gentile into the Church. It was Peter who decided a new Apostle should be chosen in the place of Judas, who had hanged himself. It was Peter who first preached to the crowds on Pentecost Sunday.

Peter ruled over the Church for some 25 years. The place he chose for his episcopal see was the city of Rome. It was in Rome that Peter was put to death, crucified upside down in about the year 67 A.D. by the Emperor Nero in his persecution of the young Christian Church. And because Peter ruled the Church from Rome, his successor as Pope was the new Bishop of Rome. It was Linus — even though several other Apostles were still alive.

And the story has been the same for over 1,900 years. Peter's successor as

Pope has ruled over the Church, and his power has been recognized. In that time there have been 262 successors. The vast majority of these have been holy and learned men: 79 of them are venerated as saints; 33 have suffered martyrdom. There is no other country, religion or organization in the history of the world that can boast of such a long line of distinguished rulers.

The Pope is the greatest spiritual authority on earth. No other leader of any religion can compare with him. No one can speak with his authority. There are many who seek the reason for this authority, but the answer is a simple one.

When Christ began his public life he one day walked along the shore of Lake Gennesaret, also called the Sea of Galilee or Tiberias. A crowd pressed upon him to hear the word of God, but our Lord saw two boats moored there and the fishermen washing their nets. Getting into one of the boats, the one that was Simon's, he asked him to put out a little from the land. And our Lord spoke to the crowd and when he had finished, he said to Simon, "Put out into the deep and lower your nets for a catch."

And Simon answered, "Master, the whole night through we have toiled and have taken nothing, but at your word I will lower the net." And when they had done so, they enclosed so many fish their net was breaking.

The miraculous catch of fish mentioned in today's gospel was the second such miracle Christ performed. It was the reason St. John recognized him to be the Lord. Later on the shore of Lake Gennesaret Christ turned to Peter and said, "From now on you will be catching men."

And Christ kept his promise. On the first Pentecost Sunday St. Peter stepped forth to preach to the crowd gathered in Jerusalem. There were Parthians, Medes and Elamites and people from every corner of the earth, and they spoke many different languages. But all heard Peter speak in their own native tongue. The result was that 3,000 people were baptized that first Pentecost Sunday. Peter had truly become a fisher of men.

But this miracle too was wrought by the grace of Christ. As he had caused the miraculous catch or fish, so too he caused this miraculous conversion.

It is the grace of Christ that gives authority to Peter's successor today. Because Christ has promised to stay with him all days, even to the end of the world, the Pope in Rome speaks with Christ's authority.

Down through the centuries apostasies have divided the Church — persecution has sapped its strength. Heresies have cut off millions of its members. But the hand of Christ has raised it back up with renewed strength, and the hand of Christ guides it still.

Let us thank God for establishing the papacy to rule his Church. Let us recognize our present Pope as the successor of St. Peter. Let us harken to his voice as the voice of Christ speaking to us. God bless you.

# "C"    Fourth Sunday of Easter

*John 10:27-30*

Today on the Fourth Sunday of Easter Holy Mother the Church places before us for our meditation the parable of the Good Shepherd. The figure of speech of viewing Christ as the Good Shepherd is one which is referred to often in Holy Scripture. Even on Holy Thursday night, the night of his Passion, Christ referred to himself in this way. He said, "It is written: "I will strike the shepherd and the sheep of the flock shall be dispersed."

After his resurrection from the dead, Christ made St. Peter the ruler over his Church and the leader of the Apostles in similar terms. He said to him, "Feed my lambs. . . . Feed my sheep."

The symbol of Christ that has been the favorite down through the centuries is that of the Good Shepherd. Christian liturgy has highly esteemed the symbol of the Good Shepherd. The figure of Christ as the Good Shepherd is a prominent one in Christian art. Christ spoke most significant words when he said, "I am the good shepherd." He added in the words of today's gospel, "My sheep hear my voice. I know them, and they follow me." Christ said in effect that he was to his Church what a shepherd was to his flock.

When Christ said, "I know them, and they follow me," he was using an expression of speech that carried a great deal of meaning to the pastoral people of the Near East to whom Christ was preaching at the time. The Jews of Palestine were well acquainted with sheep and knew their characteristics. They knew that sheep recognize their master's voice and would follow him at all times.

Recently an American tourist was traveling in Syria. On one occasion he noted three shepherds each bringing his own flock to a brook for water. The sheep of the three flocks began to mill with one another and soon one could not distinguish them apart. But finally when the sheep had drunk their full, the first shepherd began to depart. He called his sheep and at once his own left the group and followed him. The second did the same and likewise the third.

This tourist thought perhaps he could fool the sheep. He dressed in the clothing of one of the shepherds and imitating his voice called to his flock of sheep. But not a one of them moved. Through this experience the tourist became convinced that sheep know their master's voice. Thus Christ used a most meaningful expression when he said, "I know them, and they follow me."

Christ used this comparison to tell the pastoral people to whom he was preaching that he knew the members of his Church. Christ is the Second Person of the Blessed Trinity. He is the true God as well as true man. Among his many gifts, he is all-wise and all-knowing. He knows our most secret thoughts and desires. He knows our character, our strength, our weakness and our necessities even better than we do ourselves. This is the first duty of a shepherd, to know his flock.

The second duty of a shepherd is to provide for and protect his flock. Christ, the Good Shepherd, told us we should not be solicitous about what we eat or drink or what we put on to wear. Christ is interested in the welfare of each one of us. He has a deep love and concern for each and every soul in his flock.

Christ said, "I shall give them eternal life and they shall never perish." Thus he holds out to us eternal life, eternal happiness in heaven as the reward for being a faithful member of his flock. Thus to an eminent degree he fulfills the second duty of a shepherd, to provide for his flock.

Christ goes on to add, "No one shall snatch them out of my hand." With these few words he goes on to assert the notion of the Shepherd's unconquerable power — the ability to protect his flock against any and all dangers — against the physical and violent assaults of those who would attempt to wipe out his Church by persecution — against those who would attempt to poison the minds of his sheep by false teachings.

Then Christ asserts, "My Father is greater than all. . . ." This was a statement the Jews would readily accept. They knew that he was talking about almighty God, God the Father. It was their common belief that God was greater than all creatures.

Our Lord then goes on to say that because of his almighty power no one is able to snatch sheep from out of his hand. It means that the power of God is so great that it can overcome any and all adversaries. This passage of Scripture bears out the teaching of the Church that God gives sufficient grace to all men, that is, grace sufficient to resist any temptation that may come along.

This means that man, if he chooses to use his free will to oppose evil and do good, has enough grace given him by God to do just that. No one can say that the temptation was so great he had no choice but to give in to it. On the contrary, if man chooses to reject temptation, the grace to oppose it will not be wanting to him.

Christ concludes his talk with the statement, "The Father and I are one." No sooner had he said this than some of the Jews took up stones to hurl at Christ, for they clearly understood the meaning and implication of this statement. Christ was making himself equal to God the Father both in power and nature. Since the Father was God, Christ was claiming divine powers for himself.

The Jews believed that the Father was God in heaven, but most refused to believe that Christ was God also. They thought he was falsely claiming to be God. This was the sin of blasphemy, and the penalty for blasphemy was stoning. Hence, according to their consciences, they were justified in hurling stones at Jesus.

At this early point in his public ministry, Christ in an indirect way, through the parable of the Good Shepherd, claimed to be divine — to possess divine powers. He indirectly claimed to be the Messiah whom the Jews had long awaited.

Let us not be like the Jews who rejected this claim of Christ. But rather, let us hear and accept the message of Christ. Let us recognize him to be the Good Shepherd of our flock. Let us strive to be loyal sheep in his fold. Remember Christ has promised eternal life to those who follow him, and his promise is not in vain. God bless you.

# "C"    Fifth Sunday of Easter

*John 13:31-35*

The Roman Emperor Nero began to persecute the Christian Church in the year 67 A.D. This persecution of the Church continued for well over two hundred years — until the year 313 A.D. when the Edict of Constantine was issued. And what amazed their pagan persecutors was to watch the Christians walk bravely and calmly to their death. Many found joy in giving their life for their God. A comment heard everywhere from pagan lips was: "See how those Christians love one another."

But brotherly love shown by Christians should not be a surprise to anyone. In displaying love for one another and even for their persecutors, Christians were only practicing the doctrine that Christ had taught them. In his sermon on the mount Christ told his Apostles to "love your enemies, pray for your persecutors."

The words of Christ came to pass. When persecution was rampant, love became the badge of Christians. Love is the virtue that Christ taught and extolled more than any other. It is the theme of Christian living. It is the cornerstone of his Church. It is the all-pervading motive in his gospels.

Christ repudiated the philosophy of the pagan world around him which said, "Love your friends but hate your enemies." Christ taught a contrary doctrine. He said, "Love your enemies." He taught us the parable of the Good Samaritan to illustrate his point.

On one occasion one of the Scribes approached Christ and asked him what was the most important of all the commandments. Christ responded, "You shall love the Lord your God with all your heart, and with all your soul, and with all your mind, and with all your strength. This is the greatest commandment. And the second is like it: You shall love your neighbor as yourself."

These two commandments of God, the love of God and the love of neighbor, contain all the others. They oblige us to practice the virtue of charity, a synonym for love. Love or charity is an infused virtue, placed in our souls in Baptism along with sanctifying grace which enables us to so love God and our neighbor.

It is one of the three theological virtues. The three theological virtues, faith, hope and charity, are the highest of all virtues for they pertain directly to God himself. St. Paul says about them, "There remain these three — faith, hope and charity, but the greatest of these is charity."

Charity or love is the most misunderstood of all virtues. It takes in far more than mere almsgiving. Almsgiving is a part of charity when it is performed for a motive of love for one's neighbor. But often today alms are given for material reasons, for instance, to deduct from one's income tax, to impress one's neighbors or friends.

The practice of charity is obedience to the command of God, who told us to practice it. It is an expression of gratitude to God for all that he has given us.

Because God loves us with an infinite love, there is no limit to Christian charity. St. Bernard tells us that the "measure of loving God is to love him without measure."

Christ taught us charity by his preaching — by his words, but he also taught us charity by his deeds as well. Consider Christ in the Garden of Gethsemane on the first Holy Thursday night. He told his Apostles to stay behind and pray; he wanted to spare them the sight of his bloody sweat.

When the Apostle Judas betrayed him with a kiss, Christ called him friend. When St. Peter rose in his defense and cut off the ear of the servant of the high priest with a sword, Christ miraculously healed him. Christ's charity was infinite, even while knowing he was about to be put to death in the most cruel manner. Later still, while hanging on the cross, he said of his executioners, "Father, forgive them for they know not what they do."

Christ's whole life on earth was a supreme act of love. Out of love he was born in the poverty of the stable in Bethlehem. Out of love for man Christ willingly carried his cross up Mt. Calvary.

In gratitude to God for creating us, in gratitude to his divine Son for redeeming us, in gratitude for all the goods we possess in this world, we are bound to return this love to God. This we can do by keeping him uppermost in our thoughts. We can avoid any occasion of sin or anything that might separate us from him.

We too should love our neighbor for the love of God. In thinking of our neighbor, we should remember we were all created by God. We all live here on the same earth. We are descended from the same first parents. We are all traveling toward the same end — eternal happiness with God in heaven. Fraternal charity should then be a bond uniting us on this common journey and aiding us to attain our supernatural end.

When we see our fellow man, let us view him as a creature made to the image and likeness of God. We should view him as a being endowed with an immortal soul, as one who will live for all eternity.

St. Paul calls each one of us a temple of God, and this we truly are. When a person is endowed with the gift of sanctifying grace, he has the Trinity dwelling in his soul. He is a member of the mystical body of Christ. But how seldom do we stop to think of our neighbor in this regard. Consider that perhaps our neighbor may have received the body and blood of Jesus Christ into his body that very morning in the Holy Eucharist.

Remember the words of our divine Savior in this regard. Through St. John's epistle, he said, "If anyone says, 'I love God' and hates his brother, he is a liar." And again he said, "I assure you, as often as you did it for one of my least brothers, you did it for me." One person noted for his great charity was St. John of God. He dedicated his life to caring for the sick and the poor. One night as he was returning home, he saw a man near death in the street.

St. John picked up the man and carried him into the hospital. He put him in bed and bathed his hands and feet. He jumped back startled. In the sick man's hands were the wounds of nails, and likewise in his feet. Then he heard the voice of Christ speak to him, "John, you put alms in my hands, you clothed my body and you washed my feet."

A short time ago two brothers received money from their father to attend a motion picture show. When they returned home their father asked the first son how he liked the picture. He said, "I didn't. On the way to the show we met a poor boy who was crying. When I asked him why he was crying, he said he was hungry. I kept thinking about that boy all during the show, and I couldn't enjoy it a bit."

The father then asked the second son how he liked the motion picture. He replied, "It was a good movie, all right, but I didn't see it. I met the same poor boy who was crying because he was hungry. So I spent the money you gave me to buy something for him to eat. I didn't have any money left to go to the show with, so we just talked. I had a good time."

Even in this life charity has its own reward; it gives one spiritual satisfaction and peace of soul. Scripture tells us that charity covers a multitude of sins. Charity is the greatest of all the virtues. Let not a day go by without showing your love of God in some way. God bless you.

# "C"  Sixth Sunday of Easter

*John 14:23-29*

Following the institution of the Holy Eucharist on Holy Thursday night, and immediately before his suffering and death, Christ spoke to his Apostles. He delivered one of the most profound and beautiful sermons the world has seen. Part of that discourse is contained in the gospel read at today's Mass. Christ said, " 'Peace' is my farewell to you, my peace is my gift to you. . . ."

Peace is the virtue most sought after in our modern world today. It is the virtue most frequently prayed for, the virtue most fervently petitioned from heaven by Holy Mother the Church. The whole world craves peace.

The great need for peace is easily recognizable if we glance at the history of our country and of the world during this present century. We have been involved in two major wars, World War I and World War II. In addition we have fought two small localized wars since that time — the Korean War and the War in Vietnam. We call these small wars, but is any war small that lists its casualties in the tens of thousands?

The leaders of our nation and the leaders of other nations have put forth great effort toward achieving this goal of peace. We have seen the establishment of the League of Nations following World War I and the United Nations following World War II.

But as the leaders of our country have strived for peace, so too have the leaders of our Church likewise striven for peace. In this century fourteen encyclical letters on peace have been written by various Popes in Rome. Pope Benedict XV wrote three encyclicals on peace. Back in 1914 at the outbreak of World War I he pointed out that there was a lack of love in the world. This in turn brought about hatred and war. A restoration of Christian love would help bring us peace.

Pope Pius XI wrote one encyclical on peace. Pope Pius XII, the Pope of World War II, wrote nine encyclicals on the subject of peace. It was his hope that a bridge of peace could be built in the name of Christ between the peoples of the world. He said that peace primarily is an attitude of mind and secondly a harmonious equilibrium of external forces. He said the false ascendancy of materialism has caused wars and a lack of peace. He dedicated the world to Mary, Queen of Peace.

Pope John XXIII wrote perhaps the most famous of all the peace encyclicals, "Pacem in Terris." It has been one of the most widely quoted and also misquoted documents of all time. He said there can be no peace among men unless there is peace in each one of them. Peace will reign among men only when the order wished by God reigns in their hearts. He inaugurated devotions to Christ, the Prince of Peace.

Pope Paul VI has also taken up his pen in the cause of peace. He has urged us fervently to pray for peace.

True peace will come about only if it is based on justice. Peace depends upon nations and men mutually accepting the moral law. True peace must be built upon the Ten Commandments. If the Ten Commandments are taught to the youth of the world, a giant step has been taken toward achieving a lasting peace.

Peace must spring from men's hearts. It must embrace a love of God and a love of neighbor. It must link the peoples of the different countries in a bond of Christian charity.

Peace will reign among men if men possess peace within their souls. A man is at peace with himself if God's grace and God's friendship reside within his soul. The peaceful man is not disturbed by events in the material world around him. The peaceful man focuses his attention on God; other things are not in focus. Worldly events do not blot out his vision of God.

The peaceful man is serene in moments of triumph. He is calm in moments of defeat. The virtue of peace acknowledges right order in one's life. It places one's obligations to God above other things.

This divine order of things and the resulting peace which flows from it is reflected in the message of the angels on the night of Christ's birth in Bethlehem. They hovered above the stable where Christ was born and sang, "Glory to God in the highest and peace on earth to men of good will."

The virtue of peace will never be achieved simply by governments making gestures to each other. It will never come about by two large powers signing a treaty. Peace is not a virtue that any government decree can pass on to its citizens.

Rather it is a virtue that takes root and grows in the hearts of man. Only when it has blossomed in the lives of individuals can one hope to find true peace in a nation.

A man of peace is an asset to the world, a credit to mankind. Such a man was St. Francis of Assisi. On one occasion the saint arrived back at his monastery to hear that a bitter dispute had arisen between the bishop and the governor.

Moved with pity upon hearing this, St. Francis sent a group of monks to the governor's mansion instructing them to sing the Canticle of Brother Sun for the governor and his aides. He sent a second group to the residence of the bishop with similar instructions.

When the bishop heard the Brothers singing this beautiful canticle, he was moved to compassion. He said he was willing and ready to forgive the governor and all the other men who had offended him. The governor too was moved to sorrow and repented of his anger. In fact, the governor made his way to the bishop's house, and there the two apologized and became good friends once again.

On this and many other occasions St. Francis established himself as a peacemaker. He fulfilled the beatitude which our Lord gave us in his Sermon on the Mount, "Blessed are the peacemakers, for they shall be called the children of God."

In his own personal devotion St. Francis composed prayers which he said frequently — inspiring a modern prayer which bears his name. It begins:

"Lord make me an instrument of your peace.
Where there is hatred, let me sow love."

It ends:

"It is in pardoning that we are pardoned,
It is in dying that we are born to eternal life."

Holy Mother the Church in its revised liturgy has instituted the sign of peace as a part of every Mass. It is given just following the Canon and before the prayer "Lamb of God." The priest who has just finished consecrating the Sacred Eucharist conveys it either by bowing or shaking hands with those around him and it is passed throughout the Church. He conveys the greeting that Christ expresses for his Church in today's gospel, "My peace is my gift to you."

Let us accept this Christian peace in our own souls and convey it to others that we may bring peace to this world. God bless you.

# "C"    Ascension

*Luke 24:46-53*

A businessman was going away on a week's trip. As he left his house, the small boy who lived next door came up to him and asked him for a nickel to buy some candy. The man turned to the small boy and said to him, "I'll give you your choice of two things. I'll either give you a nickel for candy now or a quarter when I come home next week." The boy thought a minute and said "I'll take the nickel now."

But in a very real sense, when it comes to eternity and things that pertain to eternal life, too many of us are like that little boy. So very many people give little or no thought to the great treasures promised us in the kingdom of heaven. Many exchange these promises of eternal happiness for the fleeting pleasure of sin and selfishness here below.

This morning's gospel, my dear people, tells us of Christ's ascension into heaven. He told his Apostles to go out and make disciples of all nations. Then before their eyes he ascended up into heaven.

The Ascension of our Lord into heaven is an article of faith, which we must all believe. The fact of his Ascension has many lessons for us. It shows us, first of all, that God's permanent home is heaven. Although he came down to earth to redeem mankind, he returned to his home in heaven once his mission on earth was finished.

Also Christ's Ascension into heaven marks a clear division between things of heaven and things of earth. It points out our Lord's detachment from the things of this earth.

Christ, in coming into this world, came as God. He was the creator of the universe. He could have held as his own most or all of the goods of this earth, but he did not. He was born in the poverty of a stable. While leading his public life, he did not have a place at times where he could lay his head. He died upon the wood of a cross and was buried in the tomb of a stranger. When he ascended into heaven, he left all the goods of the earth behind him.

In imitation of Christ, we too should become detached from the possessions of this earth. We should live in the world, but our thoughts should be centered on heaven. Our goal in life should not be a temporal one, but rather an eternal one. It is on heaven that we should focus our attention.

Far too frequently on this earth, men have as their goals earthly riches. Their desires center on treasures of this earth. Thomas à Kempis warns us in his "Imitation of Christ" that the eye is not filled with seeing nor the ear with hearing. The man who possesses a small amount of riches covets more. The experience of pleasure leads to the desire for more. He tells us it is true wisdom to seek the kingdom of heaven through contempt of the world.

Our blessed Lord himself gave us this same advice in his beautiful Sermon on the Mount. He said, "Do not lay up for yourselves an earthly treasure. Moths and rust corrode; thieves break in and steal. Make it your practice instead to store up heavenly treasures which neither moths nor rust corrode nor thieves break in and steal. Remember, where your treasure is, there your heart is also."

Christ taught us, "Look at the birds in the sky. They do not sow or reap, they gather nothing into barns; yet your heavenly Father feeds them. Are you not more important than they? . . . Learn a lesson from the way the wild flowers grow. They do not work; they do not spin. Yet I assure you, not even Solomon in all his splendor was arrayed like one of these. If God can clothe in such splendor the grass of the field which blooms today and is thrown on the fire tomorrow, will he not provide much more for you, O weak in faith!"

Christ continued his Sermon on the Mount by saying, "Seek first his kingship over you, his way of holiness, and all things will be given you besides."

Christ taught detachment from the goods of the world on many occasions. On Ascension day he put these teachings into practice. He ascended into heaven and left all these goods of the world behind him.

One saint noted for his detachment from things of this earth was St. Martin, the Bishop of Tours. His life was a busy one, full of many charitable acts. He gave away nearly all of his possessions. His dying hours were notably marked with this same spirit of detachment.

For several hours prior to his death he had been lying on his back in great agony. A friend suggested that the dying bishop turn on his side to relieve the pain. St. Martin replied, "Let me contemplate heaven rather than earth. Do not disturb me as I am meditating on the path my Savior took to heaven."

On Ascension day those who were with Christ were left standing with their eyes looking up to him. This is where Christ wishes us to focus our attention. Our thoughts and aspirations should rise above the plane of this earthly life.

So important is this thought that Holy Mother the Church has set aside the Feast of the Ascension as a holy day of obligation. She compels us to come to Church and attend Holy Mass. She wishes us on this one occasion each year to stand alongside the Apostles and cast up our eyes to heaven also.

So let us resolve on this great feast day to imitate St. Martin and our Savior. Let us look to heaven not just on this one day a year, but each and every day of our life. Let us live now so that when Christ summons us in judgment, heaven will become our permanent home. God bless you.

# "C"    Seventh Sunday of Easter

*John 17:20-26*

Following the Last Supper on Holy Thursday night our blessed Lord gave a beautiful discourse to his Apostles. A part of that discourse, the seventeenth chapter of St. John's gospel, is read as the third Scripture reading of today's Mass. In it Christ reveals the mission and the unity of his Church. Christ said, "Father, all these you gave me I would have in my company. . . ."

The mission of the Church among men is to be a witness for God. Christ says later, "For this was I born, and for this I came into the world, that I should give testimony to the truth." The Church which Christ founded was the witness of his redemption of mankind and is the witness of it still. St. Peter said, "We have not, by following artificial fables, made known to you the power and presence of our Lord Jesus Christ; but we are eyewitnesses of his greatness."

Christ established his Church upon his Apostles. But it was not for their benefit alone that he did this; it was for the benefit of all men. Christ commissioned them, "Going therefore, teach all nations." Christ established his Church to save all mankind.

In the words of today's gospel, Christ said, "I do not pray for them [my disciples] alone. I pray also for those who will believe in me through their word. . . ." Christ willed that the testimony of his Apostles should descend from age to age in an unbroken chain. The will of Christ has been carried out. The testimony of the Apostles to the divine realities is as living and as fresh today as it was in the beginning of his Church.

Let us bear in mind that the will of Christ is always efficacious. Christ at all times when he was on earth was God. As God he was all powerful — omnipotent. Nothing was hard or impossible for him. If Christ willed to do something that thing was as good as done. His will always has been and always will be carried out into deed.

Christ willed that his Church should give testimony unto his name and unto the truth. This the Church has always done and will continue to do. The testimony of the Church forever triumphs in every place. The testimony that it bears to Christ will never end.

A further quality of the testimony which the Church bears to Christ is that its testimony will be one. This follows logically from Christ's teaching. Christ as God is truth personified. He embodies all truth. As truth itself is one, so the testimony of Christ is one.

But the unity of the Church's testimony follows also from the explicit prayer and will of Christ. In the words of today's gospel Christ said, "I pray . . . that all may be one, as you, Father, are in me, and I in you; I pray that they be [one] in us. . . ."

Hence the voice of the Church is one in its doctrine and one in its leadership. It is one because Christ wills it to be one — to be unified. History bears out this fact.

In the midst of all the controversies and contradictions of men, the voice of Christ's Church has been that of one divine teacher. In the face of all the errors and heresies of man, this one divine voice has perpetually declared the same immutable truths. This one divine voice is articulate, clear and piercing. It cleaves through all confusion. It is heard above the clamor of men and of nations. It is the voice of the holy Roman Catholic Church, which has taught the same immutable doctrine in every place and in every age.

This oneness of the Church's testimony is seen in its faith and doctrine. From the time of the Apostles, the content of faith in the Church has remained the same. The Church has neither added to nor subtracted from the doctrines taught by the Twelve Apostles. The Blessed Trinity, the Incarnation and Redemption of Christ and the Virgin Birth are eternal truths. They were taught when the Church was founded; they are taught now and will continue to be taught to the end of time. This oneness in faith cannot be found in any other religious sect or political body in the history of the world.

The Church possesses oneness or unity in its leadership. Christ, while here on earth, gave St. Peter the power to rule over his Church. He made him the first Pope or visible head of his Church. That power has been passed down from Peter to his successors. In an unbroken chain, two hundred sixty-three successors to his office as Bishop of Rome or Pope have ruled over the Church. Most of these have been good and holy men. History records the names of each and the years they have ruled. Our present Holy Father is the undisputed leader of the Christian world.

No other political body can make this boast. Nineteen centuries have come and gone and still the Pope rules on. Governments have risen and fallen. The Roman Empire has long since passed away. Kings and princes have ruled and died. The whole world has changed around it, but the Pope in Rome rules over the Church without change. Under him are several thousands of bishops; and under the bishops, the priests and laity of the dioceses throughout the world. Truly the Church has unity in its leadership.

Truly too, the Church of Christ has unity in its sacrifice and sacraments. From its very beginning the Apostles administered seven sacraments. These same seven sacraments are administered today without addition or subtraction. These are the same seven sacraments which Christ instituted upon this earth. The same baptism admits all to membership in the faith. Penance is the universal means of obtaining forgiveness of sin. The Holy Eucharist, which contains Christ's body and blood, is the world's source of spiritual nourishment.

From the time of its foundation the Church has had one and only one sacrifice — the Sacrifice of the Mass — the perfect religious sacrifice. It is celebrated daily in every city and hamlet throughout the world. It has been said that the sun never sets on the Holy Sacrifice of the Mass. Every minute of the day, every day of the week, the Holy Sacrifice of the Mass is being celebrated in some corner of the globe.

Each and every Sunday morning a half billion Catholics around the world kneel in adoration at the Holy Sacrifice of the Mass. They adore the Eucharist in unison as it is raised aloft at the consecration. These half billion voices are as one because this was the prayer and will of Christ.

The marvelous unity of his Church is our holy heritage. Let us thank God for the privilege of being one of these favored millions. Let us thank him for the grace of being a member of his unified Church. Let us be thankful and rejoice as did the holy psalmist centuries ago who wrote in prophecy, "Behold how good and how pleasant it is for brethren to dwell together in unity. . . ." God bless you.

# "C"      Pentecost

*John 20:19-23*

In the 19th chapter of the Acts of the Apostles we read a most interesting story about St. Paul — while passing through the city of Ephesus he ran into a group of twelve men who were associated with the Christians of that city, yet were vague in their knowledge of the religion. St. Paul asked them if they had received the Holy Spirit.

They answered no, "We have not even heard that there is a Holy Spirit." It turned out that they had been followers of John the Baptizer and had never been baptized with the Sacrament of Baptism. St. Paul lost no time in giving them these sacraments. He briefly instructed them and then baptized them. And as the Acts of the Apostles tell us, "the Holy Spirit came upon them and they began to speak in tongues and to prophesy."

The Holy Spirit is sometimes called the forgotten person of the Blessed Trinity. In comparison to our Lord Jesus Christ, who lived upon this earth as man and whose works and preaching are so familiar to us, and even in comparison to the Father, to whom is attributed the works of creation, Catholics often neglect devotion to the Holy Spirit. Nevertheless the works of sanctification are commonly attributed to him. He plays a most important part in our Catholic religion.

At the Last Supper, the night before he died, Christ told his Apostles that he was going back to the Father, that he would no longer be visibly present in their midst. In fact he had told them this on many previous occasions, but without their comprehending it. On the occasion of the Last Supper Christ repeated this same thought three times, but then he added, "It is much better for you that I go. If I fail to go, the Paraclete will never come to you, whereas if I go, I will send him to you." In these words Christ promised to send the Holy Spirit upon his Apostles.

Following his Resurrection Christ lived upon earth for forty days, but then ascended to his Father in heaven. After his Ascension, our Blessed Mother, together with his Apostles and other disciples, gathered in Jerusalem to pray and await the coming of the Holy Spirit. They prayed in the upper room for nine days.

Finally on the tenth day, on Pentecost Sunday there came a sound from heaven, as of a violent wind, and it filled the whole house where they were sitting. There appeared to them parted tongues as of fire, and they came to rest upon each of them.

It was most appropriate that the Holy Spirit should choose this means of fiery tongues to come down upon the Apostles. He chose fire for it represented the interior spiritual transformation which occurred in the souls of the Apostles. Fire, by its nature, warms, purifies and illumines objects with its light. Hence it symbolized the grace with which the Holy Spirit warmed, purified and illumined their souls.

The Holy Spirit besides giving them grace, conferred strength and courage upon the Apostles. This they were greatly in need of. Peter had denied our Lord three times. All except John had fled from the scene of Christ's crucifixion. But armed with the Holy Spirit the Apostles went forth as strong and fearless men, men willing to face death. And all of them were put to death, all except St. John, who had remained beneath the cross of Christ.

The Holy Spirit bestowed upon the Apostles the gift of tongues. For Pentecost time in Jerusalem was a great religious feast. It was their harvest time. Jews scattered all over the known world used to return to Jerusalem; they made pilgrimages there from all over the Roman Empire. As we are told in today's epistle, there were Parthians, Medes and Elamites, inhabitants of Messopotamia, Judea, Cappadocia, Pontus and Asia, Phrygia, Pamphilia and Egypt and parts of Libya around Cyrene and visitors from Rome, Jews and Proselytes. And these many people spoke many different languages.

This great crowd of people was first startled by the sound of a violent wind rushing through the streets. Then they beheld St. Peter who, inspired by the Holy Spirit, went forth to preach to this assembled crowd. Peter spoke in his native Aramaic tongue, yet every person assembled there understood him in his own language. This was the gift of tongues conferred upon him by the Holy Spirit.

He went on to tell them how they had put Christ to death, but how Christ rose from the dead. He told them that Christ had come to redeem them and take away their sins. The grace of the Holy Spirit so moved this crowd that when Peter had finished preaching, three thousand repented their sins and begged to be baptized.

This, my dear people, is the story of the first Pentecost, the birthday of the Catholic Church. This is the story of the descent of the Holy Spirit. But the Holy Spirit did not descend upon the Church on this one occasion to desert it. He reigns with it still. For in the words of Christ, "I will send you another Advocate, to dwell with you forever."

As the soul abides in the body of men, so the Holy Spirit abides in the body of the Church.

St. Augustine tells us that the voice of the Holy Spirit and the Church of Christ are identical; this divine voice has guided the Catholic Church through nineteen long centuries. It has strengthened it in the hour of persecution. In the face of the errors and heresies of men, it has perpetually declared the same immutable truth. It has been one divine voice, articulate, clear and piercing, which has cleaved through all confusion and has been heard above the clamor of men and of nations.

From sunrise to sunset he has taught the same immutable doctrine in every age. The Holy Spirit has infallibly guided 263 Popes in proclaiming the doctrines of Christ since that first Pentecost Sunday. In the words of Christ, the Holy Spirit has been the "Spirit of truth," who has taught us "all truth."

As St. Peter proclaimed in the Acts, "It has seemed good to the Holy Spirit and to us" to teach salvation to man. The Holy Spirit opened to us the way of salvation. He has put all things necessary within our reach — grace and truth. Let us then follow the leading of his grace. For they will lead us to an eternity of happiness, they will lead us to be happy in heaven with Christ forever. God bless you.

# "C"      Trinity Sunday (Sunday after Pentecost)

*John 16:12-15*

The gospel presented for our meditation on this feast of the Holy Trinity is taken from the sixteenth chapter of St. John. The words were spoken by our Lord to his Apostles at the Last Supper, the night before he died. Nevertheless, because of the message they contain, they are most appropriate for today's feast.

Christ tells his Apostles that he will soon leave them and go to his heavenly Father, but he will not leave them orphans. He will send them the Holy Spirit, the Spirit of truth.

In this text Christ refers to all three persons in the Blessed Trinity. He speaks and prays to his Father, the First Person of the Trinity. Christ, who is speaking, is the Second Person of the Trinity. The Holy Spirit, whom he promises to send upon them, is the Third Person of the Trinity. Each of these three persons are separate and distinct, but all are one and the same God.

Our human intellects are too limited to understand fully the mystery of God and his triune nature. For us it remains a mystery as to how this can exist. Yet we believe in the Trinity because of the testimony of Christ, who proved his divinity through his miracles and life on earth. We believe in the Trinity even though we cannot fully understand it.

All three persons are truly God and share in all things that God does. Nevertheless, we appropriate or associate with a certain person a particular work more than we associate it with the others. To God the Father is appropriated the work of creation. To God the Son we associate the work of our redemption here on earth. To God the Holy Ghost we appropriate the work of sanctification or guidance of the Church here on earth.

In today's gospel Christ calls the Holy Spirit the Spirit of truth, who will guide the Apostles to all truth. The Second Vatican Council states, "To men growing daily more dependent on one another, and to a world becoming more unified every day, this truth proves to be of paramount importance."

Truth is a virtue most precious to almighty God. It is conformity to fact. It is the reason why God has given us the power of speech and expression — that we might express truth.

Christ himself told us that he is the way, the truth and the life. Again St. John tells us that God is truth. In opposition to this, we are told that the devil is the father of lies.

The obligation to express the truth falls upon us from the natural law. But because the natural law was broken and overlooked, God left no doubt of this obligation. He gave us the Ten Commandments. The Eighth Commandment obliges us to speak the truth.

As an aid to know and express the truth, Christ tells us in today's gospel that he is sending the Holy Spirit, the Spirit of truth, to guide his Church. He tells us that the Holy Spirit will teach us all truth.

Christ founded his Church to teach truth upon this earth. It has continued to do this down through the centuries. His Church has been a witness of the truth; it is a guardian of the deposit of faith.

Down through the centuries the Holy Spirit has guided the Church in the way of truth. Within our own lifetime we have witnessed a new evidence of this guidance; it occurred in the convocation of the Second Vatican Council.

On January 25, 1959, Pope John XXIII spoke before the College of Cardinals in Rome. He readily admitted that he had no previous thought or intention of convoking a general council, but as he spoke, the words "Ecumenical Council" dropped from his lips. He called these words a light from heaven, clearly an inspiration of the Holy Spirit.

Truly the Holy Spirit, the Spirit of truth, was with the Council in the constitutions which it drew up. The changes brought about in the liturgy, the introduction of the vernacular languages into the Mass can be seen as an illustration of his guiding hand. It is through such media as the liturgy that the truth of revelation is brought to us.

Let us resolve to pray to the Holy Spirit daily. Let us invoke him to bestow upon us the knowledge of the truth. Let us pray that he will enlighten us to know the truth and give us the courage to follow it. God bless you.

# "C"    Corpus Christi

*Luke 9:11-17*

The ways of God are not always the ways of men. God usually accomplishes his purpose by using the simplest and most insignificant of means. An example of this can be seen in the means he chose to establish the feast we celebrate today, the feast of the Body of Christ, known in Latin as Corpus Christi.

The year was 1246. The place was Liège in Belgium. The two people involved were Bishop Robert de Thorate of Liège and a humble Augustinian Sister, Sister Juliana of Mont-Cornillon. The Sister had come to see the bishop and request him to establish a new feast to honor the Body of Christ. You can almost hear the bishop ask the Sister if she realizes the seriousness of her request.

Then Sister Juliana nervously mentioned that she had had a dream of a full moon with a dark spot in it. Later still our Lord appeared to her and explained the meaning of this dream.

People claiming to have supernatural revelations are usually regarded with suspicion, even holy Sisters. Sister Juliana was no exception. She began to explain to the bishop that Christ had revealed to her that the full moon she saw in her vision represented the liturgical year. The dark spot in the moon was the lack of a special feast to honor his precious body. He said the celebration of the Eucharist on Holy Thursday was obscured by the celebration of his passion and death. He said he desired another day to be set apart to honor his body. He gave three reasons for this.

He said he wished faith in the Eucharist to be strengthened. Secondly he wished the faithful to draw strength from the Eucharist to live a life of virtue. Lastly he wanted people to make reparation to the Eucharist for any irreverence or sacrilege shown to it.

As God so ordained, the bishop believed all these things Sister Juliana told him. Within a very short time he instituted the feast of the Body of Christ or Corpus Christi in his own diocese, as was the custom of the Church in the Middle Ages. Before long Bishop Robert was one of the most ardent devotees of this new feast. He made known to Pope Urban IV what he had done. In the year 1264 Pope Urban made Corpus Christi a universal feast of the Church, choosing the Thursday following Trinity Sunday as the day of its celebration. Thus it remained until only a few years ago, following the second Vatican

Council. In the renovation which followed this council, the feast of the Body of Christ or Corpus Christi was moved to the Sunday after Trinity Sunday, thus giving it even more prominence.

Almighty God accomplished his purpose. He brought about the establishment of a feast to show honor to his divine Son. But he did not do it through any revelation to the Pope or high Church officials. He accomplished it by making known his wishes to a humble and pious nun.

Down through the centuries there have been those who have tried to suppress this holy feast. During the Thirty Years War the Swedish armies occupied the village of Wuerzburg in Bavaria. The ruling army commander issued several orders; among them was an edict that there should not be any celebration or procession on the approaching feast of Corpus Christi.

The Carmelite monks in the village were faced with a dilemma. Almighty God has asked that this feast be celebrated to honor his divine Son. The army commander said no procession under penalty of death. The monks chose to obey almighty God. A procession with the priest carrying the Blessed Sacrament began from the Church and proceeded toward the city gates. The Swedish army drew up in battle array before them. Fearless Brother Agapytus broke from the ranks of the procession, and standing before the army, told them to kneel before God, their creator. Mechanically the army fell to its knees, unable to carry out its orders to break up the procession. The procession continued on its scheduled course. Again the will of God prevailed.

The feast of the Body of Christ commemorates the events that occurred on the first Holy Thursday night. On that occasion Christ took bread and wine into his hands and pronounced over them the words, "This is my body. . . . This is my blood." With these words the substance of the bread and wine was changed into his body and blood. Although the appearance of the bread and wine remained the same, its nature and substance were radically changed. Christ likewise passed on this power to the Apostles and their successors, for he said to them, "Do this in commemoration of me."

In giving us the Eucharist Christ gave us the supreme sacrament. He gave us his own body and blood as our food and drink. He gave us the source of grace itself. In receiving Holy Communion Christ's body becomes our own. Our nature is elevated to a supernatural level as long as the species of bread remains without our body. The Eucharist is an unbloody renewal of the sacrifice of the cross. It is the center and heart of the Catholic religion. It is the main part of the Mass which is our chief liturgical action.

Therefore, on this feast of the Body of Christ, a feast requested by Christ himself, let us show him our love and adoration. In response to his request of Sister Juliana, let us renew our faith in the Holy Eucharist. Let us draw from it the strength and grace we need to fulfill our duty as Christians. Let us make reparation for any sacrilege committed against it. In showing honor to Christ's body here on earth, we are truly following his will in heaven. God bless you.

# "C"    Second Sunday of the Year

*John 2:1-12*

On the chilly slopes of La Verna in Italy St. Francis of Assisi knelt in prayer. His prayer was most pleasing to our Lord and Savior Jesus Christ — so pleasing that he wanted to give St. Francis a sign for all to see, whereby they would know that St. Francis of Assisi had found favor with God.

Therefore, he bestowed on him the gift of stigmata, the wounds that he himself had suffered in being nailed to the cross. Christ still retained these wounds in his hands and feet after he rose from the dead, glorious and immortal on Easter Sunday. They were the same wounds that Christ showed to the unbelieving Thomas when he said, "Take your finger and examine my hands. Put your hand into my side."

These were the same scars and wounds that Christ bestowed on St. Francis of Assisi that chilly winter day on a mountainside in Italy — so that when Francis lifted his hands in prayer the world might see that Christ had stamped him with his own seal, with an indelible mark.

Thus, too, my dear people, in the wedding ceremony the groom places a ring on the bride's finger, a ring which has just been blessed by the priest.

The wedding ring becomes a bond of unity, a symbol of the mutual compact that the bride and groom enter into to take each other for better or for worse until death do they part.

Thus the wedding ring, an object of beauty, an object that is durable, an object that depicts these qualities in married life.

For marriage, my dear people, is a vocation, the primary vocation in life. It is the vocation which more people enter into than any other. You may hear some men say that their vocation in life is to be a doctor, a dentist or a lawyer. Nevertheless, these vocations are only secondary ones. Their primary vocation is to be married man, a husband and the father of a family.

And marriage too is a high vocation. Christ himself showed us this, for it was at a marriage feast, the marriage feast of Cana, that he began his public life and performed his first miracle. Cana was a small town only six miles distant from Nazareth, where Mary and Jesus lived. Most probably our Lord and our Blessed Mother knew the wedding couple well.

When the wedding party ran out of wine Mary turned to her divine Son and said to him, "They have no more wine." Then turning to the servants she said, "Do whatever he tells you."

Christ then told the servants to fill the waterpots with water and draw out some and take it to the waiter in charge of the feast. When he had tasted it, he said to the bridegroom, "People usually serve the choice wine first; then when the guests have been drinking a while, a lesser vintage. What you have done is to keep the choice wine until now."

It is significant that our Lord and his Blessed Mother were present. It is significant that he performed his first miracle and began his public life at a wedding feast. By so doing Christ showed most clearly the importance of marriage. He showed us the high place that marriage occupies in our Christian society.

Marriage is of its very nature a holy institution, for it was instituted by God himself. But Christ added to marriage an even deeper meaning and a higher beauty. He elevated it to the dignity of a sacrament. He made it a means of conferring grace on those who receive it. This grace that it gives is twofold.

Marriage bestows sanctifying grace on those who enter into it worthily. But above and beyond sanctifying grace, matrimony gives a special sacramental grace. This special sacramental grace helps a husband and wife live as children of God. It enables them to fulfill their duties to meet the problems that may arise in marriage. These graces remain with them throughout all of their married life. A husband and wife may call on them at any time, for God pledges them the lifelong support of his help.

Matrimony as a sacrament has probably been attacked more than any other. Its laws have been assaulted by individuals and by nations. This holy and lasting bond have been challenged time and time again. King Henry VIII of England attacked it and founded the Church of England when the Church ruled that his marriage to Catherine was valid and lasting.

There are many today who hold contrary to the Catholic Church that a marriage can be ended by a simple piece of legal paper. They ignore the vows of husband and wife to take each other to have and to hold until death do they part. They hold this in defiance of the words of Christ who said, "What God has joined together, let no man put asunder."

Matrimony is a sacrament of the most high God. It is a primary vocation of life. It is the means by which men and women may save their souls and gain heaven. The lasting Christian marriage is an object of admiration and splendor. By cooperating with God's graces, one can attain to this state of happiness allotted to man in this vale of tears.

The Church judges marriage to be so important that it decrees it should take place in the sanctuary of the Church. Thus a bride and groom exchange their marriage vows on the altar in the presence of the Eucharistic Christ and of his priest.

On only two occasions in all its liturgy does Holy Mother the Church permit the interruption of the Mass between the Consecration and the Communion. The first is for the ordination of a priest and the second is for the marriage ceremony. Immediately after the Our Father of the Mass the priest turns on the altar and bestows the nuptial blessing on the bride and groom.

If we should look around for models to follow in married life, we can readily turn to our Blessed Mother and St. Joseph, the two greatest saints in the Catholic Church. And they were husband and wife. Remember as St. Francis regarded the stigma of Christ a great blessing, be proud of the wedding ring upon your finger, or be proud that you have placed it there. God bless you.

# "C"     Third Sunday of the Year

*Luke 1:1-4; 4:14-21*

The gospel read at today's Mass is the prologue or the beginning of the Gospel of St. Luke. St. Luke addresses his gospel to a person named "Theophilus." Theophilus was evidently a Christian and an official in the Roman government. Yet St. Luke realized in writing this gospel that it would be read by many, many others. He wrote his gospel in the Greek language and directed it to gentile readers. It was his intention to prove to them that Jesus, the Jewish Messiah, was the divine Messiah of all mankind.

St. Luke himself was of Macedonian Greek origin; he was a native of Antioch in Syria. It is believed by many that he was also a Roman citizen. St. Luke wrote his gospel long before St. John's. The date of its composition is believed to be 63 A.D.

The Gospel of St. Luke was written with great historical accuracy. In the prologue he writes, "I . . . have carefully traced the whole sequence of events." . . . He speaks of "events . . . transmitted . . . by the original eyewitnesses . . . of the word." Since St. Luke, a Greek, was not one of the original Twelve Apostles, all of whom were Jewish, it was necessary for him to rely on the testimony of others. This he did most accurately and painstakingly. He was a close associate of St. Paul and of our Blessed Mother. He met and knew several other Apostles. The more historians have analyzed and examined the details of his gospel, the more convinced are they of his historical accuracy even down to the most minute detail.

St. Luke's is the longest of the gospels. It is twice as long as that of St. Mark and a good deal longer than St. Matthew's. Being written in 63 A.D., it was the third gospel to be written — preceded by those of Sts. Matthew and Mark, which undoubtedly St. Luke had read and had recourse to in writing his own.

Some of the miracles mentioned by Sts. Matthew and Mark are omitted by St. Luke. This was evidently because St. Luke had nothing additional to add concerning them and he did not wish to be repetitious. Of the twenty miracles which St. Luke describes in detail in his gospel, six of them are original or proper to him, unmentioned in the two earlier gospels. The remaining fourteen contain some details previously unrecorded.

The single most outstanding feature of St. Luke's gospel is his infancy narrative. He describes in detail the Annunciation, the Visitation, the Birth of Christ in Bethlehem, the Flight into Egypt, the Presentation and the Finding of Christ in the temple when he was twelve years old. St. Luke gives this information because of his acquaintance with our Blessed Mother. These events are either described briefly or entirely passed over in the two earlier gospels.

St. Luke has been called the patron of Christian art. This was not because St. Luke himself was an artist — he was not. Actually by profession he was a physician — a doctor. He was given this title because he was a literary artist. He painted beautiful pictures with words. He has greater descriptive talents than do the other evangelists. A majority of the great religious paintings which have been painted down through the centuries have been based on quotations from his gospel.

If one were to look for a theme running through his gospel, he could readily answer that St. Luke's theme is faith. He traces the growth of people's faith in Christ from his earliest disciples until the faith they put in him following his Resurrection. His theme of faith is continued in the Acts of the Apostles, of which he is also the author.

In addition to the prologue, an additional event from St. Luke's gospel is contained in the third reading from today's Mass. It is his description of our Lord's return to his native village of Nazareth during his early public life. Less than a year before this event took place, Christ left his carpenter's bench in Nazareth to begin his public life. He began to preach in communities around the Sea of Galilee and to gather his Twelve Apostles.

But now that he has entered upon his public life, he returns to preach in his home village. Christ had adopted the custom of preaching in the local synagogues. For here a preacher was sure to have an audience. A synagogue in a small village was more than just a house of prayer. It was a meeting place, a school and a courthouse. Everyone could have his turn to speak, depending only on the invitation or consent of the heads of the synagogues. Usually this was easily obtained.

Christ readily obtained this permission. At the proper time the "hazzan" or minister of the synagogue handed Christ the Old Testament, and he opened it to the words of the prophet Isaiah, the sixty-first chapter. He read the passage: "The spirit of the Lord is upon me; therefore he has anointed me. He has sent me to bring glad tidings to the poor. . . ."

When Christ had finished this prophetic passage concerning the promised Messiah, he rolled up the scroll and sat down. Then he announced to all of the native townsmen, "Today this Scripture passage is fulfilled in your hearing."

Christ was announcing that he was the anointed one of God — that he had come to preach the gospel to the poor — that he was the long-awaited Redeemer. Most people who heard Christ preach and witnessed his miracles would take him for what he was. Once he had shown his divine power, they would believe him and accept his doctrine. But not the people of Nazareth. They had grown up with Christ. He had lived in their midst as one of them for nearly thirty years. They knew him as the local carpenter. They believed him to be the son of Joseph and Mary. They found it too difficult to change their opinion of him despite the many miracles he had worked in other places and the reputation he had gained. Therefore, they refused to believe in him.

St. Luke goes on to say that Christ refused to perform any miracles in his native village of Nazareth. It had been his rule to exact an act of faith from the sick he was about to cure. But neither the sick nor the well in Nazareth would give him this act of faith. Therefore, he refused to use his miraculous power to heal any of them. They were undisposed to believe and bear witness to his gospel. They were lacking in the virtue of faith.

Faith was the theme of St. Luke in his gospel. Let us therefore read and cherish these words. Let us place our belief in them. Faith in Christ is the first step on the road to salvation. God bless you.

# "C"  Fourth Sunday of the Year

*Luke 4:21-30*

The gospel read at today's Mass, according to St. Luke, is a sequel to the gospel read last Sunday. Last Sunday's gospel told how Christ returned to his native town of Nazareth. With all the other Jews of the village he entered the synagogue on the Sabbath. When the time arrived for the reading of the Torah, that is, the books of the Law and the prophets, Christ had ascended the ambo, the pulpit for the reader, and asked to read.

The passage opened to him was the sixty-first chapter of the Prophet Isaiah, "The Spirit of the Lord is upon me; therefore he has anointed me. He has sent me to bring glad tidings to the poor. . . ." This was a passage the prophet Isaiah had written centuries before concerning the coming Messiah or Redeemer. This fact the Jewish people in the synagogue at Nazareth were most certainly aware of.

Then following his prophetical reading about the coming Messiah, Jesus calmly announced to his fellow townsmen of Nazareth, "Today this Scripture passage is fulfilled in your hearing." By this statement Christ was establishing a definite link between the Old Testament and the New. He was associating his preaching and work with the Old Testament. He was making the claim to be the long-awaited Messiah or Redeemer.

The reaction of his fellow townspeople to this was shock and surprise. They had marveled at his preaching. They were pleased with what he had to say. But they were faced with a difficult choice. They could profess their belief in this pleasing doctrine which they heard. They could take pride in the fact that the long-awaited Redeemer came from their hometown.

Or else they could let their familiarity with Christ overrule their better judgment. They could let their association with him for the past thirty years sway them from believing what was evident. This latter was the course they followed. They asked, "Is this not Joseph's son?"

One longs to speak up and insert his own words in the gospel at this point and give an answer to these incredulous people of Nazareth: "Indeed this was the son of Joseph the carpenter, but also the son of the Carpenter who made heaven and earth." Many of these people of Nazareth probably had in their homes tables and chairs and other articles of furniture made by Christ himself. Many of them may have slept in beds which he fashioned from wood and nailed together. His workmanship they accepted, but his preaching and claiming to be the Messiah they rejected. These very tables and chairs which Christ had fashioned became a stumbling block to their faith.

The atmosphere in the synagogue became charged and tense. Their question concerning his ancestry had adequately expressed their disbelief in Christ. Christ had undoubtedly returned to his home in Nazareth many times before. The reputation he had gained through his preaching and miracles in neighboring villages had preceded him. His fellow townspeople knew that he had changed water into wine at the neighboring village of Cana only six miles away. They knew that he had cured the lepers and the sick in the village of Capernaum to the north.

They were piqued and embittered that he had not performed any major miracle in their midst. Christ read their thoughts and he put them into words, "You will doubtless quote me the proverb, 'Physician heal yourself,' and say 'Do here in your own country the things we have heard you have done in Capernaum.' "

Christ then proceeded to answer these objections: ". . . no prophet gains acceptance in his own native place." Our Lord then quoted from the Old Testament again, tying a knot between the Old and the New. He mentioned the seventeenth chapter of the First Book of Kings, which tells us about the prophet Elijah whom God sent to a widow in the village of Zarephath in Syria. God directed Elijah to make his home with this poor woman. When she protested because of her poverty, the prophet directed her to make him a griddle-cake and to cook what was left in her flour jar for herself and her son, promising that there would be no lack of flour in her jar. From that day on her jar was never short of flour no matter how much she drew from it. Later still Elijah raised her son back to life after he had died. Our Lord referred to these miracles of Elijah to show what he did for a widow in a foreign land while there remained many widows in Israel.

Our Lord too made reference to a second miracle performed by the prophet Elisha recorded in the fifth chapter of the Second Book of Kings. At that time a high-ranking commander by the name of Naaman in the Syrian army contracted leprosy. His wife's maid, a Jewish girl, told him of the miraculous healing powers of the prophet Elisha in her own country. Naaman set out to see him. Elisha commanded Naaman to go and wash seven times in the Jordan River. After doing this his leprosy left him.

Christ refers to this miracle to point out that Elisha cured a foreigner of leprosy while there remained many lepers in his own country. These two examples were humiliating to the Jews of Nazareth because the beneficiaries of the miracles in both cases were gentiles. They were a foreshadowing of the direction that his gospel was to take. God was no man's debtor. His mercies would flow to others if his own rejected them. Christ was attempting to show them that his blessings and benefits would be bestowed on men because of faith and not because of race.

Christ had made it a rule to exact faith from the sick whom he meant to cure. Once he found it he would perform a miracle to confirm that faith. But not finding this disposition among the Nazarenes, he did not perform many miracles among them.

At these words of Christ the whole audience in the synagogue was filled with indignation. His fellow townspeople were exasperated at being discovered and having their lack of faith laid bare. As a body they rose up and expelled him from his home town of Nazareth, where he had lived and worked for some thirty years, where with his own hands he had built so many things for so many people.

They led Christ to the brow of the hill on which the village was built. Nazareth lies in a cup of hills. The Plain of Esdraelon lies below it, and jagged walls of rock varying in height from eighty to three hundred feet surround it. It was their intention to hurl Christ over this rocky precipice and kill him. They were acting as would a lynch mob in a western movie. They were setting themselves up as his judge and jury. They had found him guilty of performing miracles in other towns and not in their own — of correctly pointing out their lack of faith. The sentence they pronounced upon him was death — death by being hurled over the cliffs of their town.

They had asked Christ for miracles, and now he was about to grant their request. He was to show them his miraculous power, but not in a way they expected or had bargained for. When they brought him to the brink of the cliff, they were helpless. They were physically unable to carry out their wicked intention of hurling him to his death. In a similar manner the guards that surrounded his tomb were helpless on Easter Sunday morning when Christ rose from the dead.

Christ went straight through the midst of these Nazarenes and walked away. Despite their lack of faith, Christ had shown them his miraculous power. Like it or not, the townsfolk of Nazareth were forced to admit that the prophecy of Isaiah was fulfilled in their hearing. One of their own, Jesus Christ, a native Nazarene, was the Anointed One of God. The spirit of the Lord was upon him. God bless you.

# "C"     Fifth Sunday of the Year

*Luke 5:1-11*

Today's Gospel is taken from the gospel of St. Luke. It narrates in a most beautiful and interesting way how the three major Apostles, Peter, James and John, received their call or vocation from Christ.

For many centuries the people who lived along the shores of Lake Gennesaret, or the Sea of Galilee, made their living by fishing. This was the manner in which the Apostles whom our Lord called also made theirs.

Frequently a group of men would work together in a fishing venture. This was easier than working alone, for many men were needed to handle the fishing nets. Thus the two sets of brothers, Peter and Andrew and James and John, the latter two the sons of Zebedee, had entered into such an agreement.

The usual fishing gear used in Galilee consisted of three separate nets, the first of which was rather coarse and large. The second net was finer than the first, and the third finer still. These nets were suspended in the water, one before the other by cork buoys.

When the nets were suspended in place the fishermen would row their boats around them, beating the water with their oars, driving the fish into the nets.

The fishermen would fish many different spots in the lake in this manner. When the fishing in one spot proved fruitless, they would move on to another.

More often than not they would fish at night, for they found the fishing to be better at this time.

In the incident related in the gospel for today, Christ was preaching alongside the Sea of Galilee. So eager was the crowd to hear him that they were pressing upon him crowding him back into the water.

Seeing a boat tied up by the shore, our Lord stepped into it, pushed out from shore a short distance and began to preach from the boat. The boat which our Lord chose belonged to Simon Peter.

When our Lord finished preaching to the multitude, he asked Peter to push off into the deep and to lower his nets for a catch. Peter replied that he had been fishing the whole night through and had taken nothing, but at our Lord's word he would lower the nets.

Almost immediately a large catch of fish filled his nets — so many that his nets began to break. Peter and his brother called to James and John for help, and they rowed out in their boat to help them. The catch of fish was so great that it threatened to sink both boats.

Peter immediately recognized that our Lord had worked a great miracle in his behalf. He had heard our Lord preach before — most probably he had seen him work miracles for the benefit of others. But he had not been deeply moved, as the miracles had not affected him personally. But now Christ had worked a miracle for his own benefit. Peter fell down on his knees and said, "Leave me, Lord. I am a sinful man."

Jesus in turn said to Simon, "Do not be afraid. From now on you will be catching men." Jesus gave Peter a direct call to be an Apostle — a vocation to follow him. This call Peter and his companions instantly obeyed, for they left all and followed him.

To each of us in this life Christ gives a special vocation — a special call to follow some particular path of life. The vocation to which Christ calls us may differ from that of another. Not all vocations are the same. Some he calls to the religious life — others to the married state. Some people know definitely and early in life what they wish to be. Others are undecided for many years.

But whatever this call is, and whenever it comes, the important thing is to respond promptly and follow it as did St. Peter. A vocation is something one should pray fervently for every day. We should pray for the strength to accept it when it does come.

On another occasion in Holy Scripture a young man came to our Lord and asked him what he had to do to be perfect. Our Lord told him he should obey the two great commandments — to love God and love his neighbor.

But the young man replied this he had done from his youth. Our Lord then said to be perfect — to go sell what he had and give to the poor and come and follow him. This the young man refused to do because he had great possessions.

Such a person who rejects a vocation from Christ is refusing many and great graces. He will experience greater difficulty in saving his soul than he would by following the vocation Christ gave him. He is rejecting a higher place in heaven for a lower one.

One of the leaders of our Church a century ago was an English cardinal —

Herbert Cardinal Vaughan. He was one of thirteen children. His mother was a convert to the faith. Each day it was the custom of his mother to make a holy hour before the Blessed Sacrament — to pray for the proper vocations for her children. Her prayers were answered. All five of her daughters became nuns. Six of her eight sons became priests. Five of them later were made bishops and one a cardinal. She continued this daily holy hour for twenty years, and her prayers were richly rewarded.

Her example is an inspiration to all. One should pray each day to know his vocation and have the grace to follow it. For following Christ's call as did St. Peter, our Lord will reward one with great happiness in the world to come. God bless you.

# "C"     Sixth Sunday of the Year

*Luke 6:17, 20-26*

In May, 1946, President Harry Truman gave a speech at Fordham University in New York City. He was speaking about the major problems that faced the world following the end of World War II and he said he doubted whether there were any problems among the nations of the world, no matter how large, that could not be solved if they were approached in the spirit of the Eight Beatitudes.

The Eight Beatitudes, as contained in the Gospel of St. Matthew, were given by Christ in his famous Sermon on the Mount. Today's gospel presents their sequel — the four beatitudes and four woes or lamentations of St. Luke. St. Luke begins this portion of his gospel by saying that Christ had come down from the mountain and stopped at a level stretch where there were gathered a large number of his disciples. Hence this discourse of our Lord's has come to be known as his "Sermon on the Plain."

The word "beatitude" itself comes from a Latin word meaning happiness. Hence the beatitudes can be said to be conditions that bring about happiness. But in giving us these beatitudes, Christ was departing from the traditional view of happiness of his day and age. Happiness in ancient Roman times was to be acquired through the possession of material things. This meant property, money and sensual pleasures.

But Christ through his teaching pointed out there was another and better kind of happiness not found through the possession of material goods. This other and greater happiness was a spiritual one. Christ bluntly said, "My kingdom is not of this world." Happiness according to Christ is that which can make one happy or joyful in the world to come. This happiness in the world to come would be a greater happiness because it would be eternal; it would not pass away like the pleasures of this world. This heavenly or eternal happiness is the goal which Christ has in mind in presenting these four beatitudes in his "Sermon on the Plain."

The four beatitudes or benedictions which St. Luke gives us are very similar to four of the beatitudes which St. Matthew gives us in the Sermon on the Mount. This is not surprising. They may be considered to be among the chief teachings of Christ, which he often repeated.

The first of them is: "Blest are you poor; the reign of God is yours." One of Christ's main teachings was that God had special regard for the poor and the persecuted. Poverty was incorrectly regarded during the time of our Lord as a disgrace; poverty was considered a punishment for sin. The poor in that age did not accept their lot graciously. They were material-minded. Their chief ambition was to gain some wealth.

Christ tried to correct this false impression first of all by his own life. Christ was poor by choice, not by necessity. He was born poor; he lived and died in poverty. Poverty for him was self-imposed, since he was the creator of all of the goods of the world. He taught that we should be poor in spirit. Our main concern should not be for the goods of this world, but rather for treasures laid up for us in the life of heaven.

Christ said further, "Blest are you who hunger; you shall be filled." One might first suppose that the hunger Christ refers to here is a bodily hunger for food, but this hunger man has in common with all other animals. Man by his nature is superior to all other animals. He has an intellect and will. He can think and reason. Therefore, since he has a higher nature than animals, his hunger should be for higher things.

One's thirst should be for justice and the kingdom of God. When Christ was speaking about one's concern for material things He said, "Your Father in heaven knows that you have need of all these things. Seek first the kingdom of God and his justice, and all these things shall be added unto you besides."

When Christ said, "I thirst" from the cross, his thirst was for more than some liquid to drink. It was a thirst for souls. It was a burning zeal which should kindle in the heart of every Christian. It was a burning desire to see men embrace the Christian faith, to see them obey God's Ten Commandments, express their faith in the teachings of the Church and ultimately attain to eternal salvation.

Christ said, "Blest are you who are weeping; you shall laugh." It is interesting to note that Holy Scripture makes no mention of Christ laughing at any time. But it does mention his weeping and mourning on several occasions. He wept when he heard his friend Lazarus had died. He wept over the city of Jerusalem that had rejected his teachings. He suffered a bloody sweat in the Garden of Gethsemane.

Weeping or mourning is an indication of love. It shows one has concern for his fellow man. He is interested in his neighbor's welfare. It shows a desire to aid and assist others. Christ showed his concern by spending most of his public life among the poor, the sick and the crippled. He was always on the spot to speak a word of consolation, even to perform a miracle if necessary to aid his fellow men. Mourning was a means of showing his sympathy to them.

Finally Christ said, "Blest shall you be when men hate you." . . . Here Christ was speaking of persecution, of enduring suffering for the sake of Christ. The pagan world at this time viewed suffering only as a form of punishment. It was meant to arouse hatred and resentment. Christ's proposal to endure suffering for the motive of love was a radical departure from this view.

Christ gave us the example of suffering. He voluntarily endured the cruel death of crucifixion. He demanded suffering from those around him. Simeon told the Blessed Virgin that a sword of sorrow would pierce her heart, and indeed it did. St. Joseph, Christ's foster-father, had to bear suffering in this world. His hurried flight into Egypt to escape the persecution of Herod and his life of poverty testify to this. The Apostles were asked to endure martyrdom for the faith.

Why all this? Christ wanted to show us that the reward for virtue is happiness in the world to come and not in this life. True happiness will not be found here on earth. It will be found hereafter. Suffering for the sake of virtue prepares and purifies our souls to enjoy eternal happiness.

But then to these four beatitudes Christ added four woes or lamentations: woe to the rich, the full, those who laugh, those spoken well of. In declaring these woes, Christ was not condemning all those who enjoyed some of the fruits of this earth; rather, he was condemning those who made them an end in themselves.

Among the disciples of Christ could be found some prosperous men — Zacchaeus, Nicodemus, Joseph of Arimathea. They were men of high position, wealthy men by the standards of their own age. Yet they were followers of Christ. St. Luke, the author who relates this gospel passage, was himself a physician — a prominent man, a man from the upper level of society, a well-educated man. But then St. Luke left all these things behind him to become a disciple of Christ.

Those whom Christ is condemning in his woes are those who seek happiness in this life from wealth or food or fleeting pleasure — who prefer these fleeting pleasures to the eternal happiness of heaven.

In both his beatitudes and his lamentations, his blessings and his woes, Christ is holding out to us an eternal goal — the happiness of heaven hereafter. It is the goal that Christ bids us to set our sights upon — to bypass the pleasures of this world and, if need be, to suffer in this world. Heaven is unlimited happiness; heaven is eternal happiness. It is worth any worldly sacrifice we can make to get there. Christ wants us to make heaven our true and lasting home. God bless you.

# "C"    Seventh Sunday of the Year

*Luke 6:27-38*

The Jews were well acquainted with the writings of Moses in the twenty-first chapter of the Book of Exodus — to give an eye for an eye and a tooth for a tooth. This had become their guiding philosophy. Hence some were totally unprepared for what Christ had to say to them when he had descended to the plain following his Sermon on the Mount.

Christ spoke words never before heard. He said to them, "Love your enemies, do good to those who hate you; bless those who curse you. . . ." These sentiments were new and foreign to the Jewish people.

To love one's enemy was a paradox for the Jews. They had been brought up to believe that an enemy was someone you automatically hated; an enemy was one you tried to harm when the opportunity presented itself.

There were passages in the Old Testament which prescribed showing kindness to strangers. But a stranger was a foreigner, a visitor in their midst. Christ did not use the word "stranger." He used the word enemy. This was something altogether different.

Christ did not deny that we have a right to defend ourselves when our lives are in danger. He did not deny the principle of self-defense — that we can protect ourselves against grave bodily harm.

Christ does not demand the impossible. He does not order us to love our enemies to the same degree we love our friends, or to show them the same favors that we show our relatives or those near and dear to us. Instead he wants us to love them with a love of charity. He wants us to love them with a love that proceeds from our will and not our emotions. He wants us to desire their spiritual good and pray for their salvation.

Christ wants us to bestow on them the marks of interest and good will to which all members of the human family are entitled. Christ wants us to be willing to bear wrong and injury for his sake.

Christ went on to say that even sinners retaliate in kind; they do good to those who do good to them. But, he added, no merit is to be found in this. Rather merit is to be found when one returns good for evil. Merit is to be found when one suffers indignity or insult and does not stoop to return them. He raises himself above the level of his offender or enemy and shows only love and kindness in return.

Christ then holds up the example of God the Father, who bestows good on the ungrateful and the wicked. He indicated that this is the manner in which we, his followers, should act. If one can be truly good to the ungrateful and the wicked, then he deserves to be called a Christian, a son of the Most High.

Christ could well have held up himself as an example of love of enemies. He performed miracles for the benefit of many of them. He cured the ten lepers who came to him, even though he knew nine would be ungrateful. In the Garden of Olives when Peter cut off the ear of the soldier, Christ healed him, even though his avowed purpose was to arrest Christ and lead him away to be tried and crucified. Later still, upon the cross, Christ was to speak up concerning those who crucified him and say, "Father, forgive them for they know not what they do."

Christ lived and exemplified by his life the doctrine he taught us by his preaching. There is no better way of teaching a lesson to men — teaching by living. He practiced what he preached.

But still the lesson was a new one — one that caught his listeners unaware. The Jews had been told in the Old Testament to love their neighbors. But their neighbors included only those living in their proximity — those whom they knew. It did not include their enemies.

Christ was demanding of his followers a new disposition of soul — a willingness to be originators of love toward one another. Love is the theme of St. Luke the Evangelist, whose gospel we read today. Love is the predominant virtue of the New Testament. Later still the Romans were to point to the Christians, the followers of Christ, and say about them, "See how they love one another."

In saying this they were paying them a compliment. They recognized in the followers of Christ the virtue he had preached so frequently and practiced so well.

This is the virtue that all of us should strive to practice in our life today. We should practice the golden rule. The theme song of our present generation is, "Be concerned — be involved." But in reality, they are only borrowing or rephrasing a teaching of Christ. He taught this nineteen centuries ago. Christ concluded his sermon on love of neighbors by saying that "the measure you measure with will be measured back to you." God bless you.

# "C"      Eighth Sunday of the Year

*Luke 5:39-45*

The gospel read at today's Mass is taken from that of St. Luke. It is a part or continuation of Christ's Sermon on the Plain, which he delivered in Galilee after coming down from the mountain where he had preached his Sermon on the Mount.

Our Lord warns us to beware of becoming hypocrites. Hypocrites can see sin in the lives of others, but fail to see sin in their own. Christ goes on to tell us that no student is above his teacher. A student who would pretend to be better might well be called a hypocrite.

Christ asks whether a blind man can guide another blind man. He asks why one should look at the speck in his brother's eye when there is a plank in one's own eye. The implication is clearly that one should first make sure that his own life is sinless before one attempts to correct the life of one's neighbor.

Today men often make their main goal in life the pursuit of worldly honors or treasures. The honor of the world is fickle and transitory, and all the rewards the world can offer us — her riches and treasures — must end at death. The pleasure that the flesh has to offer is transitory too. It leaves one with a sense of guilt and shame and the reproach of one's conscience. Those who heed the devil will someday realize that there is an end of God's grace — that God must punish the wicked as well as reward the good.

Christ goes on to say that only the good tree can bear good fruit, while the evil tree bears evil fruit. He means that every tree bears fruit according to its nature. Thus if a tree is an apple tree, it will bring forth apples and not melons. If a tree is a cherry tree, it will bear cherries and not oranges.

The same is true of people. Those who are truly good Christians, who obey the commandments of God and practice virtue, will bear good fruit. They will have a good influence on those around them. The opposite will be true of those who lead evil lives.

An excellent example of bearing good fruit in one's life may be seen in the life of St. Felicitas and her seven sons.

St. Felicitas lived in early Roman times. Following the death of her husband, she lived the life of an ideal Christian and raised her seven sons in the practice of great faith and virtue. Her family became known far and wide for their acts of charity, their prayer and fasting.

Their edifying example bore much good fruit. Many pagan people were converted to the Christian faith because of this example. Their reputation for good aroused the jealousy of the pagan priests, who reported Felicitas and her seven sons to the emperor who was then persecuting the Church.

The Emperor Antoninus sent the prefect Publius to arrest Felicitas and her sons. This he did. Threats against this holy woman did not change her faith. Even when he threatened to torture and kill her sons she would not weaken. She expressed the belief that her sons would experience eternal life with Christ if they remained faithful, whereas they would be condemned to eternal death is they adored the Roman idols as Publius wished.

The prefect grew very angry. The following day he sent for the sons of Felicitas. One by one he examined them, and as they all remained steadfast in their Christian faith, he had each one scourged and beaten individually. Still their faith remained strong.

Following this torture the seven sons of Felicitas were sent back to prison. Again Publius examined them. Infuriated at their strong faith, he ordered each one of them to be sentenced to death by a different judge. The first of these was scourged, beaten with leather thongs studded with lead until he died. The next two were beaten to death with clubs. The fourth was thrown from a high cliff to his death. The last three were beheaded.

St. Felicitas died seven deaths herself watching her seven sons being martyred, offering their lives for the faith. Later she too was killed. But the good example of this holy woman and her sons bore much good fruit. It brought about the conversion of many in early Rome.

But Christ also warns that evil trees bear evil fruit. The evidence of this evil fruit can be seen in countless causes in the world today. The use of profanity in front of children causes untold harm to God's holy name. In this and in other instances the result is that evil trees bear evil fruit.

Let us resolve, therefore, my dear people, to lead virtuous Christian lives. God will richly reward the practice of justice and charity. This is the one way to make our lives fruitful of good. God bless you.

# "C"     Ninth Sunday of the Year

*Luke 7:1-10*

Today's gospel relates the meeting of a Roman centurion and his sending a delegation to our Lord at Capernaum. The centurion sent word that his servant was lying sick in his house and was near death.

A Roman centurion was one who was in command of a hundred soldiers. He was however a noncommissioned officer. He would correspond to a master sergeant in the American army today.

We can well imagine, too, that a centurion was not too popular a person among the Jewish people. He was an officer of an army that had conquered and was oppressing the Jewish people. But here he was milling in the crowd that surrounded our Lord in Capernaum. In fact, this particular centurion had helped the Jews build their synagogue and was well received by them.

When the opportunity presented itself his servants made the request of our divine Savior. They did this in the most direct manner and in the briefest possible way, a manner characteristic of the profession as soldier. They simply asked him to come and save the life of the servant.

This was an ordinary request, similar to the hundreds that our Lord had heard on previous occasions, from those sick of leprosy, the blind and the lame. And as usual our Lord was sympathetic to it. He set out with them.

But then the forthright centurion made an act of profound humility. He sent word on ahead to our Lord, "I am not worthy to have you enter my house." He humbled himself in the presence of Christ as did many great saints — as did St. John the Baptizer, who admitted he was unworthy to unfasten the strap of Christ's sandal and — as did St. Peter, who fell on his knees before Christ and said, "Depart from me, Lord, for I am a sinful man." This act of humility must have placed him high in the estimation of Christ.

But the centurion's message continued, "Just give the order and my servant will be cured." In these few words he made a most beautiful act of faith. The centurion was no expert in theology, but he did know a little about military discipline. He knew that when he as a commander gave an order to his soldiers it was carried out. He recognized Christ's spiritual power to cure the sick and believed that if Christ so commanded his servant would be cured even though he was a great distance away.

This act of faith of the centurion was pleasing to Christ. And our Savior replied, "I have never found so much faith among the Israelites."

Faith, my dear people, as you know, is one of the three theological virtues. It is a virtue by which we believe all those things God has revealed. St. Paul tells us in his Epistle to the Hebrews that faith is the root of all virtues.

Faith comes to us in the Sacrament of Baptism. It comes with sanctifying grace. It grows in our souls as we learn and are disposed to believe the revealed truths of God.

Faith does not depend on our completely understanding the revealed truths of our religion. Faith is not founded upon our seeing or knowing fully.

On the contrary, faith concerns itself with many things which do not appear to our senses. In faith we treat of such mysteries as the Holy Trinity, the Incarnation and the Immaculate Conception. Faith has as its object divine revelation, whatever God has revealed to man. Faith has been called the staff that supports our human reason.

Faith, however, never requires us to believe anything that is contrary to our human reason. For God is the author of them both, and they cannot contradict one another. Many mysteries of our faith are above and beyond human reason but never opposed to it.

Our authority for believing is that of God himself, who tells us what we must believe. This is the greatest authority possible. Practically every day of our life we make acts of human faith. We believe the scholars who tell us that the twinkling stars in the sky are really mighty suns. We believe the newspapers. But yet human authority can at times be wrong. They can deceive us or themselves be mistaken.

We make such acts of faith as these on human authority. The reputation of the news agencies or scholars who tell us such facts determines our intellect to make an act of assent to some particular fact. But yet the greatest of human authorities can never compare with God, who reveals to us the truths we must believe to attain salvation. For God is all-truthful and he cannot deceive us. He is all-knowing and all-wise, and he can never be deceived. God is Eternal Truth.

Faith is a gift of God — given to those whom he loves. Faith is not something we should take for granted, for God bestows it on us out of his benevolence, his goodness. It is a treasure we should thank God most dearly for possessing. We who possess it should consider it a great privilege, especially when we look around the world and see the millions who do not possess it, and also when we see many other millions who are not allowed to practice it.

And a Catholic should pray too that his faith be strengthened and increased. Certainly the centurion in today's gospel did not acquire his strong faith simply by acknowledging his belief in Christ on one occasion and then proceeding to forget about him. His strong faith was the result of renewed acts of faith. God will not fail to enliven the faith of those who fall on their knees each morning, who begin their day with the sign of the cross and who express their belief in the Trinity and the chief truths of the Catholic religion.

Let us pray that our faith be strong like the saints of old — like the Greek architect of a Christian legend. The Roman Emperor summoned him and asked him to build him a great coliseum, promising to make his name famous throughout all the world.

The architect complied with the Emperor's wishes, and in the course of time the famous Colosseum in Rome was erected. But when it was finished the emperor desecrated this beautiful structure by ordering that the Christians of Rome be fed to the hungry lions. At this the renowned architect stood before him and proudly proclaimed, "I too am a Christian." In a short time he too was thrown to the wild beasts to be torn limb from limb. In testimony of his faith, his blood flowed in the great work of art which he had created.

Let is pray daily for an increase of faith — that our faith may be strong enough to withstand the test should any challenge be hurled against it. Let us pray that our faith may be like that of the centurion — the like of which Christ said he had not seen in Israel.

Holy Mother the Church has thought so highly of these words spoken by the centurion that she has seen fit to incorporate them into the Holy Sacrifice of the Mass. Just before receiving Christ in Holy Communion, the priest holding the consecrated host says, "Lord, I am not worthy to receive you, but only say the word and I shall be healed."

These are the sentiments in which the Church wishes us to clothe our souls before receiving Christ in the Holy Eucharist, words expressing our belief that we are receiving our Lord and Savior in Holy Communion.

At each and every Mass you attend, repeat these words fervently with the priest. Tell our Lord that you are not worthy to receive him, but yet you fully believe in him. Tell him that like the centurion you are a soldier in his service and you are willing to do whatever he commands if only he will speak the word. God bless you.

# "C"     Tenth Sunday of the Year

*Luke 7:11-17*

The village of Naim, or Nain, mentioned in today's gospel, was in the southern part of Galilee, to the south of Nazareth. It was situated on the northern slope of the Hill of Moreh. Naim was more or less a small cluster of houses on the mountainside. And as one passed through it he noted a number of wells, silos and burial chambers.

Our Lord was entering the village from its southern side. As usual a crowd composed of his Apostles, disciples and others was following him. But as our Lord approached the town, another procession of people was leaving the village, passing in the opposite direction.

As this other procession approached, one first heard cries and sobs, expressions of sorrow. Then one noticed four men carrying a stretcher. They were preceded by the mourners and the flute players, indicative of those marching in a funeral procession.

In the days of our Lord burial customs were somewhat different from what they are now. A body was not buried in a coffin. Rather it was wrapped in a large band of cloth called a shroud. Neither was the body embalmed. Hence bodies could not be kept for any length of time. They were buried usually on the day of one's death.

Hence we can presume from the ancient customs of burial that the body of the young man was wrapped in a shroud and was being carried upon a stretcher by four others. These in turn were preceded by the flute players and the family and other mourners.

But as our Lord and his disciples approached and met the funeral procession, the first feeling that overcame our Lord was sympathy for the grieving mother. His first words were, "Do not weep."

Christ's sympathy then went on to remove the cause of this woman's grief — the death of her only son. The manner in which he did it was to speak to her dead son as though he were a living person. He said to him, "Young man, I bid you get up." And with that the young man sat up and began to speak.

Christ had performed other miracles on previous occasions. He had changed water into wine. He had cured the sick. But never before during his public life had he raised the dead to life. This was something new and startling.

In the Old Testament there was one instance of the prophet Elijah raising the dead to life — again in this instance the only son of a widow. But the manner in which he did it was far different. Elijah asked to be alone in the room with the dead boy. He then lay upon him and touched his hands to his hands, his mouth to his mouth, his eyes to his eyes. This process he repeated several times, in the meantime praying fervently to God. Finally, slowly, the corpse began to breathe. But the main difference in these two miracles is that Elijah raised the boy to life in the name of God. Christ did it in his own name.

Christ performed many different types of miracles here upon earth. He performed miracles over the powers of nature — miracles in curing the sick, miracles in expelling the evil spirit, and those which showed his glory. All nature obeyed him when he spoke. The sea was calmed. The fig tree withered up.

On one occasion in curing the mother-in-law of St. Peter our Lord did not speak directly to the sick person — but rather to the fever itself. The gospel tells us that our Lord rebuked the fever and it left her. Thus even germs obeyed his command. Even the most dead and mute element of nature became alive to God when he spoke and instantly obeyed him. In fact there was only one thing that did not obey him — that was man with his free will.

Thus did Christ weep over the city of Jerusalem. For although the wind and the sea and all nature obeyed him, the people of the city would not heed his teachings.

All nature, the entire universe, is alive to God. His will is obeyed instantaneously and without question. Man alone has the privilege of choosing to obey or not obey God's will. And in that decision hangs the balance of eternity.

Christ's miracles prove his divinity. His power over nature and even over life and death prove that he is God. Therefore, we who witness and hear this word have the obligation to acknowledge. We are obliged to become alive to God.

God's commands are not impossible. As he gave the water the power to sustain him when he walked upon it, he gives us grace to aid us when he commands us to obey him. God's grace is always sufficient to sustain us in whatever he asks us to do.

Therefore, let us resolve to use this grace. Let us resolve to make our minds alive to God. Our reward will not be simply life as he gave to the son of the widow of Naim, but rather eternal life in heaven. God bless you.

# "C"     Eleventh Sunday of the Year

*Luke 7:36-8:3*

The story contained in today's gospel has been called the story of the unnamed penitent, for St. Luke omits telling the name of the woman penitent who washed his feet. St. Luke was a dedicated historian and was noted for digging up many small details concerning the life of Christ to incorporate them in his gospel. It is entirely within the realm of possibility that St. Luke knew her identity but, not wishing to embarrass the woman or out of politeness, chose not to reveal her identity.

Our Lord was invited to dinner by a Pharisee named Simon. At this point in the second year of his public life, Christ had already earned the hatred of a large number of Pharisees, but not all of them. Simon's motive in inviting Christ to dinner is not revealed. One would hesitate to suspect that Simon had been converted by his preaching because of his actions and his lack of courtesy in being a host of Christ. Perhaps his motive was simply an insatiable curiosity to see and hear the man Jesus, who was so popular in Palestine, the Jesus who had helped so many by his miracles.

Back in ancient Palestine, roads were generally nothing but mud tracks from one village to another. Generally the Jews walking along them wore nothing but sandals on their feet — open sandals held on by a couple of leather straps. Hence their feet would become quite dirty in walking along these roads.

Custom demanded that when a guest entered one's house, his host would greet him by giving him the kiss of peace. He would place his hand on his guest's shoulder and touch his cheek to his. Also he would provide a basin of water for his guest to bathe and soothe his feet. And lastly he would either burn a few grams of incense or place a drop of attar of roses on his guest's head. In the case of Christ, Simon did none of these things. Simon, the Pharisee, was displaying very bad manners. He was showing that although he had invited Christ to dinner, he looked down on him; he did not regard him as an equal in his refusal to show him these ordinary courtesies.

At dinners in ancient eastern homes, the guests did not sit at table. They reclined on their left elbow on a couch near the dinner table. Their right arm was free to eat with and their feet protruded outward away from the table. Thus it was easy and convenient for the penitent woman to approach Christ and anoint his feet.

It was the custom for Jewish women to wear a small phial of concentrated perfume around their neck. Most women obtained and wore it despite the fact that it was very costly. This vase of perfumed oil probably was the woman's only valuable possession. It was probably the only gift she could give to Christ to show him her sorrow for her sin.

The penitent woman noticed the negligence of Simon — that Christ had not been extended the courtesy of washing from his feet the dust of the road. In weeping at his feet, she moistened them with her tears; she wiped them with her hair and kissed them and anointed them with precious perfumed oil.

Because all Jewish women wore their hair bound up in public, it was an act of humility on her part to let it down to use it to dry Christ's feet.

Although Simon, Christ's host, said nothing, he harbored evil thoughts. He thought Christ could not be a great prophet or else he would know that the woman doing this to him was a public sinner. But Christ, reading his thoughts, asked Simon a question — if a moneylender forgave two men their debts, one owing him five hundred coins and the other fifty, which of them was most grateful to him? Simon answered correctly, the one to whom he forgave the larger sum.

Christ then pointed out to him how as a host he had neglected the small courtesies, of kissing him, washing his feet and anointing his head. In contrast to this treatment the repentant woman had shown him great signs of love. Christ added, "Her many sins are forgiven — because of her great love. Little is forgiven the one whose love is small."

Turning to the woman he said, "Your sins are forgiven." Christ had accepted her sorrow. He was pleased with what she had done. He bestowed upon her the greatest gift one can possess in this life — the gift of sanctifying grace within her soul.

The contrast between the humble weeping woman and the proud Pharisee shows clearly the necessary conditions for penance. To be truly repentant one must be humble. One must recognize his own unworthiness. He must see himself as an ungrateful person — one who has received everything he possesses from almighty God — and yet one who turned to offend this loving and generous God by willful sin.

The repentant person must be conscious of his helplessness, of the weakness of his nature, of his inability to save himself through his own efforts. He must realize that his only hope of salvation is to throw himself on the mercy of Christ — to seek supernatural aid.

It was in this instance that the pride of the Pharisee was his downfall. He considered himself to be self-sufficient — to need no aid from God in attaining salvation. He considered himself far better than the penitent woman. In his pride he even refused to extend to Christ the common signs of courtesy that hosts are expected to show their guests.

There was little room for love in the heart of the Pharisee; there was little room for true sorrow or contrition.

In our own lives let us resolve to avoid the mistake of this proud host. Let us resolve to greet Christ with love and affection. Let us greet him each day by saying our morning and evening prayers. Let neither the dirt of the road nor the dark stain of sin mar his coming into our lives.

Let us humbly kneel at his feet as did the penitent woman. As her tears expressed her sorrow, let us pour out from our hearts our own sorrow for having offended him by sin. Let us in all humility beg his forgiveness. Only in this way can we expect forgiveness from our Savior. In the Book of Psalms we read the consoling words, "A contrite and humbled heart, O God, you will not despise." God bless you.

# "C" Twelfth Sunday of the Year

*Luke 9:18-24*

Scripture scholars divide the Gospel of St. Luke into two main parts. The first part treats of our Lord's public life, during which time he trained his Apostles until the point where they believed he was the promised Messiah. The second part is our Lord's preparation for his Passion and death.

The incident related in today's reading of Scripture represents the conclusion of this first part of Christ's public life. Altogether his public life lasted about three years. During the first eighteen months he gathered his Apostles about him and taught and trained them for their ministry. At the close of this period of training he put the question to them, "Who do the crowds say that I am?"

The answers he received were varied. Some said, "John the Baptizer," others, "Elijah," who was supposed to come back to earth, and still others thought he was a great prophet on his own right. In general they knew that he was an extraordinary man and admitted that he had the gift of prophecy. But as yet they were unwilling to admit that he was the promised and long-awaited Messiah himself.

Having ascertained this answer from the Apostles, Christ asked them a further question, "Who do you say that I am?" Peter said in reply, "The Messiah of God." Peter was the natural leader among the Apostles, and it was logical that he should have answered for them.

Hence for the first time here on earth, except for the voice of the devil, who had proclaimed Christ's identity when he had been driven out of a possessed soul, Christ was acknowledged to be the Messiah, the long-awaited Redeemer.

Christ elsewhere praises Peter's confession of his identity and makes known the source of his knowledge. Christ said that flesh and blood had not revealed this knowledge to Peter, but rather his heavenly Father. Hence Peter knew Christ's true identity, but he knew it through a direct revelation of almighty God. And since these words were spoken in front of the other Apostles, they too now knew his true identity. This revelation of his true identity culminated or brought to a close the first half of his public life.

From now on, Christ would be preparing his Apostles for another goal, to have them accept his forthcoming passion and death — to strengthen and confirm the faith he had given them. He first cautioned them not to reveal his true identity to others, for he knew the public in general was not yet ready to accept this belief.

To these words of caution he added the direct statement that the Son of Man must endure many sufferings, and be put to death and then raised up on the third day. This prophecy of his sufferings and death was a shock to them. For the Apostles as well as the other Jews of that age had an erroneous concept of what the Messiah would be. They dreamed of him as a great military leader who would liberate Israel by force of arms — a general who would be victorious in the field of battle.

This false impression Christ wanted to correct. Although gladdened by the knowledge of his true identity, they were nevertheless saddened to hear him say that he would be put to death.

The prediction of his Passion was the beginning of a severe and harsh teaching which Jesus commenced once his identity was established. It was a lesson he was to repeat time and time again until his death.

Jesus then laid down the conditions necessary to be a follower of his. He said "Whoever wishes to be my follower must deny his very self, take up his cross. . . ." Christ was demanding sacrifice of the highest type to be his disciple.

The Jews were only too familiar with the punishment of crucifixion meted out under Roman law. Varus had two thousand Jews crucified at one time. Titus was later to crucify so many there would be no more wood left for crosses. All knew that the condemned man had to carry his own cross to the place of execution. Hence Christ's use of the term "take up his cross" meant he was demanding the greatest of sacrifices from them if they wished to be his followers. He was inviting them to share the lot of suffering he was to undergo. He laid upon them a threefold condition; self-denial, sustained loyalty and obedience unto death.

Christ's next words, "Whoever would save his life will lose it," and so on, had a hidden meaning. He meant whoever would save the life of his body would lose his soul, but whoever would lose the life of his body through sacrifice would save his soul. Christ was pointing out that the life of the soul far surpasses the life of the body in value; it far surpasses that of the whole universe. No sacrifice is too great to make to save it.

From this passage in Scripture, revealing the turning point in our Lord's public life, we can learn two important lessons. The first is that we must have faith — we must believe that Christ is our Savior. The second is that once we believe in Christ, we must be willing to suffer and sacrifice to be his follower. For the true Christian, faith and sacrifice become the keys that unlocks salvation. God bless you.

# "C"     Thirteenth Sunday of the Year

*Luke 9:51-62*

The two themes of the Gospel of St. Luke are love and detachment. Both are depicted beautifully in the gospel of today's Mass. The first part of this reading relates how Christ sent disciples ahead of him to a Samaritan town to prepare for his coming. Up until this time Christ had confined his preaching to the Jewish people. It was to the chosen race that he first revealed the message of salvation. Thus the Samaritans, had they accepted Christ's teaching, would have become the first gentile or non-Jewish converts.

However, they were not disposed to do so. The Samaritans were the traditional enemies of the Jews. They watched these Jewish disciples come into their town and begin to preach; they further learned they were on their way to Jerusalem, the capital of the Jewish state of Palestine. This was enough for them. They refused to listen to them any further despite the Christian message they had to deliver.

James and John, the two sons of Zebedee, also called sons of Thunder, were most indignant at this rejection. They wanted Christ to call down fire from heaven to destroy them. Christ reprimanded these two disciples. He said in effect that he had come to save men, not to destroy them. He accepted the Samaritans' rejection with humility and showed them only love in return. Thus the first of St. Luke's two themes, that of love, is well illustrated.

His second theme is that of detachment. He alone of the four Evangelists dwells on this point. St. Luke is so filled with love for Christ, he feels that detachment from other worldly ties should follow easily. Luke's love is so great that he becomes exacting in demanding this detachment of others.

This spirit of detachment shows up clearly in his story of the three aspirants. As Christ continued his teaching in Galilee, his popularity was growing. More and more people wished to follow him. Three would-be-followers or aspirants approached him in this narrative.

The first of these was a scribe, an educated man. He said, "I will be your follower, wherever you go." To this Jesus responded, "The foxes have lairs, the birds of the sky have nests, but the Son of Man has nowhere to lay his head." Christ was pointing out to him that he had given up all claim to any kind of a permanent home in preaching the gospel. He invited this young man to estimate his own strength — to give up his home and become a wanderer in order to follow him.

Unfortunately Scripture does not give us the young man's decision. It is silent on the answer he gave to Christ. We can only hope that he had the courage and conviction to follow Christ despite these sacrifices demanded.

To a second aspirant Christ gave a direct vocation. He told him, "Come after me." The man replied, "Let me bury my father first." Jesus said to him, "Let the dead bury their dead; come away and proclaim the kingdom of God."

The favor asked by this second aspirant seems reasonable — to attend to his sick and aged father whose death was imminent. Even then it was a Jewish custom to bury one on the same day as his death. Christ's refusal to grant his request was not meant to be unjustly harsh, but simply showed that soldiers of Christ have more pressing and more important duties.

This man's vocation was a most special one. Christ summoned him, not once but twice: "Come after me," and again, "come away and proclaim the kingdom of God." Again we are not told the young man's decision. We are left in suspense and darkness as to whether he heeded his Savior's call.

Still a third aspirant said to Christ, "I will be your follower, Lord, but first let me take leave of my people at home." To this Christ answered, "Whoever, puts his hand to the plow but keeps looking back is unfit for the reign of God."

In the Old Testament when Elijah spread his mantle over Elisha to consecrate him a prophet, the young disciple begged to be allowed first to embrace his father and mother, and his aged master consented.

But a vocation to the priesthood in the New Testament is a higher vocation than that to the priesthood in the Old. Christ made more demands of his followers. Their life was of a higher order. Again the decision of this aspirant or would-be follower is left unannounced.

One may only conclude that Christ demanded extreme sacrifice from those to whom he gave a vocation. He wished to root out any imperfect dispositions. His "hard sayings" pointed out the high and honorable position it is to be a disciple of Christ.

It is well, my dear people, to pray that in our own day and age Christ will continue to care and to call young men to be his disciples — that he will call a sufficient number of young men to the priesthood to care for the needs of his Church. Let us pray that those who assume this high vocation will likewise be filled with a spirit of Christian love and detachment from worldy things. God bless you.

# "C"   Fourteenth Sunday of the Year

*Luke 10:1-12; 17-20*

In today's third Scripture reading at Mass, St. Luke tells us that our Lord sent seventy-two disciples in pairs of two into the various towns and villages he intended to visit. In reading this one should realize that our Lord's public life of preaching lasted less than three years. This incident occurred at the end of his second year of preaching. In fact, it was only about five months before Christ was to die on the cross.

Our Lord had himself visited and preached in all the towns and villages in the north of Palestine. He had traveled the length and breadth of Galilee and Samaria on the western side of the Jordan River and Decapolis on the east. He had left only Perea and Judea to cover to complete his mission of preaching on earth.

His headquarters or beginning place for this mission of preaching was the town of Bethany. In the first part of his public ministry Christ had gradually built up the faith of the people through his preaching and miracles. He increased their faith to the point where he could admit to being the Son of God, the long-awaited Messiah, and the people believed in him.

Having established this basis of faith, and with the time before his crucifixion growing short, Christ deemed it expedient to send messengers ahead of him to the towns he intended to visit to help prepare the people for the message he was to preach to them.

He sent his disciples forth in a spirit of poverty and detachment, for he said to them, "Do not carry a walking staff or traveling bag; wear no sandals. . . ." Their only weapon against their opponents was to be their meekness, for he said, "I am sending you as lambs in the midst of wolves."

He warned them not to waste time in long oriental greetings as was customary at that time. Nor should they waste time in moving from house to house when they had arrived at their destination; rather they should stay in one house, and eat and drink or take their meals there. This means of support they had a right to expect for he added, "The laborer is worth his wage." He further warned them they should be content by saying, "Eat what they set before you."

Our Lord prescribed how they should act. They should use the miraculous power he had bestowed upon them to cure the sick who were brought to them, and they should greet the people with the salutation, "The reign of God is at hand."

Their mission was not to make individual converts — that Christ himself would do later; rather, it was to reform the social and public life of the community. It was to prepare the community in general to be receptive to the preaching of Christ and prepare them to receive the means of salvation which he would offer.

Christ, in commissioning his disciples to go forth on this mission, gave them power to show their authority. They had the power of miracles, or performing miraculous cures to substantiate their preaching. He also gave them power to level sanctions or punishments. Should any town or community refuse to receive them, they were to shake the dust of that town from their feet as a witness against them. Christ said the fate of that town would be worse than Sodom.

Scripture indicates that these seventy-two disciples carried out this mission on which Christ sent them and performed it well. The disciples rejoiced that even the demons were subject to the name of Jesus. Our Lord compares this to the fall of Lucifer and the bad angels from heaven.

But Christ warns them they should not delight or take joy because of this; rather, their cause of joy should be that their names are inscribed in heaven. Our Lord was indicating to them that their mission was pleasing to God in heaven. They were doing something for which they would be richly rewarded hereafter if they persevered in the life of grace.

Their continued perseverance was necessary, for Satan was not yet conquered. He still was to succeed at invading their ranks. He was to be successful in tempting Judas to betray our Lord for thirty pieces of silver — Judas, one of the original Twelve Apostles! Satan was to succeed at weakening Peter enough to deny our Lord three times during his Passion, and cause Thomas to doubt Christ's Resurrection until he had seen the imprint of the nails in his hands and feet.

Yet Satan's fall from the high throne he had occupied, in ruling the world from the time of the original sin of Adam and Eve, was imminent. His kingdom was about to crumble, and the reign of God was about to be reestablished. The gates of heaven were soon to be reopened.

These disciples of Christ were playing an important role in Christ's plan of redemption. They were spreading the news of salvation. They would share in this reward if they persevered in their good intentions.

This was the reason for their rejoicing. Let us too rejoice that the kingdom of Satan has toppled. Let us make use of the means of salvation announced by Christ's disciples. Let us follow their leadership which will lead to eternal happiness. God bless you.

# "C" Fifteenth Sunday of the Year

*Luke 10:25-37*

A young couple decided to adopt a seven-year-old girl whose parents had mistreated and disowned her. When the couple came to the orphanage, they asked to speak to the child.

The young wife told the little girl all the things she would have at their house — her own room, playthings, and so forth. But the little girl was very suspicious. She asked, "What do I have to do for all this?"

The wife answered, "My dear, you don't have to do anything but love me and my husband."

Love, my dear people, is the predominant virtue of the Catholic religion. It is the most important force in the world. When asked by a lawyer the two most important commandments of the Law, our Lord got his questioner to reply, as contained in today's gospel, with "love the Lord your God with your whole heart and with your whole soul, and with all your strength, and with all your mind; and your neighbor as yourself."

After approving this commandment of love, our Lord then went on to exemplify it by the parable of the Good Samaritan. A man was going down from Jerusalem to Jericho, and he was attacked by robbers who stripped him and beat him and left him half dead.

A priest and a Levite came along the road, but both passed him by. Then finally a Samaritan came along. The Jews and the Samaritans were traditional enemies, but yet the Samaritan stopped and bound up the man's wounds, took him to an inn, and paid for his care.

Our Lord asked the lawyer who had been grilling him which of the three proved himself a neighbor to the victim of robbers. When he answered, "The one who showed mercy to him," our Lord answered, "Then go and do likewise."

Our Lord's command and example are most forceful and most clear. When he commands us to love our neighbor, he commands us to love everyone — even our enemies. The Jews and Samaritans were traditional enemies; yet when the Jew was robbed and beaten, the Samaritan took care of him. Our Lord told us to imitate his example.

On another occasion our Lord, commenting on the saying, "Love your neighbors and hate your enemies," said, "Love your enemies, do good to them that hate you."

Our motive for loving our neighbors is a most Christian one. We are all creatures of God. God made all men to his own image and likeness. We are showing love to God when we love our neighbor.

When Christ died on the cross he died to save all men. He told his Apostles to make disciples of all nations. Christ made us all members of his mystical body. When we love our neighbor, we show love to Christ. When we offend him, we offend Christ.

This love for our neighbor can be shown in many ways. One important way is to imitate the Good Samaritan and practice the corporal works of mercy, to feed the hungry, give drink to the thirsty, clothe the naked and so on.

Still another is to practice the spiritual works of mercy: to instruct the ignorant — for example, to assist one in learning the truths of the Catholic faith — to admonish the sinner, to counsel the doubtful, and the rest. To practice the spiritual works of mercy is to assist one in regard to his soul.

The love of neighbor shows itself in wishing good for our neighbor from our heart — in abstaining from injuring him. It does not consist merely in affectionate sentiments of good wishes. It means helping him when he needs help.

The love of our neighbor means rejoicing with him in prosperity and grieving with him in adversity. We must show respect for his life, his good name and his property.

Not long ago a young black boy, friendless, homeless and suffering from a lack of food and sleep, knocked on the door of a Catholic rectory in Dallas, Texas. When no one answered, he tried the door, and found it open and walked in. He walked into the priest's bedroom and saw an empty bed and fell asleep.

When Father DeFevere returned he found the boy in his bed fast asleep. He let him stay there for the night and made him breakfast the next morning. He allowed him to spend the next few days in the rectory and then found him a home, giving him nourishing meals in the meantime.

When the boy left the rectory he told the priest he wanted to become a Catholic. He paid the priest a high compliment saying, "I think Christ must have been something like you."

In this case a simple act of charity, of love for one's neighbor, paid a great dividend.

Remember Christ has promised a hundredfold reward for even a cup of cold water given in his name. Act so that it may be said of you as of the early Christians, "Look at these Christians, see how they love one another." God bless you.

# "C"     Sixteenth Sunday of the Year

*Luke 10:38-42*

St. Luke was a lady's man. By profession he was a doctor, a physician. Most probably he was a married man. Among the four evangelists he had the best command of the Greek language in which he was writing. He wrote with the greatest style. He wrote the longest and most complete of the four gospels.

Although not one of the original Twelve Apostles, he had a way of gaining information — facts which the other three Evangelists did not include in their gospels, for instance, the Infancy narrative. St. Luke wrote of the birth of Christ in Bethlehem, giving far more details about our Lord's birth, the Presentation, and his early life than any of the other three Evangelists. This information he must have gleaned from our Blessed Mother.

The incident mentioned in today's third reading, the meeting with Martha and Mary, is contained only in the Gospel of St. Luke. Most probably St. Luke learned of this by talking with Martha and Mary or with other eyewitnesses — proving that he had a way with women, or that he was a lady's man. We can be thankful that he did possess a facility for gaining information from women, otherwise this incident would never have been recorded in Holy Scripture.

Scripture scholars are in general agreement that the Martha and Mary mentioned were the sisters of Lazarus, whom Christ later raised from the dead, even through Lazarus is not mentioned on this occasion. Some even think that the Mary who is mentioned in today's gospel is the same person as Mary Magdalene, the converted sinner. But from Scripture there is no way of either proving or disproving this belief.

When our Lord entered Bethany, Martha invited him to her home. Undoubtedly this invitation included a number of our Lord's disciples as well. Martha, as was expected of a hostess, went about the tasks of cooking and preparing a meal, while our Lord talked and preached to those around him. Martha had a sister, Mary. The laws of hospitality dictated that she assist her sister in the chores in the kitchen. But instead Mary was so fascinated by the teaching of Christ that she sat at his feet avidly drinking in every word that fell from his lips.

Martha too evidently would have liked to listen to Christ, but circumstances did not permit it. She might be said to be somewhat envious of her sister, who heard everything he said. Her envy or irritation finally got the best of her. She spoke up and said to Christ, "Lord, are you not concerned that my sister has left me all alone to do the household tasks . . . ? Tell her to help me."

Christ said in reply, "Martha, Martha, you are anxious and upset about many things; one thing only is required. Mary has chosen the better portion and she shall not be deprived of it."

The answer of Christ has often been quoted and much discussed. There still remain some elements of ambiguity about it. For example, Christ does not explain what the one required thing is. He does not expressly state what the better part is. Many Scripture scholars think Christ was referring to a life of prayer or contemplation as being preferable to one of work or physical activity. But not all agree.

On one occasion a priest was teaching a theology class to a group of novices in a convent. He read this Scripture story to them and then asked one young novice what it meant. She stood up and said it meant that Sister Ignatius, the cook, should not spend all her time cooking up a five-course meal, that sandwiches would do just as well.

But to understand this Scripture passage more clearly, one should study the context of Holy Scripture out of which it was taken. Just before telling the story of Martha and Mary, St. Luke relates the parable of the Good Samaritan. He tells of the good Samaritan who aided the man who had been robbed and beaten. Christ praises a man who had performed a charitable deed. He concludes by saying, "Go and do in like manner."

In the following incident, Christ praises Mary for listening to his preaching. Thus the context of the gospels as well as common sense dictate that there must be a balance between prayer and physical work in everyone's life. One should not spend all his time working, neglecting prayer; nor should one spend all his time praying, neglecting other duties. Each has its time and place.

This method of contrasting two things with each other, called the diptych, is St. Luke's favorite form of teaching. He uses it frequently. Even within the same story or parable he uses it. Thus he contrasts the conduct of the priest and Levite with the Samaritan. Thus he contrasts the conduct of Martha and Mary.

From this gospel story read in today's Mass, let us learn this lesson — that we have important duties to perform in our own life, but whatever these duties, we must also spend some time in prayer. We have an obligation to give praise and thanksgiving to God for all he had given us.

There are times for hard mental and physical labor. But when our Lord should speak to us, whether it be through Holy Mass on Sunday morning or other times of prayer, we should give our attention to him. God bless you.

# "C"     Seventeenth Sunday of the Year

*Luke 11:1-13*

An Air Force pilot lost his way flying in a fog over Alaska. A dense fog covered the ground so that he could see nothing below him. In addition his compass went out of commission. The pilot began to fear for his life. He noticed too that his gas was running low.

But the pilot did make radio contact with an airfield. From the ground came this message, "Keep talking, Lieutenant, we'll try to guide you in by radio beam. But keep talking."

Without hesitation the pilot obeyed the order. He said the first words that came to his mind. And over the radio speaker on the ground below there came forth the words, "Our Father, who art in heaven, hallowed by thy name." Over and over again the words of the Lord's prayer came over the airwaves.

For not only was the pilot obeying an order of the control station on the ground, but at the same time he was asking God for help. It seemed as though his prayer was an endless stream of conversation, but through a rift in the clouds he saw the lights of the airfield. He knew then that his Our Fathers had been answered.

Some 1,900 years ago in Galilee a small group of disciples had observed our Lord in his actions. They noted that when he had gone into the desert he was absorbed in prayer — that entering the temple, he had prayed. After performing some awe-inspiring miracle, he had prayed to thank his Father in heaven. He had prayed on board ship when the Sea of Galilee had broken out in a furious storm. He had prayed for his enemies as well as his friends. They learned through watching our divine Savior of the necessity of prayer.

It was natural then that they should bring a request to him, "Lord, teach us to pray." In response to this request, Christ said, "Our Father, who art in heaven, hallowed by thy name." He taught them the Lord's Prayer.

The "Our Father," which Christ taught them, has come down to us as the best known most widely circulated of all prayers. It has often been called the perfect prayer. This title "perfect prayer" is most appropriate for several reasons. First, it was taught to us by Christ himself, who was God and all-perfect himself. Secondly, it contains all the elements essential or necessary to prayer — namely adoration, petition, thanksgiving and contrition.

The "Our Father," as a prayer, consists of an address to God, of seven petitions, and the word Amen. The address, Our Father, places the soul in the right disposition for prayer. It awakens within us confidence in God and raises our thoughts to him.

The first petition of the "Our Father," "hallowed be thy name," gives glory to God. And giving glory to God is the end of creation, the highest aid of every creature.

The next petition, "thy kingdom come," begs that his kingdom be extended throughout the world — that his Church should flourish in every land, among every people, and that all of the two billion on the earth should belong to it. It beseeches him that the pagan and infidel countries of the world come into the Church. It prays for the conversion of the Jews, and of the Communist nations of our own age.

But God's kingdom includes more than just these nations of this world. It includes also the kingdom of heaven. Hence this petition prays that we will become partakers of the joy of heaven.

The petition "thy will be done" prays that we may have the grace to know the will of God and the courage to carry it out. It prays that his will shall prevail over the wills of all those who will evil in this life.

"Give us this day our daily bread" is a prayer not only for bread but for all our needs — the needs of our body, for food, clothing, shelter and all the necessities of life. It is a prayer for health and freedom from harm and sickness. It is a prayer too for our spiritual needs, for the graces and virtues we need in this life to save our soul.

"Forgive us our trespasses" is a prayer for forgiveness. St. James in his epistle says that "in many things we all offend." Therefore, we all need to beg God's forgiveness.

But as a test of our sorrow in begging forgiveness, we pray, "as we forgive those who trespass against us." That is, we must be willing to forgive others. In the Old Testament the Jews had a law that they must be willing to forgive their enemies three times. When St. Peter asked our Lord how many times he should forgive his brother who offended him, Christ replied seventy times seven times, which meant infinitely. There was no limit.

The last petition, "deliver us from evil," means not only physical evil, but the greatest evil of all, namely sin.

These seven petitions taken together constitute the most urgent needs of man — the items we have the greatest need of praying for. They go to make up the perfect prayer.

Because the "Our Father" is the perfect prayer, because it was taught us by God himself, Holy Mother the Church has made it a part of the Mass. It is said after the Consecration and shortly before the Communion. It forms a connecting link between these two most sacred parts.

The "Our Father" is the universal prayer — the prayer known by all Christians throughout the world. Time was, when our country was founded, that our forefathers could boast that every American knew the "Our Father." But times have changed. Despite the progress made in education in this country, a recent survey taken of the children in the first and second grades of our public schools throughout the country showed that 75% of them did not know the "Our Father." The number of American adults who cannot recite the "Our Father" is also surprisingly high.

God has blessed our nation from the beginning because we were a religious people. But certainly if we wish him to continue to bless us we must continue our prayers to him.

One day a stonemason was working high up in the air constructing a skyscraper. As he worked, he noticed a small boy on the ground looking up and watching him. When he came down from his high workspot, the little boy looked up into his face and said to him, "I know why you're not afraid to work so high up in the air — it's because you said your prayers this morning." The workman thought to himself — he hadn't said his prayers that morning — in fact, he hadn't said them in quite a long time. But from that day to this he hasn't missed a day in saying an "Our Father" and some other prayers each morning.

Among our prayers, the "Our Father" is perhaps the simplest of them all, yet the richest in meaning. It is the *only* prayer that Christ ever taught us. It is a manifestation of our hope. It reaffirms our confidence in God. It contains a summary of all the requests we can make of God. It is a key that can unlock any treasure in heaven. And yet, while still being the simplest of prayers, it is at the same time profound; it provides endless subjects of meditation. Let us make the "Our Father" our prayer. Let us say it every day. God bless you.

# "C"     Eighteenth Sunday of the Year

*Luke 12:13-21*

The gospel read at today's Mass is taken from St. Luke. Our Lord was making his way south from Galilee into Judea, and he was approached by a group of Jews. One of them spoke up to Jesus: "Teacher, tell my brother to give me my share of our inheritance."

In those early times it was not at all uncommon to take unsettled property and other disputes to respected rabbis. Our Lord had proved himself to be a very highly respected teacher and prophet. Therefore this question did not seem in the least out of order. No doubt the one who asked it expected some wise and just decision to come forth from the lips of our Lord.

Instead he was given a much different answer. He said, "Friend, who has set me up as your judge or arbiter?" Christ refused to allow himself to become entangled in this legal dispute. The whole life of Christ was one which spoke of detachment from worldly possessions. Christ, who was God and the creator of all the goods of this world, was born in poverty, a voluntary and assumed poverty.

During his lifetime he renounced the goods of this world. He said the Son of Man has nowhere to lay his head. He lived his life in the spirit of poverty, of detachment from worldly goods. Therefore, he refused to allow himself to be drawn into a discussion between those who coveted and were greedy for this world's possessions. He refused to take sides.

Christ went on to make use of the opportunity, being asked this question, to give a short discourse on the subject of greed or covetousness. He said, "Avoid greed in all its forms."

In saying this he was re-echoing the Tenth Commandment which God gave to Moses 1,300 years before on Mt. Sinai, "Thou shalt not covet thy neighbor's goods." It is a sin expressly forbidden by one of the Ten Commandments.

St. Paul condemns it most sternly, for he writes in his first epistle to Timothy that "the desire of money is the root of all evils." Greed is a sin which alienates one from serving almighty God. Our prime concern on this earth should be what is pleasing and holy in the sight of almighty God. Our spiritual good should be our prime concern. But greed elevates the desire for or the accumulation of material wealth in place of the spiritual. St. Paul calls it the service of idols.

Greed brings about cruelty to others. It gives one a warped sense of values. He views things in terms of dollars and cents, how much profit it will bring to himself. He loses what sympathy and compassion he may have had for others. He is callous about the sufferings of others. The dignity of other human beings is steadily diminished.

Greed brings about discontent. If a poor man is greedy, he becomes wretched in his poverty. He hardens his heart against the rich, and soon against all his neighbors. If a rich man is greedy, then he becomes dissatisfied with any amount of wealth that he may possess. He covets and desires only more. No amount of wealth will satisfy his craving for more.

The sin of greed leads to the commission of other sins as well. At first the greedy man will use honest means to accumulate his wealth. But then the desire for wealth becomes so overpowering that when the opportunity to accumulate it by dishonest means comes along, he finally uses this too. The virtue of justice ceases to have any meaning for him. The accumulation of wealth becomes an obsession with him, whether he does it by fair means or foul. First laxity accompanies it; then untruthfulness, perhaps even impurity. Faith fades away from his soul in the light of these many abuses.

The greedy man makes one fundamental error. He tries to serve material wealth before serving his almighty Creator. Christ sums this up so beautifully when he says, "You cannot serve both God and mammon."

Christ concludes this gospel passage with a brief but poignant parable. He tells of the rich man who had a good harvest. He was distressed because he had no adequate place to store his extra grain, no further place to store his wealth. He began to make plans in the eye of his mind to tear down his barns and build bigger ones. He dreamt of the blessings and benefits he would reap for years to come because of his additional grain and wealth.

Unhesitatingly Christ speaks of such a man as "You fool!" He adds, "This very night your life shall be required of you." Death must come to all men. No one knows the exact date or hour. God chose to call to judgment the soul of this greedy man at a time when he was growing wealthy, when he was concerned only about his material possessions.

Christ, who is our God and creator, asks, "To whom will all this piled-up wealth of yours go?" The answer, of course, is that it will go to one's family or distant relatives. Perhaps in some cases, it will go to the state or some stranger. Death separates us from our material wealth; we cannot take it with us when we die. In passing from this life to the next, the only goods we can take with us are the graces and virtues we have stored within our souls and not the money we have stored in the bank.

Lest anyone miss the point of this parable, Christ draws a conclusion himself: "That is the way it works with the man who grows rich for himself instead of growing rich in the sight of God."

Almighty God and the world around us have two different concepts of what true wealth is. Wealth to the world is the accumulation of money. But true wealth in the sight of almighty God is the accumulation of grace. True wealth is stored in one's soul. It is gained through the performance of good deeds. It comes through the practice of charity. True wealth is measured in the exercise of virtue. It is measured in the amount of love one has for almighty God and the love he has for his neighbor.

No words that Christ spoke on earth have a more direct or more open meaning. They direct us most explicitly as to how we should direct our time and efforts. We should direct them toward building up grace within our souls. They coincide most perfectly with the words Christ spoke on the occasion of the Sermon on the Mount: "Blessed are the poor in spirit, for theirs is the kingdom of heaven." God bless you.

# "C"      Ninteenth Sunday of the Year

*Luke 12:32-48*

In the second year of our Lord's public life, he visited the city of Jerusalem to celebrate the Feast of Dedication. Following this feast he headed north once again toward Galilee, but the route he took was not a direct one. He detoured to the land to the east of the Jordan River, to the country of Perea. Here he spent the next four or five months preaching and performing miracles.

It is here that we find him teaching the parable contained in today's gospel of St. Luke. Our Lord had just visited the home of a leading Pharisee. Once he left his home, large crowds began to surround him. Initially, in the beginning of his public life, Christ was accustomed to preach in the synagogues in a particular village. But now, after nearly two years of preaching, his reputation had grown and the crowd around him increased so greatly no synagogue would be large enough to hold them, so Christ resorted to preaching in the open on some grassy plain or hill.

Our Lord told his listeners, who included his Apostles and disciples along with many natives of the district of Perea, that wherever your treasure lies, there your heart will be. He was telling them that the thing they should treasure most is to serve almighty God.

Christ then proceeded to tell them the parable of the farsighted and the unwise servants. But let us remember that a servant in the time of Christ was actually a slave. Wealthy men acquired slaves as the booty of war and also through the buying and selling of them. There existed in the Roman Empire a sort of refined kind of slavery. The higher class of slaves shared the household life of the master. Many of them had excellent educations, being able to read and write fluently.

In this parable our Lord tells that the master has gone to attend a wedding feast. While he is gone, the wise servant will await his return and be prepared to receive him. But the unwise servant, who does not think about his return, will be caught unprepared.

In this parable we can rightly conclude that the master represents almighty God; he represents Christ himself. The servants are those who profess the Christian faith, those who believe in Christ. The servants in responsible positions represent the Apostles, or anyone in a position of authority over others.

Christ tells his listeners that when the master returns the wise and prepared servants open the gate for him without delay and show that they are prepared for his return. The master in turn will seat them at table and begin to wait on them. This is a new and unexpected twist in the parable that his listeners did not expect to hear. Ordinarily no master of an eastern household would ever wait on his servants. He would expect them to wait on him, no matter how tired they were or how hard they had worked. Then, when they had fed and waited on the master, they would eat for themselves.

But in the new Christian concept of values, Christ is showing that he will come and be of service and wait on his servants or followers. At the Last Supper Christ would wash the feet of his Apostles. He would make his life a life of service to them, preaching to them, curing them of sickness and helping them in every way, even to the point of giving up his life for them. This was a new and startling concept for them to grasp.

In telling his followers to be vigilant and be prepared, Christ meant they should be vigilant against temptation. They should be vigilant and prepared to resist any occasion of sin. In teaching them the Lord's Prayer, he had said, "Lead us not into temptation, but deliver us from evil." Now in parable form he was instructing them in a similar vein.

But there is a positive side to this preparedness, to this vigilance against sin. It is detachment from worldly things, self-sacrifice for others. This positive practice of virtue is necessary to build up one's spiritual strength so that one will be able to resist temptation when it does come along. Detachment and sacrifice are the body-building exercises one must use to build up virtue and spiritual strength.

To further establish the necessity of preparedness, Christ uses another figure of speech; he says that we do not know when the thief will break into one's house. He adds, "Be on guard, therefore. The Son of Man will come when you least expect him." Here Christ is referring to the day of one's death, the day of particular judgment, when one must face Christ in judgment and give an account of all of his actions in this life.

The meaning of the parables of Christ was sometimes very subtle. In this case St. Peter was uncertain about it. He asked Christ directly whether he meant the parable for the Apostles or for the whole world. Christ did not answer him directly but answered by asking Peter a question — who is the far-sighted servant?

Christ was saying it had application for all of the Christian community, but in a special way for the leaders of the community. He meant it in a special way for his Apostles; he meant it for their successors, for the bishops and priests of his Church. He meant it for all those who exercise authority over others. He meant it for the parents of children.

Everyone in a position of authority will have a heavy responsibility to be spiritually prepared and to keep those in his charge prepared. Christ said, "When much has been given a man, much will be required of him. More will be asked of a man to whom more has been entrusted."

In the road of life which we follow there are many uncertainties. We do not know where it will take us. We do not know when it will end. But of one thing we can be certain; our dear Lord will meet us at the end of it. Therefore, we should always be prepared. We should live at all times in the state of sanctifying grace. For by living at all times in grace we shall be prepared to greet our Master whenever he shall come. God bless you.

# "C"    Twentieth Sunday of the Year

*Luke 12:49-53*

The words which Christ uttered, "I have come to light a fire on the earth," are words of challenge, words of division, words of supercharged meaning. They are words that breathe of violence, of battle, but then they are not words that should surprise us.

Back in the Old Testament the prophet Malachi foretold that Christ would come to purify the sons of Levi as the refiner purifies gold and silver and to purify the sons of Israel as the crucible purifies precious metals of their dross. It was a prophecy of the fire that Christ would enkindle in the midst of mankind.

A battle between the forces of good and evil was awaited and expected. From the time that Satan had successfully tempted our first parents to commit original sin, the gates of heaven had been closed to mankind. All descendents of Adam and Eve entered this world with original sin on their souls. Death and suffering had entered the world as a result of it. The devil had won a great but only a temporary battle over mankind. Speaking to the devil almighty God had said, "I will put enmities between you and the woman, and your offspring and hers." The woman referred to was the Blessed Virgin Mary and her offspring was her divine Son, Christ our Savior. Almighty God foretold of the great battle that would be waged in the future for the possession of the souls of men.

When Christ was forty days old and was presented by his mother, Mary, in the temple, the holy man Simeon said to Mary. "This child is destined to be the downfall and the rise of many in Israel, a sign that will be opposed."

When Malachi spoke of Christ purifying the sons of Israel, as the crucible purifies precious metals, he referred to the cleansing properties of fire. Fire can burn away waste and impurities. In this way precious metals are purified. In this way too Christ would help to rid the world of evil and sin.

Christ's method of doing this would not be peaceful. He did violence to his own body. He fasted in the desert for forty days and nights. He told his followers that they too should fast and pray.

Christ broke the devil's stranglehold of sin on the world by carrying his cross up the hill of Calvary, while blood, sweat and pain aggravated his every step. Christ offered himself as a sacrifice upon the cross to appease his Father's anger at the sins of men. Christ broke the lock the devil had placed on the gates of heaven, but the struggle was not an easy one.

Nor did the devil submit willingly. When Christ was fasting in the desert, three times the devil came to tempt him. The devil tempted the Apostles of Christ — and with some success, for he succeeded in persuading Judas to betray our Lord; he persuaded Peter to deny our Lord three times, and Thomas to doubt that he had truly risen.

The devil has given ground most reluctantly. Christ commissioned his Apostles to go and teach all nations. In country after country the devil had attempted to block and hinder the work of Christ's Church. The two-hundred-year-long persecution of the Roman Empire is but one example. The persecution of the Church in Communist nations today is another. Untold legions of martyrs have shed their blood for the faith when the world demanded it of them.

But the flame of our faith is a slow, steady and advancing flame. It is fanned by the breath of the Holy Spirit. It can never be extinguished. It is like the fire that St. Patrick built on the hill of Slane in defiance of commands by the druids and high priests of Ireland. They were unable to extinguish the fire that he had kindled.

Christ said, "I have come for division. From now on, a household of five will be divided three against two and two against three; father will be split against son and son against father, mother against daughter and daughter against mother. . . ." The division Christ speaks of can be a twofold division — a division here on earth and a division that will last into eternity.

Faith is a virtue by which we firmly believe in Christ. It must be made by an assent of our intellect. Faith must be affirmed by each and every person on an individual basis. Thus it becomes both possible and probable that some members of a family will give it while others will not. Within a family one or more members can firmly believe in Christ and his teachings, while others in the family do not.

Christianity is not the type of religion that will permit peaceful coexistence. Christ said not to hide your light under a basket, but rather to let it burn for all men to see. Christ commanded his Apostles to go and teach all nations. Christ commanded his followers to love their neighbors as themselves. Thus Christianity is a religion that concerns itself with one's neighbor.

Christianity regards the soul of a neighbor as a soul potentially saved. A true Christian cannot rest until he has made a sincere effort to do so. Thus as long as one member of a family believes in Christ and another does not, there will be a division between them.

It is unfortunate but true that such division may last unto eternity. Christ will judge the soul of each of us in particular judgment upon our death. Thus it is within the realm of possibility that one member of a family will save his soul while another will lose it.

Therefore, there devolves upon every Christian, every believer in Christ, the obligation of work and prayer. We must work as faithful stewards in the vineyard of Christ. We must pray that Christ will grant the gift of unity to all members of our family, to all fellow countrymen. We must pray that the divisions which Christ foretold will be healed in this world rather than maintained for eternity in the world to come. God bless you.

# "C"  Twenty-first Sunday of the Year

*Luke 13:22-30*

The story of our Lord's public life is a continuing story of small crowds following him and then building into big ones. But then some bubble would burst and the crowds would leave Christ, and the process would start again. One example of this is the crowds that followed our Lord after he had multiplied the loaves and fishes. But then following this miracle, Christ promised that he would give them his body to eat and his blood to drink. The crowd could not understand how he could do this, so most of them left our Lord.

In the incident mentioned in today's gospel of St. Luke, Christ had made his way south into Judea and Perea. But many of the people of his native Galilee had been so entranced with his preaching and miracles that they followed him into this neighboring land. Many of them held to preconceived erroneous beliefs. One such belief was that all Jews would be saved hereafter and all gentiles would be lost.

When someone in the crowd — most probably a Pharisee — approached him and asked a question, "Are they few in number who are to be saved?" Christ took this opportunity to burst another bubble, to correct another false idea. And again many of the crowd, not liking or believing what Christ told them, would leave him and return to their homes.

Christ replied, "Many . . . will try to enter and be unable." Knowing their limited understanding of this remark, Christ elaborated by giving a dialogue that might take place on the day of judgment when they beseech God to let them enter the kingdom of heaven. "Sir, open for us," they will petition.

"I do not know where you come from," he will reply.

"We ate and drank in your company. You taught in our streets," they will protest.

"I do not know where you come from," he will respond.

Christ was enunciating the principle that salvation would come to those who earned it. Faith is necessary for salvation, but in addition to faith in Christ, one must also perform good works. Both of these, faith plus good works, are necessary for salvation.

This is a subject on which volumes have been written. It has been a stumbling block to many theologians. Many false opinions have arisen concerning it. One of the main teachings that arose during the Reformation was that man was justified by faith alone. But from these words of Christ, from the Epistle of St. James, we know that good works are also necessary in addition to faith. Both are required.

When asked if there were few to be saved, Christ answered, "Try to come in through the narrow door. Many . . . will try to enter and be unable." Christ's answer was not meant to discourage one from seeking salvation or lead one into despair. On the contrary, his whole life and mission to earth was to bring salvation to man — to make it possible for man to enter heaven. He gave men the means of salvation if only they would use these means.

One may say that the gate to heaven, although narrow, is wide enough to admit any person who seeks to enter, but nothing more. Many try to enter it with bulky burdens on their shoulders — burdens such as pride, or worldliness, or greed or envy. But these burdens are too wide to permit one to enter through the narrow gate.

To enter heaven one must divest himself of these burdens. He must rid himself of pride or lust or envy. Then he will find that the gate of heaven is more than wide enough to admit him.

Christ concludes this instruction by telling that there will be great wailing and grinding of teeth. He says that people will come from the east and the west, the north and the south, and take their place in the kingdom of God. Some of the last shall be first, and some of the first shall be last.

Again primarily we may say that this passage refers to some of the Jewish people. They were the first to receive the good news of salvation, but because some of them rejected it, they shall be last. Because some of the Gentiles, who heard it last, received it, they shall be first.

But then an even wider interpretation is possible. Even among Catholics of this present day, some were baptized at birth and were taught Catholic doctrine while still in their cribs, yet in later life they may become lax in practicing it. Others, who came to know Catholic teachings only in their later life, have surged ahead of them in the practice of religion and will reach a higher place in heaven.

In religious practice one must be humble. He must continue his religious duties at every age. He must not be presumptuous about his salvation. One must practice perseverance in the practice of prayer and the performance of religious duties.

The door to heaven is a narrow one, and the road leading to it is a long one. But the happiness is worth all of our efforts to achieve it. God bless you.

# "C"    Twenty-second Sunday of the Year

*Luke 14:1, 7-14*

In today's gospel St. Luke tells us of an incident that occurred when Christ had dinner with a group of Pharisees on the Sabbath. The Pharisees as a group were strict observers of the Jewish Law. And the Jewish Law called for a strict observance of the Sabbath.

The Jewish Law compelled Jews to attend services in the synagogue on the Sabbath. Likewise the Law forbade them to perform any servile work. It also forbade the cooking of meals on the Sabbath. Hence on the Sabbath the Jews either had to eat cold meals or, as frequently was done, they would cook extra food on the day before and then by various means keep the food warm until it was served on the Sabbath.

The meal to which our Lord was invited was supposedly the main meal — served at midday — following the morning synagogue service. On previous occasions our Lord had criticized the Pharisees and their hypocrisy. Nevertheless this particular group of Pharisees had evidently heard so much about our Lord, his preaching and his miracles, they invited him to their dinner out of a spirit of curiosity, regardless of his criticism.

But at this dinner there happened to be present a man sick of the dropsy. The Pharisees had not planned to create any embarrassing situation at the meal, but seeing this sick man, our Lord himself brought up the question of whether it was lawful to heal on the Sabbath.

This question presented a dilemma to the Jews. If they answered no, it was unlawful to cure, they were going against common sense. If they answered yes, they would be violating the Sabbath Law which forbade the practice of medicine on the Sabbath. Hence they refused to answer our Lord's question.

Seven times before our Lord had cured sick people on the Sabbath. This occasion was no exception. Out of a spirit of compassion and love our Lord also healed this man sick of the dropsy. But even though the Pharisees had remained silent to his question, the looks on their faces showed their objection to it.

Our Lord then proceeded to show them how foolish their position was. He asked them which of them, if an ox fell into a pit on a Sabbath, would not draw him out. Pits, because of the numerous burial chambers and the nature of the land, were common things in Palestine. It was a commonly accepted practice to rescue any animal that fell into a pit, even on a Sabbath. Thus because the

Pharisees knew that human beings were far more valuable than animals, they could not answer his objection.

But then a second incident occurred at this meal which our Lord seized upon to instruct the Pharisees in humility. At the ceremonial banquets of the Jews, places at table were assigned to all — this was done more or less according to the prestige or reputation that one enjoyed. But at banquets other than the ceremonial ones, people were permitted to choose their own places.

It was evidently such a banquet that our Lord was then attending, for he observed how people were choosing the first places at table. He pointed out that in taking the higher places one's host may come and say, "Make room for this man," and one is humiliated in being forced to take a lower place.

Our Lord pointed out that one should take the last place and then the host may come and say, "Friend, go up higher." One then is honored in the presence of others.

Humility is one of the greatest and most important of virtues. It is a virtue in which one acknowledges his lowliness and dependence upon almighty God. It is the opposite of the vice of pride, in which one stresses his own self-importance and independence of almighty God.

Humility, in a sense, is closely identified with truth. For actually we would not exist at all if God did not create us. All we have or possess we owe to him.

Christ himself gave us the greatest possible example of humility. As our Creator and as God himself, he chose to come into this world and take on the body of man. He chose to live on this earth in the poorest and meanest of circumstances. He was born in a stable and chose a carpenter for his foster-father. He lived in an obscure town and chose poor fishermen as his Apostles. He conversed with Mary Magdalene and known sinners. He washed the feet of his Apostles. He said to "learn of me, because I am meek and humble of heart."

Our Blessed Mother also is an excellent example of the virtue of humility. Mary, in her youth, deemed herself unworthy ever to hope to become the Mother of our Savior and thus took the vow of virginity. But God recognized her humility and chose her above all other women to be his Mother.

Many saints have attained great honor in heaven because of the practice of humility. One person known for his humility was St. Chad. St. Chad lived in England in the seventh century. As a young man he decided to become a monk. Because of the holiness of his life he was looked upon as an outstanding leader of men. When the local bishop died, his fellow monks and other local Church leaders asked him to become their new bishop.

Back in those early times it was customary for a bishop to be chosen in this way rather than be chosen by the Pope in Rome. St. Chad humbly and reluctantly accepted this honor. He was duly consecrated and began to rule his diocese. But there was a mix-up.

Another priest had been asked by still other leaders to become bishop of that same diocese. He too was consecrated a bishop and showed up on the scene some time after St. Chad had begun to rule the diocese.

St. Chad could easily have contested this second bishop's appointment. But in his humility he did not. Instead he most humbly stepped aside. Even though a bishop, he retired to a monastery and there for the next few years lived as a simple monk once again.

But the story of his humility began to spread. In a few years' time, when another diocese in England needed a bishop, the king personally saw to it that St. Chad was appointed bishop of this new diocese. In this new diocese he did much for the conversion of pagans within its boundaries. He was regarded as a saint by all who knew him personally in his lifetime and is a canonized saint today.

Because St. Chad practiced humility on this one occasion, he was richly rewarded for it later on. Our Lord himself tells us the value of practicing it.

In this morning's gospel he says that "everyone who exalts himself shall be humbled, and he who humbles himself shall be exalted."

Therefore let us imitate this humble saint in our lives. Let us imitate our Lord himself and our Blessed Mother in the practice of this virtue. Christ has promised that the humble shall possess the kingdom of heaven and his promises are never made in vain. God bless you.

# "C"    Twenty-third Sunday of the Year

*Luke 14:25-33*

Today's gospel according to St. Luke tells us that a great crowd was with Jesus. On this particular occasion Christ was on his way south from Galilee into Judea on his way to Jerusalem. It was to be his last trip to the Holy City. Christ knew what was ahead of him; he knew that crucifixion lay ahead, but the crowds did not know this.

Christ turned to the crowd and said, "If anyone comes to me without turning his back on his father and mother, his wife and his children, his brothers and sisters, indeed his very self, he cannot be my follower." At first glance these words sound extremely severe! They seem harsh! But Christ is simply setting the price that one must pay to be his disciple. He is establishing the cost of discipleship. He is saying that to be his disciple one must renounce all things, even the strongest of family ties. He is saying that his disciples must have greater love for him than for any other human being.

These words of Christ tell us that there is only one absolute in our lives. Everything else is relative to that one absolute. That one absolute is our love and dedication to almighty God. Whenever a conflict arises between our devotion to God and some other creature, our choice must always be God.

Christ adds that to be his disciple one must take up his cross and follow him. The word cross had a hated and distasteful connotation to the Jewish people. It was the cruellest death they knew; it was the death meted out to the worst of their criminals. When a criminal was condemned to die on the cross he was first assigned to carry that cross, or at least the transverse beam, to the place of his crucifixion. Hence to take up a cross was to be willing to endure this cruelest of deaths — this was the price Christ was asking one to pay to be his disciple.

While Christ lived here on earth he had many distant followers but only a handful of real disciples. Only a relatively small number of their followers were willing to pay the price Christ demanded.

The same problem faces us as Christians and followers of Christ today. Christ is summoning all of us to be his disciples. The manner in which we follow Christ depends largely on the circumstances of our life. It depends on our time, our work, our family. Christ does not demand the explicit commitment of everyone to enter the religious life — that everyone should be either a priest or a Sister. The great majority of Christians follow Christ in the lay state of life. A lay Christian should be more devoted to his Creator than to any fellow creature or created object.

A person once said, "The trouble with Christianity is that it has never been practiced." In making this statement, this person had in mind the large number of Christians he knew who were Christians in name only.

We can honestly ask ourselves if there is any difference in our lives as Christians from what we find in those who are not. I'm afraid that many people have to answer that there is very little real difference. There are some non-Christians who can be found who outshine us in the practice of love of neighbor and kindness and other virtues. If this is true in one's life then perhaps one is only a distant follower of Christ and not a true disciple.

Discipleship with Christ demands a total commitment of our lives. There must be no holding back in our love and dedication to him. We cannot make any exceptions in the line of those we love most.

Christ gave two examples in today's gospel. A man building a tower must calculate the cost of it before he begins to build, to find out if he has enough money to complete it. A king going into battle must first scout the enemy and learn his strength before engaging him in battle.

In similar fashion, to be a disciple of Christ, one must first calculate the cost of it. Then, knowing the price is high, is one prepared to pay it? When King Henry VIII was king of England his chancellor, Sir Thomas More, was forced to choose between serving his king and his religious duties; he bravely chose the latter. He showed himself a true disciple of Christ. He is now a saint of God.

Let our choice be like his. Let our commitment to God be a total one. Let God be for us the absolute. The reward of being a true disciple is an eternity of happiness. God bless you.

# "C"     Twenty-fourth Sunday of the Year

*Luke 15:1-32*

One group that continually followed our Lord, but yet was very critical of him, was the Pharisees. But the Pharisees began to show their annoyance and grow critical of our Lord when the publicans or tax collectors, the extreme lowest level of Jewish society, began to crowd around him and listen to him. Their annoyance became extreme when public sinners also attached themselves to the group that followed and listened to Christ.

The Pharisees were unable to see why, if Christ were truly a king, he welcomed such people and associated with them. The Pharisees themselves were accustomed to show contempt to such people, thereby making themselves appear just and virtuous.

Our Lord on many occasions admonished the Pharisees in this regard. He had told them that sinners needed a physician. But the Pharisees failed to learn this lesson. Even on this occasion they protested.

In doing so, they were making hypocrites of themselves. They were condemning others while they themselves were guilty of many faults.

Nineteen centuries have passed since our Lord lived on earth, but human nature has changed very little. Many people follow in the footsteps of the Pharisees in looking down on their neighbors. They condemn their neighbors for vices but fail to see their own.

There are many Pharisees in our modern world today. They are the proud and self-righteous people, the type whom our Lord chastized. It was for the benefit of these people that our Lord told the parable of the lost sheep.

Our Lord told of the shepherd who had 100 sheep but lost one. He said he would leave the 99 in the flock and go in search of the lost one. Finding it, he lays it on his shoulders rejoicing, and coming home, he calls together his friends and neighbors saying to them, "Rejoice with me because I have found my lost sheep."

Our Lord then gives the moral of the parable, that similarly "there will be joy in heaven over one repentant sinner more than over ninety-nine righteous people who have no need of repentance."

Our Lord came to this earth for one prime purpose — to save sinners. He came to redeem mankind. He came to reopen to all men the gates of the kingdom of heaven.

We are all members of the flock of Christ. We stray from his fold whenever we decide to follow the path of temptation. We become lost sheep whenever we do not follow the teachings of Christ. But even then Christ does not desert us. He follows us along the treacherous paths of life with his graces.

Sometimes the lost sheep reclaimed by Christ will become great saints in his Church and will display great virtue. Thus St. Dismas, a lost sheep who was crucified beside our Lord on Calvary, gained salvation by his repentance when dying. St. Augustine, one of the great fathers and early theologians of the Church, gained sanctity even after an early life of sin.

Perhaps the greatest sculptor and painter of all time was the artist Michelangelo. One of his greatest works was the statue of David, which depicts him with his sling in the air, ready to fire a stone at the giant Goliath.

But one remarkable feature of this masterpiece is the fact that it was carved from a piece of marble which another artist had worked on and then abandoned in a field in Florence. Michelangelo came along and turned this other artist's failure into a great triumph. In a sense Michelangelo was the shepherd who had rescued the lost sheep.

But a human soul is far more valuable than a piece of marble. The sheep that are lost, who have strayed and fallen by the wayside, Christ, the Good Shepherd, is very anxious to find and bring back to the true fold.

Regardless, my dear people, what sins you may be guilty of in the past, or how often you have fallen, let us resolve not to reject the grace which Christ, the Good Shepherd, is offering us. God bless you.

# "C"    Twenty-fifth Sunday of the Year

*Luke 16:1-13*

The gospel read at today's Mass is the parable of the unjust steward, taken from St. Luke's gospel. It is one of the most interesting of all the parables taught by Christ.

In it he tells of the unjust steward or manager who squandered his master's possessions. The master became aware of this and planned to remove him from his position. When the steward heard that his master was going to remove him, he became very troubled and worried. He wondered what he would do, for he said, "I cannot dig ditches, I am ashamed to go begging."

But in the few remaining days of his stewardship he showed great prudence. He contacted his master's debtors and reduced their debts. Of the man who owed one hundred jars of oil, he accepted fifty in full payment of his debt. Of the man who owed one hundred measures of wheat, he accepted eighty in payment of his. He accepted lesser amounts from these debtors and thus gained their favor and friendship.

By doing this, the unjust steward hoped to be accepted into their houses and friendship once he was dismissed from his master's services, for he was not able to dig ditches and too ashamed to beg.

The master, seeing this, praised the unjust steward for his prudence. But the steward is like very many other people in the world today. Almighty God has placed a great trust in their hands. God has given them the gift of free will. He has placed the destiny of their souls in their hands. Sometimes he has even placed the direction of other souls in their care.

And again, like the unjust steward, many people use their talents and free will to strive after false gods. Many deny God his just rights. Many neglect to filfill their duty to God as members of his Church. Instead they use their talent and their prudence to achieve wealth and fame.

The number of men who use their God-given gift of prudence to pursue these earthly goals of wealth and fame is amazing indeed. But in so doing, they fail to realize that these goals are only temporal; in time they will fade away. They fail to realize that one's true goal should be eternity. True wisdom would direct one to using his talents to achieve eternal happiness with God. But far too few use their prudence in this way.

One outstanding example of a man who was prudent in regard to eternal life was St. Anthony of Padua. Born in 1195 in Lisbon, he was the son of a noble family of Portugal. He was also said to be a descendent of the ruling house of France. As an individual he possessed many other natural talents.

St. Anthony might well have served the throne of Portugal and been an important figure in the world. But instead he decided to enter religious life. His parents were somewhat saddened by his decision to renounce fealty to the throne, but they finally accepted it. Then they used their influence to help him pursue a career within the Church. They obtained his appointment as a canon at the Cathedral in Lisbon, Portugal. Eventually he would rise from there to become a bishop or a cardinal.

But St. Anthony also turned this down. Instead he decided to become a lay brother in the newly formed Franciscan order. This he did. He was assigned to serve in the kitchen in a small monastery in Sicily. There he spent his time peeling potatoes and performing many other menial tasks.

St. Anthony was happy in his duties, but God had other plans for him. One day at an assembly of priests his superior ordered him to speak to the assembled gathering. St. Anthony begged to be excused, saying that he was only accustomed to washing dishes and sweeping the floor, but his superior insisted and so he spoke in obedience. His great eloquence and erudition made a lasting impression on all assembled.

Following this St. Francis himself assigned Anthony to a seminary to study theology and prepare for the priesthood. In his later life as a priest he was renowned as a great preacher. But likewise he became equally well known for his practice of charity and his zeal. He lived a life of personal penance and showed great prudence in regard to the things of eternity.

The eternal prudence of this saint affords us all an example to follow. How much wiser St. Anthony was in giving up earthly honors and using his talents to serve almighty God. How different his life was from that of the unjust steward, who used his prudence only for temporal gain.

In our lives let us resolve to imitate the true prudence of this holy man. Let us resolve to use our talents for the honor and glory of almighty God. For it is in serving him rather than in serving false goals in this world that we shall become deserving of eternal reward. God bless you.

# "C"     Twenty-sixth Sunday of the Year

*Luke 16:19-31*

In the gospel read at today's Mass St. Luke relates our Lord's parable of Lazarus and the rich man. While here on earth, our Lord frequently preached in parable form. But this particular parable is unusual, for it is the only one in which our Lord mentions one of the characters by name, that is, Lazarus. Some theologians think that this must be a true story — that there really did exist a poor man named Lazarus. But nowhere in the Old Testament or in other writings can there be found any historical basis for such a conclusion.

Christ tells us that the rich man dressed in purples and linens and feasted splendidly every day. But beyond his gate lay Lazarus the beggar, covered with sores, which the dogs came to lick. Lazarus was content to eat the scraps which fell from the rich man's table.

Christ, in his description of the rich man and Lazarus, brings out the inequality between their states of life. One was living in great luxury and the other in extreme need. While one was enjoying the best of food, the other was starving.

Christ does not picture the rich man as cruel or miserly. He does not describe him as harming or mistreating Lazarus. Neither does he drive him away. Rather he only neglects him. He passes him by without bothering to help him. He is indifferent to his suffering.

But yet indifference or neglect is a great sin in itself. This we know from Christ's description of the General Judgment on the last day. On that day Christ will say to those on his left, "Out of my sight, you condemned, into that everlasting fire prepared for the devil and his angels. I was hungry and you gave me no food, I was thirsty and you gave me no drink. . . ." Then they in turn will ask: "Lord, when did we see you hungry or thirsty . . . and not attend you in your needs?"

He will answer them: "I assure you, as often as you neglected to do it to one of these least ones, you neglected to do it to me." Hence the failure to practice the common forms of charity will be sufficient reason for condemning a soul to eternal punishment. This is the sin of which the rich man is guilty.

In the parable Christ tells us that both Lazarus and the rich man died. The rich man, from the abode of the dead where he was in torment, raised his eyes, saw Abraham far off, and Lazarus resting in his bosom. He called out, "Father Abraham, have pity on me."

It is a debatable theological point whether the souls in hell can see the souls enjoying eternal happiness in heaven. It is also debatable whether the souls suffering in hell can talk to or communicate with the souls in heaven. Most probably the souls in hell have some knowledge of the identity of the souls in heaven. The devils in hell have the power to tempt man; they know the time of a man's death. They know which souls are condemned to hell and which are not.

But we must remember that our Lord was using a figure of speech to convey a message to his Jewish disciples. He was speaking in the form of a parable. In order to convey a lesson to his listeners, it served his purpose to assume that the souls in hell can see those in heaven or limbo and that they can converse back and forth.

In the parable the rich man suffering in hell asks Abraham to send Lazarus, whom he sees in his presence, to dip the tip of his finger in water and refresh his tongue. Theologians tell us that the sufferings in hell will be severe, but that sufferings will differ — that the condemned will suffer in the senses in which they have offended God. In the case of those who committed gluttony and dined sumptuously and refused to practice charity in feeding the hungry, they will suffer in their sense of taste. Thus the rich man in hell wanted but a drop of water on his tongue to relieve his suffering.

Then too the rich man in hell was tormented by envy. Knowing the former poverty and suffering of Lazarus compared to his own wealth, and then seeing Lazarus so happy while he is suffering, makes him envious of Lazarus' reward. His undue love of worldly riches and his greed for gain become a source of torment for him in hell.

The request he makes of Abraham is denied. Abraham states that there is a great abyss between them, that is, between heaven and hell, and there is no crossing between them. Here our Lord brings out a moral lesson. By this answer of Abraham he brings out the fact that there is a life hereafter. In this future life the good will be rewarded with eternal happiness and the evil punished with eternal punishment. From this punishment there will be no recourse. It will last forever.

But the rich man persists and asks a second request of Abraham — to send Lazarus to warn his five brothers on earth about the sins they are committing. Again the request is refused. Abraham responds that the living have Moses and the prophets — that if they do not listen to them, then not even one from the dead could convince them to repent.

Theologians tell us that the five brothers of the rich man represent the Jewish nation. They are the ones who have heard the preaching of Moses and the prophets. But in a broader sense they represent all men to whom the message of Christ has been preached.

Here Christ conveys the second moral lesson of his parable — that the light of Revelation is sufficient for men to save their souls — that his Church holds the key to the kingdom of heaven. If men who have heard this revelation lose their souls, it is their own fault. By their own free will they have rejected the message of Revelation — by their free wills they have chosen to reject Christianity.

Therefore, let us take to heart and apply to our own lives the lessons Christ wishes to teach us through this parable. Let us realize that a day of judgment awaits us all. On the day of death each of us will be rewarded or punished for the deeds of our lifetime.

Let us realize too that having heard the voice of Christ's Church, we have the knowledge and the means to save our souls. His grace is sufficient for us. If we should lose our souls, it will be a choice of our own free will. It will be because we have freely turned our back on Christ and his teachings.

Therefore, let us resolve to use this grace wisely; let us listen to and follow the voice of his Church, the voice of Moses and the prophets. Let us work and pray that we may spend our eternity with Lazarus and Abraham in the kingdom of heaven. God bless you.

# "C"     Twenty-seventh Sunday of the Year

*Luke 17:5-10*

Today's gospel according to St. Luke is clearly divided into two parts. The first part begins with a petition of the Apostles to our Lord to increase their faith. Faith, as we know, is the first of the three theological virtues. It is one of the greatest forces in the world. It is one of the two necessary conditions for salvation.

We say that faith is a virtue by which we firmly believe all the truths that Christ has revealed — on his authority in revealing them. Perhaps the most important aspect of faith is not what we actually believe but rather our motive in believing what we do.

Faith concerns itself with many things we cannot perceive with our senses. It concerns itself with the Blessed Trinity, the Incarnation, the presence of Christ in the Blessed Sacrament. It concerns itself with all the revealed doctrine which Christ taught here on earth.

But the important thing is that we believe in these truths because Christ taught them to us. We believe in Christ, that he is the Son of God, Second Person of the Blessed Trinity, true God and true man. Once we believe in Christ and his divinity, then it is only a short step to believe in the doctrines he taught us. Christ, as God, is all truthful. He can neither deceive nor be deceived. This is the greatest possible motive for our faith.

The Apostles, as ardent followers of our Lord, had learned the importance of faith. Hence their request to Christ to increase their faith. An ordinary person, learning the identity of Christ and his great power, might request some temporal favor of him; he might ask him for good health or some material possession. But the Apostles had passed this stage in their spiritual development. They knew that spiritual gifts were far greater than material ones. Hence their request for faith.

Christ in answering them first compared faith to the mustard seed, a seed that is extremely small in size. This comparison is a good one. Faith has a small beginning in our souls. It first comes to us when the waters of baptism are poured over our heads. It begins to grow when we reach the age of reason and begin to believe things using our own intellectual powers.

Christ continues, "If you had faith the size of a mustard seed, you could say to this sycamore, 'Be uprooted and transplanted into the sea,' and it would obey you." The sycamore was a very large tree; it would take a great force to uproot one and hurl it into the sea. But our Lord used such a figure of speech because he knew his audience. It was the custom of the Jews and other eastern peoples to speak in figures of speech and to use very vivid terms. Our Lord had in mind to convey to them the power of faith.

Christ wanted the Apostles to realize how very dependent man is upon almighty God. God has given us our very lives and everything we possess. Without him we can do nothing, but with him there is nothing we cannot do.

There is an old story that a fly lighted on the back of an elephant. The elephant walked over a wooden bridge. The fly said to the elephant, "My, didn't we shake that bridge." We can compare the fly to man and the elephant to God. It was the elephant who did most of the shaking of the bridge. Whenever we accomplish something worthwhile, it is to God that we must give most of the credit.

We can say that through faith Christ is inviting us to undertake tireless work — to undertake seemingly impossible tasks. With his help through faith, the impossible becomes possible, and the difficult easy.

In the second part of today's gospel Christ tells of the servant who comes in from ploughing and herding the sheep. The master does not tell him to sit down and take it easy. Instead he bids the servant to prepare his supper and wash the dishes. Christ is intimating that the master is not a slave driver, for the servant is only doing his duty, what is expected of him.

We can compare the master in this parable to Christ and the servant to all Christians, clergy and laity alike. Christ is telling us that the servant's work, the Christian's work is never finished. We are constantly to spread abroad the gospel of Christ, and this we can do in many different ways.

Christ, then, is laying down the duties of Christians. First, they must believe — they must have a strong faith in him. Secondly, they must work continually to spread Christ's gospel and teachings. Through faith and hard work, many seemingly impossible tasks will be accomplished. Christ will be working with us and through us. Through faith and good works we can bring about the salvation of our souls and the souls of many others. God bless you.

# "C"     Twenty-eighth Sunday of the Year

*Luke 17:11-19*

In our human society perhaps the crassest and most unforgivable of all sins is that of ingratitude. A very clear example is given of it in the true-life parable contained in this morning's gospel — that of the ten lepers.

In the time of our Lord here upon earth, leprosy — now under control as Hansen's disease — was a common affliction, also a dread one. Leprosy would eat away the hands or feet or whatever part of the body it happened to strike. It would continue eating away one's body until one died as a result. Leprosy was a slow and fatal disease, and a leper bore with him the nauseating smell of decaying flesh.

By Jewish law lepers were expelled from Jerusalem. It was a common sight to see them begging along the wayside. It was a group of ten of these that met our Lord as he was approaching Jerusalem. They had heard of his beautiful teachings and his miracles. Therefore they besought our Lord to cure them.

Our Lord had mercy on them and did as they requested. In so doing he was bestowing a great favor upon them. He cured them of a disease that ordinarily was fatal — that would have caused their death in a short time. He cured them of a disease that caused them great pain and misery — that made their flesh rot before their very eyes. He cured them of a disease that had made them outcasts of society.

Surely each one of the ten must have realized the great favor that our Lord bestowed upon them on this occasion. But yet of these ten, nine of them were not grateful enough for this favor, that of curing them of a dread disease that would take their life, to return and say thank you to our Lord. Only one of the ten did this, and this man was a Samaritan, one who was not even considered a Jew.

These nine lepers showed the greatest ingratitude. There is not another vice more severely condemned by men in general than this. God has implanted in man a natural sense of thankfulness or gratitude for favors received. When one fails to be grateful, he is rebelling against his nature.

Gratitude is one of the four main elements of prayer. Christ himself taught us the necessity of showing gratitude here upon earth. He said it is better to give than to receive. Frequently in his preaching and teaching he lifted his eyes to heaven and said, "Father, I thank you."

When Christ performed miracles he frequently thanked his Father in heaven, for instance, when he raised Lazarus from the dead. At the Last Supper and on other occasions when our Lord sat down to eat, he first gave thanks to God.

Even the holy men of the Old Testament gave thanks when the occasion arose. Tobit gave thanks when he received his sight. Noah gave thanks when the flood subsided. Even brute animals show the virtue of gratitude. The lion was most grateful when Androcles removed the thorn from his paw.

Gratitude for favors received prepares one for more favors to come. The person who thanks God for favors received prepares himself to receive more favors in the future. This is exemplified in this morning's gospel. When the one Samaritan came back to thank God for curing him, Christ forgave the man his sins.

But the ungrateful person, on the other hand, shuts off the flow of divine grace. He shuts himself off from receiving more favors in the future.

Consider for a moment what we have received from God. He has given us our gift of sight. We should thank him that we can see the color of the sunset, the beauty of a flower, the rainbow in the sky.

We should thank him for the gift of hearing — that we can hear birds sing and the sound of music — that we can hear the voices of our family and our loved ones.

We should thank God that we can walk — that we have the ability to go from place to place and are not confined to a bed or wheelchair as are many handicapped.

We should thank God for the use of our hands — that we can work, that we can use them for the thousand tasks necessary to live.

We should thank God for the gift of speech — that we can communicate and make known our thoughts to one another. In fact, we should resolve to use all these gifts for God's honor and praise.

We should thank God for the food we eat, the water we drink, the air we breathe. Were it not for the goodness of God in creating us, we should not be alive in Church today.

We should thank our Lord for the gift of faith — for coming down upon earth and redeeming us. We should thank him for the waters of baptism, by which original sin is washed from our souls. We should thank him for giving us penance, by which other sins are washed away. We should thank him for giving us his body and blood as our food and drink in the Holy Eucharist. We should thank him for dying on the cross to open to us the gates of heaven.

To thank God for these gifts is our natural duty and obligation. To neglect to thank him is the basest ingratitude. When our Lord appeared to St. Margaret Mary Alacoque, he told her his Sacred Heart suffered untold misery because of the ingratitude of man. Resolve that ingratitude on our part will never cause him pain.

Rather imitate St. Felix, who lived in the 16th century. His favorite expression was *Deo Gratias,* which means "Thanks be to God," a prayer and expression frequently found in the Holy Sacrifice of the Mass. On one occasion he found two men dueling with swords. He began to talk to them and told them of the many things they had to be grateful for. Both men put away their swords and thanked him for showing them their duty in this regard.

Another saint known for his gratitude was St. Francis of Assisi. On one occasion he was walking through the woods close to his monastery with a companion. They noticed a large number of birds chirping in the trees. St. Francis stopped to bless them and the birds flew together in a sign of the cross and hovered overhead. He then began to preach to them — telling them how grateful they should be for the streams from which to drink — the trees in which to dwell — for the mountains in which to feed.

While he was preaching the birds remained perfectly silent while hovering in the sign of the cross overhead. When Saint Francis finished his sermon they broke out in a most beautiful and loud harmony of song.

Let us, therefore, learn from these animals and creatures which God has created our obligation of gratitude. Let us not be like the nine lepers who refused to give thanks — rather let us imitate the one grateful leper. Let us imitate St. Felix and St. Francis and thank God daily for our blessings. Let us recite our grace before and after each meal. In this way we will dispose ourselves to receive many more graces from God in the future. God bless you.

# "C"    Twenty-ninth Sunday of the Year

*Luke 18:1-8*

In today's gospel St. Luke tells us explicitly that Christ was preaching a parable on the necessity of praying always and not losing heart. He then proceeds to tell us about an unjust judge who did not respect God or man, and of a widow who kept constantly appearing before him asking for justice.

The widow in this parable is the symbol of all who are poor and defenseless. She has no other hope of obtaining justice except through the judge. Even though the judge refuses her request, she pursues this one small last ray of hope. She keeps coming to him and petitioning for justice against her opponents. Her one weapon is her persistence.

In the end her persistence carries the day. The judge complains that she is wearing him out, and to be rid of her he grants her request. Thus even before a corrupt judge, her prayer, her persistent petition, is granted.

Our Lord then compares the judge to almighty God, but there is one distinction between them. Whereas the judge was corrupt and unjust, almighty God personifies justice. He is the Just Judge. Because he is just, he will hear one's petition promptly. He will act justly and quickly when prayers are addressed to him.

The lesson or moral of this parable is what St. Luke gives at its very beginning. Prayer is necessary for each one of us, and we should not lose heart when we pray.

Prayer, basically, is the lifting of our hearts and minds to almighty God. It is conversing with almighty God. It is making known to him our wants and needs. It is thanking him for the gifts he has bestowed upon us. It is begging his forgiveness for any sins or injuries we have committed against him. Prayer is showing God honor and adoration.

Prayer is to the soul what the nerves are to the body and the mind. It is a means of communication between almighty God and the souls he has created on earth. Since we are members of the Church Militant, we are struggling to attain salvation; we live in perpetual peril. Prayer is the lifeline that connects us to heaven. It is a means by which we can communicate with our creator.

Prayer for man is a precious privilege. We should be so grateful that God, our creator, has given us a means whereby we can talk to him and reveal our feelings and wants. It is a privilege for man to be able to talk to his maker.

Prayer is a duty imposed upon all Christians. God commands us through the First Commandment that we must pay him adoration and homage. Prayer is our means of accomplishing this — of fulfilling our obligation of adoring God. We do not say it would be a serious sin for one to omit his prayer on a single occasion. But it would be a serious sin for one to stop praying altogether.

Prayer is an exercise in the love of God. When we pray, we consider three persons — God, ourselves and others. When we pray we pour forth our love for God and our neighbor. But when we cease to pray we stop showing our love for God and our neighbor. To neglect praying is to sin against charity.

But one should pray not simply because God commands it, but rather because of a realization of the great power of prayer. Prayer is a pipeline that fills our souls with grace. Prayer is an access to personal sanctity. It brings an increase in holiness in our souls. Prayer is a stimulant to our spiritual lives.

Prayer holds within itself the secret of salvation. For just as in prayer we talk to God, God reveals himself and his glory to us. As the prayer of the poor widow wore out the unjust judge, the prayer of the faithful will scratch their names in the memory of almighty God. Once etched by prayer in the memory of God, they will be there on the day of judgment.

We should pray because of the great power of prayer. The prayer of Bartimaeus the blind man won him his sight. The prayer of the crippled leper won him his health. Christ said the prayer of the faithful is powerful enough to transplant huge trees — and this is the testimony of God, who is all truthful and cannot deceive us. Prayer is powerful enough to change the course of history.

One may ask, for what and whom should we pray? We answer that we may pray for anyone or everyone and for anything that is good in the sight of almighty God. Hezekiah prayed for a long life. Daniel prayed for help in the lion's den. King David prayed for mercy. St. Peter prayed for forgiveness.

We may pray at any place and at any time. Jonah prayed when he was cast into the deep. St. Peter prayed on the rooftop. St. Isidore prayed when plowing the fields. Jairus prayed on the street for Christ to heal his daughter. King David prayed in a cave. The good thief prayed when nailed to the cross. Christ prayed on a mountaintop and in the Garden of Olives.

And too, one may pray at any time. One may pray as did Daniel at noon. Certainly one appropriate time for prayer is the morning upon arising. St. Ambrose asserts, "We owe to God, our creator, the first affections of our heart, the first sound of our voice, the first words of our lips each day." Through a prayer such as the morning offering, we can turn all our daily actions into a prayer to God.

Also we should pray each night before retiring. St. Bernard asks, "If God had cured us from leprosy, would we not be grateful and pray to him each night before retiring?" But then God has given us everything. We owe him our gratitude at the end of each day.

And one quality our prayers should have is that of perseverance. Sometimes it happens that one will pray briefly for a favor and then discontinue praying when he does not receive it. The favor one is asking may be a great one, and therefore the length of time of one's prayers should be in proportion to its value.

The poor widow won justice because she persisted in her pleas. St. Monica prayed eighteen years for the conversion of her son, Augustine.

Let us remember the words of St. Paul to the Thessalonians: "Always rejoice, pray without ceasing." That means we should pray each and every day of our lives. Prayer, let us not forget, has been called the key to the kingdom of heaven. God bless you.

# "C"     Thirtieth Sunday of the Year

*Luke 18:9-14*

In today's gospel St. Luke tells the parable of the Pharisee and the publican. Pharisees, in the time of our Lord, were a sect noted for their minute observance of the Law of the Old Testament and their exterior holiness. Pharisees were not only well acquainted with the Bible itself, but also well versed in various commentaries on the Bible.

But yet in this parable and on other occasions our Lord rebuked the Pharisees. He rebuked them for praying in public and on the street corner. He chastised them for performing good works simply to be seen by men.

On the other hand the publicans were the tax-gatherers of that day. The Romans of that day collected taxes by selling the contract to collect them to others. This was sold at a very high price. But once a man had bought this contract he proceeded to collect the taxes within his province or district and keep what he collected.

Needless to say the tax collectors or publicans were regarded by the Jews as oppressors and were most unpopular.

But yet in his parable our Lord chose these two different types of people, a Pharisee, who had the reputation for external holiness, and a publican, a most unpopular person, to teach us this parable on humility.

The Pharisee in his prayer committed the sin of pride. He stood and prayed aloud and made himself better than the rest of men.

The sin of pride which he committed is the sin of the angels, of Lucifer and the others who rebelled against God — who said, "I will not serve." The proud person exaggerates his own importance. He tries to make himself more important than he is — he attempts to be independent of God. Pride is a factor in the beginning of all grave sin.

But the publican on the other hand displayed the virtue of humility. He called himself a sinner in the sight of God and begged for mercy. Humility is a virtue by which man acknowledges his lowliness and his dependence upon God.

Humility, in this sense, is closely identified with truth. For actually we would not exist if God did not create us. All we have or possess we owe to him.

Humility prompts a man to avoid seeking attention for himself. He does not attach his heart to what is transitory or passing. He has little regard for the opinion of men — either for their praise or for their criticism. Therefore, he is not dejected or downcast when they fail to praise him. He accepts this and offers it up to almighty God.

Christ himself gave us the greatest possible example of humility. As our Creator and as God himself, he chose to come into this world and take on the body of man. He chose to live on this earth in the poorest and meanest of circumstances. He was born in a stable and chose a carpenter for his foster-father. He lived in an obscure town and chose simple fishermen for his Apostles. He conversed with Mary Magdalen and known sinners; he washed his Apostles' feet. He taught us, "Learn of me because I am meek and humble of heart."

Our Blessed Mother Mary is the most honored of all human beings who ever lived. The reason for this, the reason why God chose her to be his Mother, was her humility. Mary, in her youth, deemed herself unworthy ever to hope to become the Mother of our Savior and thus took the vow of virginity. But God recognized her virtue and chose her above all others for this honor.

The beautiful prayer Mary recited, the Magnificat, tells us of this. "He [The Lord] has regarded the humility of his handmaid; for behold from henceforth all generations shall call me blessed."

Many saints have attained great honor in heaven because of their humility. One person known for his humility was the Franciscan Brother Manuel. He was born of Spanish nobility, and his parents, who were good Christians, lavished many good things upon him. Manuel grew up in this fashion. But when his parents died he began to lead a life of luxury and dissipation. He became known as a reckless gambler. Soon he lost his fortune.

He decided to board a ship and seek new fortune across the sea. But at sea his ship was wrecked in a storm. For an entire day Manuel clung to a loose plank, until he was spotted by another ship. But his joy at being rescued was short-lived, for he learned that his rescuers were pirates and his fate, as they decided, was to be a slave the rest of his life.

He lamented that one born in nobility should be treated in so vile a manner. But in his captivity he made one friend and had one source of consolation. A fellow slave and captive was a Franciscan priest. This priest gave Manuel the spiritual guidance he needed. He repented the folly of his early life and began to turn over a new spiritual leaf.

He bore his slavery with patience and humility. He offered it up to God in reparation for his sins and the sufferings Christ bore for us. Finally after several years of slave labor the Franciscan priest died as a result of the hardships. But shortly after that Manuel had an opportunity to leave the pirates, and he did. He made his way back to Europe and there entered a Franciscan monastery as a lay brother.

He was known there for his practice of humility. In our own lives let us imitate this humble Franciscan brother. Let us imitate the publican described in this morning's gospel. Let us imitate our Blessed Mother and our Lord himself in their practice of humility.

God has promised that the prayer of him who humbles himself shall pierce the clouds. He has told us also that the humble shall be exalted and that they shall possess the kingdom of heaven. His promises are never made in vain. God bless you.

# "C"     Thirty-first Sunday of the Year

*Luke 19:1-10*

St. Luke in today's gospel tells us that Christ was on his way to Jericho. Jericho in ancient times was a prosperous and important city. It was located in the fertile Jordan valley and commanded the approach to the city of Jerusalem. In its fertile soil dates, palms and balsam trees grew in abundance. Jericho exported much of its produce to the far-flung corners of the Roman empire.

But as wealth abounded in Jericho, the Roman government expected Jericho to pay a high rate of taxes to the Roman empire. In ancient times contracts to collect taxes were auctioned off to the highest bidder. Once a bidder had bought a contract he then proceeded to collect the taxes from its citizens. Whatever he managed to collect over and above the price of his contract, he was allowed to keep and put in his pocket.

The chief tax collector in a district had other tax collectors working for him; the number depended on the wealth and size of the district. These tax collectors were called publicans. In the district the chief tax collector or publican was named Zacchaeus at this particular time of our Lord's life.

Needless to say, the tax collectors were unpopular people. Frequently they would endeavor to collect more than was actually owed them. Despite their wealth and their high position in society, the publicans or tax collectors were generally despised by the other Jews.

This was the position of Zacchaeus, the chief tax collector in a prosperous city, a wealthy man. When Jesus was traveling south from Galilee toward Jerusalem, his journey led him into Jericho. His reputation as a preacher and worker of miracles had preceded him there, and large crowds turned out to see him. Zacchaeus was in their number. Curiosity had aroused him. He wanted very much to see this miracle worker and hear him preach.

But Zacchaeus had a problem: he was a short man. The crowd was very large and lined several deep along the street. One might well imagine that the other Jews, knowing Zacchaeus to be a tax collector and despising their kind, took delight in crowding in ahead of this short man and forcing him to the rear. But Zacchaeus was resourceful. In the fertile Jordan valley where Jericho was located, sycamore trees grew in abundance. They produced low leafy branches close to ground level. The short little Zacchaeus climbed up onto one of these sycamore tree branches that overlooked the road along which Jesus was coming.

When Jesus came to the spot he looked up and said, "Zacchaeus, hurry down. I mean to stay at your house today." Up to this time Zacchaeus and Christ had been complete strangers. They had never met before. But, of course, Christ, through his divine knowledge, knew who Zacchaeus was. Zacchaeus was amazed. Christ, who had never seen him before had called him by name and expressed a desire to stay at his house. Zacchaeus wasted no time in coming down from his perch in the sycamore tree.

But the crowd around Christ began to murmur in protest. They called

Zacchaeus a sinner. They said that Christ was staying as a guest at the house of a sinner. On previous occasions they had called Christ the friend of sinners. There was a distinction they could not grasp. Christ could rightfully be called the friend of sinners, but not the friend of sin. In fact, Christ died on the cross to save sinners.

But there was one thing the crowd did not know or see. Christ had moved the heart of Zacchaeus with his grace. He had prompted him with repentance. He moved him to have contrition for his sins.

When Zacchaeus climbed down from the tree he said, "I give half my belongings, Lord, to the poor. If I have defrauded anyone in the least, I pay him back fourfold."

Contrition is a virtue which moves one to sorrow for having offended God by sin. It is of two kinds: perfect and imperfect. Perfect contrition reflects on the greatness of God whom we have offended by sin. It reminds us of the benefits we have received from him — our life, our health, our food, our clothing. Perfect contrition reveals to us how ungrateful we have been, when, after receiving all these benefits from God, we then turned on him and offended him by a sinful act.

Imperfect contrition is also true sorrow, but its motive is not as noble. Imperfect contrition moves us to sorrow by recalling to mind the dreadful punishments of sin — that we are subject to the loss of eternal happiness in heaven and will be subject to painful torments in hell hereafter.

True contrition, whether perfect or imperfect, prompts us to action. It prompts us to try and avoid sin in the future. It moves us to avoid the near occasions of sin — the person, places or things that can lead us into sin. It prompts us, where one has obtained material goods in a sinful way, to make restitution of those goods.

This was true in the case of Zacchaeus. It prompted him to acts of charity even beyond this. He said he would not only return the wealth he had obtained by defrauding others, but would return it fourfold. He even promised to give half of his wealth to the poor. This was an extremely charitable act, indicative of the great sorrow for sin and love of God that had touched his heart.

The crowd had criticized Christ for staying at the house of a sinner. But Zacchaeus was not simply a sinner; he was a repentant sinner. This made all the difference in the world. Christ was ready and willing to forgive him for his sin, while the crowd was not.

Christ expressed his words of forgiveness: "Today salvation has come to this house." Christ had gladly and willingly received Zacchaeus' expression of sorrow. He granted him absolution. Christ's words indicated that Zacchaeus' sorrow had brought grace to his soul and salvation to his house. Christ implied that if Zaccheaus persevered in this newfound grace and disposition, he would enjoy eternal reward.

Christ concluded by saying that the Son of Man has come to search out and save what was lost. This was his mission on earth — to save sinners. He had entered a world hardened by the sin of our first parents. He had come to give man a way to rid himself of this sin. He came to give man the sacraments which could restore him to grace. Christ came to this world to save the lost sheep, the lost souls.

Like Zacchaeus let us elicit sorrow for our sins. Let us beg forgiveness of God, who has been so good to us, yet whom we have ungratefully offended by sin. For as Christ summoned Zacchaeus down out of the tree, he is summoning each one of us. He is willing to come and dwell in our homes if we are truly repentant. If our word and action bear our true sorrow, he will give to us as he did to Zacchaeus, the promise of eternal salvation. God bless you.

# "C"     Thirty-second Sunday of the Year

*Luke 20:27-38*

In Christ's time on earth the Jews were generally divided between two religious groups, the Pharisees and the Sadducees. The Pharisees outnumbered the Sadducees, but the Sadducees found many of their adherents among the rich and influential. The Sadducees accepted only the written law of the Old Testament. The Pharisees held as sacred not only Scripture but also many oral and ceremonial laws of the Jews. They were strict observers of all the Jewish law, whether or not it was found in Sacred Scripture.

Among other beliefs the Pharisees believed in the resurrection of the dead; they also believed in angels and spirits and life after death. The Sadducees held, however, that there was no resurrection from the dead. They said there were no angels or spirits.

The Sadducees took delight in proposing certain objections or questions the Pharisees were unable to answer. Many of these questions are contained in the Talmud, the book of oral traditions of the Jews compiled at the end of the second century. It was one of these questions of objections that they presented to Christ in today's gospel.

They asked, quoting Moses as their authority, if a man should die leaving a widow, and his brother should marry the widow and he should die, and the widow should marry in turn each of seven brothers in the family, each of whom also died, finally, when the widow died herself, whose wife would she be at the resurrection?

In quoting Moses the Sadducees were referring to the twenty-fifth verse of the book of Deuteronomy. This was the law of the "levirate" which prescribed that if a man should die leaving a widow and the man had a single brother, he must marry the brother's widow.

This question the Sadducees had proposed had stumped the Pharisees; they had been unable to answer it. But Christ had a ready and true answer for it. He said, "The children of this age marry and are given in marriage, but those judged worthy of a place in the age to come and of resurrection from the dead do not."

The answer of Christ was a most logical one. He pointed out that in heaven the relationship of marriage would cease because the purposes for which it was instituted would also cease. Marriage was made by God for a twofold reason: the propagation of the human race and the mutual love and companionship of a husband and wife here on earth.

In heaven there will be no more births. The command which God gave to Adam and Eve, "Increase and multiply and fill the earth," will no longer be valid for the earth will have passed away. At the day of last judgment when the world will have come to an end, the number of saints and angels in heaven will be constant.

The second purpose of marriage, the love and companionship a husband and wife afford each other, will no longer be needed. God said to Adam in Paradise, "It is not good for man to be alone." In heaven men and women will both enjoy the far greater happiness of the companionship of almighty God. They will enjoy the Beatific Vision. They will have no need of a lesser happiness or companionship.

In these few concise words Christ had answered a religious objection that had stumped the Jews for years and centuries. He showed that the Sadducees were wrong in denying the resurrection — there would be a resurrection. He even answered the objection based on the false assumption that the laws of marriage of this earth would be an obstacle to enjoyment of happiness hereafter.

Christ did not stop here. He explained further, "They become like angels and are no longer liable to death." Angels are pure spirits, who enjoy God's presence in heaven. The Sadducees did not believe in angels. Here again Christ was telling them that they were wrong. Christ was telling them that once a man on this earth dies and goes to heaven and becomes a saint he will be like an angel.

Like angels the future saints in heaven will also live forever and enjoy God's presence. Like angels they will possess many and great gifts. They will have great wisdom and freedom and power. Actually they differ from angels only in one respect. On the day of the last judgment the saints of this earth will be reunited with their bodies. Their glorified bodies will be taken up to heaven. There body and soul together they will enjoy the Beatific Vision.

Christ concluded his brilliant and inspiring answer to the Sadducees by quoting for them a passage from Scripture where Moses at the burning bush called the Lord, the God of Abraham, the God of Isaac and the God of Jacob. All these three holy men were long since dead. But since God can only be God of the living and since Moses called him their God, these souls must be living with him in heaven. As Christ concluded, "All are alive for him."

This argument was most forceful and meaningful to the Sadducees, for in their strict interpretation of beliefs, they did accept and believe in the Old Testament. Here was Christ proving from the words of the Old Testament itself that there was life after death — that the holy men of the Old Testament were to be alive in heaven with God.

Christ had given them an argument which they could not refute. He had given them the true interpretation of Holy Scripture. As St. Luke goes on to add in his gospel, "They no longer dared to ask him any questions."

The gospel according to St. Mark read at today's Mass is a talk Christ gave to his disciples in the week preceding his death on the cross. Our Lord had led his Apostles into the Holy City of Jerusalem to celebrate the Passover. He had completed his last visit to the temple in Jerusalem. He then led his disciples to Mount Olivet, outside the gates of the Holy City, and proceeded to speak to them about the end of the world.

He mentioned several signs that would be seen before the world came to an end: ". . . the sun will be darkened, the moon will not shed its light, stars will fall out of the skies, and the heavenly hosts will be shaken." Our Lord pointed out these phenomena to us as a sign that the end is near.

He then spoke of his parousía, his second coming, his coming in the general judgment to judge all men. He said, " . . . men will see the Son of Man coming in the clouds with great power and glory. He will . . . assemble his chosen from the four winds, from the farthest bounds of earth and sky."

Holy Mother the Church presents these words of Christ on the end of the world for our meditation today. For just as surely as the world will one day come to an end, so too will the life of each of us come to an end. At some day in the future, the soul of each one of us will depart from our body; it will appear before our Lord and Savior Jesus Christ in particular judgment. The day this will happen is the day of our death.

Death is the separation of body and soul. It is the cessation of bodily life. It is the separation of man from everyone and everything which he holds dear upon earth . . . from home, from father and mother, husband or wife. It is separation from one's friends, from one's life work, from his position in life. It is a curtain drawn down upon the play of life. Death separates us from everything we have or are, save the grace we possess in our souls the moment it strikes. Death comes like a thief in the night.

Death is the punishment for original sin. When Adam committed that first terrible sin of disobedience, God cast him forth from the garden of paradise and said, ". . . you are dust, and to dust you shall return." Adam and Eve did not at first grasp the full meaning of these words; it was not until sometime later when they discovered their beloved son Abel lying dead in a field that their meaning was brought home to them. We can picture Eve shedding bitter tears over her dead son, but death was the final victor, the result of her own first sin.

Death will come to all; of this we may be certain. St. Paul writes: "It is appointed to all men once to die, and after death to be judged." Reason demonstrates it. Experience proves it. Just as surely as the sun rises and the sun sets, and as the seasons come and go, each of us here in church today will someday meet with death.

Our entire life is a prolonged struggle against death. We are most particular to eat nourishing foods, to get plenty of sleep, fresh air and sunshine, for these things are conducive to good health. But they can only prolong our life for a few years at most, a relatively short time. When we are sick we call a doctor; through his medical care, or sometimes through surgery and hospital care, we cure a particular illness and enjoy good health for a longer time — but still only for a time

In the end death will claim each of us. No one has ever cheated death, and no one ever will. This very hour that I am speaking to you, in various parts of the world several thousand people will die. Modern statistics say that in the world today tens of thousands of people will die and face God in judgment.

Death is certain. Only the time and place are not. Who knows here at Mass today who will be the next to die? Who knows the next in his family to face death? No one except God knows these answers.

Death has been pictured as something terrible. For those who die in mortal sin, it truly is terrible. For those who have dedicated their lives to sensuality, to those who have lived dishonestly, to those who have refused to worship God at Sunday Mass, death can only mean one thing — the beginning of eternal suffering in hell. For these people have foolishly wasted their lives; they have pursued earthly pleasure; they have entered eternity without making any preparation for it. They shall have forever to regret it.

But for those who die with sanctifying grace on their souls, death holds no fear. For the just man death is but the passing into everlasting happiness. For those who have been obedient to God's laws, the Ten Commandments; for those who have shown love to both God and neighbor, death means but the passing into the beautiful and eternal mansion of heaven. Christ has told us that in his Father's house there are many mansions for those who love him.

Death should not be feared by those in the state of grace. St. Aloysius Gonzaga was playing a game of chess one day when he was asked what he would do if he knew he would die within the hour. He replied, "I would keep on playing chess." These are the sentiments of a saint. These should be the sentiments of anyone who lives in the state of grace and is in the friendship of almighty God.

The lesson death teaches is to be prepared for it at all times, to live each day as if it were going to be your last. In the words of Christ, "Watch and pray, for you know not the day nor the hour."

Christ has given us a special means of preparing for death; these are the last rites of the Church: the Sacrament of Reconciliations of Holy Eucharist, called Holy Viaticum when given at the time of death, and the Sacrament of Anointing of the Sick. These sacraments can take away serious sin, increase or restore sanctifying grace to our soul and prepare us in the last minutes of our life to pass into eternity.

Every time we say the Hail Mary we ask our Blessed Mother to pray for us now and at the hour of our death. St. Joseph has been called the patron of a happy death. But perhaps no better means of preparing for death or forceful reminder of it can be found than the prayer the priest says in the burial service: "O Lord, while we lament the departure of our brother, thy servant, out of this life, we may bear in mind that we are most certainly to follow him. Give us grace to make ready for that last hour by a devout and holy life." God bless you.

his followers, for all members of his Church. The persecution we are asked to endure may not be death; it may not be as violent as that endured by the Apostles. But still it will be real.

At times a job or promotion may be awarded to another because of our faith. One may be denied membership in some club or organization. These are not arrows like those that pierced the body of St. Sebastian, but pins that prick our skin.

Whatever persecution Christ sends us, let us endure it willingly for the sake of Christ. Christ has said, "By patient endurance you will save your lives." God bless you.

# "C" Thirty-fourth Sunday of the Year (Christ the King)

*Luke 23:35-43*

Following World War I the nation of Poland lay devastated, having been overrun by the armies of Russia and Germany. Her young men had been killed in battle. Her cities and villages had been bombed and burned. Vatican officials in Rome looked around for a suitable priest or cleric whom they might appoint to this war-torn country. Their choice fell upon a scholarly Italian priest, Msgr. Ambrose Ratti. No sooner had Msgr. Ratti assumed his post than more trouble broke out. The Russian Revolution erupted in 1917. There was much more killing and fighting and trouble for Poland.

But so well did Msgr. Ratti fulfill his post, that his good work came to the attention of the Vatican. Msgr. Ratti was recalled to Italy and made the Cardinal Archbishop of Milan. In 1922, when Pope Benedict XV died, Cardinal Ratti was elected to succeed him. He took the name Pope Pius XI. As pope he displayed the same notable qualities he had shown as priest and cardinal.

In the year 1925 Pope Pius XI instituted a new feast in the Church and wrote an encyclical about it. The feast he instituted was the Feast of Christ the King. The date he appointed for its celebration was the last Sunday in October.

The world was surprised by the establishment of this new feast, but Pope Pius gave his reasons for establishing it in his accompanying encyclical. He said he sought a true Christian peace for the world, but such a peace could only come through the reign of Christ on earth. Therefore he established the new Feast of Christ the King.

During these last few calendar years a major revision was made in the Church's liturgy. The dates of many feasts were changed; the feasts of some saints were deleted from the Church calendar and new ones added. The Feast of Christ the King has been retained, but its date of celebration has been changed. It was changed from the last Sunday of October to the last Sunday of the Church year. Since the Church year begins with the first Sunday of Advent, the Sunday before Advent begins, or the thirty-fourth or the last Sunday of the Year, is now the Feast of Christ the King. This feast we celebrate today.

It is only right and proper that we should honor Christ as our king, for he entered this world as a king and he died as a king. When Christ was born in a stable in Bethlehem the Magi from the Orient came to visit and adore him. They brought him three gifts — gold, frankincense and myrrh. But gold was a gift given only to royalty. Therefore, in his crib he was recognized as a king.

In the gospel of today's Mass we are told that when Christ was crucified an inscription was hung above his head on the cross. It was the custom with the Romans when a criminal was crucified to hang an inscription above his head on the cross listing the name of his crime. In the case of Christ, no crime was listed for Christ had been all good and guilty of no wrongdoing. Instead the inscription Pilate wrote was, "This is the King of the Jews."

Christ was acclaimed a king at other times in his life. Following the miracle of the multiplication of the loaves and fishes, the multitude wanted to seize him and make him their king. But Christ wanted no part in ruling an earthly kingdom. Therefore, he disappeared from their midst and made his way alone into the mountain district.

On Good Friday when Christ was on trial before Pontius Pilate, the Roman governor, Pilate, asked him if he were a king. Christ answered him, "It is you who say it, I am a king." Christ did not explain to Pilate of what his kingdom consisted. He did not tell him that his kingdom extended over the souls of men rather than some piece of territory, but he did admit to being a king.

Later after Christ had risen from the dead, before his Ascension into heaven, he was preaching to his Apostles on one occasion. He told them, "My kingdom is not of this world." Christ meant that his kingdom is over the hearts and souls of men.

Christ, remember, is God and our creator. He is the author of life, the ruler of life also. We as his creatures have an obligation to acknowledge him as our creator and ruler. He is the king of all men and of all times. Christ admitted to having this ruling power when he said to his Apostles, "All power is given to me in heaven and on earth." We are obliged to acknowledge his ruling power.

Christ rules over us too by right of conquest. When the devil succeeded in persuading Adam and Eve to disobey God and commit original sin, he won a temporary victory over the forces of good. Through this sin the gates of heaven were closed and man was barred from it. But Christ in coming to earth won a victory over Satan. By his death on the cross he satisfied God's justice for the sin of man and reopened the gates of heaven. By his death and resurrection he won a great victory over Satan. He wrested the control of the world from him and entrusted the spiritual rule of the world to his Church. Therefore, by his conquest over the power of Satan he claims to be our king.

In sixteenth-century England Thomas More was made Lord Chancellor of the realm. He was second in command of that country, second only to King Henry VIII. But Thomas More was an exemplary Catholic. Frequently he was seen coming out of his parish church, where it was his custom to sing in the choir. One high government official stopped him one day and upbraided him for it, claiming he was showing dishonor to his king by being a mere choir singer.

But St. Thomas disagreed with him. He said that in singing in the choir he was only paying honor to the King of Kings.

Truly Christ is the King of Kings. Let us kneel before him as Pope Pius XI urged us to do. Let us adore him as our creator and honor him as our king and ruler. Let us pray that all men will come to acknowledge Christ as their king. Christ is both the King of Kings and the Prince of Peace. If his reign extends over the hearts of all men, then we can achieve a true Christian peace. God bless you.

# "C"    Immaculate Conception

*Luke 1:26-38*

One question that is asked in the first Baltimore Catechism is: "Why did God make you?" And the answer that is given is: "God made me to know him and love him and serve him in this world and be happy with him in the next." The answer is so simple, but yet profound.

When God created us and put us on this earth, he had a plan or a purpose in so doing. Everyone was created to manifest God's glory in some small way.

When God created our first parents and placed them on this earth, he did it for a purpose. He wanted to share his eternal happiness with others.

He created them in a state of supernatural grace. God fully intended that they should live on this earth for a short while using their intellect and free will to serve him and honor him, and then he would take them into his home in heaven.

But man himself, by using the free will God had given him, created an obstacle to God's plan. Our first parents were tempted by the devil to disobey God's command — not to eat the fruit of a certain tree growing in the garden of Paradise. Man gave in to this temptation and committed original sin.

Man by his sin placed an obstacle in the path of God's plan. No longer was it possible for God to take man directly to heaven to enjoy eternal happiness. Sin blocked his way. Because of sin death entered the world, and along with death, sickness and suffering.

But still God did not desert man. He still loved him and wanted to help him. Hence God promised to send a Redeemer, who would restore grace and divine life to mankind. God determined to send his own divine Son, Jesus Christ, to bring us salvation.

Christ, our Redeemer, saved us by becoming man himself. He redeemed us by coming to earth and taking on a body like ours. He entered this world by being born as a baby. He performed the work of redemption through the consent and cooperation of a woman, and that woman was Mary. Hence it was through the Blessed Virgin Mary that Christ took his humanity through which he redeemed us. Mary clothed Christ with body and blood and helped give him his human nature. She was truly his mother.

Christ, our Savior, derived his humanity from Mary. Without Mary there would have been no Christ. Hence Mary played an essential and important part in our redemption. God placed Mary at the very center of his plan for salvation. She occupies a pre-eminent position in the work of redemption.

If we wish to honor and imitate God, we must give Mary a correspondingly important place in our lives. We must strive to know Mary better, to love her more and imitate the virtues she practiced in our own lives.

Doctrine and devotion are closely related. If we know and realize the important part Mary played in our Redemption, then we naturally have a greater devotion to her. We will show love and honor to our Blessed Mother.

One of Mary's great privileges was her Immaculate Conception. God ordained that Mary should enter this world free from the stain of original sin with which all other men are born. Almighty God bestowed this privilege on Mary not only because of her virtue but because he foresaw that one day he would choose her to be the Mother of his own divine Son.

God did not wish his divine Son born of a mother whose soul was stained with sin. Therefore he bestowed this singular privilege on Mary. She entered this world and was born free from the stain of any sin. This privilege of Mary we celebrate today, the feast of her Immaculate Conception.

The Second Vatican Council has reaffirmed the important position Mary plays in the Church and in our salvation. The Vatican Council reechoes the honor that has been paid to Mary down through the centuries. It encourages us to honor her and pray to her frequently.

Vatican II tells us that the Blessed Virgin Mary figures profoundly in the history of salvation. She unites and mirrors within herself the central truths of the faith.

Devotion to Mary was officially sanctioned by the Council of Ephesus and since then has been encouraged and fostered. Vatican II says that devotion to Mary causes her divine Son to be rightly known, loved and glorified. True devotion is shown to Mary when one comes to know her excellence and is prompted to true love of her and her divine Son. This is to be deeply encouraged.

One example of this true devotion comes out of the Protestant persecution of the Church in Scotland following the Reformation. One Catholic bishop, fleeing for his life, disguised himself as a beggar. He called at the home of a poor man whom he discovered to be lying on a pallet in a dying condition. The bishop upon entering his home spoke a few words of encouragement to him to help prepare him for death.

But the man replied, "I am at peace. I shall not die."

"Of course, I hope not," the bishop answered, "but it is always a good thing to get ready."

"I tell you I cannot possibly die," the man protested.

The bishop said, "May I ask you why you are so sure you are not going to die?"

"Are you a Catholic?" the sick man asked.

"Yes, I am," the bishop answered.

"Then," said the man, "I can tell you why I shall not die. From the day of my first Communion, I have never missed asking the Blessed Virgin every day not to let me die without a priest at my bedside, and do you think that my Mother could fail to answer my prayer? She cannot, and I shall not die."

"How good Mary is!" exclaimed the bishop. Then he opened his coat and allowed his pectoral cross to shine in the old man's eyes. "Not only does she send you a priest, but your own bishop."

The dying man's eyes filled with tears, and looking up to heaven he said, "Thank you, good Mother. I knew you had heard my prayer." Then turning to the bishop he said, "Hear my confession," and he prepared to meet Mary his Mother in heaven.

As Mary heard the prayers of this dying man, so too will she hear yours. Therefore, let us heed the words of Vatican II, and let us show true devotion to our Blessed Mother. God bless you.

# "C"    Assumption

*Luke 11:27-28*

Probably the most war-torn country in the world in recent years is Vietnam. Communists have conquered the country after waging a bloody guerrilla warfare in its jungles for more than twenty years.

But only twelve miles inside Vietnam from the Laotian border there exists a famous shrine to our Blessed Mother at the village of Lavang. Lavang has a long history. Our Blessed Mother appeared to a small group of Christians there in 1798, long before Lourdes or Fatima.

Vietnam was formerly a part of French Indo-China and was Christianized over two centuries ago. Missionaries came there and made many converts. But in the late 18th century the pagan emperors began to persecute Christians, to seek them out and put them to death. In fact 100,000 Catholics were martyred there during the latter part of the 18th century.

Catholics, to escape this persecution, went deep into the Indo-Chinese jungle at that time — into jungle infested by tigers and panthers. But they chose to face the ferocity of wild beasts rather than that of tyrannical rulers.

And in a small jungle clearing they built a chapel to our Lady and named the spot Lavang. And there they prayed fervently to our Lady for deliverance. And our Lady heard their prayer. In the year 1798 she appeared to a group of refugees. She stood on what appeared to be the moon. Rays of light emanated from her hands, and a cluster of stars circled her head.

Mary spoke to the fearful persecution victims in soothing terms. She tried to comfort them and promised them deliverance from their persecution. After the third year of severe persecution, it finally came to an end. But from that time until now Lavang has become a famous national shrine.

Located in the midst of the jungle, Lavang is in the remotest part of the country. The ground around it is most infertile; no crop will grow there. But still this remoteness does not prevent crowds from flocking to the shrine. Some 200,000 people visit there each year.

Mary is honored at Lavang under two special titles — Queen of Martyrs and Hope of Christians. She has witnessed several persecutions and hardships in the country. Even today the presence of a Hanoi-directed government in Saigon and marauding military units ravaging the country indicate the suffering of the Vietnamese people is far from at an end.

But Mary has always helped those who sought her help. The Vietnamese people in praying to Mary as Queen of Martyrs and in calling themselves Children of Martyrs — many of them are literally that — may even today claim that their grandparents or great-grandparents were put to death for the sake of the Catholic faith.

Inside the fringe of the Communist world, our Lady of Lavang is a beacon to all who trust in God. But our Lady is also a beacon to the whole world. Down through the centuries Mary has worked many miracles for those who invoke her help. She is the help of the poor and the suffering.

In her lifetime Mary was but a humble virgin; she thought herself unworthy ever to attain the great honor which all Jewish women coveted — that of becoming the mother of the Redeemer, but God rewarded her humility. He chose her above all others to be his mother.

He bestowed many other privileges on Mary too. He preserved her soul from the stain of original sin. This privilege we call her Immaculate Conception. The archangel Gabriel first announced this when he greeted her with the salutation "Rejoice, O highly favored daughter! The Lord is with you. Blessed are you among women."

Mary is the second Eve. As the disobedience of the first Eve brought misery upon the human race, so the obedience of Mary restored us to a state of grace. Through the first Eve, death entered the world; through Mary, we have eternal life.

Upon her death Mary was assumed into heaven both body and soul. For as she had never been tainted by sin in this world, God would not permit her body to corrupt into dust. In heaven today Mary reigns as its queen.

The Church in her liturgy addresses Mary as queen on many occasions. The prayer Salve Regina or Hail Holy Queen so honors her; also the hymn "Hail Holy Queen Enthroned Above." The fifth glorious mystery of the rosary is the Coronation of our Blessed Mother as Queen of Heaven. And as Pope Pius XII once said the sacred liturgy is a faultless mirror of doctrine in this regard.

Mary deserves the title of queen because of the outstanding part she played in our redemption. She willingly offered up Christ for our sake. Rightfully does she bear the title of Co-redeemer.

Pope Leo XIII proclaimed that Mary has almost immeasurable power in heaven. God has entrusted her with the honor of being the dispenser or mediatrix of all graces. She performs this function, as it were, by a mother's right. So great is her power that no grace comes to us from heaven except through her hands. As Christ granted her request at the wedding feast of Cana, he grants it as easily today. St. Bernard tells us she is all-powerful because of her intercession.

But remember Mary is our Mother too. When Christ was dying on the cross his thoughts were not of himself. Rather they were of our Blessed Mother and of us. Turning to his Mother and to St. John his beloved disciple he said, "Woman, behold your son," and to John "Behold your mother." St. John in this instance represented all mankind. Christ gave Mary to us as our Mother.

Devotion to Mary is an excellent means of attaining sanctity here below and eternal salvation hereafter. What is one to conclude, when one views the catalogue of saints who have been ardently devoted to her, and the long list of heretics and schismatics who have spurned her outstretched arms? St. Alphonsus declared it to be his persuasion that hell cannot boast of containing one single soul who ever had a true and heartfelt devotion to Mary. St. Bernard asserts that those who honor her daily will assuredly be saved. St. Francis Borgia always feared for the salvation of the soul which had little devotion to the Mother of God. In the light of such testimony can there be any doubt that devotion to Mary is most necessary?

As Queen of Martyrs, the title under which she is honored at Lavang, Mary has the greatest sympathy for the suffering and afflicted. While on earth her heart was pierced with a sword of seven sorrows. She was a witness of the greatest martyrdom of all — she witnessed her own divine Son being nailed to a cross.

As Mary herself was forced to flee into Egypt to escape the persecution of Herod, so her heart bled for the Vietnamese who had to flee their homes because of persecution. As Mary was forced to live in Egypt for several years, she sympathized with the natives enduring the terrors of wild animals and of a barren land. Mary endured her sufferings for love of her divine Son. So did the Vietnamese endure their suffering for his sake also.

When they besought her help, Mary could not refuse them. She granted them their wish — comfort in their affliction and the end of the persecution.

Mary as our mother will hear our prayers too. Let us honor her in this life as our mother, so that in the world to come, Mary may claim us as her children. God bless you.

# "C"    Nov. 1: All Saints

*Matthew 5:1-12*

In reciting the Apostles' Creed, one of the articles of faith in which we express our belief is the Communion of Saints. Our catechism calls the union of saints the union which exists between the members of the Church on earth with one another, with the blessed in heaven, and with the suffering souls in purgatory. These three groups are commonly known as the Church Militant, the Church

Triumphant and the Church Suffering. All three are governed by the Supreme Shepherd, Jesus Christ.

Thus we may say that the Church of Christ is comprised by three categories of saints. The saints already enjoying the happiness of heaven are the canonized or recognized saints. The souls in purgatory are the future saints. Someday they will be taken to heaven to enjoy its happiness. Those of us on earth are hopeful saints.

Back in the early days of the Church when the Roman Empire first began to persecute it and put Christians to death, martyrs were honored on the anniversary of their day of death. At first they were honored only within their own diocese or the city where they lived. But in the fourth century neighboring dioceses began to interchange feasts. They began to interchange relics and divide them. A few common feasts were celebrated throughout the entire Church. But their number then was not great, and each martyr or saint had his own particular feast day.

But under Diocletian in the fourth century a new and more violent persecution of the Church began. The number of martyrs increased greatly. On many occasions large numbers of Christians were put to death on the same day. It became necessary to honor many martyrs on the same day. As early as the fifth century the custom arose in many places to honor collectively all the martyrs or saints of the Church.

On May 13, 610, Pope Boniface IV officially dedicated the Pantheon in Rome as a Christian temple to honor all the saints in the Church. The Pantheon, which dated back to the golden era of Rome, was built by the emperors to honor all the Roman gods. It was the gallery of the gods. But with Rome's conversion to the Christian faith, it was given a much more meaningful purpose. It became the temple of the saints of the one true God.

But it was not until the reign of Pope Gregory IV in the early ninth century that the feast of All Saints on November 1st was made a universal feast throughout the entire Church. This is only fitting and proper. The saints are the special friends of God. They honored him by leading holy lives here upon this earth. Now they are citizens of the heavenly Jerusalem, enjoying God's presence and showing him honor for all eternity.

It is interesting to note that the saints of the Catholic Church have come from many, many different nations. They have come from practically every walk of life. But this in itself is not surprising. Christ said to the Apostles here on earth, "Go and make disciples of all nations. . . ." The Apostles literally carried out this command of Christ. The presence of saints in so many nations shows how well the Apostles carried out the command of Christ.

Of the Apostles themselves, St. Matthew was a tax collector; the remaining eleven were probably fishermen, although there is a tradition that St. Thomas like St. Joseph was a carpenter. St. Augustine was a teacher. St. Martin was a soldier. St. Isidore was a farmer.

Saints have come from practically every country the world has known — a list far too long to enumerate. St. Martin de Porres gained sainthood in caring for Negro slaves brought to America's shores. St. Isaac Joques and his companions, French Jesuits, suffered martyrdom in New York State at the hand of the Mohawk Indians. The first American citizen to be canonized a saint was Mother Cabrini. Her vocation as a nun was spent largely in the cities of New York and Chicago. And New York was the birthplace of the first American-born saint, Mother Seton.

Let us not think it impossible that some of our own relatives or ancestors may be included in the list of saints in heaven. Only a relatively small fraction of the saints and martyrs are canonized and prayed to by name; there is a multitude of unknown and unheralded ones. Today is their feast day. Let us honor and pray to them today. Let us ask them for the favors we need.

The third group of saints in the communion of saints in the Church are the future saints — the suffering souls in purgatory. Purgatory, a place of suffering, fulfills a most necessary function. Scripture tells us that nothing defiled shall enter the kingdom of heaven. A soul must be free of every stain of sin before it can enjoy eternal happiness in heaven.

But yet many souls depart this world with neither mortal sin, which would make them deserving of hell, nor with their souls entirely free from all sin, which would allow them to enter heaven. Some depart this world with small or venial sins on their souls, or with some temporal punishment not yet atoned for.

These souls are sentenced by almighty God to suffer for a time in the fires of purgatory. Purgatory, while a place of temporal punishment only, nevertheless is a place of severe punishment. A soul in purgatory is deprived of the Beatific Vision, the pleasures of seeing almighty God. He is also tortured by other severe punishments. St. Thomas Aquinas tells us that the least punishment there is greater than the greatest on this earth.

The tragic part of the souls suffering in purgatory is that they are helpless to help themselves. Their time for meriting and demeriting which they enjoyed on earth is over. Now they can only wait and suffer.

However, there is something which we here on earth can do to alleviate their sufferings. By our prayers, good works and indulgences, we can lessen their punishments and shorten their stay in this fiery prison.

Therefore, Holy Mother the Church sets aside one special day each year on which we are asked to pray for the poor suffering souls in purgatory in a special way. That day is tomorrow, November 2nd, All Souls Day.

On this day also, because the Mass is the perfect prayer and our supreme act of sacrificial worship, priests are permitted to celebrate three Masses for the intention of the poor suffering souls. If it's at all possible, attend one or more of these Masses. Pray often for the poor souls, especially during this month of November dedicated to them.

Remember your prayers can be the cause of liberating a soul from the fiery prison of purgatory. If such is the case, that soul will be eternally grateful to you. Once in heaven his prayers will benefit you in this life and in the life to come. God bless you.

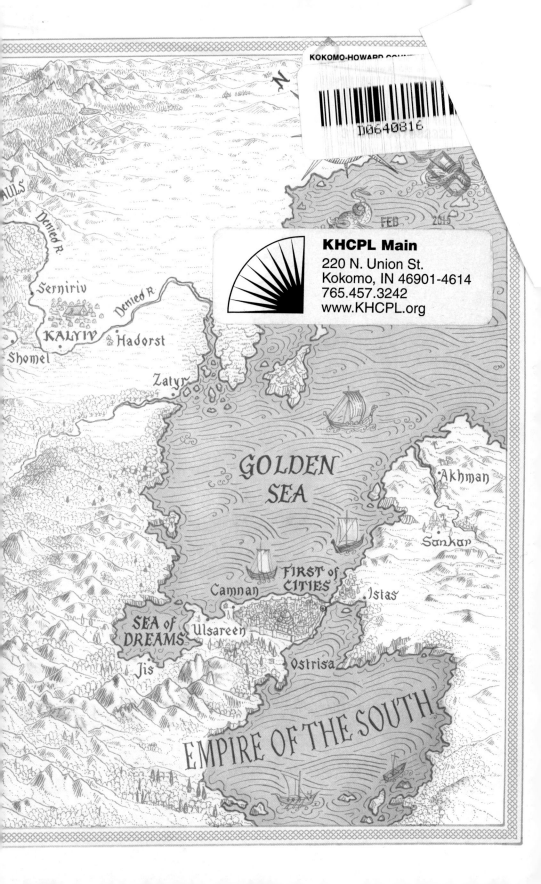

N

FEB 2015

AULS

Denied R.

Serniriv

KALYIV

Shomel

Denied R

Hadorst

Zatyr

GOLDEN
SEA

Akhman

Sankur

FIRST of
CITIES

Camnan

Istas

SEA of
DREAMS

Ulsareen

Ostrisa

Jis

EMPIRE OF THE SOUTH

By Joe Abercrombie

———

HALF A KING

HALF THE WORLD

# HALF THE WORLD

# JOE
# ABERCROMBIE

# HALF
# THE WORLD

**DEL REY • NEW YORK**

Copyright © 2015 by Joe Abercrombie

Map copyright © 2015 by Nicolette Caven

All rights reserved.

Published in the United States by Del Rey,
an imprint of Random House,
a division of Random House LLC,
a Penguin Random House Company, New York.

DEL REY and the HOUSE colophon are
registered trademarks of Random House LLC.

Published in hardcover in the United Kingdom by Harper Voyager.

LIBRARY OF CONGRESS CATALOGING-IN-PUBLICATION DATA

Abercrombie, Joe.
Half the world / Joe Abercrombie.—First U.S. edition.
pages    cm.—(Shattered sea)
ISBN 978-0-8041-7842-6 (hardcover : acid-free paper)—
ISBN 978-0-8041-7844-0 (ebook)
1. Teenage girls—Fiction.   2. First loves—Fiction.   I. Title.
PR6101 B49H35 2015
823'.92—dc23      2014038766

Printed in the United States of America on acid-free paper

www.delreybooks.com

9 8 7 6 5 4 3 2 1

First U.S. Edition

FOR EVE

CATTLE DIE,

KINDRED DIE,

EVERY MAN IS MORTAL:

BUT I KNOW ONE THING

THAT NEVER DIES,

THE GLORY OF THE GREAT DEED.

FROM *HÁVAMÁL*,
THE SPEECH OF THE HIGH ONE

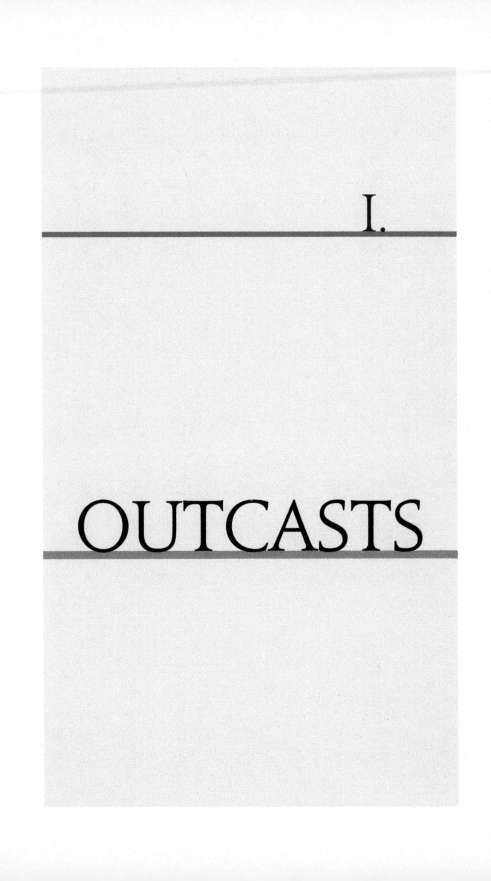

I.

OUTCASTS

# THE WORTHY

He hesitated just an instant, but long enough for Thorn to club him in the balls with the rim of her shield.

Even over the racket of the other lads all baying for her to lose, she heard Brand groan.

Thorn's father always said *the moment you pause will be the moment you die*, and she'd lived her life, for better and mostly worse, by that advice. So she bared her teeth in a fighting snarl—her favorite expression, after all—pushed up from her knees and went at Brand harder than ever.

She barged at him with her shoulder, their shields clashing and grating, sand scattering from his heels as he staggered back down the beach, face still twisted with pain. He chopped at her but she ducked his wooden sword, swept hers low and caught him full in the calf, just below his mailshirt's flapping hem.

To give Brand his due he didn't go down, didn't even cry out, just hopped back, grimacing. Thorn shook her shoulders out, waiting to see if Master Hunnan would call that a win, but he stood silent as the statues in the Godshall.

Some masters-at-arms acted as if the practice swords were real, called a halt at what would have been a finishing blow from a steel blade. But Hunnan liked to see his students put down, and hurt, and taught a hard lesson. The gods knew, Thorn had learned hard lessons enough in Hunnan's square. She was happy to teach a few.

So she gave Brand a mocking smile—her second favorite expression, after all—and screamed, "Come on, you coward!"

Brand was strong as a bull, and had plenty of fight in him, but he was limping, and tired, and Thorn had made sure the slope of the beach was on her side. She kept her eyes fixed on him, dodged one blow, and another, then slipped around a clumsy overhead to leave his side open. *The best place to sheathe a blade is in your enemy's back,* her father always said, but the side was almost as good. Her wooden sword thudded into Brand's ribs with a thwack like a log splitting, left him tottering helpless, and Thorn grinning wider than ever. There's no feeling in the world so sweet as hitting someone just right.

She planted the sole of her boot on his arse, shoved him splashing down on his hands and knees in the latest wave, and on its hissing way out it caught his sword and washed it down the beach, left it mired among the weeds.

She stepped close and Brand winced up at her, wet hair plastered to one side of his face and his teeth bloodied from the butt she gave him before. Maybe she should've felt sorry for him. But it had been a long time since Thorn could afford to feel sorry.

Instead she pressed her notched wooden blade into his neck and said, "Well?"

"All right." He waved her weakly away, hardly able to get the breath to speak. "I'm done."

"Ha!" she shouted in his face.

"Ha!" she shouted at the crestfallen lads about the square.

"Ha!" she shouted at Master Hunnan, and she thrust up her sword and shield in triumph and shook them at the spitting sky.

A few limp claps and mutters and that was it. There'd been far more generous applause for far meaner victories, but Thorn wasn't there for applause.

She was there to win.

Sometimes a girl is touched by Mother War, and put among the boys in the training square, and taught to fight. Among the smaller children there are always a few, but with each year that passes they turn to more suitable things, then are turned to them, then shouted and bullied and beaten to them, until the shameful weeds are rooted out and only the glorious flower of manhood remains.

If Vanstermen crossed the border, if Islanders landed on a raid, if thieves came in the night, the women of Gettland found blades soon enough, and fought to the death, and many of them damn well too. They always had. But the last time a woman passed the tests and swore the oaths and won a place on a raid?

There were stories. There were songs. But even Old Fen, who was the oldest person in Thorlby and, some said, the world, had never seen such a thing in all her countless days.

Not until now.

All that work. All that scorn. All that pain. But Thorn had beaten them. She closed her eyes, felt Mother Sea's salt wind kiss her sweaty face and thought how proud her father would be.

"I've passed," she whispered.

"Not yet." Thorn had never seen Master Hunnan smile. But she had never seen his frown quite so grim. "I decide the tests you'll take. I decide when you've passed." He looked over to the lads her age. The lads of sixteen, some already puffed with pride from passing their own tests. "Rauk. You'll fight Thorn next."

Rauk's brows went up, then he looked at Thorn and shrugged. "Why not?" he said, and stepped between his fellows into the square, strapping his shield tight and plucking up a practice sword.

He was a cruel one, and skillful. Not near as strong as Brand but a lot less likely to hesitate. Still, Thorn had beaten him before and she'd——

"Rauk," said Hunnan, his knobble-knuckled finger wandering on, "and Sordaf, and Edwal."

The glow of triumph drained from Thorn like the slops from a broken bath. There was a muttering among the lads as Sordaf—big, slow and with scant imagination, but a hell of a choice for stomping on someone who was down—lumbered out onto the sand, doing up the buckles on his mail with fat fingers.

Edwal—quick and narrow-shouldered with a tangle of brown curls—didn't move right off. Thorn had always thought he was one of the better ones. "Master Hunnan, three of us—"

"If you want a place on the king's raid," said Hunnan, "you'll do as you're bid."

They all wanted a place. They wanted one almost as much as Thorn did. Edwal frowned left and right, but no one spoke up. Reluctantly he slipped between the others and picked out a wooden sword.

"This isn't fair." Thorn was used to always wearing a brave face, no matter how long the odds, but her voice then was a desperate bleat. Like a lamb herded helpless to the slaughterman's knife.

Hunnan dismissed it with a snort. "This square is the battlefield, girl, and the battlefield isn't fair. Consider that your last lesson here."

There were some stray chuckles at that. Probably from some of those she'd shamed with beatings one time or another. Brand watched from behind a few loose strands of hair, one hand nursing his bloody mouth. Others kept their eyes to the ground. They all knew it wasn't fair. They didn't care.

Thorn set her jaw, put her shield hand to the pouch around her neck and squeezed it tight. It had been her against the world for longer than she could remember. If Thorn was one thing, she was a fighter. She'd give them a fight they wouldn't soon forget.

Rauk jerked his head to the others and they began to spread out, aiming to surround her. Might not be the worst thing. If she struck fast enough she could pick one off from the herd, give herself some splinter of a chance against the other two.

She looked in their eyes, trying to judge what they'd do. Edwal reluctant, hanging back. Sordaf watchful, shield up. Rauk letting his sword dangle, showing off to the crowd.

Just get rid of his smile. Turn that bloody and she'd be satisfied.

His smile buckled when she gave the fighting scream. Rauk caught her first blow on his shield, giving ground, and a second too, splinters flying, then she tricked him with her eyes so he lifted his shield high, went low at the last moment and caught him a scything blow in his hip. He cried out, twisting sideways so the back of his head was to her. She was already lifting her sword again.

There was a flicker at the corner of her eye and a sick crunch. She hardly felt as if she fell. But suddenly the sand was roughing her up pretty good, then she was staring stupidly at the sky.

There's your problem with going for one and ignoring the other two.

Gulls called above, circling.

The towers of Thorlby cut out black against the bright sky.

*Best get up*, her father said. *Won't win anything on your back.*

Thorn rolled, lazy, clumsy, pouch slipping from her collar and swinging on its cord, her face one great throb.

Water surged cold up the beach and around her knees and she saw Sordaf stamp down, heard a crack like a stick breaking.

She tried to scramble up and Rauk's boot thudded into her ribs and rolled her over, coughing.

The wave sucked back and sank away, blood tickling at her top lip, dripping pit-patter on the wet sand.

"Should we stop?" she heard Edwal say.

"Did I say stop?" came Hunnan's voice, and Thorn closed her fist tight around the grip of her sword, gathering one more effort.

She saw Rauk step toward her and she caught his leg as he kicked, hugged it to her chest. She jerked up hard, growling in his face, and he tumbled over backward, arms flailing.

She tottered at Edwal, more falling than charging, Mother Sea and Father Earth and Hunnan's frown and the faces of the watching lads all tipping and reeling. He caught her, more holding her up than trying to put her down. She grabbed at his shoulder, wrist twisted, sword torn from her hand as she stumbled past, floundering onto her knees and up again, her shield flapping at her side on its torn strap as she turned, spitting and cursing, and froze.

Sordaf stood, sword dangling limp, staring.

Rauk lay propped on his elbows on the wet sand, staring.

Brand stood among the other boys, mouth hanging open, all of them staring.

Edwal opened his mouth but all that came out was a strange squelch like a fart. He dropped his practice blade and lifted a clumsy hand to paw at his neck.

The hilt of Thorn's sword was there. The wooden blade had broken to leave a long shard when Sordaf stamped on it. The shard was through Edwal's throat, the point glistening red.

"Gods," someone whispered.

Edwal slumped down on his knees and drooled bloody froth onto the sand.

Master Hunnan caught him as he pitched onto his side. Brand and some of the others gathered around them, all shouting over each other. Thorn could hardly pick out the words over the thunder of her own heart.

She stood swaying, face throbbing, hair torn loose and whipping in her eyes with the wind, wondering if this was all a nightmare. Sure it must be. Praying it might be. She squeezed her eyes shut, squeezed them, squeezed them.

As she had when they led her to her father's body, white and cold beneath the dome of the Godshall.

But that had been real, and so was this.

When she snapped her eyes open the lads were still kneeling around Edwal so all she could see was his limp boots fallen outward. Black streaks came curling down the sand, then Mother Sea sent a wave and turned them red, then pink, then they were washed away and gone.

And for the first time in a long time Thorn felt truly scared.

Hunnan slowly stood, slowly turned. He always frowned, hardest of all at her. But there was a brightness in his eyes now she had never seen before.

"Thorn Bathu." He pointed at her with one red finger. "I name you a murderer."

# IN THE SHADOWS

"Do good," Brand's mother said to him the day she died. "Stand in the light."

He'd hardly understood what doing good meant at six years old. He wasn't sure he was much closer at sixteen. Here he was, after all, wasting what should have been his proudest moment, still trying to puzzle out the good thing to do.

It was a high honor to stand guard on the Black Chair. To be accepted as a warrior of Gettland in the sight of gods and men. He'd struggled for it, hadn't he? Bled for it? Earned his place? As long as Brand could remember, it had been his dream to stand armed among his brothers on the hallowed stones of the Godshall.

But he didn't feel like he was standing in the light.

"I worry about this raid on the Islanders," Father Yarvi was saying, bringing the argument in a circle, as ministers always seemed to. "The High King has forbidden swords to be drawn. He will take it very ill."

"The High King forbids everything," said Queen Laithlin, one hand on her child-swollen belly, "and takes everything ill."

Beside her, King Uthil shifted forward in the Black Chair. "Meanwhile he orders the Islanders and the Vanstermen and any other curs he can bend to his bidding to draw their swords against us."

A surge of anger passed through the great men and women of Gettland gathered before the dais. A week before Brand's voice would've been loudest among them.

But all he could think of now was Edwal with the wooden sword through his neck, drooling red as he made that honking pig sound. The last he'd ever make. And Thorn, swaying on the sand with her hair stuck across her blood-smeared face, jaw hanging open as Hunnan named her a murderer.

"Two of my ships taken!" A merchant's jewelled key bounced on her chest as she shook her fist toward the dais. "And not just cargo lost but men dead!"

"And the Vanstermen have crossed the border again!" came a deep shout from the men's side of the hall, "and burned steadings and taken good folk of Gettland as slaves!"

"Grom-gil-Gorm was seen there!" someone shouted, and the mere mention of the name filled the dome of the Godshall with muttered curses. "The Breaker of Swords himself!"

"The Islanders must pay in blood," growled an old one-eyed warrior, "then the Vanstermen, and the Breaker of Swords too."

"Of course they must!" called Yarvi to the grumbling crowd, his shrivelled crab-claw of a left hand held up for calm, "but when and how is the question. The wise wait for their moment, and we are by no means ready for war with the High King."

"One is always ready for war." Uthil gently twisted the pommel of his sword so the naked blade flashed in the gloom. "Or never."

Edwal had always been ready. A man who stood for the man beside him, just as a warrior of Gettland was supposed to. Surely he hadn't deserved to die for that?

Thorn cared for nothing past the end of her own nose, and her shield rim in Brand's still-aching balls had raised her no higher in his affections. But she'd fought to the last, against the odds, just as a warrior of Gettland was supposed to. Surely she didn't deserve to be named murderer for that?

He glanced guiltily up at the great statues of the six tall gods, towering in judgment over the Black Chair. Towering in judgment over him. He squirmed as though he was the one who'd killed Edwal and named Thorn a murderer. All he'd done was watch.

Watch and do nothing.

"The High King could call half the world to war with us," Father Yarvi was saying, patiently as a master-at-arms explains the basics to children. "The Vanstermen and the Throvenmen are sworn to him, the Inglings and the Lowlanders are praying to his One God, Grandmother Wexen is forging alliances in the south as well. We are hedged in by enemies and we must have friends to—"

"Steel is the answer." King Uthil cut his minister off with a voice sharp as a blade. "Steel must always be the answer. Gather the men of Gettland. We will teach these carrion-pecking Islanders a lesson they will not soon forget." On the right side of the hall the frowning men beat their approval on mailed chests, and on the left the women with their oiled hair shining murmured their angry support.

Father Yarvi bowed his head. It was his task to speak for Father Peace but even he was out of words. Mother War ruled today. "Steel it is."

Brand should've thrilled at that. A great raid, like in the songs, and him with a warrior's place in it! But he was still trapped beside the training square, picking at the scab of what he could've done differently.

If he hadn't hesitated. If he'd struck without pity, like a warrior was supposed to, he could've beaten Thorn, and there it would've ended. Or if he'd spoken up with Edwal when Hunnan set three on one, perhaps together they could've stopped it. But he hadn't spoken up. Facing an enemy on the battlefield took courage, but you had your friends beside you. Standing alone against your friends, that was a different kind of courage. One Brand didn't pretend to have.

"And then we have the matter of Hild Bathu," said Father Yarvi, the name bringing Brand's head jerking up like a thief's caught with his hand round a purse.

"Who?" asked the king.

"Storn Headland's daughter," said Queen Laithlin. "She calls herself Thorn."

"She's done more than prick a finger," said Father Yarvi. "She killed a boy in the training square and is named a murderer."

"Who names her so?" called Uthil.

"I do." Master Hunnan's golden cloak-buckle gleamed as he stepped into the shaft of light at the foot of the dais.

"Master Hunnan." A rare smile touched the corner of the king's mouth. "I remember well our bouts together in the training square."

"Treasured memories, my king, though painful ones for me."

"Ha! You saw this killing?"

"I was testing my eldest students to judge those worthy to join your raid. Thorn Bathu was among them."

"She embarrasses herself, trying to take a warrior's place!" one woman called.

"She embarrasses us all," said another.

"A woman has no place on the battlefield!" came a gruff voice from among the men, and heads nodded on both sides of the room.

"Is Mother War herself not a woman?" The king pointed up at the Tall Gods looming over them. "We only offer her the choice. The Mother of Crows picks the worthy."

"And she did not pick Thorn Bathu," said Hunnan. "The girl has a poisonous temper." Very true. "She failed the test I set her." Partly true. "She lashed out against my judgment and killed the boy Edwal." Brand blinked. Not quite a lie, but far from all the truth. Hunnan's gray beard wagged as he shook his head. "And so I lost two pupils."

"Careless of you," said Father Yarvi.

The master-at-arms bunched his fists but Queen Laithlin spoke first. "What would be the punishment for such a murder?"

"To be crushed with stones, my queen." The minister spoke calmly, as if they considered crushing a beetle, not a person, and that a person Brand had known most of his life. One he'd disliked almost as long, but even so.

"Will anyone here speak for Thorn Bathu?" thundered the king.

The echoes of his voice faded to leave the silence of a tomb. Now was the time to tell the truth. To do good. To stand in the light. Brand looked across the Godshall, the words tickling at his lips. He saw Rauk in his place, smiling. Sordaf too, his doughy face a mask. They didn't make the faintest sound.

And nor did Brand.

"It is a heavy thing to order the death of one so young." Uthil stood from the Black Chair, mail rattling and skirts rustling as everyone but the queen knelt. "But we cannot turn from the right thing simply because it is a painful thing."

Father Yarvi bowed still lower. "I will dispense your justice according to the law."

Uthil held his hand out to Laithlin, and together they came down the steps of the dais. On the subject of Thorn Bathu, crushing with rocks was the last word.

Brand stared in sick disbelief. He'd been sure among all those lads someone would speak, for they were honest enough. Or Hunnan would tell his part in it, for he was a respected master-at-arms. The king or the queen would draw out the truth, for they were wise and righteous. The gods wouldn't allow such an injustice to pass. Someone would do something.

Maybe, like him, they were all waiting for someone else to put things right.

The king walked stiffly, drawn sword cradled in his arms, his iron-gray stare wavering neither right nor left. The queen's slightest nods were received like gifts, and with the odd word she let it be known that this person or that should enjoy the favor of visiting her counting house upon some deep business. They came closer, and closer yet.

Brand's heart beat loud in his ears. His mouth opened. The queen turned her freezing gaze on him for an instant, and in shamed and shameful silence he let the pair of them sweep past.

His sister was always telling him it wasn't up to him to put the world right. But if not him, who?

"Father Yarvi!" he blurted, far too loud, and then, as the minister turned toward him, croaked far too soft, "I need to speak to you."

"What about, Brand?" That gave him pause. He hadn't thought Yarvi would have the vaguest notion who he was.

"About Thorn Bathu."

A long silence. The minister might only have been a few years older than Brand, pale-skinned and pale-haired as if the color was washed out of him, so gaunt a stiff breeze might blow him away and with a crippled hand besides, but close up there was something chilling in the minister's eye. Something that caused Brand to wilt under his gaze.

But there was no going back, now. "She's no murderer," he muttered.

"The king thinks she is."

Gods, his throat felt dry, but Brand pressed on, the way a warrior was supposed to. "The king wasn't on the sands. The king didn't see what I saw."

"What did you see?"

"We were fighting to win places on the raid—"

"Never again tell me what I already know."

This wasn't running near as smoothly as Brand had hoped. But so it goes, with hopes. "Thorn fought me, and I hesitated . . . she should've won her place. But Master Hunnan set three others on her."

Yarvi glanced toward the people flowing steadily out of the Gods-hall, and eased a little closer. "Three at once?"

"Edwal was one of them. She never meant to kill him—"

"How did she do against those three?"

Brand blinked, wrong-footed. "Well . . . she killed more of them than they did of her."

"That's in no doubt. I was but lately consoling Edwal's parents, and promising them justice. She is sixteen winters, then?"

"Thorn?" Brand wasn't sure what that had to do with her sentence. "I . . . think she is."

"And has held her own in the square all this time against the boys?" He gave Brand a look up and down. "Against the men?"

"Usually she does better than hold her own."

"She must be very fierce. Very determined. Very hard-headed."

"From what I can tell her head's bone all the way through." Brand realized he wasn't helping and mumbled weakly, "but . . . she's not a bad person."

"None are, to their mothers." Father Yarvi pushed out a heavy sigh. "What would you have me do?"

"What . . . would I what?"

"Do I free this troublesome girl and make enemies of Hunnan and the boy's family, or crush her with stones and appease them? Your solution?"

Brand hadn't expected to give a solution. "I suppose . . . you should follow the law?"

"The law?" Father Yarvi snorted. "The law is more Mother Sea than Father Earth, always shifting. The law is a mummer's puppet, Brand, it says what I say it says."

"Just thought I should tell someone . . . well . . . the truth?"

"As if the truth is precious. I can find a thousand truths under every autumn leaf, Brand: everyone has their own. But you thought no further than passing the burden of your truth to me, did you? My epic thanks, preventing Gettland sliding into war with the whole Shattered Sea gives me not enough to do."

"I thought . . . this was doing good." Doing good seemed of a sudden less a burning light before him, clear as Mother Sun, and more a tricking glimmer in the murk of the Godshall.

"Whose good? Mine? Edwal's? Yours? As we each have our own truth so we each have our own good." Yarvi edged a little closer, spoke a little softer. "Master Hunnan may guess you shared your truth with me, what then? Have you thought on the consequences?"

They settled on Brand now, cold as a fall of fresh snow. He looked up, saw the gleam of Rauk's eye in the shadows of the emptying hall.

"A man who gives all his thought to doing good, but no thought to the consequences . . ." Father Yarvi lifted his withered hand and pressed its one crooked finger into Brand's chest. "That is a dangerous man."

And the minister turned away, the butt of his elf staff tapping against stones polished to glass by the passage of years, leaving Brand to stare wide-eyed into the gloom, more worried than ever.

He didn't feel like he was standing in the light at all.

# JUSTICE

Thorn sat and stared down at her filthy toes, pale as maggots in the darkness.

She had no notion why they took her boots. She was hardly going to run, chained by her left ankle to one damp-oozing wall and her right wrist to the other. She could scarcely reach the gate of her cell, let alone rip it from its hinges. Apart from picking the scabs under her broken nose till they bled, all she could do was sit and think.

Her two least favorite activities.

She heaved in a ragged breath. Gods, the place stank. The rotten straw and the rat droppings stank and the bucket they never bothered to empty stank and the mold and rusting iron stank and after two nights in there she stank worst of all.

Any other day she would've been swimming in the bay, fighting Mother Sea, or climbing the cliffs, fighting Father Earth, or running or rowing or practicing with her father's old sword in the yard of their house, fighting the blade-scarred posts and pretending they were Gettland's enemies as the splinters flew—Grom-gil-Gorm, or Styr of the Islands, or even the High King himself.

But she would swing no sword today. She was starting to think she had swung her last. It seemed a long, hard way from fair. But then, as Hunnan said, fair wasn't a thing a warrior could rely on.

"You've a visitor," said the key-keeper, a weighty lump of a woman with a dozen rattling chains about her neck and a face like a bag of axes. "But you'll have to make it quick." And she hauled the heavy door squealing open.

"Hild!"

This once Thorn didn't tell her mother she'd given that name up at six years old, when she pricked her father with his own dagger and he called her "thorn." It took all the strength she had to unfold her legs and stand, sore and tired and suddenly, pointlessly ashamed of the state she was in. Even if she hardly cared for how things looked, she knew her mother did.

When Thorn shuffled into the light her mother pressed one pale hand to her mouth. "Gods, what did they do to you?"

Thorn waved at her face, chains rattling. "This happened in the square."

Her mother came close to the bars, eyes rimmed with weepy pink. "They say you murdered a boy."

"It wasn't murder."

"You killed a boy, though?"

Thorn swallowed, dry throat clicking. "Edwal."

"Gods," whispered her mother again, lip trembling. "Oh, gods, Hild, why couldn't you . . ."

"Be someone else?" Thorn finished for her. Someone easy, someone normal. A daughter who wanted to wield nothing weightier than a needle, dress in southern silk instead of mail, and harbor no dreams beyond wearing some rich man's key.

"I saw this coming," said her mother, bitterly. "Ever since you went to the square. Ever since we saw your father dead, I saw this coming."

Thorn felt her cheek twitch. "You can take comfort in how right you were."

"You think there's any comfort for me in this? They say they're going to crush my only child with stones!"

Thorn felt cold then, very cold. It was an effort to take a breath. As though they were piling the rocks on her already. "Who said?"

"Everyone says."

"Father Yarvi?" The minister spoke the law. The minister would speak the judgment.

"I don't know. I don't think so. Not yet."

Not yet, that was the limit of her hopes. Thorn felt so weak she could hardly grip the bars. She was used to wearing a brave face, however scared she was. But Death is a hard mistress to face bravely. The hardest.

"You'd best go." The key-keeper started to pull Thorn's mother away.

"I'll pray," she called, tears streaking her face. "I'll pray to Father Peace for you!"

Thorn wanted to say, "Damn Father Peace," but she could not find the breath. She had given up on the gods when they let her father die in spite of all her prayers, but a miracle was looking like her best chance.

"Sorry," said the key-keeper, shouldering shut the door.

"Not near as sorry as me." Thorn closed her eyes and let her forehead fall against the bars, squeezed hard at the pouch under her dirty shirt. The pouch that held her father's fingerbones.

*We don't get much time, and time feeling sorry for yourself is time wasted.* She kept every word he'd said close to her heart, but if there'd ever been a moment for feeling sorry for herself, this had to be the one. Hardly seemed like justice. Hardly seemed fair. But try telling Edwal about fair. However you shared out the blame, she'd killed him. Wasn't his blood crusted up her sleeve?

She'd killed Edwal. Now they'd kill her.

She heard talking, faint beyond the door. Her mother's voice— pleading, wheedling, weeping. Then a man's, cold and level. She couldn't quite catch the words, but they sounded like hard ones. She flinched as the door opened, jerking back into the darkness of her cell, and Father Yarvi stepped over the threshold.

He was a strange one. A man in a minister's place was almost as rare as a woman in the training square. He was only a few years Thorn's elder but he had an old eye. An eye that had seen things. They told strange stories of him. That he had sat in the Black Chair, but given it up. That he had sworn a deep-rooted oath of vengeance. That he had killed his Uncle Odem with the curved sword he always wore. They said he was cunning as Father Moon, a man rarely to be trusted and never to be crossed. And in his hands—or in his one good one, for the other was a crooked lump—her life now rested.

"Thorn Bathu," he said. "You are named a murderer."

All she could do was nod, her breath coming fast.

"Have you anything to say?"

Perhaps she should've spat her defiance. Laughed at Death. They said that was what her father did, when he lay bleeding his last at the feet of Grom-gil-Gorm. But all she wanted was to live.

"I didn't mean to kill him," she gurgled up. "Master Hunnan set three of them on me. It wasn't murder!"

"A fine distinction to Edwal."

True enough, she knew. She was blinking back tears, shamed at her own cowardice, but couldn't help it. How she wished she'd never gone to the square now, and learned to smile well and count coins like her mother always wanted. But you'll buy nothing with wishes.

"Please, Father Yarvi, give me a chance." She looked into his calm, cold, gray-blue eyes. "I'll take any punishment. I'll do any penance. I swear it!"

He raised one pale brow. "You should be careful what oaths you make, Thorn. Each one is a chain about you. I swore to be revenged on the killers of my father and the oath still weighs heavy on me. That one might come to weigh heavy on you."

"Heavier than the stones they'll crush me with?" She held her open palms out, as close to him as the chains would allow. "I swear a sun-oath and a moon-oath. I'll do whatever service you think fit."

The minister frowned at her dirty hands, reaching, reaching. He frowned at the desperate tears leaking down her face. He cocked his head slowly on one side, as though he was a merchant judging her value. Finally he gave a long, unhappy sigh. "Oh, very well."

There was a silence then, while Thorn turned over what he'd said. "You're not going to crush me with stones?"

He waved his crippled hand so the one finger flopped back and forth. "I have trouble lifting the big ones."

More silence, long enough for relief to give way to suspicion. "So . . . what's the sentence?"

"I'll think of something. Release her."

The jailer sucked her teeth as if opening any lock left a wound, but did as she was bid. Thorn rubbed at the chafe-marks the iron cuff left on her wrist, feeling strangely light without its weight. So light she wondered if she was dreaming. She squeezed her eyes shut, then grunted as the key-keeper tossed her boots over and they hit her in the belly. Not a dream, then.

She couldn't stop herself smiling as she pulled them on.

"Your nose looks broken," said Father Yarvi.

"Not the first time." If she got away from this with no worse than a broken nose she would count herself blessed indeed.

"Let me see."

A minister was a healer first, so Thorn didn't flinch when he came close, prodded gently at the bones under her eyes, brow wrinkled with concentration.

"Ah," she muttered.

"Sorry, did that hurt?"

"Just a litt—"

He jabbed one finger up her nostril, pressing his thumb mercilessly into the bridge of her nose. Thorn gasped, forced down onto her knees, there was a crack and a white-hot pain in her face, tears flooding more freely than ever.

"That got it," he said, wiping his hand on her shirt.

"Gods!" she whimpered, clutching her throbbing face.

"Sometimes a little pain now can save a great deal later." Father Yarvi was already walking for the door, so Thorn tottered up and, still wondering if this was some trick, crept after him.

"Thanks for your kindness," she muttered as she passed the key-keeper

The woman glared back. "I hope you never need it again."

"No offense, but so do I." And Thorn followed Father Yarvi along the dim corridor and up the steps, blinking into the light.

He might have had one hand but his legs worked well enough, setting quite a pace as he stalked across the yard of the citadel, the breeze making the branches of the old cedar whisper above them.

"I should speak to my mother——" she said, hurrying to catch up.

"I already have. I told her I had found you innocent of murder but you had sworn an oath to serve me."

"But . . . how did you know I'd——"

"It is a minister's place to know what people will do." Father Yarvi snorted. "As yet you are not too deep a well to fathom, Thorn Bathu."

They passed beneath the Screaming Gate, out of the citadel and into the city, down from the great rock and toward Mother Sea. They went by switching steps and narrow ways, sloping steeply between tight-crammed houses and the people tight-crammed between them.

"I'm not going on King Uthil's raid, am I?" A fool's question, doubtless, but now Thorn had stepped from Death's shadow there was light enough to mourn her ruined dreams.

Father Yarvi was not in a mourning mood. "Be thankful you're not going in the ground."

They passed down the Street of Anvils, where Thorn had spent long hours gazing greedily at weapons like a beggar child at pastries. Where she had ridden on her father's shoulders, giddy-proud as the smiths begged him to notice their work. But the bright metal set out before the forges only seemed to mock her now.

"I'll never be a warrior of Gettland." She said it soft and sorry, but Yarvi's ears were sharp.

"As long as you live, what you might come to be is in your own hands, first of all." The minister rubbed gently at some faded marks on his neck. "There is always a way, Queen Laithlin used to tell me."

Thorn found herself walking a little taller at the name alone. Laithlin might not be a fighter, but Thorn could think of no one she admired more. "The Golden Queen is a woman no man dares take lightly," she said.

"So she is." Yarvi looked at Thorn sidelong. "Learn to temper stubbornness with sense and maybe one day you will be the same."

It seemed that day was still some way off. Wherever they passed people bowed, and muttered softly, "Father Yarvi," and stepped aside to give the minister of Gettland room, but shook their heads darkly at Thorn as she skulked after him, filthy and disgraced, through the gates of the city and out onto the swarming dockside. They wove between sailors and merchants from every nation around the Shattered Sea and some much farther off, Thorn ducking under fishermen's dripping nets and around their glittering, squirming catches.

"Where are we going?" she asked.

"Skekenhouse."

She stopped short, gaping, and was nearly knocked flat by a passing barrow. She had never in her life been further than a half-day's walk from Thorlby.

"Or you could stay here," Yarvi tossed over his shoulder. "They have the stones ready."

She swallowed, then hurried again to catch him up. "I'll come."

"You are as wise as you are beautiful, Thorn Bathu."

That was either a double compliment or a double insult, and she suspected the latter. The old planks of the wharf clonked under their boots, salt water slapping at the green-furred supports below. A ship rocked beside it, small but sleek and with white-painted doves mounted at high prow and stern. Judging by the bright shields ranged down each side, it was manned and ready to sail.

"We're going now?" she asked.

"I am summoned by the High King."

"The High . . . King?" She looked down at her clothes, stiff with dungeon filth, crusted with her blood and Edwal's. "Can I change, at least?"

"I have no time for your vanity."

"I stink."

"We will haul you behind the ship to wash away the reek."

"You will?"

The minister raised one brow at her. "You have no sense of humor, do you?"

"Facing Death can sap your taste for jokes," she muttered.

"That's the time you need it most." A thickset old man was busy casting off the prow rope, and tossed it aboard as they walked up. "But don't worry. Mother Sea will have given you more washing than you can stomach by the time we reach Skekenhouse." He was a fighter: Thorn could tell that from the way he stood, his broad face battered by weather and war.

"The gods saw fit to take my strong left hand." Yarvi held up his twisted claw and wiggled the one finger. "But they gave me Rulf instead." He clapped it down on the old man's meaty shoulder. "Though it hasn't always been easy, I find myself content with the bargain."

Rulf raised one tangled brow. "D'you want to know how I feel about it?"

"No," said Yarvi, hopping aboard the ship. Thorn could only shrug at the gray-bearded warrior and hop after. "Welcome to the *South Wind.*"

She worked her mouth and spat over the side. "I don't feel too welcome."

Perhaps forty grizzled-looking oarsmen sat upon their sea chests, glaring at her, and she had no doubts what they were thinking. *What is this girl doing here?*

"Some ugly patterns keep repeating," she murmured.

Father Yarvi nodded. "Such is life. It is a rare mistake you make only once."

"Can I ask a question?"

"I have the sense that if I said no, you would ask anyway."

"I'm not too deep a well to fathom, I reckon."

"Then speak."

"What am I doing here?"

"Why, holy men and deep-cunning women have been asking that question for a thousand years and never come near an answer."

"Try talking to Brinyolf the Prayer-Weaver on the subject," grunted Rulf, pushing them clear of the wharf with the butt of a spear. "He'll bore your ears off with his talk of whys and wherefores."

"Who is it indeed," muttered Yarvi, frowning off toward the far horizon as though he could see the answers written in the clouds, "that can plumb the gods' grand design? Might as well ask where the elves went!" And the old man and the young grinned at each other. Plainly this act was not new to them.

"Very good," said Thorn. "I mean, why have you brought me onto this ship?"

"Ah." Yarvi turned to Rulf. "Why do you think, rather than taking the easy road and crushing her, I have endangered all our lives by bringing the notorious killer Thorn Bathu onto my ship?"

Rulf leaned on his spear a moment, scratching at his beard. "I've really no idea."

Yarvi looked at Thorn with his eyes very wide. "If I don't share my thinking with my own left hand, why ever would I share it with the likes of you? I mean to say, you stink."

Thorn rubbed at her temples. "I need to sit down."

Rulf put a fatherly hand on her shoulder. "I understand." He shoved her onto the nearest chest so hard she went squawking over the back of it and into the lap of the man behind. "This is your oar."

# FAMILY

"**Y**ou're late."

Rin was right. Father Moon was smiling bright, and his children the stars twinkling on heaven's cloth, and the narrow hovel was lit only by the embers of the fire when Brand ducked through the low doorway.

"Sorry, sister." He went in a stoop to his bench and sank down with a long groan, worked his aching feet from his boots and spread his toes at the warmth. "But Harper had more peat to cut, then Old Fen needed help carrying some logs in. Wasn't like she was chopping them herself, and her ax was blunt so I had to sharpen it, and on the way back Lem's cart had broke an axle so a few of us helped out—"

"Your trouble is you make everyone's trouble your trouble."

"You help folk, maybe when you need it they'll help you."

"Maybe." Rin nodded toward the pot sitting over the embers of the fire. "There's dinner. The gods know, leaving some hasn't been easy."

He slapped her on the knee as he leaned to get it. "But bless you for it, sister." Brand was fearsome hungry, but he remembered to mutter a thanks to Father Earth for the food. He remembered how it felt to have none.

"It's good," he said, forcing it down.

"It was better right after I cooked it."

"It's still good."

"No, it's not."

He shrugged as he scraped the pot out, wishing there was more. "Things'll be different now I've passed the tests. Folk come back rich from a raid like this one."

"Folk come to the forge before every raid telling us how rich they're going to be. Sometimes they don't come back."

Brand grinned at her. "You won't get rid of me that easily."

"I'm not aiming to. Fool though y'are, you're all the family I've got." She dug something from behind her and held it out. A bundle of animal skin, stained and tattered.

"For me?" he said, reaching through the warmth above the dying fire for it.

"To keep you company on your high adventures. To remind you of home. To remind you of your family. Such as it is."

"You're all the family I need." There was a knife inside the bundle, polished steel gleaming. A fighting dagger with a long, straight blade, crosspiece worked like a pair of twined snakes and the pommel a snarling dragon's head.

Rin sat up, keen to see how her gift would sit with him. "I'll make you a sword one day. For now this was the best I could manage."

"You made this?"

"Gaden gave me some help with the hilt. But the steel's all mine."

"It's fine work, Rin." The closer he looked the better it got, every scale on the snakes picked out, the dragon baring little teeth at him, the steel bright as silver and holding a deadly edge too. He hardly dared touch it. It seemed too good a thing for his dirty hands. "Gods, it's master's work."

She sat back, careless, as though she'd known that all along. "I think I've found a better way to do the smelting. A hotter way. In a clay jar, sort of. Bone and charcoal to bind the iron into steel, sand and glass to coax the dirt out and leave it pure. But it's all about the heat . . . You're not listening."

Brand gave a sorry shrug. "I can swing a hammer all right but I don't understand the magic of it. You're ten times the smith I ever was."

"Gaden says I'm touched by She who Strikes the Anvil."

"She must be happy as the breeze I quit the forge and she got you as an apprentice."

"I've a gift."

"The gift of modesty."

"Modesty is for folk with nothing to boast of."

He weighed the dagger in his hand, feeling out the fine heft and balance to it. "My little sister, mistress of the forge. I never had a better gift." Not that he'd had many. "Wish I had something to give you in return."

She lay back on her bench and shook her threadbare blanket over her legs. "You've given me everything I've got."

He winced. "Not much, is it?"

"I've no complaints." She reached across the fire with her strong hand, scabbed and calloused from forge-work, and he took it, and they gave each other a squeeze.

He cleared his throat, looking at the hard-packed earth of the floor. "Will you be all right while I'm gone on this raid?"

"I'll be like a swimmer who just shrugged her armor off." She gave him the scornful face but he saw straight through it. She was fifteen years old, and he was all the family she had, and she was scared, and that made him scared too. Scared of fighting. Scared of leaving home. Scared of leaving her alone.

"I'll be back, Rin. Before you know it."

"Loaded with treasures, no doubt."

He winked. "Songs sung of my high deeds and a dozen fine Islander slaves to my name."

"Where will they sleep?"

"In the great stone house I'll buy you up near the citadel."

"I'll have a room for my clothes," she said, stroking at the wattle wall with her fingertips. Wasn't much of a home they had, but the gods knew they were grateful for it. There'd been times they had nothing over their heads but weather.

Brand lay down too, knees bent since his legs hung way off the end of his bench these days, started unrolling his own smelly scrap of blanket.

"Rin," he found he'd said, "I might've done a stupid thing." He wasn't much at keeping secrets. Especially from her.

"What this time?"

He set to picking at one of the holes in his blanket. "Told the truth."

"What about?"

"Thorn Bathu."

Rin clapped her hands over her face. "What is it with you and her?"

"What d'you mean? I don't even like her."

"No one likes her. She's a splinter in the world's arse. But you can't seem to stop picking at her."

"The gods have a habit of pushing us together, I reckon."

"Have you tried walking the other way? She killed Edwal. She killed him. He's dead, Brand."

"I know. I was there. But it wasn't murder. What should I have done, tell me that, since you're the clever one. Kept my mouth shut with everyone else? Kept my mouth shut and let her be crushed with rocks? I couldn't carry the weight of that!" He realized he was near-shouting, anger bubbling up, and he pressed his voice back down. "I couldn't."

A silence, then, while they frowned at each other, and the fire sagged, sending up a puff of sparks. "Why does it always fall to you to put things right?" she asked.

"I guess no one else is doing it."

"You always were a good boy." Rin stared up toward the smoke-hole and the chink of starry sky showing through it. "Now you're a good man. That's your trouble. I never saw a better man for doing good things and getting bad results. Who'd you tell your tale to?"

He swallowed, finding the smoke-hole mightily interesting himself. "Father Yarvi."

"Oh, gods, Brand! You don't like half measures, do you?"

"Never saw the point of them," he muttered. "Dare say it'll all work out, though?" wheedling, desperate for her to tell him yes.

She just lay staring at the ceiling, so he picked her dagger up again, watched the bright steel shine with the colors of fire.

"Really is fine work, Rin."

"Go to sleep, Brand."

# KNEELING

"I f in doubt, kneel." Rulf's place as helmsman was the platform at the *South Wind*'s stern, steering oar wedged under one arm. "Kneel low and kneel often."

"Kneel," muttered Thorn. "Got it." She had one of the back oars, the place of most work and least honor, right beneath his ever-watchful eye. She kept twisting about, straining over her shoulder in her eagerness to see Skekenhouse, but there was a rainy mist in the air and she could make out nothing but ghosts in the murk. The looming phantoms of the famous elf-walls. The faintest wraith of the vast Tower of the Ministry.

"You might be best just shuffling around on your knees the whole time you're here," said Rulf. "And by the gods, keep your tongue still. Cause Grandmother Wexen some offense and crushing with stones will seem light duty."

Thorn saw figures gathered on the dock as they glided closer. The figures became men. The men became warriors. An honor guard, though they had more the flavor of a prison escort as the *South Wind* was tied off and Father Yarvi and his bedraggled crew clambered onto the rain-slick quay.

At sixteen winters Thorn was taller than most men but the one who stepped forward now might easily have been reckoned a giant, a full head taller than she was at least. His long hair and beard were darkened by rain and streaked with gray, the white fur about his shoulders beaded with dew.

"Why, Father Yarvi." His sing-song voice was strangely at odds with that mighty frame. "The seasons have turned too often since we traded words."

"Three years," said Yarvi, bowing. "That day in the Godshall, my king."

Thorn blinked. She had heard the High King was a withered old man, half-blind and scared of his own food. That assessment seemed decidedly unfair. She had learned to judge the strength of a man in the training square and she doubted she had ever seen one stronger. A warrior too, from his scars, and the many blades sheathed at his gold-buckled belt. Here was a man who looked a king indeed.

"I remember well," he said. "Everyone was so very, very rude to me. The hospitality of Gettlanders, eh, Mother Scaer?" A shaven-headed woman at his shoulder glowered at Yarvi and his crew as if they were heaps of dung. "And who is this?" he asked, eyes falling on Thorn.

At starting fights she was an expert, but all other etiquette was a mystery. When her mother had tried to explain how a girl should behave, when to bow and when to kneel and when to hold your key, she'd nodded along and thought about swords. But Rulf had said kneel, so she dropped clumsily down on the wet stones of the dock, scraping her sodden hair out of her face and nearly tripping over her own feet.

"My king. My high . . . king, that is—"

Yarvi snorted. "This is Thorn Bathu. My new jester."

"How is she working out?"

"Few laughs as yet."

The giant grinned. "I am but a low king, child. I am the little king of Vansterland, and my name is Grom-gil-Gorm."

Thorn felt her guts turn over. For years she had dreamed of meeting the man who killed her father. None of the dreams had worked out quite like this. She had knelt at the feet of the Breaker of Swords, the Maker of Orphans, Gettland's bitterest enemy, who even now was ordering raids across the border. About his thick neck she saw the chain, four times looped, of pommels twisted from the swords of his fallen enemies. One of them, she knew, from the sword she kept at home. Her most prized possession.

She slowly stood, trying to gather every shred of her ruined dignity. She had no sword-hilt to prop her hand on, but she thrust her chin up at him just as if it was a blade.

The King of Vansterland peered down like a great hound at a bristling kitten. "I am well accustomed to the scorn of Gettlanders, but this one has a cold eye upon her."

"As if she has a score to settle," said Mother Scaer.

Thorn gripped the pouch about her neck. "You killed my father."

"Ah." Gorm shrugged. "There are many children who might say so. What was his name?"

"Storn Headland."

She had expected taunts, threats, fury, but instead his craggy face lit up. "Ah, but that was a duel to sing of! I remember every step and cut of it. Headland was a great warrior, a worthy enemy! On chill mornings like that one I still feel the wound he gave me in my leg. But Mother War was by my side. She breathed upon me in my crib. It has been foreseen that no man can kill me, and so it has proved." He beamed down at Thorn, spinning one of the pommels idly around and around on his chain between great finger and thumb. "Storn Headland's daughter, grown so tall! The years turn, eh, Mother Scaer?"

"Always," said the minister, staring at Thorn through blue, blue narrowed eyes.

"But we cannot pick over old glories all day." Gorm swept his hand out with a flourish to offer them the way. "The High King awaits, Father Yarvi."

Grom-gil-Gorm led them across the wet docks and Thorn slunk after, cold, wet, bitter, and powerless, the excitement of seeing the Shattered Sea's greatest city all stolen away. If you could kill a man by frowning at his back, the Breaker of Swords would have fallen bloody through the Last Door that day, but a frown is no blade, and Thorn's hatred cut no one but her.

Through a pair of towering doors trudged the *South Wind*'s crew, into a hallway whose walls were covered from polished floor to lofty ceiling with weapons. Ancient swords, eaten with rust. Spears with hafts shattered. Shields hacked and splintered. The weapons that once belonged to the mountain of corpses Bail the Builder climbed to his place as the first High King. The weapons of armies his successors butchered spreading their power from Yutmark into the Lowlands, out to Inglefold and halfway around the Shattered Sea. Hundreds of years of victories, and though swords and axes and cloven helms had no voice, together they spoke a message more eloquent than any minister's whisper, more deafening than any master-at-arms' bellow.

Resisting the High King is a very poor idea.

"I must say it surprises me," Father Yarvi was saying, "to find the Breaker of Swords serving as the High King's doorman."

Gorm frowned sideways. "We all must kneel to someone."

"Some of us kneel more easily than others, though."

Gorm frowned harder but his minister spoke first. "Grandmother Wexen can be most persuasive."

"Has she persuaded you to pray to the One God, yet?" asked Yarvi.

Scaer gave a snort so explosive it was a wonder she didn't blow snot down her chest.

"Nothing will pry me from the bloody embrace of Mother War," growled Gorm. "That much I promise you."

Yarvi smiled as if he chatted with friends. "My uncle uses just those words. There is so much that unites Gettland and Vansterland. We pray the same way, speak the same way, fight the same way. Only a narrow river separates us."

"And hundreds of years of dead fathers and dead sons," muttered Thorn, under her breath.

"Shush," hissed Rulf, beside her.

"We have a bloody past," said Yarvi. "But good leaders must put the past at their backs and look to the future. The more I think on it, the more it seems our struggles only weaken us both and profit others."

"So after all our battles shall we link arms?" Thorn saw the corner of Gorm's mouth twisted in a smile. "And dance over our dead together into your brave future?"

Smiles, and dancing, and Thorn glanced to the weapons on the walls, wondering whether she could tear a sword from its brackets and stove Gorm's skull in before Rulf stopped her. There would be a deed worthy of a warrior of Gettland.

But then Thorn wasn't a warrior of Gettland, and never would be.

"You weave a pretty dream, Father Yarvi." Gorm puffed out a sigh. "But you wove pretty dreams for me once before. We all must wake, and whether it pleases us to kneel or no, the dawn belongs to the High King."

"And to his minister," said Mother Scaer.

"To her most of all." And the Breaker of Swords pushed wide the great doors at the hallway's end.

Thorn remembered the one time she had stood in Gettland's Godshall, staring at her father's pale, cold corpse, trying to squeeze her mother's hand hard enough that she would stop sobbing. It had seemed the biggest room in the world, too big for man's hands to have built. But elf hands had built the Chamber of Whispers. Five Godshalls could have fit inside with floor left over to plant a decent crop of barley. Its walls of smooth elf-stone and black elf-glass rose up, and up, and were lost in the dizzying gloom above.

Six towering statues of the tall gods frowned down, but the High

King had turned from their worship and his masons had been busy. Now a seventh stood above them all. The southerners' god, the One God, neither man nor woman, neither smiling nor weeping, arms spread wide in a smothering embrace, gazing down with bland indifference upon the petty doings of mankind.

People were crowded about the far-off edges of the floor, and around a balcony of gray elf-metal at ten times the height of a man, and a ring of tiny faces at another as far above again. Thorn saw Vanstermen with braids in their long hair, Throvenmen with silver ring-money stacked high on their arms. She saw Islanders with weathered faces, stout Lowlanders and wild-bearded Inglings. She saw lean women she reckoned Shends and plump merchants of Sagenmark. She saw dark-faced emissaries from Catalia, or the Empire of the South, or even further off, maybe.

All the people in the world, it seemed, gathered with the one purpose of licking the High King's arse.

"Greatest of men!" called Father Yarvi, "between gods and kings! I prostrate myself before you!" And he near threw himself on his face, the echoes of his voice bouncing from the galleries above and shattering into the thousand thousand whispers which gave the hall its name.

The rumors had in fact been overly generous to the greatest of men. The High King was a shrivelled remnant in his outsize throne, withered face sagging off the bone, beard a few gray straggles. Only his eyes showed some sign of life, bright and flinty hard as he glared down at Gettland's minister.

"Now you kneel, fool!" hissed Rulf, dragging Thorn down beside him by her belt. And only just in time. An old woman was already walking out across the expanse of floor toward them.

She was round-faced and motherly, with deep laughter lines about her twinkling eyes, white hair cut short, her coarse gray gown dragging upon the floor so heavily its hem was frayed to dirty tatters. About her neck upon the finest chain, crackling papers scrawled with runes were threaded.

"We understand Queen Laithlin is with child." She might have looked no hero, but by the gods she spoke with a hero's voice. Deep, soft, effortlessly powerful. A voice that demanded attention. A voice that commanded obedience.

Even on his knees, Yarvi found a way to bow lower. "The gods have blessed her, most honored Grandmother Wexen."

"An heir to the Black Chair, perhaps?"

"We can but hope."

"Convey our warm congratulations to King Uthil," scratched out the High King, no trace of either warmth or congratulation on his withered face.

"I will be delighted to convey them, and they to receive them. May I rise?"

The first of ministers gave the warmest smile, and raised one palm, and tattooed upon it Thorn saw circles within circles of tiny writing.

"I like you there," she said.

"We hear troubling tales from the north," croaked out the High King, and curling back his lip licked at a yawning gap in his front teeth. "We hear King Uthil plans a great raid against the Islanders."

"A raid, my king?" Yarvi seemed baffled by what was common knowledge in Thorlby. "Against our much-loved fellows on the Islands of the Shattered Sea?" He waved his arm so his crippled hand flopped dismissively. "King Uthil is of a warlike temper, and speaks often in the Godshall of raiding this or that. It always comes to nothing for, believe me, I am ever at his side, smoothing the path for Father Peace, as Mother Gundring taught me."

Grandmother Wexen threw her head back and gave a peal of laughter, rich and sweet as treacle, echoes ringing out as if she were a chuckling army. "Oh, you're a funny one, Yarvi."

She struck him with a snake's speed. With an open hand, but hard enough to knock him on his side. The sound of it bounced from the balconies above sharp as a whip cracks.

Thorn's eyes went wide and without thinking she sprang to her feet. Or halfway there, at least. Rulf's hand shot out and caught a fistful of her damp shirt, dragging her back to her knees, her curse cut off in an ugly squawk.

"Down," he growled under his breath.

It felt suddenly a very lonely place, the center of that huge, empty floor, and Thorn realized how many armed men were gathered about it, and came over very dry in the mouth and very wet in the bladder.

Grandmother Wexen looked at her, neither scared nor angry. Mildly curious, as though at a kind of ant she did not recognize. "Who is this . . . person?"

"A humble halfwit, sworn to my service." Yarvi pushed himself back up as far as his knees, good hand to his bloody mouth. "Forgive her impudence, she suffers from too little sense and too much loyalty."

Grandmother Wexen beamed down as warmly as Mother Sun, but the ice in her voice froze Thorn to her bones. "Loyalty can be a great blessing or a terrible curse, child. It all depends on to whom one is loyal. There is a right order to things. There *must be* a right order, and you Gettlanders forget your place in it. The High King has forbidden swords to be drawn."

"I have forbidden it," echoed the High King, his own voice dwindled to a reedy rustling, hardly heard in the vastness.

"If you make war upon the Islanders you make war upon the High King and his ministry," said Grandmother Wexen. "You make war upon the Inglings and the Lowlanders, upon the Throvenmen and the Vanstermen, upon Grom-gil-Gorm, the Breaker of Swords, whom it has been foreseen no man can kill." She pointed out the murderer of Thorn's father beside the door, seeming far from comfortable on one great knee. "You even make war upon the Empress of the South, who has but lately pledged an alliance with us." Grandmother Wexen spread her arms wide to encompass the whole vast chamber, and its legion of occupants, and Father Yarvi and his shabby crew looked a feeble flock before them indeed. "Would you make war on half the world, Gettlanders?"

Father Yarvi grinned like a simpleton. "Since we are faithful servants of the High King, his many powerful friends can only be a reassurance."

"Then tell your uncle to stop rattling his sword. If he should draw it without the High King's blessing—"

"Steel shall be my answer," croaked the High King, watery eyes bulging.

Grandmother Wexen's voice took on an edge that made the hairs on Thorn's neck prickle. "And there shall be such a reckoning as has not been seen since the Breaking of the World."

Yarvi bowed so low he nearly nosed the floor. "Oh, highest and most gracious, who would wish to see such wrath released? Might I now stand?"

"First one more thing," came a soft voice from behind. A young woman walked toward them with quick steps, thin and yellow-haired and with a brittle smile.

"You know Sister Isriun, I think?" said Grandmother Wexen.

It was the first time Thorn had seen Yarvi lost for words. "I . . . you . . . joined the Ministry?"

"It is a fine place for the broken and dispossessed. You should know that." And Isriun pulled out a cloth and dabbed the blood from the corner of Yarvi's mouth. Gentle, her touch, but the look in her eye was anything but. "Now we are all one family, once again."

"She passed the test three months ago without one question wrong," said Grandmother Wexen. "She is already greatly knowledgeable on the subject of elf-relics."

Yarvi swallowed. "Fancy that."

"It is the Ministry's most solemn duty to protect them," said Isriun. "And to protect the world from a second breaking." Her thin hands fussed one with the other. "Do you know the thief and killer, Skifr?"

Yarvi blinked as though he scarcely understood the question. "I may have heard the name . . ."

"She is wanted by the Ministry." Isriun's expression had grown even deadlier. "She entered the elf-ruins of Strokom, and brought out relics from within."

A gasp hissed around the chamber, a fearful whispering echoed among the balconies. Folk made holy signs upon their chests, murmured prayers, shook their heads in horror.

"What times are we living in?" whispered Father Yarvi. "You have my solemn word, if I hear but the breath of this Skifr's passing, my doves will be with you upon the instant."

"Such a relief," said Isriun, "Because if anyone were to strike a deal with her, I would have to see them burned alive." She twisted her fingers together, gripping eagerly until the knuckles were white. "And you know how much I would hate to see you burn."

"So we have that in common too," said Yarvi. "May I now depart, oh, greatest of men?"

The High King appeared to have nodded sideways, quite possibly off to sleep.

"I will take that as a yes." Yarvi stood, and Rulf and his crew stood with him, and Thorn struggled up last. She seemed always to be kneeling when she had better stand and standing when she had better kneel.

"It is not too late to make of the fist an open hand, Father Yarvi." Grandmother Wexen sadly shook her head. "I once had high hopes for you."

"Alas, as Sister Isriun can tell you, I have often been a sore disappointment." There was just the slightest iron in Yarvi's voice as he turned. "I struggle daily to improve."

Outside the rain was falling hard, still making gray ghosts of Skekenhouse.

"Who was that woman, Isriun?" Thorn asked as she hurried to catch up.

"She was once my cousin." The muscles worked on the gaunt side of Yarvi's face. "Then we were betrothed. Then she swore to see me dead."

Thorn raised her brows at that. "You must be quite a lover."

"We cannot all have your gentle touch." He frowned sideways at her. "Next time you might think before leaping to my defense."

"The moment you pause will be the moment you die," she muttered.

"The moment you didn't pause you nearly killed the lot of us."

She knew he was right, but it still nettled her. "It might not have come to that if you'd told them the Islanders have attacked us, and the Vanstermen too, that they've given us no choice but to—"

"They know that well enough. It was Grandmother Wexen set them on."

"How do you—"

"She spoke thunderously in the words she did not say. She means to crush us, and I can put her off no longer."

Thorn rubbed at her temples. Ministers seemed never to mean quite what they said. "If she's our enemy, why didn't she just kill us where we knelt?"

"Because Grandmother Wexen does not want her children dead. She wants them to obey. First she sends the Islanders against us, then the Vanstermen. She hopes to lure us into rash action and King Uthil is about to oblige her. It will take time for her to gather her forces, but only because she has so many to call on. In time, she will send half the world against us. If we are to resist her, we need allies."

"Where do we find allies?"

Father Yarvi smiled. "Among our enemies, where else?"

# DEAD MAN'S
# MAIL

The boys were gathered.

The *men* were gathered, Brand realized. There might not be much beard among them, but if they weren't men now they'd passed their tests and were about to swear their oaths, when would they be?

They were gathered one last time with Master Hunnan, who'd taught them, and tested them, and hammered them into shape like Brand used to hammer iron at Gaden's forge. They were gathered on the beach where they'd trained so often, but the blades weren't wooden now.

They were gathered in their new war-gear, bright-eyed and breathless at the thought of sailing on their first raid. Of leaving Father Peace at their backs and giving themselves guts and sinew to his red-mouthed wife, Mother War. Of winning fame and glory, a place at the king's table and in the warriors' songs.

Oh, and coming back rich.

Some were buckled up prettily as heroes already, blessed with family who'd bought them fine mail, and good swords, and new gear all aglitter. Though he counted her more blessing than he deserved,

Brand had only Rin, so he'd borrowed his mail from Gaden in return for a tenth share of aught he took—dead man's mail, tarnished with use, hastily resized and still loose under the arms. But his ax was good and true and polished sharp as a razor, and his shield that he'd saved a year for was fresh painted by Rin with a dragon's head and looked well as anyone's.

"Why a dragon?" Rauk asked him, one mocking eyebrow high.

Brand laughed it off. "Why not a dragon?" It'd take more than that fool's scorn to spoil the day of his first raid.

And it wasn't just any raid. It was the biggest in living memory. Bigger even that the one King Uthrik led to Sagenmark. Brand went up on tiptoe again to see the gathered men stretched far off down the shore, metal twinkling in the sun and the smoke from their fires smudging the sky. Five thousand, Hunnan had said, and Brand stared at his fingers, trying to reckon each a thousand men. It made him as dizzy as looking down a long drop.

Five thousand. Gods, how big the world must be.

There were men well-funded by tradesmen or merchants and ragged brotherhoods spilled down from the mountains. There were proud-faced men with silvered sword-hilts and dirty-faced men with spears of flint. There were men with a lifetime of scars and men who'd never shed blood in their lives.

It was a sight you didn't see often, and half of Thorlby was gathered on the slopes outside the city walls to watch. Mothers and fathers, wives and children, there to see off their boys and husbands and pray for their safe and enriched return. Brand's family would be there too, no doubt. Which meant Rin, on her own. He bunched his fists, staring up into the wind.

He'd make her proud. He swore he would.

The feeling was more of wedding-feast than war, the air thick with smoke and excitement, the clamor of songs, and jests, and arguments. Prayer-Weavers wove their own paths through the throng speaking blessings for a payment, and merchants too, spinning lies about how all great warriors carried an extra belt to war. It wasn't just warriors hoping to turn a coin from King Uthil's raid.

"For a copper I'll bring you weaponluck," said a beggar-woman, selling lucky kisses, "for another I'll bring you weatherluck too. For a third—"

"Shut up," snapped Master Hunnan, shooing her off. "The king speaks."

There was a clattering of gear as every man turned westward. Toward the barrows of long-dead rulers above the beach, dwindling away to the north into wind-flattened humps.

King Uthil stood tall before them on the dunes, the long grass twitching at his boots, cradling gently as a sick child his sword of plain gray steel. He needed no ornaments but the scars of countless battles on his face. Needed no jewels but the wild brightness in his eye. Here was a man who knew neither fear nor mercy. Here was a king that any warrior would be proud to follow to the very threshold of the Last Door and beyond.

Queen Laithlin stood beside him, hands on her swollen belly, golden key upon her chest, golden hair taken by the breeze and torn like a banner, showing no more fear or mercy than her husband. They said it was her gold that bought half these men and most of these ships, and she wasn't a woman to take her eye off an investment.

The king took two slow, swaggering steps forward, letting the breathless silence stretch out, excitement building until Brand could hear his own blood surging in his ears.

"Do I see some men of Gettland?" he roared.

Brand and his little knot of newly-minted warriors were lucky to be close enough to hear him. Further off the captains of each ship passed on the king's words to their crews, wind-blown echoes rippling down the long sweep of the shore.

A great clamor burst from the gathered warriors, weapons thrust up toward Mother Sun in a glittering forest. All united, all belonging. All ready to die for the man at their shoulder. Perhaps Brand had only one sister, but he felt then he had five thousand brothers with him on the sand, a sweet mixture of rage and love that wetted his eyes and warmed his heart and seemed in that moment a feeling worth dying for.

King Uthil raised his hand for silence. "How it gladdens me to see so many brothers! Wise old warriors often tested on the battlefield, and bold young warriors lately tested in the square. All gathered with good cause in the sight of the gods, in the sight of my forefathers." He spread his arms toward the ancient barrows. "And can they ever have looked on so mighty a host?"

"No!" someone screamed, and there was laughter, and others joined him, shouting wildly, "No!" Until the king raised his hand for silence again.

"The Islanders have sent ships against us. They have stolen from us, and made our children slaves, and spilled our blood on our good soil." A muttering of anger began. "It is they who turned their backs on Father Peace, they who opened the door to Mother War, they who made her our guest." The muttering grew, and swelled, an animal growling that found its way to Brand's own throat. "But the High King says we of Gettland must not be good hosts to the Mother of Crows! The High King says *our* swords must stay sheathed. The High King says we must suffer these insults in silence! Tell me, men of Gettland, what should be our answer?"

The word came from five thousand mouths as one deafening roar, Brand's voice cracking with it. "Steel!"

"Yes." Uthil cradled his sword close, pressing the plain hilt to his deep-lined cheek as if it was a lover's face. "Steel must be the answer! Let us bring the Islanders a red day, brothers. A day they will weep at the memory of!"

With that he stalked toward Mother Sea, his closest captains and the warriors of his household behind him, storied men with famous names, men Brand dreamed of one day joining. Folk whose names had yet to trouble the bards crowded about the king's path for a glimpse of him, for a touch of his cloak, a glance of his gray eye. Shouts came of, "The Iron King!" and "Uthil!" until it became a chant, "Uthil! Uthil!" each beat marked with the steely clash of weapons.

"Time to choose your futures, boys."

Master Hunnan shook a canvas bag so the markers clattered within. The lads crowded him, shoving and honking like hogs at feeding time, and Hunnan reached inside with his gnarled fingers and one by one pressed a marker into every eager palm. Discs of wood, each with a sign carved into it that matched the prow-beasts on the many ships, telling each boy—or each man—which captain he'd swear his oath to, which crew he'd sail with, row with, fight with.

Those given their signs held them high and whooped in triumph, and some argued over who'd got the better ship or the better captain, and some laughed and hugged each other, finding the favor of Mother War had made them oarmates.

Brand waited, hand out and heart thumping. Drunk with excitement at the king's words, and the thought of the raid coming, and of being a boy no more, being poor no more, being alone no more. Drunk on the thought of doing good, and standing in the light, and having a family of warriors always about him.

Brand waited as his fellows were given their places—lads he liked and lads he didn't, good fighters and not. He waited as the markers grew fewer in the bag, and let himself wonder if he was left till last because he'd won an oar on the king's own ship, no place more coveted. The more often Hunnan passed him over, the more he allowed himself to hope. He'd earned it, hadn't he? Worked for it, deserved it? Done what a warrior of Gettland was supposed to?

Rauk was the last of them, forcing a smile onto his crestfallen face when Hunnan brought wood from the bag for him, not silver. Then it was just Brand left. His the only hand still out, the fingers trembling. The lads fell silent.

And Hunnan smiled. Brand had never seen him smile before, and he felt himself smile too.

"This for you," said the master-at-arms as he slowly, slowly drew out his battle-scarred hand. Drew out his hand to show . . .

Nothing.

No glint of the king's silver. No wood neither. Only the empty bag, turned inside out to show the ragged stitching.

"Did you think I wouldn't know?" said Hunnan.

Brand let his hand drop. Every eye was upon him now and he felt his cheeks burning like he'd been slapped.

"Know what?" he muttered, though he knew well enough.

"That you spoke to that cripple about what happened in my training square."

A silence, while Brand felt as if his guts dropped into his arse. "Thorn's no murderer," he managed to say.

"Edwal's dead and she killed him."

"You set her a test she couldn't pass."

"I set the tests," said Hunnan. "Passing them is up to you. And you failed this one."

"I did the right thing."

Hunnan's brows went up. Not angry. Surprised. "Tell yourself that if it helps. But I've my own right thing to look to. The right thing for the men I teach to fight. In the training square we pit you against each other, but on the battlefield you have to stand together, and Thorn Bathu fights everyone. Men would have died so she could play with swords. They're better off without her. And they're better off without you."

"Mother War picks who fights," said Brand.

Hunnan only shrugged. "She can find a ship for you, then. You're a good fighter, Brand, but you're not a good man. A good man stands for his shoulder-man. A good man holds the line."

Maybe Brand should've snarled, "It isn't fair," as Thorn had when Hunnan broke her hopes. But Brand wasn't much of a talker, and he had no words then. No anger in him when he actually needed it. He didn't make even a mouse's squeak while Hunnan turned and walked away. Didn't even bunch his fists while the lads followed their master-at-arms toward the sea. The lads he'd trained with these ten years.

Some looked at him with scorn, some with surprise. One or two even gave him a sorry pat on the shoulder as they passed. But they all passed. Down the beach, toward the breaking waves and their hard-won places on the ships that rocked there. Down to their oaths of loyalty and off on the raid that Brand had dreamed of all his life. It was Rauk who went last, one hand slack on the hilt of his fine new sword, grinning over his shoulder.

"See you when we get back."

Brand stood alone for a long time, not moving. Alone, in his borrowed mail, with the gulls crying over that vast stretch of sand, empty apart from the bootprints of the men he'd thought his brothers. Alone, long after the last ship had pushed off from the shore and out to sea, carrying Brand's hopes away with it.

So it goes, with hopes.

# POISON

She Who Sings the Wind sang one hell of a wind on the way over from Skekenhouse and they were washed leagues off-course.

They rowed like fury while Rulf roared abuse at them until his voice was hoarse and their oars were all tangled and every one of them was blowing like a fish and soaked with Mother Sea's salt spray. Thorn was quite extremely terrified but she put a brave face on. The only faces she had were brave, though this was a green one, as the thrashing of the ship like an unbroken horse soon made her sick as she'd never been sick in her life. It felt as if everything she'd ever eaten went over the side, over her oar, or over her knees, and half that through her nose.

Thorn had a fair storm blowing on the inside too. The giddy wave of gratitude at being given back her life had soon soaked away, leaving her chewing over the bitter truth that she had traded a future as a proud warrior for one as a minister's slave, collared by her own over-hasty oath, for purposes Father Yarvi had no intention of sharing.

To make matters even worse, she could feel her blood coming and her guts were stabbed through with aches and her chest was sore and she had a rage in her even beyond the usual. The mocking laughter of the crew at her puking might've moved her to murder if she could've unpeeled her death-gripping fingers from the oar.

So it was on wobbling legs she staggered onto the wharf at Yaletoft, the stones of Throvenland pocked with puddles from last night's storm, twinkling in this morning's sun. She blundered through the crowds with her shoulders hunched around her ears, every hawker's squawk and seagull's call, every wagon's rattle and barrel's clatter a knife in her, the over-hearty slaps on the back and snide chuckles of the men who were supposed to be her fellows cutting deeper still.

She knew what they were thinking. *What do you expect if you put a girl in a man's place?* And she muttered curses and swore elaborate revenges, but didn't dare lift her head in case she spewed again.

Some revenge that would be.

"Don't be sick in front of King Fynn," said Rulf, as they approached the looming hall, its mighty roof beams wonderfully carved and gilded. "The man's famous for his temper."

But it was not King Fynn but his minister, Mother Kyre, who greeted them at the dozen steps, each one cut of a different-colored marble. She was a handsome woman, tall and slender with a ready smile that did not quite reach her eyes. She reminded Thorn of her mother, which was a dark mark against her from the off. Thorn trusted few enough people, but hardly any had ready smiles and none at all looked like her mother.

"Greetings, Father Yarvi," said King Fynn's handsome minister. "You are ever welcome in Yaletoft, but I fear the king cannot see you."

"I fear you have advised him not to see me," answered Father Yarvi, planting one damp boot on the lowest step. Mother Kyre did not deny it. "Perhaps I might see Princess Skara? She can have been no more than ten years old when we last met. We were cousins then, before I took the Minister's Test—"

"But you did take the test," said Mother Kyre, "and gave up all your family but the Ministry, as did I. In any case, the princess is away."

"I fear you sent her away when you heard I was coming."

Mother Kyre did not deny that either. "Grandmother Wexen has sent me an eagle, and I know why you are here. I am not without sympathy."

"Your sympathy is sweet, Mother Kyre, but King Fynn's help in the trouble that comes would be far sweeter yet. It might prevent the trouble altogether."

Mother Kyre winced the way someone does who has no intention of helping. The way Thorn's mother used to wince when Thorn spoke of her hero's hopes.

"You know my master loves you and his niece Queen Laithlin," she said. "You know he would stand against half the world to stand with you. But you know he cannot stand against the wishes of the High King." A sea of words, this woman, but that was ministers for you. Father Yarvi was hardly a straight talker. "So he sends me, wretched with regret, to deny you audience, but to humbly offer you all food, warmth, and shelter beneath his roof."

Which, apart from the food, sounded well enough to Thorn.

King Fynn's hall was called the Forest for it was filled with a thicket of grand columns, said to have been floated down the Divine River from Kalyiv, beautifully carved and painted with scenes from the history of Throvenland. Somewhat less beautiful were the many, many guards, closely watching the *South Wind*'s disheveled crew as they shuffled past, Thorn most disheveled of all, one hand clutched to her aching belly.

"Our reception in Skekenhouse was . . . not warm." Yarvi leaned close to Mother Kyre and Thorn heard his whisper. "If I didn't know better I might say I am in danger."

"No danger will find you here, Father Yarvi, I assure you." Mother Kyre gestured at two of the most unreassuring guards Thorn had ever seen, flanking the door to a common room that stank of stale smoke.

"Here you have water." She pointed out a barrel as if it was the highest of gifts. "Slaves will bring food and ale. A room for your crew to sleep in is made ready. No doubt you will wish to be away with the first glimpse of Mother Sun, to catch the tide and carry your news to King Uthil."

Yarvi scrubbed unhappily at his pale hair with the heel of his twisted hand. "It seems you have thought of everything."

"A good minister is always prepared." And Mother Kyre shut the door as she left them, lacking only the turning of a key to mark them out as prisoners.

"As warm a welcome as you thought we'd get," grunted Rulf.

"Fynn and his minister are predictable as Father Moon. They are cautious. They live in the shadow of the High King's power, after all."

"A long shadow, that," said Rulf.

"Lengthening all the time. You look a little green, Thorn Bathu."

"I'm sick with disappointment to find no allies in Throvenland," she said.

Father Yarvi had the slightest smile. "We shall see."

THORN'S EYES SNAPPED OPEN in the fizzing darkness.

She was chilly with sweat under her blanket, kicked it off, felt the sticky wetness of blood between her legs and hissed a curse.

Beside her Rulf gave a particularly ripping snore then rolled over. She could hear the rest of the crew breathing, wriggling, muttering in their sleep, squashed in close together on dirty mats, tight as the fresh catch on market day.

They had made no special arrangements for her and she had asked for none. She wanted none. None except a fresh cloth down her trousers, anyway.

She stumbled down the corridor, hair in a tangle and guts in an aching knot, her belt undone with the buckle slapping at her thighs and one hand shoved down her trousers to feel how bad the bleeding was. All she needed to stop the mocking was a great stain around her crotch, and she cursed He Who Sprouts the Seed for inflicting this stupid business on her, and she cursed the stupid women who thought it was something to celebrate, her stupid mother first among them, and she cursed—

There was a man in the shadows of the common room.

He was dressed in black and standing near the water butt. In one hand he held its lid. In the other a little jar. As if he'd just poured something in. The place was lit by only one guttering candle and he had a bad squint, but Thorn got the distinct feeling he was staring right at her.

They stood unmoving, he with his jar over the water, she with her hand down her trousers, then the man said, "Who are you?"

"Who am I? Who are you?"

*Know where your nearest weapon is,* her father used to tell her, and her eyes flickered to the table where the wreckage of their evening meal was scattered. An eating knife was wedged into the wood, short blade faintly gleaming. Hardly a hero's blade, but when surprised at night with your belt open you take what you can get.

She gently eased her hand out of her trousers, gently eased toward the table and the knife. The man gently eased the jar away, eyes fixed on her, or at least somewhere near her.

"You're not supposed to be here," he said.

"*I'm* not? What're you putting in our water?"

"What're you doing with that knife?"

She wrenched it from the table and held it out, somewhat shaky, her voice high. "Is that poison?"

The man tossed down the barrel's lid and stepped toward her. "Now don't do anything stupid, girl." As he turned she saw he had a sword at his belt, his right hand reaching for the hilt.

Perhaps she panicked then. Or perhaps she thought more clearly than she ever had. Before she knew it she sprang at him, caught his wrist with one hand and drove the knife into his chest with the other.

It wasn't hard to do. Much easier than you'd think.

He heaved in a wheezing breath, sword no more than quarter drawn, eyes more crossed than ever, pawing at her shoulder.

"You . . ." And he crashed over on his back, dragging her on top of him.

Thorn tore his limp hand away and struggled up. His black clothes turned blacker as blood soaked them, the eating knife wedged in his heart to the handle.

She squeezed her eyes shut, but when she opened them, he was still there.

Not a dream.

"Oh, gods," she whispered.

"They rarely help." Father Yarvi stood frowning in the doorway. "What happened?"

"He had poison," muttered Thorn, pointing weakly at the fallen jar. "Or . . . I think he did . . ."

The minister squatted beside the dead man. "You have a habit of killing people, Thorn Bathu."

"That's a bad thing," she said in a voice very small.

"It does rather depend on who you kill." Yarvi slowly stood, looked about the room, walked over to her, peering at her face. "He hit you?"

"Well . . . no—"

"Yes." He punched her in the mouth and she sprawled against the table. By then he was already throwing the door wide. "Bloodshed in King Fynn's Hall! To arms! To arms!"

First came Rulf, who blinked down at the corpse and softly said, "That works."

Then came guards, who blinked down at the corpse and made their weapons ready.

Then came the crew, who shook their shaggy heads and rubbed their stubbled jaws and murmured prayers.

And finally came King Fynn.

Thorn had moved among the powerful since she killed Edwal. She had met five ministers and three kings, one of them High, and the only one to impress her was the one who killed her father. Fynn might have been famed for his anger, but the first thing that struck Thorn was what a strangely shapeless man the King of Throvenland was. His chin melted into his neck, his neck into his shoulders, his shoulders into his belly, his sparse gray hairs in wafting disarray from the royal bed.

"Kneeling isn't your strength, is it?" hissed Rulf, dragging Thorn down along with everyone else. "And for the gods' sake fasten your damn belt!"

"What happened here?" roared the king, spraying his wincing guards with spit.

Thorn kept her eyes down as she fumbled with her buckle. Crushing with rocks looked inevitable now. Certainly for her. Possibly for the rest of the crew too. She saw the looks on their faces. *This is what happens if you give a girl a blade. Even a little one.*

Mother Kyre, immaculate even in her nightclothes, took up the fallen jar between finger and thumb, sniffed at it and wrinkled her nose. "Ugh! Poison, my king."

"By the gods!" Yarvi put his hand on Thorn's shoulder. The same hand he had just punched her with. "If it wasn't for this girl's quick thinking, I and my crew might have passed through the Last Door before morning."

"Search every corner of my hall!" bellowed King Fynn. "Tell me how this bastard got in!"

A warrior who had knelt to root through the dead man's clothes held out his palm, silver glinting. "Coins, my king. Minted in Skekenhouse."

"There is altogether too much from Skekenhouse in my hall of late." Fynn's quivering jowls had a pink flush. "Grandmother Wexen's coins, Grandmother Wexen's eagles, Grandmother Wexen's demands too. Demands of me, the King of Throvenland!"

"But think of your people's welfare, my king," coaxed Mother Kyre, still clinging to her smile, but it hardly touched her mouth now, let alone her eyes. "Think of Father Peace, Father of Doves, who makes of the fist—"

"I have suffered many indignities on behalf of Father Peace." The flush had spread to King Fynn's cheeks. "Once the High King was the first among brothers. Now he gives a father's commands. How men should fight. How women should trade. How all should pray. Temples to the One God spring up across Throvenland like mushrooms after the rains, and I have held my tongue!"

"You were wise to do so," said Mother Kyre, "and would be wise to—"

"Now Grandmother Wexen sends assassins to my land?"

"My king, we have no proof at all—"

Fynn bellowed over his minister, doughy face heating from pink to blazing crimson. "To my very house? To poison my guests?" He stabbed at the corpse with one sausage of a finger. "Beneath my own roof and under my protection?"

"I would counsel caution—"

"You always do, Mother Kyre, but there is a limit on my forbearance, and the High King has stepped over it!" With face now fully purple he seized Father Yarvi's good hand. "Tell my beloved niece Queen Laithlin and her honored husband that they have a friend in me. A friend whatever the costs! I swear it!"

Mother Kyre had no smile ready for this moment, but Father Yarvi certainly did. "Your friendship is all they ask for." And he lifted King Fynn's hand high.

The guards cheered this unexpected alliance between Throvenland and Gettland with some surprise, the *South Wind*'s crew with great relief, and Thorn Bathu should no doubt have applauded loudest of all. Killing a man by accident had made her a villain. Killing another on purpose had made her a hero.

But all she could do was frown at the body as they dragged it out, and feel there was something very odd in all this.

# LOST AND FOUND

Brand was proper drunk.

He often had been, lately.

Lifting on the docks was the best work he could find, and a day of that was thirsty work indeed. So he'd started drinking, and found he'd a real gift for it. Seemed he'd inherited something from his father after all.

The raid had been a mighty success. The Islanders were so sure the High King's favor would protect them they were taken unawares, half their ships captured and half the rest burned. Brand had watched the warriors of Gettland swagger up through the twisting streets of Thorlby when they landed, laden with booty and covered in glory and cheered from every window. He heard Rauk took two slaves, and Sordaf got himself a silver arm-ring. He heard Uthil dragged old King Styr naked from his hall, made him kneel and swear a sun-oath and a moon-oath never to draw a blade against another Gettlander.

All heroes' news, like something from the songs, but there's nothing like others' successes to make your own failures sting the worse.

Brand walked the crooked walk down some alley or other, between some houses or other, and shouted at the stars. Someone shouted back. Maybe the stars, maybe from a window. He didn't care. He didn't know where he was going. Didn't seem to matter anymore.

He was lost.

"I'm worried," Rin had said.

"Try having all your dreams stolen," he'd spat at her.

What could she say to that?

He tried to give her the dagger back. "I don't need it and I don't deserve it."

"I made it for you," she'd said. "I'm proud of you whatever." Nothing made her cry but she had tears in her eyes then, and they hurt worse than any beating he'd ever taken and he'd taken plenty.

So he asked Fridlif to fill his cup again. And again. And again. And Fridlif shook her gray head to see a young life wasted and all, but it was hardly the first time. Filling cups was what she did.

At least when he was drunk Brand could pretend other people were to blame. Hunnan, Thorn, Rauk, Father Yarvi, the gods, the stars above, the stones under his feet. Sober, he got to thinking he'd brought this on himself.

He blundered into a wall in the darkness and it spun him about, the anger flared up hot and he roared, "I did good!" He threw a punch at the wall and missed, which was lucky, and fell in the gutter, which wasn't.

Then he was sick on his hands.

"Are you Brand?"

"I was," he said, rocking back on his knees and seeing the outline of a man, or maybe two.

"The same Brand who trained with Thorn Bathu?"

He snorted at that, but his snorting tasted of sick and nearly made him spew again. "Sadly."

"Then this is for you."

Cold water slapped him in the face and he spluttered on it, tried to scramble up and slipped over in the gutter. An empty bucket skittered away across the cobbles. Brand scraped the wet hair out of his eyes, saw a strip of lamplight across an old face, creased and lined, scarred and bearded.

"I should hit you for that, you old bastard," he said, but getting up hardly seemed worth the effort.

"But then I'd hit you back, and a broken face won't mend your troubles. I know. I've tried it." The old man put hands on knees and leaned down close. "Thorn said you were the best she used to train with. You don't look like the best of anything to me, boy."

"Time hasn't been kind."

"Time never is. A fighter keeps fighting even so. Thought you were a fighter?"

"I was," said Brand.

The old man held out his broad hand. "Good. My name's Rulf, and I've got a fight for you."


THEY'D MADE THE TORCHLIT storehouse up like a training square, ropes on the old boards marking the edge. There wasn't as big an audience as Brand was used to, but what there was made him want to be sick again.

On one of the stools, with the key to the kingdom's treasury gleaming on her chest, sat Laithlin, Golden Queen of Gettland. Beside her was the man who had once been her son and was now her minister, Father Yarvi. Behind them were four silver-collared slaves—two huge Inglings with hard axes at their belts and even harder frowns on their rock-chiselled faces, and two girls like as the halves of a walnut, each with braids so long they had them looped around and around one arm.

And leaning against the far wall with one boot up on the stonework and that mocking little lop-sided smile on her lips was Brand's least favorite sparring partner, Thorn Bathu.

And the strange thing was, though he'd spent long drunk hours blaming her for all his woes, Brand was happy to see her face. Happier than he'd been in a long while. Not because he liked her so much, but because the sight of her reminded him of a time when he liked himself. When he could see his future, and liked what he saw. When his hopes stood tall and the world seemed full of dares.

"Thought you'd never get here." She worked her arm into the straps of a shield and picked out a wooden sword.

"Thought they crushed you with rocks," said Brand.

"It's still very much a possibility," said Father Yarvi.

Rulf gave Brand a shove between the shoulderblades and sent him tottering into the square. "Get to it, then, lad."

Brand knew he didn't have the fastest mind, and it was far from its fastest then, but he got the gist. He walked almost a straight line to the practice weapons and picked out a sword and shield, keenly aware of the queen's cold eyes judging his every movement.

Thorn was already taking her mark. "You're a sorry bloody sight," she said.

Brand looked down at his vest, soaked and somewhat sick-stained, and had to nod. "Aye."

That wrinkle to her mouth twisted into a full sneer. "Weren't you always telling me you'd be a rich man after your first raid?"

That stung. "I didn't go."

"Hadn't marked you for a coward."

That stung more. She'd always known how to sting him. "I didn't get picked," he grunted.

Thorn burst out laughing, no doubt showing off in front of the queen. She'd never tired of spouting how much she admired the woman. "Here's me full of envy, expecting you all puffed up like a hero, and what do I find but some drunk beggar-boy?"

Brand felt a cold flush through him then, sweeping the drink away more surely than any ice water. He'd done more than his share of begging, that was true. But it's the true ones that sting.

Thorn was still chuckling at her cleverness. "You always were an idiot. Hunnan stole my place, how did you toss yours away?"

Brand would've liked to tell her how he'd lost his place. He would've liked to scream it in her face, but he couldn't get the words out because he'd started growling like an animal, growling louder and louder until the room throbbed with it, and his chest hummed with it, his lips curled back and his jaw clenched so hard it seemed his teeth would shatter, and Thorn was frowning at him over the rim of her shield like he'd gone mad. Maybe he had.

"Begin!" shouted Rulf, and he was on her, hacked her sword away, struck back so hard he sent splinters from her shield. She twisted, quick, she'd always been deadly quick, made enough space to swing but he wasn't hesitating this time.

He shrugged the blow off his shoulder, barely felt it, bellowed as he pressed in blindly, driving her staggering back, shield-rims grinding together, almost lifting her as she tripped over the rope and crashed into the wall. She tried to twist her sword free but he still had it pinned useless over his shoulder, and he caught her shield with his left hand and dragged it down. Too close for weapons, he flung his practice blade away and started punching her, all his anger and his disappointment in it, as if she was Hunnan, and Yarvi, and all those so-called friends of his who'd done so well from doing nothing, stolen his place, stolen his future.

He hit her in the side and heard her groan, hit her again and she folded up, eyes bulging, hit her again and she went down hard, coughing and retching at his feet. He might've been about to set to kicking her when Rulf caught him around the neck with one thick forearm and dragged him back.

"That's enough, I reckon."

"Aye," he muttered, going limp. "More'n enough."

He shook the shield off his arm, shocked of a sudden at what he'd done and nowhere near proud of it, knowing full well what it felt like on the other side of a beating like that. Maybe there was more than one thing he'd inherited from his father. He didn't feel like he was standing in the light right then. Not at all.

Queen Laithlin gave a long sigh, Thorn's coughing and dribbling in the background, and turned on her stool. "I was wondering when you'd arrive."

And it was only then Brand noticed another watcher, slouched in the shadows of a corner in a cloak of rags every shade of gray. "Always when I am sorest needed and least expected." A woman's voice from within the hood and a strange accent on it. "Or hungry."

"Did you see it?" asked Yarvi.

"I had that questionable privilege."

"What do you think?"

"She is wretched. She is all pride and anger. She has too much confidence and too little. She does not know herself." The figure pushed back her hood. A black-skinned old woman with a face lean as famine and hair shaved to gray fuzz. She picked her nose with one long forefinger, carefully examined the results, then flicked them away. "The girl is stupid as a stump. Worse. Most stumps have the dignity to rot quietly without causing offense."

"I'm right here," Thorn managed to hiss from her hands and knees.

"Just where the drunk boy put you." The woman flashed a smile at Brand that seemed to have too many teeth. "I like him, though: he is pretty and desperate. My favorite combination."

"Can anything be done with her?" asked Yarvi.

"Something can always be done, given enough effort." The woman peeled herself away from the wall. She had the strangest way of walking—wriggling, jerking, strutting—as though she was dancing to music only she could hear. "How much effort will you pay for me to waste upon her worthless carcass, is the question? You owe me already, after all." A long arm snaked from her cloak with something in the hand.

It was a box perhaps the size of a child's head—dark, square, perfect, with golden writing etched into the lid. Brand found his eyes drawn to it. It took an effort not to step closer, to look closer. Thorn was staring too. And Rulf. And the queen's thralls. All fascinated and afraid at once, as if by the sight of a terrible wound. None of them could read, of course, but you did not have to be a minister to know those were elf-letters on the box. Letters written before the Breaking of God.

Father Yarvi swallowed, and with the one finger of his crippled hand eased the box open. Whatever was inside, a pale light shone from it. A light that picked out the hollows of the minister's face as his mouth fell open, that reflected in Queen Laithlin's widening eyes which a moment before Brand had thought nothing could surprise.

"By the gods," she whispered. "You have it."

The woman gave an extravagant bow, the hem of her cloak sending up a wash of straw-dust from the storehouse floor. "I deliver what I promise, my most gilded of queens."

"Then it still works?"

"Shall I make it turn?"

"No," said Father Yarvi. "Make it turn for the Empress of the South, not before."

"There is the question of—"

Without taking her eyes from the box, the Queen held out a folded paper. "Your debts are all canceled."

"The very question I had in mind." The black-skinned woman frowned as she took it between two fingers. "I have been called a witch before but here is sorcery indeed, to trap such a weight of gold in a scrap of paper."

"We live in changing times," murmured Father Yarvi, and he snapped the box shut, putting the light out with it. Only then Brand realized he'd been holding his breath, and slowly let it out. "Find us a crew, Rulf, you know the kind."

"Hard ones, I'm guessing," said the old warrior.

"Oarsmen and fighters. The outcasts and the desperate. Men who don't get weak at the thought of blood or the sight of it. The journey is long and the stakes could not be higher. I want men with nothing to lose."

"My kind of crew!" The black-skinned woman slapped her thigh. "Sign me up first!" She slipped between the stools and strutted over toward Brand, and for a moment her cloak of rags came open and he saw the glint of steel. "Can I buy you a drink, young man?"

"I think the boy has drunk enough." Queen Laithlin's gray eyes were on him, and the eyes of her four slaves as well, and Brand swallowed, his sick-tasting mouth suddenly very dry. "Though my first husband gave me two sons, for which I will always be grateful, he drank too much. It spoils a bad man. It ruins a good one."

"I . . . have decided to stop, my queen," mumbled Brand. He knew then he wasn't going back. Not to the ale-cup, nor to begging, nor to lifting on the docks.

The black woman puffed out her cheeks in disappointment as she made for the door. "Young people these days have no ambition in them."

Laithlin ignored her. "The way you fight reminds me of an old friend."

"Thank you—"

"Don't. I had to kill him." And the queen of Gettland swept out, her slaves following in her wake.

"I've a crew to gather." Rulf took Brand under the arm. "And no doubt your gutter's missing you—"

"It'll manage without me." Rulf was strong but Brand wouldn't be moved. He'd remembered how it felt to fight, and how it felt to win, and he was more sure of the good thing to do than he'd ever been in his life. "Luck's with you, old man," he said. "Now you need to gather one less."

Rulf snorted. "This ain't no two-day jaunt, boy, nor even a raid to the Islands. We're headed far up the Divine River and down the Denied, over the tall hauls and beyond. We go to speak to the Prince of Kalyiv. To seek an audience with the Empress of the South in the First of Cities, even! All kinds of dangers on that journey, even if you're not seeking allies against the most powerful man in the world. We'll be gone months. If we come back at all."

Brand swallowed. Dangers, no doubt, but opportunities too. Men won glory on the Divine. Men won fortunes beyond it. "You need oarsmen?" he said. "I can pull an oar. You need loads lifted? I can lift a load. You need fighters?" Brand nodded toward Thorn, who'd managed to stand, wincing as she kneaded at her battered ribs. "I can fight. You want men with nothing to lose? Look no further."

Rulf opened his mouth but Father Yarvi spoke over him. "The way may be hard, but we go to smooth the path for Father Peace. We go to find allies." The minister gave Brand the slightest nod. "We might need one man aboard who spares some thought for doing good. Give him a marker, Rulf."

The old warrior scratched at his gray beard. "Yours'll be the lowest place, boy. The worst work for the thinnest rewards. Back oar." He jerked his head over at Thorn. "Opposite that article."

Thorn gave Brand a long, hard frown and spat, but it only made him smile wider. He saw his future once again, and he liked what he saw. Compared to lifting loads on the docks, he liked it a lot.

"Looking forward to it." He plucked the marker from Rulf's hand, the minister's dove carved into the face, and he wrapped his fingers painfully tight about it.

It seemed Mother War had found a crew for him after all. Or Father Peace had.

II.

DIVINE
AND DENIED

# THE FIRST
# LESSON

The *South Wind* rocked on the tide, boasting new oars and a new sail, freshly painted and freshly provisioned, lean and sleek as a racing dog and with minister's doves gleaming white at high prow and stern. It was, without doubt, a beautiful ship. A ship fit for high deeds and heroes' songs.

Sadly, her new crew were not quite of that caliber.

"They seem a . . ." Thorn's mother always found a pretty way to put things, but even she was stumped. "*Varied* group."

" 'Fearsome' is the word I'd have reached for," grunted Thorn.

She might well have tripped over "desperate," "disgusting" or "axbitten" on the way. All three seemed apt for the gathering of the damned crawling over the *South Wind* and the wharf beside it, hefting sacks and barrels, hauling at ropes, shoving, bellowing, laughing, threatening, all under Father Yarvi's watchful eye.

Fighting men, these, but more like bandits than warriors. Men with many scars and few scruples. Men with beards forked and braided and shaved in strange patches and dyed hair chopped into spikes. Men whose clothes were ragged but whose muscled arms and thick necks and calloused fingers glittered with gold and silver ring-money, proclaiming to the world the high value they put on themselves.

Thorn wondered what mountain of corpses this lot might have heaped up between them, but she wasn't one to be easily intimidated. Especially when she had no choice. She set down her sea-chest, everything she had inside, her father's old sword wrapped in an oilcloth on top. She put on her bravest face, stepped up to the biggest man she could see and tapped him on the arm.

"I'm Thorn Bathu."

"I am Dosduvoi." She found herself staring sharply up at one of the biggest heads she ever saw, tiny features squeezed into the center of its doughy expanse, looming so high above her that at first she thought its owner must be standing on a box. "What bad luck brings you here, girl?" he asked, with a faintly tragic quiver to his voice.

She wished she had a different answer, but snapped out, "I'm sailing with you."

His face retreated into an even tinier portion of his head as he frowned. "Along the Divine River, to Kalyiv and beyond?"

She thrust her chin up at him in the usual manner. "If the boat floats with so much meat aboard."

"Reckon we'll have to balance the benches with some little ones." This from a man small and hard as Dosduvoi was huge and soft. He had the spikiest shag of red hair and the maddest eyes, bright blue, shining wet and sunken in dark sockets. "My name is Odda, famed about the Shattered Sea."

"Famed for what?"

"All kinds of things." He flashed a yellow wolf-smile and she saw his teeth were filed across the front with killer's grooves. "Can't wait to sail with you."

"Likewise," Thorn managed to croak, stepping back despite herself and nearly tripping over someone else. He looked up as she turned and, brave face or no, she shrank back the other way. A huge scar started at the corner of one eye, all dragged out of shape to show the pink lid, angled across his stubbled cheek and through both lips. To make matters worse, she realized from his hair, long and braided back around his face, that they would be sailing with a Vansterman.

He met her ill-concealed horror with a mutilated blankness more terrible than any snarl and said mildly, "I am Fror."

It was either bluster or look weak and Thorn reckoned that no choice at all, so she puffed herself up and snapped out, "How did you get the scar?"

"How did *you* get the scar?"

Thorn frowned. "What scar?"

"That's the face the gods gave you?" And with the faintest of smiles the Vansterman went back to coiling rope.

"Father Peace protect us," squeaked Thorn's mother as she edged past. "Fearsome is a fair word for them."

"They'll be the ones scared of me soon enough," said Thorn, wishing, and not for the first time, that saying a thing firmly enough makes it so.

"That's a good thing?" Her mother stared at a shaven-headed man with runes stating his crimes tattooed on his face, laughing jaggedly with a bony fellow whose arms were covered in flaking sores. "To be feared by men like these?"

"Better to be feared than afraid." Her father's words and, as always, her mother was ready for them.

"Are those life's only two choices?"

"They're a warrior's two choices." Whenever Thorn traded more than ten words with her mother she somehow ended up defending an indefensible position. She knew what came next. *Why fight so hard to be a warrior if all you can win is fear?* But her mother only shut her mouth, and looked pale and scared, and piled guilt on Thorn's simmering anger. As ever.

"You can always go back to the house," snapped Thorn.

"I want to see my only child on her way. Can't you give me that? Father Yarvi says you might be gone a year." Her mother's voice took on an infuriating quiver. "If you come back at all—"

"Fear not, my doves!" Thorn jumped as someone flung an arm

around her shoulders. The strange woman who had watched Thorn fight Brand a few days before thrust her gray-stubbled skull between her and her mother. "For the wise Father Yarvi has placed your daughter's education in my dextrous hands."

Thorn hadn't thought her spirits could drop any lower, but the gods had found a way. "Education?"

The woman hugged them tighter, her smell a heady mix of sweat, incense, herbs and piss. "It's where I teach and you learn."

"And who . . ." Thorn's mother gave the ragged woman a nervous look, "or what . . . are you?"

"Lately, a thief." When that sharpened nervousness into alarm she added brightly, "but also an experienced killer! And navigator, wrestler, stargazer, explorer, historian, poet, blackmailer, brewer . . . I may have forgotten a few. Not to mention an accomplished amateur prophet!"

The old woman scraped a spatter of fresh bird-droppings from a post, tested its texture with her thumb, smelled it closely, seemed on the point of tasting it, then decided against and wiped the mess on her ragged cloak.

"Inauspicious," she grunted, peering up at the wheeling gulls. "Add to all that my unchallenged expertise in . . ." she gave a suggestive wiggling of the hips, "*the romantic arts* and you can see, my doves, there are few areas of interest to the modern girl in which I am not richly qualified to instruct your daughter."

Thorn should have enjoyed the rare sight of her mother rendered speechless, but was, for once, speechless herself.

"Thorn Bathu!" Rulf shouldered his way through the bustle. "You're late! Get your skinny arse down the wharf and start shifting those sacks. Your friend Brand has already . . ." He swallowed. "I didn't know you had a sister."

Thorn sourly worked her tongue. "Mother."

"Surely not!" Rulf combed at his beard with his fingers in a vain attempt to tame the brown-and-gray tangle. "If you can suffer a compliment from a plain old fighting man, your beauty lights these docks up like a lamp at twilight." He glanced at the silver key on her chest. "Your husband must be—"

Thorn's mother could suffer the compliment. Indeed she clutched it with both hands. "Dead," she said quickly. "Eight years, now, since we howed him up."

"Sorry to hear that." Though Rulf sounded, in fact, anything but sorry. "I'm Rulf, helmsman of the *South Wind*. The crew may seem rough but I've learned never to trust a smooth one. I picked these men and each knows his business. Thorn'll be rowing right beneath my beard and I'll treat her with just as soft a heart and firm a hand as I would my own daughter."

Thorn rolled her eyes, but it was wasted effort. "You have children?" her mother asked.

"Two sons, but it's years since I saw them. The gods parted me from my family for too long."

"Any chance they could part you from mine?" grunted Thorn.

"Shush," hissed her mother, without taking her eyes from Rulf, and the thick-linked golden chain he wore in particular. "It will be a great comfort to know that a man of your quality looks to my daughter's welfare. Prickly though she may be, Hild is all I have."

A lot of strong wind and no doubt not a little strong ale had rendered Rulf ruddy about the cheeks already, but Thorn thought she saw him blush even so. "As for being a man of quality you'll find many to disagree, but as to looking to your daughter's welfare I promise to do my best."

Thorn's mother flashed a simpering smile. "What else can any of us promise?"

"Gods," hissed Thorn, turning away. The one thing she hated worse than being fussed over was being ignored.

Brinyolf the Prayer-Weaver had wrought murder on some unwitting animal and was daubing its blood on the *South Wind*'s prow-beast, red to the wrists as he wailed out a blessing to Mother Sea and She Who Finds the Course and He Who Steers the Arrow and a dozen other small gods whose names Thorn had never even heard before. She'd never been much for prayers and had her doubts the weather was that interested in them either.

"How does a girl end up on a fighting crew?"

She turned to see a young lad had stolen up on her. Thorn judged him maybe fourteen years, slight, with a bright eye and a twitchy quickness to him, a mop of sandy hair and the first hints of beard on his sharp jaw.

She frowned back. "You saying I shouldn't be?"

"Not up to me who gets picked." He shrugged, neither scared nor scornful. "I'm just asking how you did."

"Leave her be!" A small, lean woman gave the lad a neat cuff around the ear. "Didn't I tell you to make yourself useful?" Some bronze weights swung on a cord around her neck while she herded him off toward the *South Wind,* which made her a merchant, or a storekeeper, trusted to measure fairly.

"I'm Safrit," she said, planting her hands on her hips. "The lad with all the questions is my son Koll. He's yet to realize that the more you learn the more you understand the size of your own ignorance. He means no harm."

"Nor do I," said Thorn, "but I seem to cause a lot even so."

Safrit grinned. "It's a habit with some of us. I'm along to mind the stores, and cook, and watch the cargo. Fingers off, understand?"

"I thought we were aiming to win friends for Gettland? We're carrying cargo too?"

"Furs and tree-tears and walrus ivory among . . . other things." Safrit frowned toward an iron-shod chest chained up near the mast. "Our first mission is to talk for Father Peace but Queen Laithlin paid for this expedition."

"Ha! And there's a woman who never in her life missed out on a profit!"

"Why would I?"

Thorn turned again to find herself looking straight into the queen's face at a distance of no more than a stride. Some folk are more impressive from far off but Laithlin was the opposite, as radiant as

Mother Sun and stern as Mother War, the great key to the treasury shining on her chest, her thralls and guards and servants in a disapproving press behind her.

"Oh, gods . . . I mean, forgive me, my queen." Thorn wobbled down to one knee, lost her balance and nearly caught Laithlin's silken skirts to steady herself. "Sorry, I've never been much good at kneeling—"

"Perhaps you should practice." The queen was about as unlike Thorn's mother as was possible for two women of an age—not soppy soft and circumspect but hard and brilliant as a cut diamond, direct as a punch in the face.

"It's an honor to sail with you as patron," Thorn blathered. "I swear I'll give your son the very best service—Father Yarvi, that is," realizing he wasn't supposed to be her son any longer. "I'll give your minister the very best service—"

"You are the girl who swore to give that boy a beating just before he gave you one." The Golden Queen raised a brow. "Fools boast of what they will do. Heroes do it." She summoned one of her servants with a snap of her fingers and was already murmuring instructions as she swept past.

Thorn might never have got off her knees had Safrit not hooked her under the arm and dragged her up. "I'd say she likes you."

"How does she treat folk she doesn't like?"

"Pray you never find out." Safrit clutched at her head as she saw her son had swarmed up the mast nimbly as a monkey and was perched on the yard high above, checking the knots that held the sail. "Gods damn it, Koll, get down from there!"

"You told me to be useful!" he called back, letting go the beam with both hands to give an extravagant shrug.

"And how useful will you be when you plummet to your doom, you fool?"

"I'm so pleased to see you're joining us." Thorn turned once more to find Father Yarvi at her side, the old bald woman with him.

"Swore an oath, didn't I?" Thorn muttered back.

"To do whatever service I think fit, as I recall."

The black woman chuckled softly to herself. "Oooh, but that wording's awfully vague."

"Isn't it?" said Yarvi. "Glad to see you're making yourself known to the crew."

Thorn glanced around at them, worked her mouth sourly as she saw her mother and Rulf still deep in conversation. "They seem a noble fellowship."

"Nobility is overrated. You met Skifr, did you?"

"You're Skifr?" Thorn stared at the black-skinned woman with new eyes. "The thief of elf-relics? The murderer? The one sorely wanted by Grandmother Wexen?"

Skifr sniffed at her fingers, still slightly smeared with gray, and frowned as though she could not guess how bird droppings might have got there. "As for being a thief, the relics were just lying in Strokom. Let the elves impeach me! As for being a murderer, well, the difference between murderer and hero is all in the standing of the dead. As for being wanted, well, my sunny disposition has made me always popular. Father Yarvi has hired me to do . . . various things, but among them, for reasons best known to himself," and she pressed her long forefinger into Thorn's chest, "to teach you to fight."

"I can fight," growled Thorn, drawing herself up to her most fighting height.

Skifr threw back her shaved head and laughed. "Not that risible stomping about I saw. Father Yarvi is paying me to make you deadly." And with blinding speed Skifr slapped Thorn across the face, hard enough to knock her against a barrel.

"What was that for?" she said, one hand to her stinging cheek.

"Your first lesson. Always be ready. If I can hit you, you deserve to be hit."

"I suppose the same would go for you."

Skifr gave a huge smile. "Of course."

Thorn dived at her but caught only air. She stumbled, her arm suddenly twisted behind her, and the slimy boards of the wharf smashed her in the face. Her fighting scream became a wheeze of shock and then, as her little finger was savagely twisted, a long moan of pain.

"Do you still suppose I have nothing to teach you?"

"No! No!" whimpered Thorn, writhing helplessly as fire shot through every joint in her arm. "I'm keen to learn!"

"And your first lesson?"

"If I can be hit I deserve it!"

Her finger was released. "Pain is the best schoolmaster, as you will soon discover."

Thorn clambered to her knees, shaking out her throbbing arm, to find her old friend Brand standing over her, a sack on his shoulder and a grin on his face.

Skifr grinned back. "Funny, eh?"

"Little bit," said Brand.

Skifr slapped him across the cheek and he tottered against a post, dropped his sack on his foot, and was left stupidly blinking. "Are you teaching me to fight?"

"No. But I see no reason you shouldn't be ready too."

"Thorn?" Her mother was offering a hand to help her up. "What happened?"

Thorn pointedly didn't take it. "I suppose you'd know if you'd been seeing your daughter off instead of snaring our helmsman."

"Gods, Hild, you've no forgiving in you at all, have you?"

"My father called me Thorn, damn it!"

"Oh, your father, yes, him you'll forgive anything—"

"Maybe because he's dead."

Thorn's mother's eyes were already brimming with tears, as usual. "Sometimes I think you'd be happier if I joined him."

"Sometimes I think I would be!" And Thorn dragged up her sea-chest, her father's sword rattling inside as she swung it onto her shoulder and stomped toward the ship.

"I like that contrary temperament of hers," she heard Skifr saying behind her. "We'll soon have that flowing down the right channels."

One by one they clambered aboard and set their sea-chests at their places. Much to Thorn's disgust Brand took the other back oar, the two of them wedged almost into each other's laps by the tapering of the ship's sides.

"Just don't jog my elbow," she growled, in a filthier mood than ever.

Brand wearily shook his head. "I'll just throw myself in the sea, shall I?"

"Could you? That'd be perfect."

"Gods," muttered Rulf, at his place on the steering platform above them. "Will I have to listen to you two snap at each other all the way up the Divine like a pair of mating cats?"

"More than likely," said Father Yarvi, squinting up. The sky was thick with cloud, Mother Sun barely even a smudge. "Poor weather for picking out a course."

"Bad weatherluck," moaned Dosduvoi, from his oar somewhere near the middle of the boat. "Awful weatherluck."

Rulf puffed out his grizzled cheeks. "Times like this I wish Sumael was here."

"Times like this and every other time," said Father Yarvi, with a heavy sigh.

"Who's Sumael?" muttered Brand.

Thorn shrugged. "How the hell should I know who he is? No one tells me anything."

Queen Laithlin watched them push away with one palm on her child-swollen belly, gave Father Yarvi a terse nod, then turned and was gone toward the city, her gaggle of thralls and servants scurrying after. This crew were men who blew with the wind, so there was only a sorry little gathering left to wave them off. Thorn's mother was one, tears streaking her cheeks and her hand raised in farewell until the wharf was a distant speck, then the citadel of Thorlby only a jagged notching, then Gettland fading into the gray distance above the gray line of Mother Sea.

The thing about rowing, you face backward. Always looking into the past, never the future. Always seeing what you're losing, never what you've got to gain.

Thorn put a brave face on it, as always, but a brave face can be a brittle thing. Rulf's narrowed eyes were fixed ahead on the horizon. Brand kept to his stroke. If either of them saw her dashing the tears on her sleeve they had nothing to say about it.

# THE SECOND
# LESSON

Roystock was a reeking spew of wooden shops, piled one on the other and crammed onto a rotting island at the mouth of the Divine River. The place spilled over with yammering beggars and swaggering raiders, rough-handed dockers and smooth-talking merchants. Its teetering wharves were choked by strange boats with strange crews and stranger cargoes, taking on food and water, selling off goods and slaves.

"Gods damn it I need a drink!" snarled Odda, as the *South Wind* scraped alongside her wharf and Koll sprang ashore to make her fast.

"I might be persuaded to join you," said Dosduvoi. "As long as there are no dice involved. I have no luck at dice." Brand could have sworn the *South Wind* rose a few fingers in the water when he heaved himself ashore. "Care to join us, boy?"

It was a sore temptation after the hell of hard work and hard words, bad weather and bad tempers they'd been through on the way across the Shattered Sea. Brand's hopes for the wondrous voyage had so far proved a great deal more wondrous than the voyage itself, the crew less a family bound tight by a common goal than a sackful of snakes, spitting poison at each other as though their journey was a struggle that could have only one winner.

Brand licked his lips as he remembered the taste of Fridlif's ale going down. Then he caught sight of Rulf's disapproving face, and remembered the taste of Fridlif's ale coming back up, and chose to stand in the light. "I'd best not."

Odda spat in disgust. "One drink never hurt anyone!"

"One didn't," said Rulf.

"Stopping at one is my problem," said Brand.

"Besides, I have a better use for him." Skifr slipped between Brand and Thorn, one long arm hooking each of their necks. "Fetch weapons, my sprouts. It is past time the education began!"

Brand groaned. The last thing he wanted to do was fight. Especially to fight Thorn, who'd been jostling his oar at every stroke and sneering at his every word since they left Thorlby, no doubt desperate to even the score. If the crew were snakes, she was the most venomous of the lot.

"I want you all back here before midday!" yelled Yarvi as most of his crew began to melt away into the mazy alleys of Roystock, then muttered under his breath to Rulf, "We stop overnight we'll never get this lot started again. Safrit, make sure none of them kill anyone. Especially not each other."

Safrit was in the midst of buckling on a knife only just this side of a sword, and a well-used one at that. "A man bent on self-destruction will find his way there sooner or later."

"Then make sure it's later."

"Don't suppose you've a notion how I do that?"

"Your tongue's sharp enough to goad a tree to movement." Which brought a mad giggle from Koll as he knotted the rope. "But if that fails you, we both know you're not too shy to stick them with your dagger instead."

"All right, but I swear no oaths." Safrit nodded to Brand. "Try and keep my Death-flirting son off that mast, will you?"

Brand looked at Koll, and the lad flashed him a mischief-loving grin. "Don't suppose you've a notion how I do that?"

"If only," snorted Safrit, and with a sigh she headed into town, while Rulf set a few who'd drawn short lots to scrubbing down the deck.

Brand clambered onto the wharf, firm boards seeming treacherous after so long on the shifting water, groaning as he stretched out muscles stiff from rowing and shook out clothes stiff with salt.

Skifr was frowning at Thorn with hands on hips. "Do we need to strap down your chest?"

"What?"

"A woman's chest can make trouble in a fight, swinging about like sacks of sand." Skifr snaked her hand out and before Thorn could wriggle away gave her chest an assessing squeeze. "Never mind. That won't be a problem for you."

Thorn glared at her. "Thanks for that."

"No need for thanks, I am paid to teach you!" The old woman hopped back aboard the *South Wind*, leaving Brand and Thorn facing each other once again, wooden weapons in hand, he nearest to the town, she with the sea at her back.

"Well, children? Do you await an invitation by eagle?"

"Here?" Thorn frowned down at the few paces of narrow wharf between them, cold Mother Sea slapping at the supports below.

"Where else? Fight!"

With a growl Thorn set to work, but with so little space all she could do was jab at him. It was easy for Brand to fend her efforts off with his shield, pushing her back a quarter-step each time.

"Don't tickle him!" barked Skifr, "Kill him!"

Thorn's eyes darted about for an opening but Brand gave her no room, easing forward, herding her toward the end of the wharf. She came at him with her usual savagery, their shields clashing, grating, but he was ready, used his weight to doggedly shove her back. She snarled and spat, her boots scraping at the mossy boards, flailed at him with her sword but the blows were weak.

It was inevitable. With a despairing cry Thorn toppled off the end of the wharf and splashed into the welcoming arms of Mother Sea. Brand winced after her, very much doubting this would make a year of rowing beside her any easier.

Kalyiv was a long, long way off, but it was starting to seem farther than ever.

The crew chuckled to each other over the result. Koll, who'd shinned up to the *South Wind*'s yard as usual in spite of his mother's warnings, whooped from above.

Skifr put long finger and thumb to her temples and gently rubbed at them. "Inauspicious."

Thorn flung her shield onto the wharf and dragged herself up by a barnacle-crusted ladder, soaked to the skin and white with fury.

"You seem distressed," said Skifr. "Is the test not fair?"

Thorn forced through her clenched teeth, "The battlefield is not fair."

"Such wisdom in one so young!" Skifr offered out Thorn's fallen practice sword. "Another go?"

The second time she went into the sea even faster. The third she ended up on her back tangled with the *South Wind*'s oars. The fourth she beat at Brand's shield so hard she broke off the end of her practice sword. Then he barged her off the wharf again.

By now a merry crowd had gathered on the docks to watch. Some crew from their ship, some crew from others, some folk from the town come to laugh at the girl being knocked into the sea. There was even some lively betting on the result.

"Let's stop," begged Brand. "Please." The only outcomes he could see were enraging her further or going into the sea himself, and neither particularly appealed.

"Damn your please!" snarled Thorn, setting herself for another round. No doubt she'd still have been tumbling into the sea by the light of Father Moon if she'd been given the chance, but Skifr steered her broken sword down with a gentle fingertip.

"I think you have entertained the good folk of Roystock enough. You are tall and you are strong."

Thorn stuck her jaw out. "Stronger than most men."

"Stronger than most boys in the training square, but . . ." Skifr flopped one lazy hand out toward Brand. "What is the lesson?"

Thorn spat on the boards, and wiped a little stray spit from her chin, and kept sullen silence.

"Do you like the taste of salt so much you wish to try him again?" Skifr walked to Brand and seized him by the arms. "Look at his neck. Look at his shoulders. What is the lesson?"

"That he is stronger." Fror stood with his forearms dangling over the *South Wind*'s rail, rag and block in his hands. Might've been the first time Brand had heard him speak.

"Exactly so!" called Skifr. "I daresay this tight-lipped Vansterman knows battle. How did you get that scar, my dove?"

"I was milking a reindeer and she fell on me," said Fror. "She was ever so sorry afterward, but the damage was done." And Brand wondered if he winked his misshapen eye.

"Truly a hero's mark, then," grunted Thorn, curling her lip.

Fror shrugged. "Someone must bring in the milk."

"And someone must hold my coat." Skifr whipped off her cloak of rags and tossed it to him.

She was lean as a whip, narrow-waisted as a wasp, wound about with strips of cloth, coiled with belts and straps, bristling with knives and hooks, pouches and picks, scrags, rods, papers and devices Brand could not guess at the purpose of.

"Have you never seen a grandmother without her cloak before?" And from behind her back she brought an ax with a shaft of dark wood and a thin, bearded blade. A beautiful weapon, snakes of strange letters etched into the bright steel. She held up her other hand, thumb folded in and fingers pressed together. "Here is my sword. A blade fit for the songs, no? Put me in the sea, boy, if you can."

Skifr began to move. It was a baffling performance, lurching like a drunkard, floppy as a doll, and she swung that ax back and forth, knocking the boards and striking splinters. Brand watched her over his shield's rim, trying to find some pattern to it, but he'd no idea where her next footstep might fall. So he waited for the ax to swing wide, then aimed a cautious swipe at her.

He could hardly believe how fast she moved. His wooden blade missed her by a hair as she darted in, caught the rim of his shield with that hooked ax and dragged it away, slipped past his sword arm and jabbed him hard in the chest with her fingertips, making him grunt and stagger back on his heels.

"You are dead," she said.

The ax flashed down and Brand jerked his shield up to meet it. But the blow never came. Instead he winced as Skifr's fingers jabbed him in the groin, and looking down saw her smirking face beneath the bottom rim of his shield.

"You are dead twice."

He tried to barge her away but he might as well have barged the breeze. She somehow slipped around him, fingers jabbing under his ear and making his whole side throb.

"Dead."

She chopped him in the kidneys with the edge of her hand as he tried to turn.

"Dead."

He reeled around, teeth bared, sword flashing at neck height but she was gone. Something trapped his ankle, turning his war cry to a gurgle of shock, and he kept spinning, balance gone, lurching off the edge of the wharf—

He stopped, choking as something caught him around the neck.

"You are the deadest boy in Roystock."

Skifr had one foot on his heel, the bearded blade of her ax hooked into his collar to keep him from falling, leaning sharply away to balance his weight. He was held helpless, teetering over the cold sea. The watching crowd had fallen silent, almost as dumbstruck at Skifr's display as Brand was.

"You will not beat a strong man with strength any more than I will beat you with youth," Skifr hissed at Thorn. "You must be quicker to strike and quicker when you do. You must be tougher and cleverer, you must always look to attack, and you must fight without honor, without conscience, without pity. Do you understand?"

Thorn slowly nodded. Of all those in the training square, she'd been the one who hated most being taught. But she'd been the one quickest to learn.

"Whatever happened here?" Dosduvoi had strolled up and stood staring at Brand as he dangled spluttering over the water.

"They're training," called Koll, who'd leaned out from the mast to flip a copper coin nimbly across his knuckles. "Why are you back so soon?"

"I lost terribly at dice." He rubbed sadly at his great forearm, where a couple of silver rings had gone missing. "Awful luck, it was."

Skifr gave a disgusted hiss. "Those with bad luck should at least attempt to balance it with good sense." She twisted her wrist. The ax blade tore through Brand's shirt collar and it was his turn to plunge flailing into cold water. His turn to drag himself up the ladder. His turn to stand dripping under the scorn of the crowd.

He found he enjoyed his turn even less than he had Thorn's.

The Vansterman threw Skifr's ragged cloak back to her. "An impressive performance."

"Like magic!" Koll tossed his coin high but fumbled it on the way back so it flickered down toward the sea.

"Magic?" The old woman darted out a hand to pluck Koll's coin from the air between finger and thumb. "That was training, and experience, and discipline. Perhaps I will show you magic another day, but let us all hope not." She flicked the coin spinning far into the air and Koll laughed as he caught it. "Magic has costs you will not wish to pay."

Skifr shrugged her coat back on with a snapping of cloth. "This style of fighting you have learned," she said to Thorn, "standing in a row with shield and mail and heavy blade, it does not suit you. It is not meant to suit you." Skifr dragged the shield from Thorn's arm and tossed it rattling among the chests on the *South Wind*. "You will fight with lighter, quicker weapons. You will fight in lighter armor."

"How will I stand in the shield wall without a shield?"

"Stand?" Skifr's eyes went wide as cups. "You are a killer, girl! You are the storm, always moving! You rush to meet your enemy, or you trick him into meeting you, and on the ground of your choosing, in the manner of your choosing, you *kill him*."

"My father was a famous warrior, he always said—"

"Where is your father?"

Thorn frowned for a moment, mouth half open, then touched her hand to a lump in her damp shirt, and slowly shut it. "Dead."

"So much for his expertise." Skifr tossed over the long ax and Thorn plucked it from the air, and weighed it in her hand, and swished it cautiously one way and the other. "What do the letters on the blade mean?"

"They say in five languages, 'to the fighter everything must be a weapon.' Good advice, if you are wise enough to take it."

Thorn nodded, frowning. "I am the storm."

"As yet, more of a drizzle," said Skifr. "But we are only beginning."

# THE THIRD
# LESSON

The Divine River.

Thorn remembered listening entranced to her father's stories of journeys up it and down its sister, the Denied, his eyes bright as he whispered of desperate battles against strange peoples, and proud brotherhoods forged in the crucible of danger, and hoards of gold to be won. Ever since she had dreamed of her own voyage, the names of those far places like the words of a magic spell, bursting with power and mystery: the tall hauls, Kalyiv, the First of Cities.

Strange to say, her dreams had not included arse and hands chafed raw from rowing, nor endless clouds of biting midges, nor fog so thick you only got fleeting glimpses of the fabled land, and those of bitter bog and tangled forest, the joys of which were hardly rare in Gettland.

"I was hoping for more excitement," grunted Thorn.

"So it is with hopes," muttered Brand.

She was a long way from forgiving him for humiliating her in front of Queen Laithlin, or for all those drops into Roystock's cold harbor, but she had to give a grim snort of agreement.

"There'll be excitement enough before we're back this way," said

Rulf, giving a nudge to the steering oar. "Excitement enough you'll be begging for boredom. If you live through it."

Mother Sun was sinking toward the ragged treetops when Father Yarvi ordered the *South Wind* grounded for the night and Thorn could finally ship her oar, flinging it roughly across Brand's knees and rubbing at her blistered palms.

They dragged the ship from the water by the prow rope in a stumbling, straining crowd, the ground so boggy it was hard to tell where river ended and earth began.

"Gather some wood for a fire," called Safrit.

"Dry wood?" asked Koll, kicking through the rotten flotsam clogged on the bank.

"It does tend to burn more easily."

"Not you, Thorn." Skifr was leaning on one of the ship's spare oars, the blade high above her head. "In the day you belong to Rulf, but at dawn and dusk you are mine. Whenever there is light, we must seize every chance to train."

Thorn squinted at the gloomy sky, huddled low over the gloomy land. "You call this light?"

"Will your enemies wait for morning if they can kill you in the dark?"

"What enemies?"

Skifr narrowed her eyes. "The true fighter must reckon everyone their enemy."

The sort of thing Thorn used to airily proclaim to her mother. Heard from someone else, it sounded like no fun at all. "When do I rest, then?"

"In the songs of great heroes, do you hear often of resting?"

She watched Safrit tossing flat loaves among the crew, and her mouth flooded with spit. "You sometimes hear of eating."

"Training on a full stomach is unlucky."

Even Thorn had precious little fight left after a long day competing with Brand at the oar. But she supposed the sooner they started, the sooner they'd finish. "What do we do?"

"I will try to hit you. You will try not to be hit."

"With an oar?"

"Why not? To hit and not be hit is the essence of fighting."

"There's no way I could work this stuff out on my own," grunted Thorn.

She didn't even gasp when Skifr darted out a hand and cuffed her across the cheek. She was getting used to it.

"You will be struck, and when you are, the force of it must not stagger you, the pain of it must not slow you, the shock of it must not cause you to doubt. You must learn to strike without pity. You must learn to be struck without fear." Skifr lowered the oar so that the blade hovered near Thorn's chest. "Though I advise you to get out of the way. If you can."

She certainly tried. Thorn dodged, wove, sprang, rolled, then she stumbled, lurched, slipped, floundered. To begin with she hoped to get around the oar and bring Skifr down, but she soon found just staying out of its way took every grain of wit and energy. The oar darted at her from everywhere, cracked her on the head, on the shoulders, poked her in the ribs, in the stomach, made her grunt, and gasp, and whoop as it swept her feet away and sent her tumbling.

The smell of Safrit's cooking tugged at her groaning belly, and the crew ate and drank, spreading their fingers to the warmth of the fire, propping themselves easily on their elbows, watching, chuckling, making bets on how long she could last. Until the sun was a watery glow on the western horizon and Thorn was soaked through and mud-caked from head to toe, throbbing with bruises, each breath ripping at her heaving chest.

"Would you like the chance to hit me back?" asked Skifr.

If there was one thing that could have made Thorn enthusiastic about holding an oar again, it was the chance to club Skifr with one.

But the old woman had other ideas. "Brand, bring me that bar."

He scraped the last juice from his bowl, stood up wrapped in a blanket and brought something over, licking at his teeth. A bar of rough-forged iron, about the length of a sword but easily five times the weight.

"Thanks," said Thorn, voice poisonous with sarcasm.

"What can I do?"

All she could think of was him wearing that same helpless look on the beach below Thorlby, as Hunnan sent three lads to kill her dreams. "What do you ever do?" Not fair, maybe, but she wasn't feeling too fair. Wasn't as if anyone was ever fair to her.

His brow furrowed, and he opened his mouth as if to snap something at her. Then he seemed to think better of it, and turned back to the fire, dragging his blanket tight over his hunched shoulders.

"Aye!" she called after him, "you go and sit down!" A feeble sort of jibe, since she would have liked nothing better.

Skifr slid a shield onto her arm. "Well, then? Hit me."

"With this?" It took an effort just to lift the damn thing. "I'd rather use the oar."

"To a fighter, everything must be a weapon, remember?" Skifr rapped Thorn on the forehead with her knuckles. "Everything. The ground. The water. That rock. Dosduvoi's head."

"Eh?" grunted the giant, looking up.

"Dosduvoi's head would make a fearsome weapon, mark you," said Odda. "Hard as stone and solid right through."

Some chuckling at that, though laughter seemed a foreign tongue to Thorn as she weighed that length of iron in her hand.

"For now, that is your weapon. It will build strength."

"I thought I couldn't win with strength."

"You can lose with weakness. If you can move that bar fast enough to hit me, your sword will be quick as lightning and just as deadly. Begin." Skifr opened her eyes very wide and said in a piping mimicry of Thorn's voice. "Or is the task not fair?"

Thorn set her jaw even harder than usual, planted her feet, and with a fighting growl went to work. It was far from pretty. A few swings and her arm was burning from neck to fingertips. She reeled about after the bar, struck great clods of mud from the ground, one landing in the fire and sending up a shower of sparks and a howl of upset from the crew.

Skifr danced her lurching dance, dodging Thorn's clumsy efforts with pitiful ease and letting her lumber past, occasionally knocking the bar away with a nudge of her shield, barking out instructions Thorn could barely understand, let alone obey.

"No, you are trying to lead the way, you must follow the weapon. No, more wrist. No, elbow in. The weapon is part of you! No, angled, angled, like so. No, shoulder up. No, feet wider. This is your ground! Own it! You are queen of this mud! Try again. No. Try again. No. Try again. No, no, no, no, no. No!"

Thorn gave a shriek and flung the bar to the wet earth, and Skifr shrieked back, crashed into her with the shield, and sent her sprawling. "Never lower your guard! That is the moment you die. Do you understand?"

"I understand," Thorn hissed back through her gritted teeth, tasting a little blood.

"Good. Let us see if your left hand has more spice in it."

By the time Skifr called a grudging halt Father Moon was smiling in the sky and the night was noisy with the strange music of frogs. Apart from a handful keeping watch the crew was sleeping soundly, bundled in blankets, in furs and fleeces, and in the luckiest cases bags of seal-skin, sending up a thunder of snores and a smoking of breath in the ruddy light of the dying fire.

Safrit sat crosslegged, Koll sleeping with his head in her lap and her hand on his sandy hair, eyelids flickering as he dreamed. She handed up a bowl. "I saved you some."

Thorn hung her head, face crushed up tight. Against scorn, and pain, and anger she was well-armored, but that shred of kindness brought a sudden choking sob from her.

"It'll be all right," said Safrit, patting her knee. "You'll see."

"Thanks," whispered Thorn, and she smothered her tears and crammed cold stew into her face, licking the juice from her fingers.

She thought she saw Brand's eyes gleaming in the dark as he shifted up to leave a space, shoving Odda over and making him mew like a kitten in his fitful sleep. Thorn would have slept happily among corpses then. She didn't even bother to take her boots off as she dropped onto ground still warm from Brand's body.

She was almost asleep when Skifr gently tucked the blanket in around her.

# THE GODS'
# ANGER

The days were lost in a haze of rowing, and wood creaking, and water slopping against the *South Wind*'s flanks, Thorn's jaw muscles bunching with every stroke, Rulf's eyes narrowed to slits as he gazed upriver, Father Yarvi's withered hand clutched behind his back in his good one, Koll's endless questions and Safrit's scolding, stories told about the fire, shadows shifting over the scarred faces of the crew, the constant muttering of Skifr's instructions and the rattle, grunt and clatter of Thorn's training as Brand drifted off to sleep.

He couldn't say he liked her, but he had to admire the way she kept at it, always fighting no matter the odds, always getting up no matter how often she was put down. That was courage. Made him wish he was more like her.

From time to time they came ashore at villages belonging to no land or lord. Turf-roofed fishers' huts huddling in loops of the river, wattle hovels shepherds shared with their animals under the eaves of the silent forest, which made the one Brand had shared with Rin seem a palace indeed and brought a surge of sappy homesickness welling up in him. Father Yarvi would trade for milk and ale and still-bleating goats, knowing every tongue spoken by men or beasts, it seemed, but there were few smiles traded on either side. Smiles might be free, but they were in short supply out there on the Divine.

They passed boats heading north, and sometimes their crews were dour and watchful, and sometimes they called out cautious greetings. Whichever they did Rulf kept careful eyes on them until they were well out of sight with his black bow ready in one hand, a fearsome thing near as tall as a man, made from the great ridged horns of some beast Brand had never seen and never wanted to.

"They seemed friendly enough," he said, after one almost-merry encounter.

"An arrow from a smiling archer kills you just as dead," said Rulf, setting his bow back beside the steering oar. "Some of these crews will be heading home with rich cargo, but some will have failed, and be looking to make good on their trip by taking a fat ship, and selling her pretty young pair of back oars for slaves."

Thorn jerked her head toward Brand. "They'll only find one pretty back oar on this boat."

"You'd be prettier if you didn't scowl so much," said Rulf, which brought a particularly ugly scowl, just as it was meant to.

"Might be the minister's prow keeps the raiders off," said Brand, wedging his ax beside his sea-chest.

Thorn snorted as she slid her sword back into its sheath. "More likely our ready weapons."

"Aye," said Rulf. "Even law-abiding men forget themselves in lawless places. There's a limit on the reach of the Ministry. But the authority of steel extends to every port. It's a fine sword you have there, Thorn."

"My father's." After a moment of considering, she offered it up to him.

"Must've been quite a warrior."

"He was a Chosen Shield," said Thorn, puffing with pride. "He was the one made me want to fight."

Rulf peered approvingly down the blade, which was well-used and well-kept, then frowned at the pommel, which was a misshapen lump of iron. "Don't reckon this can be its first pommel."

Thorn stared off toward the tangled trees, jaw working. "It had a better, but it's strung on Grom-gil-Gorm's chain."

Rulf raised his brows, and there was an awkward silence as he passed the sword back. "How about you, Brand? Your father a fighting man?"

Brand frowned off toward a heron wading in the shallows of the other bank. "He could give a blow or two."

Rulf puffed out his cheeks, clear that subject was firmly buried. "Let's row, then!"

Thorn spat over the side as she worked her hands about her oar. "Bloody rowing. I swear, when I get back to Thorlby I'll never touch an oar again."

"A wise man once told me to take one stroke at a time." Father Yarvi was just behind them. There were many bad things about being at the back oar, but one of the worst was that you never knew who might be at your shoulder.

"Done a lot of rowing, have you?" Thorn muttered as she bent to the next stroke.

"Oy!" Rulf kicked at her oar and made her flinch. "Pray you never have to learn what he knows about rowing!"

"Let her be." Father Yarvi smiled as he rubbed at his withered wrist. "It's not easy being Thorn Bathu. And it's only going to get harder."

The Divine narrowed and the forest closed in dark about the banks. The trees grew older, and taller, and thrust twisted roots into the slow-flowing water and held gnarled boughs low over it. So while Skifr knocked Thorn over with an oar the rest of the crew rolled up the sail, and took down the mast, and laid it lengthways between the sea-chests on trestles. Unable to climb it, Koll pulled out his knife and set to carving on it. Brand was expecting childish hackings and was amazed to see animals, plants, and warriors all intertwined and beautifully wrought spreading steadily down its length.

"Your son's got talent," he said to Safrit when she brought around the water.

"All kinds of talent," she agreed, "but a mind like a moth. I can't keep it on one thing for two moments together."

"Why is it even called Divine?" grunted Koll, sitting back to stare off upriver, spinning his knife around and around in his fingers and somewhat proving his mother's point. "I don't see much holy about it."

"I've heard because the One God blessed it above all other waters," rumbled Dosduvoi.

Odda raised a brow at the shadowy thicket that hemmed them in on both banks. "This look much blessed to you?"

"The elves knew the true names of these rivers," said Skifr, who'd made a kind of bed among the cargo to drape herself on. "We call them Divine and Denied because those are as close as our clumsy human tongues can come."

The good humor guttered at the mention of elves, and Dosduvoi mumbled a prayer to the One God, and Brand made a holy sign over his heart.

Odda was less pious. "Piss on the elves!" He leapt from his sea-chest, dragging his trousers down and sending a yellow arc high over the ship's rail. Some laughter, and some cries of upset from men behind who took a spattering as a gust blew up.

One man going often made others feel the need, and soon Rulf was ordering the boat held steady mid-stream while half the crew stood at the rail with hairy backsides on display. Thorn shipped her oar, which meant flinging it in Brand's lap, and worked her trousers down to show a length of muscled white thigh. It was hardly doing good to watch but Brand found it hard not to, and ended up peering out the corner of his eye as she slithered up and wedged her arse over the ship's side.

"I'm all amazement!" called Odda at her as he sat back down.

"That I piss?"

"That you do it sitting. I was sure you were hiding a prick under there." A few chuckles from the benches at that.

"Thought the same about you, Odda." Thorn dragged her trousers back up and hooked her belt. "Reckon we're both disappointed."

A proper laugh swept the ship. Koll gave a whooping snigger, and Rulf thumped at the prow-beast in appreciation, and Odda laughed loudest of all, throwing his head back to show his mouthful of filed teeth. Safrit slapped Thorn on the back as she dropped grinning back on her sea-chest and Brand thought Rulf had been right. There was nothing ugly about her when she smiled.

The gust that wetted Odda's oarmates was the first of many. The heavens darkened and She Who Sings the Wind sent a cold song swirling about the ship, sweeping ripples across the calm Divine and whipping Brand's hair around his face. A cloud of little white birds clattered up, a flock of thousands, twisting and swirling against the bruised sky.

Skifr slid one hand into her ragged coat to rummage through the mass of runes and charms and holy signs about her neck. "That is an ill omen."

"Reckon a storm's coming," muttered Rulf.

"I have seen hail the size of a child's head drop from a sky like that."

"Should we get the boat off the river?" asked Father Yarvi.

"Upend her and get under her." Skifr kept her eyes on the clouds like a warrior watching an advancing enemy. "And quickly."

They grounded the *South Wind* at the next stretch of shingle, Brand wincing as the wind blew colder, fat spots of rain stinging his face.

First they hauled out mast and sail, then stores and sea-chests, weapons and shields. Brand helped Rulf free the prow-beasts with wedges and mallet, wrapped them carefully in oiled cloth while Koll helped Thorn wedge the oars in the rowlocks so they could use them as handles to lift the ship. Father Yarvi unlocked the iron-bound chest from its chains, the veins in Dosduvoi's great neck bulging as he hefted its weight onto his shoulder. Rulf pointed out the spots and six stout barrels were rolled into place around their heaped-up gear, Odda wielding a shovel with marvelous skill to make pits that the tall prow and stern would sit in.

"Bring her up!" bellowed Rulf, Thorn grinning as she vaulted over the side of the ship.

"You seem happy enough about all this," said Brand, gasping as he slid into the cold water.

"I'd rather lift ten ships than train with Skifr."

The rain came harder, so it scarcely made a difference whether they were in the river or not, everyone soaked through, hair and beards plastered, clothes clinging, straining faces beaded with wet.

"Never sail in a ship you can't carry!" growled Rulf through gritted teeth. "Up! Up! Up!"

And with each shout there was a chorus of grunting, growling, groaning. Every man, and woman too, lending all their strength, the cords standing out stark from Safrit's neck and Odda's grooved teeth bared in an animal snarl and even Father Yarvi dragging with his one good hand.

"Tip her!" roared Rulf as they heaved her from the water. "But gently now! Like a lover, not a wrestler!"

"If I tip her like a lover do I get a kiss?" called Odda.

"I'll kiss you with my fist," hissed Thorn through her clenched teeth.

It had grown dark as dusk, and He Who Speaks the Thunder grumbled in the distance as they heaved the *South Wind* over, prow and stern digging deep into the boggy earth. Now they took her under the top rail, upside down, and carried her up the bank, boots mashing the ground to sliding mud.

"Easy!" called Father Yarvi. "Gently! A little toward me! Yes! And down!"

They lowered the ship onto the barrels, and Odda shrieked and flapped his hand because he'd got it caught, but that was the only injury and the *South Wind* was steady on her back. Soaked, sore and gasping they slipped under the hull and crouched huddled in the darkness.

"Good work," said Rulf, his voice echoing strangely. "Reckon we might make a crew of this crowd of fools yet." He gave a chuckle, and others joined him, and soon everyone was laughing, and slapping each other, and hugging each other, for they knew they'd done a fine job, each working for one another, and were bound together by it.

"She makes a noble hall," said Dosduvoi, patting at the timbers above his head.

"One I am exceedingly grateful for in this weather," said Odda.

The rain was pelting now, coming in sheets and curtains, coursing from the *South Wind*'s top rail which had become the eaves of their roof. They heard thunder crackle close by and the wind howled icy-chill around the barrels. Koll huddled up tighter and Brand put his arm around him, like he might've round Rin when they were children and had no roof at all. He felt Thorn pressed tight against him on the other side, the woody hardness of her shoulder against his, shifting as she breathed, and he wanted to put his arm around her too but didn't much fancy her fist in his face.

Probably he should've taken the chance to tell her that he'd been the one went to Father Yarvi. That he'd lost his place on the king's raid over it. Might've made her think twice before digging him with her oar again, at least, or with her insults either.

But the gods knew he wasn't much good at telling things, and the gods knew even better she wasn't easy to tell things to, and the further it all dwindled into the past the harder it got. Didn't seem like doing good, to put her in his debt that way.

So he stayed silent, and let her shoulder press against his instead, then felt her flinch as something heavy banged against the hull.

"Hail," whispered Skifr. The rattling grew louder, and louder yet, blows like axes on shields, and the crew peered fearfully up, or shrank against the ground, or put hands over their heads.

"Look at this." Fror held up a stone that had rolled under the boat, a spiked and knobbled chunk of ice the size of a fist. In the gloom outside the ship Brand could see the hail pounding the wet earth, bouncing and rolling.

"You think the gods are angry with us?" asked Koll.

"It is frozen rain," said Father Yarvi. "The gods hate those who plan badly, and help those with good friends, good swords, and good sense. Worry less about what the gods might do and more about what you can, that's my advice."

But Brand could hear a lot of prayers even so. He'd have given it a go himself, but he'd never been much good at picking out the right gods.

Skifr was yammering away in at least three languages, not one of which he understood. "Are you praying to the One God or the many?" he asked.

"All of them. And the fish god of the Banyas, and the tree spirits of the Shends, and great eight-armed Thopal that the Alyuks think will eat the world at the end of time. One can never have too many friends, eh, boy?"

"I . . . suppose?"

Dosduvoi peered out sadly at the downpour. "I went over to the worship of the One God because her priests said she would bring me better luck."

"How's that worked out?" asked Koll.

"Thus far, unluckily," said the big man. "But it may be that I have not committed myself enough to her worship."

Odda spat. "You can never bow low enough for the One God's taste."

"In that she and Grandmother Wexen are much alike," murmured Yarvi.

"Who are you praying to?" Brand muttered at Thorn, her lips moving silently while she clung to something on a thong around her neck.

He saw her eyes gleam as she frowned back. "I don't pray."

"Why?"

She was silent for a moment. "I prayed for my father. Every morning and every night to every god whose name I could learn. Dozens of the bastards. He died anyway." And she turned her back on him and shifted away, leaving darkness between them.

The storm blew on.

# READY OR DEAD

"Gods," whispered Brand.

The elf-ruins crowded in on both sides of the river, looming towers and blocks and cubes, broken elf-glass twinkling as it caught the watery sun.

The Divine flowed so broad here it was almost a lake, cracked teeth of stone and dead fingers of metal jutting from the shallows. All was wreathed with creeper, sprouting with sapling trees, choked with thickets of ancient bramble. No birds called, not even an insect buzzed over water still as black glass, only the slightest ripple where the oar-blades smoothly dipped, yet Thorn's skin prickled with the feeling of being watched from every empty window.

All her life she had been warned away from elf-ruins. It was the one thing on which her mother and father had always stood united. Men daily risked shipwreck hugging the coast of Gettland to keep their distance from the haunted island of Strokom, where the Ministry had forbidden any man to tread. Sickness lurked there, and death, and things worse than death, for the elves had wielded a magic powerful enough to break God and destroy the world.

And here they went, forty little people in a hollow twig, rowing through the midst of the greatest elf-ruins Thorn had ever seen.

"Gods," breathed Brand again, twisting to look over his shoulder.

There was a bridge ahead, if you could call a thing built on that scale a bridge. It must once have crossed the river in a single dizzying span, the slender roadway strung between two mighty towers, each one dwarfing the highest turret of the citadel of Thorlby. But the bridge had fallen centuries before, chunks of stone big as houses hanging from tangled ropes of metal, one swinging gently with the faintest creak as they rowed beneath.

Rulf gripped the steering oar, mouth hanging wide as he stared up at one of the leaning towers, crouching as if he expected it to topple down and crush the tiny ship and its ant-like crew into nothingness. "If you ever needed reminding how small you are," he muttered, "here's a good spot."

"It's a whole city," whispered Thorn.

"The elf-city of Smolod." Skifr lounged on the steering platform, peering at her fingernails as though colossal elf-ruins were hardly worthy of comment. "In the time before the Breaking of God it was home to thousands. Thousands of thousands. It glittered with the light of their magic, and the air was filled with the song of their machines and the smoke of their mighty furnaces." She gave a long sigh. "All lost. All past. But so it is with everything. Great or small, the Last Door is life's one certainty."

A sheet of bent metal stuck from the river on rusted poles, arrows sweeping across it in flaking paint, bold words written in unknowable elf-letters. It looked uncomfortably like a warning, but of what, Thorn could not say.

Rulf tossed a twig over the side, watched it float away to judge their speed and gave a grudging nod. For once he had to bellow no encouragements—meaning insults—to get the *South Wind* moving at a pretty clip. The ship itself seemed to whisper with the prayers, and oaths, and charms of its crew, spoken in a dozen languages. But

Skifr, who had something for every god and every occasion, for once let the heavens be.

"Save your prayers for later," she said. "There is no danger here."

"No danger?" squeaked Dosduvoi, fumbling a holy sign over his chest and getting his oar tangled with the man in front.

"I have spent a great deal of time in elf-ruins. Exploring them has been one of my many trades."

"Some would call that heresy," said Father Yarvi, looking up from under his brows.

Skifr smiled. "Heresy and progress often look much alike. We have no Ministry in the south to meddle with such things. Rich folk there will pay well for an elf-relic or two. The Empress Theofora herself has quite a collection. But the ruins of the south have often been picked clean. Those about the Shattered Sea have much more to offer. Untouched, some of them, since the Breaking of God. The things one can find there . . ."

Her eyes moved to the iron-shod chest, secured by chains near the setting of the mast, and Thorn thought of the box, and the light from inside it. Had that been dug from the forbidden depths of a place like this one? Was there magic in it that could break the world? She gave a shiver at the thought.

But Skifr only smiled wider. "If you go properly prepared into the cities of elves, you will find less danger than in the cities of men."

"They say you're a witch." Koll blew a puff of wood-chips from his latest patch of carving and looked up.

"They say?" Skifr widened her eyes so the white showed all the way around. "True and false are hard to pick apart in the weave of what *they say*."

"You said you know magic."

"And so I do. Enough to cause much harm, but not enough to do much good. So it is, with magic."

"Could you show it to me?"

Skifr snorted. "You are young and rash and know not what you ask, boy." They rowed in the shadow of a vast wall, its bottom sunk in the river, its top broken off in a skein of twisted metal. Rank upon rank of great windows yawned empty. "The powers that raised this city also rendered it a ruin. There are terrible risks, and terrible costs. Always, there are costs. How many gods do you know the names of?"

"All of them," said Koll.

"Then pray to them all that you never see magic." Skifr frowned down at Thorn. "Take your boots off."

Thorn blinked. "Why?"

"So you can take a well-deserved break from rowing."

Thorn looked at Brand and he shrugged back. Together they pulled their oars in and she worked off her boots. Skifr slipped out of her coat, folded it and draped it over the steering oar. Then she drew her sword. Thorn had never seen it drawn before, and it was long, and slender, and gently curved, Mother Sun glinting from a murderous edge. "Are you ready, my dove?"

The break from rowing suddenly did not seem so appealing. "Ready for what?" asked Thorn, in a voice turned very small.

"A fighter is either ready or dead."

On the barest shred of instinct Thorn jerked her oar up, the blade of Skifr's sword chopping into it right between her hands.

"You're mad!" she squealed as she scrambled back.

"You're hardly the first to say so." Skifr jabbed left and right and made Thorn hop over the lowered mast. "I take it as a compliment." She grinned as she swished her sword back and forth, oarsmen jerking fearfully out of her way. "Take everything as a compliment, you can never be insulted."

She sprang forward again and made Thorn slither under the mast, breath whooping as she heard Skifr's sword rattle against it once, twice.

"My carving!" shouted Koll.

"Work around it!" snarled Skifr.

Thorn tripped on the chains that held the iron-bound chest and toppled into Odda's lap, tore his shield from its bracket, blocked a blow with both hands before Skifr ripped it from her and kicked her over backwards.

Thorn clawed up a coil of rope and flung it in the old woman's face, lunged for Fror's sword but he slapped her hand away. "Find your own!"

"It's in my chest!" she squealed, rolling over Dosduvoi's oar and grabbing the giant from behind, peering over his great shoulder.

"God save me!" he gasped as Skifr's blade darted past his ribs on one side then the other, nicking a hole in his shirt, Thorn dodging desperately, running out of room as the carved prow and Father Yarvi, smiling as he watched the performance, grew mercilessly closer.

"Stop!" shouted Thorn, holding up a trembling hand. "Please! Give me a chance!"

"Do the berserks of the Lowlands stop for their enemies? Does Bright Yilling pause if you say please? Does Grom-gil-Gorm give chances?"

Skifr stabbed again and Thorn leapt past Yarvi, teetered on the top strake, took one despairing stride and sprang, clear off the ship and onto the shaft of the front oar. She felt it flex under her weight, the oarsman straining to keep it level. She tottered to the next, bare foot curling desperately around the slippery wood, arms wide for balance. To hesitate, to consider, to doubt, was doom. She could only run on in great bounds, the water flickering by beneath, oars creaking and clattering in their sockets and the cheering of the crew ringing in her ears.

She gave a shrill whoop at the sheer reckless excitement of it, wind rushing in her open mouth. Running the oars was a noble feat, often sung of but rarely attempted. The feeling of triumph was short-lived, though. The *South Wind* had only sixteen oars a side and she was quickly running out. The last came rushing at her, Brand reaching over the rail, fingers straining. She made a despairing grab at his outstretched hand, he caught her sleeve—

The oar struck her hard in the side, her sleeve ripped and she tumbled headfirst into the river, surfaced gasping in a rush of bubbles.

"A creditable effort!" called Skifr, standing on the steering plat-form with her arm draped around Rulf's shoulders. "And swimming is even better exercise than rowing! We will make camp a few miles further on and wait for you!"

Thorn slapped her hand furiously into the water. "Miles?"

Her rage did not slow the *South Wind*. If anything it caused it to quicken. Brand stared from the stern with that helpless look, his arm still hanging over the side, and shrugged.

Skifr's voice floated out over the water. "I'll hold on to your boots for you!"

Snarling curses, Thorn began to swim, leaving the silent ruins in her wake.

# ITCHING

**B**rand went down hard, practice sword spinning from his hand, tumbled grunting down the slope and flopped onto his back with a groan, the jeering of the crew echoing in his ears.

Lying there, staring into the darkening sky with his many bruises throbbing and his dignity in shreds, he guessed she must have hooked his ankle. But he'd seen no hint it was coming.

Thorn stuck her own sword point-down in the knobbled turf where they'd set out their training square and offered him her hand. "Is that three in a row now, or four?"

"Five," he grunted, "as you well know." He let her haul him up. He'd never been able to afford much pride and sparring with her was taking an awful toll on what little he had. "Gods, you got quick." He winced as he arched his back, still aching from her boot. "Like a snake but without the mercy."

Thorn grinned wider at that, and wiped a streak of blood from under her nose, the one mark he'd put on her in five bouts. He hadn't meant it as a compliment but it was plain she took it as one, and Skifr did too.

"I think young Brand has taken punishment enough for one day," the old woman called to the crew. "There must be a ring-crusted hero among you with the courage to test themselves against my pupil?"

Wasn't long ago they'd have roared with laughter at that offer. Men who'd raided every bitter coast of the Shattered Sea. Men who'd lived by the blade and the feud and called the shield wall home. Men who'd spilled blood enough between them to float a longship, fighting some sharp-tongued girl.

No one laughed now.

For weeks they'd watched her training like a devil in all weathers. They'd watched her put down and they'd watched her get up, over and over, until they were sore just with the watching of it. For a month they'd gone to sleep with the clash of her weapons as a lullaby and been woken by her warcries in place of a cock's crow. Day by day they'd seen her grow faster, and stronger, and more skillful. Terrible skillful, now, with ax and sword together, and she was getting that drunken swagger that Skifr had, so you could never tell where she or her weapons would be the next moment.

"Can't recommend it," said Brand as he lowered himself wincing beside the fire, pressing gently at a fresh scab on his scalp.

Thorn spun her wooden ax around her fingers as nimbly as you might a toothpick. "None of you got the guts for it?"

"Gods damn it, then, girl!" Odda sprang up from the fire. "I'll show you what a real man can do!"

Odda showed her the howl a real man makes when a wooden sword whacks him right in the groin, then he showed her the best effort Brand had ever seen at a real man eating his own shield, then he showed her a real man's muddy backside as he went sprawling through a bramble-bush and into a puddle.

He propped himself on his elbows, caked head to toe with mud, and blew water out of his nose. "Had enough yet?"

"I have." Dosduvoi stooped slowly to pick up Odda's fallen sword and drew himself up to his full height, great chest swelling. The wooden blade looked tiny in his ham of a fist.

Thorn's jaw jutted as she scowled up at him. "The big trees fall the hardest." Splinter in the world's arse she might be, but Brand found himself smiling. However the odds stood against her, she never backed down.

"This tree hits back," said Dosduvoi as he took up a fighting stance, big boots wide apart.

Odda sat down, kneading at a bruised arm. "It'd be a different story if the blades were sharpened, I can tell you that!"

"Aye," said Brand, "a short story with you dead at the end."

Safrit was busy cutting her son's hair, bright shears click-clicking. "Stop squirming!" she snapped at Koll. "It'll be over the faster."

"Hair has to be cut." Brand set a hand on the boy's shoulder. "Listen to your mother." He almost added *you're lucky to have one,* but swallowed it. Some things are better left unsaid.

Safrit waved the shears toward Brand. "I'll give that beard of yours a trim while I'm about it."

"Long as you don't bring the shears near me," said Fror, fingering one of the braids beside his scar.

"Warriors!" snorted Safrit. "Vainer than maidens! Most of these faces are best kept from the world, but a good-looking lad like you shouldn't be hidden in all that undergrowth."

Brand pushed his fingers through his beard. "Surely has thickened up these past few weeks. Starting to itch a little, if I'm honest."

A cheer went up as Dosduvoi lifted his sword high and Thorn dived between his wide-set legs, spun, and gave him a resounding kick in the arse, sending the big man staggering.

Rulf scratched at a cluster of raw insect bites on the side of his neck. "We're all itching a little."

"No avoiding some passengers on a voyage like this." Odda had a good rummage down the front of his trousers. "They're only striving to find the easiest way south, just as we are."

"They fear a war is brewing with the High King of lice," said Safrit, "and seek allies among the midges." And she slapped one against the back of her neck.

Her son scrubbed a shower of sandy clippings from his hair, which still seemed wild as ever. "Are there really allies to be found out here?"

"The Prince of Kalyiv can call on so many riders the dust of their horses blots out the sun," said Odda.

Fror nodded. "And I hear the Empress of the South has so many ships she can fashion a footbridge across the sea."

"It's not about ships or horses," said Brand, rubbing gently at the callouses on his palms. "It's about the trade that comes up the Divine. Slaves and furs go one way, silver and silk come the other. And it's silver wins wars, just as much as steel." He realized everyone was looking at him and trailed off, embarrassed. "So Gaden used to tell me . . . at the forge . . ."

Safrit smiled, toying with the weights strung about her neck. "It's the quiet ones you have to watch."

"Still pools are the deepest," said Yarvi, his pale eyes fixed on Brand. "Wealth is power. It is Queen Laithlin's wealth that is the root of the High King's jealousy. He can shut the Shattered Sea to our ships. Cut off Gettland's trade. With the Prince of Kalyiv and the empress on his side, he can close the Divine to us too. Throttle us without drawing a blade. With the prince and the empress as our allies, the silver still flows."

"Wealth is power," muttered Koll to himself, as though testing the words for truth. Then he looked over at Fror. "How did you get the scar?"

"I asked too many questions," said the Vansterman, smiling at the fire.

Safrit bent over Brand, tugging gently at his beard, shears snipping. It was strange, having someone so close, fixed on him so carefully, gentle fingers on his face. He always told Rin he remembered their mother, but it was only stories told over and over, twisted out of shape by time until he remembered the stories but not the memories themselves. It was Rin who'd always cut his hair, and he touched the knife she'd made for him then and felt a sudden longing for home. For the hovel they'd worked so hard for, and the firelight on his sister's face, and worry for her rushed in so sharp he winced at the sting of it.

Safrit jerked back. "Did I nick you?"

"No," croaked Brand. "Missing home is all."

"Got someone special waiting, eh?"

"Just my family."

"Handsome lad like you, I can hardly believe it."

Dosduvoi had finally put a stop to Thorn's dodging by grabbing a handful of her unruly hair, and now he caught her belt with his other hand, jerked her up like a sheaf of hay and flung her bodily into a ditch.

"Some of us are cursed with bad love-luck," said Rulf mournfully, as Skifr called a halt to the bout and peered into the ditch after her pupil. "I was gone from my farm too long and my wife married again."

"Bad love-luck for you, maybe," muttered Safrit, tossing a tuft of Brand's beard into the fire, "but good for her."

"Bad love-luck is swearing an oath not to have any love at all." Father Yarvi gave a sigh. "The older I get, the less the tender care of Grandmother Wexen seems a good trade for romance."

"I did have a wife," said Dosduvoi, lowering himself beside the fire and gingerly seeking out a comfortable position for his bruised buttocks, "but she died."

"It's not bad luck if she's crushed by your bulk," said Odda.

"That is not funny," said the giant, though judging from the sniggering many of the crew disagreed.

"No wife for me," said Odda. "Don't believe in 'em."

"I doubt they're any more convinced by you," said Safrit. "Though I feel sorry for your hand, forced to be your only lover all this time."

Odda grinned, filed teeth shining with the firelight. "Don't be. My hand is a sensitive partner, and always willing."

"And, unlike the rest of us, not put off by your monstrous breath." Safrit brushed some loose hairs from Brand's now close-cropped beard and sat back. "You're done."

"Might I borrow the shears?" asked Skifr.

Safrit gave the gray fuzz on her skull a look over. "Doesn't seem you've much to cut."

"Not for me." The old woman nodded at Thorn, who'd dragged herself out of the ditch and was limping over, grimacing as she rubbed at her sore head, loose hair torn free and shooting off at all angles. "I think another of our lambs needs shearing. Dosduvoi has proved that mop a weakness."

"No." Thorn tossed down her battered wooden weapons and tidied a few strands back behind her ear, a strange gesture from her, who never seemed to care the least for how she looked.

Skifr raised her brows. "I would not have counted vanity among your many shortcomings."

"I made my mother a promise," said Thorn, snatching up a flat loaf and stuffing half of it in her mouth with dirty fingers in one go. She might not have outfought three men at once but Brand had no doubt she could have out-eaten them.

"I had no notion you held your mother in such high regard," said Skifr.

"I don't. She's always been a pain in my arse. Always telling me the right way to do things and it's never the way I want to do them." Thorn ripped at the loaf with her teeth like a wolf at a carcass, eating and speaking at once, spraying crumbs. "Always fussing over what folk think of me, what they'll do to me, how I might be hurt, how I might embarrass her. Eat this way, talk this way, smile this way, piss this way."

All the while she talked Brand was thinking about his sister, left alone with no one to watch over her, and the anger stole up on him. "Gods," he growled. "Is there a blessing made you couldn't treat like a curse?"

Thorn frowned, cheeks bulging as she chewed. "What does that mean?"

He barked the words, suddenly disgusted with her. "That you've a mother who gives a damn about you, and a home waiting where you're safe, and you still find a way to complain!"

That caused an uncomfortable silence. Father Yarvi narrowed his eyes, and Koll widened his, and Fror's brows crept up in surprise. Thorn swallowed slowly, looking as shocked as if she'd been slapped. More shocked. She got slapped all the time.

"I bloody hate *people*," she muttered, snatching another loaf from Safrit's hand.

It was hardly the good thing to say but for once Brand couldn't keep his mouth shut. "Don't worry." He dragged his blanket over one shoulder and turned his back on her. "They feel much the same about you."

# DAMN THEM

Thorn's nose twitched at the smell of cooking. She blinked awake, and knew right off something was odd. She could scarcely remember the last time she had woken without the tender help of Skifr's boot.

Perhaps the old witch had a heart after all.

She had dreamt a dog was licking at the side of her head, and she tried to shake the memory off as she rolled from her blankets. Maybe dreams were messages from the gods, but she was damned if she could sieve the meaning from that one. Koll was hunched at the water's edge, grumbling as he washed the pots out.

"Morning," she said, giving an almighty stretch and almost enjoying the long ache through her arms and across her back. The first few days she'd hardly been able to move in the mornings from the rowing and the training together, but she was hardening to the work now, getting tough as rope and timber.

Koll glanced up and his eyes went wide. "Er . . ."

"I know. Skifr let me sleep." She grinned across the river. For the first time, Divine seemed an apt name for it. The year was wearing on and Mother Sun was bright and hot already, birds twittering in the forest and insects floating lazy over the water. The trailing branches of the trees about the bank were heavy with white flowers and Thorn took a long, blossom-scented breath in through her nose and let it sigh away. "I've a feeling it'll be a fine day." And she ruffled Koll's hair, turned around, and almost walked into Brand.

He stared at her, that helpless look of his splattered all over his face. "Thorn, your—"

"Go and die." Half the night she'd been lying awake thinking of harsh things to say to him, but when the moment came that was the best she could manage. She shouldered past and over to the embers of the fire where the crew were gathered.

"Eat well," Rulf was saying. "Might be later today we'll reach the tall hauls. You'll need all the strength you've got and more besides when we carry . . . the . . ." He trailed off, staring, as Thorn walked up, grabbing a spare a bowl and peering into the pot.

"No need to stop for me," she said. They were all staring at her and it was starting to make her nervous.

Then Odda chuckled, spluttering food. "She looks like a brush with half the bristles plucked!"

"A lamb half-sheared," said Dosduvoi.

"A willow with half the branches lopped," murmured Fror.

"I like that one," said Odda. "That has poetry. You should speak more."

"You should speak less, but things are as they are."

A breeze floated up from the river, strangely cold against the side of Thorn's head, and she frowned down, and saw her shoulder was covered in hair. She touched one hand to her scalp, afraid of what she might find. On the right side her hair was muddled into its usual incompetent braid. The left was shaved to patchy stubble, her fingertips trembling as they brushed the unfamiliar knobbles of her skull.

"You sleep on your right." Skifr leaned past her shoulder, plucking a piece of meat from the pot between long thumb and forefinger. "I did the best I could without waking you. You look so peaceful when you sleep."

Thorn stared at her. "You said you wouldn't make me do it!"

"Which is why I did it." And the old woman smiled as though she'd done Thorn quite the favor.

So much for the witch having a heart, and the fine day too. Thorn hardly knew then whether she wanted to weep, scream, or bite Skifr's face. In the end all she could do was stalk off toward the river, the crew's laughter ringing in her ears, clenching her teeth and clutching at her half-tangled, half-bald head.

Her mother's most treasured possession was a little mirror set in silver. Thorn always teased her that she loved it because she was so vain, but knew really it was because it had been a gift from her father, brought back long ago from the First of Cities. Thorn had always hated to look at herself in it. Her face too long and her cheeks too hollow, her nose too sharp and her eyes too angry. But she would happily have traded that reflection for the lopsided mockery that peered from the still water at the river's edge now.

She remembered her mother singing softly as she combed Thorn's hair, her father smiling as he watched them. She remembered the laughter and the warmth of arms about her. Her family. Her home. She gripped the pouch she wore and thought what a pitiful thing it was to carry your father's fingerbones around your neck. But it was all she had left. She bitterly shook her head as she stared at her ruined reflection and another appeared behind her—tall and lean and colorless.

"Why did you bring me out here?" she asked, slapping both reflections angrily from the water.

"To make allies of our enemies," said Father Yarvi. "To bring help to Gettland."

"In case you hadn't noticed, I've no touch for making friends."

"We all have our shortcomings."

"Why bring me, then? Why pay Skifr to teach me?"

The minister squatted beside her. "Do you trust me, Thorn?"

"Yes. You saved my life." Though looking into his pale blue eyes she wondered how far one should trust a deep-cunning man. "And I swore an oath. What choice do I have?"

"None. So trust me." He glanced up at the wreckage of her hair. "It might take a little getting used to, but I think it suits you. Strange and fierce. One of a kind."

She snorted. "It's unusual, that I'll grant you."

"Some of us are unusual. I always thought you were happy to stand out. You seem to thrive on mockery like a flower on dung."

"Harder work than it seems," she muttered. "Always finding a brave face."

"That I know, believe me."

They stayed there, beside the water, for a while, in silence.

"Would you help me shave the other side?"

"I say leave it."

"Like this? Why?"

Yarvi nodded over toward the crew. "Because damn them, that's why."

"Damn them," muttered Thorn, scooping up water with her hand and pushing back the hair she still had. She had to admit she was getting a taste for the idea. Leaving it half-shaved, strange and fierce, a challenge to everyone who looked at her. "Damn them." And she snorted up a laugh.

"It's not as though you'll be the only odd-looking one on this crew. And anyway," Yarvi brushed some of the clippings gently from her shoulder with his withered hand, "hair grows back."


THAT WAS A TOUGH DAY'S WORK at the oar, fighting an angry current as the Divine narrowed and its banks steepened, Rulf frowning as he nudged the ship between rocks frothing with white water. That evening, as the sunset flared pink over the forested hills, they reached the tall hauls.

There was a strange village at the shore where no two houses were the same. Some built of timber, some of stone, some from turf like the barrows of dead heroes. It was home to folk of the Shattered Sea who had stopped on the way south, and folk from Kalyiv and the empire who had stopped on the way north, and folk from the forest tribes and the Horse People too who must have stuck on journeys east or west. Seeds blown from half the world away and chosen by some weird luck to put their roots down here.

Whatever their clothes and their customs, though, however sharp they had grown at spinning coins from passing crews, Father Yarvi had the Golden Queen's blood in his veins and knew the best way to fleece them. He bargained with each in their own tongue, baffled them now with charming smiles and now with stony blankness, until he had them bickering over the chance to offer him the lowest prices. When he finally rented eight great bearded oxen from the village's headwoman, he left her blinking down bewildered at the few coins in her palm.

"Father Yarvi is no fool," said Brand as they watched him work his everyday magic.

"He's the most deep-cunning man I ever met," answered Rulf.

There was a graveyard of abandoned timber by the river—rollers and runners, broken masts and oars, even a warped old keel with some strakes still on it, the bones of a ship that must have come down off the hills too damaged and been broken up for parts. The crew busied themselves with axes and chisels and by the time Father Moon was showing himself they had the *South Wind* ashore with good runners mounted alongside her keel and all her cargo packed on two rented wagons.

"Do we train now?" asked Thorn, as she watched the crew settle to their usual evening merry-making about the fire, Koll causing waves of laughter by copying one of Odda's less-than-likely stories.

Skifr looked at her, one eye gleaming in the fading light. "It is late, and there will be hard work tomorrow. Do you want to train?"

Thorn pushed some wood-shavings around with her toe. "Maybe just a little?"

"We will make a killer of you yet. Fetch the weapons."

—

RULF KICKED THEM ALL grumbling from their beds at the first glimmer of dawn, his breath steaming on the damp air.

"Up, you turds! You've got the hardest day of your lives ahead of you!"

There had been no easy days since they set off from Thorlby, but their helmsman was right. Carrying a ship over a mountain is exactly as hard as it sounds.

They heaved groaning at ropes, dragged snarling at oars switched about to make handles, set their shoulders to the keel when the runners snagged, gripping at each other in a straining, stinking, swearing tangle. Even with four of the oxen yoked to the prow they were soon all bruised from falls and raw from rope, whipped by twigs and riddled with splinters.

Safrit went ahead to clear the track of fallen branches. Koll darted in and out below the keel with a bucket of pitch and pig fat to keep the runners sliding. Father Yarvi shouted to the drovers in their tongue, who never used the goad but only crooned to the oxen in low voices.

Uphill, always uphill, the track faint and full of stones and roots. Some prowled armed through the trees about the ship, watching for bandits who might wait in the woods for crews to ambush, and rob, and sell as slaves.

"Selling a ship's crew is much more profitable than selling things to a ship's crew, that's sure." Odda's sigh implied he spoke from experience.

"Or than dragging a ship through a wood," grunted Dosduvoi.

"Save your breath for the lifting," Rulf forced through clenched teeth. "You'll need it."

As the morning wore on Mother Sun beat down without mercy and fat flies swarmed about the toiling oxen and the toiling crew. The sweat ran down Thorn's stubbled scalp in streaks, dripped from her brows and soaked her vest so that it chafed her nipples raw. Many of the crew stripped to their waists and a few much further. Odda struggled along in boots alone, sporting the hairiest arse ever displayed by man or beast.

Thorn should have been watching where she put her feet but her eyes kept drifting across the boat to Brand. While the others grumbled and stumbled and spewed curses he kept on, eyes ahead and wet hair stuck to his clenched jaw, thick muscles in his sweat-beaded shoulders working as he hefted all that weight with no complaints. That was strength right there. Strength like Thorn's father had, solid and silent and certain as Father Earth. She remembered Queen Laithlin's last words to her. *Fools boast of what they will do. Heroes do it.* And Thorn glanced across at Brand again and found herself wishing she was more like him.

"Yes, indeed," murmured Safrit as she held the waterskin to Thorn's cracked lips so she could drink without letting go her rope. "That is a well-made lad."

Thorn jerked her eyes away, got half her mouthful down her windpipe and near choked on it. "Don't know what you're speaking of."

"Course not." Safrit pushed her tongue into her cheek. "That must be why you keep not looking."

Once they even passed a ship being hauled the other way by a crowd of sweat-bathed Lowlanders, and they nodded to each other but wasted no breath on greetings. Thorn had no breath to spare, chest on fire and every muscle aching. Even her toenails hurt.

"I'm no great enthusiast . . . for rowing," she snarled, "but I'd damn sure rather . . . row a ship . . . than carry it."

With one last effort they heaved the *South Wind* over a stubborn brow and onto the flat, the runners grinding to a halt.

"We'll rest here for now!" called Father Yarvi.

There was a chorus of grateful groans, and men tied their ropes off around the nearest trees, dropping among the knotted roots where they stood.

"Thank the gods," whispered Thorn, pushing her hands into her aching back. "The downslope'll be easier. It has to be."

"Guess we'll see when we get there," said Brand, shading his eyes.

The ground dropped away ahead but, further on, indistinct in the haze, it rose again. It rose in forested slopes, higher, and higher, to a ridge above even the one they stood on now.

Thorn stared at it, jaw hanging open in sick disbelief. "More and more, crushing with stones seems like it might have been the less painful option."

"It's not too late to change your mind," said Father Yarvi. "We may be short of comforts out here, but I'm sure we can find stones."

# THE MAN
# WHO
# FOUGHT A
# SHIP

I t was a grim and weary crew who struggled groaning from their beds, all wracked with aches and bruises from yesterday's labor and looking forward to as hard a day ahead. Even Odda had no jokes as he contemplated the long drop down the forested hillside, the hint of water glimmering in the misty distance.

"Least it's downhill," said Brand.

Odda snorted as he turned away. "Ha."

Brand soon found out his meaning. Uphill, the challenge had been dragging the *South Wind* on. Downhill, it was stopping her running off, which meant just as much work but a lot more danger. Not enough width on the crooked track for any help from the oxen, a dozen of the crew wrapped rags around sore hands, looped check-ropes around raw forearms and across aching shoulders padded with blankets and struggled along beside the ship, six of them on each side. They strained to keep her straight as she lurched down that lumpy hillside, Koll creeping ahead with his bucket, slipping in to daub the runners whenever they set to smoking.

"Steady," grumbled Rulf, holding up a hand. "Steady!"

"Easier said than bloody done," groaned Brand. He'd been given a rope, of course. The trouble with being able to lift heavy things is that when heavy things need lifting folk step out of the way and smile at you. He'd done some tough jobs to earn a crust for him and Rin but he'd never worked this hard in his life, hemp wet with sweat wound around one forearm, over his shoulders, then around the other, cutting at him with every step, legs all aquiver, boots scuffing at the loose earth and the slick leaves and the fallen pine needles, coughing on the dust Odda scuffled up ahead of him and flinching at the curses of Dosduvoi behind.

"When do we get to that damn river?" snarled Odda over his shoulder as they waited for a fallen tree to be heaved from the path.

"We'll soon be able to float the boat in the one flowing out of me." Brand shook his head and the sweat flew in fat drops from his wet hair.

"As soon as Safrit brings the water it's straight out of my back and down my crack," said Dosduvoi from behind him. "Are you going to tell us how you got the scar, Fror?"

"Cut myself shaving," the Vansterman called from the other side of the ship, then left a long pause before adding, "Never shave with an ax."

Thorn was one of five carrying the part-carved mast. Brand could feel her eyes sharp as arrows in his back and guessed she was still furious over what he'd said about her mother. He hardly blamed her. Wasn't Thorn who'd trotted off and left Rin to fend for herself, was it? Seemed whenever Brand lost his temper it was really himself he was angry at. He knew he ought to say sorry for it but words had never come easy to him. Sometimes he'd spend days picking over the right ones to say, but when he finally got his mouth open the wrong ones came drooling straight out.

"Reckon I'd be better off if I never said another word," he grunted to himself.

"You'd get no bloody complaints from me," he heard Thorn mutter, and was just turning to give her a tongue-lashing he'd no doubt soon regret when he felt a jolt through his rope that dragged him floundering into a heap of leaves, only just keeping his feet.

"Easy!" roared Dosduvoi, and hauled back hard on his own rope. A knot slipped with a noise like a whip cracking and he gave a shocked yelp and went flying over backwards.

Odda squealed out, "Gods!" as he was jerked onto his face, knocking the next man over so he lost his grip on his own rope, the loose end snapping like a thing alive.

There was a flurry of wingbeats as a bird took to the sky and the *South Wind* lurched forward, one of the men on the other side shrieking as his rope tore across his shoulders and spun him around, knocking Fror sideways, the sudden weight dragging the rest of the men over like skittles.

Brand saw Koll leaning in with his pitch, staring up in horror as the high prow shuddered over him. He tried to scramble clear, slipped on his back under the grinding keel.

No time for first thoughts, let alone second ones. Maybe that was a good thing. Brand's father had always told him he wasn't much of a thinker.

He bounded off the track in a shower of old leaves, dragging his rope around the nearest tree, a thick-trunked old beast with gnarled roots grasping deep into the hillside.

Folk were screaming over each other, timbers groaning, wood snapping, but Brand paid them no mind, wedged one boot up against the tree and then the other. With a grunt he forced his legs and his back out straight, leaning into the rope across his shoulders, hauling it taut so he was standing sideways from the trunk like one of the branches.

If only he'd been made of wood too. The rope twanged like a harpstring and his eyes bulged at the force of it, hemp grating against bark, slipping in his hands, biting into his arms. He clenched his teeth and closed his eyes and gripped at the rags around the rope. Gripped them tight as Death grips the dying.

Too much to lift. Way too much, but once the load's on you what choice do you have?

More grinding in his ears as the *South Wind* shifted and the weight grew, and grew, and crushed a slow groan out of him, but he knew if he let his knees, or his back, or his arms bend once the rope would fold him in half.

He opened his eyes for an instant. Sunlight flickered through leaves. Blood on his quivering fists. The rope smoking about the trunk. Voices echoed far away. He hissed as the rope twitched and pinged then slipped again, biting into him surely as a saw.

Couldn't let go. Couldn't fail his crew. Bones creaking as the hemp cut into his shoulders, his arms, his hands, sure to rip him apart, the jagged breath tearing at his chest and snorting from his clenched teeth.

Couldn't let go. Couldn't fail his family. His whole body trembling, every last thread of muscle on fire with the effort.

Nothing in the world but him and the rope. Nothing but effort and pain and darkness.

And then he heard Rin's voice, soft in his ear. "Let go."

He shook his head, whimpering, straining.

"Let go, Brand!"

An ax thudded into wood and he was falling, the world turning over. Strong arms caught him, lowered him, weak as a child, floppy as rags.

Thorn, with Mother Sun behind her, glowing in the fuzz on the side of her head.

"Where's Rin?" he whispered, but the words were just a croak.

"You can let go."

"Uh." His fists were still gripping. Took a mighty effort to make his pulsing fingers come open, enough for Thorn to start unwinding the rope, hemp dark with blood.

She winced, and shrieked out, "Father Yarvi!"

"I'm sorry," he croaked.

"What?"

"Shouldn't have said that . . . about your mother—"

"Shut up, Brand." There was a pause, then, a babble of voices in the distance, a bird sending up a trilling call in the branches above. "Thing that really burns is I'm starting to think you were right."

"I was?"

"Don't get carried away. Doubt it'll happen again."

There were people gathering about them, blurry outlines looking down.

"You ever see the like o' that?"

"He had her whole weight for a moment."

"A feat to sing of, all right."

"Already setting it to a verse," came Odda's voice.

"You saved my life," said Koll, staring down with wide eyes, pitch smeared up his cheek.

Safrit put the neck of the waterskin to Brand's lips. "The ship would have crushed him."

"The ship might've crushed herself," said Rulf. "We'd have brought no help to Gettland then."

"We'd have needed a stack of help ourselves."

Even swallowing was an effort. "Just . . . done what anyone would do."

"You remind me of an old friend of ours," said Father Yarvi. "Strong arm. Strong heart."

"One stroke at a time," said Rulf, voice a little choked.

Brand looked down at what the minister was doing and felt a surge of sickness. The rope-burns coiled up his arms like red snakes around white branches, raw and bloody.

"Does it hurt?"

"Just a tingle."

"Just a damn tingle!" bellowed Odda. "You hear that? What rhymes with tingle?"

"It'll hurt soon enough," said Father Yarvi. "And leave you some scars."

"Marks of a great deed," murmured Fror who, when it came to scars, had to be reckoned an expert. "Hero's marks."

Brand winced as Yarvi wound the bandages around his forearms, the cuts burning like fury now. "Some hero," he muttered, as Thorn helped him sit up. "I fought a rope and lost."

"No." Father Yarvi slid a pin through the bandages and put his withered hand on Brand's shoulder. "You fought a ship. And won. Put this under your tongue." And he slipped a dried leaf into Brand's mouth. "It'll help with the pain."

"The knot slipped," said Dosduvoi, blinking at the frayed end of his rope. "What kind of awful luck is that?"

"The kind that afflicts men who don't check their knots," said Father Yarvi, glaring at him. "Safrit, make space for Brand in the wagon. Koll, you stay with him. Make sure he's moved to perform no further heroics."

Safrit made a bed among the supplies from the crew's blankets. Brand tried to tell her he could walk but they could all see he couldn't.

"You'll lie there and you'll like it!" she snapped, her pointed finger in his face.

So that was that. Koll perched on a barrel beside him and the wagon set lurching off down the slope, Brand wincing at every jolt.

"You saved my life," muttered the lad, after a while.

"You're quick. You'd have got out of the way."

"No I wouldn't. I was looking through the Last Door. Let me thank you, at least."

They looked at each other for a moment. "Fair enough," said Brand. "I'm thanked."

"How did you get that strong?"

"Work, I guess. On the docks. At the oar. In the forge."

"You've done smith work?"

"For a woman named Gaden. She took her husband's forge on when he died and turned out twice the smith he'd been." Brand remembered the feel of the hammer, the ringing of the anvil, the heat of the coals. Never thought he'd miss it, but he did. "It's a good trade, working iron. Honest."

"Why'd you stop?"

"Always dreamed of being a warrior. Winning a place in the songs. Joining a crew." Brand watched Odda and Dosduvoi squabbling under the weight of their ropes, Fror shaking his head in disgust, and smiled. "It was a cleaner crew than this I had in mind, but you have to take the family you're given." The pain was less but it seemed Yarvi's leaf had loosened his tongue. "My mother died when I was little. Told me to do good. My father didn't want me . . ."

"My father died," said Koll. "Long time ago."

"Well, now you've got Father Yarvi. And all these brothers around you." Brand caught Thorn's eye for an instant before she frowned off sideways into the trees. "And Thorn for a sister too, for that matter."

Koll gave his quick grin. "Mixed blessing, that."

"Most blessings are. She's prickly, but I reckon she'd fight to the death for any one of us."

"She certainly does like fighting."

"She certainly does."

The wagon's wheels squealed, the cargo rattled, the straining crew bellowed at one another. Then Koll said, quietly, "Are you my brother, then?"

"Guess so. If you'll have me."

"Reckon I could do worse." The lad shrugged, as if it didn't matter much either way. But Brand got the feeling it did.


WITH ONE LAST HEAVE the *South Wind* slid into the churning waters of the Denied and a ragged cheer went up.

"We made it," said Brand, hardly believing it. "Did we make it?"

"Aye. You can all tell your grandchildren you carted a ship over the tall hauls." Rulf wiped the sweat from his forehead on one thick forearm. "But we've some rowing still to do today!" he called, bringing the celebrations to a quick end. "Let's get her loaded up and make a few miles before sundown!"

"On your feet, idler." Dosduvoi swung Brand down from the wagon and onto his still-shaky legs.

Father Yarvi was talking to the leader of the drovers in the gods knew what strange tongue, then they both broke into laughter and gave each other a long hug.

"What did he say?" asked Brand.

"Beware of the Horse People," said Father Yarvi, "for they are savage and dangerous."

Thorn frowned toward the oxen, finally freed of their burden. "I don't see the joke."

"I asked him what he says to the Horse People, when he trades with them."

"And?"

"Beware of the Boat People, for they are savage and dangerous."

"Who are the Boat People?" asked Koll.

"We are," said Brand, grimacing as he clambered back aboard the *South Wind*. Every joint and sinew was aching and he went stooped in an old man's shuffle to his place at the stern, flopping onto his sea chest the moment Thorn thumped it down for him.

"You sure you can row?"

"I'll keep stroke with you all right," he muttered back at her, though it felt like a hero's effort just to sit up.

"You can barely keep stroke with me healthy," she said.

"We'll see if you can keep stroke with me, you mouthy string of gristle." Rulf was standing behind them. "You're in my place, lad."

"Where do I go?"

Rulf nodded toward the steering oar on its platform above them. "Thought for this evening you might take the helm."

Brand blinked. "Me?"

"Reckon you earned it." And Rulf slapped him on the back as he helped him up.

Grunting at the pain, Brand turned, one arm over the steering oar, and saw the whole crew watching him. Safrit and Koll with the cargo, Odda and Dosduvoi and Fror at their oars, Father Yarvi standing with Skifr near the dove-carved prow and beyond it the Denied flowing away south, Mother Sun scattering gold upon the water.

Brand grinned wide. "I like the view from here."

"Don't get used to it," said Rulf.

And all at once the crew started thumping at their oars, hammering, pounding, a thunder of flesh on wood. A drumming of respect. For him. For him who all his life had been nothing.

"To be fair, it was quite a thing you did up there." Thorn had the hint of a grin, eyes glinting as she slapped at her oar. "Quite a thing."

Brand felt pride swelling in him then like he'd never known before. He'd come a long road since Hunnan left him alone on the beach below Thorlby. He might not have sworn a warrior's oath, but he'd found a crew even so. A family to be part of. He wished Rin was there to see it, and pictured her face if she had been, and had to sniff and pretend he'd got something in his eye. Felt like standing in the light, and no mistake.

"Well don't just hit 'em, you lazy bastards!" he shouted in a broken voice. "Pull 'em!"

The crew laughed as they set to their oars, and the *South Wind* pulled smoothly off into the swift Denied, rowing with the current at last, leaving the oxen and their drivers to wait on the bank for a new burden.

# STRANGE TIMES

The forest gave way to the open steppe. Terribly open. Ruthlessly flat. Mile upon mile of lush, green, waving grass.

To Thorn, brought up among the hills and mountains and cliffs of Gettland, there was something crushing in all that emptiness, all that space, stretching off under a bottomless sky to the far, far horizon.

"Why does no one farm it?" asked Koll, straddling the downed mast with the wind whipping the shavings from under his knife.

"The Horse People graze it," said Dosduvoi. "And don't like finding other folk out here."

Odda snorted. "They like it so little they skin 'em alive, indeed."

"A practice the Prince of Kalyiv taught them."

"Who learned it in the First of Cities," said Fror, wiping his misshapen eye with a fingertip.

"Though I understand it was taken there by travellers from Sagenmark," said Rulf.

"Who were taught it when Bail the Builder first raided them," said Yarvi.

"So are the skinners skinned," mused Skifr, watching the wind sweep patterns in the grass, "and the bloody lessons turn in circles."

"Well enough." Rulf scanned the river ahead, and behind, and the flat land around with eyes more fiercely narrowed than ever. "Long as we take no instruction."

"Why are you so worried?" asked Thorn. "We haven't seen a ship for days."

"Exactly. Where are they?"

"Here are two," said Father Yarvi, pointing downriver.

He had sharp eyes. It wasn't until they came much closer that, straining over her shoulder, Thorn could see what the black heaps on the river's bank were. The charred skeletons of a pair of small ships in a wide patch of trampled grass. The blackened circle of a spent fire. A fire just like the one they warmed their hands at every night.

"It doesn't look good for the crews," muttered Brand, with a knack for saying what everyone could already see.

"Dead," said Skifr brightly. "Perhaps some lucky ones are enslaved. Or unlucky ones. The Horse People are not known as gentle masters."

Odda frowned out across the expanse of flat grass. "You think we'll make their acquaintance?"

"Knowing my luck," murmured Dosduvoi.

"From now on we look for high ground to camp on!" bellowed Rulf. "And we double the guard! Eight men awake at all times!"

So it was with everyone nervous, frowning out across the steppe and startling at every sound, that they caught sight of a ship rowing upriver.

She was of a size with the *South Wind*, sixteen oars a side or so. Her prow-beast was a black wolf, so Thorn guessed her crew to be Throvenlanders, and by the scars on the shields at the rail, men ready for a fight. Maybe even hungry for one.

"Keep your weapons close!" called Rulf, his horn bow already in his hand.

Safrit watched nervously as men struggled to manage oar-blades and war-blades at once. "Shouldn't we smooth the path for Father Peace?"

"Of course." Father Yarvi loosened his own sword in its sheath. "But the words of an armed man ring that much sweeter. Well met!" he called across the water.

A mailed and bearded figure stood tall at the prow of the other ship. "And to you, friends!" It would have sounded more peaceable if he hadn't had men with drawn bows on either side of him. "Our ship is the *Black Dog*, come up the Denied from the First of Cities!"

"The *South Wind*, come down the Divine from Roystock!" Yarvi shouted back.

"How were the tall hauls?"

"Thirsty work for those who did the lifting." Yarvi held up his crippled hand. "But I got through it."

The other captain laughed. "A leader should share his men's work, but take a fair share and they'll lose all respect for him! May we draw close?"

"You may, but know we are well armed."

"In these parts it's the unarmed men who cause suspicion." The captain signalled to his crew, a weathered-looking group, all scars, beards, and bright ring-money, who skilfully drew the *Black Dog* into the middle of the current and alongside the *South Wind*, prow to stern.

Their captain burst out in disbelieving laughter. "Who's that old bastard you have at the helm there? Bad Rulf or I'm a side of ham! I was sure you were dead and had lost no sleep over it!"

Rulf barked out a laugh of his own. "A side of ham and a rotten one at that, Blue Jenner! I was sure you were dead and had tapped a keg in celebration!"

"Bad Rulf?" muttered Thorn.

"Long time ago." The old helmsman waved it away as he set his bow down. "Folk generally get less bad with age."

The crew of the *Black Dog* tossed their prow-rope across the water and, in spite of some cursing at their tangling oars, the crews dragged the two ships together. Blue Jenner leaned across and clasped Rulf's arm, both men beaming.

Thorn did not smile, and kept her own hand on her father's sword.

"How the hell did you get clear of that mess Young Halstam got us into?" Rulf was asking.

Jenner pulled off his helmet and tossed it back to his men, scrubbing at a tangle of thin gray hair. "I'm ashamed to say I took my chances with Mother Sea and swam for it."

"You always had fine weaponluck."

"Still took an arrow in my arse, but despite being a bony man I've been blessed with a fleshy arse and it's done no lasting harm. I counted the arrow good luck, for it surely pricked me free of a thrall collar."

Rulf fingered gently at his neck, and Thorn saw marks she'd never noticed there, below his beard. "I was less lucky. But thanks to Father Yarvi I find myself a free man again."

"Father Yarvi?" Jenner's eyes went wide. "Gettland's minister? Who was once the son of the Golden Queen Laithlin?"

"The same," said Yarvi, threading his way between the sea-chests to the back of the boat.

"Then I'm honored, for I've heard you named a deep-cunning man." Blue Jenner raised his brows at Thorn. "You've got women pulling your oars now?"

"I've got whoever moves my boat," said Rulf.

"Why the mad hair, girl?"

"Because damn you," growled Thorn, "that's why."

"Oh, she's a fierce one! Never mind the oar, I daresay she could break a man in half."

"I'm willing to give it a go," she said, not a little flattered.

Jenner showed his teeth, a yellowing set with several gaps. "Were I ten years younger I'd leap at the chance, but age has brought caution."

"The less time you have, the less you want to risk what's left," said Rulf.

"That's the truth of it." Jenner shook his head. "Bad Rulf back from beyond the Last Door and girls pulling oars and heaven knows what else. Strange times, all right."

"What times aren't?" asked Father Yarvi.

"There's the truth of that too!" Blue Jenner squinted up at the muddy sun. "Getting towards dinner. Shall we put ashore and swap news?"

"By swap news do you mean drink?" asked Rulf.

"I do, and that excessively."

THEY FOUND AN EASILY-DEFENDED loop of the river, set a strong guard and built a great fire, the flames whipped sideways by the ceaseless wind, showering sparks across the water. Then each crew tapped a keg of their ale and there was much singing of ever more tuneless songs, telling of ever more unbelievable tales, and making of ever more raucous merriment. Someone ill-advisedly gave Koll beer, and he got quite a taste for it, then shortly afterward was sick and fell asleep, much to his mother's profound disgust and everyone else's profound amusement.

Merry-making had never made Thorn especially merry, though. In spite of the smiles everyone kept blades to hand and there were several men who laughed as little as she did. The *Black Dog*'s helmsman, called Crouch and with a white streak in his balding hair, seemed to be nursing some particular grudge against the world. When he got up to piss in the river Thorn noticed him giving the *South Wind*'s contents a thorough look-over, that iron-bound chest of Father Yarvi's in particular.

"I don't like the look of him," she muttered to Brand.

He peered at her over the rim of his cup. "You don't like the look of anyone."

She'd never had any objection to the look of Brand at all, but she kept that to herself. "I like his look less than most, then. One of those people with nought in them but hard stares and hard words. Face like a slapped arse."

He grinned into his ale at that. "Oh, I hate those people."

She had to grin herself. "Beneath my forbidding exterior I've got hidden depths, though."

"Well hidden," he said, as he lifted his cup. "But I might be starting to plumb 'em."

"Bold of you. Plumbing a girl without so much as a by your leave."

He blew ale out of his nose, fell into a coughing fit and had to be clapped on the back by Odda, who seized the chance to honk out his ill-made verse on Brand lifting the ship. The slope got steeper and the danger greater and the feat more impressive with every telling, Safrit beaming at Brand and saying, "He saved my son's life." The only one to dispute the questionable facts was Brand himself, who couldn't have looked less comfortable at all the praise if he'd been sitting on a spike.

"How are things around the Shattered Sea?" Blue Jenner asked when the song was over. "It's been a year since we've seen home."

"Much as they were," said Yarvi. "Grandmother Wexen makes ever greater demands on behalf of the High King. The latest talk is of taxes."

"A pox on him and his One God!" snapped Jenner. "A fellow should own what he takes, not have to rent it from some other thief just because he has the bigger chair."

"The more some men get the more they want," said Yarvi, and folk on both sides of the fire murmured their agreement.

"Was the Divine clear?"

"We found no trouble, anyway," said Rulf. "And the Denied?"

Jenner sucked at the gaps in his teeth. "The damn Horse People are stirred up like angry bees, attacking boats and caravans, burning steadings within sight of Kalyiv."

"Which tribe?" asked Yarvi. "Uzhaks? Barmeks?"

Jenner stared back blankly. "There are tribes?"

"All with their own ways."

"Well, they mostly shoot the same kind of arrows, far as I can see, and the Prince of Kalyiv isn't making much distinction between 'em either. He's grown sick of their taunting, and means to teach them a bloody lesson."

"The best kind," said Odda, baring his filed teeth.

"Except he's not planning to do it with his own hands."

"Princes rarely do," said Yarvi.

"He's strung a chain across the Denied and is letting no fighting crew pass until we Northerners have helped him give the Horse People their proper chastisement."

Rulf puffed up his broad chest. "Well he won't be stopping the Minister of Gettland."

"You don't know Prince Varoslaf and no sensible man would want to. There's no telling what that bald bastard will do one moment to the next. Only reason we got away is I spun him a tale about spreading the news and bringing more warriors from the Shattered Sea. If I was you I'd turn back with us."

"We're going on," said Yarvi.

"Then the very best of weatherluck to you all, and let's hope you don't need weaponluck." Blue Jenner took a long draft from his cup. "But I fear you might."

"As might anyone who takes the tall hauls." Skifr lay on her back, arms behind her head, bare feet toward the fire. "Perhaps you should test yours while you can?"

"What did you have in mind, woman?" growled Crouch.

"A friendly test of arms with practice blades." Skifr yawned wide. "My pupil has beaten everyone on our crew and needs new opponents."

"Who's your pupil?" asked Jenner, peering over at Dosduvoi, who seemed a mountain in the flickering shadows.

"Oh, no," said the giant. "Not me."

Thorn put on her bravest face, stood, and stepped into the firelight. "Me."

There was a silence. Then Crouch gave a disbelieving cackle, soon joined by others.

"This half-haired waif?"

"Can the girl even heft a shield?"

"She could heft a needle, I reckon. I need someone to stitch a hole in my sock!"

"You'll need someone to stitch a hole in you after she's done," growled Odda.

A lad maybe a year older than Thorn begged for the chance to give her the first beating and the two crews gathered in a noisy circle with torches to light the contest, shouting insults and encouragement, making wagers on their crew-mate. He was a big one with great thick wrists, fierce in the eyes. Thorn's father always said, *fear is a good thing. Fear keeps you careful. Fear keeps you alive.* That was just as well because Thorn's heart was thudding so hard she thought her skull might burst.

"Bet on this scrap of nothing?" yelled Crouch, chopping one of his armrings in half with a hatchet and betting it against Thorn. "Might as well throw your money in the river! You having a piece of this?"

Blue Jenner quietly stroked his beard so his own armrings rattled. "I like my money where it is."

The nerves vanished the moment their wooden blades first clashed and Thorn knew she had the lad well beaten. She dodged his second blow, steered away the third and let him stumble past. He was strong but he came at her angrily, blindly, his weight set all wrong. She ducked under a heedless sweep, almost laughing at how clumsy it was, hooked his shield down and struck him across the face with a sharp smack. He sat down hard in the dirt, blinking stupidly with blood pouring from his nose.

"You are the storm," she heard Skifr murmur over the cheering. "Do not wait for them. Make them fear. Make them doubt."

She sprang screaming at the next man the instant Jenner called for the fight to start, barged him into his shocked friends, chopped him across the stomach with her practice sword, and put a dent in his helmet with a ringing blow of her wooden ax. He stumbled drunkenly for a moment while the *South Wind*'s crew laughed, trying to pry the rim back up over his brows.

"Men used to fighting in the shield wall tend to think only ahead. The shield becomes a weakness. Use the flanks."

The next man was short but thick as a tree-trunk, cautious and watchful. She let him herd her back with his shield long enough for the boos of the *Black Dog*'s crew to turn to cheers. Then she came alive, feinted left and darted right, went high with her sword and, as he raised his shield, hooked his ankle with her ax, dragged him squealing over and left her sword's point tickling at his throat.

"Yes. Be never where they expect you. Always attack. Strike first. Strike last."

"You useless dogs!" snapped Crouch. "I'm shamed to be one of you!" And he snatched up the fallen sword, took up a shield with a white arrow painted on it and stepped into the circle.

He was a vicious one, and fast, and clever, but she was faster and cleverer and far more vicious and Skifr had taught her tricks he never dreamed of. She danced about him, wore him down, rained blows on him until he hardly knew which way he was facing. Finally she slipped around a lunge and gave him a smack across the arse with the flat of her sword they might have heard in Kalyiv.

"This was no fair test," he growled as he stood up. It was plain he desperately wanted to rub his stinging buttocks but was forcing himself not to.

Thorn shrugged. "The battlefield isn't fair."

"On the battlefield we fight with steel, girl." And he flung the practice sword down. "It'd be a different outcome with real blades."

"True," said Thorn. "Rather than nursing a bruised pride and a bruised backside you'd be spilling guts out of your split arse."

Laughter from the *South Wind*'s crew at that, and Jenner tried to calm his helmsman with an offer of more ale but he shook him off. "Get me my ax and we'll see, bitch!"

The laughter guttered out, and Thorn curled her lip and spat at his feet. "Get your ax, sow, I'm ready!"

"No," said Skifr, putting her arm across Thorn's chest. "The time will come for you to face death. This is not it."

"Hah," spat Crouch. "Cowards!"

Thorn growled in her throat, but Skifr pushed her back again, eyes narrowed. "You are a hatful of winds, helmsman. You are a hollow man."

Odda stepped past her. "Far from being hollow, he is full to the crown with turds." Thorn was surprised to see a drawn knife gleaming in his hand. "I never had a braver oarmate, man or woman. At your next insult I will take it upon myself to kill you."

"You'll have to beat me to it," rumbled Dosduvoi, tossing aside his blanket and drawing himself up to his full height.

"And me." And Brand was beside her with his bandaged hand on that fine dagger of his.

Many fingers were tickling at weapons on both sides and—what with the ale, and the injured pride, and the lost silver—things might quickly have turned exceeding ugly. But before a blow was landed Father Yarvi sprang nimbly between the two bristling crews.

"We all have enemies enough without making more among our friends! Blood shed here would be blood wasted! Let us make of the fist an open hand. Let us give the Father of Doves his day. Here!" And he reached into a pocket and tossed something glinting to Crouch.

"What's this?" growled the helmsman.

"Queen Laithlin's silver," said Yarvi, "and with her face upon it." The minister might have been lacking fingers but the ones he had were quick indeed. Coins spun and glittered in the firelight as he flicked them among the *Black Dog*'s crew.

"We don't want your charity," snarled Crouch, though many of his oarmates were already scrambling on their knees for it.

"Consider it an advance, then!" called Yarvi. "On what the queen will pay you when you present yourselves at Thorlby. She and her husband King Uthil are always seeking bold men and good fighters. Especially those who have no great love for the High King."

Blue Jenner raised his cup high. "To the beautiful and generous Queen Laithlin, then!" As his crew cheered, and charged their cups, he added more softly, "and her deep-cunning minister," and even more softly yet, with a wink at Thorn, "not to mention his formidable back oar."

"What's happening?" cried Koll, staggering up wild-eyed, wild-haired and tangled with his blanket, then he fell over and was promptly sick again, to gales of helpless laughter.

Within a few moments the two crews were once more exchanging tales, and finding old comrades in common, and arguing over whose was the better knife while Safrit dragged her son away by the ear and dunked his head in the river. Crouch was left nursing his grudge alone, standing with fists on hips and glaring daggers at Thorn.

"I've a feeling you've made an enemy there," muttered Brand, sliding his dagger back into its sheath.

"Oh, I'm always doing that. What does Father Yarvi say? Enemies are the price of success." She threw one arm around his shoulders, the other about Odda's, and hugged the two of them tight. "The shock is that I've made some friends besides."

# A RED DAY

"Shields!" bellowed Rulf.

And Brand was hooked by panic and torn from happy dreams of home, scrambling from the comfort of his blankets and up into a chill dawn the color of blood.

"Shields!"

The crew were stumbling from their beds, bouncing off one another, charging about like startled sheep, half-dressed, half-armed, half-awake. A man kicked the embers of the fire as he ran past and sent sparks whirling. Another bellowed as he tried to struggle into his mail shirt, tangled with the sleeves.

"Arm yourselves!"

Thorn was up beside him. The unshaved side of her head was chaos these days, braids and snarls and matted worms bound up with rings of silver clipped from coins, but her weapons were oiled and polished to a ready gleam and her face was set hard. Made Brand feel braver, to see her brave. The gods knew, he needed courage. He needed courage and he needed to piss.

They'd pitched camp on the only hill for miles, a flat-topped knoll in a bend of the river, broken boulders jutting from its flanks, a few stunted trees clinging to the top. Brand hurried to the eastern crest where the crew were gathering, stared down the slope and across the flat ocean of grass that stretched away into the sunrise. As he scraped sleep from his eyes with trembling fingers he saw figures out there, ghostly riders wriggling in the dawn haze.

"Horse People?" he croaked out.

"Uzhaks, I think," Father Yarvi shaded his pale eyes against Mother Sun, a bloody smudge on the far horizon, "but they live on the shores of the Golden Sea. I don't know what's brought them here."

"A deep desire to kill us?" said Odda as the riders took shape out of the murk, red sun glinting on metal, on the blades of spears and curved swords, on helmets made to look like the heads of beasts.

"How many are there?" muttered Thorn, jaw-muscles working on the shaved side of her head.

"Eighty?" Fror watched them as calmly as a man might watch a neighbor weed his garden. "Ninety?" He opened up a pouch and spat in it, started mixing something inside with a fingertip. "A hundred?"

"Gods," whispered Brand. He could hear the sound of hooves as the Horse People circled closer, yells and yips and strange warbles echoing across the plain, above the rattle and growl of the crew making ready their own war-gear and calling on their chosen gods for weaponluck. One rider swerved close, long hair streaming, to try an arrow. Brand shrank back but it was just a ranging shot, a taunting shot, dropping into the grass halfway up the slope.

"An old friend once told me the greater the odds the greater the glory," said Rulf, plucking at his bowstring with calloused fingers and making it angrily hum.

Dosduvoi slipped the oil-cloth from the head of his great ax. "The chances of death also increase."

"But who wants to meet Death old, beside the fire?" And Odda's teeth shone with spit as he flashed his mad grin.

"Doesn't sound such a bad outcome." Fror pushed his hand into his pouch and pulled it out covered in blue paint, pressed it onto his face with the fingers spread to leave a great palm-print. "But I am ready."

Brand wasn't. He gripped his shield that Rin had painted with a dragon, it seemed a hundred years ago and half the world away. He gripped the haft of his ax, palms still sore with the rope burns underneath their bandages. The Horse People were ever-moving, their troop breaking apart and coming back together, flowing across the plain like swift-running water but always working their way closer, a white banner streaming under a horned skull. He caught glimpses of brave faces, beast faces, battle faces, teeth bared and eyes rolling. So many of them.

"Gods," he whispered. Had he really chosen this? Instead of a nice, safe, boring life at Gaden's forge?

"Skifr!" called Father Yarvi, low and urgent.

The old woman was sitting behind them, crosslegged beneath one of the trees, frowning into the dead fire as though the solution to their troubles might be hidden among the embers. "No!" she snapped over her shoulder.

"Arrows!" someone screeched and Brand saw them, black splinters sailing high, drifting with the wind. One flickered down near him, the feathered flights twitching. What change in the breeze might have wafted that little thing of wood and metal through his chest, and he'd have died out here under a bloody sky and never seen his sister again, or the docks, or the middens of Thorlby. Even things you always hated seem wonderful when you look back on them from a place like this.

"Get a wall together you lazy dogs!" Rulf roared, and Brand scrambled between Odda and Fror, wood and metal grating as they locked their shields together, rim behind the one on the left and in front of the one on the right. A thousand times he'd done it in the training square, arms and legs moving by themselves. Just as well, since his head felt full of mud. Men with spears and bows crowded behind them, thumping the front rank on their backs and snarling encouragements, those without shields waiting to kill anyone who broke through, to plug the gaps when men fell. When men died. Because men would die here, today, and soon.

"Before breakfast too, the bastards!" snapped Odda.

"If I had it in mind to kill a man I'd want him hungry," grunted Fror.

Brand's heart was beating as if it would burst his chest, his knees shaking with the need to run, jaw clenched tight with the need to stand. To stand with his crew, his brothers, his family. He wriggled his shoulders to feel them pressed tight against him. Gods, he needed to piss.

"How did you get the scar?" he hissed.

"Now?" growled Fror.

"I'd like to die knowing something about my shoulder-man."

"Very well." The Vansterman flashed a mad grin, good eye white in the midst of that blue handprint. "When you die, I'll tell you."

Father Yarvi squatted in the shadow of the shield wall, yelling words in the Horse People's tongue, giving Father Peace his chance, but no answer came but arrows, clicking on wood, flickering overhead. Someone cried out as a shaft found his leg.

"Mother War rules today," muttered Yarvi, hefting his curved sword. "Teach them some archery, Rulf."

"Arrows!" shouted the helmsman and Brand stepped back, angling his shield to make a slot to shoot through, Rulf stepping up beside him with his black bow full-drawn, string whining in fury. Brand felt the wind of the flying shaft on his cheek as he stepped back and locked his rim with Fror's again.

A shrill howl echoed out as the arrow found its mark and the crew laughed and jeered, stuck out their tongues and showed their brave faces, beast faces, battle faces. Brand didn't feel much like laughing. He felt like pissing.

The Horse People were known for darting in and out, tricking their enemies and wearing them down with their bows. A well-built shield wall is hard to pierce with arrows alone, though, and that horn bow of Rulf's was even more fearsome than it looked. With the height of their little hill he had the longer reach and, in spite of the years washed by him, his aim was deadly. One by one he sent arrows whistling down the grassy slope, calm as still water, patient as stone. Twice more the crew cheered as he brought down a horse then knocked a rider from his saddle to tumble through the grass. The others fell back out of his bow's reach and began to gather.

"They can't get around us because of the river." Father Yarvi pressed between them to glance over Odda's shield. "Or make use of their horses among the boulders, and we have the high ground. My left hand picked a good spot."

"It's not my first dance," said Rulf, sliding out another arrow. "They'll come on foot, and they'll break on our wall like Mother Sea on the rocks."

Rocks feel no pain. Rocks shed no blood. Rocks do not die. Brand went up on his toes to peer over the wall, saw the Uzhaks sliding from their saddles, readying for a charge. So many of them. The *South Wind*'s crew was outnumbered two to one by his reckoning. Maybe more.

"What do they want?" whispered Brand, scared by the fear in his own voice.

"There is a time for wondering what a man wants," said Fror, no fear at all in his. "And there is a time for splitting his head. This is that second time."

"We hold 'em here!" roared Rulf, "and when I cry 'heave' we drive these bastards down the slope. Drive 'em, and cut 'em down, and trample 'em, and keep mercy for another day, you hear? Arrow."

The shields swung apart and Brand caught a glimpse of men running. Rulf sent his shaft flitting down the hill into the nearest one's ribs, left him crawling, wailing, pleading to his friends as they charged on past.

"Hold now, boys!" called Rulf, tossing aside his bow and lifting a spear. "Hold!"

Around him men growled and spat and muttered prayers to Mother War, breath echoing from the wood in front of them. The odd speckle of rain was falling, a dew on helmets and shield rims, and Brand needed to piss worse than ever.

"Oh, true God!" shouted Dosduvoi, as they heard the quick footsteps of their enemies, howling war cries coming ever closer. "All-powerful! All-knowing God! Smite these heathens!"

"I'll smite the bastards myself!" screamed Odda.

And Brand gasped at the impact, staggered back a half-step, then forwards, putting all his weight to his shield, boots sliding at the wet grass. Metal clanged and rattled and battered against wood. A storm of metal. Something pinged against the rim of his shield and he ducked away, splinters in his face, a devil's broken voice shrieking on the other side.

Fror's misshapen eye bulged as he bellowed words from the *Song of Bail*. "Hand of iron! Head of iron! Heart of iron!" And he lashed blindly with his sword over the shield wall. "Your death comes, sang the hundred!"

"Your death comes!" roared Dosduvoi. Some time for poetry, but others took up the cry, fire in their throats, fire in their chests, fire in their maddened eyes. "Your death comes!"

Whether it was the Horse People's death or theirs they didn't say. It didn't matter. Mother War had spread her iron wings over the plain and cast every heart into shadow. Fror lashed again and caught Brand above the eye with the pommel of his sword, set his ears ringing.

"Heave!" roared Rulf.

Brand ground his teeth as he pushed, shield grinding against shield. He saw a man fall yelling as a spear darted under a rim and ripped into his leg, kept shoving anyway. He heard a voice on the other side, so clear the words, so close the enemy, just a plank's thickness from his face. He jerked up, chopping over his shield with his ax, and again, a grunt and a gurgle, the blade caught on something. A spear jabbed past, scraped against his shield rim and a man howled.

Fror butted someone, their nose popping against his forehead. Men growled and spluttered, stabbing and pushing, all tangled one with another.

"Die, you bastard, die!"

An elbow caught Brand's jaw and made him taste blood. Mud flicked in his face, half-blinded him, and he tried to blink it away, and snarled, and cursed, and shoved, and slipped, and spat salt, and shoved again. The slope was with them and they knew their business and slowly but surely the wall began to shift, driving their enemies back, forcing them down the hill the way they'd come.

"Your death comes, sang the hundred!"

Brand saw an oarsman biting at an Uzhak's neck. He saw Koll stabbing a fallen man with a knife. He saw Dosduvoi fling a figure tumbling with a sweep of his shield. He saw the point of a blade come out of a man's back. Something bounced from Brand's face and he gasped. At first he thought it was an arrow, then realized it had been a finger.

"Heave, I said! Heave!"

They pressed in harder, a hell of snarling and straining bodies, crowded too tight to use his ax and he let it fall, snaked his arm down and slid out the dagger Rin forged for him.

"Hand of iron! Heart of iron!"

The feel of its grip in his hand made him think of Rin's face, firelit in their little hovel. These bastards were between him and her and a rage boiled up in him. He saw a face, rough metal rings in braided hair, and he jerked his shield up into it, snapped a head back, stabbed under the rim, metal squealing, stabbed again, hand sticky-hot. The man fell and Brand trampled over him, stumbling and stomping, dragged up by Odda, spitting through his clenched teeth.

"Your death comes!"

How often had he listened breathless to that song, mouthing the words, dreaming of claiming his own place in the wall, winning his own glory? Was this what he'd dreamed of? There was no skill here, only blind luck. No matching of noble champions, only a contest of madness. No room for tricks or cleverness or even courage, unless courage was to be carried helpless by the surge of battle like a storm washes driftwood. Perhaps it was.

"Kill them!"

The noise of it was horrifying, a clamor of rattling metal and battering wood and men swearing at the tops of their broken voices. Sounds Brand couldn't understand. Sounds that had no meaning. The Last Door stood wide for them all and each of them faced it as best he could.

"Your death comes!"

The rain was getting heavier, boots ripping the grass and churning the red earth to mud and he was tired and sore and aching but there was no stopping. Gods, he needed to piss. Something smashed against his shield, near tore it from his arm. A red blade darted past his ear and he saw Thorn beside him.

The side of her face was spotted with blood and she was smiling. Smiling like she was home.

# BATTLE-JOY

Thorn was a killer. That, no one could deny.

The muddied and bloodied and boot-trampled stretch of grass behind the shifting shield wall was her ground, and to anyone who trod there she was Death.

With a hammering louder than the hail on the *South Wind*'s hull the shield wall edged down the hillside, shoving, hacking, trampling over men and dragging them between their shields, swallowing them up like a hungry serpent. One tried to get up and she stabbed him in the back with her father's sword, his bloodied face all fear and pain and panic as he fell.

It should have been harder than with a practice blade, but it was so much easier. The steel so light, so sharp, her arm so strong, so quick. Her weapons had minds of their own. Ruthless minds, fixed on murder.

She was a killer. Skifr had said so and here was the proof, written in blood on the skins of her enemies. She wished her father had been there to see it. Maybe his ghost was, cheering her on at her shoulder.

She wished Hunnan had been there, so she could shove his face in the blood she'd spilled. So she could dare him to deny her a place. So she could kill him too.

The Horse People didn't understand this way of fighting and they swarmed at the wall in a mess, in ones and twos, their own courage their undoing. Thorn saw one clumsily angling a spear over the shields, aiming to stab at Brand. She darted forward, hooked him around the back with her ax, its pointed beard sinking deep into his shoulder, dragged him between the shields and into her arms.

They tottered in a hug, snapping at each other, his long hair in her mouth, digging with knees and elbows, then Father Yarvi slashed him across the back of his legs and she screamed as she tore her ax free, hacked it into the side of his skull, ripping off his helmet and sending it bouncing up the ruined hillside.

She'd heard her father speak of the battle-joy. The red joy Mother War sends her most favored children. She'd listened to his tales wide-eyed and dry-mouthed beside the fire. Her mother had told him those were no stories for a daughter's ear but he'd leaned close and spoken on in a throaty whisper, so close she felt his warm breath on her cheek. She'd heard him speak of the battle-joy, and now she felt it.

The world burned, blazed, danced, her ripping breath a furnace in her throat as she rushed to the end of the wall, which was flexing now, twisting, threatening to break apart. Two Uzhaks had clambered up between the boulders on the hill's flank and got around Dosduvoi. She hacked one in the side, folded him double. The spear of the other seemed to move as slowly as if it came through honey and she laughed as she slipped around it, chopped his legs away with her ax, sent him reeling.

An arrow flickered past her and Dosduvoi snatched her behind his shield, two shafts already lodged near its rim. The wall was buckling in the center, faces twisted as men strained to hold it together. There was a crash, a crewman fell, drooling teeth, and the wall split apart. A huge Uzhak stood in the gap, wearing a mask made from a walrus jaw with the tusks on either side of his leering face, snorting like a bull as he swung a great toothed club in both fists, sending men staggering, tearing the breach wider.

Thorn had no fear in her. Only the battle-joy, fiercer than ever.

She raced at the giant, blood surging like Mother Sea. His maddened eyes rolled toward her and she dropped, slid on her side between his great boots, turned, slashed as his club thudded into the ground behind her, caught him across the back of his leg, blood frozen in black spots as he lurched onto his knees. Fror stepped forward and hacked him down with thudding blows, one, two, three, the blue hand on his face red-speckled.

Thorn saw the Horse People scattering, bounding away down the slope toward the open plain and their waiting horses and she held her weapons high and screamed, burning to the tips of her fingers. Her father's ghost urged her on and she sprang after her fleeing enemies like a hound after hares.

"Stop her!" roared Rulf, and someone dragged her back, cursing and struggling, the hair she still had tangled across her face. It was Brand, his beard scratching her cheek and his left arm under hers so that his shield was across her. Beyond the running Uzhaks she saw others stalking forward through the grass, bows drawn and faces eager. Lots of them, and close behind the ebbing battle-joy a wave of fear washed in on her.

"Close up the wall!" roared Rulf, spit flecking from his teeth. The men edged back, shuffled together, stopping up the gaps, shields wobbling and rattling and the daylight flickering between them. Thorn heard arrows click against lime-wood, saw one spin from the rim of Brand's shield and over his shoulder. Odda was down, a shaft in his side, spewing curses as he dragged himself up the hill.

"Back! Back! Steady, now!"

She caught Odda under his arms and started to haul him away, while he grunted and kicked and blew bloody bubbles. She fell with him on top of her, nearly cut herself with her own ax, struggled up and dragged him on, then Koll was there to help and between them they pulled him back to the crest of the hill, the shield wall edging after them. Back to where they'd stood a few mad moments ago, the river at their backs and the plain stretching away before them.

Thorn stood there dumb, numb, not sure how many of the crew were dead. Three? Four? Everyone had scratches and some were hurt bad. Didn't know if she was hurt. Didn't know whose blood was on her. From the look of that arrow she held no high hopes for Odda. She held no high hopes for anything. Through the gaps in the battered shields she could see the trampled slope scattered with bodies, some still moving, groaning, pawing at their wounds.

"Push it through or pull it out?" snapped Safrit, kneeling beside Odda, gripping his bloody hand tight.

Father Yarvi only stared down, and rubbed at his lean jaw, fingertips leaving red streaks across his cheek.

The fury was gone as though it had never been, the fire in her guttered to ashes. Thorn's father never told her that the battle-joy is borrowed strength and must be repaid double. She gripped the pouch with his fingerbones in it but there was no comfort there. She saw the leaking wounds and the men moaning and the slaughter they'd done. The slaughter she'd done.

She was a killer, that there was no denying.

She hunched over as if she'd been punched in the guts and coughed thin puke into the grass, straightened shivering, and staring, with the world too bright and her knees all a-wobble and her eyes swimming.

She was a killer. And she wanted her mother.

She saw Brand staring at her over his shoulder, his face all grazed down one side and his neck streaked with blood into the collar of his shirt and the tattered bandages flapping about the red dagger in his hand.

"You all right?" he croaked at her.

"Don't know," she said, and was sick again, and if she'd eaten anything she might never have stopped.

"We have to get to the *South Wind*," someone said in a voice squeaky with panic.

Father Yarvi shook his head. "They'd rain down arrows on us from the bank."

"We need a miracle," breathed Dosduvoi, eyes turned toward the pink sky.

"Skifr!" shouted Yarvi, and the old woman winced as though a fly was bothering her, muttering and hunching her shoulders. "Skifr, we need you!"

"They're coming again!" someone called from the ragged wall.

"How many?" asked Yarvi.

"More than last time!" shouted Rulf, nocking an arrow to his black bow.

"How many more?"

"A lot more!"

Thorn tried to swallow but for once could find no spit. She felt so weak she could hardly lift her father's sword. Koll was bringing water to the shield wall and they were drinking, and snarling, and wincing at their wounds.

Fror swilled water around his mouth and spat. "Time to sell our lives dearly, then. Your death comes!"

"Your death comes," a couple of men muttered, but it was more lament than challenge.

Thorn could hear the Horse People coming, could hear their war-cries and their quick footsteps on the hillside. She heard the growling of the crew as they made ready to meet the charge and, weak though she was, she clenched her teeth and hefted her red-speckled ax and sword. She walked toward the wall. Back to that trampled stretch of mud behind it, though the thought gave her anything but joy.

"Skifr!" screamed Father Yarvi.

With a shriek of anger the old woman sprang up, throwing off her coat. "Be damned, then!" And she began to chant, soft and low at first but growing louder. She strode past, singing words Thorn did not understand, had never heard the like of. But she guessed the language and it was no tongue of men.

These were elf-words, and this was elf-magic. The magic that had shattered God and broken the world, and as if at a chill wind every hair on Thorn's body bristled.

Skifr chanted on, higher and faster and wilder, and from the straps about her body she drew two studded and slotted pieces of dark metal, sliding one into the other with a snap like a closing lock.

"What is she doing?" said Dosduvoi but Father Yarvi held him back with his withered hand.

"What she must."

Skifr held the elf-relic at arm's length. "Stand aside!"

The wavering shield wall split in two and Thorn stared through the gap. There were the Horse People, a crawling mass of them, weaving between the bodies of their fallen, springing swift and merciless with death in their eyes.

There was a clap like thunder close at hand, a flash of light and the nearest of the Uzhaks was flung tumbling down the hillside as though flicked by a giant finger. Another crack and a disbelieving murmur went up from the crew, another man sent spinning like a child's toy, his shoulder on fire.

Skifr's wailing went higher and higher, splinters of shining metal tumbling from the elf-relic in her hand and falling to smoke in the grass at her feet. Men whimpered, and gaped, and clutched at talismans, more fearful of this sorcery than they were of the Uzhaks. Six strokes of thunder rolled across the plain and six men were left ruined and burning and the rest of the Horse People ran squealing in terror.

"Great God," whispered Dosduvoi, making a holy sign over his heart.

There was a silence then. The first in some time. Only the whisper of the wind in the grass and the rough clicking of Odda's breath. There was a smell like burning meat. One of the fallen splinters had caught fire in the grass. Skifr stepped forward grimly and ground the flame out under her boot.

"What have you done?" whispered Dosduvoi.

"I have spoken the name of God," said Skifr. "Written in fire and caught in elf-runes before the Breaking of the World. I have torn

Death from her place beside the Last Door and sent her to do my bidding. But there is always a price to be paid."

She walked over to where Odda was slumped pale against one of the stunted trees, Safrit bent over him trying to tease out the arrow.

"The name of God has seven letters," she said, and she pointed that deadly piece of metal at him. "I am sorry."

"No!" said Safrit, trying to put herself between them, but Odda pushed her gently away.

"Who wants to die old?" And he showed his mad grin, the filed lines in his teeth turned red with blood. "Death waits for us all."

There was another deafening crack, and Odda arched his back, trembling, then fell still, smoke rising from a blackened hole in his mail.

Skifr stood looking down. "I said I would show you magic."

# NOT LIKE
# THE SONGS

"They're running." The wind whipped Thorn's hair about her bloody face as she stared after the Uzhaks, the riders, and the horses without their riders, dwindling specks now far out across the ocean of grass.

"Can't say I blame 'em," muttered Brand, watching Skifr wrap her coat tight about herself and slump again crosslegged, gripping at the holy signs around her neck, glowering at the embers of the fire.

"We fought well," said Rulf, though his voice sounded hollow.

"Hands of iron." Fror nodded as he wiped the paint from his face with a wetted rag. "We won a victory to sing of."

"We won, anyway." Father Yarvi picked up one of the bits of metal Skifr had left in the grass and turned it this way and that so it twinkled in the sun. A hollow thing, still with a little smoke curling out. How could that reach across the plain and kill a man?

Safrit was frowning toward Skifr as she wiped her bloody hands clean. "We won using some black arts."

"We won." Father Yarvi shrugged. "Of the two endings to a fight that is the better. Let Father Peace shed tears over the methods. Mother War smiles upon results."

"What about Odda?" Brand muttered. The little man had seemed invincible, but he was gone through the Last Door. No more jokes.

"He would not have survived the arrow," said Yarvi. "It was him or all of us."

"A ruthless arithmetic," said Safrit, her mouth set in a hard line.

The minister did not look at her. "Such are the sums a leader must solve."

"What if this sorcery brings a curse on us?" asked Dosduvoi. "What if we risk a second Breaking of God? What if we—"

"We won." Father Yarvi's voice was as cold and sharp as drawn steel, and he curled the fingers of his good hand about that little piece of elf-metal and made a white-knuckled fist of it. "Thank whatever god you believe in for your life, if you know how. Then help with the bodies."

Dosduvoi shut his mouth and walked away, shaking his great head.

Brand pried open his sore fingers and let his shield drop, Rin's painted dragon all hacked and gouged, the rim bright with new scratches, the bandages on his palm blood-spotted. Gods, he was bruised and grazed and aching all over. He hardly had the strength to stand, let alone to quibble over the good thing to have done. The more he saw, the less sure he was of what the good thing might be. There was a burning at his neck, wet when he touched it. A scratch there, from friend or enemy he couldn't say. The wounds hurt just as much whoever dealt them.

"Lay them out with dignity," Father Yarvi was saying, "and fell these trees for pyres."

"Those bastards too?" Koll pointed to the Horse People scattered torn and bloody down the slope, several of the crew picking over their bodies for anything worth the taking.

"Them too."

"Why give them a proper burning?"

Rulf caught the lad by the arm. "Because if we beat beggars here, we're no better than beggars. If we beat great men, we're greater still."

"Are you hurt?" asked Safrit.

Brand stared at her as if she was speaking a foreign tongue. "What?"

"Sit down."

That wasn't hard to do. He was so weak at the knees he was near falling already. He stared across the windswept hilltop as the crew put aside their weapons and started dragging the corpses into lines, others setting about the stunted trees with axes to make a great pyre. Safrit leaned over him, probing at the cut on his neck with strong fingers.

"It's not deep. There's plenty worse off."

"I killed a man," he muttered, to no one in particular. Maybe it sounded like a boast, but it surely wasn't meant to be. "A man with his own hopes, and his own worries, and his own family."

Rulf squatted beside him, scratching at his gray beard. "Killing a man is nowhere near so light a matter as the bards would have you believe." He put a fatherly hand on Brand's shoulder. "You did well today."

"Did I?" muttered Brand, rubbing his bandaged hands together. "Keep wondering who he was, and what brought him here, and why we had to fight. Keep seeing his face."

"Chances are you'll be seeing it till you step through the Last Door yourself. That's the price of the shield wall, Brand." And Rulf held out a sword to him. A good sword, with silver on the hilt and a scabbard stained from long use. "Odda's. But he'd have wanted you to take it. A proper warrior should have a proper blade."

Brand had dreamed of having his own sword, now looking at it made him feel sick. "I'm no warrior."

"Yes y'are."

"A warrior doesn't fear."

"A fool doesn't fear. A warrior stands in spite of his fear. You stood."

Brand plucked at his damp trousers. "I stood and pissed myself."

"You won't be the only one."

"The hero never pisses himself in the songs."

"Aye, well." Rulf gave his shoulder a parting squeeze, and stood. "That's why those are songs, and this is life."

Mother Sun was high over the steppe when they set off, the pyre-smoke slowly rising. Though the blood had drained from the sky and left only a clear and beautiful blue, it was still crusted dark under Brand's fingernails, and in his bandages, and at his throbbing neck. It was still a red day. He felt every day he lived would be a red day now.

Four oars lay still beside the mast, the ashes of the men who'd pulled them already whirling out across the plains. Skifr sat brooding among the cargo, hood drawn up, the nearest oarsmen all shuffled as far from her as they could get without falling out of the boat.

Brand glanced across at Thorn as they settled to rowing and she looked back, her face as pale and hollow as Odda's had been when they stacked the wood around him. He tried to smile, but his mouth wouldn't find the shape of it.

They'd fought in the wall. They'd stood at the Last Door. They'd faced Death and left a harvest for the Mother of Crows. Whatever Master Hunnan might've said, they were both warriors now.

But it wasn't like the songs.

# WHAT GETTLAND NEEDS

Kalyiv was a sprawling mass, infesting one bank of the Denied and spreading like a muddy sickness onto the other, the bright sky above smudged with the smoke of countless fires and dotted with scavenging birds.

The prince's hall stood on a low hill over the river, gilded horses carved upon its vast roof beams, the wall around it made as much from mud as masonry. Crowding outside that was a riot of wooden buildings ringed by a fence of stout logs, the spears of warriors glinting at the walkway. Crowding outside that, a chaos of tents, yurts, wagons, shacks and temporary dwellings of horrible wretchedness sprawled out over the blackened landscape in every direction.

"Gods, it's vast," muttered Brand.

"Gods, it's ugly," muttered Thorn.

"Kalyiv is as a slow-filling bladder," said Skifr, thoughtfully picking her nose, considering the results, then wiping them on the shoulder of the nearest oarsman so gently he didn't even notice. "In spring it swells with northerners, and folk from the empire, and Horse People from across the steppe all swarming here to trade. In summer it splits its skin and spills filth over the plains. In winter they all move on and it shrivels back to nothing."

"It surely smells like a bladder," grunted Rulf, wrinkling his nose.

Two huge, squat towers of mighty logs had been thrown up on either side of the river and a web of chains strung between them, links of black iron spiked and studded, bowing under the weight of frothing water, snarled up with driftwood and rubbish, stopping dead all traffic on the Denied.

"Prince Varoslaf has fished up quite a catch with his iron net," said Father Yarvi.

Thorn had never seen so many ships. They bobbed on the river, and clogged the wharves, and had been dragged up on the banks in tight-packed rows stripped of their masts. There were ships from Gettland and Vansterland and Throvenland. There were ships from Yutmark and the Islands. There were strange ships which must have come up from the south, dark-hulled and far too fat-bellied for the trip over the tall hauls. There were even two towering galleys, each with three ranks of oars, dwarfing the *South Wind* as they glided toward the harbor.

"Look at those monsters," murmured Brand.

"Ships from the Empire of the South," said Rulf. "Crews of three hundred."

"It's the crews he's after," said Father Yarvi. "To fight his fool's war against the Horse People."

Thorn was far from delighted at the thought of fighting more Horse People. Or for that matter of staying in Kalyiv for the summer. It had smelled a great deal better in her father's stories. "You think he'll want our help?"

"Certainly he'll want it, as we want his." Yarvi frowned up toward the prince's hall. "Will he demand it, is the question."

He had demanded it of many others. The harbor thronged with sour-faced men of the Shattered Sea, all mired in Kalyiv until Prince Varoslaf chose to loosen the river's chains. They lazed in sullen groups about slumping tents and under rotten awnings, and played loaded dice, and drank sour ale, and swore at great volume, and stared at everything with hardened eyes, the newest arrivals in particular.

"Varoslaf had better find enemies for these men soon," murmured Yarvi, as they stepped from the *South Wind*. "Before they find some nearer to hand."

Fror nodded as he made fast the prow-rope. "Nothing more dangerous than idle warriors."

"They're all looking at us." Brand's bandages had come off that morning and he kept picking nervously at the rope-scabs snaking up his forearms.

Thorn dug him with her elbow. "Maybe your hero's fame goes ahead of us, Ship-lifter."

"More likely Father Yarvi's does. I don't like it."

"Then pretend you do," said Thorn, putting her bravest face on and meeting every stare with a challenge. Or the most challenge she could manage with a hot wind whipping grit in her eyes and flapping her shirt against her sweaty back.

"Gods, it stinks," choked Brand as they made it off the creaking wharves and onto Father Earth, and Thorn could not have disagreed even if she could have taken a full breath to do it. The crooked streets were scattered with baking dung, dogs squabbling over rubbish, dead animals skewered on poles beside doorways.

"Are they selling those?" muttered Brand.

"They're offering them up," answered Father Yarvi, "so their gods can see which houses have made sacrifices and which have not."

"What about those?" Thorn nodded toward a group of skinned carcasses dangling from a mast raised in the middle of a square, gently swinging and swarming with flies.

"Savages," murmured Rulf, frowning up at them.

With an unpleasant shifting in her stomach, Thorn realized those glistening bodies were man-shaped. "Horse People?" she croaked.

Father Yarvi grimly shook his head. "Vanstermen."

"What?" The gods knew there were few people who liked Vanster-men less than Thorn, but she could see no reason for the Prince of Kalyiv to skin them.

Yarvi gestured toward some letters scraped into a wooden sign. "A crew that defied Prince Varoslaf's wishes and tried to leave. Other men of the Shattered Sea are discouraged from following their example."

"Gods," whispered Brand, only just heard over the buzzing of the flies. "Does Gettland want the help of a man who does this?"

"What we want and what we need may be different things."

A dozen armed men were forcing their way through the chaos of the docks. The prince might have been at war with the Horse People, but his warriors did not look much different from the Uzhaks Thorn had killed higher up the Denied. There was a woman in their midst, very tall and very thin, coins dangling from a silk headscarf wound around her black, black hair.

She stopped before them and bowed gracefully, a satchel swinging from her slender neck. "I am servant to Varoslaf, Great Prince of Kalyiv."

"Well met, and I am—"

"You are Father Yarvi, Minister of Gettland. The prince has given me orders to conduct you to his hall."

Yarvi and Rulf exchanged a glance. "Should I be honored or scared?"

The woman bowed again. "I advise you to be both, and prompt besides."

"I have come a long way for an audience and see no reason to dawdle. Lead on."

"I'll pick out some men to go with you," growled Rulf, but Father Yarvi shook his head.

"I will take Thorn and Brand. To go lightly attended, and by the young, is a gesture of trust in one's host."

"You trust Varoslaf?" muttered Thorn, as the prince's men gathered about them.

"I can pretend to."

"He'll know you pretend."

"Of course. On such twisted foundations are good manners built."

Thorn looked at Brand, and he stared back with that helpless expression of his.

"Have a care," came Skifr's voice in her ear. "Even by the ruthless standards of the steppe Varoslaf is known as a ruthless man. Do not put yourself in his power."

Thorn looked to the great chains strung across the river, then to those dangling bodies swinging, and could only shrug. "We're all in his power now."

THE PRINCE OF KALYIV'S HALL seemed even bigger on the inside, its ribs fashioned from the trunks of great trees still rooted in the hard-packed earth, shafts of sunlight filled with floating dust spearing down from windows high above. There was a long firepit but the flames burned low and the echoing space seemed almost chill after the heat outside.

Varoslaf, Prince of Kalyiv, was much younger than Thorn had expected. Only a few years older than Yarvi, perhaps, but without a hair on his head, nor his chin, nor even his brows, all smooth as an egg. He was not raised up on high, but sat on a stool before the firepit. He was not a big man, and he wore no jewels and boasted no weapon. He had no terrible frown upon his hairless face, only a stony blankness. There was nothing she could have described to make him seem fearsome to a listener, and yet he was fearsome. More so, and more, the closer they were led across that echoing floor.

By the time she and Brand stood at Father Yarvi's shoulders a dozen strides from his stool, Thorn feared Prince Varoslaf more than anyone she had ever met.

"Father Yarvi." His voice was dry and whispery as old papers and sent a sweaty shiver down her back. "Minister of Gettland, high is our honor at your visit. Welcome all to Kalyiv, Crossroads of the World."

His eyes moved from Brand, to Thorn, and back to Yarvi, and he reached down to stroke the ears of a vast hound curled about the legs of his stool. "It is a well-judged compliment that a man of your standing comes before me so lightly attended."

Thorn did indeed feel somewhat lonely. As well as that bear of a dog there were many guards scattered about the hall, with bows and curved swords, tall spears and strange armor.

But if Yarvi was overawed, the minister did not show a grain of it. "I know I will want for nothing in your presence, great prince."

"Nor will you. I hear you have that witch Scarayoi with you, the Walker in the Ruins."

"You are as well-informed as a great lord should be. We call her Skifr, but she is with us."

"Yet you keep her from my hall." Varoslaf's laugh was harsh as a dog's bark. "That was well-judged too. And who are these young gods?"

"The back oars of my crew. Thorn Bathu, who killed six Uzhaks in a skirmish on the Denied, and Brand who took the whole weight of our ship across his shoulders as we crossed the tall hauls."

"Slayer of Uzhaks and Lifter of Ships." Brand shifted uncomfortably as the prince gave the two of them a searching gaze. "It warms me to see such strength, and skill, and bravery in those so young. One could almost believe in heroes, eh, Father Yarvi?"

"Almost."

The prince jerked his head toward his willow-thin servant. "A token for tomorrow's legends."

She drew something from the satchel around her neck and pressed it into Brand's palm, then did the same to Thorn. A big, rough coin, crudely stamped with a prancing horse. A coin of red gold. Thorn swallowed, trying to judge its value, and guessed she had never held so much in her hand before.

"You are too generous, great prince," croaked Brand, staring down with wide eyes.

"Great deeds deserve great rewards from great men. Or else why raise men up at all?" Varoslaf's unblinking gaze shifted back to Yarvi. "If they are your back oars what wonders might the others perform?"

"I daresay some of them could make the rest of your gold vanish before your eyes."

"No good crew is without a few bad men. We cannot all be righteous, eh, Father Yarvi? Those of us who rule especially."

"Power means having one shoulder always in the shadows."

"So it does. How is the jewel of the north, your mother, Queen Laithlin?"

"She is my mother no more, great prince, I gave up my family when I swore my oath to the Ministry."

"Strange customs, you northerners have," and the prince fiddled lazily with the ears of his hound. "I think the bonds of blood cannot be severed with a word."

"The right words can cut deeper than swords, and oaths especially. The queen is with child."

"An heir to the Black Chair perhaps? News rich as gold in these unhappy times."

"The world rejoices, great prince. She speaks often of her desire to visit Kalyiv again."

"Not too soon, I pray! My treasury still bears the scars of her last visit."

"Perhaps we can forge an agreement that will mend those scars and make your treasury swell besides?"

A pause. Varoslaf looked to the woman and she shook herself gently, the coins dangling from her scarf twisting and twinkling on her forehead. "Is that why you have come so far, Father Yarvi? To make my treasury swell?"

"I have come seeking help."

"Ah, you too desire the bounty of great men." Another pause. Thorn felt a game was played between these two. A game of words, but no less skillful than the exercises in the training square. And even more dangerous. "Only name your desire. As long as you do not seek allies against the High King in Skekenhouse."

Father Yarvi's smile did not slip by so much as a hair. "I should have known your sharp eyes would see straight to the heart of the matter, great prince. I—and Queen Laithlin, and King Uthil—fear Mother War may spread her wings across the Shattered Sea in spite of all our efforts. The High King has many allies, and we seek to balance the scales. Those who thrive on the trade down the Divine and the Denied may need to pick a side—"

"And yet I cannot. As you have seen I have troubles of my own, and no help to spare."

"Might I ask if you have help to spare for the High King?"

The prince narrowed his eyes. "Ministers keep coming south with that question."

"I am not the first?"

"Mother Scaer was here not a month ago."

Father Yarvi paused at that. "Grom-gil-Gorm's minister?"

"On behalf of Grandmother Wexen. She came before me with a dozen of the High King's warriors and warned me not to paddle in the Shattered Sea. One might almost say she made threats." The hound lifted its head and gave a long growl, a string of drool slipping from its teeth and spattering the ground. "Here. In my hall. I was sore tempted to have her skinned in the public square but . . . it did not seem politic." And he stilled his dog with the slightest hiss.

"Mother Scaer left with her skin, then?"

"It would not have fit me. She headed southward in a ship bearing the High King's prow, bound for the First of Cities. And though I much prefer your manners to hers, I fear I can only give you the same promise."

"Which was?"

"To help all my good friends about the Shattered Sea equally."

"Meaning not at all."

The Prince of Kalyiv smiled, and it chilled Thorn even more than his frown. "You are known as a deep-cunning man, Father Yarvi. I am sure you need no help to sift out my meaning. You know where I sit. Between the Horse People and the great forests. Between the High

King and the empress. At the crossroads of the world and with perils all about me."

"We all have perils to contend with."

"But a prince of Kalyiv must have friends in the east, and the west, and the north, and the south. A prince of Kalyiv thrives on balance. A prince of Kalyiv must keep a foot over every threshold."

"How many feet do you have?"

The dog pricked up its ears and gave another growl. Varoslaf's smile faded as slowly as melting snow. "A word of advice. Stop this talk of war, Father Yarvi. Return to Gettland and smooth the way for Father Peace, as I understand a wise minister should."

"I and my crew are free to leave Kalyiv, great prince?"

"Force Uthil's minister to stay against his will? That would not be politic either."

"Then I thank you humbly for your hospitality and for your advice, well meant and gratefully received. But we cannot turn back. We must go on with all haste to the First of Cities, and seek help there."

Thorn glanced across at Brand, and saw him swallow. To go on to the First of Cities, half the world away from home. She felt a flicker of excitement at that thought. And a flicker of fear.

Varoslaf merely snorted his disdain. "I wish you luck. But I fear you will get nothing from the empress. She has grown ever more devout in her old age, and will have no dealings with those who do not worship her One God. The only thing she hungers after more than priest-babble is spilled blood. That and elf-relics. But it would take the greatest ever unearthed as a gift to win her favor."

"Oh, great prince, wherever would I find such a thing?" Father Yarvi bowed low, all innocence and humility.

But Thorn saw the deep-cunning smile at the corner of his mouth.

# III.

# FIRST
OF CITIES

# LUCK

The gods knew, there'd been a stack of disappointments on that journey high as Brand's head. Plenty of things sadly different from the tales whispered and the songs sung back in Thorlby. And plenty of things folk tended to leave out altogether.

The vast bogs about the mouth of the Denied, for one—clouds of stinging insects haunting banks of stinking sludge where they'd woken to gray mornings soaked with marshwater and bloated with itching bites.

The long coast of the Golden Sea, for another—mean little villages in mean little fences where Father Yarvi argued in strange tongues with shepherds whose faces were tanned to leather by the sun. Beaches of pebbles where the crew pitched rings of spitting torches and lay watching the night, startling at every sound, sure bandits were waiting just beyond the light.

The memory of the battle with the Horse People prowled in their wake, the face of the man Brand killed haunting his thoughts, the hammering of steel on wood finding him in his sleep.

"Your death comes!"

Jerking awake in the sticky darkness to nothing but the quick thud of his heart and the slow chirp of crickets. There was nothing in the songs about regrets.

The songs were silent on the boredom too. The oar, the oar, and the buckled shoreline grinding by, week after week. The homesickness, the worry for his sister, the weepy nostalgia for things he'd always thought he hated. Skifr's endless barking and Thorn's endless training and the endless beatings she gave out to every member of the crew and Brand especially. Father Yarvi's endless answers to Koll's endless questions about plants, and wounds, and politics, and history, and the path of Father Moon across the sky. The chafing, the sickness, the sunburn, the heat, the flies, the thirst, the stinking bodies, the worn-through seat of his trousers, Safrit's rationing, Dosduvoi's toothache, the thousand ways Fror got his scar, the bad food and the running arses, the endless petty arguments, the constant fear of every person they saw and, worst of all, the certain knowledge that, to get home, they'd have to suffer through every mile of it again the other way.

Yes, there'd been a stack of frustrations, hardships, hurts, and disappointments on that journey.

But the First of Cities exceeded every expectation.

It was built on a wide promontory that jutted miles out into the straits, covered from sea to sea with buildings of white stone, with proud towers and steep roofs, with lofty bridges and strong walls within strong walls. The Palace of the Empress stood on the highest point, gleaming domes clustered inside a fortress so massive it could have held the whole of Thorlby with room for two Roystocks left over.

The whole place blazed with lights, red and yellow and white, so many they tinged the blue evening clouds with welcoming pink and set a thousand thousand reflections dancing in the sea, where ships from every nation of the world swarmed like eager bees.

Perhaps they'd seen greater buildings up there on the silence of the Divine, but this was no elf-ruin but the work of men alone, no crumbling tomb to lost glories but a place of high hopes and mad dreams, bursting with life. Even this far distant Brand could hear the city's call. A hum at the edge of his senses that set his very fingertips tingling.

Koll, who'd swarmed up the half-carved mast to cling to the yard for the best view, started flailing his arms and whooping like a madman. Safrit clutched her head below muttering, "I give up. I give up. He can plunge to his death if he wants to. Get down from there, you fool!"

"Did you ever see anything like it?" Brand whispered.

"There is nothing like it," said Thorn, a crazy grin on a face grown leaner and tougher than ever. She had a long pale scar through the stubble on the shorn side of her head, and rings of red gold to go with the silver in her tangled hair, clipped from the coin Varoslaf had given her. A hell of an indulgence to wear gold on your head, Rulf had said, and Thorn had shrugged and said it was as good a place to keep your money as any.

Brand kept his own in a pouch around his neck. It was a new life for Rin, and he didn't plan on losing that for anything.

"There she is, Rulf!" called Father Yarvi, clambering between the smiling oarsmen toward the steering platform. "I've a good feeling."

"Me too," said the helmsman, a cobweb of happy lines cracking the skin at the corners of his eyes.

Skifr frowned up at the wheeling birds. "Good feelings, maybe, but poor omens." Her mood had never quite recovered from the battle on the Denied.

Father Yarvi ignored her. "We will speak to Theofora, the Empress of the South, and we will give her Queen Laithlin's gift, and we shall see what we shall see." He turned to face the crew, spreading his arms, tattered coat flapping in the breeze. "We've come a long and dangerous way, my friends! We've crossed half the world! But the end of the road is ahead!"

"The end of the road," murmured Thorn as the crew gave a cheer, licking her cracked lips as if she was a drunk and the First of Cities a great jug of ale on the horizon.

Brand felt a childish rush of excitement and he splashed water from his flask all over Thorn, spray sparkling as she slapped it away and shoved him off his sea-chest with her boot. He punched her on the shoulder, which these days was like punching a firmly-held shield, and she caught a fistful of his frayed shirt, the two of them falling in a laughing, snarling, sour-smelling wrestle in the bottom of the boat.

"Enough, barbarians," said Rulf, wedging his foot between them and prying them apart. "You are in a civilized place, now! From here on we expect civilized behavior."

THE DOCKS WERE ONE vast riot.

Folk shoved and tugged and tore at each other, lit by garish torch-light, the crowd surging like a thing alive as fights broke out, fists and even blades flashing above the crowd. Before a gate a ring of warriors stood, dressed in odd mail like fishes' scales, snarling at the mob and occasionally beating at them with the butts of their spears.

"Thought this was a civilized place?" muttered Brand as Rulf guided the *South Wind* toward a wharf.

"The most civilized place in the world," murmured Father Yarvi. "Though that mostly means folk prefer to stab each other in the back than the front."

"Less chance of getting blood on your fine robe that way," said Thorn, watching a man hurry down a wharf on tiptoe holding his silken skirts above his ankles.

A huge, fat boat, timbers green with rot, was listing badly in the harbor, half its oars clear of the water, evidently far overloaded and with panicked passengers crammed at its rail. While Brand pulled in his oar two jumped—or were pushed—and tumbled flailing into the sea. There was a haze of smoke on the air and a smell of charred wood, but stronger still was the stink of panic, strong as hay-reek and catching as the plague.

"This has the feel of poor luck!" called Dosduvoi as Brand clambered onto the wharf after Thorn.

"I'm no great believer in luck," said Father Yarvi. "Only in good planning and bad. Only in deep cunning and shallow." He strode to a grizzled northerner with a beard forked and knotted behind his neck, frowning balefully over the loading of a ship much like theirs.

"A good day to—" the minister began.

"I don't think so!" the man bellowed over the din. "And you won't find many who do!"

"We're with the *South Wind*," said Yarvi, "come down the Denied from Kalyiv."

"I'm Ornulf, captain of the *Mother Sun*." He nodded toward his weatherbeaten vessel. "Came down from Roystock two years hence. We were trading with the Alyuks in spring, and had as fine a cargo as you ever saw. Spices, and bottles, and beads, and treasures our womenfolk would've wept to see." He bitterly shook his head. "We had a storehouse in the city and it was caught up in the fire last night. All gone. All lost."

"I'm sorry for that," said the minister. "Still, the gods left you your lives."

"And we're quitting this bloody place before we lose those too."

Yarvi frowned at a particularly blood-curdling woman's shriek. "Are things usually like this?"

"You haven't heard?" asked Ornulf. "The Empress Theofora died last night."

Brand stared at Thorn, and she gave a grimace and scratched at the scar on her scalp.

The news sucked a good deal of the vigor from Father Yarvi's voice. "Who rules, then?"

"I hear her seventeen-year-old niece Vialine was enthroned as thirty-fifth Empress of the South this morning." Ornulf snorted. "But I received no invitation to the happy event."

"Who rules, then?" asked Yarvi, again.

The man's eyes swiveled sideways. "For now, the mob. Folk taking it upon themselves to settle scores while the law sleeps."

"Folk love a good score down here, I understand," said Rulf.

"Oh, they hoard 'em up for generations. That's how that fire got started, I hear, some merchant taking vengeance on another. I swear they could teach Grandmother Wexen a thing or two about old grudges here."

"I wouldn't bet on that," muttered Father Yarvi.

"The young empress's uncle, Duke Mikedas, is having a stab at taking charge. The city's full of his warriors. Here to keep things calm, he says. While folk adjust."

"To having him in power?"

Ornulf grunted. "I thought you were new here."

"Wherever you go," murmured the minister, "the powerful are the powerful."

"Perhaps this duke'll bring order," said Brand, hopefully.

"Looks like it'd take five hundred swords just to bring order to the docks," said Thorn, frowning toward the chaos.

"The duke has no shortage of swords," said Ornulf, "but he's no lover of northerners. If you've a license from the High King you're among the flowers but the rest of us are getting out before we're taxed to a stub or worse."

Yarvi pressed his thin lips together. "The High King and I are not on the best of terms."

"Then head north, friend, while you still can."

"Head north now you'll find yourself in Prince Varoslaf's nets," said Brand.

"He's still fishing for crews?" Ornulf grabbed his forked beard with both fists as though he'd tear it from his jaw. "Gods damn it, so many wolves! How's an honest thief to make a living?"

Yarvi passed him something and Brand saw the glint of silver. "If he has sense, he presents himself to Queen Laithlin of Gettland, and says her minister sent him."

Ornulf stared down at his palm, then at Yarvi's shrivelled hand, then up, eyes wide. "You're Father Yarvi?"

"I am." The line of warriors had begun to spread out from their gate, shoving folk ahead of them though there was nowhere to go. "And I have come for an audience with the empress."

Rulf gave a heavy sigh. "Unless Theofora can hear you through the Last Door, it'll have to be this Vialine we speak to."

"The empress dies the very day we turn up," Brand leaned close to mutter. "What do you think about luck now?"

Father Yarvi gave a long sigh as he watched a loaded cart heaved off the docks and into the sea, the uncoupled horse kicking out wildly, eyes rolling with terror. "I think we could use some."

# BEHIND THE THRONE

"I look like a clown," snapped Thorn, as she wove through the teeming streets after Father Yarvi.

"No, no," he said. "Clowns make people smile."

He'd made her wash, and put some bitter-smelling herb in the searing water to kill off her lice, and she felt as raw under her chafing new clothes as the skinned men on the docks of Kalyiv. Safrit had clipped half her hair back to stubble, then hacked at the matted side with a bone comb but given up in disgust once she broke three teeth off it. She'd given Thorn a tunic of some blood-colored cloth with gold stitching about the collar, so fine and soft it felt as if you were wearing nothing, then when Thorn demanded her old clothes back Safrit had pointed out a heap of burning rags in the street and asked if she was sure.

Thorn might've been a head taller but Safrit was as irresistible as Skifr in her way and would not be denied. She had ended up with jingling silver rings on her arms and a necklace of red glass beads wound around and around her neck. The sort of things that would have made her mother clasp her hands with pride to see her daughter wearing, but had always felt as comfortable as slave's chains to Thorn.

"People here expect a certain . . ." Yarvi waved his crippled hand at a group of black-skinned men whose silks were set with flashing splinters of mirror. "Theater. They will find you fascinatingly fearsome. Or fearsomely fascinating. You look just right."

"Huh." Thorn knew she looked an utter fool because when she finally emerged in all her perfumed absurdity Koll had sniggered, and Skifr had puffed out her cheeks, and Brand had just stared at her in silence as if he'd seen the dead walk. Thorn's face had burned with the humiliation and had hardly stopped burning since.

A man in a tall hat gaped at her as she passed. She would have liked to show him her father's sword but foreigners weren't allowed to carry weapons in the First of Cities. So she leaned close and snapped her teeth at him instead, which proved more than enough armament to make him squeak in fear and scurry off.

"Why haven't you made any effort?" she asked, catching up to Yarvi. He seemed to have a knack of slipping unnoticed through the press while she had to shoulder after him leaving a trail of anger in her wake.

"I have." The minister brushed down his plain black coat, not a trace of adornment anywhere. "Among these gaudy crowds I will stand out for my humble simplicity, a trustworthy servant of the Father of Doves."

"You?"

"I said I'd look like one, not that I'd be one." Father Yarvi shook his head as she dragged at the over-tight seat of her new trousers yet again. "Honestly, Brand was right when he said there is no blessing you cannot treat like a curse. Most people would be thankful for fine new clothes. I can scarcely take you to the palace reeking like a beggar, can I?"

"Why are you taking me to the palace at all?"

"Should I go alone?"

"You could take someone who won't say the worst thing at the worst time. Safrit, or Rulf, or Brand, even? He's got one of those faces folk trust."

"He's got one of those faces folk take advantage of. And not to dismiss the towering diplomatic talents of Safrit, or Rulf, or Brand, but there's always the chance the young Empress Vialine will warm to a woman her own age."

"Me? Folk never warm to me!" Thorn remembered the contempt of the girls in Thorlby, the dagger-stares and the poison-laughter and, even though she'd killed eight men, she shivered at the thought. "Women my age least of all."

"This will be different."

"Why?"

"Because you will be keeping your tongue still and smiling ever so sweetly."

Thorn raised her brows at that. "Doesn't sound much like me. You sure?"

Yarvi's narrowed eyes slid across to hers. "Oh, I am sure. Wait, now."

Thorn's jaw dropped at the sight of six strange monsters crossing the street, each fastened to the one behind by a silver chain, necks long as a man was tall swaying mournfully.

"We're a long way from Gettland," she muttered as she watched them plod off between white buildings so high the crooked lane was like a shadowy canyon. She remembered the damp, dark stone of Gettland, the morning mist over gray Mother Sea, her breath smoking on the dawn chill, huddling about the fire for warmth in the long evening, her mother's voice crooning out the night prayer. It seemed another life. It seemed another world. One Thorn had never thought she might miss.

"Yes we are," said Yarvi, setting briskly off through the sticky, stinking heat of the First of Cities. Thorn knew the year was wearing on, but autumn here was far hotter than midsummer in Thorlby.

She thought of the hard miles they'd traveled. The months of rowing. The slaving over the tall hauls. The constant danger of the steppe. Not to mention the brooding presence of Prince Varoslaf across the path. "Could the empress give us any help even if she chose to try?"

"Perhaps not in steel, but in silver, most definitely." Yarvi murmured an apology in some unknown language as he stepped around a group of women in dark veils, their paint-rimmed eyes following Thorn as if she was the strange one.

"The odds at home will still be long." Thorn counted the enemies off on her calloused fingers. "The High King's own men in Yutmark, and the Inglings, and the Lowlanders, and the Vanstermen, and the Islanders—"

"You may be surprised to learn I had thought of this already."

"And we've got only the Throvenlanders on our side."

Yarvi snorted. "That alliance is milk left in the noon heat."

"Eh?"

"Won't last."

"But King Fynn said—"

"King Fynn is a bloated bag of guts with little authority even in his own kingdom. Only his vanity will bind him to us, and that will melt before Grandmother Wexen's wrath in due course like snow before Mother Sun. That little trick only bought us time."

"Then . . . we'll stand alone."

"My uncle Uthil would stand alone against the world and insist that steel is the answer."

"That sounds brave," said Thorn.

"Doubtless."

"But . . . not wise."

Yarvi gave her a smile. "I'm impressed. I expected you to learn swordsmanship, but never prudence. Don't worry, though. I hope to find other ways to shorten the odds."


AS SOON AS THEY stepped through the towering bronze doors of the palace Thorn went from embarrassment at being dressed like a princess to shame at being dressed like a peasant. The slaves here looked like queens, the guards like heroes of legend. The hall in which they were received was crowded with jewel-encrusted courtiers as brightly colored, as pompous and, as far as Thorn could tell, every bit as useless as the peacocks that swaggered about the immaculate gardens outside.

She would happily have shrivelled away into her new boots but they had great thick soles, and she had grown the past few months, and she stood taller than Father Yarvi now, who was taller than most himself. As always she was left with no choice but to push her shoulders back and her chin up and put on that bravest face of hers, however much the coward behind it might be sweating through her absurd crimson tunic.

Duke Mikedas sat above them in a golden chair on a high dais, one leg slung casually over its carven arm, his fabulous armor covered with gilded swirls. He was one of those handsome men who fancies himself more handsome than he is, dark-skinned and with a twinkling eye, his black hair and beard streaked with silver.

"Greetings, friends, and *welcome* to the First of Cities!" He flashed a winning smile, though it won nothing from Thorn but the deepest suspicion. "How is my mastery of your tongue?"

Father Yarvi bowed low and Thorn followed. Bow when I bow, he had said, and that seemed to mean whenever possible. "Flawless, your grace. A most welcome and impressive—"

"Remind me of your names again, I have the most *abysmal* memory for names."

"He is Father Yarvi, Minister of Gettland."

The woman who spoke was long and lean and very pale, her head close shaven. Elf-bangles rattled on one tattooed forearm, ancient steel, and gold, and broken crystal glittering. Thorn curled her lips back from her teeth, and only just remembered in time not to spit on the highly polished floor.

"Mother Scaer," said Yarvi. "Every time our paths cross it is a fresh delight."

The Minister of Vansterland, who whispered in the ear of Grom-gil-Gorm, and had been sent south by Grandmother Wexen to warn Prince Varoslaf not to paddle in the Shattered Sea.

"I wish I could say the same," said Mother Scaer. "But none of our three meetings has been altogether pleasant." She moved her ice-blue gaze to Thorn. "This woman I do not know."

"In fact you met in Skekenhouse. She is Thorn Bathu, daughter of Storn Headland."

Thorn was somewhat gratified to see Mother Scaer's eyes widen. "Whatever have you been feeding her?"

"Fire and whetstones," said Yarvi, smiling, "and she has quite the appetite. She is a proven warrior now, tested against the Uzhaks."

"What curious warriors you have!" Duke Mikedas sounded more amused than impressed and his courtiers tittered obediently. "I'd like to see her matched against a man of my household guard."

"How about two of 'em?" snapped Thorn, before she even realized her mouth was open. The voice hardly sounded like hers, a grating challenge echoing loud and savage from the silver-fretted marble walls.

But the duke only laughed. "Wonderful! The exuberance of the young! My niece is the same. She thinks anything can be done, in spite of tradition, in spite of the feelings of others, in spite of . . . *realities*."

Yarvi bowed again. "Those who rule, and those beside them, must be always mindful of realities."

The duke wagged his finger. "I like you already."

"I believe, in fact, we have a friend in common."

"Oh?"

"Ebdel Aric Shadikshirram."

The duke's eyes widened, and he swung his leg down from the chair and sat forward. "How is she?"

"I am sorry to tell you she has passed through the Last Door, your grace."

"Dead?"

"Killed by a treacherous slave."

"Merciful God." The duke slumped back. "She was a singular woman. I asked her to marry me, you know. I was a young man then, of course, but . . ." He shook his head in wonderment. "She *refused* me."

"A singular woman indeed."

"The years trickle like water through our fingers. It seems only yesterday . . ." The duke gave a long sigh, and his eyes hardened. "But, to the matter."

"Of course, your grace." Father Yarvi bowed again. His head was bobbing like an apple in a bucket. "I come as emissary from Queen Laithlin and King Uthil of Gettland, and seek an audience with her radiance Vialine, Empress of the South."

"Hmmmm." The duke propped himself on one elbow and rubbed unhappily at his beard. "Where is Guttland again?"

Thorn ground her teeth but Father Yarvi's patience was steel-forged. "Gettland is on the western shore of the Shattered Sea, your grace, north of the High King's seat at Skekenhouse."

"So many little countries up there it takes a scholar to keep track of them!" A tinkling of laughter from the courtiers and Thorn felt a powerful urge to put her fist in their faces. "I wish I could honor *every* supplicant with an audience, but you must understand this is a difficult time."

Yarvi bowed. "Of course, your grace."

"So many enemies to be tamed and friends to be reassured. So many alliances to tend to and some . . . less important than others, no disrespect intended." His brilliant smile exuded disrespect like the stink from an old cheese.

Yarvi bowed. "Of course, your grace."

"The Empress Vialine is not a woman of . . ." he gestured at Thorn as if at an unpromising horse in his stable, "*this* type. She is little more than a girl. Impressionable. Innocent. She has so very much to learn about how things truly *are*. You understand I must be cautious. You understand you must be patient. For a nation as wide and varied as ours to ford the river from one ruler to another is always . . . a *bumpy* crossing. But I will send for you in due course."

Yarvi bowed. "Of course, your grace. Might I ask when?"

The duke waved him away with a flourish of his long fingers. "Due course, Father, er . . ."

"Yarvi," hissed out Mother Scaer.

Thorn was no diplomat, but she got the strong impression due course meant never.

Mother Scaer was waiting for them in the statue-lined hallway outside with two warriors of her own, a scowling Vansterman and a great Lowlander with a face like a stone slab. Thorn was in a black mood and set straight away to bristling, but neither seemed willing to be stared down.

Nor did their mistress. "I am surprised to see you here, Father Yarvi."

"And I you, Mother Scaer." Though neither of them looked surprised in the least. "We both find ourselves half the world from our proper places. I thought you would be beside your king, Grom-gil-Gorm. He needs you to speak for Father Peace, before Mother War drags him to ruin against Gettland."

Mother Scaer's look grew even icier, if that was possible. "I would be with him, had Grandmother Wexen not chosen me for this mission."

"A high honor." The slightest curl at the corner of Yarvi's mouth suggested it was closer to a sentence of exile, and they both knew it. "You must truly have delighted Grandmother Wexen to earn it. Did you speak up for your country? Did you stand for your king and his people, as a minister should?"

"When I make an oath I keep it," snapped Scaer. "A loyal minister goes where her grandmother asks her."

"Just like a loyal slave."

"You are the expert there. Does your neck still chafe?"

Yarvi's smile grew strained at that. "The scars are quite healed."

"Are they?" Scaer leaned close, her thin lips curling from her teeth. "If I were you, I would return to the Shattered Sea before you pick up some more." And she brushed past, Thorn and the Vansterman exchanging one more lingering scowl before he strode away.

"She's trouble," whispered Thorn once they were out of earshot.

"Yes."

"And she's close with the duke."

"Yes."

"And was sent here ahead of us."

"Yes."

"So . . . Grandmother Wexen guessed what you'd do long before you did it."

"Yes."

"I've a feeling we're not going to get an audience with anything this way."

Yarvi looked sourly across at her. "See? You're a diplomat after all."

# OLD FRIENDS

Gods, she was quick now. Brand was twice the fighter he'd been when they left Thorlby just from fighting her, but every day he was less her equal. He felt like a lumbering hog against her, always three steps behind. Alone he had no chance at all, whatever the ground. Even with two comrades beside him he was starting to feel outnumbered. Less and less she was on the defensive, more and more she was the hunter and they the helpless prey.

"Koll," called Brand, jerking his head, "take the left." They started to spread out about the courtyard of the crumbling palace Yarvi had found for them, trying to trap her, trying to tempt her with the gaps between them. "Dosduvoi, get—"

Too late he realized Thorn had lured the big man into the one bright corner of the yard and Dosduvoi cringed as Mother Sun stabbed him suddenly in the eyes.

Thorn was on him like lightning, staggered him in spite of his size with a splintering ax-blow on the shield, slid her sword under the rim and rammed the point into his considerable gut. She reeled away laughing as Brand lashed at the air where she'd stood a moment before, making sure one of the flaking pillars that ringed the yard was between her and Koll.

"Oh, God," wheezed Dosduvoi as he folded up, clutching at his belly.

"Promising," said Skifr, circling them with her hands clasped behind her back. "But don't let your own wind sweep you away. Treat every fight as if it is your last. Every enemy as though they are your worst. The wise fighter seems less than they are, however mean the opposition."

"Thanks for that," Brand forced through gritted teeth, trying to wipe some trickling sweat off on his shoulder. Gods, it was hot. Sometimes it didn't seem there was a breath of wind anywhere in this cursed city.

"My father used to say never get proud." Thorn's eyes darted from Brand to Koll and back as they tried to herd her into a corner. "He said great warriors start believing their own songs, start thinking it'll have to be a great thing that kills them. But a little thing can kill anyone."

"Scratch gone bad," said Safrit, watching with hands on hips.

"Frayed shield strap," grunted Brand, trying to keep his eyes on Thorn's weapons but finding her clinging vest something of a distraction.

"Slip on a sheep's turd," said Koll, nipping in and jabbing at Thorn but giving her the chance to land a crashing blow on his shield and slip around him into space again.

"Your father sounds a sensible man," said Skifr. "How did he die?"

"Killed in a duel with Grom-gil-Gorm. By all accounts, he got proud."

Thorn changed direction in an instant and, fast as Koll was getting, she was far faster. Fast as a scorpion and less merciful. Her ax thudded into the lad's leg, made it buckle and he gasped as he staggered sideways. Her sword slapped into his side and he went tumbling across the courtyard with a despairing cry.

But that gave Brand his chance. Even off-balance she managed to turn his sword away so it thudded hard into her shoulder. Gods, she was tough, she didn't even flinch. He crashed into her with his shield, drove her snarling back against the wall, rim gouging out a shower of loose plaster. They staggered in an ungainly tussle and, for a moment, he was sure he had her. But even as he was forcing her back she somehow twisted her foot behind his, growled as she switched her weight and sent him tumbling over it.

They went down hard, him on the bottom. Gods, she was strong. It was like Bail wrestling the great eel in the song, but more than likely with a worse outcome.

"You're supposed to be killing him!" called Skifr, "not coupling with him! That you can do on your own time."

They rolled in a tangle and came out with Thorn on top, teeth bared as she tried to work her forearm up under his jaw to choke him, he with a grip on her elbow, straining to twist it away, both snarling in each other's faces.

So close her two eyes blurred into one. So close he could see every bead of sweat on her forehead. So close her chest pressed against him with each quick, hot, sour-sweet breath.

And for a moment it felt as if they weren't fighting at all, but something else.

Then the heavy door shuddered open and Thorn sprang off him as quickly as if she'd been slapped.

"Another win?" snapped Father Yarvi, stepping over the threshold with Rulf frowning at his shoulder.

"Of course," said Thorn, as if there was nothing in her mind but giving Brand a beating. What else would there be?

He clambered up, brushing himself off, pretending his skin wasn't burning from his face to his toes. Pretending he was hunching over because of an elbow in the ribs rather than any swelling lower down. Pretending everything was the same as ever. But something had changed that day she stepped into the courtyard in her new clothes, the same but so, so different, the light catching the side of her frown and making one eye gleam, and he couldn't speak for staring at her. Everything had fallen apart all of a sudden. Or maybe it had fallen together. She wasn't just his friend or his rival or his oarmate any more, one of the crew. She still was, but she was something else as well, something that excited and fascinated but mostly scared the hell out of him. Something had changed in the way he saw her and now when he looked at her he couldn't see anything else.

They were sleeping on the floor of the same crumbling room. Hadn't seemed anything strange about it when they moved in, they'd been sleeping on top of each other for months. Only now he lay awake half the sticky-hot night thinking about how close she was. Listening to the endless sounds of the city and trying to make out her slow breath. Thinking how easy it would be to reach out and touch her . . .

He realized he was looking sidelong at her arse again, and forced his eyes down to the floor. "Gods," he mouthed, but he'd no idea which one you prayed to for help with a problem like this.

"Well I'm tremendously glad someone's winning," snapped Yarvi.

"No luck at the palace?" croaked out Brand, still bent over and desperate to find a distraction.

"The palace has no luck in it at all," said Rulf.

"Another day wasted." Yarvi sank down on a bench with his shoulders slumped. "We'll be lucky if we get another chance to be insulted by Duke Mikedas, let alone his niece."

"I thought you didn't believe in luck?" asked Thorn.

"Right now, I'm down to hoping it believes in me."

Father Yarvi looked rattled, and Brand had never seen that before. Even when they fought the Horse People, he had always seemed certain of what to do. Now Brand wondered whether that was a mask the minister had made himself. A mask which was starting to crack. For the first time he was painfully aware Yarvi was only a few years older than he was, and had the fate of Gettland to carry, and only one good hand to do it.

"I wonder what they're doing in Thorlby right now?" murmured Koll wistfully, shaking out his hurt leg.

"Coming close to harvest time, I reckon," said Dosduvoi, who'd rolled his shirt up to check his own bruises.

"Fields golden with swaying barley," said Skifr.

"Lots of traders coming to the markets." Safrit toyed with the merchant's weights around her neck. "Docks swarming with ships. Money being made."

"Unless the crops have been burned by the Vanstermen's raids," snapped Yarvi. "And the merchants have been held at Skekenhouse by Grandmother Wexen. Fields black stubble and the docks sitting empty. She could have roused the Lowlanders by now. The Inglings too, with Bright Yilling at their head. Thousands of them, marching on Gettland."

Brand swallowed, thinking of Rin in their fragile little hovel outside the walls. "You think so?"

"No. Not yet. But soon, maybe. Time drains away and I do nothing. There's always a way." The minister stared down at the ground, good fingers fussing with the nail on his twisted thumb. "Half a war is fought with words, won with words. The right words to the right people. But I don't have either."

"It'll come right," muttered Brand, wanting to help but with no idea what he could do.

"I wish I could see how." Yarvi put his hands over his pale face, the bad one like a twisted toy next to the good. "We need a damn miracle."

And there was a thumping knock on the door.

Skifr raised an eyebrow. "Are we by any chance expecting visitors?"

"We're hardly overburdened with friends in the city," said Thorn.

"You're hardly overburdened with friends anywhere," said Brand.

"It could be that Mother Scaer has sent a welcoming party," said Yarvi.

196 | JOE ABERCROMBIE

"Weapons," growled Rulf. He tossed Thorn's sword to her and she snatched it from the air.

"By God, I'm happy to fight anyone," said Dosduvoi, seizing a spear, "as long as it's not her."

Brand drew the blade that had been Odda's, the steel frighteningly light after the practice sword. Fear had quickly solved the problem in his trousers, if nothing else.

The door shuddered from more knocks, and it was not a light door.

Koll crept over to it, going up on tiptoe to peer through the spy-hole.

"It's a woman," he hissed. "She looks rich."

"Alone?" asked Yarvi.

"Yes, I'm alone," came a muffled voice through the door. "And I'm a friend."

"That's just what an enemy would say," said Thorn.

"Or a friend," said Brand.

"The gods know we could use one," said Rulf, but nocking an arrow to his black bow even so.

"Open it," said Yarvi.

Koll whipped back the bolt as though it might burn him and sprung away, a knife at the ready in each hand. Brand crouched behind his shield, fully expecting a flight of arrows to come hissing through the archway.

Instead the door creaked slowly open and a face showed itself at the crack. A woman's face, dark-skinned and dark-eyed with black hair loosely twisted up and held with jewelled pins. She had a little scar through her top lip, a notch of white tooth showing as she smiled.

"Knock, knock," she said, slipping through and pushing the door shut behind her. She wore a long coat of fine white linen and around her neck a golden chain, each link worked to look like an eye. She raised one brow at all the sharpened steel and slowly put up her palms. "Oh, I surrender."

Rulf gave a great whoop, and flung his bow skittering across the floor, rushed over to the woman and gathered her in a great hug.

"Sumael!" he said, squeezing her tight. "Gods, how I've missed you!"

"And I you, Rulf, you old bastard," she wheezed, slapping him on the back, then groaning as he lifted her off her feet. "Had my suspicions when I heard a ship called the *South Wind* had landed. Nice touch, by the way."

"It reminds us where we came from," said Yarvi, good hand rubbing at his neck.

"Father Yarvi," said Sumael, slipping free of the helmsman's embrace. "Look at you. Lost at sea and desperately in need of someone to pick out the course."

"Some things never change," he said. "You look . . . prosperous."

"You look awful."

"Some things never change."

"No hug for me?"

He gave a snort, almost a sob. "I'm worried if I do I might never let go."

She walked over, their eyes fixed on each other. "I'll take the risk." And she put her arms around him, going up on her toes to hold him close. He put his head on her shoulder, and tears glistened on his gaunt cheeks.

Brand stared at Thorn, and she shrugged back. "I guess now we know who Sumael is."

"SO THIS IS THE EMBASSY of Gettland?" Sumael poked at a lump of mold-speckled plaster and it dropped from the wall and scattered across the dusty boards. "You've an eye for a bargain."

"I am my mother's son," said Yarvi. "Even if she's not my mother anymore." The crumbling hall they ate in could have seated forty but most of the crew had gone their own ways and the place had a hollow echo to it now. "What are you doing here, Sumael?"

"Apart from catching up with old friends?" She sat back in her chair and let one stained boot, strangely at odds with her fine clothes, drop onto the scarred tabletop. "I helped my uncle build a ship for the Empress Theofora and one thing led to another. Much to the annoyance of several of her courtiers, she made me inspector of her fleet." A strand of hair fell across her face and she stuck her bottom lip out and blew it back.

"You always had a touch with boats." Rulf was beaming at her as if at a favorite daughter unexpectedly come home. "And annoying people."

"The empire's boats were rotting in the harbor of Rugora, down the coast. Which, as it happens, was also where the empress's niece Vialine was being educated." That strand of hair fell loose again and she blew it back again. "Or imprisoned, depending how you look at it."

"Imprisoned?" asked Brand.

"There's little trust within the royal family here." Sumael shrugged. "But Vialine wanted to understand the fleet. She wants to understand everything. We became friends, I suppose. When Theofora fell ill and Vialine was called back to the First of Cities, she asked me to go with her, and . . ." She lifted the chain of eyes with a fingertip and let it fall clinking. "By some strange magic I find myself counselor to the Empress of the South."

"Talent floats to the top," said Rulf.

"Like turds," grunted Thorn.

Sumael grinned back. "You must be buoyant, then."

Brand laughed, and Thorn gave him a glare, and he stopped.

"So you sit at the right hand of the most powerful woman in the world?" asked Rulf, shaking his balding head.

"By no means alone." That strand fell again and Sumael gave a twitch of annoyance and started pulling the pins from her hair. "There's a council of dozens, and most of them belong to Duke Mikedas. Vialine may be empress in name but he holds the power, and has no intention of sharing."

"He shared nothing with us," said Yarvi.

"I heard." The hair fell in a black curtain across half of her face, the other eye twinkling. "At least you came away with your heads."

"You think we'll keep them if we stay?" asked Yarvi.

Sumael's eye slid across to Thorn. "That depends on how diplomatic you can be."

"I can be diplomatic," snarled Thorn.

Sumael only smiled the wider. She seemed immune to intimidation. "You remind me of a ship's captain Yarvi and I used to sail with."

Yarvi burst out laughing, and so did Rulf, and Thorn frowned through it. "Is that an insult or a compliment?"

"Call it a little of both." Yarvi sat forward, elbows on the table and his shrivelled hand clasped in the other. "The High King is making ready for war, Sumael. Who knows, war might already have started."

"What allies do you have?" she asked, sweeping her hair up with both hands and gathering it in a knot.

"Fewer than we need."

"Some things never change, eh, Yarvi?" Sumael slid the pins back with nimble fingers. "The duke is not so taken with the One God as Theofora was, but he means to honor the alliance with Grandmother Wexen, even so. He can pick a winner."

"We shall see," said Yarvi. "I need to speak to the empress."

Sumael puffed out her cheeks. "I can try. But more than a hearing I cannot promise."

"You don't owe me anything."

She held his eye as she flicked the last pin home, its jewelled end glittering. "It's not a question of debts. Not between us."

Yarvi looked to be caught between laughing and crying, and in the end he sat back, and gave a ragged sigh. "I thought I'd never see you again."

Sumael smiled, that notch of white tooth showing, and Brand found he was starting to like her. "And?"

"I'm glad I was wrong."

"So am I." That strand of hair fell into her face again and she frowned cross-eyed at it a moment, and blew it back.

# HOPES

Thorn pushed through a grumbling throng flooding into a temple for prayers. So many temples here, and so much crowding into them to pray.

"Worshipping this One God takes up a lot of time," grunted Brand, trying to work his broad shoulders through the press.

"The tall gods and the small gods have their own business to be about. The One God only seems to care for meddling in everyone else's."

"And bells." Brand winced at another clanging peel from a white tower just above them. "If I never hear another bloody bell I won't complain." He leaned close to whisper. "They bury their dead unburned. Bury them. In the ground. Unburned."

Thorn frowned at the overgrown yard beside the temple, crammed with marking stones wonky as a beggar's teeth, each one, she guessed, with a corpse beneath it, rotting. Hundreds of them. Thousands. A charnel pit right inside the city.

She gave a sweaty shudder at the thought, squeezing at the pouch that held her father's fingerbones. "Damn this city." He might have loved talking about the place, but she was starting to hate it. Far too big, the size of it was crushing. Far too noisy so you couldn't think straight. Far too hot, always sticky and stinking day or night. Rubbish and flies and rot and beggars everywhere, it made her dizzy. So many people, and all of them passing through, no one knowing each other, or wanting anything from each other but to claw out a profit.

"We should go home," she muttered.

"We only just got here."

"Best time to leave a place you hate."

"You hate everything."

"Not everything." She glanced sideways and caught Brand looking at her, and felt that tingling in her stomach again as he quickly looked away.

Turned out he didn't just have the puzzled look and the helpless look, he had another, and now she was catching it all the time. Eyes fixed on her, bright behind a few stray strands of hair. Hungry, almost. Scared, almost. The other day, when they'd been pressed together on the ground, so very close, there'd been . . . something. Something that brought the blood rushing to her face, and not just her face either. In her guts she was sure. Just below her guts, even more so. But the doubts crowded into her head like the faithful into their temples at prayer time.

Could you just ask? I know we used to hate each other but I've come to think I might like you quite a lot. Any chance you like me, at all? Gods, it sounded absurd. All her life she'd been pushing folk away, she had no idea where to start at pulling one in. What if he looked at her as if she was mad? The thought yawned like a pit at her feet. What do you mean *like*? Like, *like* like? Should she just take hold of him and kiss him? She kept thinking about it. She hardly thought about anything else anymore. But what if a look was just a look? What if it was like her mother said—what man would want someone as strange and difficult and contrary as she was? Not one like Brand who was well-made and well-liked and what a man should be and could have anyone he wanted—

Suddenly his arm was around her, herding her back into a doorway. Her heart was in her mouth, she even gave a little girlish squeak as he pressed up tight against her. Then everyone was scrambling to the sides of the lane as horses clattered by, feathers on their bridles thrashing and gilded armor glinting and tall riders in tall helmets caring nothing for those who cowered to either side. Duke Mikedas's men, no doubt.

"Someone could get hurt," Brand muttered, frowning after them.

"Aye," she croaked. "Someone could."

She was fooling herself. Had to be. They were friends. They were oarmates. That was all they needed to be. Why ruin it by pushing for something she couldn't have, didn't deserve, wouldn't get . . . then she caught his eye, and there was that damn look again that set her heart going as if she'd rowed a hard mile. He jerked away from her, gave an awkward half-smile, strode on as the crowds pressed back in after the horsemen.

What if he felt the same as her, wanting to ask but scared to ask and not knowing how to ask? Every conversation with him felt dangerous as a battle. Sleeping in the same room was torture. They'd just been oarmates on one floor when they first threw their blankets down, laughing at the state of the great ruin Yarvi had bought, daylight showing through the roof. But now she only pretended to sleep while she thought about how close he was, and sometimes she thought he was pretending too, could swear his eyes were open, watching her. But she was never sure. The thought of sleeping next to him made her miserable, and the thought of not sleeping next to him made her miserable.

Do you . . . *like* me? Like? *Like?*

The whole thing was a bloody riddle in a language she couldn't speak.

Brand puffed out his cheeks and wiped sweat from his forehead, no doubt blissfully unaware of the trouble he was causing. "Guess we'll be gone soon as we strike a deal with the empress."

Thorn tried to swallow her nerves and talk normally, whatever that meant. "I'm thinking that won't happen."

Brand shrugged. Calm and solid and trusting as ever. "Father Yarvi'll find a way."

"Father Yarvi's deep-cunning all right but he's no sorcerer. If you'd been at the palace, seen that duke's face . . ."

"Sumael will find a way for him, then."

Thorn snorted. "You'd think Mother Sun was up that woman's arse for the light she's shining into everyone's lives."

"Not yours, I reckon."

"I don't trust her."

"You don't trust anyone."

She almost said, "I trust you," but swallowed it at the last moment and settled for a grunt.

"And Rulf trusts her," Brand went on. "With his life, he told me. Father Yarvi too, and he's hardly the trusting type."

"Wish I knew more about what happened with those three," said Thorn. "There's a story there."

"Sometimes you'll be happier for knowing less."

"That's you. Not me." She glanced over at him and caught him looking back. Hungry almost, scared almost, and she felt that tingle deep in her stomach and would have been off on a mad argument with herself yet again if they hadn't come to the market.

One of the markets, anyway. The First of Cities had dozens, each one big as Roystock. Places of mad bustle and noise, cities of stalls choked with people of every shape and color. Great scales clattered and abacuses rattled and prices were screamed in every tongue over the braying and clucking and honking of the livestock. There was a choking reek of cooking food and sickly-sweet spice and fresh dung and the gods knew what else. Everything else. Everything in the world for sale. Belt buckles and salt. Purple cloth and idols. Monstrous, sad-eyed fishes. Thorn squeezed her eyes shut and forced them open, but the every-colored madness still boiled before her.

"Just meat," said Thorn plaintively, weighing Father Yarvi's purse in her hand. "We just want meat." Safrit hadn't even asked for a certain kind. She dodged as a woman in a stained apron strode past with a goat's head under her arm. "Where the hell do we start?"

"Hold up." Brand had stopped at a stall where a dark-skinned merchant was selling strings of glass beads and lifting one so Mother Sun sparkled through the yellow glass. "Pretty, ain't they? Sort of thing a girl likes as a gift."

Thorn shrugged. "I'm no expert on pretty. Girls neither, for that matter."

"You are one, aren't you?"

"So my mother tells me." She added in a mutter, "Opinion's divided."

He held up another necklace, green and blue this time. "Which ones would you want?" And he grinned sideways. "For a gift?"

Thorn felt that tingling in her stomach, stronger than ever. Close to actual vomiting. If ever she was going to get proof then here it was. A gift. For her. Hardly the one she would have chosen but with luck that might be next. If she picked out the right words. What to say? Gods, what to say? Her tongue seemed twice its usual size of a sudden.

"Which ones would I want, or . . ." She kept her eyes on him and let her head drop to one side, tried to make her voice soft. Winsome, whatever that sounded like. She couldn't have been soft more than three times in her life and winsome never, and it came out a clumsy growl. "Which ones *do* I want?"

The puzzled look, now. "I mean, which ones would you want brought back? If you were in Thorlby."

And in spite of the cloying heat a coldness spread out, starting in Thorn's chest and creeping slowly to her very fingertips. Not for her. For someone back in Thorlby. Of course they were. She'd let herself get blown away on her own wind, in spite of Skifr's warnings.

"Don't know," she croaked, trying to shrug as if it was nothing, but it wasn't nothing. "How should I know?" She turned away, her face burning as Brand talked prices with the merchant, and she wished the ground would open up and eat her unburned like the southern dead.

She wondered what girl those beads were for. Wasn't as if there were that many in Thorlby the right age. More than likely Thorn knew her. More than likely Thorn had been laughed at and pointed at and sneered at by her. One of the pretty ones her mother always told her to be more like. One of the ones who knew how to sew, and how to smile, and how to wear a key.

She thought she'd made herself tough right through. Slaps and punches and shield blows hardly hurt her. But everyone has chinks in their armor. Father Yarvi might have stopped them crushing her with stones, but casually as that Brand crushed her just as flat with a string of beads.

He was still grinning as he slipped them into a pocket. "She'll like them, I reckon."

Thorn's face twisted. Never even occurred to him she might think they were for her. Never even occurred to him to think of her the way she'd come to think of him. It was as if all the color had drained out of the world. She'd spent a lot of her life feeling shamed and foolish and ugly, but never so much as this.

"I'm such a stupid shit," she hissed.

Brand blinked at her. "Eh?"

The helpless look, this time, and the temptation to sink her fist into it was almost overpowering, but she knew it wasn't his fault. It was no one's fault but her own, and punching yourself never solves anything. She tried to put a brave face on but she couldn't find it right then. She wanted just to get away. To get anywhere, and she took one step and stopped dead.

The scowling Vansterman who had stood beside Mother Scaer in the palace was blocking her path, his right hand hidden in a rolled up cloak where, she had no doubt, it held a blade. There was a rat-faced little man at his shoulder and she could feel someone moving over on her left. The big Lowlander, she guessed.

"Mother Scaer wants a word with you," said the Vansterman, showing his teeth, and far from a pretty set. "Be best if you came quietly."

"Better yet, we'll go our own way quietly," said Brand, plucking at Thorn's shoulder.

She shook him off, hot shame turned to chill rage in an instant. She needed to hurt someone, and these idiots had come along at just the right moment.

Right for her. Wrong for them.

"I'll be doing nothing quietly." And she flicked one of Father Yarvi's silver coins to the holder of the nearest stall, covered in tools and timber.

"What's this for?" he asked as he caught it.

"The damage," said Thorn, and she snatched up a hammer, flung it underhand so it bounced from the Vansterman's skull, sending him stumbling back, all amazement.

She grabbed a heavy jug from another stall and smashed it over his head before he could get his balance, spraying them both with wine. She caught him as he fell and dug the jagged remains of the handle into his face.

A knife came at her and she dodged it on an instinct, jerking back from the waist so the blade hissed by her, eyes wide as she followed the flashing metal. The rat-faced man stabbed again and she reeled sideways, lurched over a stall, its owner wailing about his goods. She came up clutching a bowl of spice, flung it at Rat-face in a sweet-smelling orange cloud. He coughed, spat, lunged at her blindly. She used the bowl like a shield, the knife-blade buried itself in the wood and she wrenched it from his hand.

He came at her with a clumsy punch but she got her arm inside it, felt his fist scuff her cheek as she stepped in and kneed him full in the gut, then again between the legs and made him squeal. She caught him around the jaw, arching back, and butted him with all her strength in his rat face. The jolt of it dizzied her for a moment, but not half as much as it did him. He flopped onto his hands and knees, drooling blood, and she stepped up with a wild swing of her boot and kicked him onto his back, a table going over and half-burying him in an avalanche of glistening fish.

She turned, saw Brand being forced backward over a stall stacked with fruit, the big Lowlander trying to push a knife into his face, Brand's tongue wedged between his teeth, eyes crossed as he stared at the bright point.

When you're training, fighting your oarmates, there's always a little held back. Thorn held back nothing now. She caught the Lowlander's thick wrist with one hand and hauled his arm straight behind him, screamed as she drove the heel of her other hand down into his elbow. There was a crunch and his arm bent the wrong way, knife tumbling from his flopping hand. He screamed until Thorn chopped him in the neck just the way Skifr taught her and he fell jerking onto the next stall, sending broken pottery flying.

"Come on!" she spat, but there was no one left to fight. Only the shocked stall-holders and the scared bystanders and a mother holding her hand over her daughter's eyes. "Go quietly, will I?" she shrieked, lifting her boot to stomp on the Lowlander's head.

"No!" Brand caught her under the arm and dragged her through the wreckage, folk scrambling to give them room as they half-walked, half-ran into the mouth of a side-street.

"Did you kill them?" he was squeaking.

"With any luck," snarled Thorn, tearing herself free of him. "Why? Did you plan to buy 'em beads, did you?"

"What? We were sent to get meat, not make corpses!" They took a quick turn, past a group of surprised beggars and on through the shadows of a rotten alley, the commotion fading behind them. "Don't want to cause trouble for Father Yarvi. Don't want to see you crushed with rocks either if I can help it."

She saw he was right, and that made her angrier than ever. "You're such a coward," she hissed, which surely wasn't fair but she wasn't feeling very fair right then. There was something tickling her eye, and she wiped it, and her hand came away red.

"You're bleeding," he said, reaching out, "here—"

"Get your hand off me!" She shoved him against the wall, then, when he bounced off, shoved him again even harder. He shrank back, one hand up as she stood over him with her fists clenched, and he looked confused, and hurt, and scared.

It was a look that gave her a tingle, all right, but not in a good way. In that look she saw her silly bloody hopes as twisted and broken as she'd left that Lowlander's arm, and it was no one's fault but her own. She shouldn't have let herself hope, but hopes are like weeds: however often you root them out they keep on springing up.

She gave a growl of frustration, and stalked off down the alleyway.

# RUINS

He'd ruined it.

Brand leant against the crumbling wall of the courtyard between Rulf and Father Yarvi, watching Thorn give Fror a pasting. He'd spent half his time watching her, since they reached the First of Cities. But now he did it with the mournful longing of an orphan at a baker's stall, taunting himself with the sight of treats he knows he'll never have. A feeling Brand knew all too well. A feeling he'd hoped never to have again.

There'd been something good between them. A friendship, if nothing else. A friendship a long, hard time in the making.

Like the blundering oaf he was, he'd ruined it.

He'd come back to their room and her things were gone and she was sleeping with Safrit and Koll and she hadn't said why. She hadn't said one word to him since that day in the market. She must've seen how he was looking at her, guessed what he was thinking. Wasn't as though he was any good at hiding it. But judging by the way she looked at him now, or rather the way she didn't, the thought made her flesh crawl. Of course it did.

Why would someone like her—so strong, and sharp, and confident—want a dullard like him? Anyone could see at one glance she was something truly special and he was nothing, and would always be nothing, just like his father used to tell him. A cringing dunce who'd begged for scraps, and picked through rubbish, and dragged sacks around the docks for a pittance and been grateful to get it.

He wasn't sure exactly how he'd done it, but he'd found a way to let everyone down. His crew. His family. Himself. Thorn. He'd ruined it.

Koll slid back the bolt on the door and Sumael stepped into the courtyard. She had two others with her: a small servant in a hooded cloak and a big-shouldered man with a watchful frown and a scar through one gray brow.

The servant pushed her hood back. She was slight and dark-haired, with quick eyes that missed no detail as she watched the fight. If you could call it a fight. Fror was one of the best warriors on the crew, but it only took Thorn a few more moments to put him down and she wasn't even breathing hard afterward.

"I'm done," he groaned, clutching at his ribs with one hand while he held the other up for mercy.

"Most encouraging," said Skifr, catching the wooden blade of Thorn's ax before she could hit him again regardless. "I delight in the way you are fighting today, my dove. No doubts, no conscience, no mercy. Who will be next to face you . . . ?"

Dosduvoi and Koll found the corners of the courtyard suddenly fascinating. Brand held up helpless palms as Skifr's eyes fell on him. The mood Thorn was in, he wasn't sure he'd come through a bout alive. The old woman gave a sigh.

"I fear you have nothing left to learn from your oarmates. The time has come for stiffer opposition." She pulled her coat off and tossed it over Fror's back. "How did you get that scar, Vansterman?"

"I kissed a girl," he grunted, crawling toward the wall, "with a very sharp tongue."

"Further proof that romance can be more dangerous than sword-play," said Skifr, and Brand could only agree with that. She pulled out a wooden sword and ax of her own. "Now, my dove, we shall truly see what you have learned—"

"Before you begin," said Sumael, "I've—"

"Red-toothed war waits for nothing!" Skifr sprang, weapons darting out quick and deadly as striking snakes, Thorn twisting and writhing as she dodged and parried. Brand could hardly count how many crashing blows they traded in the time it took him to take a breath. Eight? Ten? They broke apart as suddenly as they met, circling each other, Thorn weaving between the columns in a prowling crouch, Skifr swaggering sideways, weapons drifting in lazy circles.

"Oh, this is something," murmured Rulf, grinning wide.

Fror winced as he rubbed at his ribs. "It's a lot more fun than fighting her yourself, that's sure."

Sumael's frowning companion murmured something under his breath, and Father Yarvi smiled.

"What did he say?" whispered Brand.

"He said the girl is extraordinary."

Brand snorted. "That's bloody obvious."

"Very good," Skifr was saying. "But do not wait for me to hand you an opening. I am no gift-giver."

"I'll cut my own, then!" Thorn darted forward so fast Brand took a wobbly step back, her ax and sword flashing in circles, but Skifr twisted, reeled, somehow finding a path between them and away to safety.

"Please," said Sumael, louder. "I need to—"

"There is no place for please on the battlefield!" screamed Skifr, unleashing another blinding flurry, wood clattering on wood, herding Thorn into the corner of the yard then her blade raking stone as Thorn ducked under it, rolled away and came up swinging. Skifr gasped as she stumbled back, Thorn's sword missing the end of her nose by a finger's breadth.

Koll gave a disbelieving titter. Father Yarvi puffed out his cheeks, eyes bright. Rulf shook his balding head in disbelief. "I never saw the like."

"Excellent," said Skifr, eyes narrowed. "I am glad to see my wisdom has not been wasted." She spun her ax in her fingers so quickly it became a blur. "Truly excellent, but you will find—"

"Stop!" screamed Sumael, dragging every face sharply toward her. To Brand's surprise she sank to one knee, sweeping her arm toward her servant. "May I present her radiance Vialine, Princess of the Denied, Grand Duke of Napaz, Terror of the Alyuks, Protector of the First of Cities and Thirty-fifth Empress of the South."

For a moment Brand thought it some elaborate joke. Then he saw Father Yarvi drop to one knee, and everyone else in the yard just afterward, and any hint of laughter quickly died.

"Gods," he whispered, getting his own knee to the paving so fast it hurt.

"Sorry," croaked Thorn, hastily doing the same.

The empress stepped forward. "Don't be. It was a most instructive display." She spoke the Tongue with a heavy accent, but her voice was rich and full of confidence.

"Your radiance—" said Yarvi.

"Do I seem all that radiant to you?" The empress laughed. An open, friendly laugh that echoed about the courtyard. "I would rather we speak plainly. I get very little plain speaking at the palace. Except from Sumael, of course."

"I find Sumael's speaking just a little too plain at times." Father Yarvi brushed off his knees as he stood. "We are truly honored by your visit."

"It is I who should be honored. You have traveled across half the world to speak with me, after all. I would hate to be the sort of person who would not walk half a mile from my palace gate to speak with you."

"I will try not to waste your time, then, empress." The minister

took a step toward her. "Do you understand the politics of the Shattered Sea?"

"I know a little. Sumael has told me more."

Yarvi took another step. "I fear Mother War will soon spread her
bloody wings across its every shore."

"And you seek my help. Even though we pray to different gods?
Even though my aunt made an alliance with the High King?"

"Her alliance, not yours."

The empress folded her arms and stepped sideways. She and the
minister began to circle each other warily, very much as Thorn and
Skifr had done a few moments before. "Why should I forge a new one
with Gettland?"

"Because you wish to favor the winning side."

Vialine smiled. "You are too bold, Father Yarvi."

"King Uthil would say there is no such thing as *too* bold."

"Gettland is a small nation, surrounded by enemies—"

"Gettland is a rich nation surrounded by paupers. Queen Laithlin
has made sure of it."

"The Golden Queen," murmured Vialine. "Her fame as a merchant has spread even this far. Is it true she has found a way to catch
gold and silver in paper?"

"She has. One of many wonders, the secrets of which she would
happily share with her allies."

"You offer me gold and silver, then?"

"The High King offers nothing but prayers."

"Is gold and silver everything to you, Father Yarvi?"

"Gold and silver is everything to everyone. Some of us have
enough of it to pretend otherwise."

The empress gave a little gasp at that.

"You asked for honesty." Yarvi snapped his fingers toward Thorn
and she stood up. "But as it happens my mother has sent something
made of neither gold nor silver. A gift, brought the long, hard road
down the Divine and the Denied from the darkest corners of the Shat-

tered Sea." And he slid the black box from inside his coat and handed it to Thorn.

"An elf-relic?" said the empress, scared and curious at once.

The frowning man moved closer to her, frowning even deeper.

Thorn held the box out awkwardly. They might have been of an age, but Vialine looked like a child next to her. Her head barely came to Thorn's chest, let alone her shoulder. As though realizing how strange a pair they made, Thorn dropped to one knee so she could hold the gift at a more fitting angle, the elf-letters etched on the lid glinting as they caught the light. "Sorry."

"Don't be. I wish I was tall." Vialine pushed back the lid of the box, and that pale light flooded out, and her eyes went wide. Brand felt Rulf stiffen beside him, heard Koll give a gasp of amazement, Fror murmuring a breathless prayer. He'd seen the light before and still he strained forward, longing to see what made it. The lid of the box was in the way, though.

"It is beautiful," breathed the empress, reaching out. She gasped as she touched whatever was inside, the light on her face shifting from white to pink and back as she jerked her hand away. "Great God! It still turns?"

"It does," said Skifr. "It senses you, Empress, and shifts to match your mood. It was brought from the elf-ruins of Strokom, where no man has trodden since the Breaking of God. There may not be another like it in the world."

"Is it . . . safe?"

"No truly wonderful thing can be entirely safe. But it is safe enough."

Vialine stared into the box, her wide eyes reflecting its glow. "It is too grand a gift for me."

"How could any gift be too grand for the Empress of the South?" asked Yarvi, taking a gentle step toward her. "With this upon your arm, you will seem radiant indeed."

"It is beautiful beyond words. But I cannot take it."

"It is a gift freely given—"

Vialine looked up at him through her lashes. "I asked you to speak honestly, Father Yarvi." And she snapped the box shut, and put the light out with it. "I cannot help you. My aunt Theofora made promises I cannot break." She lifted her small fist high. "I am the most powerful person in the world!" Then she laughed, and let it fall. "And there is nothing I can do. Nothing I can do about anything. My uncle has an understanding with Mother Scaer."

"A ruler must plow her own furrow," said Yarvi.

"Easier said than done, Father Yarvi. The soil is very stony hereabouts."

"I could help you dig it over."

"I wish you could. Sumael says you are a good man."

"Above average." Sumael had a little smile at the corner of her mouth. "I've known worse men with both their hands."

"But you cannot help me. No one can." Vialine drew up her hood, and with one last glance toward Thorn, still kneeling in the middle of the courtyard with the box in her hand, the Empress of the South turned to leave. "And I am sorry, but I cannot help you."

It was hardly what they'd all been hoping for. But so it goes, with hopes.

# SOME
# BLOODY
# DIPLOMAT

Skifr came at her again but this time Thorn was ready. The old woman grunted in surprise as Thorn's ax caught her boot and sent her lurching. She parried the next blow but it rocked her on her heels and the one after tore her sword from her hand and knocked her clean on her back.

Even on the ground Skifr was dangerous. She kicked dust in Thorn's face, rolled and flung her ax with deadly accuracy. But Thorn was ready for that too, hooked it from the air with her own and sent it skittering into the corner, pressing on, teeth bared, and pinning Skifr against one of the pillars, the point of her sword tickling the old woman's sweat-beaded throat.

Skifr raised her gray brows. "Auspicious."

"I won!" bellowed Thorn, shaking her notched wooden weapons at the sky. It had been months since she dared hope she might ever get the better of Skifr. Those endless mornings being beaten with the oar as Mother Sun rose, those endless evenings trying to hit her with the bar by the light of Father Moon, those endless blows and slaps and slides into the mud. But she had done it. "I beat her!"

"You beat her," said Father Yarvi, nodding slowly.

Skifr winced as she clambered up. "You have beaten a grand-mother long years past her best. There will be sterner challenges ahead for you. But . . . you have done well. You have listened. You have worked. You have become deadly. Father Yarvi was right—"

"When am I wrong?" The minister's smile vanished at a hammer-ing on the door. He jerked his head toward Koll and the boy slid back the bolt.

"Sumael," said Yarvi, smiling as he did whenever she visited. "What brings—"

She was breathing hard as she stepped over the threshold. "The empress wishes to speak to you."

Father Yarvi's eyes widened. "I'll come at once."

"Not you." She was looking straight at Thorn. "You."

BRAND HAD SPENT MOST of his life feeling out of place. Beggar among the rich. Coward among the brave. Fool among the clever. But a visit to the Palace of the Empress opened up whole new gulfs of crippling inadequacy.

"Gods," he whispered, every time he crept around another corner after Thorn and Sumael into some new marbled corridor, or gilded stairway, or cavernous chamber, each richer than the last. He tiptoed down a hallway lit with candles tall as a man. Dozens of them, each worth more in Thorlby than he was, left burning on the chance that someone might happen by. Everything was jewelled or silvered, pan-elled or painted. He looked at a chair inlaid with a dozen kinds of wood, and thought how much more it must have cost than everything he had earned in his life. He wondered if he was dreaming it, but knew he didn't have a good enough imagination.

"Wait here," said Sumael, as they reached a round room at the top of a flight of steps, every bit of the marble walls carved as finely as Koll's mast with scenes from some story. "Touch nothing." And she left Brand alone with Thorn. The first time since that day in the market.

And look how that turned out.

"Quite a place," he muttered.

Thorn stood with her back to him, turning her head to show a sliver of frown. "Is that why Father Yarvi sent you along? To say what anyone could see?"

"I don't know why he sent me along." Chill silence stretched out. "I'm sorry if I dragged you back. The other day. You're far the better fighter, I should've let you take the lead."

"You should've," she said, without looking at him.

"Just . . . seems like you're angry with me, and whatever I—"

"Does now seem like the time?"

"No." He knew some things were better left unsaid but he couldn't stand thinking she hated him. He had to try and put things right. "I just—" He glanced across at her, and she caught him looking, the way she had dozens of times the last few weeks, but now her face twisted.

"Just shut your bloody mouth!" she snarled, white with fury, and looked ready to give him a bloody mouth as well.

He looked down at the floor, so highly polished he could see his own stricken face staring stupidly back, and had nothing to say. What could you say to that?

"If you love-birds are quite finished," said Sumael from the doorway, "the empress is waiting."

"Oh, we're finished," snapped Thorn, stalking off.

Sumael shrugged her shoulders at Brand, and two frowning guards shut the doors on him with a final-sounding *click*.


THE GARDENS WERE LIKE something from a dream, all lit in strange colors by the purple sunset and the shifting torchlight, flames flickering from cages of coals that sent sparks dancing with every breath of wind. Nothing was the way the gods had made it, everything tortured by the hands of man. Grass shaved as carefully as a romancer's jaw. Trees clipped into unnatural shapes and bowing under the weight of their own bloated, sweet-smelling blossom. Birds too, twittering from the twisted branches, and Thorn wondered why they didn't fly away until she saw they were all tethered to their perches with silver chains fine as spider's threads.

Paths of white stone twisted between statues of impossibly stern, impossibly slender women wafting scrolls, books, swords. Empresses of the past, Thorn reckoned, and all wondering why this half-shaved horror had been allowed among them. The guards looked as if they had the same question. Lots of guards, every mirror-bright sword and spear making her acutely aware of how unarmed she was. She sloped after Sumael around a star-shaped pool, crystal water tinkling into it from a fountain carved like snakes coiled together, up to the steps of a strange little building, a dome set on pillars with a curved bench beneath it.

On the bench sat Vialine, Empress of the South.

She had undergone quite a transformation since she visited Father Yarvi's crumbling house. Her hair was twisted into a shining coil netted with golden wire and hung with jewels. Her bodice was set with tiny mirrors that twinkled blue and pink with the fading light, red and orange with the torch-flames. From a streak of dark paint across the bridge of her nose, her eyes gleamed brightest of all.

Thorn wasn't sure she'd ever felt so far out of her depth. "What do I say?"

"She's just a person," said Sumael. "Talk to her like she's a person."

"What the hell do I know about talking to a person?"

"Just be honest." Sumael slapped Thorn on the back and sent her stumbling forward. "And do it now."

Thorn edged onto the lowest stair. "Your radiance," she croaked out, trying to go down on one knee then realizing it couldn't really be done on a set of steps.

"Vialine, and please don't kneel. A week ago I was nobody much. It still makes me nervous."

Thorn froze awkwardly halfway down, and wobbled back to an uncertain stoop. "Sumael says you sent for—"

"What is your name?"

"Thorn Bathu, your—"

"Vialine, please. The Thorn seems self-explanatory. The Bathu?"

"My father won a famous victory there the day I was born."

"He was a warrior?"

"A great one." Thorn fumbled for the pouch about her neck. "Chosen Shield to a queen of Gettland."

"And your mother?"

"My mother . . . wishes I wasn't me." Sumael had told her to be honest, after all.

"My mother was a general who died in battle against the Alyuks."

"Good for her," said Thorn, then instantly thought better of it. "Though . . . not for you." Worse and worse. "I suppose, your radiance . . ." She trailed off into mortified silence. Some bloody diplomat.

"Vialine." The empress patted the bench beside her. "Sit with me."

Thorn stepped up into the little pavilion, around a table, a silver platter on it heaped with enough perfect fruit to feed an army, and to a waist-high rail.

"Gods," she breathed. She had scarcely thought about how many stairs she climbed, but now she saw they were on the palace roof. There was a cliff-like drop to more gardens far below. The First of Cities was spread out under the darkening sky beyond, a madman's maze of buildings, lights twinkling in the blue evening, as many as stars in the sky. In the distance, across the black mirror of the straight, other clusters of lights. Other towns, other cities. Strange constellations, faint in the distance.

"And all this is yours," Thorn whispered.

"All of it and none of it." There was something in the set of Vialine's jaw, jutting proudly forward, that Thorn thought she recognized. That she had seen in her mother's mirror, long ago. That made her think the empress was used to wearing a brave face of her own.

"That must be quite a weight to carry," she said.

Vialine's shoulders seemed to sag a little. "Something of a burden."

"Empress, I don't know anything about politics." Thorn perched herself on the bench in a manner she hoped was respectful, whatever that looked like, she'd never been too comfortable sitting unless it was at an oar. "I don't know anything about anything. You'd be much better talking to Father Yarvi—"

"I don't want to talk about politics."

Thorn sat in prickling awkwardness. "So . . ."

"You're a woman." Vialine leaned forward, her hands clasped in her lap and her eyes fixed on Thorn's face. Disarmingly close. Closer than Thorn was used to having anyone, let alone an empress.

"So my mother tells me," she muttered. "Opinion's divided . . ."

"You fight men."

"Yes."

"You beat men."

"Sometimes . . ."

"Sumael says you beat them three at a time! Your crew respect you. I could see it in their faces. They *fear* you."

"Respect, I don't know. Fear, maybe, your—"

"Vialine. I never saw a woman fight like you. Can I?" Before Thorn could answer the empress had put her hand on Thorn's shoulder and squeezed at it. Her eyes went wide. "Great God, you're like wood! You must be so strong." She let her hand drop, much to Thorn's relief, and stared down at it, small and dark on the marble between them. "I'm not."

"Well, you won't beat a strong man with strength," murmured Thorn.

The empress's eyes flickered to hers, white in the midst of that black paint, torch flames gleaming in the corners. "With what, then?"

"You must be quicker to strike and quicker when you do. You must be tougher and cleverer, you must always look to attack, and you must fight without honor, without conscience, without pity." Skifr's words, and Thorn realized only then how completely she had learned them, how totally she had taken them in, how much the old woman had taught her. "So I'm told, anyway—"

Vialine snapped her fingers. "*That* is why I sent for you. To learn how to fight strong men. Not with swords, but the principles are the same." She propped her chin on her hands, a strangely girlish gesture in a woman who ruled half the world. "My uncle wants me to be nothing more than prow-beast for his ship. Less, if anything. The prow-beast at least goes at the keel."

"Our ships have one at the stern as well."

"Marvelous. He wants me to be that one, then. To sit in the throne and smile while he makes the choices. But I refuse to be his puppet." Vialine clenched her fist and thumped the table, scarcely even making the tiny fruit knife rattle on the platter. "I refuse, do you hear me?"

"I do, but . . . I'm not sure my hearing will make much difference."

"No. It's my uncle's ears I need to open." The empress glared off across the darkening gardens. "I stood up to him again in the council today. You should have seen his face. He couldn't have been more shocked if I'd stabbed him."

"You can't know that for sure until you stab him."

"Great God, I'd like to!" Vialine grinned across at her. "I bet no one makes a puppet of you, do they? I bet no one dares! Look at you." She had an expression Thorn wasn't used to seeing. Almost . . . admiring. "You're, you know—"

"Ugly?" muttered Thorn.

"No!"

"Tall?"

"No. Well, yes, but, *free*."

"Free?" Thorn gave a disbelieving snort.

"Aren't you?"

"I'm sworn to serve Father Yarvi. To do whatever he thinks necessary. To make up for . . . what I did."

"What did you do?"

Thorn swallowed. "I killed a boy. Edwal was his name, and I don't reckon he deserved to die, but . . . I killed him, all right."

Vialine was just a person, as Sumael had said and, in spite of her clothes and her palace, or maybe because of them, there was something in her even, earnest gaze that drew the words out.

"They were all set to crush me with stones for it, but Father Yarvi saved me. Don't know why, but he did. It was Skifr taught me to fight." Thorn smiled as she touched her fingers to the shaved side of her head, thinking how strong she'd thought herself back then and how weak she'd been. "We fought Horse People on the Denied. Killed a few of them, then I was sick. And we fought men in the market, the other day. Me and Brand. Not sure whether I killed those, but I wanted to. Angry, about those beads . . . I reckon . . ." She trailed off, realizing she'd said a lot more than she should have.

"Beads?" asked Vialine, the painted bridge of her nose crinkled with puzzlement.

Thorn cleared her throat. "Wouldn't worry about it."

"I suppose freedom can be dangerous," said the empress.

"I reckon."

"Perhaps we look at others and see only the things we don't have."

"I reckon."

"Perhaps we all feel weak, underneath."

"I reckon."

"But you fight men and win, even so."

Thorn sighed. "At that, I win."

Vialine counted the points off on her small fingers. "So, quickness to strike, and cleverness, and aggression without conscience, honor or pity."

Thorn held up her empty hands. "They've got me everything I have."

The empress laughed. A big laugh, from such a small woman, loud and joyous with her mouth wide open. "I like you, Thorn Bathu!"

"You're joining a small group, then. Sometimes feels like it's shrinking all the time." And Thorn eased out the box, and held it between them. "Father Yarvi gave me something for you."

"I told him I could not take it."

"He told me I had to give it to you even so." Thorn bit her lip as she eased the box open and the pale light spilled out, more strange and more beautiful than ever in the gathering darkness. The perfect edges of the elf-bangle gleamed like dagger-blades, glittering metal polished and faceted, winking with the lamplight, dark circles within circles shifting in the impossible depths beneath its round window. A relic from another world. A world thousands of years gone. A thing beside which the priceless treasures of the palace seemed petty baubles, worthless as mud.

Thorn tried to make her voice soft, persuasive, diplomatic. It came out rougher than ever. "Father Yarvi's a good man. A deep-cunning man. You should speak to him."

"I did." Vialine looked from the bangle to Thorn's eyes. "And you should be careful. Father Yarvi is a man like my uncle, I think. They give no gift without expecting something in return." She snapped the box closed, then took it from Thorn's hand. "But I will take it, if that is what you want. Give Father Yarvi my thanks. But tell him I can give him no more."

"I will." Thorn looked out at the garden as it sank into gloom, fumbling for something else to say, and noticed that where the guard had stood beside the fountain there were only shadows. All of them were gone. She and the empress were alone. "What happened to your guards?"

"That's odd," said Vialine. "Ah! But here are more."

Thorn counted six men climbing the steps at the far end of the gardens. Six imperial soldiers, fully armed and armored, clattering quickly down the path through pools of orange torchlight toward the empress's little house. Another man followed them. A man with gold on his breastplate and silver in his hair and a smile brighter than either upon his handsome face.

Duke Mikedas, and as he saw them he gave a jaunty wave.

Thorn had a feeling, then, as though the guts were draining out of her. She reached for the silver plate and slipped the little fruit knife between her fingers. A pitiful weapon, but better than none at all.

She stood as the soldiers stepped smartly around the fountain and between two statues, felt Vialine stand at her shoulder as they spread out. Thorn recognized one of them as the breeze caught the glowing coals and light flared across his face. The Vansterman she had fought in the market, cuts and purple bruises down one cheek and a heavy ax in his fist.

Duke Mikedas bowed low, but with a twist to his mouth, and his men did not bow at all. Vialine spoke in her own language and the duke answered, waving a lazy hand toward Thorn.

"Your grace," she forced through clenched teeth. "What an honor."

"My apologies," he said in the Tongue. "I was telling her radiance that I simply *could* not miss your visit. A gift, indeed, to find the two of you alone!"

"How so?" asked Vialine.

The duke raised his brows high. "Northern interlopers have come to the First of Cities! *Barbarians,* from Guttland, or wherever. Set on exporting their petty squabbles to our shores! They have tried to drive a wedge between us and our ally, the High King, who has accepted our One God into his heart. When that failed . . ." He sternly shook his head. "They have sent an *assassin* to the palace. An unnatural murderer, hoping to prey upon the innocent good nature of my idiot niece."

"I suppose that'd be me?" growled Thorn.

"Oh, *fiend* in woman's shape! Roughly woman's shape, anyway, you're rather too . . . muscular for my taste. I seem to remember you wanted to try two of my guards?" Mikedas grinned, and all the while his men edged forward, steel glimmering as it caught the light. "How d'you feel about six of 'em?"

Always look less than you are. Thorn cringed back, hunched her

226 I JOE ABERCROMBIE

shoulders, made herself look small and full of fear even though a strange calm had come on her. As if the Last Door did not yawn at her heels, but she saw it all from outside. She judged the distances, noted the ground, the statues, the torches, the table, the pillars, the steps, the long drop behind them.

"An empress really shouldn't take such chances with her safety," the duke was saying, "but do not despair, my dear niece, I shall avenge you!"

"Why?" whispered Vialine. Thorn could feel her fear, and that was useful. Two weak, and scared, and helpless girls, and behind her back she curled her fingers tight around that tiny knife.

The duke's lip curled. "Because you prove to be an utter pain in my arse. We all like a girl with spirit, don't we?" He stuck out his bottom lip and shook his head in disappointment. "But there is a limit. Really there is."

Thorn's father used to tell her, *if you mean to kill, you kill, you don't talk about it.* But fortunately for her the duke was no killer, prating and boasting and savoring his power, giving Thorn time to judge her enemy, time to choose her best chance.

She reckoned the duke himself a small threat. He wore a sword and dagger but she doubted they had ever been drawn. The others knew their business, though. Good swords out, and good shields on their arms, and good daggers at their belts. Good armor too, scaled mail twinkling in the twilight, but weak at the throat. The insides of the elbows. The backs of the knees. That was where she had to strike.

She alone, against seven. She almost laughed then. Absurd odds. Impossible odds. But the only ones she had.

"Theofora could never do as she was told," the duke blathered on, "but then she was too old a horse to learn obedience. I really had hoped a seventeen-year-old empress could be led by the nose." He gave a sigh. "Some ponies just chafe at the bridle, though. They kick and bite and refuse to be ridden. Better to destroy them before they throw their master. The throne will pass to your cousin Asta next." He showed those perfect teeth of his. "She's four. Now that's a woman you can work with!" Finally tiring of his own cleverness, he sent two of his men forward with a lazy gesture. "Let's get it done."

Thorn watched them come. One had a big, often-broken nose. The other a pocked and pitted face, smiling in a faintly uninterested way. Swords drawn but not raised as they came onto the first step. You couldn't blame them for being confident. But they were so confident they never even considered she might give them a fight.

And Thorn would give them a fight.

"Careful, your grace," said the Vansterman. "She's dangerous."

"Please," scoffed the duke, "she's just a girl. I thought you northerners were all fire and—"

The wise wait for their moment, as Father Yarvi had often told her, but never let it pass. The big-nosed man took the next step, squinting as the light from the torches in the pavilion shone into his eyes, then looking mildly surprised when Thorn darted forward and slit his throat with the fruit knife.

She angled the cut so blood sprayed the pock-faced man beside and he flinched. Just for an instant, but long enough for Thorn to jerk Big Nose's knife from his belt as he stumbled backward and ram it under the rim of Pockmark's helmet, into the shadow between his neck and his collarbone, all the way to the grip.

She planted her boot against his chest as he made a strangled groan and kicked him back, toppling from the first step and tangling with the two men behind. She caught his sword, cutting her hand on the blade but tearing it from his slack grip, bloody fingers around the crosspiece so she held it overhand like a dagger. She screamed as she ripped it upward, scraping the rim of the next man's shield and catching him under the jaw, the point raking across his face and knocking his helmet askew.

He reeled away screeching, blood bubbling between his clutching fingers, tottering into the duke who gasped and shoved him into the bushes, staring at the black specks down his breastplate as though they were a personal affront.

Big Nose was stumbling drunkenly back, looking even more surprised than before, desperately trying to hold his neck together but his whole left side was already dark with blood. Thorn reckoned she could put him out of her mind.

To deal with three that quickly was fine weaponluck indeed, but surprise had been her one advantage. It was spent, and the odds still four to one.

"God damn it!" bellowed the duke, wiping at his blood-spattered cloak. "Kill them!"

Thorn shuffled back, keeping a pillar close on her left like a shield, eyes darting back and forth as the men closed in, shields and swords and axes plenty ready now, hard steel and hard eyes all gleaming red with the torchlight. She could hear Vialine behind her, almost whimpering with each breath.

"Brand!" she screamed at the top of her lungs. "Brand!"

# RAGE

**B**rand stood there, staring at the jug of water on the table, and the goblets beside it, thinking they must be there for visitors but not daring to touch them even though he was thirsty as a man lost in the desert.

What if they were meant for better visitors than him?

He twisted his shoulders in a vain effort to peel his clinging shirt from his sticky skin. Gods, the heat, the endless, strangling heat, even as night crept in. He went to the window, closed his eyes and took a long breath, feeling the warm breeze on his face and wishing it was the salt wind of Thorlby.

He wondered what Rin was doing now. Rolled his eyes to the twilit skies and sent a prayer up to Father Peace to keep her well. In his eagerness to be a warrior, and find a crew, and make himself a new family he'd forgotten about the one he had. He was a man you could rely on, all right. To make a damn mess of things. He heaved up a heavy sigh.

And then he heard it, faint. Like someone calling his name. Thought he was dreaming it at first, then it came again, and he was sure. It sounded like Thorn, and the way things were between them she wouldn't be calling him without a reason.

He shoved the door open, thinking to rouse the guards.

But the guards were gone. Only the empty corridor, shadowy steps up at the far end. He thought he heard fighting, felt a stab of worry. Metal, and cries, and his name screamed out again.

He started running.

THORN SNATCHED UP THE SILVER PLATTER, fruit tumbling, shrieked as she flung it at the Vansterman and he ducked behind his big ax, stumbling away as the plate bounced from his shoulder and spun off into the bushes.

Tethered songbirds flapped and squawked and fluttered in a helpless panic and Thorn wasn't much better off, penned behind the pillars of the pavilion as if it was a cage. Beside the Vansterman there were two soldiers still standing—one tall and rangy with a hell of a reach, one short and beefy with a neck thick as a tree. The duke loitered at the back, pointing at Thorn with his dagger and shouting in a broken voice. A clever man, maybe, but a man used to everything going his way.

"Got blood on your shoes have I?" she snarled at him. "Y'old bastard?"

She made a grab for one of the torches, ripping it from its sconce, ignoring the sparks that scattered searing up her arm.

Thick Neck darted toward her and she blocked his sword with hers, steel clashing, chopped at him and struck splinters from his shield, stepped away, trying to give herself room to think of something, slipped on fallen fruit in the darkness and lurched against the table. A sword chopped into her leg. The meat of her left thigh, above the knee. She gave a kind of swallowing yelp as the tall soldier pulled it free of her, readying for a thrust.

*You will be struck, and when you are the force of it must not stagger you, the pain of it must not slow you, the shock of it must not cause you to doubt.* She lashed at the tall soldier with the torch and he brought his shield up just in time, tottering down the steps as red coals spilled from the cage and across his back in a shower of glowing dust.

She ducked on an instinct, Thick Neck's sword whistling by and clanging against the nearest pillar, splinters of marble spinning, fighting shadows flickering, dodging, stabbing all around them. Thorn swung for him but her leg had no strength in it, her sword bounced from his armored shoulder, only checked him for a moment.

She saw her blood, gleaming black in the torchlight, a trail of spots and spatters leading to the point of the tall man's sword. She saw the duke's face twisted with rage. She heard the empress screaming something over the rail. Calling for help, but there was no help coming. Thick Neck had his front foot on the top step, hard eyes fixed on her over his shield rim. Tall was clawing at his back, trying to brush the coals from his smoldering cloak.

She had to fight, while she still had blood to fight with. Had to attack, and it had to be now.

She shoved herself from the table as Thick Neck stabbed at her and sprang down the steps, over a fallen body. Her wounded thigh gave as she came down but she was ready for that, fell forward, rolled under Tall's hard-swung sword, the wind from the blade catching her hair, came up on her good side, slashing at him as she passed.

She caught Tall behind the knee and he grunted, trying to turn and falling to all fours in front of her. She lifted the sword high, arching back, brought it crashing down on his helmet. The force of it jolted her arm so hard it made her teeth buzz. The blade shattered, shards of steel bouncing away. But it left a mighty dent, one of Tall's legs kicking wildly as he flopped on his face, mouth open in a silent yawn. Thorn tottered against a statue, broken sword still clutched in her fist.

Good weaponluck, Odda would've said, because the Vansterman chose that moment to swing his ax and it missed her by a hair, heavy blade knocking a great chunk of marble loose. Thorn shoved him away with the torch, a few last sparks whirling on the breeze. Her leg was throbbing, pulsing, no strength in it at all.

Thick Neck stepped carefully toward her, shield up. There's always a way, Father Yarvi used to say, but Thorn couldn't see it. She was too hurt. The odds were too long. She clutched hard to that broken sword, bared her teeth, showed him her bravest face. She could smell flowers. Flowers and blood.

"Your death comes," she whispered.

Vialine shrieked as she leapt between the pillars and onto the short man's back, grabbing him around his bull neck, clutching at the wrist of his sword arm. He tried to throw her off, shield flailing, but that left a gap. Thorn dived at him, her left knee buckled, pain stabbing through her leg but she caught his armor as she fell and dragged herself up, snarled as she drove the broken sword blade up under his jaw. He spoke blood, the empress squealing as they crashed down on top of her.

Thorn rolled just in time, the Vansterman's heavy ax flashing past, thudding through Thick Neck's mail and deep into his chest. Thorn half-scrambled, half hopped up as he struggled to drag his ax free, the breath burning in her heaving chest.

"Brand!" she screamed in a broken voice. She heard a step behind her, lurched around and saw a flash of metal. The duke punched her in the cheek, made her head jolt, but it was a feeble sort of blow, barely even staggering her.

She clutched at his gilded breastplate. "That your best?" she hissed, but the words were blood, drooling down her chin. There was something in her mouth. Cold, and hard, across her tongue. That was when she realized he'd stabbed her. He'd stabbed her and the dagger was right through her face, between her jaws, his hand still around the grip.

They stared at each other in the darkness, neither quite believing what had happened. Neither quite believing she was still standing. Then, by the glimmering of torchlight, she saw his eyes go hard.

She felt the blade shift in her mouth as he tried to tear it free and she bit down on it, kneed him in his side with her wounded leg, twisted her head, twisting the bloody grip of the dagger out of his limp hand. She shoved him clumsily away, staggering sideways as the Vansterman swung at her, his ax grazing her shoulder and ripping a shower of leaves from the bushes as she hopped back toward the fountain.

Everyone's got a plan until they start bleeding and she was bleeding now. Her leg was hot with it, her face sticky with it. No plans any more. She snorted and blew a red mist.

She caught the grip and dragged the dagger out of her face. Came out easy enough. Might have been a tooth came with it, though. Gods, she was dizzy. Her leg had stopped throbbing. Just numb. Numb and wet and her knee trembling. She could hear it flapping inside her blood-soaked trousers.

Drowsy.

She shook her head, trying to shake the dizziness out but it only made things worse, the blurry gardens tipping one way then back the other.

Duke Mikedas had drawn his sword, was dragging the corpse of the thick-necked man away so he could get at the empress.

Thorn waved the knife around but it was so heavy. As if there was an anvil hanging off the point. The torches flashed and flickered and danced.

"Come on," she croaked, but her tongue was all swollen, couldn't get the words around it.

The Vansterman smiled as he herded her back toward the fountain.

She tripped, clutched at something, knee buckling, just staying upright.

Kneeling in water. Fish flitting in the darkness.

Vialine screamed again. Her voice was getting hoarse from it.

The Vansterman wafted his ax back and forward and the big blade caught the light and left orange smears across Thorn's blurred sight.

The empress said *don't kneel* but she couldn't get up.

She could hear her own breath, wheezing, wheezing.

234 | JOE ABERCROMBIE

Didn't sound too good.

Gods, she was tired.

"Brand," she mumbled.

HE CAME UP THE steps running.

Caught a glimpse of a darkened garden, a path of white stones between flowering trees, and statues, and dead men scattered in the shadows about a torchlit fountain—

He saw Thorn kneeling in it, clutching at wet stone carved like snakes, a dagger in her other hand. Her face was tattered red and her clothes torn and stuck to her dark and the water pink with blood.

A man stood over her with an ax in his hand. The Vansterman from the market.

Brand made a sound like a boiling kettle. A sound he never made before and never heard a man make.

He tore down that path like a charging bull and as the Vansterman turned, eyes wide, Brand caught him, snatched him off his feet like the north gale snatches up a leaf and rammed him at a full sprint into a statue.

They hit it so hard the world seemed to shake. So hard it rattled Brand's teeth in his head. So hard the statue broke at the waist and the top fell in dusty chunks across the grass.

Brand might've heard the Vansterman's shattered groan if it wasn't for the blood pounding in his skull like Mother Sea on a storm day, blinding him, deafening him. He seized the Vansterman's head with both hands and rammed it into the marble pedestal, two times, three, four, chips of stone flying until his skull was bent and dented and flattened and Brand flung him down ruined onto the path.

Thorn was slumped against the fountain, her face all the wrong colors, skin waxy pale and streaked with blood and her torn cheeks and her mouth and her chin all clotted black.

"Stay back!" someone shrieked. An older man in a gilded breast-plate with a sheen of sweat across his face. He had the Empress Vialine about the neck, a jewelled sword to her throat, but it was too long for the task. "I am Duke Mikedas!" he bellowed, as if the name was a shield.

But a name's just a name. Brand's lips curled back and he took a step forward, the growling in his throat hot as dragon's fire, kicking a corpse out of his way.

The duke whipped the sword from Vialine's neck and pointed it wobbling toward Brand. "I'm warning you, stay—"

The empress grabbed his hand and bit it, twisting free as he screamed. He raised his sword but Brand was on him, making that sound again, that shrieking, keening, gurgling sound, not thinking of doing good, or of standing in the light, or anything but breaking this man apart with his hands.

The sword grazed his head and bounced off his shoulder. Maybe it cut him and maybe it didn't and Brand didn't care. His arms closed tight about the duke like a lock snapping shut. He was a big man, but Brand once held the weight of a ship across his shoulders. He hoisted Duke Mikedas into the air as if he was made of straw.

Four charging steps he took, thudding across the dark lawn, lifting the duke higher and higher.

"You can't—" he screeched, then Brand flung him into space. Over the stone rail he tumbled. He seemed to hang there for a moment against the dusky sky, astonished, sword still in his hand. His screech turned to a coughing gurgle and he plummeted flailing out of sight.

"God," croaked Vialine.

There was a crunch far below as her uncle hit the ground. Then a long clatter.

Then silence.

# DEBTS AND
# PROMISES

Thorn's eyes opened and it was dark.

The darkness beyond the Last Door?

She tried to move, and gasped at the pain.

Surely the one good thing about death was that the pain stopped?

She felt bandages across her face, remembered the jolt as Duke Mikedas's knife punched through her mouth, gave a rusty groan, her throat dry as old bones.

She squinted toward a slit of brightness, fumbled back blankets and slowly, ever so slowly, swung her legs down, everything bruised and battered and stabbed through with cramps. She moaned as she tried to put weight on her left leg, pain catching fire in her thigh, creeping up into her back, down through her knee.

She hopped and she shuffled, clutching at the wall. Gods, the pain in her leg, but when she winced at that, gods, the pain in her face, and when she whimpered at that, gods, the pain in her chest, up her throat, in her eyes as the tears flowed, and she made it to that strip of light, the light under a door, and pawed it open.

She shuffled forward with one hand up to shield her sore eyes, like staring into the blinding sun even though it was only a single candle. A thick candle with long, jewelled pins stuck into the wax. She saw crumbling plaster, fallen clothes casting long shadows across the boards, the dark folds on a rumpled bed—

She froze. A dark-skinned back, a bare back, lean muscles shifting. She heard a slow grunting, a woman's voice and a man's, together, and Thorn saw a pale arm slip up that back, a long, wasted arm and on the end was a shrivelled hand with just one stump of a finger.

"Uh," she croaked, eyes wide, and the woman's head jerked around. Black hair across her face, and a scar through her top lip, and a notch of white tooth showing. Sumael, and with Father Yarvi underneath her.

"Uh." Thorn couldn't go forward, couldn't go back, and she stared at the floor, burning with pain and embarrassment, trying to swallow but feeling as if she'd never have spit again in the aching hole of her mouth.

"You're awake." Father Yarvi scrambled from the bed and into his trousers.

"Am I?" she wanted to ask, but it came out, "Uh."

"Back to bed before you set that leg bleeding." And the minister slipped his arm around her and started helping her to hop and shuffle back toward the dark doorway.

Thorn couldn't help glancing over her shoulder as they passed the threshold, saw Sumael stretched out naked as though nothing could be more ordinary, looking sideways at her through narrowed eyes.

"In pain?" asked Father Yarvi as he lowered her onto the bed.

"Uh," she grunted.

Water sloshed into a cup, a spoon rattled as he mixed something in. "Drink this."

It tasted beyond foul and her ripped mouth and her swollen tongue and her dry throat burned from it, but she fought it down, and at least she could make words afterward.

"I thought," she croaked, as he swung her legs back into the bed and checked the bandages around her thigh, "you swore . . . an oath."

"I swore too many. I must break some to keep another."

"Who decides which ones you keep?"

"I'll keep my first one." And he closed the fingers of his good hand and made a fist of it. "To be revenged upon the killers of my father."

She was growing drowsy. "I thought . . . you did that . . . long ago."

"On some of them. Not all." Yarvi pulled the blankets over her. "Sleep, now, Thorn."

Her eyes drifted closed.

"DON'T GET UP."

"Your radiance—"

"For God's sake: Vialine." The empress had some scratches across her cheek, but no other sign of her brush with Death.

"I should—" Thorn winced as she tried to sit and Vialine put her hand on her shoulder, and gently but very firmly pushed her back onto the bed.

"Don't get up. Consider that an imperial edict." For once, Thorn decided not to fight. "Are you badly hurt?"

She thought about saying no, but the lie would hardly have been convincing. She shrugged, and even that was painful. "Father Yarvi says I'll heal."

The empress looked down as though she was the one in pain, her hand still on Thorn's shoulder. "You will have scars."

"They're expected on a fighter."

"You saved my life."

"They would have killed me first."

"Then you saved both our lives."

"Brand played his part, I hear."

"And I have thanked him. But I have not thanked you." Vialine took a long breath. "I have dissolved the alliance with the High King. I have sent birds to Grandmother Wexen. I have let her know that, regardless of what gods we pray to, the enemy of Gettland is my enemy, the friend of Gettland is my friend."

Thorn blinked. "You're too generous."

"I can afford to be, now. My uncle ruled an empire within the empire, but without him it has fallen like an arch without its keystone. I have taken your advice. To strike swiftly, and without mercy. Traitors are being weeded out of my council. Out of my guard." There was a hardness in her face, and just then Thorn was glad she was on Vialine's right side. "Some have fled the city, but we will hunt them down."

"You will be a great empress," croaked Thorn.

"If my uncle has taught me anything, it is that an empress is only as great as those around her."

"You have Sumael, and you—"

Vialine's hand squeezed her shoulder, and she looked down with that earnest, searching gaze. "Would you stay?"

"Stay?"

"As my bodyguard, perhaps? Queens have them, do they not, in the North? What do you call them?"

"A Chosen Shield," whispered Thorn.

"As your father was. You have proved yourself more than qualified."

A Chosen Shield. And to the Empress of the South. To stand at the shoulder of the woman who ruled half the world. Thorn fumbled for the pouch around her neck, felt the old lumps inside, imagining her father's pride to hear of it. What songs might be sung of that in the smoky inns, and in the narrow houses, and in the high Godshall of Thorlby?

And at that thought a wave of homesickness surged over Thorn, so strong she nearly choked. "I have to go back. I miss the gray cliffs. I miss the gray sea. I miss the *cold*." She felt tears in her eyes, then, and blinked them away. "I miss my mother. And I swore an oath."

"Not all oaths are worth keeping."

"You keep an oath not for the oath but for yourself." Her father's words, whispered long ago beside the fire. "I wish I could split myself in half."

Vialine sucked at her teeth. "Half a bodyguard would be no good to me. But I knew what your answer would be. You are not one to be held, Thorn Bathu, even with a gilded chain. Perhaps one day you will come back of your own accord. Until then, I have a gift for you. I could only find one worthy of the service you have done me."

And she brought out something that cast pale light across her face, and struck a spark in her eyes, and stopped Thorn's breath in her throat. The elf-bangle that Skifr had dug from the depths of Strokom, where no man had dared tread since the Breaking of God. The gift the *South Wind* had carried all the long road down the Divine and the Denied. A thing too grand for an empress to wear.

"Me?" Thorn wriggled up the bed in an effort to get away from it. "No! No, no, no!"

"It is mine to give, well-earned and freely given."

"I can't take it—"

"One does not refuse the Empress of the South." Vialine's voice had iron in it, and she raised her chin and glared down her nose at Thorn with an authority that was not to be denied. "Which hand?"

Thorn mutely held out her left, and Vialine slipped the elf-bangle over it and folded the bracelet shut with a final sounding click, the light from its round window glowing brighter, shifting to blue-white, metal perfect as a cut jewel gleaming, and circles within circles slowly shifting beneath the glass. Thorn stared at it with a mixture of awe and horror. A relic beyond price. Beautiful beyond words. Sitting now, on her ridiculous bony wrist, with the bizarre magnificence of a diamond on a dung-heap.

Vialine smiled, and finally let go of her shoulder. "It looks well on you."

THE SHEARS CLICK-CLICKED OVER the left side of Thorn's scalp and the hair fluttered down onto her shoulder, onto her bandaged leg, onto the cobbles of the yard.

"Do you remember when I first clipped your head?" asked Skifr. "You howled like a wolf cub!"

Thorn picked up a tuft of hair and blew it from her fingers. "Seems you can get used to anything."

"With enough work." Skifr tossed the shears aside and brushed the loose hair away. "With enough sweat, blood, and training."

Thorn worked her tongue around the unfamiliar inside of her mouth, rough with the stitches, and leaned forward to spit pink. "Blood I can give you." She grimaced as she stretched her leg out, the elf-bangle flaring angry purple with her pain. "But training might be difficult right now."

Skifr sat, one arm about Thorn's shoulders, rubbing her hand over her own stubbled hair. "We have trained for the last time, my dove."

"What?"

"I have business I must attend to. I have ignored my own sons, and daughters, and grandsons, and granddaughters too long. And only the most wretched of fools would dare now deny that I have done what Father Yarvi asked of me, and made you deadly. Or helped you make yourself deadly, at least."

Thorn stared at Skifr, an empty feeling in her stomach. "You're leaving?"

"Nothing lasts forever. But that means I can tell you things I could not tell you before." Skifr folded her in a tight, strange-smelling hug. "I have had twenty-two pupils in all, and never been more proud of one than I am of you. None worked so hard. None learned so fast. None had such courage." She leaned back, holding Thorn at arm's length. "You have proved yourself strong, inside and out. A loyal companion. A fearsome fighter. You have earned the respect of your friends and the fear of your enemies. You have demanded it. You have *commanded* it."

"But . . ." muttered Thorn, rocked far more by compliments than blows, "I've still got so much to learn . . ."

"A fighter is never done learning. But the best lessons one teaches oneself. It is time for you to become the master." And Skifr held out her ax, letters in five languages etched on the bearded blade. "This is for you."

Thorn had dreamed of owning a weapon like that. A thing fit for a hero's song. Now she took it numbly, and laid it on her lap, and looked down at the bright blade. "To the fighter, everything must be a weapon," she muttered. "What will I do without you?"

Skifr leaned close, her eyes bright, and gripped her tight. "Anything! Everything! I am no mean prophet and I foresee great things for you!" Her voice rose higher and higher, louder and louder, and she pointed one clawing finger toward the sky. "We will meet again, Thorn Bathu, on the other side of the Last Door, if not on this one, and I will thrill to the tales of your high deeds, and swell with pride that I played my own small part in them!"

"Damn right you will," said Thorn, sniffing back her tears. She had held this strange woman in contempt. She had hated her, and feared her, and cursed her name all down the Divine and the Denied. And now she loved her like a mother.

"Be well, my dove. Even more, be ready." Skifr's hand darted out but Thorn caught it by the wrist before it could slap her and held it trembling between them.

Skifr smiled wide. "And always strike first."

FATHER YARVI SMILED AS he peeled away the bandages. "Good. Very good." He pressed gently at the sore flesh of her cheeks with his fingertips. "You are healing well. Walking already."

"Lurching like a drunk already."

"You are lucky, Thorn. You are very lucky."

"Doubtless. Not every girl gets to be stabbed through the face."

"And by a duke of royal blood too!"

"The gods have smiled on me, all right."

"It could have been through your eye. It could have been through your neck." He started to bathe her face with a flannel that smelled of bitter herbs. "On the whole I would prefer to be scarred than dead, wouldn't you?"

Thorn pushed her tongue into the salty hole her missing tooth had left. It was hard to think of herself as lucky just then. "How are the scars? Tell me the truth."

"They will take time to heal, but I think they will heal well. A star on the left and an arrow on the right. There must be some significance in that. Skifr might have told us, she had an eye for portents—"

Thorn did not need Skifr to see into her face's future. "I'll be monstrous, won't I?"

"I know of people with uglier deformities." And Yarvi put his withered hand under her nose and let the one finger flop back and forth. "Next time, avoid the blade."

She snorted. "Easily said. Have you ever fought seven men?"

Drops trickled into the steaming bowl as he wrung out the flannel, the water turning a little pink. "I could never beat one."

"I saw you win a fight once."

He paused. "Did you indeed?"

"When you were king, I saw you fight Keimdal in the square." He stared at her for a moment, caught for once off-balance. "And when you lost, you asked to fight him again, and sent your mother's Chosen Shield in your place. And Hurik ground Keimdal's face into the sand on your behalf."

"A warrior fights," murmured Yarvi. "A king commands."

"So does a minister."

He started to smear something on her face that made the stitches sting. "I remember you now. A dark-haired girl, watching."

"Even then you were a deep-cunning man."

"I have had to be."

"Your trip to the First of Cities has turned out better than anyone could've hoped."

"Thanks to you." He unwound a length of bandage. "You have

done what no diplomat could achieve, and made an ally of the Empire of the South. Almost enough to make me glad I didn't crush you with rocks. And you have your reward." He tapped at the elf-bangle, its faint light showing through her sleeve.

"I'd give it back if I could open it."

"Skifr says it cannot be opened. But you should wear it proudly. You have earned it, and more besides. I may not be my mother's son any longer, but I still have her blood. I remember my debts, Thorn. Just as you remember yours."

"I've had a lot of time for remembering, the last few days. I've been remembering Throvenland."

"Another alliance that no one could have hoped for."

"You have a habit of coming away with them. I've been thinking about the man who poisoned the water."

"The man you killed?"

Thorn fixed his pale blue eye with hers. "Was he your man?"

Father Yarvi's face showed no surprise, no confirmation and no denial. He wound the bandages around her head as if she had not spoken.

"A deep-cunning man," she went on, "in need of allies, knowing King Fynn's ready temper, might have staged such a thing."

He pushed a pin gently through the bandages to hold them firm. "And a hot-headed girl, a thorn in the world's arse, not knowing anything, might have got herself caught up in the gears of it."

"It could happen."

"You are not without some cunning of your own." Father Yarvi put the bandages and the knife carefully away in his bag. "But you must know a deep-cunning man would never lay bare his schemes. Not even to his friends." He patted her on the shoulder, and stood. "Keep your lies as carefully as your winter grain, my old teacher used to tell me. Rest, now."

"Father Yarvi?" He turned back, a black shape in the bright outline of the door. "If I hadn't killed that poisoner . . . who would have drunk the water?"

A silence, then, and with the light behind him she could not see his face. "Some questions are best not asked, Thorn. And certainly best not answered."

"RULF'S BEEN GETTING THE CREW back together." Brand pushed some invisible dust around with the toe of his boot. "Few new men but mostly the same old faces. Koll can't wait to get started carving the other side of the mast, he says. And Dosduvoi's thinking of preaching the word of the One God up north. Fror's with us too."

Thorn touched a finger to her bandages. "Reckon folk'll be asking me how I got the scars, now, eh?"

"Hero's marks," said Brand, scratching at the ones that snaked up his own forearms. "Marks of a great deed."

"And it's hardly like my looks were ever my strongest point, is it?" Another awkward silence. "Father Yarvi says you killed Duke Mikedas."

Brand winced as though the memory was far from pleasant. "The ground killed him. I just made the introduction."

"You don't sound proud of it."

"No. Not sure I'm touched by Mother War like you are. Don't have your . . ."

"Fury?"

"I was going to say courage. Anger I've got plenty of. Just wish I didn't."

"Father Yarvi says you carried me back. He says you saved my life."

"Just what an oarmate does."

"Thanks for doing it, even so."

He stared at the ground, chewing at his lip, and finally looked up at her. "I'm sorry. For whatever I did. For . . ." He had that helpless look of his again, but rather than making her want to hold him, it made her want to hit him. "I'm sorry."

"Not your fault," she grated out. "Just the way things are."

"I wish they were a different way."

"So do I." She was too tired, too sore, too hurting inside and out to try and make it pretty. "Not as if you can make yourself like someone, is it?"

"Guess not," he said in a meek little voice that made her want to hit him even more. "Been through a lot together, you and me. Hope we can be friends, still."

She made her voice cold. Cold and sharp as a drawn blade. It was that or she might set to crying and she wouldn't do it. "Don't think that'll work for me, Brand. Don't see how this just goes back the way it was."

His mouth gave a sorry twist at that. As if he was the one hurt. Guilt, more than likely, and she hoped it stung. Hoped it stung half as much as she did. "Up to you." He turned his back on her. "I'll be there. If you need me."

The door shut, and she bared her teeth at it, and that made her face ache, and she felt tears in her eyes, and dashed them hard away. Wasn't fair. Wasn't fair at all, but she guessed love's even less fair than the battlefield.

To fool herself once was once too often. She had to rip those hopes up before they could take root. She had to kill the seeds. As soon as she could she limped off to find Rulf and asked for a different oar to pull on the way back home.

Owed her that much, didn't they?

# STRANGE
# BEDFELLOWS

"So you're leaving?" asked Sumael, her heavy footsteps echoing down the corridor.

"Within the week," said Father Yarvi. "We may not make it home before the Divine freezes as it is. You could always come with us. Don't pretend you don't miss the northern snows."

She laughed. "Oh, every balmy day here I wish I was frozen near to death again. You could always stay with us. Don't you enjoy the southern sun?"

"I am a little too pale. I burn before I brown." He gave a ragged sigh. "And I have an oath to keep."

Her smile faded. "I didn't think you took your oaths that seriously."

"This one I do," said Father Yarvi.

"Will you break the world to keep it?"

"I hope it won't come to that."

Sumael snorted. "You know how it is, with hopes."

"I do," murmured Brand. He got the feeling there were two conversations going on. One in plain sight and one hidden. But he'd never been much good with conversations, or with things he couldn't see, so he said no more.

Sumael swung a gate open with a squealing of rusted hinges, rough steps dropping into darkness. "She's down there."

The vaulted passage at the bottom was caked with mold, something scurrying away from the flickering light of Brand's torch.

"Just follow my lead," said Yarvi.

Brand gave a weary nod. "What else would I do?"

They stopped before a barred opening. Brand saw the glimmer of eyes in the shadows and stepped close, raising his torch.

Mother Scaer, once minister of Vansterland, then emissary of Grandmother Wexen, now sat against a wall of mossy rock with her shaved head on one side, her tattooed forearms on her knees and her long hands dangling. She had five elf-bangles stacked on one wrist, gold and glass and polished metal glinting. Brand would've been awestruck at the sight of them once but now they seemed petty, gaudy, broken things beside the one Thorn wore.

"Ah, Father Yarvi!" Scaer stretched a long leg toward them, chains rattling from an iron band about her bare ankle. "Have you come to gloat?"

"Perhaps a little. Can you blame me? You did conspire to murder the Empress Vialine, after all."

Mother Scaer gave a hiss. "I had no part of that. Grandmother Wexen sent me here to stop that puffed-up bladder of arrogance Duke Mikedas from doing anything foolish."

"How did that work out?" asked Yarvi.

Mother Scaer held up a length of chain to show them, and let it drop in her lap. "You should know better than anyone, a good minister gives the best advice they can, but in the end the ruler does what the ruler does. Did you bring this one to frighten me?" Mother Scaer's blue eyes fell on Brand, and even through the bars he felt a chill. "He is not frightening."

"On the contrary, I brought him to make you feel comfortable. My frightening one picked up a scratch killing seven men when she saved the empress and ruined all your plans." Brand didn't point out that he'd killed two of those men. He took no pride in it, and he was getting the feeling that wasn't the story everyone wanted to tell. "But she's healing nicely. Perhaps she can frighten you later."

Mother Scaer looked away. "We both know there is no later for me. I should have killed you at Amwend."

"You wanted to leave my guts for the crows, I remember. But Grom-gil-Gorm said, why kill what you can sell?"

"His first mistake. He made a second when he trusted you."

"Well, like King Uthil, Gorm is a warrior, and warriors tend to prefer action to thought. That is why they need ministers. That is why he needs your advice so very badly. That, I suspect, is why Grandmother Wexen was so keen to prize you from his side."

"He will get no help from me now," said Mother Scaer. "You, and Grandmother Wexen, and Duke Mikedas between you have made sure of that."

"Oh, I don't know," said Yarvi. "I am heading back up the Divine within the week. Back to the Shattered Sea." He pushed out his lips and tapped at them with his forefinger. "To send a passenger on to Vulsgard would not be too much trouble, eh, Brand?"

"Not too much," said Brand.

Yarvi raised his brows as though the idea had just occurred. "Perhaps we could find room for Mother Scaer?"

"We've lost one mysterious bald woman." Brand shrugged. "We've space for another."

Gorm's minister frowned up at them. Interested, but not wanting to seem interested. "Don't toy with me, boy."

"Never been much good at toying," said Brand. "I had a short childhood."

Mother Scaer slowly unfolded her long limbs and stood, bare feet flapping on damp stone as she walked to the bars until the chains were taut, then leaned a little farther, shadows shifting in the hollows of her gaunt face.

"Are you offering me my life, Father Yarvi?"

"I find it in my hands, and have no better use for it."

"Huh." Mother Scaer raised her brows very high. "What tasty bait. And no hook in it, I suppose?"

Yarvi leaned closer to the bars himself, so the two minister's faces were no more than a foot's length apart. "I want allies."

"Against the High King? What allies could I bring you?"

"There is a Vansterman on our crew. A good man. Strong at the oar. Strong in the wall. Would you say so, Brand?"

"Strong at the oar." Brand remembered Fror bellowing out the *Song of Bail* on that hill above the Denied. "Strong in the wall."

"Seeing him fight beside men of Gettland made me realize again how much alike we are," said Yarvi. "We pray to the same gods under the same skies. We sing the same songs in the same tongue. And we both struggle under the ever-weightier yoke of the High King."

Mother Scaer's lip curled. "And you would free Vansterland from her bondage, would you?"

"Why not? If at the same time I can free Gettland from hers. I did not enjoy wearing a galley captain's thrall-collar. I enjoy being slave to some drooling old fool in Skekenhouse no more."

"An alliance between Gettland and Vansterland?" Brand grimly shook his head. "We've been fighting each other since before there was a High King. Since before there was a Gettland. Madness, surely."

Yarvi turned to look at him, a warning in his eye. "The line between madness and deep-cunning has ever been a fine one."

"The boy is right." Mother Scaer pushed her arms through the bars and let them dangle. "There are ancient feuds between us, and deep hatreds—"

"There are petty squabbles between us, and shallow ignorance. Leave the wrathful words to the warriors, Mother Scaer, you and I know better. Grandmother Wexen is our true enemy. She is the one who tore you from your place to do her slave-work. She cares nothing for Vansterland, or Gettland, or any of us. She cares only for her own power."

Mother Scaer let her head fall on one side, blue eyes narrowed. "You will never win. She is too strong."

"Duke Mikedas was too strong, and both his power and his skull lie in ruins."

They narrowed further. "King Uthil will never agree."

"Let me worry about King Uthil."

Further still. "Grom-gil-Gorm will never agree."

"Do not underestimate yourself, Mother Scaer, I do not doubt your own powers of persuasion are formidable."

Blue slits, now. "Less so than yours, I think, Father Yarvi." Of a sudden she opened her eyes wide, and pushed her hand out through the bars so fast that Brand flinched back and nearly dropped his torch. "I accept your offer."

Father Yarvi took her hand and, stronger than she looked, she pulled him close by it. "You understand I can promise nothing."

"I am less interested in promises than I used to be. The way to bend someone to your will is to offer them what they want, not to make them swear an oath." Yarvi twisted his hand free. "It will be cold on the Divine, as the year grows late. I'd pack something warm."

As they walked off into the darkness, Father Yarvi put his hand on Brand's shoulder. "You did well."

"I scarcely said a thing."

"No. But the wise speaker learns first when to stay silent. You'd be surprised how many clever people never take the lesson."

Sumael was waiting for them at the gate. "Did you get what you wanted?"

Yarvi stopped in front of her. "Everything I wanted and far more than I deserved. But now it seems I must leave it behind."

"Fate can be cruel."

"It usually is."

"You could stay."

"You could come."

"But in the end we must all be what we are. I am counselor to an empress."

"I am minister to a king. We both have our burdens."

Sumael smiled. "And when you've a load to lift . . ."

"You're better lifting than weeping."

"I will miss you, Yarvi."

"It will be as if I left the best piece of myself behind."

They looked at each other for a moment longer, then Sumael dragged in a sharp breath. "Good luck on the journey." And she strode away, shoulders back.

Father Yarvi's face twisted and he leaned against the gate as if he might fall. Brand was on the point of offering his hand, but the wise speaker learns first when to stay silent. Soon enough the minister drew himself up without help.

"Gather the crew, Brand," he said. "We've a long way to go."

# IV.

# HIGH
# DEEDS

# FAREWELLS

Thorn gently slid her oar from its port and gave the sweat-polished wood a fond final stroke with her fingertips.

"Fare you well, my friend." The oar was all indifference, though, so with a parting sigh she hefted her sea-chest rattling onto the wharf and sprang up after it.

Mother Sun smiled down on Thorlby from a clear sky, and Thorn closed her eyes and tipped her face back, smiling as the salt breeze kissed her scarred cheeks.

"Now that's what weather should be," she whispered, remembering the choking heat of the First of Cities.

"Look at you." Rulf paused in tying off the prow-rope to shake his balding head in wonder. "Hard to believe how you've grown since you first sat at my back oar. And not just in height."

"From girl to woman," said Father Yarvi, clambering from the *South Wind*.

"From woman to hero," said Dosduvoi, catching Thorn in a crushing hug. "Remember that crew of Throvenmen singing a song about you on the Divine? The she-devil who killed ten warriors and saved the Empress of the South! A woman who breathes fire and looks lightning!"

"Snake for a tail, wasn't it?" grunted Fror, winking his smaller eye at her.

"All that time spent staring at your arse," mused Koll, "and I never noticed the tail—ow!" As his mother clipped him around the head.

Dosduvoi was still chuckling over the Throvenmen. "Their faces when they realized you were sitting right in front of them!"

"And then they begged to fight you." Rulf laughed with him. "Bloody fools."

"We warned 'em," grunted Fror. "What did you say, Safrit?"

"She might not breathe fire, but you'll get burned even so."

"And she kicked their white arses one after another and dumped their captain in the river!" shouted Koll, springing up onto the ship's rail and balancing there with arms spread wide.

"Lucky he didn't drown with all that ice," said Rulf.

In spite of the warmth, Thorn shivered at the memory. "Gods, but it was cold up there on the Divine."

The ice had come early, crackling against the keel, and just a week north of the tall hauls it had locked the river tight. So they'd dragged the South Wind over and made a hall of her again, and lived there huddled like a winter flock for two freezing months.

Thorn still trained as hard as if she could hear Skifr's voice. Harder, maybe. She fought Dosduvoi and Fror and Koll and Rulf, but though she saw him watching, she never asked for Brand.

She still woke when Skifr would've woken her. Earlier, maybe. She'd look down in the chill darkness through the smoke of her breath and see him lying, chest slowly shifting, and wish she could drop down beside him in the warmth the way she used to. Instead she'd force herself out into the bitter chill, teeth clenched against the aching in her leg as she ran across a white desert, the elf-bangle glowing chill white at her wrist, the streak of the crew's campfire the one feature in the great white sky.

She had what she'd always wanted. Whatever Hunnan and his like might say she had proved herself a warrior, with a favored place on a minister's crew and songs sung of her high deeds. She had sent a dozen men through the Last Door. She had won a prize beyond price from the most powerful woman in the world. And here was the harvest.

A thousand miles of lonely nothing.

Thorn had always been happiest in her own company. Now she was as sick of it as everyone else was. So she stood on the docks of Thorlby and hugged Safrit tight, and dragged Koll down from the rail and scrubbed his wild hair while he squirmed in embarrassment, then caught Rulf and kissed him on his balding pate, and seized hold of Dosduvoi and Fror and hauled them into a struggling, sour-smelling embrace. A frowning giant and a scarred Vansterman, foul as dung and frightening as wolves when she met them, grown close to her as brothers.

"Gods damn it but I'll miss you horrible bastards."

"Who knows?" said Mother Scaer, still stretched out among their supplies where she had spent most of the homeward voyage. "Our paths may cross again before too long."

"Let's hope not," Thorn muttered under her breath, looked over those familiar faces, and gave it one last try. "How'd you get the scar, Fror?"

The Vansterman opened his mouth as if to toss out one of his jokes. He always had one ready, after all. Then his eyes flickered to her scarred cheeks and he stopped short, thinking. He took a long breath, and looked her straight in the eye.

"I was twelve years old. The Gettlanders came before dawn. They took most of the villagers for slaves. My mother fought and they killed her. I tried to run, and their leader cut me with his sword. Left me for dead with nothing but this scar."

There was the truth, then, and it was ugly enough. But there was something else in the way Fror looked at her. Something that made the hairs stand on Thorn's neck. Her voice cracked a little when she asked the question. "Who was their leader?"

"They called him Headland."

Thorn stared down at the sword she wore. The sword that had been her father's. "This sword, then?"

"The gods cook strange recipes."

"But you sailed with Gettlanders! You fought beside me. Even though you knew I was his daughter?"

"And I'm glad I did." Fror shrugged. "Vengeance only walks a circle. From blood, back to blood. Death waits for us all. You can follow your path to her bent under a burden of rage. I did, for many years. You can let it poison you." He took a long breath, and let it sigh away. "Or you can let it go. Be well, Thorn Bathu."

"You too," she muttered, hardly knowing what to say. Hardly knowing what to think.

She took a last look at the *South Wind*, tame now, at the wharf, the paint flaking on the white doves mounted at prow and stern. That ship had been her home for a year. Her best friend and her worst enemy, every plank and rivet familiar. Seemed a different ship to the one they set out in. Weathered and worn, scarred and seasoned. A little bit like Thorn. She gave it a final, respectful nod, jerked her sea-chest up onto her shoulder, turned—

Brand stood behind her, close enough that she could almost smell his breath, sleeves rolled up to show the snaking scars about his forearms, stronger and quieter and better-looking than ever.

"Reckon I'll be seeing you, then," he said.

His eyes were fixed on her, gleaming behind those strands of hair across his face. It seemed she'd spent most of the last six months trying not to think about him, which was every bit as bad as thinking about him but with the added frustration of failing not to. Hard to forget someone when they're three oars in front of you. His shoulder moving with the stroke. His elbow at his oar. A sliver of his face as he looked back.

"Aye," she muttered, putting her eyes to the ground. "I reckon." And she stepped around him, and down the bouncing planks of the wharf, and away.

Maybe it was hard, to leave it at that after all they had been through. Maybe it was cowardly. But she had to put him behind her, and leave her disappointment and her shame and her foolishness along with him. When something has to be done, there's nothing to be gained by putting it off but pain.

Damn, but she was starting to sound like Skifr.

That thought rather pleased her.

Thorlby was changed. Everything so much smaller than she remembered. Grayer. Emptier. The wharves were nowhere near so crowded as they used to be, a sorry few fisherman working at their squirming catches, scales flashing silver. Warriors stood guard on the gate, but young ones, which made Thorn wonder what the rest were busy at. She knew one from the training square, his eyes going wide as ale cups as she strutted past.

"Is that her?" she heard someone mutter.

"Thorn Bathu," a woman whispered, voice hushed as if she spoke a magic spell.

"The one they're singing of?"

Her legend had marched ahead of her, would you believe? So Thorn put her shoulders back, and her bravest face on, and she let her left arm swing, the elf-bangle shining. Shining in the sunlight, shining with its own light.

Up the Street of Anvils she went, and the customers turned to stare, and the hammering ceased as the smiths looked out, and Thorn whistled a song as she walked. The song those Throvenmen had sung, about a she-devil who saved the Empress of the South.

Why not? Earned it, hadn't she?

Up the steep lanes she'd walked down with Father Yarvi when he led her from the citadel's dungeons and off to Skekenhouse, to Kalyiv, to the First of Cities. A hundred years ago it seemed, as she turned down a narrow way where every stone was familiar.

She heard muttering behind and saw she'd picked up a little gaggle of children, peering awestruck from around the corner. Just like the ones that had followed her father when he was in Thorlby. Just as he used to she gave them a cheery wave. Then just as he used to she bared her teeth and hissed, scattered them screaming.

Skifr always said that history turns in circles.

The narrow house, the step worn in the middle, the door her father badly carved, all the same, yet somehow they made her nervous. Her heart was hammering as she reached up to shove the door wide, but at the last moment she bunched her fist and knocked instead. She stood waiting, awkward as a beggar even though this was her home, fingers clutched tight around the pouch at her neck, thinking about what Fror had told her.

Maybe her father hadn't been quite the hero she always reckoned him. Maybe her mother wasn't quite the villain either. Maybe no one's all one or all the other.

It was her mother who answered. Strange, to see her looking just the same after all that had happened. Just another hair or two turned gray, and for a moment Thorn felt like a child again, clamping a brave face over her anger and her fear.

"Mother . . ." She tried to tame the tangled side of her head, plucking at the gold and silver rings bound up in her matted hair. A fool's effort, as she couldn't have combed that thicket with an ax. She wondered what her mother's tongue would stab at first: the madness of her hair or the ugliness of her scars or the raggedness of her clothes, or the—

"Hild!" Her face lit up with joy and she caught Thorn in her arms and held her so tight she made her gasp. Then she jerked her out to arm's length and looked her up and down, beaming, then clutched her tight again. "I'm sorry, Thorn—"

"You can call me Hild. If you like." Thorn snorted out a laugh. "It's good to hear you say it."

"You never used to like it."

"There's a lot changed this past year."

"Here too. War with the Vanstermen, and the king ill, and Grandmother Wexen keeping ships from the harbor . . . but there'll be time for that later."

"Aye." Thorn slowly pushed the door shut and leaned back against it. It was only then she realized how tired she was. So tired she nearly slid down onto her arse right there in the hall.

"You were expected back weeks ago. I was starting to worry. Well, I started worrying the day you left——"

"We got caught in the ice."

"I should've known it would take more than half the world to keep my daughter away. You've grown. Gods, how you've grown!"

"You're not going to say anything about my hair?"

Her mother reached out, and tidied a loose worm of it behind Thorn's ear, touched her scarred cheek gently with her fingertips. "All I care about is that you're alive. I've heard some wild stories about—— Father Peace, what's that?" Her mother caught Thorn's wrist and lifted it, the light from the elf-bangle falling across her face, eyes glittering with golden reflections as she stared down.

"That . . ." muttered Thorn, "is a long story."

# GREETINGS

Brand said he'd help them unload.

Maybe because that was the good thing to do. Maybe because he couldn't bear to leave the crew quite yet. Maybe because he was scared to see Rin. Scared she'd come to harm while he was gone. Scared she might blame him for it.

So he said as long as he didn't have to lift the ship he'd help them unload it, and told himself it was the good thing to do. There aren't many good things don't have a splinter of selfishness in them somewhere, after all.

And when the unloading was done and half the crew already wandered their own ways he hugged Fror, and Dosduvoi, and Rulf, and they laughed over things Odda had said on the way down the Divine. Laughed as Mother Sun sank toward the hills behind Thorlby, shadows gathering in the carvings that swirled over the whole mast from its root to its top.

"You did one hell of a job on that mast, Koll," said Brand, staring up at it.

"It's the tale of our voyage." Koll had changed a deal since they set out, twitchy-quick as ever but deeper in the voice, stronger in the face, surer in the hands as he slid them gently over the carved trees, and rivers, and ships, and figures all wonderfully woven into one another. "Thorlby's here at the base, the Divine and Denied flow up this side and down the other, the First of Cities at the mast-head. Here we cross the Shattered Sea. There Brand lifts the ship. There we meet Blue Jenner."

"Clever boy, isn't he?" said Safrit, hugging him tight. "Just as well you didn't fall off the bloody yard and smash your brains out."

"Would've been a loss," murmured Brand, gazing up at the mast in more wonder than ever.

Koll pointed out more figures. "Skifr sends Death across the plain. Prince Varoslaf chains the Denied. Thorn fights seven men. Father Yarvi seals his deal with the empress, and . . ." He leaned close, made a few more cuts to a kneeling figure at the bottom with his worn-down knife and blew the chippings away. "Here's me, now, finishing it off." And he stepped back, grinning. "Done."

"It's master's work," said Father Yarvi, running his shrivelled hand over the carvings. "I've a mind to have it mounted in the yard of the citadel, so every Gettlander can see the high deeds done on their behalf, and the high deed of carving it not least among them."

The smiles faded then and left them dewy-eyed, because they all saw the voyage was over, and their little family breaking up. Those whose paths had twined so tight together into one great journey would each be following their own road now, scattered like leaves on a gale to who knew what distant ports, and it was in the hands of the fickle gods whether those paths would ever cross again.

"Bad luck," murmured Dosduvoi, slowly shaking his head. "You find friends and they wander from your life again. Bad, bad luck—"

"Oh, stop prating on your luck you huge fool!" snapped Safrit. "My husband had the poor luck to be stolen by slavers but he never stopped struggling to return to me, never gave up hope, died fighting to the last for his oarmates."

"That he did," said Rulf.

"Saved my life," said Father Yarvi.

"So you could save mine and my son's." Safrit gave Dosduvoi's arm a shove which made the silver rings on his wrist rattle. "Look at all you have! Your strength, and your health, and your wealth, and friends who maybe one day wander back into your life!"

"Who knows who you'll pass on this crooked path to the Last Door?" murmured Rulf, rubbing thoughtfully at his beard.

"That's good luck, damn it, not bad!" said Safrit. "Give praise to whatever god you fancy for every day you live."

"I never thought of it like that before," said Dosduvoi, forehead creased in thought. "I'll endeavor to think on my blessings." He carefully rearranged the ring-money on his great wrist. "Just as soon as I've had a little round of dice. Or two." And he headed off toward the town.

"Some men never bloody learn," muttered Safrit, staring after him with hands on hips.

"None of 'em do," said Rulf.

Brand held out his hand to him. "I'll miss you."

"And I you," said the helmsman, clasping him by the arm. "You're strong at the oar, and strong at the wall, and strong there too." And he thumped Brand on his chest, and leaned close. "Stand in the light, lad, eh?"

"I'll miss all of you." Brand looked toward Thorlby, the way that Thorn had gone, and had to swallow the lump in his throat. To walk off with scarcely a word that way, as if he was nothing and nobody. That hurt.

"Don't worry." Safrit put her hand on his shoulder and gave it a squeeze. "There are plenty of other girls about."

"Not many like her."

"That's a bad thing?" asked Mother Scaer. "I know of a dozen back in Vulsgard who'd tear each other's eyes out for a lad like you."

"That's a good thing?" asked Brand. "On balance, I'd prefer a wife with eyes."

Mother Scaer narrowed hers, which made him more nervous still. "That's why you pick the winner."

"Always sensible," said Father Yarvi. "It is time you left us, Mother

Scaer." He frowned toward the warriors standing at the city's gate. "Vanstermen are less popular even than usual in Thorlby, I think."

She growled in her throat. "The Mother of Crows dances on the border once again."

"Then it is our task as ministers to speak for the Father of Doves, and make of the fist an open hand."

"This alliance you plan." Scaer scrubbed unhappily at her shaved head. "To sponge away a thousand years of blood is no small deed."

"But one that will be worth singing of."

"Men prefer to sing of the making of wounds, fools that they are." Her eyes were blue slits as she stared into Yarvi's. "And I fear you stitch one wound so you can carve a deeper. But I gave my word, and will do what I can."

"What else can any of us do?" The elf-bangles rattled on Mother Scaer's long arm as Yarvi clasped her hand in farewell. Then his eyes moved to Brand, cool and level. "My thanks for all your help, Brand."

"Just doing what you paid me for."

"More than that, I think."

"Just trying to do good, then, maybe."

"The time may come when I need a man who is not so concerned about the greater good, but just the good. Perhaps I can call on you?"

"It'd be my honor, Father Yarvi. I owe you for this. For giving me a place."

"No, Brand, I owe you." The minister smiled. "And I hope soon enough to pay."

BRAND HEADED ACROSS THE hillside, threading between the tents and shacks and ill-made hovels sprouted up outside the gates like mushrooms after the rains. Many more than there used to be. There was war with the Vanstermen, and folk had fled homes near the border to huddle against Thorlby's walls.

Lamplight gleamed through chinks in wattle, voices drifting into the evening, a fragment of a sad song echoing from somewhere. He passed a great bonfire, pinched faces of the very old and very young lit by whirling sparks. The air smelled strong of smoke and dung and unwashed bodies. The sour stink of his childhood, but it smelled sweet to him then. He knew this wouldn't be his home much longer.

As he walked he felt the pouch shifting underneath his shirt. Heavy it was, now. Red gold from Prince Varoslaf and yellow gold from the Empress Vialine and good silver with the face of Queen Laithlin stamped upon it. Enough for a fine house in the shadow of the citadel. Enough that Rin would never want for anything again. He was smiling as he shoved the door of their shack rattling open.

"Rin, I'm—"

He found himself staring at a clutch of strangers. A man, a woman, and how many children? Five? Six? All crushed tight about the firepit where he used to warm his aching feet and no sign of Rin among them.

"Who the hell are you?" Fear clutched at him, and he put his hand on his dagger.

"It's all right!" The man held up his palms. "You're Brand?"

"Damn right I am. Where's my sister?"

"You don't know?"

"If I knew would I be asking? Where's Rin?"

IT WAS A FINE HOUSE in the shadow of the citadel.

A rich woman's house of good cut stone with a full second floor and a dragon's head carved into its roof beam. A homely house with welcoming firelight spilling around its shutters and into the evening. A handsome house with a stream gurgling through a steep channel beside it and under a narrow bridge. A well-kept house with a door new-painted green, and hanging over the door a shingle in the shape of a sword, swinging gently with the breeze.

"Here?" Brand had labored up the steep lanes with crates and barrels to the homes of the wealthy often enough, and he knew the street. But he'd never been to this house, had no notion why his sister might be inside.

"Here," answered the man, and gave the door a beating with his knuckles.

Brand stood there wondering what sort of pose to strike, and was caught by surprise halfway between two when the door jerked open.

Rin was changed. Even more than he was, maybe. A woman grown, she seemed now, taller, and her face leaner, dark hair cut short. She wore a fine tunic, clever stitching about the collar, like a wealthy merchant might.

"You all right, Hale?" she asked.

"Better," said the man. "We had a visitor." And he stepped out of the way so the light fell across Brand's face.

"Rin . . ." he croaked, hardly knowing what to say, "I'm—"

"You're back!" And she flung her arms around him almost hard enough to knock him over, and squeezed him almost hard enough to make him sick. "You just going to stand on the step and stare?" And she bundled him through the doorway. "Give my love to your children!" she shouted after Hale.

"Be glad to!"

Then she kicked the door shut and dragged Brand's sea-chest from his shoulder. As she set it on the tiled floor a chain hung down, a silver chain with a silver key gleaming on it.

"Whose key's that?" he muttered.

"Did you think I'd get married while you were gone? It's my own key to my own locks. You hungry? You thirsty? I've got—"

"Whose house is this, Rin?"

She grinned at him. "It's yours. It's mine. It's ours."

"This?" Brand stared at her. "But . . . how did—"

"I told you I'd make a sword."

Brand's eyes went wide. "Must've been a blade for the songs."

"King Uthil thought so."

Brand's eyes went wider still. "King Uthil?"

"I found a new way to smelt the steel. A hotter way. The first blade cracked when we quenched it, but the second held. Gaden said we had to give it to the king. And the king stood up in the Godshall and said steel was the answer, and this was the best steel he ever saw. He's carrying it now, I hear." She shrugged, as if King Uthil's patronage was no great honor. "After that, everyone wanted me to make them a sword. Gaden said she couldn't keep me. She said I should be the master and she the apprentice." Rin shrugged. "Blessed by She who Strikes the Anvil, like we used to say."

"Gods," whispered Brand. "I was going to change your life. You did it by yourself."

"You gave me the chance." Rin took his wrist, frowning down at the scars there. "What happened?"

"Nothing. Rope slipped going over the tall hauls."

"Reckon there's more to that story."

"I've got better ones."

Rin's lip wrinkled. "Long as they haven't got Thorn Bathu in 'em."

"She saved the Empress of the South from her uncle, Rin! The Empress! Of the South."

"That one I've heard already. They're singing it all over town. Something about her beating a dozen men alone. Then it was fifteen. Might've even been twenty last time I heard it. And she threw some duke off a roof and routed a horde of Horse People and won an elf-relic and lifted a ship besides, I hear. Lifted a ship!" And she snorted again.

Brand raised his brows. "I reckon songs have a habit of outrunning the truth."

"You can tell me the truth of it later." Rin took down the lamp and drew him through another doorway, stairs going up into the shadows. "Come and see your room."

"I've got a room?" muttered Brand, eyes going wider than ever. How often had he dreamed of that? When they hadn't a roof over their heads, or food to eat, or a friend in the world besides each other?

She put her arm around his shoulders and it felt like home. "You've got a room."

# WRONG
# IDEAS

"Reckon I need a new sword."

Thorn sighed as she laid her father's blade gently on the table, the light of the forge catching the many scratches, glinting on the deep nicks. It was worn almost crooked from years of polishing, the binding scuffed to greasy shreds, the cheap iron pommel rattling loose.

The apprentice gave Thorn's sword one quick glance and Thorn herself not even that many. "Reckon you're right." She wore a leather vest scattered with burns, gloves to her elbow, arms and shoulders bare and beaded with sweat from the heat, hard muscles twitching as she turned a length of metal in the glowing coals.

"It's a good sword." Thorn ran her fingers down the scarred steel. "It was my father's. Seen a lot of work. In his day and in mine."

The apprentice didn't so much as nod. Somewhat of a gritty manner she had, but Thorn had one of those herself, so she tried not to hold it too much against her.

"Your master about?" she asked.

"No."

Thorn waited for more, but there wasn't any. "When will he be back?"

The girl just snorted, slid the metal from the coals, looked it over, and rammed it hissing back in a shower of sparks.

Thorn decided to try starting over. "I'm looking for the blade-maker on Sixth Street."

"And here I am," said the girl, still frowning down at her work.

"You?"

"I'm the one making blades on Sixth Street, aren't I?"

"Thought you'd be . . . older."

"Seems thinking ain't your strength."

Thorn spent a moment wondering whether to be annoyed by that, but decided to let it go. She was trying to let things go more often. "You're not the first to say so. Just not common, a girl making swords."

The girl looked up then. Fierce eyes, gleaming with the forge-light through the hair stuck across her strong-boned face, and some-thing damned familiar about her but Thorn couldn't think what. "Almost as uncommon as one swinging 'em."

"Fair point," said Thorn, holding out her hand. "I'm—"

The sword-maker slid the half-made blade from the forge, glow-ing metal passing so close Thorn had to snatch her hand back. "I know who y'are, Thorn Bathu."

"Oh. Course." Thorn guessed her fame was running off ahead of her. She was only now starting to see that wasn't always a good thing.

The girl took up a hammer and Thorn watched her knock a fuller into the blade, watched her strike the anvil-music, as the smiths say, and quite a lesson it was. Short, quick blows, no wasted effort, all au-thority, all control, each one perfect as a master's sword thrust, glow-ing dust scattering from the die. Thorn knew a lot more about using swords than making them, but an idiot could've seen this girl knew her business.

"They say you make the best swords in Thorlby," said Thorn.

"I make the best swords in the Shattered Sea," said the girl, hold-ing up the steel so the glow from it fell across her sweat-shining face.

"My father always told me never get proud."

"Ain't a question of pride. It's just a fact."

"Would you make me one?"

"No. Don't think I will."

Folk who are the best at what they do sometimes forego the niceties, but this was getting strange. "I've got money."

"I don't want your money."

"Why?"

"I don't like you."

Thorn wasn't usually slow to rise to an insult but this was so unexpected she was caught off-guard. "Well . . . I guess there are other swords to be found."

"No doubt there are."

"I'll go and find one, then."

"I hope you find a long one." The swordmaker on Sixth Street leaned down to blow ash from the metal with a gentle puff from her pursed lips. "Then you can stick it up your arse."

Thorn snatched her old sword up, gave serious thought to clubbing the girl across the head with the flat, decided against and turned for the door. Before she quite made it to the handle, though, the girl spoke again.

"Why'd you treat my brother that way?"

She was mad. Had to be. "Who's your damn brother?"

The girl frowned over at her. "Brand."

The name rocked Thorn surely as a kick in the head. "Not Brand who was with me on—"

"What other Brand?" She jabbed at her chest with her thumb. "I'm Rin."

Thorn surely saw the resemblance, now, and it rocked her even more, so it came out a guilty squeak when she spoke. "Didn't know Brand had a sister . . ."

Rin gave a scornful chuckle. "Why would you? Only spent a year on the same boat as him."

"He never told me!"

"Did you ask?"

"Of course! Sort of." Thorn swallowed. "No."

"A year away." Rin rammed the blade angrily back into the coals. "And the moment he sees me, do you know what he sets to talking about?"

"Er . . ."

She started pounding at the bellows like Thorn used to pound Brand's head in the training square. "Thorn Bathu ran the oars in the middle of an elf-ruin. Thorn Bathu saved his life in the shield wall. Thorn Bathu made an alliance that'll put the world to rights. And when I could've bitten his face if I heard your name one more time, what do you think he told me next?"

"Er . . ."

"Thorn Bathu scarcely spoke a word to him the whole way back. Thorn Bathu cut him off like you'd trim a blister. I tell you what, Thorn Bathu sounds something of a bloody bitch to me, after all he's done for her and, no, I don't much fancy making a sword for—"

"Hold it there," snapped Thorn. "You don't have the first clue what happened between me and your brother."

Rin let the bellows be and glared over. "Enlighten me."

"Well . . ." Last thing Thorn needed was to rip that scab off again just when there was a chance of letting it heal. She wasn't about to admit that she made a fool's mistake, and burned herself bad, and had to make herself not look at Brand or talk to Brand or have anything to do with Brand every moment of every day in case she burned herself again. "You got it back to front is all!"

"Strange how people are always getting the wrong idea about you. How often does that have to happen, 'fore you start thinking maybe they got the right idea?" And Rin dragged the iron from the forge and set it back on the anvil.

"You don't know me," growled Thorn, working up the bellows on some anger of her own. "You don't know what I've been through."

"No doubt we've all had our struggles," said Rin, lifting her hammer. "But some of us get to weep over 'em in a big house our daddy paid for."

Thorn threw up her hands at the fine new forge behind the fine home near the citadel. "Oh, I see you and Brand have barely been scraping by!"

Rin froze, then, muscles bunching across her shoulders, and her eyes flicked over, and she looked angry. So angry Thorn took a little step back, a cautious eye on that hovering hammer.

Then Rin tossed it rattling down, pulled her gloves off and flung them on the table. "Come with me."

"MY MOTHER DIED WHEN I was little."

Rin had led them outside the walls. Downwind, where the stink of Thorlby's rubbish wouldn't bother the good folk of the city.

"Brand remembers her a little. I don't."

Some of the midden heaps were years covered over and turned to grassy mounds. Some were open and stinking, spilling bones and shells, rags and the dung of men and beasts.

"He always says she told him to do good."

A mangy dog gave Thorn a suspicious eye, as though it considered her competition, and went back to sniffing through the rot.

"My father died fighting Grom-gil-Gorm," muttered Thorn, trying to match ill-luck for ill-luck. Honestly, she felt a little queasy. From the look of this place, and the stink of it, and the fact she had scarcely even known it was here because her mother's slaves had always carted their rubbish. "They laid him out in the Godshall."

"And you got his sword."

"Less the pommel," grunted Thorn, trying not to breathe through her nose. "Gorm kept that."

"You're lucky to have something from your father." Rin didn't seem bothered by the stench at all. "We didn't get much from ours. He liked a drink. Well. I say *a* drink. He liked 'em all. He left when

Brand was nine. Gone one morning, and maybe we were better off without him."

"Who took you in?" asked Thorn in a small voice, getting the sense she was far outclassed in the ill-luck contest.

"No one did." Rin let that sink in a moment. "There were quite a few of us living here, back then."

"Here?"

"You pick through. Sometimes you find something you can eat. Sometimes you find something you can sell. Winters." Rin hunched her shoulders and gave a shiver. "Winters were hard."

Thorn could only stand there and blink, feeling cold all over even if summer was well on the way. She'd always supposed she'd had quite the tough time growing up. Now she learned that while she raged in her fine house because her mother didn't call her by the name she liked, there had been children picking through the dung for bones to chew. "Why are you telling me this?"

"Cause Brand didn't say and you didn't ask. We begged. I stole." Rin gave a bitter little smile. "But Brand said he had to do good. So he worked. He worked at the docks and the forges. He worked anywhere folk would give him work. He worked like a dog and more than once he was beaten like one. I got sick and he got me through it and I got sick again and he got me through it again. He kept on dreaming of being a warrior, and having a place on a crew, a family always around him. So he went to the training square. He had to beg and borrow the gear, but he went. He'd work before he trained and he'd work after, and even after that if anyone needed help he'd be there to help. Do good, Brand always said, and folk'll do good for you. He was a good boy. He's become a good man."

"I know that," growled Thorn, feeling the hurt all well up fresh, sharper than ever for the guilt that welled up with it, now. "He's the best man I know. This isn't bloody news to me!"

Rin stared at her. "Then how could you treat him this way? If it wasn't for him I'd be gone through the Last Door, and so would you, and this is the thanks—"

Thorn might have been wrong about a few things, and she might not have known a few others she should have, and she might have been way too wrapped up in herself to see what was right under her nose, but there was a limit on what she'd take.

"Hold on, there, Brand's secret sister. No doubt you've opened my eyes wider than ever to my being a selfish arse. But me and him were oarmates. On a crew you stand with the men beside you. Yes, he was there for me, but I was there for him, and—"

"Not that! Before. When you killed that boy. Edwal."

"What?" Thorn felt queasier still. "I remember that day well enough and all Brand did was bloody stand there."

Rin gaped at her. "Did you two talk at all that year away?"

"Not about Edwal, I can tell you that!"

"Course you didn't." Rin closed her eyes and smiled as though she understood it all. "He'd never take the thanks he deserves, the stubborn fool. He didn't tell you."

Thorn understood nothing. "Tell me what, damn it?"

"He went to Father Yarvi." And Rin took Thorn gently but firmly by the shoulder and let the words fall one by one. "He told him what happened on the beach. Even though he knew it'd cost him. Master Hunnan found out. So it cost him his place on the king's raid, and his place as a warrior, and everything he'd hoped for."

Thorn made a strange sound then. A choked-off cluck. The sound a chicken makes when its neck gets wrung.

"Brand went to Father Yarvi," she croaked.

"Yes."

"Brand saved my life. And lost his place for it."

"Yes."

"Then I mocked him over it, and treated him like a fool the whole way down the Divine and the Denied and the whole way back up again."

"Yes."

"Why didn't he just bloody *say*—" And that was when Thorn saw something gleaming just inside the collar of Rin's vest. She reached out, hooked it with a trembling finger, and eased it into the light.

Beads. Glass beads, blue and green.

The ones Brand bought that day in the First of Cities. The ones she'd thought were for her, then for some other lover back in Thorlby. The ones she now saw were for the sister she'd never bothered to ask if he had.

Thorn made that squawking sound again, but louder.

Rin stared at her as if she'd gone mad. "What?"

"I'm such a stupid shit."

"Eh?"

"Where is he?"

"Brand? At my house. Our house—"

"Sorry." Thorn was already backing away. "I'll talk to you about the sword later!" And she turned and started running for the gate.


HE LOOKED BETTER THAN ever. Or maybe she just saw him differently, knowing what she knew.

"Thorn." He looked surprised to see her and she could hardly blame him. Then he looked worried. "What's wrong?"

She realized she must look worse even than usual and wished she hadn't run all the way, or at least waited to knock until she'd caught her breath and wiped the sweat from her forehead. But she'd been dancing around this far too long. Time to face it, sweaty or not.

"I talked to your sister," she said.

He looked more worried. "What about?"

"About you having a sister, for one thing."

"That's no secret."

"That might not be."

He looked even more worried. "What did she tell you?"

"That you saved my life. When I killed Edwal."

He winced. "I told her not to say anything!"

"Well, that didn't work."

"Reckon you'd best come in. If you want to." He stepped back from the door and she followed him into the shadowy hallway, heart pounding harder than ever. "You don't have to thank me."

"Yes," she said. "I do."

"I wasn't trying to do anything noble, just . . . something good. And I wasn't sure, and it took me too long, and I made a bloody mess of it—"

She took a step toward him. "Did you go to Father Yarvi?"

"Yes."

"Did Father Yarvi save my life?"

"Yes."

"Did you lose your place because of it?"

He worked his mouth as though looking for a way to deny it, but couldn't. "I was going to tell you, but . . ."

"I'm not easy to tell things to."

"And I'm not much good at telling." He pushed his hair back and scrubbed at his head as though it hurt. "Didn't want you feeling in my debt. Wouldn't have been fair."

She blinked at that. "So . . . you didn't just risk everything for my sake, you kept it to yourself so I wouldn't feel bad about it."

"One way of putting it . . . maybe." And he looked at her from under his brows, eyes gleaming in the shadows. That look, as if there was nothing he would rather be looking at. And however she'd tried to weed those hopes away they blossomed in a riot, and the want came up stronger than ever.

She took another little step toward him. "I'm so sorry."

"You don't have to be."

"But I am. For how I treated you. On the way back. On the way out, for that matter. I'm sorry, Brand. I've never been sorrier. I've never been sorry at all, really. Got to work on that. Just . . . I got the wrong idea about . . . something."

He stood there, silent. Waiting. Looking. No bloody help at all.

Just say it. How hard could it be? She'd killed men. Just say it. "I stopped talking to you . . . because . . ." But getting the words out was like hauling anvils out of a well. "I . . . like . . ." It was as if she tottered out onto a frozen lake, not knowing whether the next step might send her plunging to an icy doom. "I've always . . . liked . . ." She couldn't make the "you." She couldn't have made the "you" if it was that or die. She squeezed her eyes shut. "What I'm trying to say is— Whoa!"

She snapped her eyes open. He'd touched her cheek, fingertips brushing the scar there.

"You've got your hand on me." Stupidest thing she'd ever said and that with some fierce competition. They could both see he had his hand on her. Wasn't as if it fell there by accident.

He jerked it away. "I thought—"

"No!" She caught his wrist and guided it back. "I mean . . . Yes." His fingertips were warm against her face, hers sliding over the back of his hand, pressing it there and it felt . . . Gods. "This is happening, is it?"

He stepped a little closer, the knobble on his neck bobbing as he swallowed. "I reckon." He was looking at her mouth. Looking at it as though there was something really interesting in there and she wasn't sure she'd ever been so scared.

"What do we do?" she found she'd squeaked out, voice running away from her, higher and higher. "I mean, I know what we *do* . . . I guess." Gods, that was a lie, she hadn't a clue. She wished now Skifr had taught her a little less about swords and a bit more about the arts of love, or whatever. "I mean, what do we do *now* we know that, you know—"

He put his thumb gently across her lips. "Shut up, Thorn."

"Right," she breathed, and she realized she had her hand up between them, as if to push him away. So used to pushing folk away, and him in particular, and she forced it to go soft, laid it gently on his chest, hoped he couldn't feel it trembling.

Closer he came, and she was taken suddenly with an urge to run for it, and then with an urge to giggle, and she made a stupid gurgle swallowing her laughter, and then his lips were touching hers. Gently, just brushing, one way, then the other, and she realized she had her eyes open and snapped them shut. Couldn't think what to do with her hands. Stiff as a woman made of wood, she was, for a moment, but then things started to go soft.

The side of his nose nudged hers, ticklish.

He made a noise in his throat, and so did she.

She caught his lip between hers, tugged at it, slipped that hand on his chest up around his neck, and pulled him closer, their teeth knocked awkwardly together and they broke apart.

Not much of a kiss, really. Nothing like she'd imagined it would be, and the gods knew she'd imagined it enough, but it left her hot all over. Maybe that was just the running, but she'd done a lot of running and never felt quite like this.

She opened her eyes and he was looking at her. That look, through the strands of hair across his face. Wasn't the first kiss she ever had, but the others had felt like children playing. This was as different from that as a battle from the training square.

"Oh," she croaked. "That . . . wasn't so bad."

She let go of his hand and caught a fistful of his shirt, started dragging him back toward her, caught the smile at the corner of his mouth and smiled herself—

There was a rattle outside the door.

"Rin," muttered Brand, and as if that was the starting word on a race they both took off running. Pelted down the corridor like thieves caught in the act, tangling on a stairway, giggling like idiots as they scrambled into a room and Brand wrestled the door shut, leaning back against it as if there were a dozen angry Vanstermen outside.

They hunched in the shadows, their breath coming quick.

"Why did we run?" he whispered.

"I don't know," Thorn whispered back.

"You think she can hear us?"

"What if she can?" asked Thorn.

"I don't know."

"So this is your room, is it?"

He straightened up, grinning like a king who'd won a victory. "I have a room."

"Quite the distinguished citizen," she said, strolling around in a circle, taking it in. Didn't take long. There was a pallet bed in one corner with Brand's worn-out old blanket on it, and his sea chest sitting open in another, and the sword that used to be Odda's leaning against the wall, and aside from that just bare boards and bare walls and a lot of shadows. "Ever wonder if you've overdone the furniture?"

"It's not quite finished."

"It's not quite started," she said, the circle taking her back toward him.

"If it's not what you were used to at the empress's palace, I won't keep you."

She snorted. "I lived under a boat with forty men in it. Reckon I can stand this a while."

His eyes were on her as she came close. That look. Little bit hungry, little bit scared. "Staying, then?"

"I've got nothing else pressing."

And they were kissing again, harder this time. She wasn't worrying about Brand's sister anymore, or about her mother, or about anything. There was nothing on her mind but her mouth and his. Not to begin with, at least. But soon enough some other parts started making themselves known. She wondered what was prodding at her hip and stuck her hand down there to check and then she realized what was prodding at her hip and had to break away she felt so foolish, and scared, and hot, and excited, and hardly knew what she felt.

"Sorry," he muttered, bending over and lifting one leg as if he was trying to hide the bulge and looking so ridiculous she spluttered with laughter.

He looked hurt. "Ain't funny."

"It is kind of." She took his arm and pulled him close, then she hooked her leg around his and he gasped as she tripped him, put him down hard on his back with her on top, straddling him. Familiar territory in its way, but everything was different now.

She pressed her hips up against his, rocking back and forward, gently at first, then not so gently. She had her hand tangled in his hair, dragging his face against hers, his beard prickling at her chin, their open mouths pressed together so her head seemed to be full of his rasping breath, hot on her lips.

She was fair grinding away at him now and liking the feel of it more than a bit, then she was scared she was liking the feel of it, then she decided just to do it and worry later. She was grunting in her throat with each breath and one little part of her thinking that must sound pretty foolish but a much bigger part not caring. One of his hands slipped up her back under her shirt, the other up her ribs, one by one, and made her shiver. She pulled away, breathing hard, looking down at him, propped up on one elbow.

"Sorry," he whispered.

"For what?" She ripped her shirt open and dragged it off, got it caught over the elf-bangle on her wrist, finally tore it free and flung it away.

She felt a fool for a moment, knew she was nothing like a woman should be, knew she was pale and hard and nothing but gristle. But he looked anything but disappointed, slid his hands up her sides and around her back, pulled her down against him, kissing at her, nipping at her lips with his teeth. The pouch with her father's fingerbones fell in his eye and she slapped it back over her shoulder. She set to pulling his shirt open, pushing her hand up his stomach, fingers through the hairs on his chest, the bangle glowing soft gold, reflected in the corners of his eyes.

He caught her hand. "We don't have to . . . you know . . ."

No doubt they didn't have to, and no doubt there were a hundred reasons not to, and right then she couldn't think of one she gave a damn about.

"Shut up, Brand." She twisted her hand free and started dragging his belt open. She didn't know what she was doing, but she knew some right idiots who'd done it.

How hard could it be?

# SORT OF ALONE

They'd gone to sleep holding each other but it hadn't lasted long. Brand never knew anyone to thrash about so much in the night. She twitched and twisted, jerked and shuddered, kicked and rolled until she kicked him awake and rolled him right out of his own bed.

So he was left sitting on his sea chest, the lid polished to a comfortable gloss by hundreds of miles of his own rowing backside, watching her.

She'd ended up facedown with her arms spread wide, a strip of sunlight from the narrow window angled across her back, one hand hanging off the bed and the elf-bangle casting a faint glow on the floor. One long leg poked out from under the blanket, a puckered scar across the thigh, hair bound with rings of silver and gold, tangled across her face so all he could see was half of one shut eye and a little piece of cheek with that arrow-shaped mark on it.

To begin with he'd sat with a stupid smile on his face, listening to her snore. Thinking how she'd snored in his ear all the way down the Divine and the Denied. Thinking how much he liked hearing it. Hardly able to believe his luck that she was there, now, naked, in his bed.

Then he'd started worrying.

What would people think when they found out they'd done this? What would Rin say? What would Thorn's mother do? What if a child came? He'd heard it wasn't likely but it happened, didn't it? Sooner or later she'd wake. What if she didn't want him anymore? How could she want him anymore? And, lurking at the back of his mind, the darkest worry of all. What if she woke and she did want him still? What then?

"Gods," he muttered, blinking up at the ceiling, but they'd answered his prayers by putting her in his bed, hadn't they? He could hardly pray for help getting her out.

With a particularly ripping snort Thorn jerked, and stretched out, clenching her fists, and stretching her toes, her muscles shuddering. She blew snot out of one nostril, wiped it on the back of her hand, rubbed her eyes on the back of the other and dragged her matted hair out of her face. She froze, and her head jerked around, eyes wide.

"Morning," he said.

She stared at him. "Not a dream, then?"

"I'm guessing no." A nightmare, maybe.

They looked at each other for a long moment. "You want me to go?" she asked.

"No!" he said, too loud and too eager. "No. You want to go?"

"No." She sat up slowly, dragging the blanket around her shoulders, knobbled knees toward him, and gave a huge yawn.

"Why?" he found he'd said. She stopped halfway through, mouth hanging open. "Wasn't like last night went too well did it?"

She flinched at that like he'd slapped her. "What did I do wrong?"

"You? No! You didn't . . . it's me I'm talking of." He wasn't sure what he was talking of, but his mouth kept going even so. "Rin told you, didn't she?"

"Told me what?"

"That my own father didn't want me. That my own mother didn't want me."

She frowned at him. "I thought your mother died."

"Same bloody thing isn't it?"

"No. It isn't."

He was hardly listening. "I grew up picking through rubbish. I had to beg to feed my sister. I carted bones like a slave." He hadn't meant to say any of it. Not ever. But it just came puking out.

Thorn shut her mouth with a snap. "I'm an arse, Brand. But what kind of arse would I be if I thought less of you for that? You're a good man. A man who can be trusted. Everyone who knows you thinks so. Koll worships you. Rulf respects you. Even Father Yarvi likes you, and he doesn't like anyone."

He blinked at her. "I never speak."

"But you listen when other people speak! And you're handsome and well-made as Safrit never tired of telling me."

"She did?"

"She and Mother Scaer spent a whole afternoon discussing your arse."

"Eh?"

"You could have anyone you wanted. Specially now you don't live in a midden. The mystery is why you'd want me."

"Eh?" He'd never dreamed she had her own doubts. Always seemed so damn sure about everything.

But she drew the blanket tight around her shoulders and looked down at her bare feet, mouth twisted with disgust. "I'm selfish."

"You're . . . ambitious. I like that."

"I'm bitter."

"You're funny. I like that too."

She rubbed gently at her scarred cheek. "I'm ugly."

Anger burned up in him then, so hot it took him by surprise. "Who bloody said so? Cause first they're wrong and second I'll punch their teeth out."

"I can punch 'em myself. That's the problem. I'm not . . . you know." She stuck a hand out of the blanket and scrubbed her nails against the shaved side of her head. "I'm not how a girl should be. Or a woman. Never have been. I'm no good at . . ."

"What?"

"Smiling or, I don't know, sewing."

"I don't need anything sewed." And he slid off his sea chest and knelt down in front of her. His worries had faded. Things had got ruined before somehow and he wouldn't let them get ruined again. Not for lack of trying. "I've wanted you since the First of Cities. Since before, maybe." He reached out and put his hand on hers where it rested on the bed. Clumsy, maybe, but honest. "Just never thought I'd get you." He looked into her face, groping for the right words. "Looking at you, and thinking you want me, makes me feel like . . . like I won."

"Won something no one else would want," she muttered.

"What do I care what they want?" he said, that anger catching fire again and making her look up. "If they're too damn stupid to see you're the best woman in the Shattered Sea that's my good luck, isn't it?" He fell silent, and felt his face burning, and thought for sure he'd ruined the whole thing again.

"That might be the nicest thing anyone ever said to me." She reached up and pushed the hair out of his face. Gentle as a feather, her touch. He hadn't realized she could be so gentle. "No one ever says anything nice to me, but even so." The blanket slipped off her bare shoulder and he set his hand on it, slid it down her side and around her back, skin hissing on skin, warm, and smooth, her eyes closing, and his—

A thumping echoed through the house. Someone beating on the front door, and knocks that weren't to be ignored. Brand heard the bolt drawn back, voices muttering.

"Gods," said Thorn, eyes wide. "Could be my mother."

They hadn't moved so fast even when the Horse People came charging across the steppe, grabbing up clothes and tossing them to each other, pulling them on, him fumbling with his belt and getting it all messed up because he was watching her wriggle her trousers over her arse out of the corner of his eye.

"Brand?" came his sister's voice.

They both froze, he with one boot on, she with none, then Brand called out a cracked, "Aye?"

"You all right?" Rin's voice coming up the steps.

"Aye!"

"You alone?" Just outside the door now.

"Course!" Then, when he realized she might come in, he followed up with a guilty, "Sort of."

"You're the worst liar in Gettland. Is Thorn Bathu in there with you?"

Brand winced. "Sort of."

"She's in there or she's not. Are you bloody in there, Thorn Bathu?"

"Sort of?" said Thorn at the door in a tiny voice.

A long pause. "That was Master Hunnan."

The name was like a bucket of cold water down Brand's trousers and no mistake.

"He said a dove came with news of a raid at Halleby, and with all the men gone north to fight, he's gathering what's left to go and see to it. Some who are training, some who are wounded, some who failed a test. They're meeting on the beach."

"He wants me?" called Brand, a quiver in his voice.

"He says Gettland needs you. And he says for any man who does his duty there'll be a warrior's place."

A warrior's place. Always to have brothers at your shoulder. Always to have something to fight for. To stand in the light. And quick as that the ashes of old dreams that had seemed for months burned out flared up hot and bright again. Quick as that he was decided.

"I'll be down," called Brand, heart suddenly beating hard, and he heard his sister's footsteps move away.

"You're going with that bastard?" asked Thorn. "After what he did to you? What he did to me?"

Brand pulled the blanket off the bed. "Not for his sake. For Gettland."

She snorted. "For you."

"All right, for me. Don't I deserve it?"

Her jaw worked for a moment. "I notice he didn't ask for me."

"Would you have followed him?" he asked, putting his few things onto the blanket and making a bundle of it.

"Course I would. Then I'd have kicked his face in."

"Maybe that's why he didn't ask for you."

"Hunnan wouldn't ask for me if I was holding a bucket of water and he was on fire. None of them would. Warriors of Gettland. There's a bloody joke! Not a funny one, mind." She paused halfway through dragging one boot on. "You're not so keen to go just so you can get away from me, are you? Cause if you're thinking better of this just tell me. I reckon we've had enough secrets—"

"That's not it," he said, even though he wondered if it was part of it. Just get some room to breathe. Just get some time to think.

"Sometimes I wish I'd stayed in the First of Cities," she said.

"You'd never have bedded me then."

"When I died rich and storied that could've been my life's one great regret."

"Just give me a week," he said, strapping on Odda's sword. "I'm not thinking better of anything, but I have to do this. I might never get another chance."

She curled her lips back and made a long hiss. "One week. Then I go after the next man I find who can lift a ship."

"Done." And he kissed her one more time. Her lips were scummy, and her mouth was sour, and he didn't care. He slung his shield over his shoulder, and hefted the little bundle he'd made with his blanket, and he took a long breath, and headed off to the iron embrace of Mother War.

Something stopped him in the doorway, though, and he took one last look back. As if to make sure she was really there. She was, and smiling at him. They were rare, her smiles, but that made them precious. Precious as gold, it seemed, and he was mightily pleased with himself for being the cause of it.

# THE CHOSEN
# SHIELD

The citadel of Thorlby had not been happy ground for Thorn. The last time she visited it had been as a murderer, herded in chains to the cells. The time before it had been to see her father laid out in the Godshall, pale and cold beneath the dome, her mother sobbing beside her, and she'd looked up at the hard faces of the tall gods and known her prayers had all been wasted. She had to swallow a shadow of the anger she'd felt then, the anger that had burned at her ever since, gripping at the pouch that held her father's fingerbones as she frowned toward the great doors of the Godshall.

There were boys training in the yard, beneath the ancient cedar. Training in the square, the way Thorn used to, their master-at-arms barking out orders as they scrambled into a rickety shield wall. They seemed so young now. So slow and so clumsy. She could hardly believe she had ever been one of them as Koll led her past.

"You are Thorn Bathu?"

An old man sat at the corner of the square, swathed in a thick black fur in spite of the warmth, a drawn sword cradled in his arms. He seemed so withered, and hunched, and pale, that even with the golden circle on his brow it took Thorn a moment to recognize him.

She wobbled down onto one knee beside Koll, staring at the grass. "I am, my king."

King Uthil cleared his throat. "I hear unarmed you killed seven men, and forged an alliance with the Empress of the South. I did not believe it." He narrowed his watery eyes as he looked her up and down. "Now I begin to."

Thorn swallowed. "It was only five men, my king."

"Only five, she says!" And he gave a throaty chuckle to the old warriors about him. A couple just about cracked smiles. The faces of the others grew more dour with every word. No deed would ever be high enough to raise her in their estimation: she was as much an object of contempt as ever. "I like you, girl!" said the king. "We should practice together."

So she could practice with him, as long as she didn't presume to fight for him. Thorn lowered her eyes in case she let her anger show and ended up visiting the citadel's dungeons for a second time. "That would be a high honor," she managed to say.

Uthil broke into a coughing fit, and drew his cloak tight about his shoulders. "Once my minister's potions have worked their magic and I am past this illness. I swear those dung-tasting brews only make me weaker."

"Father Yarvi is a deep-cunning healer, my king," said Thorn. "I would have died without his wisdom."

"Aye," murmured Uthil, staring off into the distance. "I hope his wisdom works soon for me. I must go north, and teach these Vanstermen a lesson. The Breaker of Swords has questions for us." His voice had withered to a crackling wheeze. "What should be our answer?"

"Steel!" hissed Thorn, and the other warriors about the king murmured the word as one.

Uthil's pale hand trembled as he clutched his drawn sword close, and Thorn did not think she would be practicing with the king any time soon. "Steel," he breathed, and settled slowly into his fur, wet eyes fixed on the boys in the square, as if he had forgotten Thorn was there.

"Father Yarvi's waiting," murmured Koll. He led her away across the grass, into a shadowy hall and up a long flight of steps, the scraping of their boots echoing in the darkness, the shouts of the training boys fading behind them.

"Is Brand all right?"

"How the hell should I know?" Thorn snapped, and felt guilty right away. "I'm sorry. I hope he is."

"Are you and him . . ." Koll peered at her sideways. "You know."

"I don't know what me and him are," she snapped, another wave of temper and another slow wash of guilt. "Sorry."

"You're bored."

"I'm idle," she growled, "while high deeds are being done."

Her mood had been filthy for days and the scorn of Uthil's warriors hadn't helped. She had nothing to do but worry. Worry that Brand wouldn't want her when he came back or that she wouldn't want him when he came back or that he wouldn't come back at all. She had more doubts and frustrations spinning faster around her head than before she'd bedded him and there was nothing she could do about any of it.

"Bloody men," she muttered. "We'd be better off without them."

"What did I do?" asked Koll.

"You don't count." She grinned, and ruffled his hair. "Yet."

A heavy door squealed open on a cave of wonders. A round room, ill-lit by flickering lamps, smelling of spice and fust and lined with shelves, the shelves stacked with books, with jars of dried leaves and colored dust, with animals' skulls and broken sticks, with bunches of herbs and stones glittering with crystals.

Safrit stood in there, beckoning Thorn up some steps toward another archway. She leaned close to whisper. "Don't worry."

"Eh?"

"It'll work out fine, whatever you decide."

Thorn stared at her. "Now I'm worried."

Father Yarvi sat on a stool by a firepit in the room beyond, the elf-metal staff that leaned beside him gleaming with reflected fire.

Safrit knelt so low at the threshold she nearly butted the floor, but Thorn snorted as she swaggered forward.

"Having good folk kneel before you, Father Yarvi? I thought you gave up being a king—" The rest of the room came into view and Thorn saw Queen Laithlin sitting on the other side of the fire. Her robe was shrugged back, one pale shoulder bare, and she clasped a bundle of fur to her chest. Prince Druin, Thorn realized, heir to the Black Chair.

"Gods." Thorn was being ambushed by royalty around every corner. She scrambled down to one knee, knocked a jar off a shelf with her elbow, dislodged another when she shot out a hand to catch it, ended up clumsily crowding the clinking mess back with her chest. "Sorry, my queen. I've never been much good at kneeling." She remembered she had said the very same thing the last time they met, on the docks of Thorlby before the *South Wind* left, and she felt her face burning just as hot as it had then.

But Laithlin did not seem to notice. "The best people aren't." She gestured to another stool beside the firepit. "Sit instead."

Thorn sat, but that was no more comfortable. Queen and minister both tipped their heads back and looked at her through narrowed gray eyes. The resemblance between them was uncanny. Mother and son still, whatever oaths he might have sworn to give up all family but the Ministry. They both gazed at her in calm silence. A double assessment that made Thorn feel the size of a pinhead, and all the while the infant prince sucked, sucked, sucked, and a tiny hand slipped from the fur and pulled at a strand of yellow hair.

"Last time we met," said Laithlin, in the end, "I told you that fools boast of what they will do, while heroes do it. It seems you took my words to heart."

Thorn tried to swallow her nerves. Thorlby might have seemed smaller after all she had seen, famed warriors feeble after all she had done, but the Golden Queen was as awe-inspiring as ever. "I've tried to, my queen."

"Father Yarvi tells me you have become most deadly. He tells me you killed six Horse People in battle on the Denied. That seven men came for the Empress of the South and you fought them alone, unarmed, and won."

"I had help. The best of teachers, and a good man beside me— men, that is. Good men beside me."

Laithlin gave the slightest smile. "You have learned humility, then."

"Thanks to Father Yarvi I've learned many things, my queen."

"Tell me about the Empress of the South."

"Well . . ." All Thorn could think of then was how very different she was from Queen Laithlin. "She is young, and small, and clever—"

"And generous." The queen glanced down at the elf-bangle on Thorn's wrist, which flared with it own pink as she blushed again.

"I tried not to take it, my queen, but—"

"It was meant to break an alliance. It helped forge a new one. I could not have hoped for a better return on my investment. Do you wish you had stayed in the First of Cities?"

Thorn blinked. "I . . ."

"I know the empress asked you to. To stand at her shoulder, and protect her from her enemies, and help steer the course of a great nation. Few indeed will ever receive such an offer."

Thorn swallowed. "Gettland is my home."

"Yes. And here you languish in Thorlby while Grandmother Wexen closes the Shattered Sea to our ships and the Vanstermen swarm across the border, a storied warrior sitting on her strong hands while unripe boys and doddering old men are called upon to fight. My husband the king must seem quite a fool to you. Like a man who goes to mow his meadow with a spoon, and leaves his fine new scythe to rust upon the shelf." The queen peered down at her infant son. "The world changes. It must. But Uthil is a man of iron, and iron does not bend easily to new ways."

"He does not seem himself," murmured Thorn.

The minister and queen exchanged a glance she could not plumb the meaning of. "He is not well," said Yarvi.

"And he must soothe the feelings of older and even more rigid men," said Laithlin.

Thorn licked her lips. "I've done too many foolish things to accuse anyone else of folly, least of all a king."

"But you would like to fight?"

Thorn lifted her chin and held the queen's eye. "It's what I'm made for."

"It must grate on your warrior's pride to be ignored."

"My father told me never to get proud."

"Fine advice." The prince had fallen asleep and Laithlin eased him from her breast and passed him up to Safrit, shrugging her robe closed. "Your father was a Chosen Shield for a time, I understand."

"To King Uthil's mother," murmured Yarvi.

"What became of him?" asked the queen, while Safrit rocked the prince in her arms and gently cooed to him.

Thorn felt the pouch weigh against her chest as she shifted uncomfortably. "He was killed in a duel with Grom-gil-Gorm."

"The Breaker of Swords. A fearsome warrior. A terrible enemy to Gettland. And now we face him again. I once had a Chosen Shield of my own."

"Hurik," said Thorn. "I saw him fight in the training square. He was a great warrior."

"He betrayed me," said the queen, her cold eyes on Thorn. "I had to kill him."

She swallowed. "Oh . . ."

"I have never found one worthy to take his place." There was a long and pregnant silence. "Until now."

Thorn's eyes went wide. She looked at Yarvi, and back to the queen. "Me?"

Yarvi held up his crippled hand. "Not me."

Thorn's heart was suddenly hammering. "But . . . I never passed my warrior's test. I never swore a warrior's oath—"

"You've passed far sterner tests," said the queen, "and the only oath a Chosen Shield must swear is to me."

Thorn slid off her stool and knelt at Laithlin's feet, this time without knocking anything into the fire. "Tell me the words, my queen."

"You are a brave one." Laithlin leaned forward, putting her fingertips gently on Thorn's scarred cheek. "But you should not be rash."

"You should be careful what oaths you swear," said Father Yarvi.

"This is a burden as well as an honor. You might have to fight for me. You might have to die for me."

"Death waits for us all, my queen." Thorn did not have to think. It felt more right than anything she had ever done. "I've dreamed of this since I could hold a sword. I am ready. Tell me the words."

"Father Yarvi?" Koll hurried into the room, flushed with excitement and greatly out of breath.

"Not now, Koll—"

"A crow's come!" And he held out a little scrap of paper, tiny marks scrawled across it.

"Mother Scaer replies, at last." Yarvi spread it out upon his knees, eyes flickering over the signs. Thorn watched in wonder. To capture words in lines on a scrap of nothing seemed like magic to her as surely as what Skifr had done out on the steppe.

"What does it say?" asked Laithlin.

"Grom-gil-Gorm accepts King Uthil's challenge. His raids will cease until midsummer's day. Then the warriors of Vansterland and Gettland will meet in battle at Amon's Tooth." Yarvi turned the paper over, and narrowed his eyes.

"What else?"

"The Breaker of Swords makes a challenge of his own. He asks if King Uthil will meet him in the square, man against man."

"A duel," said Laithlin.

"A duel."

"The king is not well enough to fight." Laithlin looked over at her son. Her minister. "He cannot be well enough to fight."

"With the favor of Father Peace, it will never come to that."

"Your circles move, Father Yarvi."

He crumpled up the paper and tossed it into the firepit. "They move."

"Then we must be ready to ride north within the week." Queen Laithlin stood, tall and stern, wise and beautiful, and kneeling at her feet Thorn thought there could never have been a woman more worth following. "Teach her the words."

# HALLEBY

It had rained, and the fire was gone. Everything was gone, more or less. A few charred uprights. A few tottering chimney stacks. The rest of the village of Halleby was mud-churned ash and splinters. A few people picking through for anything worth saving and not finding much. A few others gathered around some fresh turned earth, heads hanging.

"A sorry place at the best of times," muttered Brand.

"And these ain't them," said Rauk.

An old man knelt in the wreckage of a house, all smeared with soot and his wispy hair blowing, croaking at the sky, "They took my sons. They took my sons. They took my sons," over and over.

"Poor bastard." Rauk wiped his running nose on the back of one hand and winced again as he hefted his shield. He'd been wincing ever since they left Thorlby.

"Your arm hurt?" asked Brand.

"Took an arrow a few weeks back. I'm all right." He didn't look all right. He looked thin, and drained out, and his watery eyes held none of the challenge they used to. Brand would never have thought he might miss that. But he did.

"You want me to haul your shield awhile?"

A flicker of that old pride, then Rauk seemed to sag. "Thanks." He let his shield drop, groaned through clenched teeth as he worked his arm around in a circle. "Didn't look much of a wound but, gods, it hurts."

"No doubt it's on the mend already," said Brand, swinging the extra shield across his back.

Didn't look like they'd need it today, the Vanstermen were long gone. Just as well, because it was some sorry scrapings Hunnan had gathered. A couple dozen boys with gear that didn't fit, hardly older than Koll and a lot less use, staring at the burned-out wreckage with big, scared eyes. A handful of greybeards, one without a tooth in his head, another without a hair on his, a third with a sword speckled hilt to blunt point with rust. Then there were the wounded. Rauk, and a fellow who'd lost an eye whose bandages kept leaking, and another with a bad leg who'd slowed them down the whole way, and Sordaf, who'd nothing wrong with him at all far as Brand could tell. Apart from being as big an idiot as ever, of course.

He puffed his cheeks out and gave a weary sigh. He'd left Thorn. Naked. In his bed. No clothes at all. For this. The gods knew he'd made some awful decisions but that had to be the worst. Damn standing in the light, he should've been lying in the warm.

Rauk was kneading his shoulder with his pale hand. "Hope it heals soon. Can't stand in the shield wall with a bad arm. You stood in the wall?" There'd have been a barb in that question, once, but now there was only a hollow dread in his voice.

"Aye, on the Denied." There'd have been a pride in that, once, but now all Brand could think of was the feel of his dagger sinking into flesh and he'd a dread of his own as he spoke. "We fought the Horse People there. Don't know why, really, but . . . we fought 'em. You?"

"I have. A skirmish against some Vanstermen, few months back."

Rauk gave another long sniff, both of 'em chewing at memories they didn't much like the taste of. "You kill anyone?"

"I did." Brand thought of the man's face, still so clear. "You?"

"I did," said Rauk, frowning at the ground.

"Thorn killed six." Brand said it far too loud and far too jolly, but desperate to talk about anything but his own part in it. "Should have seen her fight! Saved my life."

"Some folk take to it." Rauk's watery eyes were still fixed on the mud. "Seemed to me most just get through it though, best they can."

Brand frowned at the burned out wreckage that used to be a village. Used to be some folks' lives. "Being a warrior . . . not all brotherhood and back-slapping, is it?"

"It's not like the songs."

"No." Brand pulled the two shields higher up his shoulder. "No it isn't."

"They took my sons. They took my sons. They took my sons . . ."

Master Hunnan had been talking to a woman who'd got away when the Vanstermen came. Now he strode back over with the thumb of his sword-hand tucked in his belt, gray hair flicked by the wind about a frown harder even than usual.

"They came at sunset two days ago. She thinks two dozen but she's not sure and I reckon fewer. They had dogs with 'em. They killed two men, took ten for slaves, and five or so were sick or old they let burn in their houses."

"Gods," whispered one of the boys, and he made a holy sign over his chest.

Hunnan narrowed his eyes. "This is what war is, boy. What were you expecting?"

"They've been gone two days, then." Brand cast an eye over the old men, and that young lad with the bad leg. "And we're not the fastest moving crew you ever saw. We'll never catch 'em now."

"No." Hunnan's jaw worked as he stared off hard-eyed toward the north. Toward Vansterland. "But we can't let this pass either. There's a Vanstermen's village not far from here. Just over the river."

"Rissentoft," said Sordaf.

"You know it?"

He shrugged. "It's got a good sheep-market. Used to drive lambs there with my uncle in the spring. I know a ford nearby."

"Won't it be watched?" asked Brand.

"We weren't watching it."

"There we go, then." Hunnan worked his sword hilt from the sheath then slapped it back in. "We cross at this ford and head for Rissentoft. Get your skinny arses moving!" And the master-at-arms put his head down and started walking.

Brand hurried after him, speaking low, not wanting to start an argument in front of the others, they'd got doubts enough as it was. "Master Hunnan, wait. If it was wrong when they did it to us, how's it right if we do it to them?"

"If we can't hurt the shepherds, we'll have to hurt the flock."

"It wasn't sheep did this, nor shepherds neither. It was warriors."

"This is war," said Hunnan, his mouth twisting. "Right's got nothing to do with it. King Uthil said steel is the answer, so steel it has to be."

Brand waved his hand toward the miserable survivors, picking over the wreckage of their homes. "Shouldn't we stay and help them? What good will burning some other village do just 'cause it's across a river—"

Hunnan rounded on him. "Might help the next village, or the one after that! We're warriors not nursemaids! You got a second chance, boy, but I'm starting to think I was right after all, and you've got more Father Peace than Mother War in you." Looking at Mother War's handiwork behind them, Brand wondered whether that was such a bad thing. "What if it was your family died here, eh? Your house burned? Your sister made some Vansterman's slave? Would you be for vengeance then?"

Brand looked over his shoulder toward the other lads, following in a meager straggle. Then he gave a sigh and hefted the two shields.

"Aye," he said. "I guess I would."

But he couldn't see how any good would come of this.

# FIRE

"Reckon I need a new sword."

Thorn tossed her father's rattling down on the table.

Rin gave the blade she was working on another grating stroke with the polishing stone and frowned over at her. "This seems familiar."

"Very. But I'm hoping for a different answer this time around."

"Because you bedded my brother?"

"Because there's going to be a battle, and Queen Laithlin wants her Chosen Shield suitably armed."

Rin set her stone aside and walked over, slapping dust from her hands. "The Queen's Chosen Shield? You?"

Thorn raised her chin and stared back. "Me."

They watched each other for a long moment, then Rin picked up Thorn's sword, spun it over, rubbed at the cheap pommel with her thumb, laid it back down and planted her hands on her hips. "If Queen Laithlin says it's so, I guess it's so."

"It's so," said Thorn.

"We'll need some bone."

"What for?"

"To bind with the iron and make steel." Rin nodded over at the bright blade clamped to the bench, gray steel-dust gathered under it. "I used a hawk's for that one. But I've used a wolf's. A bear's. Do it right, you trap the animal's spirit in the blade. So you pick something strong. Something deadly. Something that means something to you."

Thorn thought about that for a moment, then the idea came and she started to smile. She pulled the pouch from around her neck and tipped the smooth and yellowed little lumps out across the table. She'd worn them long enough. Time to put them to better use. "How about a hero's bones?"

Rin raised her brows at them. "Even better."

THEY STOPPED IN AN ash-scattered clearing by the river, a ring of stones in the center blackened as if it had held one hell of a fire.

Rin swung the big bag of tools down from her shoulder. "We're here."

"Did we have to come so far?" Thorn dumped the coal sacks, stretching out her back and wiping her sweating face on her forearm.

"Don't want my secrets stolen. Talking of which, tell anyone what happens here I'll have to kill you." Rin tossed Thorn a shovel. "Now get in the river and dig out some clay."

Thorn frowned sideways, sucking at the hole in her teeth. "I'm starting to think Skifr was an easier master."

"Who's Skifr?"

"Never mind."

She waded out to her waist in the stream, the water so cold it made her gasp in spite of the summer warmth, and set to cutting clay from the bed and slopping it onto the bank in gray shovelfuls.

Rin put some dull lumps of iron-stone in a jar, along with the black ash of Thorn's father's bones, and a sprinkle of sand, and two glass beads, then she started smearing clay around the lid, sealing it shut.

"What's the glass for?" asked Thorn.

"To trick the dirt out of the iron," murmured Rin, without looking up. "The hotter we get the furnace the purer the steel and the stronger the blade."

"How did you learn all this?"

"I was apprentice to a smith called Gaden. I watched some others. I talked to some sword-merchants from down the Divine." Rin tapped at the side of her head and left a smear of clay there. "The rest I worked out for myself."

"You're a clever girl, aren't you?"

"When it comes to steel." Rin set the clay jar carefully in the middle of the ring of stones. "Back in the river, then."

So Thorn sloshed out shivering into the stream again while Rin built the furnace. She heaped coal up inside, stones outside, and mortared them with clay until she'd built a thing looked like a great domed bread-oven, chest high, with an opening at the bottom.

"Help me seal it." Rin dug up clay with her hands and Thorn did the same, smearing it thick over the outside. "What's it like? Being a Chosen Shield?"

"Dreamed of it all my life," said Thorn, puffing herself up. "And I can't think of anyone I'd rather serve than Queen Laithlin."

Rin nodded. "They don't call her the Golden Queen for nothing."

"It's a high honor."

"No doubt. But what's it like?"

Thorn sagged. "So far, boring. Since I swore the oath I've spent most of my time standing in the queen's counting house, frowning at merchants while they ask her for favors that might as well be in a foreign tongue for all I understand them."

"Wondering if you made a mistake?" asked Rin, digging up another handful of gray mush.

"No," snapped Thorn, and then, after a moment spent squashing more clay into the cracks, "Maybe. It'd hardly be my first."

"You ain't at all as tough you make out, are you?"

Thorn took a long breath. "Who is?"

———

RIN BLEW GENTLY ON her shovel, the coals rustling as they glowed bright, then she got on her belly and rammed them deep into the mouth of the furnace, puffing out her cheeks as she blew hard, over and over. Finally she rocked back on her heels, watching the fire taking the coal, flame flickering orange inside the vent.

"What's happening between you and Brand?" she asked.

Thorn had known it was coming, but that didn't make it any more comfortable. "I don't know."

"Not that complicated a question, is it?"

"You wouldn't think so."

"Well, are you done with him?"

"No," said Thorn, surprised by how firm she sounded.

"Did he say he was done with you?"

"We both know Brand's not much at saying things. But I wouldn't be surprised. Not exactly what men dream of, am I?"

Rin frowned at her for a moment. "I reckon different men dream of different things. Just like different women."

"Couldn't have taken off running much sooner, though, could he?"

"He's wanted to be a warrior a long time. That was his chance."

"Aye." Thorn took a long breath. "Thought it'd get simpler when . . . you know."

"But it didn't get simpler?"

Thorn scrubbed at her shaved head, feeling the bald scar in the stubble. "No, it bloody didn't. I don't know what we're doing, Rin. I wish I did but I don't. I've never been any good at anything but fighting."

"You never know. You might find a talent at working bellows too." And Rin dropped them beside the mouth of the furnace.

"When you've a load to lift," muttered Thorn as she knelt, "you're better lifting than weeping." And she gritted her teeth and made those bellows wheeze until her shoulders were aching and her chest was burning and her vest was soaked through with sweat.

"Harder," said Rin. "Hotter." And she started singing out prayers, soft and low, to He Who Makes the Flame, and She Who Strikes the Anvil, and Mother War too, the Mother of Crows, who gathers the dead and makes the open hand a fist.

Thorn worked until that vent looked like a gate to hell in the gathering darkness, like a dragon's maw in the twilight. Worked until, even though she'd helped carry a ship each way over the tall hauls, she wasn't sure she'd ever worked harder.

Rin snorted. "Out of the way, killer, I'll show you how it's done."

And she set to, as calm and strong and steady at the bellows as her brother at the oar. The coals glowed up hotter yet as the stars came out above, and Thorn muttered out a prayer of her own, a prayer to her father, and reached for the pouch around her neck but his bones were gone into the steel, and that felt right.

She sloshed out into the river and drank, soaked to the skin, and sloshed back out to take another turn, imagining the bellows were Grom-gil-Gorm's head, on and on until she was dried out by the furnace then soaked with sweat again. Finally they worked together, side by side, the heat like a great hand pressing on Thorn's face, red-blue flames flickering from the vent and smoke pouring from the baked clay sides of the furnace and sparks showering up into the night where Father Moon sat big and fat and white above the trees.

Just when it seemed Thorn's chest was going to burst and her arms come right off her shoulders Rin said, "Enough," and the pair of them flopped back, soot-smeared and gasping.

"What now?"

"Now we wait for it to cool." Rin dragged a tall bottle out of her pack and pulled out the stopper. "And we get a little drunk." She took a long swig, soot-smeared neck shifting as she swallowed, then handed the bottle to Thorn, wiping her mouth.

"You know the way to a woman's heart." Thorn closed her eyes, and smelled good ale, and soon after tasted it, and soon after swallowed it, and smacked her dry lips. Rin was setting the shovel in the shimmering haze on top of the furnace, tossed bacon hissing onto the metal.

"You've got all kinds of skills, don't you?"

"I've done a few jobs in my time." And Rin cracked eggs onto the shovel that straight away began to bubble. "There's going to be a battle, then?"

"Looks that way. At Amon's Tooth."

Rin sprinkled salt. "Would Brand fight in it?"

"I guess we both would. Father Yarvi's got other ideas, though. He usually does."

"I hear he's a deep-cunning man."

"No doubt, but he's not sharing his cleverness."

"Deep-cunning folk don't tend to," said Rin, flipping the bacon with a knife blade.

"Gorm's offered a challenge to King Uthil to settle it."

"A duel? There's never been a finer swordsman than Uthil, has there?"

"Not at his best. But he's far from his best."

"I heard a rumor he was ill." Rin pulled the shovel from the furnace and dropped down on her haunches, laying it between them, the smell of meat and eggs making Thorn's mouth flood with spit.

"Saw him in the Godshall yesterday," said Thorn. "Trying to look like he was made of iron but, in spite of Father Yarvi's plant-lore, I swear, he could hardly stand."

"Doesn't sound good, with a battle coming." Rin pulled a spoon out and offered it to Thorn.

"No. It doesn't sound good."

They started stuffing food in and, after all that work, Thorn wasn't sure she'd ever tasted better. "Gods," she said around a mouthful, "a woman who can make fine eggs and fine swords *and* brings fine ale with her? It doesn't work out with Brand I'll marry you."

Rin snorted. "If the boys show as much interest as they've been doing I might count that a fine match."

They laughed together at that, and ate, and got a little drunk, the furnace still hot on their faces.

"YOU SNORE, DO YOU know that?"

Thorn jerked awake, rubbing her eyes, Mother Sun just showing herself in the stony sky. "It has been commented on."

"Time to break this open, I reckon. See what we've got."

Rin set to knocking the furnace apart with a hammer, Thorn raking the still smoking coals away, hand over her face as a tricking breeze sent ash and embers whirling. Rin delved in with tongs and pulled the jar out of the midst, yellow hot. She swung it onto a flat stone, broke it open, knocking white dust away, pulling something from inside like a nut from its shell.

The steel bound with her father's bones, glowing sullen red, no bigger than a fist.

"Is it good?" asked Thorn.

Rin tapped it, turned it over, and slowly began to smile. "Aye. It's good."

# RISSENTOFT

In the songs, Angulf Clovenfoot's Gettlanders fell upon the Vanstermen like hawks from an evening sky.

Master Hunnan's misfits fell on Rissentoft like a herd of sheep down a steep flight of steps.

The lad with the game leg could hardly walk by the time they reached the river and they'd left him sore and sorry on the south bank. The rest of them got soaked through at the ford and one lad had his shield carried off by the current. Then they got turned around in an afternoon mist and it wasn't until near dark, all worn-out, clattering and grumbling, that they stumbled on the village.

Hunnan cuffed one boy around the head for quiet then split them up with gestures, sent them scurrying in groups of five down the streets, or down the hardened dirt between the shacks, at least.

"Stay close!" Brand hissed to Rauk, who was straggling behind, shield dangling, looking more pale and tired than ever.

"The place is empty," growled the toothless old-timer, and he looked to have the right of it. Brand crept along a wall and peered through a door hanging open. Not so much as a dog moving anywhere. Apart from the stink of poverty, an aroma he was well familiar with, the place was abandoned.

"They must've heard us coming," he muttered.

The old man raised one brow. "You think?"

"There's one here!" came a scared shriek, and Brand took off running, scrambled around the corner of a wattle shack, shield up.

An old man stood at the door of a house with his hands raised. Not a big house, or a pretty house. Just a house. He had a stoop to his back, and gray hair braided beside his face the way the Vanstermen wore it. Three of Hunnan's lads stood in a half-circle about him, spears levelled.

"I'm not armed," he said, holding his hands higher. They had something of a shake to them and Brand hardly blamed him. "I don't want to fight."

"Some of us don't," said Hunnan, stepping between the lads with his sword drawn. "But sometimes a fight finds us anyway."

"I got nothing you want." The old man stared about nervously as they gathered around him. "Please. Just don't want my house burned. Built it with my wife."

"Where's she?" asked Hunnan.

The old man swallowed, his gray-stubbled throat shifting. "She died last winter."

"What about those in Halleby? You think they wanted their houses burned?"

"I knew folk in Halleby." The man licked his lips. "I didn't have nought to do with that."

"Not surprised to hear about it, though, are you?" And Hunnan hit him with his sword. It opened a great gash in his arm and he yelped, staggered, clutched at his doorframe as he fell.

"Oh," said one of the boys.

Hunnan stepped up with a snarl and chopped the old man in the back of the head with a sound like a spade chopping earth. He rolled over, shuddering, tongue stuck out rigid. Then he lay still, blood spreading across his door-stone, pooling in the deep-cut runes of the gods that guarded his house.

Same gods that guarded the houses in Thorlby. Seemed they weren't watching right then.

Brand stared, cold all over. Happened so fast he'd no time to stop it. No time to think about whether he wanted to stop it, even. Just happened, and they all stood there and watched.

"Spread out," said Hunnan. "Search the houses, then burn 'em. Burn 'em all." The bald old man shook his head, and Brand felt sick inside, but they did as they were bid.

"I'll stay here," said Rauk, tossing down his shield and sitting on it.

Brand shouldered open the nearest door and froze. A low room, much like the one he and Rin used to share, and by the firepit a woman stood. A skinny woman in a dirty dress, couple of years older than Brand. She stood with one hand on the wall, staring at him, breathing hard. Scared out of her wits, he reckoned.

"You all right?" called Sordaf from outside.

"Aye," said Brand.

"Well, bloody hell!" The fat lad grinned as he ducked his head under the low doorway. "Not quite empty, I reckon." He uncoiled some rope, sawed off a length with his knife, and handed it over. "Reckon she'll get a decent price, you lucky bastard."

"Aye," said Brand.

Sordaf went out shaking his head. "War's all bloody luck, I swear . . ."

The woman didn't speak and neither did Brand. He tied the rope around her neck, not too tight, not too loose, and she didn't so much as twitch. He made the other end fast around his wrist, and all the while he felt numb and strange. This was what warriors did in the songs, wasn't it? Take slaves? Didn't seem much like doing good to Brand. Didn't seem anywhere near it. But if it wasn't him took her it'd be one of the others. That was what warriors did.

Outside they were already torching the houses. The woman made a sort of moan when she saw the dead old man. Another when the thatch on her hovel went up. Brand didn't know what to say to her, or to anyone else, and he was used to keeping silent, so he said nothing. One of the boys had tears streaking his face as he set his torch to the houses, but he set it to them all the same. Soon the air was thick with the smell of burning, wood popping and crackling as the fire spread, flaming straw floating high into the gloom.

"Where's the sense in this?" muttered Brand.

But Rauk just rubbed at his shoulder.

"One slave." Sordaf spat with disgust. "And some sausages. Not much of a haul."

"We didn't come for a haul," said Master Hunnan, frown set tight. "We came to do good."

And Brand stood, holding on to a rope tied around a woman's neck, and watched a village burn.


THEY ATE STALE BREAD in silence, stretched out on the chill ground in silence. They were still in Vansterland and could afford no fire, every man alone with his thoughts, all darkling strangers to each other.

Brand waited for the faintest glimmer of dawn, gray cracks in the black cloud overhead. Wasn't as if he'd been sleeping, anyway. Kept thinking about that old man. And the boy crying as he set fire to the thatch. Kept listening to the woman breathing who was now his slave, his property, because he'd put a rope around her neck and burned her house.

"Get up," hissed Brand, and she slowly stood. He couldn't see her face but there was a slump to her shoulders like nothing mattered any more.

Sordaf was on watch, now, blowing into his fat hands and rubbing them together and blowing into 'em again.

"We're going off a bit," said Brand, nodding toward the treeline not far away.

Sordaf gave him a grin. "Can't say I blame you. Chilly night."

Brand turned his back on him and started walking, tugged at the rope and felt the woman shuffling after. Under the trees and through the undergrowth they went, no words said, sticks cracking under Brand's boots, until the camp was far behind. An owl hooted somewhere and he dragged the woman down into the brush, waiting, but there was no one there.

He wasn't sure how long it took them to reach the far side of the wood, but Mother Sun was a gray smudge in the east when they stepped from the trees. He pulled out the dagger Rin made for him and cut the rope carefully from around the woman's neck.

"Go, then," he said. She just stood staring. He pointed out the way. "Go."

She took one step, and looked back, then another, as if she expected some trick. He stood still.

"Thanks," she whispered.

Brand winced. "I don't deserve thanking. Just go."

She took off fast. He watched her run back the way they'd come, through the wet grass, down the gentle slope. As Mother Sun crawled higher he could see Rissentoft in the distance, a black smear on the land, still smoldering.

He reckoned it must've looked a lot like Halleby before the war started.

Now it did again.

# FROZEN
# LAKES

The king's household halted in the spitting rain above the camp, a thousand fires sprawling under the darkening sky, pinprick torches trickling into the valley as the warriors of Gettland gathered. Thorn sprang down and offered the queen her hand. Not that Laithlin needed any help, she was twice the rider Thorn was. But Thorn was desperate to be useful.

In the songs, Chosen Shields protected their queens from assassins, or carried secret messages into the mouth of danger, or fought duels on which the fates of nations rested. Probably she should have learned by now not to take songs too seriously.

She found herself lost among an endlessly shifting legion of slaves and servants, trailing after the Golden Queen like the tail after a comet, besieging her with a thousand questions to which, whether she was nursing the heir to the throne at the time or not, she always had the answers. King Uthil might have sat in the Black Chair but, after a few days in Laithlin's company, it was plain to Thorn who really ruled Gettland.

There was no trace of the easy companionship she'd had with Vi-aline. No earnest talks or demands to be called by her first name. Laithlin was more than twice Thorn's age: a wife and mother, a peer-less merchant, the mistress of a great household, as beautiful as she was deep-cunning as she was masterfully controlled. She was every-thing a woman should be and more. Everything Thorn wasn't.

"My thanks," Laithlin murmured, taking Thorn's hand and mak-ing even sliding down from a saddle look graceful.

"I want only to serve."

The queen did not let go of her hand. "No. You were not born to stand in dusty meetings and count coins. You want to fight."

Thorn swallowed. "Give me the chance."

"Soon enough." Laithlin leaned close, gripping Thorn's hand tight. "An oath of loyalty cuts both ways. I forgot that once, and never will again. We shall do great things together, you and I. Things to sing of."

"My king?" Father Yarvi's voice, and sharp with worry.

Uthil had stumbled climbing from his own saddle and now he was leaning heavily on his minister, gray as a ghost, chest heaving as he clutched his drawn sword against it.

"We will speak later," said Laithlin, letting go of Thorn's hand.

"Koll, boil water!" called Father Yarvi. "Safrit, bring my plants!"

"I saw that man walk a hundred miles through the ice and never falter," said Rulf, standing beside Thorn with his arms folded. "The king is not well."

"No." Thorn watched Uthil shamble into his tent with one arm over his minister's shoulders. "And with a great battle coming. Poor luck indeed."

"Father Yarvi doesn't believe in luck."

"I don't believe in helmsmen, but they dog me even so."

Rulf chuckled at that. "How's your mother?"

Thorn frowned across at him. "Unhappy with my choices, as al-ways."

"Still striking sparks from each other?"

"Since you ask, not near so much as we used to."

"Oh? I reckon one of you must have grown up a little."

Thorn narrowed her eyes. "Maybe one of us had a wise old warrior to teach them the value of family."

"Everyone should be so lucky." Rulf peered down at the ground, rubbing at his beard. "I've been thinking, perhaps . . . I should pay her a visit."

"You asking my permission?"

"No. But I'd like to have it, still."

Thorn gave a helpless shrug. "Far be it from me to come between a pair of young lovers."

"Or me." Rulf gave a meaningful look past her from under his brows. "Which is why I'll be dwindling into the west, I think . . ."

Thorn turned, and Brand was walking toward her.

She had been hoping she might see him, but as soon as she did she felt a surge of nerves. As if she was stepping into the training square for the first time and he was her opponent. They should have been familiar to each other now, surely? But of a sudden she had no idea how to be with him. Prickly-playful, like one oar-mate with another? Simpering soft, like a maiden with a suitor? Frosty-regal, like Queen Laithlin with a debtor? Creepy-cautious, like a clever gambler keeping her dice well hidden?

Each step he came closer felt like a step back out onto that frozen lake, ice creaking under her weight, no notion what the next footfall might bring.

"Thorn," he said, looking her in the eye.

"Brand," she said, looking back.

"Couldn't stand to wait for me any longer, eh?"

Prickly-playful, then. "The suitors were queued up outside my house all the way to the bloody docks. There's only so much of men weeping over my beauty I can stand." And she pressed a fingertip to one side of her nose and blew snot into the mud out of the other.

"You've a new sword," he said, looking down at her belt.

She hooked a finger under the plain crosspiece and drew it halfway so he could draw it the rest with the faintest ringing. "From the best blade-maker in the Shattered Sea."

"Gods, she's got good." He brushed Rin's mark on the fuller with his thumb, swished the blade one way and the other, lifted it to peer with one eye down the length, Mother Sun flashing along the bright steel and glinting on the point.

"Didn't have time to do anything fancy with it," said Thorn, "but I'm getting to like it plain."

Brand softly whistled. "That is fine steel."

"Cooked with a hero's bones."

"Is that so?"

"Reckon I'd had my fathers fingers about my neck for long enough."

He grinned as he offered the sword back to her, and she found she was grinning too. "I thought Rin said no to you?"

"No one says no to Queen Laithlin."

Brand had that old puzzled look of his. "Eh?"

"She wanted her Chosen Shield suitably armed," she said, slapping the sword back into its scabbard.

He gaped at her in silence while that sank in.

"I know what you're thinking." Thorn's shoulders slumped. "I don't even have a shield."

He snapped his mouth shut. "I'm thinking you are the shield, and none better. If I was a queen I'd pick you."

"Hate to crush your hopes, but I doubt you'll ever be queen."

"None of the gowns would suit me." He slowly shook his head, starting to smile again. "Thorn Bathu, Chosen Shield."

"What about you? Did you save Gettland, yet? Saw you gathering on the beach. Quite the crowd of young champions. Not to mention a couple of ancient ones."

Brand winced. "Can't say we saved much of anything. We killed an old farmer. We stole some sausages. We burned a village 'cause it was on the wrong side of a river. We took a slave." Brand scratched at his head. "I let her go."

"You just can't help doing good, can you?"

"Don't think Hunnan sees it that way. He'd like to tell everyone I'm a disgrace but he'd have to admit his raid was a disgrace, so . . ." He puffed out his cheeks, looking more puzzled than ever. "I'm swearing my warrior's oath tomorrow. Along with some lads never swung a blade in anger."

Thorn put on Father Yarvi's voice. "Let Father Peace spill tears over the methods! Mother War smiles upon results! You must be pleased."

He looked down at the ground. "I suppose so."

"You're not?"

"Do you ever feel bad? About those men you've killed?"

"Not a lot. Why should I?"

"I'm not saying you should. I'm just asking if you do."

"I don't."

"Well, you're touched by Mother War."

"Touched?" Thorn snorted. "She's slapped me purple."

"Being a warrior, brothers at my shoulder, it's what I always wanted . . ."

"There's no disappointment like getting what you've always wanted."

"Some things are worth the wait," he said, looking her in the eye.

She had no doubts at all what that look meant now. She was starting to wonder if getting across this frozen lake of theirs might not be so hard. Maybe you just took one step at a time, and tried to enjoy the thrill of it. So she took a little pace closer to him. "Where are you sleeping?"

He didn't back off. "Under the stars, I reckon."

"A Chosen Shield gets a tent."

"You trying to make me jealous?"

"No, it's only a small one." She moved another little step. "But it's got a bed."

"I'm getting to like this story."

"Bit cold, though." She moved another little step, and they were both smiling. "On my own."

"I could have a word with Sordaf for you, reckon he could warm a blanket with one fart."

"Sordaf's everything most women could ask for, but I've always had odd tastes." She reached up, using her fingers like a comb, and pushed the hair out of his face. "I had someone else in mind."

"There's a lot of folk watching," said Brand.

"Like I care a damn."

# COWARDICE

They knelt in a line. Three of the young lads and Brand. Two had pointed spears at an old farmer. One had cried as he set fire to some houses. The last had let the only slave they took go.

Some warriors.

Yet here they were, with the fighting men of Gettland gathered about them in an armed and armored crowd, ready to welcome them into their brotherhood. Ready to have them at their shoulders when they met Grom-gil-Gorm and his Vanstermen at the appointed place. Ready to carry them into the iron embrace of Mother War.

King Uthil had changed a lot in the year since Brand saw him last, and not for the better. His skin had turned the same iron-gray as his hair, rheumy eyes sunken in dark shadows. He seemed shrivelled in his chair, scarcely moving, as though the King's Circle on his brow was a crushing weight, hands trembling as he hugged his naked sword.

Father Yarvi perched on a stool at the king's side, Queen Laithlin sat bolt upright on the other, shoulders back, fists clenched on her knees, sweeping the crowd with her pale stare as though she could make up for her husband's weakness with her strength.

Thorn stood at the queen's shoulder, pointed chin up and with a challenge in her eyes, arms folded and the elf-bangle burning a chill white on her wrist. She looked like something from the songs, a Chosen Shield from her toes to her half-shaved scalp. Brand could hardly believe he'd clambered out of her bed an hour before. At least he had one thing to feel pleased about.

The king looked slowly down the line of boys to Brand, and cleared his throat.

"You are young," he said, voice so crackly quiet it could hardly be heard over the wind flapping the tent cloth. "But Master Hunnan has judged you worthy, and Gettland is beset by enemies." He raised himself a little in his seat, a glimpse of the man whose speech Brand had thrilled to on the beach before Thorlby. "We march to Amon's Tooth to meet the Vanstermen in battle, and we need every shield!" He was caught by a coughing fit, and croaked out, "Steel is the answer." Then slumped back in his chair, Father Yarvi leaning close to whisper in his ear.

Master Hunnan stepped up with sword in hand and frown on face to stand over the first of the boys. "Do you swear loyalty to Gettland?"

The lad swallowed. "I do."

"Do you swear to serve your king?"

"I do."

"Do you swear to stand by your shoulder-man in the shield wall, and obey your betters?"

"I do."

"Then rise a warrior of Gettland!"

The boy did, looking a lot more scared than happy, and all about him men drummed fists on their chests, clattered ax-hafts on shield rims, thumped boots on the earth in approval.

It took a moment's struggle for Brand to swallow. Soon it would be his turn. Should have been the proudest day of his life. But as he thought of the ashes of Halleby and Rissentoft, of the old man bleeding on his doorstep and the woman with the rope around her neck, pride wasn't his first feeling.

The crowd cheered as the second boy said his third "I do" and the man behind jerked him to his feet like a fish from a pond.

Brand caught Thorn's eye, and her mouth curled up in the faintest smile. He would've smiled back, if he hadn't been churning with doubts. Do good, his mother told him with her dying breath. What good had they done at Rissentoft the other night?

The third lad had tears in his eyes again as he swore his oaths, but the warriors took them for tears of pride and gave him the loudest cheer so far, the clashing of weapons cutting at Brand's jangling nerves.

Hunnan worked his jaw, frown hardening even further as Brand stepped up to him, and the men fell silent.

"Do you swear loyalty to Gettland?"

"I do," croaked Brand, his mouth dry.

"Do you swear to serve your king?"

"I do," croaked Brand, heart thumping in his ears.

"Do you swear to stand by your shoulder-man in the shield wall, and obey your betters?"

Brand opened his mouth, but the words didn't come. Silence stretched out. Smiles faded. He felt every eye on him. There was a faint scraping of metal as warriors stirred uneasily.

"Well?" snapped Hunnan.

"No."

The silence stretched for a pregnant moment longer, like the silence before a cloudburst, then a disbelieving mutter started up.

Hunnan stared down, astonished. "What?"

"Stand, boy," came the king's rasping voice, the noise growing angrier as Brand got to his feet. "I never heard of such a thing before. Why will you not swear your oath?"

"Because he's a coward," snarled Hunnan.

More muttering, angrier still. The boy beside Brand stared at him with wide eyes. Rulf bunched his fists. Father Yarvi raised one brow. Thorn took a step forward, her mouth twisting, but the queen stopped her with a raised finger.

With a wincing effort the king held up one bony hand, eyes on Brand, and his warriors fell silent. "I asked him."

"Maybe I am a coward," said Brand, though his voice sounded out a good deal more boldly than usual. "Master Hunnan killed an old farmer the other night, and I was too coward to stop him. We burned a village and I was too coward to speak out. He set three students on one as a test and I was too coward to stand for the one. Standing for the weak against the strong. Isn't that what a warrior should be?"

"Damn you for a liar!" snarled Hunnan, "I'll—"

"You'll hold your tongue!" growled Father Yarvi, "until the king asks you to speak."

The master-at-arms' frown was murderous, but Brand didn't care. He felt as if a load was lifted. As if he'd had the *South Wind*'s weight across his shoulders again, and suddenly let go. He felt, for the first time since he left Thorlby, as if he was standing in the light.

"You want someone with no fear?" He stuck his arm straight out. "There she stands. Thorn Bathu, the Queen's Chosen Shield. In the First of Cities she fought seven men alone and saved the Empress of the South. They're singing songs of it all about the Shattered Sea! And yet you'd rather take boys who scarcely know which end of a spear to hold. What mad pride is that? What foolishness? I used to dream of being a warrior. To serve you, my king. To fight for my country. To have a loyal brother always at my shoulder." He looked Hunnan right in the eye, and shrugged. "If this is what it means to be a warrior, I want no part of it."

The anger burst out once again, and once again King Uthil had to lift a trembling hand for silence.

"Some here might not care for your words," he said. "But they are not the words of a coward. Some men are touched by Father Peace." His tired eyes swiveled toward Yarvi, and then toward Thorn, and one eyelid began to flicker. "Just as some women are touched by Mother War. Death . . . waits for us all." The hand upon his sword was suddenly trembling worse than ever. "We each must find our own . . . right path . . . to her door . . ."

He keeled forward. Father Yarvi darted from his stool and caught the king before he fell, his sword sliding from his lap and clattering in the mud. Between him and Rulf they lifted Uthil from his chair and walked him back into his tent. His head lolled. His feet dragged in the dirt. The muttering came up stronger than ever, but shocked and fearful now.

"The king dropped his sword."

"An ill omen."

"Poor weaponluck."

"The favor of the gods is elsewhere . . ."

"Calm yourselves!" Queen Laithlin stood, sweeping the crowd with icy scorn. "Are these warriors of Gettland or prattling slave-girls?" She had taken the king's sword from the dirt, hugging it to her chest as he had done, but there was no quiver to her hand, no dampness in her eye, no weakness in her voice. "This is no time for doubts! The Breaker of Swords waits for us at Amon's Tooth! The king may not be with us, but we know what he would say."

"Steel is the answer!" barked Thorn, the elf-bangle flaring hot red.

"Steel!" roared Master Hunnan, holding high his sword, and metal hissed as more blades were drawn, and stabbed toward the sky.

"Steel! Steel! Steel!" came the chant from a hundred throats.

Brand was the only one who stayed silent. He'd always thought doing good meant fighting alongside his brothers. But maybe doing good meant not fighting at all.

# THE APPOINTED PLACE

The armies of Vansterland and Gettland glared at each other across a shallow valley of lush, green grass.

"A fine spot to graze a herd of sheep," said Rulf.

"Or to fight a battle." Thorn narrowed her eyes and scanned the ridge opposite. She had never in her life seen a host half the size, the warriors picked out black on the crest against the bright sky, here or there a blade flashing as it caught the light of Mother Sun. The Vanstermen's shield wall was drawn up loose, their shields blobs of bright-painted color and their spears a bristling forest behind. Grom-gil-Gorm's dark banner hung limp over the center, a dusting of archers thrust out in front, more lightly armed skirmishers on each wing.

"So like our own army we might be looking in a great mirror," murmured Yarvi.

"Apart from that damn elf-tower," said Thorn.

Amon's Tooth rose from a rocky outcrop at the far end of the Vanstermen's line, a hollow tower thirty times a man's height, tall and slender as a tapering sword blade, made from hollow cobwebs of elf-metal bars.

"What did it used to be?" asked Koll, gazing up at it in wonder.

"Who can say now?" said the minister. "A signal tower? A monument to the arrogance of the elves? A temple to the One God they broke into many?"

"I can tell you what it will be." Rulf gazed grimly at the host gathered in its shadow. "A grave-marker. A grave for many hundreds."

"Many hundreds of Vanstermen," snapped Thorn. "I reckon our host the larger."

"Aye," said Rulf. "But it's seasoned warriors win battles, and the numbers there are much the same."

"And Gorm is known for keeping some horsemen out of sight," said Father Yarvi. "Our strength is closely matched."

"And only one of us has our king." Rulf glanced back toward the camp. Uthil had not left his sick bed since the previous evening. Some said the Last Door stood open for him, and Father Yarvi had not denied it.

"Even a victory will leave Gettland weakened," said the minster, "and Grandmother Wexen well knows it. This battle is all part of her design. She knew King Uthil could never turn down a challenge. The only victory here is if we do not fight at all."

"What elf-spell have you worked to make that happen?" asked Thorn.

Father Yarvi gave his brittle smile. "I hope a little minister's magic may do the trick."

Koll plucked at his sparse shadow of a beard as he looked across the valley. "I wonder if Fror's among them."

"Maybe," said Thorn. A man they had trained with, laughed with, fought beside, rowed beside.

"What will you do if you meet him in the battle?"

"Probably kill him."

"Let's hope you don't meet, then." Koll lifted an arm to point. "They're coming!"

Gorm's banner was on the move, a party of horsemen breaking from the center of his host and coming down the slope. Thorn nudged her way through the king's most favored warriors to Laithlin's side, but the queen waved her away. "Keep to the back, Thorn, and stay hooded."

"My place is beside you."

"Today you are not my shield but my sword. Sometimes a blade is best hidden. If your moment comes, you will know it."

"Yes, my queen."

Reluctantly, Thorn pulled up her hood, waited until the rest of the royal party had set off, then slouching in her saddle like a thief, in a place no songs are sung of, followed at the back. Down the long slope they trotted, hooves flicking mud from the soft ground. Two standard-bearers went with them, Laithlin's gold and Uthil's iron-gray bravely snapping as the breeze took them.

Closer drew the Vanstermen, and closer. Twenty of their most storied warriors, high-helmed, stern-frowned, braids in their hair and gold rings forged into their mail. And at the fore, the necklace of pommels twisted from the swords of his fallen enemies four-times looped about his great neck, came the man who killed Thorn's father. Grom-gil-Gorm, the Breaker of Swords, in his full battle glory. On his left rode his standard-bearer, a great Shend slave with a garnet-studded thrall collar, black cloth flapping behind him. On his right rode two stocky white-haired boys, one with a mocking smile and Gorm's huge shield upon his back, the other with a warlike sneer and Gorm's great sword. Between them and the king, her jaw working so hard that her shaved scalp squirmed, rode Mother Scaer.

"Greetings, Gettlanders!" The hooves of Gorm's towering horse squelched as he pulled it up in the valley's marshy bottom and grinned into the bright sky. "Mother Sun smiles upon our meeting!"

"A good omen," said Father Yarvi.

"For which of us?" asked Gorm.

"For both of us, perhaps?" Laithlin nudged her own mount forward. Thorn itched to ride up close beside where she could protect her, but forced her heels to be still.

"Queen Laithlin! How can your wisdom and beauty so defy the passing years?"

"How can your strength and courage?" asked the queen.

Gorm scratched thoughtfully at his beard. "When last I was in Thorlby I did not seem to be held in such high regard."

"The gods give no finer gift than a good enemy, my husband always says. Gettland could ask for no better enemy than the Breaker of Swords."

"You flatter me, and I enjoy it hugely. But where is King Uthil? I was so looking forward to renewing the friendship we forged in his Godshall."

"I fear my husband could not come," said Laithlin. "He sends me in his place."

Gorm gave a disappointed pout. "Few warriors so renowned. The battle will be the lesser for his absence. But the Mother of Crows waits for no man, whatever his fame."

"There is another choice." Yarvi eased his horse up beside the queen's. "A way in which bloodshed could be spared. A way in which we of the north could free ourselves from the yoke of the High King in Skekenhouse."

Gorm raised a brow. "Are you a magician as well as a minister?"

"We both pray to the same gods, both sing of the same heroes, both endure the same weather. Yet Grandmother Wexen turns us one against the other. If there is a battle at Amon's Tooth today, whoever is the victor, only she will win. What could Vansterland and Gettland not achieve together?" He leaned eagerly forward in his saddle. "Let us make of the fist an open hand! Let there be an alliance between us!"

Thorn gave a gasp at that, and she was not alone. A muttering went through the warriors on both sides, breathed oaths and angry glances, but the Breaker of Swords held up his hand for quiet.

"A bold idea, Father Yarvi. No doubt you are a deep-cunning man. You speak for Father Peace, as a minister should." Gorm worked his mouth unhappily, took a long breath through his nose, and let it sigh away. "But I fear it cannot be. My minister is of a different mind."

Yarvi blinked at Mother Scaer. "She is?"

"My new minister is."

"Greetings, Father Yarvi." Gorm's young white-haired sword-and shield-bearers parted to let a rider through, a cloaked rider upon a pale horse. She pushed her hood back and the wind blew up chill, lashing the yellow hair about her gaunt face, eyes fever-bright as she smiled. A smile so twisted with bitterness it was hard to look upon.

"You know Mother Isriun, I think," murmured Gorm.

"Odem's brat," hissed Queen Laithlin, and it was plain from her voice that this was no part of her plans.

"You are mistaken, my queen." Isriun gave her a crooked smile. "My only family now is the Ministry, just as Father Yarvi's is. Our only parent is Grandmother Wexen, eh, *brother?* After her abject failure in the First of Cities, she did not feel Sister Scaer could be trusted." Scaer's face twitched at that title. "She sent me to take her place."

"And you allowed it?" muttered Yarvi.

Gorm worked his tongue sourly around his mouth, clearly a long stride from pleased. "I have an oath to the High King to consider."

"The Breaker of Swords is wise as well as strong," said Isriun. "He remembers his proper place in the order of things." Gorm looked sourer yet at that, but kept a brooding silence. "Something you of Gettland have forgotten. Grandmother Wexen demands you be chastised for your arrogance, your insolence, your disloyalty. Even now the High King raises a great army of Lowlanders and Inglings in their countless thousands. He summons his champion, Bright Yilling, to command them! The greatest army the Shattered Sea has ever seen! Ready to march on Throvenland for the glory of the One God!"

Yarvi snorted. "And you stand with them, do you, Grom-gil-Gorm? You kneel before the High King? You prostrate yourself before his One God?"

The long hair fluttered across Gorm's scarred face in the wind, his frown carved from stone. "I stand where my oaths have put me, Father Yarvi."

"Still," said Isriun, her thin hands twisting eagerly together, "the

Ministry speaks always for peace. The One God offers always for-giveness, however little it may be deserved. To spare bloodshed is a noble desire. We stand by our offer of a duel of kings to settle the issue." Her lip curled. "But I fear Uthil is too old, and weak, and riddled with sickness to fight. No doubt the One God's punishment for his disloyalty."

Laithlin glanced across at Yarvi, and the minister gave the slightest nod. "Uthil sends me in his place," she said, and Thorn felt her heart, already beating hard, begin to thud against her ribs. "A challenge to a king must be a challenge to his queen also."

Mother Isriun barked scornful laughter. "Will you fight the Breaker of Swords, gilded queen?"

Laithlin's lip curled. "A queen does not fight, child. My Chosen Shield will stand for me."

And Thorn felt a terrible calm settle upon her, and inside her hood she began to smile.

"This is trickery," snapped Isriun, her own smile vanished.

"This is law," said Yarvi. "As minister to a king you should under-stand it. You gave the challenge. We accept."

Gorm waved a great hand as though at a bothersome fly. "Trick-ery or law, it is the same. I will fight anyone." He sounded almost bored. "Show me your champion, Laithlin, and at dawn tomorrow we will meet on this ground, and I will kill him, and break his sword, and add its pommel to my chain." He turned his dark eyes on the warriors of Gettland. "But your Chosen Shield should know that Mother War breathed on me in my crib, and it has been foreseen no man can kill me."

Laithlin gave a chill smile, and it was as if all things slotted smoothly into place like the workings of a lock, and the gods' purpose for Thorn Bathu was suddenly revealed.

"My Chosen Shield is not a man."

So it was time for the sword to be drawn. Thorn pulled off the cloak and flung it away. In silence Gettland's warriors parted and she nudged her horse between them, her gaze fixed on the King of Vansterland.

And as he saw her come his great brow furrowed with doubt.

"Grom-gil-Gorm," she said softly as she rode between Laithlin and Yarvi. "Breaker of Swords." Mother Isriun's horse shied back out of her way. "Maker of Orphans." Thorn reined in beside him, his frowning face lit red by the blazing light of her elf-bangle, and she leaned from her saddle to whisper.

"Your death comes."

# A BRAVE
# FACE

For a while afterward they didn't move. Her hair tickling his face, her ribs pressing on his with each hot breath. She kissed his open mouth, nuzzled his face, and he lay still. She slid off him, stretched out beside him with a contented grunt, and he lay still. She wriggled against him, working her head into his shoulder, breath getting slower, softer, and he lay still.

No doubt he should've been holding her like a miser clutches his gold, making the most of every moment they had.

But instead Brand felt sore, and surly, and scared. Instead her clammy skin against his felt as if it was trapping him, her heat smothering him, and he twisted free of her and stood, caught his head on the canvas in the darkness and thrashed it away with his hand, cursing, making the fabric flap and wobble.

"You surely taught my tent a lesson," came Thorn's voice.

He could hardly see any sign of her. Maybe a little crescent of light on her shoulder as she propped herself on one elbow. A gleam at the corners of her eyes. A glint of gold in her hair.

"You're going to fight him, then?" he said.

"I reckon."

"Grom-gil-Gorm."

"Unless he's so scared he decides not to turn up."

"The Breaker of Swords. The Maker of Orphans." The names dropped dead in the darkness. Names great warriors quailed at. Names mothers scared their children with. "How many duels has he fought?"

"They say a score."

"How many have you?"

"You know how many, Brand."

"None."

"It's around that number."

"How many men has he killed?"

"Pits full of them." Her voice was getting hard, now, a fiery glow under the blanket from her elf-bangle. "More than any man around the Shattered Sea, maybe."

"How many pommels on that chain of his? A hundred? Two?"

"And my father's is one of them."

"You looking to follow in his footsteps?"

That glow grew brighter, showing him the lines of her scowl. "Since you ask, I'm hoping to kill the big bastard and leave his corpse for the crows."

Silence between them, and someone passed outside with a torch, orange flaring across the side of Thorn's face, the star-shaped scar on her cheek. Brand knelt, level with her. "We could just go."

"No, we can't."

"Father Yarvi, he twisted you into this. A trick, a gamble, like that poisoner in Yaletoft. This is all his plan—"

"What if it is? I'm not a child, Brand, my eyes were open. I swore an oath to him and another to the queen and I knew what they meant. I knew I might have to fight for her. I knew I might have to die for her."

"If we took horses we could be ten miles off by dawn."

She kicked angrily at the blanket and lay back, hands over her face. "We're not running, Brand. Neither one of us. I told Gorm his death comes. Be a bit of a let-down for everyone if I never even arrived, wouldn't it?"

"We could go south to Throvenland, join a crew and go down the Divine. On to the First of Cities. Vialine would give us a place. For the gods' sake, Thorn, he's the Breaker of Swords—"

"Brand, stop!" she snarled, so suddenly that he jerked back. "You think I don't know all this? You think my head isn't buzzing with it already like a nest of bloody wasps? You think I don't know everyone in our camp is working at the same sums and coming to the same answer?" She leaned farther forward, eyes gleaming. "I'll tell you what you could do for me, Brand. You could be the one man in fifty miles who thinks I can win. Or at least pretends I can. This isn't your choice, it's mine, and I've made it. Your choice is to be my shoulder-man or go."

He knelt there naked, blinking for a moment as if he'd been slapped. Then he took a long, shuddering breath, and blew it out. "I'll always be your shoulder-man. Always."

"I know you will. But I'm meant to be the one terrified."

"I'm sorry." He reached out, touched her face in the darkness and she pressed her cheek into his hand. "It's just . . . It took us a long time getting here. I don't want to lose you."

"I don't want to be lost. But you know I was born to do this."

"If anyone can beat him, you can." He wished he believed it.

"I know. But I might not have much time left." She took his wrist, and dragged him into the bed. "I don't want to spend it talking."

BRAND SAT WITH THORN'S sword across his knees and polished it.

He'd polished it plain hilt to bright point a dozen times already. As the stars were snuffed out, and the sky brightened, and Mother Sun showed herself behind Amon's Tooth. The steel couldn't be any cleaner, the edge any keener. But still he scrubbed, muttering prayers to Mother War. Or the same prayer, over and over.

". . . let her live, let her live, let her live . . ."

You want a thing when you can't have it. When you get it you suddenly sprout doubts. Then when you think you might lose it you find you need it worse than ever.

Father Yarvi was muttering some prayers of his own while he tended to a pot over the fire, from time to time tossing a few dried leaves from one pouch or another into a brew that smelled like feet.

"You could probably stop polishing," he said.

"I can't stand in the square with her." Brand flipped the sword over and set furiously to work on the other side. "All I can do is polish and pray. I plan to do both the best I can."

Brand knew Thorn would show no fear. But she even had the hint of a smile as she sat, elbows on her knees and her hands calmly dangling, the elf-bangle on her wrist glowing bright. She had a steel guard on her left arm but otherwise no armor, just leather stitched in places with steel rings, bound tight with straps and belts so there was nothing left loose to catch a hold of. Queen Laithlin stood at her side, binding her tangled hair tight against her skull, fingers moving sure and steady as if it was for a wedding feast rather than a duel. Two brave faces there, and no mistake. The bravest in the camp, for all they were the two with most to lose.

So when Thorn glanced over at him, Brand did his best to nod back with a brave face of his own. That much he could do. That, and polish, and pray.

"Is she ready?" murmured Father Yarvi.

"It's Thorn. She's always ready. Whatever these idiots might think."

The warriors had been gathering since first light and now there was a whispering crowd looking on, pressed in about the tents, peering over one another's shoulders. Master Hunnan was in the front rank, and couldn't have frowned any harder without tearing the deep-creased skin on his forehead. Brand could see the dismay and disgust on their faces. That some girl should be fighting for Gettland's honor while the sworn warriors stood idle. A girl who'd failed a test and been named a murderer. A girl who wore no mail and carried no shield.

Thorn showed no sign of giving a damn for their opinion as she stood, though. She looked as long and lean as a spider, the way Skifr used to but taller, and broader, and stronger, and she spread her arms wide and worked the fingers, her jaw set hard and her narrowed eyes fixed on the valley.

Queen Laithlin set a hand on her shoulder. "May Mother War stand with you, my Chosen Shield."

"She always has, my queen," said Thorn.

"It's nearly time." Father Yarvi poured some of his brew into a cup and held it out with his good hand. "Drink this."

Thorn sniffed at it and jerked back. "Smells foul!"

"The best brews do. This will sharpen your senses, and quicken your hands and dull any pain."

"Is that cheating?"

"Mother Isriun will be using every trick she can devise." And Yarvi held out the steaming cup again. "A champion must win, the rest is dust."

Thorn held her nose, swallowed it down, and spat with disgust.

Rulf stepped up, shield held like a tray with two knives laid on it, freshly sharpened. "Sure you don't want mail?"

Thorn shook her head. "Speed will be my best armor and my best weapon. Speed, and surprise, and aggression. These might come in handy too, though." She took the blades and slid them into sheaths at her chest and her side.

"One more for luck." Brand held out the dagger that Rin made him, the one he'd carried up and down the Divine and the Denied. The one that saved his life out on the steppe.

"I'll keep it safe." Thorn slid it through her belt at the small of her back.

"I'd rather it kept you safe," murmured Brand.

"A lot of blades," said Father Yarvi.

"Got caught without any once and didn't enjoy the experience," said Thorn. "I won't be dying for lack of stabbing back, at least."

"You won't be dying." Brand made sure his voice held no doubts, even if his heart was bursting with them. "You'll be killing the bastard."

"Aye." She leaned close. "I feel like my guts are going to drop out of my arse."

"I'd never know."

"Fear keeps you careful," she muttered, hands opening and closing. "Fear keeps you alive."

"No doubt."

"I wish Skifr was here."

"You've got nothing left to learn from her."

"A little of that elf-magic might not hurt, though. Just in case."

"And rob you of the glory? No." Brand showed her both sides of the sword, a frosty glint to the edges he'd been polishing since the first hint of light. "Don't hesitate."

"Never," she said, as she slid the blade through the clasp at her side and held her hand out for the ax. "Why did you? That day on the beach?"

Brand thought back, back down a long, strange year to the training square on the sand. "I was thinking about doing good." He spun the ax around, steel etched with letters in five tongues flashing. "Looking at both sides of the case, like the fool I am."

"You'd have beaten me if you hadn't."

"Maybe."

Thorn slid the ax through its loop. "I would've failed my test and Hunnan would never have given me another. I wouldn't have killed Edwal. I wouldn't have been called a murderer. I wouldn't have been trained by Skifr, or rowed down the Divine, or saved the empress, or had songs sung of my high deeds."

"I wouldn't have lost my place on the king's raid," said Brand. "I'd be a proud warrior of Gettland now, doing just as Master Hunnan told me."

"And my mother would have married me off to some old fool, and I'd be wearing his key all wrong and sewing very badly."

"You wouldn't be facing Grom-gil-Gorm."

"No. But we'd never have had . . . whatever we've got."

He looked into her eyes for a moment. "I'm glad I hesitated."

"So am I." She kissed him, then. One last kiss before the storm. Her lips soft against his. Her breath hot in the dawn chill.

"Thorn?" Koll was standing beside them. "Gorm's in the square."

Brand wanted to scream, then, but he forced himself to smile instead. "The sooner you start, the sooner you kill him."

He drew Odda's sword and started beating on Rulf's shield with the hilt, and others did the same with their own weapons, their own armor, noise spreading out through the ranks, and men began to shout, to roar, to sing out their defiance. She was nowhere near the champion they'd have picked, but she was Gettland's champion even so.

And Thorn strode tall through a thunder of clashing metal, the warriors parting before her like the earth before the plow.

Striding to her meeting with the Breaker of Swords.

# STEEL

"I have been waiting for you," said Grom-gil-Gorm in his sing-song voice.

He sat upon a stool with his white-haired blade- and shield-bearers kneeling to either side, one of them smiling at Thorn, the other scowling as if he might fight her himself. Behind them, along the eastern edge of the square, twenty of Gorm's closest warriors were ranged, Mother Isriun glaring from their midst, hair stirred about her gaunt face by a breath of wind, Sister Scaer sullen beside her. Behind them were hundreds more fighting men, black outlines along the top of the ridge, Mother Sun bright as she rose beyond Amon's Tooth.

"Thought I'd give you a little more time alive." Thorn put on her bravest face as she stepped between Queen Laithlin and Father Yarvi. Stepped out in front of Gettland's twenty best and into that little plot of close-cut grass. A square just like the many she'd trained in, eight strides on a side, a spear driven into the ground at each corner.

A square where either she or Grom-gil-Gorm would die.

"No gift to me." The Breaker of Swords shrugged his great shoulders and his heavy mail, forged with zigzag lines of gold, gave an iron whisper. "Time drags when the Last Door stands so near."

"Perhaps it stands nearer for you than for me."

"Perhaps." He toyed thoughtfully with one of the pommels on his chain. "You are Thorn Bathu, then?"

"Yes."

"This one they sing the songs of?"

"Yes."

"The one who saved the Empress of the South?"

"Yes."

"The one who won a priceless relic from her." Gorm glanced down at the elf-bangle, glowing red as a burning coal on Thorn's wrist, and raised his brows. "I had taken those songs for lies."

She shrugged. "Some of them."

"However grand the truth, it is never enough for the skalds, eh?" Gorm took his shield from the smiling boy, a mighty thing, painted black with a rim scored and dented by a hundred old blows. Gifts from the many men he had killed in squares like this one. "I think we met before."

"In Skekenhouse. Where you knelt before the High King."

His cheek gave the faintest twitch of displeasure. "We all must kneel to someone. I should have known you sooner, but you have changed."

"Yes."

"You are Storn Headland's daughter."

"Yes."

"That was a glorious duel." The frowning boy offered Gorm's sword and he curled his great fingers about the grip and drew it. A monstrous blade, Thorn would have needed both hands to swing it but he carried it lightly as a willow switch. "Let us hope ours will make as jolly a song."

"Don't count on the same outcome," said Thorn, watching Mother Sun's reflection flash down his steel. He would have the reach, the strength, the armor but, weighed down by all that metal, she would have the speed. She would last the longer. Who would have the upper hand in the contest of wits, it remained to be seen.

"I have fought a score of duels, and put a score of brave men in their howes, and learned one thing. Never count on the outcome." Gorm's eyes moved over her clothes, her weapons, judging her as she was judging him. She wondered what strengths he saw. What weaknesses. "I never fought a woman before, though."

"Nor will you again. This is your last fight." She raised her chin at him. "Mother War's breath will not shield you from me."

She had hoped for anger, some sign he might be taunted into rashness, but all the King of Vansterland gave her was a sad little smile. "Ah, the confidence of the young. It was foreseen no man could kill me." And he stood, his great shadow stretching toward her across the stubbled grass, a giant stepped out from the songs. "Not that you could."


"MOTHER WAR, LET HER LIVE," mouthed Brand, both fists clenched aching tight. "Mother War, let her live . . ."

An eerie silence fell across the valley as the fighters took their places. Only the stirring of the wind in the grass, a bird calling high and harsh in the iron sky, the faint jingle of war-gear as one man or another shifted nervously. Mother Isriun stepped out into the lonely space between the two champions.

"Are you ready to kill? Are you ready to die?" She held up her hand, a curl of white goose-down in her fingers. "Are you ready to face the One God's judgment?"

Gorm stood straight and tall, huge as a mountain, his broad shield held before him, his long sword out behind. "Mother War will be my judge," he growled.

Thorn crouched low, teeth bared in a vicious grin, tense as a full-bent bow. "Whichever." She turned her head and spat. "I'm ready."

"Then begin!" called Mother Isriun, and let the feather fall, and hurried back, out of the short grass and into the rank of warriors opposite.

Down that feather drifted, slow, slow, every eye on both sides fixed upon it. It was caught by an eddy, whirled and spun. Down it drifted, and down, every breath on both sides held.

"Mother War, let her live, Mother War, let her live . . ."

THE INSTANT THAT SCRAP of down touched the close-cropped grass Thorn sprang. She had not forgotten Skifr's lessons. They were in her flesh. Always attack. Strike first. Strike last.

One stride and the wind rushed at her. Gorm stayed rigid, watching. Two strides and she crushed the feather into the dirt beneath her heel. Still he was frozen. Three strides and she was on him, screaming, swinging high with Skifr's ax, low with the sword forged from her father's bones. Now he moved, moved to meet her, and her blade crashed on his, and the ax chopped splinters from his shield.

In that instant she knew she had never fought anyone so strong. She was used to a shield giving when she hit it, used to staggering a man with the weight of her blows. But striking Gorm's shield was like striking a deep-rooted oak. Striking his sword jarred her from her palm to the tip of her nose and left her bared teeth rattling.

Thorn had never been one to get discouraged at the first reverse, though.

Gorm had thrust his heavy left boot recklessly forward and she dropped low, trying to hook it with her ax and bring him down. He stepped back nimbly for all his mountainous bulk and she heard him grunt, felt the great sword coming, whipping at her like a scorpion's tail. She only just lurched under as it ripped past at a vicious angle, a blow to split shields, to split helms, to split heads, the wind of it cold on her face.

She twisted, watching for the opening a swing like that must leave, but there was none. Gorm handled that monstrous blade as neatly as

Thorn's mother might a needle, no rage or madness in it, all control. His eyes stayed calm. His door of a shield never drifted.

That first exchange she judged a draw, and she danced back into room to wait for another chance. To seek out a better opening.

Slowly, carefully, the Breaker of Swords took one step toward the center of the square, twisting his great left boot into the sod.

"YES!" HISSED RULF AS Thorn darted in, letting go a flurry of blows. "Yes!" Blades clattered as they scarred Gorm's shield, Brand clenching his fists so tight the nails bit at his palms.

He gasped as Thorn rolled under the shining arc of Gorm's sword, came up snarling to hack at his shield, pushed a great thrust scornfully away and danced back out of range, using the full width of the square. She went in a drunken swagger, weapons drifting, the way that Skifr used to, and Gorm studied her over the rim of his shield, trying to find some pattern in the chaos.

"He is cautious," hissed Queen Laithlin.

"Stripped of the armor of his prophecy," muttered Father Yarvi. "He fears her."

The King of Vansterland took one more slow step, twisting his boot into the ground again as though he were laying the foundation stone of a hero's hall. He was all stillness, Thorn all movement.

"Like Mother Sea against Father Earth," murmured Rulf.

"Mother Sea always wins that battle," said Laithlin.

"Given time," said Father Yarvi.

Brand winced, unable to look, unable to look away. "Mother War, let her live . . ."

GORM'S SHIELD WAS SOLID as a citadel's gate. Thorn couldn't have broken it down with a ram and twenty strong men. And getting around it would hardly be easier. She'd never seen a shield handled so cleverly. Quick to move it, he was, and even quicker to move behind it, but he held it high. Each step he took that big left boot of his crept too far forward, more of his leg showing below the bottom rim than was prudent. Each time she saw it happen it seemed more a weakness.

Tempting. So tempting.

Too tempting, maybe?

Only a fool would think a warrior of his fame would have no tricks, and Thorn was no one's fool. Be quicker, tougher, cleverer, Skifr said. She had tricks of her own.

She let her eyes rest on that boot, licking her lips as if she watched the meat brought in, long enough to make sure he saw her watching, then she moved. His sword darted out but she was ready, slipped around it, Skifr's ax whipping across, but shoulder-high, not low where he expected it. She saw his eyes go wide. He lurched back, jerking up the shield, caught her ax with the rim, but the bearded blade still thudded into his shoulder, mail rings flying like dust from a beaten carpet.

She expected him to drop back, maybe even fall, but he shrugged her ax off as if it was a harsh word, pressed forward, too close for his sword or hers. The rim of his shield caught her in the mouth as she tumbled away and sent her staggering. No pain, no doubt, no dizziness. The shock of it only made her sharper. She heard Gorm roar, saw Mother Sun catch steel and dodged back as his blade whistled past.

That exchange she had to judge a draw as well, but they were both marked now.

Blood on his mail. Blood on his shield rim. Blood on her ax. Blood in her mouth. She bared her teeth at him in a fighting snarl and spat red onto the grass between them.

# BLOOD

Like a pack of dogs, the sight of blood brought the gathered warriors suddenly to life, and the noise couldn't have been more deafening if they'd had the battle after all.

From the ridge in front the Vanstermen screeched prayers and bellowed curses, from the ridge behind the Gettlanders roared out futile encouragements, pointless advice. They rattled axes on shields, swords on helmets, sent up a din of lust and fury to wake the dead in their howes, to wake the gods from slumber.

Of all things, men most love to watch others face Death. It reminds them they yet live.

Across the square, among the snarling, snapping Vanstermen, Brand saw Mother Isriun, livid with fury, and Mother Scaer beside her, eyes calmly narrowed as she watched the contest.

Gorm swung a great overhead and Thorn twitched away, his sword missing her by a hand's breadth and opening a huge wound in the ground, grass and earth showering up. Brand bit his knuckle, painful hard. It would only take one of those to find her and that heavy steel could cut her clean in half. It felt as if it was a day since the fight began and he hadn't taken a breath the whole time.

"Mother War, let her live . . ."

THORN STRUTTED ABOUT THE SQUARE. It was her grass. She owned it. Queen of this mud. She hardly heard the screaming warriors on the high ground, barely saw Laithlin, or Isriun, or Yarvi, or even Brand. The world had shrunk to her, and the Breaker of Swords, and the few short strides of short grass between them, and she was starting to like what she saw.

Gorm was breathing hard, sweat across his furrowed forehead. The weight of all that gear was bound to tell, but she hadn't hoped it would be so soon. His shield was beginning to droop. She almost laughed. She could have done this for hours. She had done it for hours, for days, for weeks, down the Divine and the Denied and back.

She sprang in, aiming high with her sword. Too high, so he could duck, and duck he did, but just as she had planned his shield tipped forward. It was an easy thing to step around it, hook the top rim with the bearded head of Skifr's ax, marked with letters in five tongues. She meant to drag it down, leave him open, maybe tear it from his arm altogether, but she misjudged him. He roared, ripping his shield upwards, tearing the ax from her grip and sending it spinning high into the air.

That left his body unguarded for a moment, though, and Thorn had never been one to hesitate. Her sword hissed in below his shield and struck him in the side. Hard enough to fold him slightly, to make him stumble. Hard enough to cut through mail and find the flesh beneath.

Not hard enough to stop him, though.

He snarled, swung once and made her stagger back, thrust and made her dance away, chopped again, even harder, steel hissing at the air, but she was already backing off, watchful, circling.

As he turned toward her she saw the ragged tear in his mail, links flapping free, blood glistening. She saw how he favored that side as he took up his stance, and she began to smile as she filled her empty left hand with her longest dagger.

She might have lost her ax, but that round was hers.

NOW, THORN WAS ONE of them. Now she'd bloodied Grom-gil-Gorm and Master Hunnan thrust his fist in the air, roared his support. Now the warriors who'd sneered at her made a deafening din in admiration of her prowess.

No doubt those with the gift were already setting the song of her triumph in verse. They tasted victory, but all Brand could taste was fear. His heart thudded as loud as Rin's hammer. He twitched and gasped with every movement in the square. He'd never felt so helpless. He couldn't do good. He couldn't do bad. He couldn't do anything.

Thorn darted forward, going low with her sword, so fast Brand could hardly follow it. Gorm dropped his shield to block but she was already gone, slashing across the top of his shield with her dagger. Gorm jerked his head back, staggered a step, a red line across his cheek, across his nose, under his eye.

THE BATTLE JOY WAS on her now. Or maybe Father Yarvi's brew was.

The breath ripped at her chest, she danced on air. The blood sweet in her mouth, her skin on fire. She smiled, smiled so wide it seemed her scarred cheeks might split.

The cut below Gorm's eye was leaking, streaks of blood down his face, out of his slit nose, into his beard.

He was tiring, he was hurt, he was growing careless. She had his measure and he knew it. She could see the fear in his eyes. Could see the doubt, ever growing.

His shield had drifted up even higher to guard his wounded face.

His stance had loosened, his heavy sword wilting in his grip. That left leg slipped still farther forward, all exposed, knee wobbling.

Perhaps it had been a trick, in the beginning, but what trick could stop her now? She breathed fire and spat lightning. She was the storm, always moving. She was Mother War made flesh.

"Your death comes!" she screamed at him, words even she could hardly hear over the noise.

She would kill the Breaker of Swords, and avenge her father, and prove herself the greatest warrior about the Shattered Sea. The greatest warrior in the world! The songs they would sing of this!

She led him in a circle, led him around until her back was to the Vanstermen, until her back was to the east. She saw Gorm narrow his eyes as Mother Sun stabbed at them, twisting away, leaving his leg unguarded. She feinted high, tightening her fingers about the grip, ducked under an ill-timed chop and screamed out as she swept her sword in a great, low circle.

The blade forged with her father's bones struck Gorm's leg above the ankle with all Thorn's strength, and anger, and training behind it. The moment of her victory. The moment of her vengeance.

But instead of slicing through flesh and bone the bitter edge clanged on metal, jarred in Thorn's hand so badly she stumbled forward, off-balance.

Hidden armor. Steel glinting beneath the slit leather of Gorm's boot.

He moved quick as a snake, not near so tired nor so hurt as he had made her think, chopping down, catching her blade with his and tearing it from her numbed fingers.

She lashed at him with her knife but he caught it on his shield and rammed the boss into her ribs. It was like being kicked by a horse and she tottered back, only just staying on her feet.

Gorm glared at her over his shield rim, and it was his turn to smile. "You are a worthy opponent," he said. "As dangerous as any I have fought." He stepped forward, planting that armored boot on her fallen sword and grinding it into the sod. "But your death comes."

———

"OH, GODS," CROAKED BRAND, cold right through to his bones.

Thorn was fighting with two knives now, no reach, and Gorm was herding her around the square with shining sweeps of his great sword, seeming stronger than ever.

The men of Gettland had fallen suddenly quiet, while the noise from across the valley redoubled.

Brand prayed Thorn would stay away but knew her only chance was to close with him. Sure enough, she ducked under a high cut and flung herself forward, stabbed with her right, a vicious, flashing over-hand, but Gorm heaved his shield up, her blade thudding deep be-tween two boards and lodging tight.

"Kill him!" hissed Queen Laithlin.

Thorn slashed at Gorm's sword-arm with her left as he brought it back, dagger scraping down his mail and catching his hand, blood spattering as the great sword tumbled from his grip.

Or perhaps he let it fall. As she stabbed at him again he caught her arm, his fingers closing about her wrist with a smack that was like a punch in Brand's stomach.

"Oh, gods," he croaked.

# BREATH

Thorn snatched for Brand's dagger but her elbow tangled with Gorm's loose shield and he stepped close, smothering her. He had her left wrist tight and he wrenched it up, the elf-bangle grinding into her flesh. He let go the handle of his shield and caught her right sleeve.

"I have you!" he snarled.

"No!" She twisted back as if she was trying to wriggle free and he dragged her closer. "I have you!"

She jerked forward, using his strength against him, butted him full in the jaw and snapped his head up. She set her knee against his ribs, screamed as she ripped her right arm free.

He kept his crushing grip on her left wrist, though. She had one nce. Just one. She tore Brand's dagger from the small of her back, ed at Gorm's neck as his eyes came back toward her.

jerked his shield hand up to ward her off and the blade punched the meat of it, snake-worked crosspiece smacking against his snarled as she drove his hand back, his shield flopping loose ps, but with a trembling effort he stopped the bright point just short of his throat, held it there, pink spit flecking from his bared teeth.

Then, even though his hand was stabbed right through, the great fingers closed about her right fist and trapped her tight.

Thorn strained with every fiber to push the red blade into his neck, but you will not beat a strong man with strength, and there was no man as strong as the Breaker of Swords. He had both her hands pinned and he set his shoulder, let go a growl, and pressed her trembling back, back toward the edge of the square, hot blood leaking from his punctured palm and down the hilt of the dagger, wetting her crushed fist.

BRAND GAVE A SICK GROAN as Gorm forced Thorn down onto her knees in front of the jeering warriors of Vansterland.

Her elf-bangle glowed red through the flesh of his clutching sword hand, bones showing black inside, squeezing, squeezing. She gasped through her gritted teeth as the knife toppled from the loose fingers of her left hand, bounced from her shoulder and away into the grass, and Gorm let go her wrist and caught her tight around the throat.

Brand tried to take a step into the square but Father Yarvi had him by one arm, Rulf by the other, wrestling him back.

"No," hissed the helmsman in his ear.

"Yes!" shrieked Mother Isriun, staring down in delight.

NO BREATH.

Thorn's every hard-trained muscle strained but Gorm was too strong, and back he twisted her, and back. His grip crushed her right hand around the handle of Brand's dagger, bones groaning. She fumbled in the grass with the other for her knife but couldn't find it, punched at his knee but there was no strength in it, tried to reach his face but could only tear weakly at his bloody beard.

"Kill her!" shouted Mother Isriun.

Gorm forced Thorn toward the ground, blood dripping from his snarl and pattering on her cheek. Her chest heaved, but all that happened was a dead squelching in her throat.

No breath. Her face was burning. She could hardly hear the storm of voices for the surging of blood in her head. She plucked at Gorm's hand with her numb fingertips, tore at it with her nails but it was forged from iron, carved from wood, ruthless as the roots of trees that over years will burst the very rock apart.

"Kill her!" Even though she could see Mother Isriun's face, twisted in triumph above her, she could only just hear her shriek. "The High King decrees it! The One God ordains it!"

Gorm's eyes flickered sideways to his minister, his cheek twitching. His grip seemed to loosen, but perhaps that was Thorn's grip on life, slipping, slipping.

No breath. It was growing dark. She faced the Last Door, no tricks left to play. Death slid the bolt, pushed it wide. She teetered on the threshold.

But Gorm did not push her over.

As if through a shadowy veil she saw his forehead crease.

"Kill her!" screeched Mother Isriun, her voice going higher and higher, wilder and wilder. "Grandmother Wexen demands it! Grandmother Wexen *commands* it!"

And Gorm's bloody face shuddered again, a spasm from his eye down to his jaw. His lips slipped back over his teeth and left his mouth a straight, flat line. His right hand relaxed, and Thorn heaved in a choking breath, the world tipping over as she flopped onto her side.


BRAND WATCHED IN DISBELIEF as Gorm let Thorn fall and turned slowly to stare at Isriun. The hungry snarls of his warriors began to fade, the crowds above fell silent, the noise all guttering out to leave a shocked quiet.

"I am the Breaker of Swords." Gorm put his right hand ever so gently on his chest. "What madness makes you speak to me in such a fashion?"

Isriun pointed down at Thorn, rolling onto her face, coughing puke into the grass. "Kill her!"

"No."

"Grandmother Wexen commands—"

"I tire of Grandmother Wexen's commands!" roared Gorm, eyes near-popping from his bloody face. "I tire of the High King's arrogance! But most of all, Mother Isriun . . ." He bared his teeth in a horrible grimace as he twisted Brand's dagger from his shield hand. "I tire of your voice. Its constant bleating grates upon me."

Mother Isriun's face had turned deathly pale. She tried to shrink back but Scaer's tattooed arm snaked about her shoulders and held her tight. "You would break your oaths to them?" muttered Isriun, eyes wide.

"Break my oaths?" Gorm shook the scarred shield from his arm and let it clatter down. "There is less honor in keeping them. I shatter them. I spit on them. I shit on them." He loomed over Isriun, the knife glinting red in his hand. "The High King decrees, does he? Grandmother Wexen commands, does she? Old goat and old sow, I renounce them! I defy them!"

Isriun's thin neck fluttered as she swallowed. "If you kill me there will be war."

"Oh, there will be war. The Mother of Crows spreads her wings, girl." Grom-gil-Gorm slowly raised the knife that Rin had forged, Isriun's eyes rooted to the bright point. "Her feathers are swords! Hear them rattle?" And a smile spread across his face. "But I do not need to kill you." He tossed the knife skittering through the grass to end beside Thorn where she hunched on hands and knees, retching. "After all, Mother Scaer, why kill what you can sell?"

Gorm's old minister, and now his new one, gave a smile chill as the winter sea. "Take this snake away and put a collar on her."

"You'll pay!" shrieked Isriun, eyes wild. "You'll pay for this!" But Gorm's warriors were already dragging her up the eastern slope.

The Breaker of Swords turned back, blood dripping from the dangling fingers of his wounded hand. "Does your offer of alliance still stand, Laithlin?"

"What could Vansterland and Gettland not achieve together?" called the Golden Queen.

"Then I accept."

A stunned sigh rippled around the square, as if the held breath of every man was suddenly let out.

Brand twisted free of Rulf's limp hands and ran.


"THORN?"

The voice seemed to echo from a long way away, down a dark tunnel. Brand's voice. Gods, she was glad to hear it.

"You all right?" Strong hands at her shoulder, lifting her.

"I got proud," she croaked, throat raw, mouth stinging. Tried to get to her knees, so weak and dizzy she nearly fell again, but he caught her.

"But you're alive."

"I reckon," she whispered, more than a little surprised as Brand's face drifted gradually out of the bright blur. Gods, she was glad to see it.

"That's enough." He stretched her arm over his shoulders and she groaned as he lifted her gently to her feet. She couldn't have taken a step on her own, but he was strong. He wouldn't let her fall. "You need me to carry you?"

"It's a fine thought." She winced as she looked toward the warriors of Gettland gathered on the crest ahead of them. "But I'd better walk. Why didn't he kill me?"

"Mother Isriun changed his mind."

Thorn took one look back as they shuffled up the slope toward the camp. Grom-gil-Gorm stood in the middle of the square, bloodied but unbeaten. Mother Scaer was already working at his wounded shield hand with needle and thread. His sword-hand was gripping

Queen Laithlin's, sealing the alliance between Vansterland and Gettland. Bitter enemies made friends. At least for now.

Beside them, with arms folded, Yarvi smiled.

In spite of all the prayers to Mother War, it seemed Father Peace made the judgment that day.

# IN THE
# LIGHT

Brand gave the billet a few more ringing blows with his hammer then shoved it back into the coals in a shower of sparks.

Rin gave a disgusted click of her tongue. "You've not got what they call a gentle touch, have you?"

"That's what you're here for." Brand grinned at her. "Got to make you feel special, don't I?"

But she was looking past him, toward the door. "You've a visitor."

"Father Yarvi, what an honor." Brand set down his hammer and wiped his forehead on his forearm. "Come to buy a blade?"

"A minister should stand for Father Peace," said Yarvi as he stepped into the forge.

"A good one stays friendly with Mother War too," said Rin.

"Wise words. And now more than ever."

Brand swallowed. "It's going to be war, then?"

"The High King will take time gathering his warriors. But I think it will be war. Still. War is a fine thing for a swordsmith's business."

Rin raised her brows at Brand. "We'd settle for a poorer peace, I reckon. I hear King Uthil's on the mend, at least."

"His strength rushes back," said Yarvi. "Soon he will be terrorizing his warriors once again at sword practice, and using your fine steel to do it."

"Father Peace be praised," said Rin.

"Father Peace and your skills," said Brand.

Yarvi humbly bowed. "I do what I can. And how do the gods treat you, Brand?"

"Well enough." He nodded at his sister. "If it wasn't for my tyrant of a master I'd be enjoying the job. Turns out I like working with metal a lot more than I remembered."

"Easier than working with people."

"Steel is honest," said Brand.

Father Yarvi looked sideways at him. "Is there somewhere we can speak alone?"

Brand looked over at Rin, already pounding at the bellows. She shrugged. "Steel is patient too."

"You're not, though."

"Go have your talk." She narrowed her eyes at him. "Before I change my mind."

Brand pulled his gloves off and led Yarvi out into the little yard, noisy with the sound of running water. He sat on the bench Koll had carved for them in the dappled shade of the tree, breeze cool on his sweat-sheened face, and offered Father Yarvi the place beside him.

"A pleasant spot." The minister smiled up at Mother Sun, flashing and flickering through the leaves. "It's a fine life you and your sister have made for yourselves."

"She made it. I just happened along."

"You've always played your part. I remember you taking the weight of the *South Wind* across your shoulders." Yarvi looked down at the scars snaking up Brand's forearms. "There was a feat to sing of."

"I find I care less for songs than I used to."

"You are learning. How is Thorn?"

"Already back to training three-quarters of every day."

"She is carved from wood, that one."

"No woman firmer touched by Mother War."

"And yet she has been the needle that stitched two great alliances together. Perhaps she was touched by Father Peace too."

"Don't tell her that."

"The two of you are still . . . together?"

"Aye." Brand had a sense the minister knew these answers, but that every question had another hidden in it. "You could call it that."

"Good. That's good."

"I suppose so," he said, thinking of the screaming argument they'd had that morning.

"It's not good?"

"It's good," he said, thinking of how they'd made up afterward. "It's just . . . I always thought of being together as the end of the work. Turns out it's where the work starts."

"No road worth traveling is easy," said Father Yarvi. "Each of you has strengths the other lacks, weaknesses the other makes up for. It is a fine thing, a rare thing, to find someone who . . ." He frowned up at the shifting branches, as though he thought of something far away, and the thought was painful. "Makes you whole."

Took a little while for Brand to gather the courage to speak. "I've been thinking about melting down that coin Prince Varoslaf gave me."

"To make a key?"

Brand pushed a couple of fallen leaves around with the side of his boot. "Probably she'd prefer a dagger but . . . a key's traditional. What do you think Queen Laithlin would think of it?"

"The queen has had three sons and no daughters. I think she is becoming very much attached to her Chosen Shield. But I'm sure she could be persuaded."

Brand gave those leaves another push. "No doubt folk think I'm the one should wear the key. I'm none too popular in Thorlby."

"The king's warriors are not all admirers of yours, it is true. Master Hunnan in particular. But I have heard it said enemies are the price of success. Perhaps they are the price of conviction too."

"The price of cowardice, maybe."

"Only a fool would reckon you a coward, Brand. To stand up before the warriors of Gettland and speak as you did?" Father Yarvi put his lips together and gave a faint whistle. "People may sing no hero's songs of it, but that was rare courage."

"You think so?"

"I do, and courage is not your only admirable quality."

Brand hardly knew what to say to that, so he said nothing.

"Did you know Rulf melted down his earnings from our voyage and made a key of his own?"

"For who?"

"Thorn's mother. They are being married in the Godshall next week."

Brand blinked. "Oh."

"Rulf is getting old. He would never say so, but he is keen to step back." Yarvi looked sideways. "I think you would do well in his place."

Brand blinked again. "Me?"

"I told you once that I might need a man beside me who thinks of doing good. I think so more than ever."

"Oh." Brand couldn't think of anything else to say.

"You could join Safrit, and Koll, and be part of my little family." Every word Father Yarvi let drop was carefully weighed out and these did not fall by accident. He knew just what to offer. "You would be close to me. Close to the queen. Close to the queen's Chosen Shield. The helmsman of a minister's ship." He remembered that day on the steering platform, the crew thumping at their oars, the sunlight bright on the water of the Denied. "You would stand at the right hand of the man who stands at the right hand of the king."

Brand paused, rubbing at his fingertips with his thumbs. No doubt he should've leapt at the chance. A man like him couldn't expect too many like it. Yet something held him back. "You're a deep-cunning man, Father Yarvi, and I'm not known for my wits."

"You could be, if you used them. But it's your strong arm and your strong heart I want you for."

"Can I ask you a question?"

"You can ask. But make sure you want the answer."

"How long had you planned for Thorn to fight a duel with Grom-gil-Gorm?"

Yarvi narrowed his pale eyes a little. "A minister must deal in like-lihoods, in chances, in possibilities. That one occurred to me long ago."

"When I came to you in the Godshall?"

"I told you then the good thing is a different thing for every man. I considered the possibility that a woman who could use a sword might one day find a way to challenge Gorm. Great and storied war-rior that he is, he would not be able to turn down a woman's chal-lenge. And yet he would fear one. More than any man."

"You believe that prophecy?"

"I believe that he believes it."

"That was why you had Skifr train her."

"One reason. The Empress Theofora loved rare things, and also loved to watch blood spilled, and I thought a fighting girl from the far north might excite her curiosity long enough for me to speak to her, and present my gift. Death ushered Theofora through the Last Door before I got the chance." Yarvi gave a sigh. "A good minister strives to look ahead, but the future is a land wrapped in fog. Events do not always flow down the channel you dig for them."

"Like your deal with Mother Scaer."

"Another hope. Another gamble." Father Yarvi sat back against the trunk of the tree. "I needed an alliance with the Vanstermen, but Mother Isriun spoiled that notion. She gave the challenge, though, and a duel was better than a battle." He spoke calmly, coldly, as though he spoke of pieces on a board rather than people he knew.

Brand's mouth felt very dry. "If Thorn had died, what then?"

"Then we would have sung sad songs over her howe, and happy songs over her high deeds." Yarvi's were the eyes of a butcher who looks at livestock, judging where the profit is. "But we and the Vanstermen would not have wasted our strength fighting each other. Queen Laithlin and I would have prostrated ourselves at the feet of Grandmother Wexen and made golden apologies. King Uthil would have recovered, free of dishonor. In time we might have thrown the dice again."

Something in Father Yarvi's words niggled at Brand, like a hook in his head, tickling, tickling. "We all thought King Uthil was at the Last Door. How could you be sure he'd recover?"

Yarvi paused for a moment, his mouth half-open, then carefully shut it. He looked toward the doorway, the clanging of Rin's hammer echoing from beyond, and back to Brand. "I think you are a more cunning man than you pretend."

Brand had a feeling he stood on spring ice, cracks spreading beneath his boots, but there was no going back, only forward. "If I'm to stand at your shoulder I should know the truth."

"I told you once that the truth is like the good thing, each man has his own. My truth is that King Uthil is a man of iron, and iron is strong, and holds a fine edge. But iron can be brittle. And sometimes we must bend."

"He would never have made peace with the Vanstermen."

"And we had to make peace with the Vanstermen. Without them we stand alone against half the world."

Brand slowly nodded, seeing the pieces of it slide into place. "Uthil would have accepted Gorm's duel."

"He would have fought Gorm in the square, for he is proud, and he would have lost, for each year leaves him weaker. I must protect my king from harm. For his good, and the good of the land. We needed allies. We went seeking allies. I found allies."

Brand thought of the minister bent over the fire, throwing dried leaves into the brew. "You poisoned him. Your own uncle."

"I have no uncle, Brand. I gave my family up when I joined the

Ministry." Yarvi's voice held no guilt. No doubt. No regret. "Sometimes great rights must be stitched from little wrongs. A minister does not have the luxury of doing what is simply good. A minister must weigh the greater good. A minister must choose the lesser evil."

"Power means having one shoulder always in the shadows," muttered Brand.

"It does. It must."

"I understand. I don't doubt you, but . . ."

Father Yarvi blinked, and Brand wondered whether he'd ever seen him look surprised before. "You refuse me?"

"My mother told me to stand in the light."

They sat there for a moment, looking at one another, then Father Yarvi slowly began to smile. "I admire you for it, I truly do." He stood up, laying his good hand on Brand's shoulder. "But when Mother War spreads her wings, she may cast the whole Shattered Sea into darkness."

"I hope not," said Brand.

"Well." Father Yarvi turned away. "You know how it goes, with hopes." And he walked into the house, and left Brand sitting in the shade of the tree, wondering, as ever, if he'd done a good thing or a bad.

"A little help here!" came his sister's voice.

Brand started up. "On my way!"

# A STORM
# COMING

Thorn strode across the sand with her stool on her shoulder. The tide was far out and the wind blew hard over the flats, tattered clouds chasing each other across a bruised sky.

They were packed in tight about the training square, the shouts turning to grunts as she pushed through the warriors, the grunts to silence as she set her stool next to the spear that marked one corner. Even the two lads who were meant to be sparring came to an uncertain halt, staring at her as she stepped over her stool and planted her arse on it.

Master Hunnan frowned over. "I see the queen's Chosen Shield is among us."

Thorn held up one hand. "Don't worry, you needn't all applaud."

"The training square is for warriors of Gettland, and for those who would be warriors."

"Aye, but there's probably some half-decent fighters down here even so. Don't let me stop you."

"You won't," snapped Hunnan. "Heirod, you're next." It was a great big lad that stood, pink blotches on his fat cheeks. "And you,

Edni." She was maybe twelve years old, and a skinny scrap, but she sprang up bravely enough, her chin thrust out as she took her mark, even though the shield was way too big for her and wobbled in her hand.

"Begin!"

There was no art to it at all. The boy went charging in, puffing like a bull, shrugged Edni's sword off his thick shoulder, barrelled into her and sent her sprawling, the shield coming off her arm and rolling away on its edge.

The boy looked at Hunnan, waiting for him to call the bout, but the master-at-arms only stared back. Heirod swallowed, and stepped forward, and gave Edni a couple of reluctant kicks before Hunnan raised his hand for a halt.

Thorn watched the girl clamber up, wiping blood from under her nose, clinging tight to her brave face, and thought of all the beatings she'd taken in this square. Thought of all the kicks and the scorn and the sand she'd eaten. Thought of that last day, and Edwal with her wooden sword through his neck. No doubt nudging her memory had been what Master Hunnan had in mind.

He gave a rare, thin little smile. "What did you think of that?"

"I think the boy's a clumsy thug." She pressed her thumb on one side of her nose and blew snot onto the sand. "But it's not his fault. He learned from one, and so did she. The one who got shamed in that bout was their teacher."

A muttering went through the warriors, and Hunnan's smile sprang back into a frown. "If you think you know better, why don't you give a lesson?"

"That's why I'm here, Master Hunnan. I've nothing to learn from you, after all." She pointed to Edni. "I'll take her," Then she pointed out an older girl, big and solemn. "And her." And then another with pale, pale eyes. "And her. I'll give them a lesson. I'll give them one a day, and in a month we'll come back, and we'll see what we'll see."

"You can't just come here and take my pupils where you please!"

"Yet here I am, and with King Uthil's blessing."

Hunnan licked his lips, wrong-footed, but he soon rallied, and fixed on attack. "Hild Bathu," his lip curled with disgust. "You failed your test in this square. You failed to become a warrior. You lost to the Breaker of Swords—"

"I lost to Gorm, true." Thorn rubbed at one scarred cheek as she grinned up at him. "But he never broke my sword." She stood, one hand slack on the pommel. "And you're not Gorm." She stepped across the sand toward him. "Reckon you're better than me?" And she stepped so close she almost planted her boots on his. "Fight me." She leaned in, so their noses were near touching, and hissed it over and over. "Fight me. Fight me. Fight me. Fight me. Fight me. Fight me. Fight me."

Hunnan flinched each time she said it, but he kept his silence.

"Good choice," she said. "I'd snap you like an old twig."

She shouldered past him, calling out to the rest of the warriors. "Maybe you're thinking that wasn't fair. The battlefield isn't fair, but I'll grant you old Hunnan's a few years past his best. So anyone thinks he can fill Gorm's boots, I'll fight him. I'll fight any of you." She swaggered in a circle, taking in each side of the square, staring the warriors in their eyes one after another.

Silence. Only the wind sighing across the beach.

"No one?" She snorted. "Look at you, sulking because you didn't get a battle. There'll be more battle than you know what to do with soon enough. I hear the High King gathers his warriors. Lowlanders, and Islanders, and Inglings. Thousands of them. There's a storm coming, and Gettland will need every man. Every man and every woman. You three, come with me. We'll be back in a month." She lifted her arm to point at Hunnan. "And your boys better be ready."

Thorn swung the stool up onto her shoulder and stalked from the square, off across the sand toward Thorlby. She didn't look back.

But she heard the footsteps of the girls behind her.

# ACKNOWLEDGMENTS

As always, four people without whom:
Bren Abercrombie, whose eyes are sore from reading it.
Nick Abercrombie, whose ears are sore from hearing about it.
Rob Abercrombie, whose fingers are sore from turning the pages.
Lou Abercrombie, whose arms are sore from holding me up.

Then, because no man is an island, especially this one, my heartfelt
   thanks:
For planting the seed of this idea: Nick Lake.
For making sure the sprout grew to a tree: Robert Kirby.
For making sure the tree bore golden fruit: Jane Johnson.

Then, because the fruit metaphor has run its course, all those who've
   helped make, market, publish, publicize, illustrate, translate and
   above all *sell* my books wherever they may be around the world
   but, in particular: Natasha Bardon, Emma Coode, Ben North,
   Jaime Frost, Tricia Narwani, Jonathan Lyons, and Ginger Clark.

To the artists and designers somehow rising to the impossible challenge of making me look classy: Nicolette and Terence Caven, Mike Bryan and Dominic Forbes.

For endless enthusiasm and support in all weathers: Gillian Redfearn.

And to all the writers whose paths have crossed mine on the Internet, at the bar, or in some cases even on the printed page, and who've provided help, advice, laughs and plenty of ideas worth the stealing.

You know who you are . . .

## ABOUT THE AUTHOR

JOE ABERCROMBIE is the *New York Times* bestselling author of *Half a King*, *Red Country*, and the First Law trilogy: *The Blade Itself*, *Before They Are Hanged*, and *Last Argument of Kings*. He spent ten years as a freelance film editor, but is now a full-time writer who lives in Bath, England, with his wife, two daughters, and son.

joeabercrombie.com

Facebook.com/joeabercrombieauthor

@LordGrimdark

ABOUT THE TYPE

This book was set in Fournier, a typeface named for Pierre-Simon Fournier (1712–68), the youngest son of a French printing family. He started out engraving woodblocks and large capitals, then moved on to fonts of type. In 1736 he began his own foundry and made several important contributions in the field of type design; he is said to have cut 147 alphabets of his own creation. Fournier is probably best remembered as the designer of St. Augustine Ordinaire, a face that served as the model for the Monotype Corporation's Fournier, which was released in 1925.